Lecture Notes in Computer Science 4001

Commenced Publication in 1973
Founding and Former Series Editors:
Gerhard Goos, Juris Hartmanis, and Jan van Leeuwen

Editorial Board

David Hutchison
  Lancaster University, UK
Takeo Kanade
  Carnegie Mellon University, Pittsburgh, PA, USA
Josef Kittler
  University of Surrey, Guildford, UK
Jon M. Kleinberg
  Cornell University, Ithaca, NY, USA
Friedemann Mattern
  ETH Zurich, Switzerland
John C. Mitchell
  Stanford University, CA, USA
Moni Naor
  Weizmann Institute of Science, Rehovot, Israel
Oscar Nierstrasz
  University of Bern, Switzerland
C. Pandu Rangan
  Indian Institute of Technology, Madras, India
Bernhard Steffen
  University of Dortmund, Germany
Madhu Sudan
  Massachusetts Institute of Technology, MA, USA
Demetri Terzopoulos
  University of California, Los Angeles, CA, USA
Doug Tygar
  University of California, Berkeley, CA, USA
Moshe Y. Vardi
  Rice University, Houston, TX, USA
Gerhard Weikum
  Max-Planck Institute of Computer Science, Saarbruecken, Germany

T0181322

Eric Dubois   Klaus Pohl (Eds.)

Advanced Information Systems Engineering

18th International Conference, CAiSE 2006
Luxembourg, Luxembourg, June 5-9, 2006
Proceedings

 Springer

Volume Editors

Eric Dubois
Centre de Recherche Public Henri Tudor
29, Avenue John F. Kennedy, 1855 Luxembourg-Kirchberg, Luxembourg
E-mail: eric.dubois@tudor.lu

Klaus Pohl
Lero - The Irish Software Engineering Research Center
University of Limerick
Ireland
and
University of Duisburg-Essen
Software Systems Engineering
ICB - Institute of Computer Science and Business Information Sysems
Schützenbahn 70, 45117 Essen, Germany
E-mail: Pohl@sse.uni-essen.de

Library of Congress Control Number: 2006926432

CR Subject Classification (1998): H.2, H.3-5, J.1, K.4.3-4, K.6, D.2, I.2.11

LNCS Sublibrary: SL 3 – Information Systems and Application,
incl. Internet/Web and HCI

ISSN   0302-9743
ISBN-10   3-540-34652-X Springer Berlin Heidelberg New York
ISBN-13   978-3-540-34652-4 Springer Berlin Heidelberg New York

Preface

Welcome to CAiSE 2006 – the 18th International Conference on Advanced Information Systems Engineering. The goal of the CAiSE conference series is to bring together the R&D community concerned with the development of information systems so as to take advantage of emerging methods and technologies that both facilitate innovation and create business opportunities.

The conference theme of CAiSE 2006 was "Trusted Information Systems." Ambient, pervasive and ubiquitous computing are enabling the use of information systems almost everywhere. Consequently, the impact of information systems on the everyday life of organizations as well as individuals is rapidly increasing. Individuals and organizations find themselves depending on information systems that they did not develop themselves, that they do not fully understand, or that they do not manage and control themselves.

Under these rapidly changing circumstances, trust in information systems is clearly becoming a central issue for organisations and individuals. Three important aspects of trust in information systems were addressed by the invited keynotes of CAiSE 2006:

- Trusted Interaction: User Control and System Responsibilities in Interaction Design for Information Systems by Larry Constantine (Constantine & Lockwood, Ltd., and University of Madeira)
- Dealing with Trust in eGov Services by Vassily Kritis (Intrasoft International)
- Trust: from Cognition to Conceptual Models and Design by Alistair Sutcliffe (The Centre for HCI Design, University of Manchester)

The accepted papers and the panels, as well as the CAiSE Forum, addressed additional facets of trust such as business/IT alignment, queries and Web services, knowledge engineering and ontologies, change management, conceptual modelling and requirements management.

For CAiSE 2006, we received 189 submissions in the five categories mentioned in the call for papers: case studies, experience reports, experimental reports, problem statements and research papers. The largest number of submissions came from China (21 papers) followed by Spain (19 papers) and Germany (13 papers). Overall, one third of the submissions came from outside Europe. In an extensive review process, the Programme Committee of CAiSE 2006 accepted 33 papers out of the 189 submissions – an acceptance rate of 17%. In addition, the Programme Committee recommended 18 papers for acceptance in the CAiSE 2006 Forum. The programme of CAiSE 2006 was complemented by 12 workshops, 1 working conference, a PhD consortium and 9 tutorials.

CAiSE 2006 would not have been possible without the efforts and expertise of a number of people who selflessly offered their time and energy to help make this conference a success. We would like to thank all the people on the Organisation

Committee. Special thanks are due to Sacha Reis and Richard van de Stadt for their responsive and helpful support during the paper evaluation and selection process, as well as during the preparation of the proceedings.

We also offer our sincere thanks to the members of the CAiSE 2006 Programme Committee for devoting their time and knowledge to reviewing and discussing the submitted papers. We would especially like to thank the members of the Programme Committee who attended the two-day Programme Committee meeting, held in Essen on January 30-31, 2006.

Finally, we thank the main conference sponsors: Research National Fund of Luxembourg Public Research Centre Henri Tudor (Luxembourg), University of Luxembourg, Lero (University of Limerick), University of Duisburg-Essen, University of Namur, Intrasoft International, Sun Microsystems and other national research authorities.

We hope you enjoy the CAiSE 2006 the proceedings.

Eric Dubois
Klaus Pohl

Organisation

Advisory Committee	Janis Bubenko Jr. Royal Institute of Technology, Sweden Colette Rolland Université Paris 1 - Sorbonne, France Arne Sølvberg Norwegian University of Science and Technology, Norway
General Chair	Eric Dubois Public Research Centre Henri Tudor, Luxembourg
Programme Chair	Klaus Pohl Lero - The Irish Software Engineering Research Centre, Ireland, and University of Duisburg-Essen, Germany
Organising Chair	Pascal Bouvry University of Luxembourg
Workshop Chairs	Michael Petit University of Namur, Belgium Thibaud Latour Public Research Centre Henri Tudor, Luxembourg
Tutorial Chairs	Djamel Khadraoui Public Research Centre Henri Tudor, Luxembourg Patrick Heymans University of Namur, Belgium
Doctoral Consortium Chairs	Colette Rolland Université Paris 1 - Sorbonne, France Pedro F. Campos University of Madeira, Portugal
Forum Chairs	Nicolas Guelfi University of Luxembourg, Luxembourg Nacer Boudjlida University Henri Poincaré Nancy I, LORIA, France

Publicity Chairs   Riad Aggoune
University of Luxembourg, Luxembourg
Thorsten Weyer
University of Duisburg-Essen, Germany

Programme Committee

Jean-Claude Asselborn	Luxembourg
Sjaak Brinkkemper	The Netherlands
Silvana Castano	Italy
Jaelson Castro	Brazil
Johann Eder	Austria
Hans-Dieter Ehrich	Germany
Stefan Eicker	Germany
João Falcão e Cunha	Portugal
Xavier Franch	Spain
Paolo Giorgini	Italy
Claude Godart	France
Jaap Gordijn	The Netherlands
Jean-Luc Hainaut	Belgium
Terry Halpin	USA
Brian Henderson-Sellers	Australia
Matthias Jarke	Germany
Manfred Jeusfeld	The Netherlands
Paul Johannesson	Sweden
Gerti Kappel	Austria
Dimitris Karagiannis	Austria
Roland Kaschek	New Zealand
John Krogstie	Norway
Julio Leite	Brazil
Michel Lemoine	France
Michel Léonard	Switzerland
Pericles Loucopoulos	UK
Kalle Lyytinen	USA
Neil Maiden	UK
Florian Matthes	Germany
Heinrich Mayr	Austria
Jean-Pol Michel	Luxembourg
Michele Missikoff	Italy
Ana Moreira	Portugal
Moira Norrie	Switzerland
Andreas Oberweis	Germany
Antoni Olivé	Spain
Andreas L. Opdahl	Norway

Oscar Pastor Lopez	Spain
Barbara Pernici	Italy
Anne Persson	Sweden
Yves Pigneur	Switzerland
Klaus Pohl	Germany
Jolita Ralyte	Switzerland
Colette Rolland	France
Kevin Ryan	Ireland
Motoshi Saeki	Japan
Camille Salinesi	France
Guttorm Sindre	Norway
Monique Snoeck	Belgium
Janis Stirna	Sweden
Alistair Sutcliffe	UK
Bernhard Thalheim	Germany
Juha-Pekka Tolvanen	Finland
Aphrodite Tsalgatidou	Greece
Yannis Vassiliou	Greece
Gottfried Vossen	Germany
Yair Wand	Canada
Roel Wieringa	The Netherlands
Eric Yu	Canada

Additional Referees

Birger Andersson	Hans-Georg Fill	Lyubov Kolos-Maruryk
João Araújo	Anna Formica	Henk Koning
Danilo Ardagna	Virginia Nunes	Hartmut König
George Athanasopoulos	Leal Franqueira	Eleni Koutrouli
Maria Bergholtz	Walid Gaaloul	Gerhard Kramler
Paola Bertolazzi	Andrew Gemino	Andreas Kupfer
Aliaksandr Birukou	Miguel Goulão	Jens Lechtenboerger
Enrico Blanzieri	Sabine Graf	Marek Lehmann
Rik Bos	Fabio Grandi	Norbert Luttenberger
Volha Bryl	Michael Grossniklaus	Sergio Mascetti
Andrew Burton-Jones	Peter Höfferer	Brigitte Mathiak
Hock Chan	Stephan Hagemann	Michele Melchiori
François Charoy	Martin Henkel	Elke Michlmayr
Dolors Costal	Sandra Hintringer	Pascal Molli
Marcin Czenko	Slinger Jansen	Stefano Montanelli
Fulvio D'Antonio	Marijke Janssen	Marion Murzek
Daniel Dahl	Rim Samia Kaabi	Enrico Mussi
Silke Eckstein	Kinshuk	Martin Nemetz
Joerg Evermann	Marite Kirikova	Karl Neumann
Alfio Ferrara	Maik Kollmann	Antonio De Nicola

Nunzia Osimi
Michael Pantazoglou
Lia Patrício
Olivier Perrin
Horst Pichler
Thomi Pilioura
Manfred Reichert
Boriana Rukanova
Andrea Schauerhuber
Peter M. Schuler
Joachim Schwieren
Vladimir Shekhovtsov
Hala Skaf

Eriks Sneiders
Mehdi Snene
Pnina Soffer
Jurriaan Souer
Jorge Pinho de Sousa
Veronika Stefanov
Xiaomeng Su
Francesco Taglino
Nick Tahamtan
Philippe Thiran
Alexei Tretiakov
Slim Turki
Christina Tsagkani

Jan Herman Verpoorten
Johan Versendaal
Inge van de Weerd
Nadir Weibel
Liu Fu Wen
Peter Westerkamp
Manuel Wimmer
Andreas Wombacher
Lai Xu
Nicola Zannone
Jane Zhao
Sergiy Zlatkin

Sponsors

In Cooperation with

 SSE Software Systems Engineering
Prof. Dr. Klaus Pohl
ICB (Institute for Computer Science &
Business Information Systems)
University of Duisburg-Essen

 *lero* THE IRISH SOFTWARE
ENGINEERING RESEARCH CENTRE

Corporate Sponsors

Table of Contents

Keynotes

Security

Conceptual Modelling

Queries

Agent Orientation

Requirements Management

Keynotes

Trust: From Cognition to Conceptual Models and Design

Alistair Sutcliffe

School of Informatics, University of Manchester,
PO Box 88, Manchester, UK
ags@manchester.ac.uk

Abstract. Trust as a design issue for information systems has appeared in e-commerce, e-science, and a wide variety of collaborative applications. Much discussion has centred around trust in computational artefacts such as protocols, encryption and security mechanisms; however, little research has focused on exactly what trust means in human terms. In this presentation I will review the psychology literature on trust as a product of reasoning processes, and describe a cognitive model to explain and predict inter-personal and inter-organisational trust. I argue that sound design should be based on cognitive models of users, and these should inform the semantics of conceptual modelling as well as guiding the design process. I will explore the implications of the cognitive model of trust for conceptual modelling in requirements specification languages such as i*. The final part will be more speculative. After a brief review of the implementations of trust-enhancing mechanisms in collaborative and e-science systems, focusing on user interface features rather than encryption, etc. middleware, I will discuss the design challenges for future trustworthy systems. This will cover how trust can be communicated, and issues of honesty when users may not always have the best intentions.

1 Introduction

Since trust has frequently been associated only with connotations of security and privacy (Haley, Laney et al., 2004; Giorgini, Massacci et al., 2005), the scope and interaction of trust-related issues in information systems development needs to be investigated. This leads to investigating how trust as a phenomenon can be interpreted in conceptual models and requirements specifications of systems. Modelling and designing for trustworthy or trust-promoting systems necessitates understanding and applying psychological and socio-psychological theories that explain trust and related phenomena. Trust has a social dimension in its role of governing personal relationships; it also has implications for how we make decisions, when we decide how to react to objects and people, as trustworthy or not. However, to realise the value in modelling trust, design implications should be discovered. To make some progress in this direction I will propose a framework for modelling trust-related issues, and then apply the framework in a case study of e-science. Trust has been highlighted as a social issue in the UK e-science programme; however, to date there has been little research that defines what trust means in e-science or how it should be interpreted in designing collaborative software.

E. Dubois and K. Pohl (Eds.): CAiSE 2006, LNCS 4001, pp. 3–17, 2006.
© Springer-Verlag Berlin Heidelberg 2006

The paper is organised as follows; a brief review of cognitive and social psychological models of trust is followed by a description of the framework of trust-related issues. The subsequent section applies the framework to analysing trust-related problems in e-science. Finally, a research agenda for trust-motivated research in information systems is discussed.

2　Cognitive and Social Models of Trust

In sociology, trust models have considered economic viewpoints of trust between organisations as well as social attitudes governing trust towards institutions and between groups. In transaction cost theory (Williamson, 1993), trust is viewed as a consequence of inter-organisational relationships and the evolution of markets. The nature of the transaction and value of the goods influences trust between the purchasers and vendor and trust is regarded as a means of reducing transaction costs (e.g. legal fees) in contracts. Thoburn and Takashima (1993) argue that the existence of contracts should not inevitably be taken to mean that trust is absent, and note that in highly interdependent relationships contracts must be supplemented by other measures such as relationship building and the development of transparent accounting procedures between alliance partners. This includes the development of a no-blame culture to encourage truthful reporting and an open and honest dialogue (Tomkins, 2001).

Korczynski (2000) developed a model to illustrate the multiple types of trust that underlie relationships in economic activity, and pointed out that trust has a "political" as well as an economic aspect. For example, those who act out of social and ethical motives will be trusted more than opportunistic individuals. In associations where the participants have a long "time horizon" developed through personal associations and shared vision, there is less likelihood that incumbents will be narrowly rational in calculating trust. The "political" aspects of trust involve aspects such as legitimacy, reputation, status and knowledge.

Sociological studies of trust follow the perspective of society as a whole (Barber, 1983) or from individual perspectives of personal trust (Lewis & Weigert, 1985; Luhmann, 1979; Shapiro, 1987; Zucker, 1986). The primary definition used in the sociological literature is that of Barber (1983, p. 165), who defines trust as two expectations: "[that] of technically competent performance and ... of fiduciary obligation and responsibility". Generally sociologists consider trust to be developed over time and influenced by personality traits, social experiences, or commonly shared norms and values (Fukuyama, 1995). Risk is implied in trust, but the risk is a calculated one, so individuals may choose not to trust if the risk is too great.

Drawing upon the literature of several disciplines, Hupcey et al. (2001) propose a three-component model that contains (i) *antecedents*: a need which cannot be met without help from another; prior knowledge and/or experience of the other, and assessment of risk; (ii) *attributes* composed of dependency upon another to meet the need, choice or willingness to take some risk; expectation that the trusted individual will behave in a certain way; focus upon the behaviour related to the need and testing the trustworthiness of the individual; (iii) *boundaries* when trust ceases to exist if there is a perception of no choice or the risks outweigh the benefits.

In psychology the emphasis is upon interpersonal relationships as defined by Rotter (1971, p. 444): "an expectancy held by an individual or a group that the word, promise, verbal or written statement of another individual or group can be relied on". However, trusting an individual places the trustor at risk (Kramer, 1999), and therefore relies upon encountering consistent and benevolent behaviour in others (Larzelere & Huston, 1980). Cannon, Doney and Mullen (1998) define trust as a willingness to rely on another party, and therefore to make oneself vulnerable to that party.

Formal socio-cognitive models of trust have been proposed (Castelfranchi & Falcone, 1998) with equations that attempt to evaluate the various factors that influence trusting relationships, such as the degree of delegation between the two parties, the motivations, risks and goals shared by the parties to establish the need for a relationship, and properties which can be evaluated to establish their reputations. The role of the environment and experience also influence how trust may be assessed within groups, although no clear means of assessing the impact of experience is given. The socio-cognitive theory of trust (Falcone & Castelfranchi, 2001a, 2001b) represents a considerable synthesis of the literature; however, the equations and premises contain many assumptions which are not based on empirical evidence. Furthermore, the predictions of the model have not been validated in case studies or experiments.

Studies of trust in technology have investigated how people assess the trustworthiness of websites and have proposed guidelines for trust enhancing design (Neilsen, Molich et al., 2000). Empirical studies in e-commerce environments reviewed by Grabner-Krauter and Kaluscha (2003), focus on assessment of trustworthiness of websites as well as the web as an institution. Guidelines for promoting trust are reported with questionnaire inventories for assessing reputation of trustees. Corritore, Kracher and Wiedenbeck (2003) propose a model of trust oriented to assessment of websites and interactive products, which assesses quality factors such as usability and credibility balanced against the risk of entering into transactions on the web. A more comprehensive model (Riegelsberger, Sasse & McCarthy, 2003) analyses trusting relationships and trust-enforcing institutions and proposes mechanisms for promoting trust in communities, with design guidelines to facilitate evaluation of intrinsic trust of the reputation of the trustee, as well as feedback from experience. However, Riegelsberger et al. note that external manifestations of trust can be subject to mimicry by ill-intentioned agents, so trust relies on well regulated communities.

The concept of trust has been elaborated into credibility in studies of websites (Fogg, Marshall et al., 2001), where trust is an attribute assigned to websites based on the user's assessment of several factors such as usability, accuracy of information, brand and persuasive features. However, Fogg proposed no specific model of trust *per se*. A more elaborate model based on qualitative and quantitative research is the two-process model of trust in which first impressions, based on the interface look and feel, are distinguished from more detailed evaluations, based on the analysis of source credibility, personalisation and predictability (Briggs, Burford et al., 2002). The relationship between trust, personalisation and brand was further investigated in a large-scale experiment which also addressed methodological issues concerning the extent to which planned and actual behaviours converge (Briggs, Burford & De Angeli, 2004).

Although the diversity in trust theories and models can be daunting, a common set of components appears in several theories. First there must be some motivation for one party to trust another. The fact that one party has a need which can potentially be met by the other implies a degree of vulnerability. This is because the trustor is placing themselves at some risk *vis-à-vis* the potentially more powerful party. A trustor has to feel some confidence in the past performance and reliability of the trusted party to assess whether they are likely to fulfil their part of the bargain. The trustor relies on the trusted, or trustee, to share their commitment towards achieving a goal. The boundaries of trust are reached when one party perceives that the risks in trusting the other party outweigh the potential benefits.

3 Modelling Trust

At the social level, trust is a relationship between the trustor and the trustee. There is an implicit asymmetry in the relationship between the latter, who is more powerful, and the trustor who is in some way more dependent on the trustee. Trust is associated with power (i.e. authority and perceived power), vulnerability and risk. Indeed trust can be seen as a type of insurance policy for making relationships manageable when there is some doubt about the intentions of the other party. If one individual perceives some risk or vulnerability which could be exploited in the relationship, the courses of action are either to abandon the relationship, or to adopt risk reduction via legal contracts, financial insurance, etc., or to trust the other party and hope for the best. Trust has the added advantage of being cheap; if it works it reduces the overhead of relationship management and promotes a better *modus operandi*.

In information systems, trust may be modelled as a relationship between individual agents, or organisations, as illustrated figure 1.

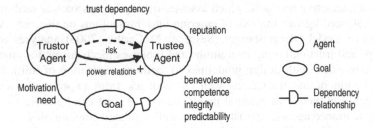

Fig. 1. Trust modelling conventions illustrated in an adaptation of i* notation

Trust relationships are associated with a goal dependency in which the trustor relies on the trustee. The trustees' suitability depends on their competence to fulfil the goal, their benevolence not to exploit the trustor's vulnerability, their ethical integrity and predictability of their behaviour. The semantics of power relationships are worth modelling explicitly, since power asymmetry is invariably associated with trust; an evaluation function is required to assess the agent's reputation from its properties. The properties will vary between applications, individual agents and organisations; however, some generic properties which give an indication of domain specifics are honesty, history of trustworthiness, association with reliable agents, openness in negotiation, and membership of trustworthy organisations. Reputation assessment is accompanied by power asymmetry or vulnerability analysis; hence the overall assessment depends on each agent's need for trust, which is a combination of their goals and motivation for entering into the relationship, and vulnerability or risk exposure. The need for trust defines the requirements for the relationship, i.e. a highly asymmetric relationship implies a need for a higher level of trust than does a more symmetric relationship. Trust develops over time, so in the initial stages the trustee's reputation is evaluated either in depth or more superficially depending on the trustor's predisposition and the availability of information. As the relationship matures trust becomes a default assumption unless unpleasant experience triggers a review of the relationship.

4 Cognitive Model of Trust

Cognitive models place trust as in the context of theories of decision making, such as the theory of reasoned action (Klein, 1989) which asserts that decisions are influenced by a combination of the events and situation at a point in time combined with the user's prior memory and attitude towards the decision problem. Trust is a specialisation of such models in which the decision is to enter into a relationship with an agent depending on the situation and prior knowledge. The following cognitive model of trust considers both the reputation and experience components of trust. A four-stage process is proposed elaborating concepts in earlier phase models (Briggs et al., 2004) as illustrated in figure 2.

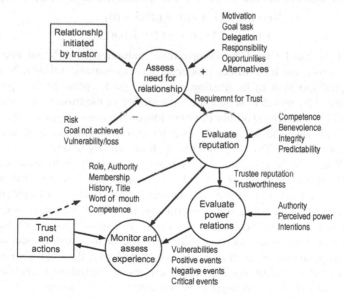

Fig. 2. Process model of trust-related decision making

The first stage is assessment of the need for trust. The trustor agent has a goal which requires the cooperation of another to achieve it. The importance of the goal is evaluated in light of the options available and the potential loss if the goal is not achieved. This assessment may be complex, involving trade-offs of recruiting multiple relationships, the degree of explicitness in the relationship (i.e. overt delegation or not), and alternatives to trust such as legal contracts, economic incentives, etc. While assessment details will be domain and situation specific, the essence is a motivation and risk calculation, expressed in equation 1. It creates a "need for trust" metric (Nt) as a function of need, motivation and potential loss.

$$Nt = (M + G + env + (r.p)) \tag{1}$$

Where

$M =$ motivation for entering the relationship

$G =$ goal that one party wishes to achieve expressed as importance ranking

$env =$ environment factor that represents the degrees of freedom available to the trustor

$r =$ risk exposure

$p =$ perceived power difference between the parties.

Risk exposure and degree of choice available increase the need for trust value if the risk is high and there are few alternatives. Env is assessed as higher if fewer choices exist. As the risk and power asymmetry increases, the need for trust increases. The formula can be converted into a metric by estimating M, G, env and r on a 10-point (low to high) scale, with p expressed on a 0 to 1 scale where equal power = 0.5 and 1.0 = complete asymmetry in favour of the trustee. A constant of 0.5 modulates the effect of power on risk exposure. So with a high motivation and an important goal for the trustor, but with considerable risk and few options, the need for trust might be:

$$Nt = (M + G + env + r.(0.5 + p))$$
$$28.1 = 6 + 7 + 6 + 7.(0.5 + 0.8) \tag{1}$$

These metrics can be used for comparative evaluation of different need for trust situations; however, the trust values produced have no intrinsic validity. Motivation is the agent's predisposition to be trusting, while the goal represents the specific need. Risk is modulated by power to reflect the vulnerability of the trustor, i.e. a more powerful trustee will have increased ability to inflict loss on the trustor without repercussions.

In the second stage the opportunity to enter into a trusting relationships is evaluated in light of the need. This may involve a choice among several suitors so the risk exposure will need to be evaluated for each suitor agent. Reputations of each trustor are assessed from their perceived benevolence, competence, integrity and predictability. Assessment criteria will vary by domain and the availability of evidence for the trustor. However, typical reputation properties are the trustee's competence to achieve the goal, honesty, past trustworthiness, reputation as vouched for by others, membership of trusted organisations, and socio-demographic factors such as occupation, age, and gender. Reputations of the trustees are compared with the trustor's requirements for entering into the relationship. Equation 2 creates an "initial trust" metric as a function of needs and risk, balanced against the reputation of the trustee.

$$T^i = R - N^t \tag{2}$$

Where

$T^i =$ Initial trustworthiness level

$R =$ Reputation of the trustee

$N^t =$ trustor's need level from equation (1).

The formula can be converted into a metric by estimating reputation on 40 point scale to balance with the need for trust. If the trustee's reputation is high and the trustor's need for trust does not exceed it, the starting level of trust will be positive. Alternatively, if the trustee has a poor reputation or it is exceeded by a high need for trust, then the starting trust level will be negative reflecting low confidence and mistrust. The value can be calculated in both directions in a relationship, although for asymmetric relationships the trustee is the focus of attention. A confidence metric may also be calculated based on the knowledge available to the trustor, risk exposure, and previous reputation history of the trustee. The level of confidence is fed into the threshold which determines when trust will switch into distrust.

Trusting relationships may change over time, so assessment of reputation only models the initial starting point between the two parties. Events influence the evolution of trust. Adverse events may be tolerated for a while but sooner or later, trust will rapidly decline into mistrust, from which there is no quick escape, as demonstrated by empirical studies on the effect of errors on trust in computer applications (Lee & Moray, 1992). Once this initial trust value has been established, the experience component of the model predicts change over time, as described in equation 3:

$$T^i = T^{i-1} f^{th}(E.w)$$ (3)

Where

T^i = level of trust in time interval i and the previous interval i-1

E = experiences which may be either positive, confirming or increasing trust; or negative and leading to suspicion about trustworthiness of the trustee

w = weighting factor for the criticality of each event

f = function determining trust increase or decrease

th = threshold that influences the trend function of the initial reputation-based trust.

The threshold function controls the four separate trend patterns according to the initial reputation and history of the experience:

1. an initial high level of trust survives several adverse experiences but if the negative events continue once a critical threshold is exceeded trust will rapidly decrease into distrust
2. a low level of initial trust will experience gradual improvement with positive experience and a similar decrease in trust with adverse experience
3. a relationship that started with high trust and descended into mistrust has a very poor recovery function, so a large number of positive events are required before trust is regained
4. mid-range trust values have an increasing gradient with positive experience and a rapid decrease with adverse experience.

A screen dump of the computational tool that embeds the theory is illustrated in figure 3.

The model is controlled by parameters and thresholds which determine when the functions change for ascending or descending trust, as well as allowing the model to be tailored for a specific domain, e.g. the number and strength of positive and negative

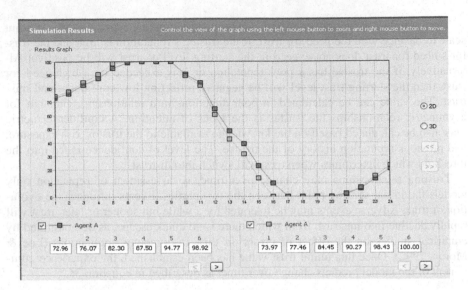

Fig. 3. Screen dump of tool that models Dynamic Trust Theory, showing a simulated time course of a relationship (pattern 1 followed by 3)

events that will precipitate rapid descent to mistrust, etc. Event criticality is reflected in the weighting factor as well as the input value assigned to each event. Assessment of experience also depends on domain-specific interpretation of the number and valency of events necessary and how the significance of events is determined. Typical events in inter-organisational relationships are meeting deadlines, compliance with commitments, provision of information, prompt responses, willingness to help the other party, etc. Failure to fulfil obligations without any reason, and deceit in covering up failure, are typical critical negative experiences. The agent's reputation parameters are entered as the settings for variables 1 to 6 and the plot shows the change in trust with an experience scenario that starts with positive events followed by critical negative events leading to rapid decline in trust.

5 Framework for Trust Modelling

So far, the model has assumed agents (individual or organisational) were involved as both parties; however, we also trust artefacts, products, information, processes, and data. The relationship motivation and vulnerability analysis still apply. The risk exposure of using the object is assessed to determine the need for trust. The object's reputation can be assessed as before; furthermore, for products the attribute of brand is an important component of trust, as it is for inter-organisational relationships. The problem space of trust issues and relationships is summarised in figure 4.

The nature of experience with trusted objects depends on whether they are active or passive. Active objects, for example mobile phones, exhibit behaviour resulting in the user's experience, which may be favourable or not. Any device which causes frequent

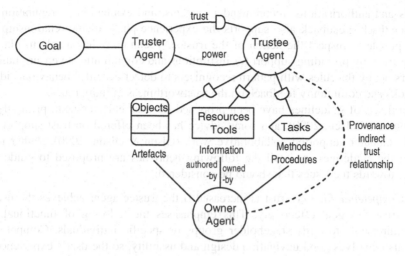

Fig. 4. Framework of trust issues and relationships

errors will rapidly become distrusted. A passive object such as a book has no inherent behaviour but can be experienced through reading. Trust in an author's work may develop if the reader feels the plots are consistently well constructed. Finally, some passive objects may not be directly experienced in use; for instance, a painting is appreciated aesthetically but not actually used. Trust in this case depends on the quality of the perceptual experience. Hence trust is closely related to use and possibly aesthetics. In HCI there has been considerable interest in assessing qualities of use including usability, aesthetics and the user's experience (Hassenzahl, 2004; Lavie & Tractinsky, 2004; Sutcliffe & De Angeli, 2005). However, these measures have not been correlated with the development of trust between users and a software product, although some authors have argued that the quality of experience and aesthetic appeal are critical determinants of a product's success because the experience creates a positive emotional response (i.e. pleasure) and this fosters trust (McCarthy & Wright, 2005; Norman 2004).

5.1 Design Implications

Modelling trust may illuminate our understanding of a socio-technical system; however, without any design implications its utility will be limited. Design and trust intersect in two ways. First, software products need to be designed so users trust them and have a positive experience. Secondly, technology is a mediator of trust between people, organisations or products. The first role is fulfilled by good design, e.g. usability, appropriate functionality, professional aesthetic look and feel, as well as design to facilitate trust through ownership via customisation and adaptation to the user's needs. In the second role, technology should reduce the uncertainty in relationships and thereby increase trust by making information more accessible, and by communicating status, identity, intent and processes transparently. Better quality functions can help evaluating reputations to promote trust, e.g. display of status information, memberships and authorisations, recommender systems, and evaluation of reputation berships and authorisations, recommender systems, and evaluation of reputation by social feedback. Feedback also supports the experience phase of the relationship allowing people to inspect the action of the trustee. Technology has a role to play in policing trust, by providing support for institutions and communities to ensure human members act by the rules with pattern recognisers to detect deceitful behaviour, identity checks and community feedback on the trustworthiness of individuals.

Several sets of guidelines have been proposed for trust enhancement, primarily in e-commerce (Nielsen, 2000), and some advice has been offered on trust support for general computer supported collaborative work (Olson & Olson, 2000). Rather than reiterate the guidelines in detail the following heuristics are proposed to guide the designer towards the issues that should be considered:

- *Competence factors*: trust is increased if the trustee agent achieves the user's (trustor's) goal effectively. This emphasises the tailoring of functional requirements towards stakeholder groups or specific individuals. Competence also involves good navigation design and usability, so the user's experience is positive. Poor usability has a negative impact on trust.
- *Benevolence*: this property reflects more directly on the developer or owner of the application. Favourable predispositions can be communicated by statements of honesty, access to the people who operate the application, and provision of information about the developers/owners. In e-commerce applications this is reflected in guidelines for "contact us" and "about us" information, and statements of fair trading policies, etc.
- *Integrity*: this reflects the ethical standards of the developers/owners and can be conveyed by brand images, membership of trustworthy organisations, compliance with standards, and certification authorities.
- *Predictability*: this is a consistent experience related to good usability, reliable applications, and prevention of errors.

Trust is also enhanced by good design for related non-functional requirements such as accuracy (of information), privacy, security and reliability. Usability reduces uncertainty by making interaction predictable with clear feedback, hence building confidence in an application.

Design for trust may also involve fostering relationships between human and organisational parties more directly by processes to facilitate matching of trustors and trustees, and vetting services for reputation management. Recommender systems, brokers, and social feedback facilities such as eBay's vendor reputation management are examples of functions for trust relationship management. Workflow, version control, and coordination tools help build trust by efficient relationship management. Logging and monitoring tools can track experience and make processes transparent by shared data and models, while status displays can help build confidence in relationships, thereby building trust. Provision of more information about individuals and the ability to query claims and identities reduce the opportunities for deceit. In the next section the framework and process model of trust is applied to an e-science domain to investigate how design for trust might be deployed.

6 Case Study: Modelling Trust in e-Science

E-science is the collaboration between remote groups of scientists mediated by CSCW (Computer Supported Collaborative Work) technology and GRID computing over the Internet. Although e-science is proposed as an empowering form of re-organising work practice, evidence of successful e-science collaboration is hard to find, and furthermore, the few evaluations that have been carried out (Cummings & Kiesler, in press) point to several reasons why collaborations have been unsuccessful. Although several causal factors were cited such as clash of time zones, organisational cultures, and inadequate technology, the lack of trust between teams was a contributing factor.

6.1 Applying the Framework

Trust in relationships between individuals and between teams is an important aspect of improving relationships. Socio-psychological theories of group working (Arrow, McGrath & Berdahl, 2000) emphasise the importance of frequent social contacts that build a network of relationships between group members and hence create trust. The role of CSCW and GRID video conference technology in promoting good social bonds is poor, hence there may be no substitute for face-to-face interaction to build this aspect of trust. However, the reputation of individuals and groups can be assessed and this might provide an indicator of the trust requirements, when considered with the needs of each group to enter into a collaboration.

The following example is based on e-science collaboration in genomic research in which teams of biomedical researchers are trying to understand the complicated process by which genes (DNA) are transcribed into an intermediate form (RNA) which is then used to produce proteins in cells by complicated bio-chemical processes. Unfortunately the mapping of genes (segments of DNA) to protein (sequences of amino acids) is not 1 to 1. A common approach is to segment chromosomes into gene fragments, provide the *in vivo* environment for protein synthesis using the gene (DNA sequence) fragments, assay the proteins produced, then try the experiment with different inhibitor chemicals and DNA segments to see when the inhibitors stop production of the protein, thus confirming that DNA segment x is responsible for producing protein y. This process is time consuming and could benefit from a combined approach where teams try different inhibitors on the same sequence, etc. The model of the collaboration, illustrated in figure 5, is produced by applying the trust analysis method as follows:

Motivation Analysis: the motivation for the relationship is not strong since each team can continue to work incrementally as before. However, the risk exposure of collaboration is relatively low since each team will still have results to publish, although there is the possible loss of not being the team to make the scientific breakthrough. This creates a moderate need for trust.

Reputation Analysis: the reputation of each group depends on their host universities and publication record; in this case reputation was approximately equal and both teams were relatively well funded so the power balance is almost symmetrical. Reputation is reinforced by the need for trust, so e-science technology has to lower the cost of collaboration and foster trust. The teams trust the artefacts produced by their experimental processes, e.g. microarrays, chromatography gels; the procedures they follow which are set by conventions and the refereeing process in the biomedical research community; and the analytic instruments they use (DNA and protein sequence auto-analysers) which involves trusting the manufacturers. The trust relationships are all interdependent. The teams trust their own results and artefacts, but that depends on following procedures accurately and tools performing correctly. For each team to trust the other they not only have to assess their mutual interests and respective reputations, but also the second order trust relationships with procedures, etc. in each group.

Experience Analysis: in e-science CSCW technology can promote trust and manage experience by making the experimental artefacts and procedures shareable. This allows each team to inspect each other's progress, working methods and results to build confidence in the collaboration. However, as noted in the motivation analysis, such sharing does involve some risk, so security and privacy have to be guaranteed, and visibly so. Frequent communication via video conferencing can help to build trust by facilitating social interaction. However, there are limitations in the ability of collaborative technology to promote trust. The benevolence of each team, their competence and integrity are human properties that can be communicated but not enhanced by technology.

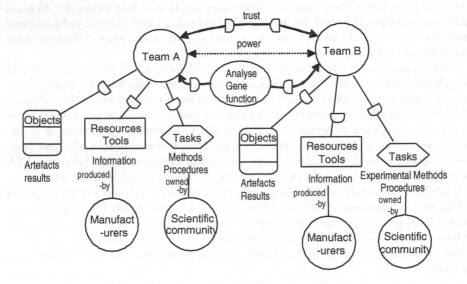

Fig. 5. Model of e-science collaboration

Promoting trust in e-science has to overcome the problem of low motivation or adopting the technology by lowering the cost of establishing trust. This can be achieved by enhancing the shareability and visibility of the methods, procedures and results between teams to build confidence. Increasing the visibility of each team's experimental procedures helps build confidence in the competence and integrity of each team, and may have the side benefit of facilitating sharing of workflows for experimental procedures. Since social interaction is an important influence for building trust between groups (Arrow et al., 2000), use of video conference facilities as well as e-mail can enhance relationship building. Since e-science collaborations are agreements in communities with little formal regulation, technology does not have a trust policing role. Trust in e-science tools and collaborative technology is also a function of usability in design (predictability in interaction), as well as fulfilling users' requirements (competence).

7 Conclusions

Trust is a complicated topic which is difficult to pin down, since it can be viewed from many perspectives. A plethora of models have been proposed, unfortunately exceeding the volume of empirical evidence to justify their assumptions. The model proposed in this paper takes a process perspective to draw attention to how trust can be evaluated, as well as pointing out the components of trust synthesised from other theories.

As systems move into the social domain on the Internet and Cyber communities, where use become discretionary, understanding and designing for trust-promoting facilities will be a growing concern. Further research is necessary to improve the link between trust and uncertainty by better provision of information, and to understand how trust in applications can be promoted by good design (competence). A more significant challenge lies in developing trust management systems. The easy design options of certificates for membership and identity, logging behaviours and social feedback have already been implemented. However, the role of active agents, recommender systems and brokers still needs to be explored in depth. The penalty here lies in bad experience when intelligent systems make poor guesses, leading users to distrust them.

Trust modelling is still in its infancy. Although some modelling languages such as i* have been used to analyse trust and more formal models have been proposed, these do not address the complexities of trust in socio-technical systems. Modelling methods and tools are required to better understand how risk, trust and power interact. There are considerable opportunities for tool development to evaluate trust; however, given that evaluation details will frequently be domain dependent, such tools will need to be configurable.

Finally, trust is but one facet of the complexity of human social relationships that needs to be approached within a wider, theoretically sound framework. Theories of decision making (Klein, 1996; Payne, Bettman & Johnson, 1993) or socio-psychological models of group behaviour (Arrow et al., 2000) may provide the answer. Integrating such theories into conceptual modelling languages is the grand challenge for information systems engineering, and trust may well provide the stimulus.

References

Arrow, H., McGrath, J. E., & Berdahl, J. L. (2000). *Small groups as complex systems: Formation, coordination, development and adaptation.* Thousand Oaks CA: Sage Publications.

Barber, B. (1983). *The logic and limits of trust.* New Brunswick NJ: Rutgers University Press.

Briggs, P., Burford, B., & De Angeli, A. (2004). Personalisation and trust: A reciprocal relationship? In K. Karat, J. O. Blom, & J. Karat (Eds.), *Designing personalised user experiences in e-commerce* (pp. 39-55). Norwell MA: Kluwer Academic Publishers.

Briggs, P., Burford, B., De Angeli, A., & Lynch, P. (2002). Trust in online advice. *Social Science Computer Review*, *20*(3), 321-332.

Cannon, J., Doney, P., & Mullen, M. (1998). National culture and the development of trust: The need for more data and more theory. *Academy of Management Review*, *24*(1), 8-11.

Castelfranchi, C., & Falcone, R. (1998). Social trust: Cognitive anatomy, social importance, quantification and dynamics. *Proceedings: Autonomous Agents '98 Workshop on Deception, Fraud and Trust in Agent Societies, Minneapolis/St Paul*, (pp. 35-49).

Corritore, C. L., Kracher, B., & Wiedenbeck, S. (2003). On-line trust: Concepts, evolving themes, a model. *International Journal of Human-Computer Studies*, *58*, 737-758.

Cummings, J., & Kiesler, S. (in press). Collaborative research across disciplinary and organizational boundaries. *Social Studies of Science*.

Falcone, R., & Castelfranchi, C. (2001a). Social trust: A cognitive approach. In C. Castelfranchi, & Y. Tan (Eds.), *Trust and deception in virtual societies* (pp. 55-90). Boston MA: Kluwer Academic Publishers.

Falcone, R., & Castelfranchi, C. (2001b). The socio-cognitive dynamics of trust: Does trust create trust? In R. Falcone, M. Singh, & Y. Tan (Eds.), *Trust in cybersocieties: Integrating the human and artificial perspectives* (pp. 55-72). Berlin: Springer.

Fogg, B. J., Marshall, J., Laraki, O., Osipovish, A., Varma, C., et al. (2001). What makes web sites credible? A report on a large quantitative study. In J. A. Jacko, A. Sears, M. Beaudouin-Lafon, & R. J. K. Jacob, (Eds). *CHI 2001 Conference Proceedings: Conference on Human Factors in Computing Systems, Seattle 31 March-5 April 2001*. New York: ACM Press.

Fukuyama, F. (1995). *Trust: The social virtues and the creation of prosperity*. New York: Free Press.

Giorgini, P., Massacci, F., Mylopoulos, J., & Zannone, N. (2005). Modeling security requirements through ownership, permission, and delegation. *Proceedings: 13th IEEE International Conference on Requirements Engineering, Paris 29 August - 2 September 2005*, (pp. 167-176). Los Alamitos CA: IEEE Computer Society Press.

Grabner-Krauter, S., & Kaluscha, E. A. (2003). Empirical research in online-trust: A review and critical assessment. *International Journal of Human-Computer Studies*, *58*, 783-821.

Haley, C. B., Laney, R., Moffett, J. D., & Nuseibeh, B. (2004). The effect of trust assumptions on the elaboration of security requirements. *Proceedings: 12th IEEE International Conference on Requirements Engineering, Kyoto 6-10 September 2004*,. Los Alamitos CA: IEEE Computer Society Press.

Hassenzahl, M. (2004). The interplay of beauty, goodness and usability in interactive products. *Human-Computer Interaction*, *19*(4), 319-349.

Hupcey, J. E., & et al. (2001). An exploration and advancement of the concept of trust. *Journal of Advanced Nursing*, *36*(2), 282-293.

Klein, G. A. (1989). Recognition-primed decisions. In W. B. Rouse (Ed.), *Advances in man-machine systems research (Vol. 5)* (pp. 47-92). Greenwich CT: JAI Press.

Klein, S. (1996). The configuration of inter-organisational relations. *European Journal of Information Systems*, *5*, 92-102.

Korczynski, M. (2000). The political economy of trust. *Journal of Management Studies*, *37*(1), 1-22.

Kramer, R. M. (1999). Trust and distrust in organizations: Emerging perspectives, enduring questions. *Annual Review of Psychology*, *50*, 556-557.

Larzelere, R. J., & Huston, T. L. (1980). The dyadic trust scale: Toward understanding interpersonal trust in close relationships. *Journal of Marriage and the Family*, *42*(August), 595-604.

Lavie, T., & Tractinsky, N. (2004). Assessing dimensions of perceived visual aesthetics of web sites. *International Journal of Human-Computer Studies*, *60*(3), 269-298.

Lee, J., & Moray, N. (1992). Trust, control strategies and allocation of function in human machine systems. *Ergonomics*, *35*(1), 1243-1270.

Lewis, J., & Weigert, A. (1985). Trust as a social reality. *Social Forces*, *63*, 967-985.

Luhmann, N. (1979). *Trust and power*. New York: Wiley.

McCarthy, J., & Wright, P. (2005). *Technology as experience*. Cambridge MA: MIT Press.

Nielsen, J. (2000). *Designing web usability: The practice of simplicity*. New Riders.

Nielsen, J., Molich, R., Snyder, S., & Farell, C. (2000). *E-commerce user experience: Trust*. Nielsen Norman Group.

Norman, D. A. (2004). *Emotional design: Why we love (or hate) everyday things*. New York: Basic Books.

Olson, G. M., & Olson J.S. (2000). Distance matters. *Human-Computer Interaction, 15*(2), 139-178.

Payne, J. W., Bettman, J. R., & Johnson, E. J. (1993). *The adaptive decision maker*. Cambridge: Cambridge University Press.

Riegelsberger, J., Sasse, M. A., & McCarthy, J. D. (2003). Shiny happy people building trust? Photos on e-commerce websites and consumer trust. In V. Bellotti, T. Erickson, G. Cockton, & P. Korhonen, (Eds). *CHI 2003 Conference Proceedings: Conference on Human Factors in Computing Systems, Fort Lauderdale FL 5-10 April 2003*, (pp. 121-128). New York: ACM Press.

Rotter, J. B. (1971). Generalised expectancies for interpersonal trust. *American Psychologist, 26*, 443-452.

Shapiro, S. (1987). The social control of interpersonal trust. *American Journal of Sociology, 93*, 623-658.

Sutcliffe, A. G., & De Angeli, A. (2005). Assessing interaction styles in web user interfaces. In M. F. Costabile, & F. Paterno, (Eds). *Proceedings: Human Computer Interaction - Interact 2005, Rome*, (pp. 405-417). Berlin: Springer Verlag.

Thoburn, J. T., & Takashima, M. (1993). Industrial performance: Lessons from Japanese subcontracting. *National Westminster Bank Quarterly Review* (February), 2-11.

Tomkins, C. (2001). Interdependencies, trust and information in relationships, alliances and networks. *Accounting, Organizations and Society, 26*(2), 161-191.

Williamson, O. E. (1993). Calculativeness, trust and economic organization. *Journal of Law and Economics, 36*, 453-486.

Zucker, L. G. (1986). The production of trust: Institutional sources of economic structure, 1840-1920. In B. M. Staw, & L. L. Cummings (Eds.), *Research in Organizational Behaviour* (pp. 8:55-111). Greenwich CT: JAI Press.

Dealing with Trust in eGov Services

Vassily Kritis

Intrasoft International, Chief Operation Officer, 40, rue Montoyer straat,
B-1000 Brussels, Belgium
Vassily.Kritis@intrasoft-intl.com

Public Organisations are generally concerned with delivery of services to taxpayers and members of a sovereign state, or with delivery and maintenance of frameworks that benefit the general public (traffic networks, protection against criminals, education, protection from foreign perpetrators, etc.). Traditionally and in most states, Public Organizations have been early adopters of Information and Communication Technologies (ICT) in their effort to increase efficiency and quality of services delivered to the public.

Typically, trust in general purpose public sector Computerised Information Systems is established by ensuring integrity, confidentiality, availability, authentication and non-repudiation of the various constituents. This applies to software, communications, data, hardware, as well as the physical/environmental aspects, staff, and remaining administrative/organisational aspects. It must however be observed that, in recent years, contemporary Public Sector Information Systems increasingly expand their scope into the management of public funds. In this particular area though, the process of establishing trust in related Public Information Systems must extend beyond the five trust elements mentioned above, and also address the prevention of fraud.

Fraud detection is the first step in building a Public Organisation's Information System fraud-prevention shield. Intelligent fraud detection is necessary so that additional overhead introduced, that might have a damaging effect on the relationship between citizens and the State, is kept to the minimum. Also, continuous fraud detection is necessary to identify (a) new cases previously unknown, (b) variants of previously detected frauds, or (c) cases which ceased to be relevant to the organisation. Fraud may have many guises, be that of (a) individual public administrators abusing their access authority on potential system loopholes, (b) multiple public administrators colluding in an institutionalised privilege, or (c) collusion between public administrators and outsiders.

In order to deal with fraud, a Public Organisation must identify and evaluate which fraud cases could be potentially conducted through its Information Systems. We address the need to monitor and fight fraud in an intelligent and continuous way by employing the process of Data Mining. By analysing information within an Information System, data mining helps identify patterns, relationships and recognisable indicators of fraudulent activities. To fight fraud successfully requires an understanding of both, (a) the fraud mechanisms themselves and (b) the potential of data mining in an Information System. Data mining techniques may be used proactively to review a business process to identify anomalies or operational risks and reactively to assist law enforcement agencies in their investigations.

E. Dubois and K. Pohl (Eds.): CAiSE 2006, LNCS 4001, pp. 18–19, 2006.
© Springer-Verlag Berlin Heidelberg 2006

By building data mining based fraud-detection systems within Governmental Information Systems we increase fraud deterrence and therefore enhance trust. We can further prevent fraud which cannot be easily deterred and promptly detect fraud which cannot be obviously prevented. Additionally we enable analysis and investigation of detected fraud to substantiate legal action against those responsible.

Trusted Interaction:
User Control and System Responsibilities in Interaction Design for Information Systems

Larry L. Constantine, IDSA

University of Madeira, Laboratory for Usage-centered Software Engineering
Constantine & Lockwood Ltd, 58 Kathleen Circle, Rowley, MA 01969, USA
lconstantine@foruse.com

Abstract. Trust emerges from interaction. If trust in information systems is to be promoted, then attention must be directed, at least in part, to interaction design. This presentation will explore issues of trust in the interactions between users and systems from the perspective of interaction design. It will consider a variety of pragmatic aspects in interaction design that impact user trust, including, predictability, interface stability, user control, and the match between expectations and performance. It will critically examine contemporary design practices, such as adaptive interfaces, in terms of their impact on user trust.

1 Introduction

Trust has long been recognized as a crucial element shaping human relationships and human interaction of all kinds. Where there is trust, activities proceed more smoothly, actions are more decisive, and people work with greater confidence. By reducing uncertainty under conditions of interdependence, trust engenders more efficient collaboration [1]. The absence of trust, in contrast, introduces inefficiencies, demanding added vigilance, encouraging protective and unproductive actions, and complicating interaction.

Trust, then, is a potentially important factor in human performance, not only in interpersonal relations but in our relationships with the technology we use in our everyday personal and work lives. When we do not trust the system we are using, we proceed more cautiously and hesitantly. We take additional time, often unnecessary, to think through and plan actions before proceeding, then double-check our actions. We protect ourselves from untrustworthy software with redundant copies of data or take circuitous and inefficient but seemingly safe paths to achieve our goals. Unable to count on "good behavior" from the software, we are reluctant to explore new features that might well prove useful to us.

It is not the purpose of this paper to offer yet another survey of the extensive literature on trust in human relations nor even to review that subset concerned with trust in commercial transactions. Rather the intent to is to explore the interconnected issues of user trust and user performance from the perspective of a designer, to gain insights from the broader field of human trust to draw implications regarding how we can design the interface between system and user to promote and sustain trust on the part

E. Dubois and K. Pohl (Eds.): CAiSE 2006, LNCS 4001, pp. 20–30, 2006.
© Springer-Verlag Berlin Heidelberg 2006

of users, and thereby enhance user performance. With this objective in mind, it is appropriate to begin with a focus on the problems of user interface design.

2 Designing Interaction

Although there is wide variability in how applicable terms are defined and employed, the design of user interfaces ultimately encompasses two broad areas, which may conveniently be referred to as presentation design and interaction design. Presentation design covers what is presented to the user, where it is presented, and how it is presented. As such, it involves the designer in decisions about what information and capabilities--the tools and materials available for use--are to be present, how these will be arranged or organized, and how they will look, feel, or sound to the user. For the graphical user interfaces of modern information systems, this often largely reduces to visual design, although other modalities of communication, such as sound, may also play some role. To an industrial designer devising products for consumer, business, or industrial use, many other factors may come into play, such as, weight and shape of devices and the tactile response of manual controls.

In recent years, professional interaction designers have laid claim to virtually the entire territory of external design, but, strictly speaking, interaction design is concerned with the design or planning of the interaction between user and system by way of the user interface. Thus interaction design covers not only how the user will interact with the system but how the system will respond to the user, including how the behavior of the various elements or pieces of the user interface are coupled or interdependent.

2.1 Designing for User Performance

User performance refers to the ability of users of a system to satisfy their intentions and achieve their objectives efficiently and reliably. One would expect that user performance would be at the heart of user interface design, and that was certainly the case with early work in ergonomics and human factors. However, throughout recent decades, a different perspective has dominated the design world, particularly for the Web and in products aimed at the general consumer population. Under the broad rubric of user-centered [2] or human-centered design, this perspective makes users and user satisfaction the central focus of design activities. Its purest and most extreme manifestations can be found in participatory design, which actively involves users as collaborators in the design process, and in user experience design, which broadens the focus of design to encompass every aspect of the user's experience with a system.

User-centered design elevates user satisfaction and user experience to primary importance. Potentially every aspect of users as human participants in use is of interest, including personality, attitudes, feelings, social context, cultural background, personal and work experience, and the like. Although user-centered design methods and techniques vary widely, the essence of all user-centered approaches is iterative design refinement grounded in a rich understanding of users gained through substantial initial user studies and driven through successive rounds of redesign by extensive feedback from user evaluations and user testing.

Growing dissatisfaction with the end results of this process has led to recent calls for a shift in focus from users to usage, from actors to activities [3]. Even the originator of the term "user-centered design," Donald Norman, has suggested in a highly controversial critique [4] that the current interpretation of user-centered design is flawed and even potentially harmful. He has called for an activity-centered design philosophy that looks more closely at what people are doing and are trying to do.

Activity-centered design in the sense used by Norman and usage-centered design [5] both seek to enhance user performance by devising user interfaces better fitted to the activities, tasks, and operations carried out by users. Users are primarily of interest for the roles they play in relationship to the system being design and for the parts they play in activities. The goal of the designer is to fully understand the tasks of users within these activities and to find the most effective way to support these tasks-broadly, in combination, and in detail.

From this point of view, trust in itself is of little interest except insofar as it improves performance in interaction with the system being designed. While this orientation may seem cold hearted to those steeped in the humanistic traditions of user-centered design, in truth it gets to the heart of why people use systems at all, namely, to accomplish something.

3 Elements of Human Trust

In human social contexts, trust is recognized as complex and variable, but it is, at least in part, an expression of individual propensity. Some of us are more prone to trust from the outset than are others. Trust also clearly depends on the specific interpersonal relationship. We trust some people more than we do others. It can also depend on the situation. You may trust a close colleague with sensitive commercial information but not with your personal health history. Finally, it may depend on particular kinds of social contexts. We are required by the setting to put our trust into certain people at certain times, such as when being treated by medical personnel in an emergency facility. Trust, then, is an attribute of the individual, the relationship, the situation, and the context.

Trust can be viewed from many different perspectives, and many disciplines in the human sciences have weighed in on the matter, including psychology, sociology, and economics. Some recent attempts have tried to distill the essence of this vast literature for various purposes [6, 7].

With an eye to application in electronic commerce, McKnight and Chervany [6] combined the sundry perspectives of diverse fields into an interdisciplinary model of trust concepts that includes dispositional trust, institutional trust (referring to both situations and social structures), and interpersonal trust. They developed a typology of trust based on analysis of some 65 definitions of trust from varied disciplines. These they ultimately distilled down to 16 characteristics organized into four conceptual categories--competence, predictability, benevolence, and integrity--plus a miscellaneous category of otherwise unclassified characteristics, of which the most salient is openness.

Also addressing the domain of electronic commerce on the Web, MIT trust guru Glen Urban advocates for trustworthy Web sites based on eight imperatives [8]:

transparency, quality of products and services, alignment with customers, helping customers help themselves, putting customers to work, comparing products to competitors, trust-based supply chain, and trust as top priority. While some of these clearly relate to business policy and practice rather than interaction design, others might be conceptually linked to interaction design.

Although commerce-oriented Web sites are certainly a special case of information systems, there is considerable overlap with work in other areas of application, such as the Tschannen-Moran and Hoy [8] catalog of facets of trust validated through factor analysis. These facets include: willingness to risk vulnerability, confidence, benevolence, reliability (consistency or predictability), competence, honesty, and openness.

4 Trust in User Interaction

Among the many facets of trust in human social situations, not all are equally salient for human-computer interaction or as likely to yield rich insights for interaction design. Some, like predictability, can be applied directly. Others, such as benevolence or integrity, require a certain amount of creative interpretation. Still others, such as, comparing products to competitors or trust-based supply chain, are limited to very specific contexts. And some, such as, alignment with customers or trust as top priority, are clearly beyond the ken of interaction design.

By reorganizing the elements of the theoretical models and focusing on those of clearest salience and most closely coupled to interaction design, four factors (Table 1) emerge as important in design for trusted interaction: predictability, transparency, competence, and benevolence.

Table 1. Salient factors in interaction design for trusted interaction

Factor	Characteristics
predictability	consistency, reliability, dependability
transparency	openness, visibility, accessibility, directness, clarity
competence	capability, completeness, reliability, accuracy, performance
benevolence	responsiveness, responsibility, safety

4.1 Predictability

"At its most basic level trust has to do with predictability, that is, consistency of behavior and knowing what to expect from others," [7]. A close reading of numerous sources suggests that predictability is arguably the most important single factor in promoting trust in interaction. We are apt to trust a system that does what we expect and what we ask, that is reliable and behaves as we anticipate, that does not suddenly do something different when we take a particular action. The behavior most damaging to trust is when a system does something unpredictable and unexplainable, particularly if it is unwanted or unasked.

Predictability is often conflated with consistency or even repetitiveness, but predictability is more than mere consistency. Even completely novel features and unprecedented functions can promote trust in the system and encourage exploration if they behave as the user predicts or anticipates [9].

4.2 Transparency

Transparency is the user interface parallel to honesty in human relationships. An interface is transparent when its content and organization are evident to the user, when features and information are visible or readily available where and when needed. Transparency means directness of communication, without obfuscation, misdirection, or disguise. It means that representations are direct, that What You See Is What You Get (WYSIWYG) [5].

Openness is the extent to which relevant information is not withheld [10, 11]. Does an application expose information to the user or keep it hidden? Is important information easily accessed, particularly information needed by users to make decisions and exercise their options? Is the underlying model or structure of the information evident? Does the user interface attempt to hide what is happening or what it does or does it expose these to the user?

Transparency is very closely related to the widely accepted design principle of visibility [5, 12] which admonishes designers to make clear to users what options are available and what actions are possible as what are the results of their actions.

4.3 Competence

Trust is affected by whether the other party possesses the competence or relevant capability to carry out their responsibilities in a relationship. In the context of information systems, competence means that the system is capable of doing what the user needs it to do, that it performs reliably and delivers accurate results. To be considered competent by the user, the system must be complete in the functionality that the user reasonably expects, without flaws or holes in functionality that would render it ineffective. It must perform with sufficient speed and dispatch to meet user needs with respect to timeliness.

4.4 Benevolence

In human relationships, trust depends to some degree on the perception of benevolence, that the other has our best interests at heart or at least is not malevolent. While the application of this concept to interaction design may seem to be a stretch, some aspects of benevolence carry over into human-computer interaction. Benevolence is dependent on respect, on respect for possessions, for boundaries, and for privacy. It has been described as "the confidence that one's well-being, or something one cares about, will be protected and not harmed" by the other [7]. Benevolence in this sense is obviously connected to the sense of safety and security, the assurance that the system will not bring harm to the user by discarding, corrupting, or destroying the user's data. Thus the manner in which a system handles user input and possessions, such as data files, is clearly an important contributor to perceived benevolence. A trustworthy system acts responsibly in handling user information. It does not require re-entry of already provided data. It does not unduly penalize the user for mistakes or make recovery from error difficult.

Benevolence also includes responsiveness (McKnight and Chervany). A system that is responsive to user needs, as expressed in user actions and choices, is, in an important sense, benevolent. Benevolence, like predictability, is linked to user control, the perception that the system will respond as directed and desired, taking responsibility for doing what the user asks when asked.

5 The Process of Trust

How is trust engendered or eroded? How do we, as users, come to trust or distrust the technology we use? For that matter, how do we, as colleagues, come to trust—or distrust—each other? Trust in tools or artifacts is not the same as trust in persons or institutions, but it does, to some large degree, emerge from the same foundations.

A precondition of trust is interdependence, where each party to an interaction depends on the other in some manner [13]. This is clearly the case in human-computer interaction: the system obviously depends on the user for input and direction, while the user depends on the system to perform as requested and provide feedback and the desired results.

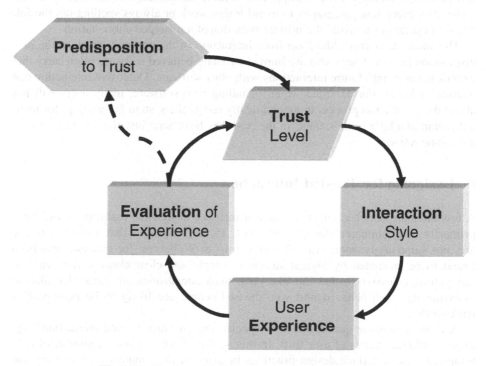

Fig. 1. Feedback model of trust in user-system interaction

Apart from any pre-existing propensity, trust emerges from experience. The evolution of trust in human-computer interaction can be expressed in a simple feedback model with five elements: predisposition, trust level, interaction style, user experience, and evaluation. As represented in Figure 1, the level of trust at any given time is a function of the evaluation of experience in interaction with the system as influenced by the prior level of trust.

Users bring to their first encounter with any system a predisposition to trust that is compounded of many factors, including personality, habitual orientation, and prior experience with other software. This predisposition to trust determines the initial level of trust and shapes the style of early interaction. Level of trust in turn influences interaction experience, as it affects such things as the speed of interaction, propensity to explore new or alternative paths, and use of self-protective mechanisms, all of which can impact system behavior and, consequently, user experience. High levels of initial distrust may slow or even preclude the development of trust.

It is unlikely that most users consciously or deliberately evaluate their experience and thereby alter their level of trust, yet it seems evident that users are typically aware of their level of trust regarding specific software or software in general. ("I find Excel very unpredictable. I can never trust it to do what I expect." "In general, I don't trust new releases." "I think that [XYZ] is a firewall I can trust.")

One manifestation of distrust is the emergence of defensive interaction involving self-protective measures. An example of defensive interaction is compulsively saving a file after every few paragraphs to avoid losing work or always spelling out the full name of operations to avoid the misinterpretation of a mistyped abbreviation.

The model also closes the loop from interaction in the particular back to the predisposition to trust. Users who are burned by badly behaved software often carry that experience over into future interactions with other software. Defensive interaction can become habitual. For example, when installing new software, many users will not allow the installation process to automatically restart the system but will opt for manual restart at a later time because in the past they have seen installations hang during automatic restart.

6 Designing for Trusted Interaction

A few attempts have been made to tie user interface design and usability to user trust, primarily in e-commerce (for example, [14, 15, 16]). Systems that are easier to use are, not surprisingly, more trusted. Initial trust in Web sites, for example, has been found to be promoted by logical structure, simple and clear classification, ease of navigation, consistency, and the like [16]. Such conclusions are somewhat akin to asserting that well-behaved and well-dressed people are likely to be perceived as trustworthy.

A more interesting question is how specific design practices and interaction techniques influence facets of user trust. In this section, I will consider a number of contemporary user interface design practices in terms of their impact on user trust and user performance.

6.1 Adaptive and Adaptable Interfaces

Stability of the user interface is a critical contributor to predictability. When the same elements are always located in the same place and do the same thing, the interface is prima facie more predictable, contributing to user trust and thus enhancing user performance. This is not just a matter of consistency in the traditional sense of similarity of appearance and consistent placement of objects within the user interface; it is also a matter of interaction design.

Adaptive user interfaces are a popular modern style of interaction design. Adaptive interfaces change form and behavior automatically in response to user actions, in principle to adapt dynamically to ever changing tasks and context of use. Adaptable interfaces, by way of contrast, support end-user tailoring of the user interface. Where adaptive user interfaces attempt to anticipate user needs and configure the user interface for the user, adaptable user interfaces leave changes in the configuration under the control of the user.

The popular application suite Microsoft Office provides examples of both kinds of designs. In addition to being able to alter dozens of predetermined options, such as whether or not to check spelling and grammar continuously, users can also enter a special mode that allows them to customize the configuration of menus and toolbars, even to define new toolbars. This is an example of an adaptable interface.

The adaptive menu feature of Microsoft Office is an example, as the name suggests, of adaptive interface design. On initial installation, the default behavior of Office menus is to display short, incomplete lists of commands when a menu is opened, as seen in Figure 2(a). After a short delay or when the user clicks at the bottom of the menu, the complete list of available commands appears, as in Figure 2(b). Which commands display when a menu is first opened depends on what selections the user has made previously. Selecting a command not initially displayed will promote it to the initial list. Commands that are used infrequently automatically disappear from the short list. Thus, not only does each menu change between two distinct forms, short and long, with different arrangements of commands, but the contents and arrangement of the short form seen first can vary from use to use, as seen in Figure 2(c).

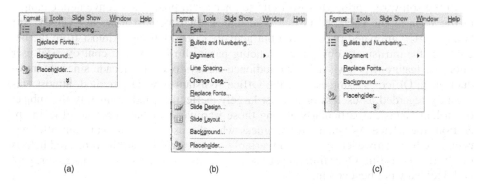

(a)   (b)   (c)

Fig. 2. Adaptive menus in Microsoft Office. Initial short list *(a)*, full list *(b)*, and short list after some use *(c)*.

The design rationale for this approach is that it is supposed to simplify use by adjusting the menu content to the user's actual pattern of usage. The impact on user trust and performance is quite different, however. Adaptive interfaces not only reduce stability and predictability, but they usurp user control. Users describe their experience with adaptive menus in terms of what to them is utter unpredictability. ("I never know what I am going to see when I open a menu. Something that was one place the last time I used it is now suddenly someplace else or hidden where I have to wait for it.")

Performance is degraded because users must actually read down the menu list on every use in order to select the right command. Moreover, they never gain the efficiencies of learned reflexes, such as clicking halfway down the Tools menu to track changes. The constantly changing content and organization also reduces the reliability of interaction by significantly increasing the likelihood of making the wrong selection.

In informal audience surveys of thousands of students, professionals, and business people over recent years, only a handful of regular Office users report finding the feature to be useful. The vast majority have turned it off, and not a few have reported trying unsuccessfully to stop the behavior. (The feature was not originally indexed as such within the help system, and the is not where most users expect it within the Tools | Options... dialog but under Tools | Customize... on the Options tab.)

6.2 Wizards, Agents, and Pseudo-intelligence

Leaving aside the issue of predictability and interface stability, to be effective, adaptive interfaces must correctly anticipate user needs. Often this requires some manner of software intelligence, usually in the form of rules-based or heuristic inference. In principle, a sufficiently intelligent software agent might successfully analyze user actions and anticipate needs. In practice, the limited pseudo-intelligence provided by the software is rarely if ever helpful. The problem is, of course, that not even human beings are very good at anticipating the real needs of others, even in relatively simple situations. For that matter, in the real physical world and in real human relationships, accurate anticipation is not always experienced as a good thing. ("I'd rather do it myself.") People can find it disconcerting to have their every need or intention anticipated through behind-the-scenes manipulation [17].

In the software world, Microsoft Office once again provides a convenient example in the form of the so-called Office Assistant, known to most users as "Clippy" (or "that (*)#@^ animated paper clip") but actually named Clippit. Almost from the beginning, the intrusively obsequious dancing paper clip has been a controversial user interface feature. My own informal audience surveys over the decade since its introduction in Office '97 suggest that the Office Assistant is widely reviled, almost universally regarded as useless or at least largely ineffective, and frequently the subject of violent fantasies, particularly among those who were unable to get rid of it. In operation, the Office Assistant tries to guess what the user is doing and then offer appropriate help. However, it almost invariably guesses wrong and the proffered help is rarely if ever useful. Over time, most users come to see most such agents as arrogant and decidedly not benevolent.

Even where users are highly dependent on pseudo-intelligent agents, such as in automatic email spam filters, there remains a high level of distrust, particularly as false positives, in which legitimate and potentially important messages get classified as spam, require manual review and recovery by the user.

7 Paternalism and User Control

To some extent, many modern user interface design practices are experienced by users as arrogant, manifesting an attitude of "we know better than you." Modern information systems often hoard information and hide it from the user. They bury controls under layers of wizards and dialogs, menus and property sheets, all in the name of protecting users from themselves.

Truly benevolent design is not paternalistic. It is built on trust and grounded in respect, respect for the integrity and the ability of the user. It manifests itself in not only the architecture of interaction but also small details of design and programming practices, such as never discarding user input. Nothing erodes trust more quickly than for users to click on the back button within a browser only to discover a form newly cleared of all their personal data so carefully entered. To treat with cavalier disrespect what the user has worked hard to create not only violates trust but obviously contributes to inefficiency, inaccurate or incomplete data, and even lost customers.

Trust is reciprocal. If users are to trust systems, system designers need to learn how to trust users, to return control to users and allow them to make their own decisions about what to do, where to do it, and how. This is not a call for a return to the intimidating and confusing tabula rasa of the command-line interface of yesteryear. Rather it is a suggestion that designers and developers may have become too arrogant in assuming that users are stupid and incapable, and that "we" know best.

In truth, all too often users have been made stupid and incapable by the ill-conceived tools we have given them. Rather than "dumbing down" interfaces with so-called wizards that work no magic or arrogating user prerogatives by embedding in software more so-called intelligence that is at best profoundly naïve and at worst maliciously misguided, we should instead be designing better tools. Tools do not do the work of the user. Good tools serve the user—and thereby earn the user's trust—by allowing and enabling activity, use, performance. To this end, to design trustworthy interaction, we must better understand and apply knowledge of how tools are used in the activities of users.

References

1. Arrow, K. J.: The Limits of Organization. Norton, New York (1974)
2. Norman, D., and Draper, S.: User Centered System Design: New Perspectives on Human-Computer Interaction. Erlbaum (1986)
3. Constantine, L. L.: Beyond User-Centered Design and User Experience. Cutter IT Journal, Vol. 17 No. 2, (2004)
4. Norman D.: Human-Centered Design Considered Harmful. Interactions, Vol. 12, No. 4, (2005) 14-19
5. Constantine, L. L., and Lockwood, L. A. D.: Software for Use: A Practical Guide to the Models and Methods of Usage-Centered Design. Addison-Wesley Reading, MA (1999)

6. McKnight, D. H., Chervany, N. L.: What Trust Means in E-Commerce Customer Relationships: An Interdisciplinary Conceptual Typology. International Journal of Electronic Commerce, Vol. 6, No. 2, (2001) 35–59

7. Tschannen-Moran, M. and Hoy, W. K.: A conceptual and empirical analysis of trust in schools. Review of Educational Research, Vol. 71 (2000) 547-593.

8. Urban, G. L. The Trust Imperative. MIT Sloan School of Management Working Paper 4302-03 (2003)

9. Constantine, L. L., and Lockwood, L. A. D.: Instructive Interaction: Making Innovative Interfaces Self-Teaching. User Experience, Vol. 1, No. 3, Winter (2002)

10. Butler, J. K. & Cantrell, R.S.: A Behavioral Decision Theory Approach to Modeling Dyadic Trust in Superiors and Subordinates. Psychological Reports, Vol. 55 (1984), 81-105

11. Hosmer, L.T.: Trust: The Connecting Link Between Organizational Theory and Philosophical Ethics. Academy of Management Review, Vol. 20, (1995) 379–403.

12. Norman, D.: The Psychology of Everyday Things.

13. Rousseau, D., Sitkin, S. B., Burt, R., and Camerer, C.: Not So Different After All: A Cross-Discipline View of Trust. The Academy of Management Review, Vol. 23, No. 3 (1998) 393-404

14. Kim, J. Towards the Construction of Customer Interfaces for Cyber-Shopping Malls. Electronic Markets, Vol. 7, No. 2 (1997) 12-15

15. Egger, F. N.: Consumer Trust in E-Commerce: From Psychology to Interaction Design. In J. Prins (ed.) Trust in Electronic Commerce. Kluwer International (2002)

16. Zhou, X., and Liu, X.: Effective User Interface Design for Consumer Trust: Two Case Studies. Masters Thesis. Lulea University of Technology, Lulea, Sweden (2005)

17. Johnson, A.: Hotels Take 'Know Your Customer' to New Level. The Wall Street Journal, February 8, D1 (2006)

Security

Designing Security Requirements Models Through Planning*

Volha Bryl, Fabio Massacci, John Mylopoulos, and Nicola Zannone

Department of Information and Communication Technology,
University of Trento - Italy
{bryl, massacci, jm, zannone}@dit.unitn.it

Abstract. The quest for designing secure and trusted software has led to refined Software Engineering methodologies that rely on tools to support the design process. Automated reasoning mechanisms for requirements and software verification are by now a well-accepted part of the design process, and model driven architectures support the automation of the refinement process. We claim that we can further push the envelope towards the automatic exploration and selection among design alternatives and show that this is concretely possible for Secure Tropos, a requirements engineering methodology that addresses security and trust concerns. In Secure Tropos, a design consists of a network of actors (agents, positions or roles) with delegation/permission dependencies among them. Accordingly, the generation of design alternatives can be accomplished by a planner which is given as input a set of actors and goals and generates alternative multiagent plans to fulfill all given goals. We validate our claim with a case study using a state-of-the-art planner.

1 Introduction

The design of secure and trusted software that meets stakeholder needs is an increasingly hot issue in Software Engineering (SE). This quest has led to refined Requirements Engineering (RE) and SE methodologies so that security concerns can be addressed during the early stages of software development (e.g. Secure Tropos vs i*/Tropos, UMLsec vs UML, etc.). Moreover, industrial software production processes have been tightened to reduce the number of existing bugs in operational software systems through code walkthroughs, security reviews etc. Further, the complexity of present software is such that all methodologies come with tools for automation support.

The tricky question in such a setting is what kind of automation? Almost fifty years ago the idea of actually deriving code directly from the specification (such as that advocated in [22]) started a large programme for deductive program synthesis,[1] that is still

---

* We thank Alfonso Gerevini and Alessandro Saetti for the support on the use of LPG-td. This work was partly supported by the projects RBNE0195K5 FIRB-ASTRO, RBAU01P5SS FIRB-SECURITY, 016004 IST-FP6-FET-IP-SENSORIA, 27587 IST-FP6-IP-SERENITY, 27004 IST-FP6-STREP-S3MS, 2003-S116-00018 PAT-MOSTRO, 1710SR-B/P PAT-STAMPS.

[1] A system goal together with a set of axioms are specified in a formal specification language. Then the system goal is proved from the axioms using a theorem prover. A program for achieving the goal is extracted from the proof of the theorem.

E. Dubois and K. Pohl (Eds.): CAiSE 2006, LNCS 4001, pp. 33–47, 2006.
© Springer-Verlag Berlin Heidelberg 2006

active now [5, 11, 25, 29]. However, proposed solutions are largely domain-specific, require considerable expertise on the part of their users, and in some cases do not actually guarantee that the synthesized program will meet all requirements stated up front [11].

Another approach is to facilitate the work of the designer by supporting tedious aspects of software development by automating the design refinement process. This approach underlies Model Driven Architectures (MDA) [27], which focuses on the (possibly automatic) transformation from one system model to another. Tools supporting MDA exist and are used in the Rational Unified Process for software development in UML. Yet, the state-of-the-art is still not satisfactory [30].

Such approaches only cover part of the work of the designer. We advocate that there is another activity where the support of automation could be most beneficial [20]:

> "Exploring alternative options is at the heart of the requirements and design processes."

Indeed, in most SE methodologies the designer has tools to report and verify the final choices (be it goal models in KAOS, UML classes, or Java code), but not actually the possibility of automatically exploring design alternatives (i.e. the *potential choices* that the designer may adopt for the fulfillment of system actors' objectives) and finding a satisfactory one. Conceptually, this automatic selection of alternatives is done in deductive program synthesis: theorem provers select appropriate axioms to establish the system goal. Instead, we claim that the automatic selection of alternatives should and indeed can be done during the very early stages of software development. After all, the automatic generation of alternatives is most beneficial and effective during these stages.

There are good reasons for this claim. Firstly, during early stages the design space is large, and a good choice can have significant impact on the whole development project. Supporting the selection of alternatives could lead to a more thorough analysis of better quality designs with respect to security and trust. Secondly, requirements models are by construction simpler and more abstract than implementation models (i.e. code). Therefore, techniques for automated reasoning about alternatives at the early stages of the development process may succeed where automated software synthesis failed.

Since our overall goal is to design a secure system we have singled out the Secure Tropos methodology [16] as the target for our work. Its primitive concepts include those of Tropos and i* [7], but also concepts that address security concerns, such as ownership, permission and trust. Further, the framework already supports the designer with automated reasoning tools for the verification of requirements as follows:

1. Graphical capture of the requirements for the organization and the system-to-be,
2. Formal verification of the functional and security requirements by
   – completion of the model drawn by the designer with axioms (a process hidden to the designer)
   – checking the model for the satisfaction of formal properties corresponding to specific security or design patterns

In this framework (as in many other similar RE and SE frameworks) the selection of the alternatives is left to the designer. We will show that we can do better.

Indeed, in Tropos (resp. Secure Tropos) requirements are conceived as networks of functional dependencies (resp. delegation of execution) among actors (organizational/ human/software agents, positions and roles) for goals, tasks and resources. Every dependency (resp. delegation of execution) also involves two actors, where one actor depends on the other for the delivery of a resource, the fulfillment of a goal, or the execution of a task. Intuitively, these can be seen as *actions* that the designer has ascribed to the members of the organization and the system-to-be. As suggested by Gans et al. [14] the task of designing such networks can then be framed as a planning problem for multi-agent systems: selecting a suitable possible design corresponds to selecting a plan that satisfies the prescribed or described goals of human or system actors. Secure Tropos adds to the picture also the notion of delegation of permission and various notions of trust.

In this paper we show that it is possible to use an off-the-shelf planner to select among the potential dependencies the actual ones that will constitute the final choice of the requirements engineer. If a planner is already able to deliver good results then this looks a promising avenue for transferring the technique to complex industry-level case studies where a customized automated reasoning tool might be very handy. At the same time, if the problem is not trivial, not all planners will be able to deliver and indeed this turned out to be the case. The techniques we use are sufficiently powerful to cope with security requirements as well as functional requirements, but we concentrate here on their applicability to a security setting where an automated support for the selection of potentially conflicting alternatives is more urgent. The application of the same planning techniques to the overall software development phases can be found in [3].

In this work we have not focused on optimal designs: after all, human designers do not aim for optimality in their designs. As noted by Herbert Simon in his lecture on a "Science of Design" [31] what makes humans effective (in comparison to machines) is their ability to identify a satisficing design as opposed to an optimal one.

Of course, we assume that the designer remains in the loop: designs generated by the planner are suggestions to be refined, amended and approved by the designer. The planner is a(nother) support tool intended to facilitate the design process.

The rest of the paper is structured as follows. Section 2 explains Secure Tropos concepts and describes the requirements verification process. In Sections 3, 4 and 5 the planning approach to the system design is introduced and explained, , while in Section 6 the implementation of our approach is presented. Finally, in Sections 7 and 8 a brief overview of related work is presented and conclusions are drawn.

2 Secure Tropos

Secure Tropos [16] is a RE methodology for modeling and analyzing functional and security requirements, extending the Tropos methodology [7]. This methodology is tailored to describe both the system-to-be and its organizational environment starting with early phases of the system development process. The main advantage of this approach is that one can capture not only the *what* or the *how*, but also the *why* a security mechanism should be included in the system design. In particular, Secure Tropos deals with business-level (as opposed to low-level) security requirements. The focus of such requirements includes, but is not limited to, how to build trust among different partners in a virtual organization and trust management. Although their name does *not* mention security, they are generally regarded as part of the overall security framework.

Secure Tropos uses the concepts of actor, goal, task, resource and social relations for defining entitlements, capabilities and responsibilities of actors. An *actor* is an intentional entity that performs actions to achieve goals. A *goal* represents an objective of an actor. A *task* specifies a particular sequence of actions that should be executed for satisfying a goal. A *resource* represents a physical or an informational entity.

Actors' desires, entitlements, capabilities and responsibilities are defined through social relations. In particular, Secure Tropos supports *requesting, ownership, provisioning, trust*, and *delegation*. Requesting identifies desires of actors. Ownership identifies the legitimate owner of a goal, a task or a resource, that has full authority on access and disposition of his possessions. Provisioning identifies actors who have the capabilities to achieve a goal, execute a task or deliver a resource. We demonstrate the use of these concepts through the design of a Medical IS for the payment of medical care.[2]

Example 1. The Health Care Authority (HCA) is the "owner" of the goal provide medical care; that is, it is the only one that can decide who can provide it and through what process. On the other hand, Patient wants this goal fulfilled. This goal can be AND-decomposed into two subgoals: provisioning of medical care and payment for medical care. The Healthcare Provider has the capability for the provisioning of medical care, but it should wait for authorization from HCA before doing it.

Delegation of execution is used to model situations where an actor (the delegator) delegates the responsibilities to achieve a goal, execute a task, or delivery a resource to another actor (the delegatee) since he does not have the capability to provide one of above by himself. It corresponds to the actual choice of the design. *Trust of execution* represents the belief of an actor (the trustor) that another actor (the trustee) has the capabilities to achieve a goal, execute a task or deliver a resource. Essentially, delegation is an action due to a decision, whereas trust is a mental state driving such decision. Tropos dependency can be defined in terms of trust and delegation [17]. Thus, a Tropos model can be seen as a particular Secure Tropos model. In order to model both functional and security requirements, Secure Tropos introduces also relations involving permission. *Delegation of permission* is used when in the domain of analysis there is a formal passage of authority (e.g. a signed piece of paper, a digital credential, etc.). Essentially, this relation is used to model scenarios where an actor authorizes another actor to achieve a goal, execute a task, or deliver a resource. It corresponds to the actual choice of the design. *Trust of permission* represents the belief of an actor that another actor will not misuse the goal, task or resource.

Example 2. The HCA must choose between different providers for the welfare management for executives of a public institution. Indeed, since they have a special private-law contract, they can qualify for both the INPDAP and INPDAI[3] welfare schemes. The

---

[2] An extended description of the example is provided in [4].

[3] INPDAP (Istituto Nazionale di Previdenza per i Dipendenti dell'Amministrazione Pubblica) and INPDAI (Istituto Nazionale di Previdenza per i Dirigenti di Aziende Industriali) are two Italian national welfare institutes.

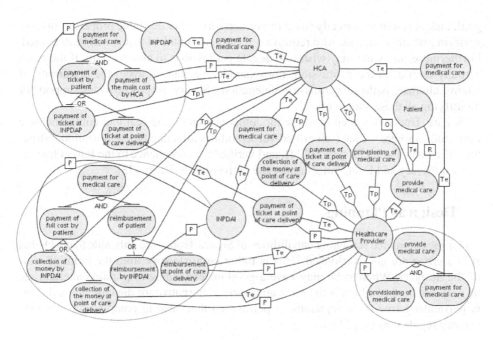

Fig. 1. Secure Tropos model

INPDAP scheme requires that the Patient partially pays for medical care (with a ticket) and the main cost is directly covered by the HCA. On the contrary, the INPDAI scheme requires that the Patient pays in advance the full cost of medical care and then gets reimbursed. Once an institution has decided the payment scheme, this will be part of the requirements to be passed onto the next stages of system development. Obviously, the choice of the alternative may have significant impacts on other parts of the design.

Figure 1 summarizes Examples 1 and 2 in terms of a Secure Tropos model. In this diagram, actors are represented as circles and goals as ovals. Labels **O**, **P** and **R** are used for representing ownership, provisioning and requesting relations, respectively. Finally, we represent trust of permission and trust of execution relationships as edges respectively labelled **Tp** and **Te**.

Once a stage of the *modeling phase* is concluded, Secure Tropos provides mechanisms for the verification of the model [16]. This means that the design process iterates over the following steps:

- model the system;
- translate the model into a set of clauses (this is done automatically);
- verify whether appropriate design or security patterns are satisfied by the model.

Through this process, we can verify the compliance of the model with desirable properties. For example, it can be checked whether the delegator trusts that the delegatee will achieve a goal, execute a task or deliver a resource (trust of execution), or will use a goal, task or resource correctly (trust of permission). Other desirable properties involve verifying whether an actor who requires a service, is confident that it will be delivered. Furthermore, an owner may wish to delegate permissions to an actor only if the latter actually does need the permission. For example, we want to avoid the possibility of having alternate paths of permission delegations. Secure Tropos provides support for identifying all these situations.

Secure Tropos has been used for modeling and analyzing real and comprehensive case studies where we have identified vulnerabilities affecting the organizational structure of a bank and its IT system [24], and verified the compliance to the Italian legislation on Privacy and Data Protection by the University of Trento [23].

3   Design as Planning

So far the automated reasoning capabilities of Secure Tropos are only able to check that subtle errors are not overlooked. This is rather unsatisfactory from the point of view of the designer. Whereas he may have a good understanding of possible alternatives, he may not be sure which is the most appropriate alternative for the case at hand. This is particularly true for delegations of permission that need to comply with complex privacy regulations (see [23]).

Example 3. Figures 2(a) and 2(c) present fragments of Figure 1, that point out the potential choices of the design. The requirements engineer has identified trust relations between the HCA and INPDAP and INPDAI. However, when passing the requirements onto the next stage only one alternative has to be selected because that will be the system that is chosen. Figures 2(b) and 2(d) present the actual choices corresponding to the potential choices presented in Figures 2(a) and 2(c), respectively.

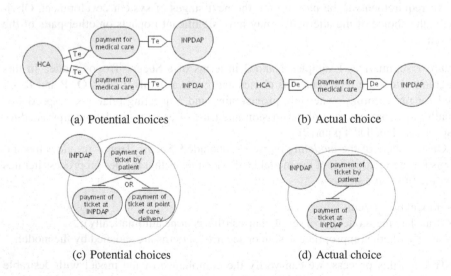

(a) Potential choices   (b) Actual choice

(c) Potential choices   (d) Actual choice

Fig. 2. Design Alternatives

Here, we want to support the requirements engineer in the selection of the best alternative by changing the design process as follows:

- Requirements analysis phase
  - Identify system actors along with their desires, capabilities and entitlements, and possible ways of goal decomposition.
  - Define trust relationships among actors both in terms of execution and permission.
- Design phase
  - The space of design alternatives is automatically explored to identify delegation of execution/permission.
  - Depending on the time/importance of the goal the designer may settle for satisficing solutions [31] or ask for an optimal solution.

To support the designer in the process of selecting the best alternative we advocate a planning approach which recently has proved to be applicable in the field of automatic Web service composition [6].

The basic idea behind the planning approach is to automatically determine the course of actions (i.e. a plan) needed to achieve a certain goal where an action is a transition rule from one state of the system to another [34, 28]. Actions are described in terms of preconditions and effects: if the precondition is true in the current state of the system, then the action is performed. As consequence of the action, the system will be in a new state where the effect of the action is true. Thus, once we have described the initial state of the system, the goal that should be achieved (i.e. the desired final state of the system), and the set of possible actions that actors can perform, the solution of the planning problem is the (not necessarily optimal) sequence of actions that allows the system to reach the desired state from the initial state.

In order to cast the design process as a planning problem, we need to address the following question: *which are the "actions" in a software design?* When drawing the Secure Tropos model, the designer assigns the execution of goals from one actor to another, delegates permission and – last but not least – identifies appropriate goal refinements among selected alternatives. These are the actions to be used by the planner in order to fulfill all initial actor goals.

4   Planning Domain

The planning approach requires a specification language to represent the planning domain and the states of the system. Different types of logics could be applied for this purpose, e.g. first order logic is often used to describe the planning domain with conjunctions of literals[4] specifying the states of the system. We find this representation particularly useful for modeling real case studies. Indeed, when considering security requirements at enterprise level, one must be able to reason both at the class level (e.g. the CEO, the CERT team member, the employee of the HR department) and at the instance level (e.g. John Doe and Mark Doe playing those roles).

---

[4] Let p be a predicate symbol with arity n, and $t_1, \ldots, t_n$ be its corresponding arguments. $p(t_1, \ldots, t_n)$ is called an *atom*. The expression *literal* denotes an atom or its negation.

Table 1. Primitive Predicates

Goal Properties
AND_decomposition$_n$(g : goal, g$_1$: goal, . . . , g$_n$: goal)
OR_decomposition$_n$(g : goal, g$_1$: goal, . . . , g$_n$: goal)
Actor Properties
provides(a : actor, g : goal)
requests(a : actor, g : goal)
owns(a : actor, g : goal)
Actor Relations
trustexe(a : actor, b : actor, g : goal)
trustper(a : actor, b : actor, g : goal)

Table 2. Actions

Basic Actions
DelegateExecution(a : actor, b : actor, g : goal)
DelegatePermission(a : actor, b : actor, g : goal)
Satisfy(a : actor, g : goal)
AND_Refine$_n$(a : actor, g : goal, g$_1$: goal, . . . , g$_n$: goal)
OR_Refine$_n$(a : actor, g : goal, g$_1$: goal, . . . , g$_n$: goal)
Absence of Trust
Negotiate(a : actor, b : actor, g : goal)
Contract(a : actor, b : actor, g : goal)
DelegateExecution_under_suspicion(a : actor, b : actor, g : goal)
Fulfill(a : actor, g : goal)
Evaluate(a : actor, g : goal)

The planning domain language should provide support for specifying:

– the initial state of the system,
– the goal of the planning problem,
– the actions that can be performed,
– the axioms of background theory.

Table 1 presents the predicates used to describe the *initial state of the system* in terms of actor and goal properties, and social relations among actors. We use

– AND/OR_decomposition to describe the possible decomposition of a goal;
– provides, requests and owns to indicate that an actor has the capabilities to achieve a goal, desires the achievement of a goal, and is the legitimate owner of a goal, respectively;
– trustexe and trustper to represent trust of execution and trust of permission relations, respectively.

The desired state of the system (or *goal of the planning problem*) is described through the conjunction of predicates done derived from the requesting relation in the initial state. Essentially, for each request(a,g) we need to derive done(g).

By contrast, an *action* represents an activity to accomplish a goal. We list them in Table 2 and define them in terms of preconditions and effects as follows:

Satisfy. The satisfaction of goals is an essential action. Following the definition of goal satisfaction given in [16], we say that an actor satisfies a goal only if the actor wants and is able to achieve the goal, and – last but not least – he is entitled to achieve it. The effect of this action is the fulfillment of the goal.

DelegateExecution. An actor may not have enough capabilities to achieve assigned goals by himself, and so he has to delegate their execution to other actors. We represent this passage of responsibilities through action **DelegateExecution.** It is performed only if the delegator requires the fulfillment of the goal and trusts that the delegatee will achieve it. Its effect is that the delegator does not worry any more about the fulfillment of this goal after delegating it since he has delegated its execution to a trusted actor. Furthermore, the delegatee takes the responsibility for the fulfillment of the goal and so it becomes a his own desire. Notice that we do not care how the delegatee satisfies the goal (e.g. by his own capabilities or by further delegation). It is up to the delegatee to decide it.

DelegatePermission. In the initial state of the system, only the owner of a goal is entitled to achieve it. However, this does not mean that he wants it or has the capabilities to achieve it. On the contrary, in the system there may be some actors that want that goal and others that can achieve it. Thus, the owner could decide to authorize trusted actors to achieve the goal. The formal passage of authority takes place when the owner issues a certificate that authorizes another actor to achieve the goal. We represent the act of issuing a permission through action **Delegate-Permission** which is performed only if the delegator has the permission on the goal and trusts that the delegatee will not misuse the goal. The consequence of this action is to grant rights (on the goal) to the delegatee, that, in turn, can re-delegate them to other trusted actors.

AND/OR_Refine. An important aspect of Secure Tropos is goal refinement. In particular, the framework supports two types of refinement: OR_decomposition, which suggests the list of alternative ways to satisfy the goal, and AND-decomposition, which refines the goals into subgoals which all are to be satisfied in order to satisfy the initial goal. We introduce actions **AND_Refine** and **OR_Refine**. Essentially, **AND_Refine** and **OR_Refine** represent the action of refining a goal along a possible decomposition. An actor refines a goal only if he actually need it. Thus, a precondition of **AND_Refine** and **OR_Refine** is that the actor requests the fulfillment of the initial goal. A second precondition determines the way in which the goal is refined. The effect of **AND_Refine** and **OR_Refine** is that the actor who refines the goal focuses on the fulfillment of subgoals instead of the fulfillment of the initial goal.

In addition to actions we define *axioms* in the planning domain. These are rules that hold in every state of the system and are used to complete the description of the current state. They are used to propagate actors and goal properties along goal refinement: a goal is satisfied if all its AND-subgoals or at least one of the OR-subgoals are satisfied. Moreover, axioms are used to derive and propagate entitlements. Since the owner is entitled to achieve his goals, execute his tasks and access his resources, we need to propagate actors' entitlements top-down along goal refinement.

5 Delegation and Contract

Many business and social studies have emphasized the key role played by trust as a necessary condition for ensuring the success of organizations [9]. Trust is used to build collaboration between humans and organizations since it is a necessary antecedent for cooperation [1]. However, common sense suggests that fully trusted domains are simply idealizations. Actually, many domains require that actors who do not have the capabilities to fulfill their objectives, must delegate the execution of their goals to other actors even if they do not trust the delegatees. Accordingly, much work in recent years has focused on the development of frameworks capable of coping with lack of trust, sometimes by introducing an explicit notion of distrust [14, 17].

The presence (or lack) of trust relations among system actors particularly influences the strategies to achieve a goal [21]. In other words, the selection of actions to fulfill a goal changes depending on the belief of the delegator about the possible behavior of the delegatee. In particular, if the delegator trusts the delegatee, the first is confident that the latter will fulfill the goal and so he does not need to verify the actions performed by the delegatee. On the contrary, if the delegator does not trust the delegatee, the first wants some form of control on the behavior of the latter.

Different solutions have been proposed to ensure for the delegator the fulfillment of his objectives. A first batch of solutions comes from transaction cost economics and contract theories that view a contract as a basis for trust [35]. This approach assumes that a delegation must occur only in the presence of trust. This implies that the delegator and the delegatee have to reach an agreement before delegating a service. Essentially, the idea is to use a contract to define precisely what the delegatee should do and so establish trust between the delegator and the delegatee. Other theories propose models where effective performance may occur also in the absence of trust [12]. Essentially, they argue that various control mechanisms can ensure the effective fulfillment of actors's objectives.

In this paper we propose a solution for delegation of execution that borrows ideas from both approaches. The case for delegation of permission is similar. The process of delegating in the absence of trust is composed of two phases: *establishing trust* and *control*. The establishing trust phase consists of a sequence of actions, namely Negotiate and Contract. In Negotiate the parties negotiate the duties and responsibilities accepted by each party after delegation. The postcondition is an informal agreement representing the initial and informal decision of parties to enter into a partnership. During the execution of Contract the parties formalize the agreement established during negotiation. The postcondition of Contract is a trust "under suspicion" relation between the delegator and the delegatee. Once the delegator has delegated the goal and the delegatee has fulfilled the goal, the first wants to verify if the latter has really satisfied his objective. This control is performed using action Evaluation. Its postcondition is the "real" fulfillment of the goal. To support this solution we have introduced some additional actions (last part of Table 2) to distinguish the case in which the delegation is based on trust from the case in which the delegator does not trust the delegatee.

Sometimes establishing new trust relations might be more convenient than extending existing trust relations. A technical "side-effect" of our solution is that it is possible to control the length of trusted delegation chains. Essentially, every action has a unit cost. Therefore, refining an action into sub-actions corresponds to increasing the cost associated with the action. In particular, refining the delegation action in absence of trust guarantees that the framework first tries to delegate to trusted actors, but if the delegation chain results too long the system can decide to establish a new trust relation rather than to follow the entire trust chain.

Need-to-know property of a design decision states that the owner of a goal, a task or a resource wants that only the actors who need permission on its possession are authorized to access it. Essentially, only the actor that achieves a goal, executes a task or delivers a resource, and the actors that belong to the delegation of permission chain from the owner to the provider should be entitled to access this goal, task or resource. Thus, we want to obtain a plan where only the actions that contribute to reaching the desired state occur, so that if any action is removed from the plan it no longer satisfies the goal of the planning problem. This approach guarantees the absence of alternative paths of permission delegations since a plan does not contain any redundant actions.

6 Using the Planner

In the last years many planners have been proposed (Table 3). In order to choose one of them we have analyzed the following requirements:

1. The planner should produce solution that satisfy need-to-know property by construction, that is, the planner should not produce redundant plans. Under non-redundant plan we mean that, by deleting an arbitrary action of the plan, the resulting plan is no more a "valid" plan (i.e. it does not allow to reach the desired state from the initial state).
2. The planner should use PDDL (Planning Domain Definition Language) [15], since it is becoming the "standard" planning language and many research groups work on its implementation. In particular, the planner should use PDDL 2.2 specifications [10], since this version support features, such as derived predicates, that are essential for implementing our planning domain.
3. The planner should be available on both Linux and Windows platforms as our previous Secure Tropos reasoning tool works on both.

Table 4 presents a comparison among the planners we have considered with respect to above requirements. Based on such requirements, we have chosen LPG-td, a fully

Table 3. Comparison among planners

Planner	Release	URL
DLV^K	2005-02-23	http://www.dbai.tuwien.ac.at/proj/dlv/K/
IPP 4.1	2000-01-05	http://www.informatik.uni-freiburg.de/ koehler/ipp.html
CPT 1.0	2004-11-10	http://www.cril.univ-artois.fr/ vidal/cpt.en.html
SGPLAN	2004-06	http://manip.crhc.uiuc.edu/programs/SGPlan/index.html
SATPLAN	2004-10-19	http://www.cs.washington.edu/homes/kautz/satplan/
LPG-td	2004-06	http://zeus.ing.unibs.it/lpg/

Table 4. Comparison among planners

Requirement \ Planner	DLV^K	IPP	CPT	SGPLAN	SATPLAN	LPG-td
1		X	X	X	X	X
2				X	X	X
3	X	X	X			X

```
(: action Satisfy
  : parameters (?a − actor ?g − goal)
  : precondition (and
       (provides ?a ?g)
       (requests ?a ?g)
       (has_per ?a ?g))
  : effect (and
       (done ?g)
       not (requests ?a ?g)))
```

```
(: action DelegatePermission
  : parameters (?a ?b − actor ?g − goal)
  : precondition (and
       (trustper ?a ?b ?g)
       (has_per ?a ?g))
  : effect (and
       (has_per ?b ?g)))
```

(a) Satisfy   (b) DelegatePermission

Fig. 3. Actions' Specification

```
DelegateExecution Pat HP ProvideMC
AND_Refine HP ProvideMC ProvisioningMC PaymentMC
DelegatePermission HCA HP ProvisioningMC
Satisfy HP ProvisioningMC
DelegateExecution HP HCA PaymentMC
DelegateExecution HCA INPDAP PaymentMC
AND_Refine INPDAP PaymentMC PaymentTicket PaymentHCA
DelegateExecution HCA INPDAP PaymentHCA
Satisfy HCA PaymentHCA
OR_Refine INPDAP PaymentTicket PaymentTicketINPDAP PaymentTicketHP
DelegatePermission HCA INPDAP PaymentTicketINPDAP
Satisfy INPDAP PaymentTicketINPDAP
```

Fig. 4. The optimal solution

automated system for solving planning problems, supporting PDDL 2.2. Figure 3 shows the specification of actions Satisfy and DelegatePermission in PDDL 2.2.

We have applied our approach to the Medical IS presented in Figure 1. The desired state of the system is obviously one where the patient gets medical care. The PDDL 2.2 specification of the planning problem is given in [4].

Figure 4 shows the optimal solution (i.e. the plan composed of the fewer number of actions than any other plan) proposed by LPG-td. However, this was not the first choice of the planner. Before selecting this plan, the planner proposed other two sub-optimal alternatives (see [4] for a discussion). It is interesting to see that the planner has first provided a solution with INPDAP, then a solution with INPDAI, and then, finally, a revised solution with INPDAP. A number of other experiments were conduced to test the scalability of our approach. The results are reported in [4].

7 Related Work

In recent years many efforts have addressed the integration of security with the system development process, in particular during early requirements analysis. In this setting, many researchers have recognized trust as an important aspect of this process since trust influences the specification of security and privacy policies. However, very few requirements engineering methodologies introduce trust concerns during the system development process. Yu et al. [36] model trust by using the concept of softgoal, i.e. goal having no clear definition for deciding whether it is satisfied or not. However, this approach considers trust as a separate concept from security and does not provide a complete framework to consider security and trust throughout the development process. Haley et al. [18] propose to use trust assumptions, problem frames, and threat descriptions to aid requirements engineers to define and analyze security requirements, and to document the decisions made during the process.

Other approach focus on security requirements without taking into account trust aspect. van Lamsweerde et al introduce the notion of antigoals for representing the goals of attackers [33]. McDermott et al. define abuse case model [26] to specify the interactions among actors, whose the results are harmful to some actors. Similarly, Sindre et al. define the concept of a misuse case [32], the inverse of a use case, which describes a function that the system should block.

Model Driven Architecture (MDA) approach [27], proposed by Object Management Group, is a framework for defining software design methodologies. Its central focus is on the model transformation, for instance from the platform-independent model of the system to platform-specific models used for implementation purposes. Models are usually described in UML, and the transformation is performed in accordance with the set of rules, called mapping. Transformation could be manual, or automatic, or mixed. Among the proposals on automating a software design process the one of Gamma et al. on design patterns [13] has been widely accepted. A design pattern is a solution (commonly observed from practice) to the certain problem in the certain context, so it may be thought as a problem-context-solution triple. Several design patterns can be combined to form a solution. Notice that it is still the designer who makes the key decision on what pattern to apply to the given situation.

The field of AI planning have been making advances during the last decades, and has found a number of applications (robotics, process planning, autonomous agents, Web services, etc.). There two basic approaches to the solution of planning problems [34]. One is graph-based planning algorithms [2] in which a compact structure called a Planning Graph is constructed and analyzed. While in the other approach [19] the planning problem is transformed into a SAT problem and a SAT solver is used. An application of the planning approach to requirements engineering is proposed by Gans et al. [14]. Essentially, they propose to map trust, confidence and distrust described in terms of i* models [36] to delegation patterns in a workflow model. Their approach is inspired by and implemented in ConGolog [8], a logic-based planning language. In this setting, tasks are implemented as ConGolog procedures where preconditions correspond to conditionals and interrupts. Also monitors are mapped into ConGolog procedures. They run concurrently to the other agent tasks waiting for some events such as task completion and certificate expiration. However, their focus is on modeling and reasoning about trust in social networks, rather than on secure design.

8 Conclusions

We have shown that in our extended Secure Tropos framework it is possible to automatically support the designer of secure and trusted systems also in the automatic selection of design alternatives. Our enhanced methodology allows one to:

1. Capture through a graphical notation of the requirements for the organization and the system-to-be.
2. Verify the correctness and consistency of functional and security requirements by
   - completion of the model drawn by the designer with axioms (a process hidden to the designer),
   - checking the model for the satisfaction of formal properties corresponding to specific security or design patterns.
3. Automatically select alternative solutions for the fulfillment of functional and security requirements by
   - transformation of the model drawn by the designer into a planning problem (a process hidden to the designer),
   - automatic identification of an alternative satisficing the goals of the various actors by means of planner.

In this paper we show that this is possible with the use of an off-the-shelf planner to generate possible designs for not trivial security requirements. Of course, we assume that the designer remains in the design loop, so the designs generated by the planner are seen as suggestions to be refined, amended and approved by the designer. In other words, the planner is a(nother) support tool intended to facilitate the design process.

Our future work includes extending the application of this idea to other phases of the design and towards progressively larger industrial case studies to see how far can we go without using specialized solvers.

References

1. R. Axelrod. *The Evolution of Cooperation*. Basic Books, 1984.
2. A. Blum and M. L. Furst. Fast Planning Through Planning Graph Analysis. *Artif. Intell.*, 90(1-2):281–300, 1997.
3. V. Bryl, P. Giorgini, and J. Mylopoulos. Requirements Analysis for Socio-technical Systems: Exploring and Evaluating Alternatives, 2006. Submitted to RE'06.
4. V. Bryl, F. Massacci, J. Mylopoulos, and N. Zannone. Designing Security Requirements Models through Planning. Technical Report DIT-06-003, University of Trento, 2006.
5. J. Caldwell. Moving Proofs-as-Programs into Practice. In *Proc. of ASE'97*, pages 10–17. IEEE Press, 1997.
6. M. Carman, L. Serafini, and P. Traverso. Web service composition as planning. In *Proc. of the 2003 Workshop on Planning for Web Services*, 2003.
7. J. Castro, M. Kolp, and J. Mylopoulos. Towards Requirements-Driven Information Systems Engineering: The Tropos Project. *Inform. Sys.*, 27(6):365–389, 2002.
8. G. de Giacomo, Y. Lespérance, and H. J. Levesque. ConGolog, a concurrent programming language based on the situation calculus. *Artif. Intell.*, 121(1-2):109–169, 2000.
9. P. Drucker. *Managing the Non-Profit Organization: Principles and Practices*. HapperCollins Publishers, 1990.
10. S. Edelkamp and J. Hoffmann. Pddl2.2: The language for the classical part of the 4th international planning competition. Technical Report 195, University of Freiburg, 2004.
11. T. Ellman. Specification and Synthesis of Hybrid Automata for Physics-Based Animation. In *Proc. of ASE'03*, pages 80–93, 2003.
12. M. J. Gallivan. Striking a balance between trust and control in a virtual organization: a content analysis of open source software case studies. *ISJ*, 11(2):277, 2001.

13. E. Gamma, R. Helm, R. Johnson, and J. Vlissides. *Design Patterns: Elements of Reusable Object-Oriented Software*. Addison-Wesley, 1995.

14. G. Gans, M. Jarke, S. Kethers, and G. Lakemeyer. Modeling the Impact of Trust and Distrust in Agent Networks. In *Proc. of AOIS'01*, pages 45–58, 2001.

15. M. Ghallab, A. Howe, C. Knoblock, D. McDermott, A. Ram, M. Veloso, D. Weld, and D. Wilkins. PDDL – The Planning Domain Definition Language. In *Proc. of AIPS'98*, 1998.

16. P. Giorgini, F. Massacci, J. Mylopoulos, and N. Zannone. Modeling Security Requirements Through Ownership, Permission and Delegation. In *Proc. of RE'05*, pages 167–176. IEEE Press, 2005.

17. P. Giorgini, F. Massacci, J. Mylopoulos, and N. Zannone. Modelling Social and Individual Trust in Requirements Engineering Methodologies. In *Proc. of iTrust'05, LNCS 3477*, pages 161–176. Springer-Verlag, 2005.

18. C. B. Haley, R. C. Laney, J. D. Moffett, and B. Nuseibeh. Using Trust Assumptions with Security Requirements. *Requirements Eng. J.*, 11:138–151, 2006.

19. H. Kautz and B. Selman. Planning as satisfiability. In *Proc. of ECAI'92*, pages 359–363. John Wiley & Sons, Inc., 1992.

20. E. Letier and A. van Lamsweerde. Reasoning about partial goal satisfaction for requirements and design engineering. *ACM SIGSOFT Software Eng. Notes*, 29(6):53–62, 2004.

21. N. Luhmann. *Trust and Power*. Wisley, 1979.

22. Z. Manna and R. Waldinger. A Deductive Approach to Program Synthesis. *TOPLAS*, 2(1):90–121, 1980.

23. F. Massacci, M. Prest, and N. Zannone. Using a Security Requirements Engineering Methodology in Practice: The compliance with the Italian Data Protection Legislation. *Comp. Standards & Interfaces*, 27(5):445–455, 2005.

24. F. Massacci and N. Zannone. Detecting Conflicts between Functional and Security Requirements with Secure Tropos: John Rusnak and the Allied Irish Bank. Technical Report DIT-06-002, University of Trento, 2006.

25. M. Matskin and E. Tyugu. Strategies of Structural Synthesis of Programs and Its Extensions. *Comp. and Informatics*, 20:1–25, 2001.

26. J. McDermott and C. Fox. Using Abuse Case Models for Security Requirements Analysis. In *Proc. of ACSAC'99*, pages 55–66. IEEE Press, 1999.

27. Object Management Group. Model Driven Architecture (MDA). http://www.omg.org/docs/ormsc/01-07-01.pdf, July 2001.

28. J. Peer. Web Service Composition as AI Planning - a Survey. Technical report, University of St. Gallen, 2005.

29. S. Roach and J. Baalen. Automated Procedure Construction for Deductive Synthesis. *ASE*, 12(4):393–414, 2005.

30. R. K. Runde and K. Stølen. What is model driven architecture? Technical Report UIO-IFI-RR304, Department of Informatics, University of Oslo, March 2003.

31. H. A. Simon. *The Science of the Artificial*. MIT Press, 1969.

32. G. Sindre and A. L. Opdahl. Eliciting security requirements with misuse cases. *Requirements Eng. J.*, 10(1):34–44, 2005.

33. A. van Lamsweerde, S. Brohez, R. De Landtsheer, and D. Janssens. From System Goals to Intruder Anti-Goals: Attack Generation and Resolution for Security Requirements Engineering. In *Proc. of RHAS'03*, pages 49–56, 2003.

34. D. S. Weld. Recent Advances in AI Planning. *AI Magazine*, 20(2):93–123, 1999.

35. R. K. Woolthuis, B. Hillebrand, and B. Nooteboom. Trust, Contract and Relationship Development. *Organization Studies*, 26(6):813–840, 2005.

36. E. S. K. Yu and L. Liu. Modelling Trust for System Design Using the i* Strategic Actors Framework. In *Proc. of the Workshop on Deception, Fraud, and Trust in Agent Societies, LNCS 2246*, pages 175–194. Springer-Verlag, 2001.

Towards a Comprehensive Framework for Secure Systems Development

Haralambos Mouratidis[1], Jan Jürjens[2], and Jorge Fox[2]

[1] Innovative Informatics, School of Computing and Technology, University of East London, UK
haris@uel.ac.uk
[2] Software and Systems Engineering, TU Munich, Germany
juerjens@in.tum.de, fox@in.tum.de

Abstract. Security involves technical as well as social challenges. In the development of security-critical applications, system developers must consider both the technical and the social parts. To achieve this, security issues must be considered during the whole development life-cycle of an information system. This paper presents an approach that allows developers to consider both the social and the technical dimensions of security through a structured and well defined process. In particular, the proposed approach takes the high-level concepts and modelling activities of the secure Tropos methodology and enriches them with a low level security-engineering ontology and models derived from the UMLsec approach. A real case study from the e-commerce sector is employed to demonstrate the applicability of the approach.

1 Introduction

Security related challenges and problems fall into two categories: *technical challenges*, i.e. those related to the available technology and the infrastructure of information systems, and *social challenges*, i.e. those related to the impact of the human factor on the security of a system. To be able to develop secure information systems, both dimensions should be considered simultaneously. Consider for instance, a typical social engineering attack on health information systems. Social engineering is a non-technical kind of intrusion that relies on human interaction and involves tricking other people (doctors, or nurses in the case of medical records) to break normal security procedures. A private detective (or someone interested in obtaining personal health information) calls in a health professional's office or a hospital, introduces herself as a doctor in an emergency hospital and asks information about the medical record of a particular patient [22]. This example shows that considering only the technical dimension of security, will not produce the desirable output.

To enable developers to deal with both dimensions, research has shown that security should not be considered in isolation but within the context of the development process employed to develop the system [7][13][16][8]. However, it has remained true over the last 30 years, since the seminal paper [16], that no coherent and complete methodology to ensure security in the construction of large general-purpose systems exists yet, in spite of very active research and many useful results addressing particular subgoals [17], as well as a large body of security engineering

E. Dubois and K. Pohl (Eds.): CAiSE 2006, LNCS 4001, pp. 48–62, 2006.
© Springer-Verlag Berlin Heidelberg 2006

knowledge accumulated [1]. In contrast, today ad hoc development leads to many deployed systems that do not satisfy important security requirements. Thus a sound methodology supporting secure systems development is needed. Such a methodology should take into account not only the technical problems but also the social dimension of developing secure information systems.

Our goal is to work towards the development of such methodology. This paper presents an approach for modelling secure information systems, which takes the high-level concepts and modelling activities of the secure Tropos methodology [3] and enriches them with a low level security-engineering ontology and models derived from the UMLsec [11] approach. More concretely, we present an approach that integrates two complementing security-oriented approaches: secure Tropos and UMLsec. Section 2 provides an overview of secure Tropos and UMLSec, and section 3 discusses their integration. Section 4 illustrates the enhanced framework with the aid of a use case, and section 5 concludes the paper.

2 An Overview of Secure Tropos and UMLsec

Secure Tropos [13][14] is a security-oriented extension of the well known[1] Tropos methodology. Tropos provides support for four phases [3]: *Early Requirements Analysis*, aimed at defining and understanding a problem by studying its existing organizational setting; *Late Requirements Analysis*, conceived to define and describe the system-to-be, in the context of its operational environment; *Architectural Design*, that deals with the definition of the system global architecture in terms of subsystems; and the *Detailed Design* phase, aimed at specifying each architectural component in further detail, in terms of inputs, outputs, control and other relevant information.

Secure Tropos introduces security related concepts to the Tropos methodology, to enable developers to consider security issues throughout the development of information systems. A *security constraint* is defined as a restriction related to security issues, such as privacy, integrity, and availability, which can influence the analysis and design of the information system under development by restricting some alternative design solutions, by conflicting with some of the requirements of the system, or by refining some of the system's objectives [13]. Additionally, secure Tropos defines secure dependencies. A *secure dependency* introduces security constraint(s) that must be fulfilled for the dependency to be satisfied [14]. Secure Tropos uses the term *secure entity* to describe any goals and tasks related to the security of the system. A *secure goal* represents the strategic interests of an actor with respect to security. Secure goals are mainly introduced in order to achieve possible security constraints that are imposed to an actor or exist in the system. However, a secure goal does not particularly define how the security constraints can be achieved, since alternatives can be considered. The precise definition of how the secure goal can be achieved is given by a secure task. A *secure task* is defined as a task that represents a particular way for satisfying a secure goal.

UMLsec is an extension of UML [15] for secure systems development. Recurring security requirements, such as secrecy, integrity, and authenticity are offered as

---

[1] In the requirements engineering area.

specification elements by the UMLsec extension. These properties and its associated semantics are used to evaluate UML diagrams of various kinds and indicate possible security vulnerabilities. One can thus verify that the desired security requirements, if fulfilled, enforce a given security policy. One can also ensure that the requirements are actually met by the given UML specification of the system. UMLsec encapsulates knowledge on prudent security engineering and thereby makes it available to developers who may not be experts in security. The extension is given in form of a UML profile using the standard UML extension mechanisms. *Stereotypes* are used together with *tags* to formulate security requirements and assumptions on the system environment. *Constraints* give criteria that determine whether the requirements are met by the system design, by referring to a precise semantics mentioned below.

The tags defined in UMLsec represent a set of desired properties. For instance, "freshness" of a value means that an attacker can not guess what its value was. Moreover, to represent a profile of rules that formalise the security requirements, the following are some of the stereotypes that are used: «critical», «high», «integrity», «internet», «encrypted», «LAN», «secrecy», and «secure links». The definition of the stereotypes allows for model checking and tool support. As an example consider «secure links». This stereotype is used to ensure that security requirements on the communication are met by the physical layer. More precisely, when attached to a UML subsystem, the constraint enforces that for each dependency d with stereotype $s \in \{<< secrecy >>, << integrity >>, << high >>\}$ between subsystems or objects on different nodes, according to each of the above stereotypes, there shall be no possibilities of an attacker reading, or having any kind of access to the communication, respectively. A detailed explanation of the tags and stereotypes defined in UMLsec can be found in [11]. The extension has been developed based on experiences on the model-based development of security-critical systems in industrial projects involving German government agencies and major banks, insurance companies, smart card and car manufacturers, and other companies. There have been several applications of UMLsec in industrial development projects.

3 Integration of Secure Tropos and UMLsec

There are various reasons for selecting secure Tropos and UMLsec from the large number of different existing methodologies and modelling languages. Secure Tropos considers the social dimension of security as well as the high-level technical dimension of it. Firstly, an analysis regarding social aspects of security takes place in which the security requirements of the stakeholders, users and the environment of the system are analysed and identified. Then, the methodology continues to a more technical dimension by considering the system and identifying its secure requirements, and allowing developers to identify the architecture of their systems with respect to the identified requirements. However, the developers of the methodology do not focus on the detailed security specification of each component of the system. The UMLsec approach is on the other side of the spectrum. It does not consider the social dimension, since the only analysis that it offers at the early stages of the development (stages at which the social issues are introduced) is use case diagrams, which do not consider the social security requirements of the system's stakeholders. We believe that integrating these two approaches will lead us to a complementary approach for secure information systems development, which will consider the two dimensions of security. In particular, we have identified individual strengths of such integration, which indicate what makes each of these approaches suitable for our purpose, as well as combinational strengths, which indicate why these two approaches are suitable for integration. *Individually*, secure Tropos considers security issues throughout the development stage, from the early requirements analysis down to implementation. Moreover, it allows developers not only to identify security issues but also to reason about them, and it provides a security pattern language to assist developers without much security knowledge to specify the architecture of the system according to its security requirements. On the other hand, UMLsec encapsulates established rules of prudent security engineering in the context of widely known notations, and thus makes them available to developers without extensive training in security. In addition, UMLsec supports automatic validation/verification of security properties. *Combinational*, both of the approaches are extensions of well-known approaches (Tropos and especially UML) and this makes the approach easier accessible to a large number of researchers/developers. Also, the strength of secure Tropos (requirements analysis) is complementary to the strengths of UMLsec (design) and vice versa, therefore providing a complete solution. In addition, the use of UML models during the design stage of the Tropos methodology makes the integration of secure Tropos and UMLsec more natural.

As mentioned above, secure Tropos is particularly focused on the *Early Requirements Analysis*, *Late Requirements Analysis*, and *Architectural Design*, whereas for the *Detailed Designed* stage the methodology is mainly based on UML diagrams with minor extensions to indicate some security issues [13]. On the other hand, the strength of UMLsec can be found on the *architectural* and *detailed* design stages, while some weak support for *late requirements* can be introduced using use case diagrams. Therefore, the integration of the two methods provides a framework of particular strength throughout all the development stages as shown in Figure 1.

However, the integration of secure Tropos and UMLsec is not straightforward and we had to deal with various challenges. To overcome these, a set of mapping guidelines and steps were defined and the secure Tropos development process was redefined and enriched with extra methods and procedures.

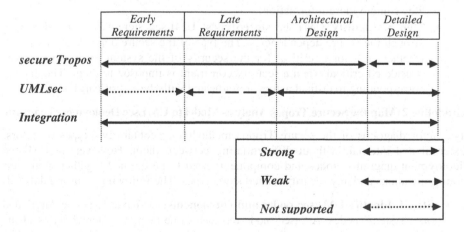

Fig. 1. Secure Tropos and UMLsec coverage of development phases

3.1 Mapping the Secure Tropos Models to UMLsec Models

As it was mentioned above, the appropriate stage of the secure Tropos development process for the integration is the *architectural design* stage. However, different concepts and notations are used by secure Tropos and UMLsec. So, the first challenge involved the definition of a set of guidelines to map the secure Tropos analysis and early design models to UMLsec models. The following guidelines and steps were identified towards this direction.

Guideline 1: Map the Secure Tropos Analysis Model to UMLsec Class Diagram

- **Step 1. Identify the UMLsec classes:** For every actor on the secure Tropos actor diagram a class is created on the UMLsec class diagram. In case there are sub-actors, these are mapped into the UMLsec class diagram as an inheritance relationship pointing from the sub-actor class to the main actor class.
- **Step 2. Identify the operations of the UMLsec classes:** The capabilities of each of the actors mapped into the UMLsec classes are added on the corresponding class as operations.
- **Step 3. Identify the attributes of the UMLsec classes:** Resources related to each of the actors are mapped to attributes on the UMLsec diagram. This is not a 1-to-1 mapping, meaning that a UMLsec class will not have exactly the same number of attributes as the secure Tropos actor counterpart. The reason for this is that Tropos models are mainly analysis models, whereas the UMLsec model is a design model. Therefore, it is up to the developers to identify additional attributes according to the identified operations, by following the same process followed when identifying attributes for a class on any class diagram.
- **Step 4. Identify associations:** In order to identify any associations between the UMLsec classes, the dependencies of the secure Tropos actor diagram are taken into account. Each dependency might provide an association. However, this is not a strict rule, and in fact in some cases developers will identify one association for a number of dependencies. This is again due to the reason that secure Tropos models are analysis models and UMLsec are design models so they contain more information.
- **Step 5. Identify UMLsec stereotypes:** UMLsec stereotypes are identified through the secure dependencies. The type of the secure dependency indicates whether an actor is critical for the security of the system or not. Actors are considered critical when a security constraint is imposed to them. The classes corresponding to critical actors are indicated with the <<critical>> stereotype.

Guideline 2: Map the Secure Tropos Analysis Model to UMLsec Deployment Diagram

The actor diagrams of the secure Tropos methodology contain two types of actors, external and internal, without differentiating between them. However, in UMLsec deployment diagrams, nodes and components need to be defined together with their communications and any security related stereotypes. The following steps are defined:

- **Step 1. Identify UMLsec nodes and components:** Define at least one "user" and one "system" nodes. A "user" node represents one or more external actors of the system, whereas the "system" node represents the system. External actors should be modelled as components on the appropriate "user" node, whereas system's internal actors must be modelled as components of the "system" node.

- **Step 2. Mode of communication:** Identify the mode of communication between the different nodes and use UMLsec stereotypes to denote that mode. For example, if the internet is used as the mode of communication between user node X and system node Y, then the <<internet>> UMLsec stereotype should be employed to denote that communication.
- **Step 3. Identify the necessary security stereotypes:** Consider the security constraints from the secure Tropos model. At least one UMLsec stereotype should be identified for each security constraint. It should be noted that the mapping is not one-to-one, meaning that more than one stereotypes will, usually, result from one security constraint.

3.2 The New Process

In a nutshell, the redefined secure Tropos process, allows developers initially to employ secure Tropos concepts and modelling activities to identify and analyse the security requirements of the system-to-be. Then, a combination of secure Tropos and UMLsec is employed to determine a suitable architecture for the system with respect to the identified security requirements, and identify the components of the system along with their secure capabilities, protocols, and properties. During the last stage UMLsec is used to specify in detail the components, which were identified in the previous stage, with respect to security.

In particular, during the *Early Requirements Analysis* the security needs of the stakeholders are analysed and a set of security constraints are imposed to the actors that satisfy the identified security needs. Moreover, security goals and entities are identified, for each of the participating actors, to satisfy the imposed security constraints. To achieve this, developers employ a set of different, but related, modelling activities defined by secure Tropos and its diagrammatic notations, such as actor's and the goal diagrams [13]. During the *Late Requirements Analysis,* the security requirements of the system are identified taking into account the security needs of the stakeholders as well as their security constraints (identified during the analysis of the previous stage). The output of this stage will be the definition of the system's security requirements together with a set of security constraints, along with the system's security goals and tasks that allow the satisfaction of the security requirements of the system.

The main aim of the *Architectural Design* is to define the architecture of the system with respect to its security requirements. To achieve this, initially secure Tropos notation together with a set of security patterns [13] are used to determine the general architecture and the components of the system, then the secure Tropos models are mapped to UMLsec models and in particular UMLsec Class and Deployment diagrams. These are used to model the security protocols and properties of the architecture.

During *Detailed design,* UMLsec is used to specify in detail the components of the system identified in the previous stage. For this reason, UMLsec activity diagrams are used to define explicitly the security of the components, UMLsec sequence diagrams are used to model the secure interactions of the system's components, e.g., to determine if cryptographic session keys exchange in a key exchanged protocol remain confidential in considering possible adversaries. UMLsec statechart diagrams are used to specify the security issues on the resulting sequences of states and the interaction with the component's environment. Figure 2 illustrates the redefined development process. Highlighted in italic are the new activities due to the integration of the two approaches.

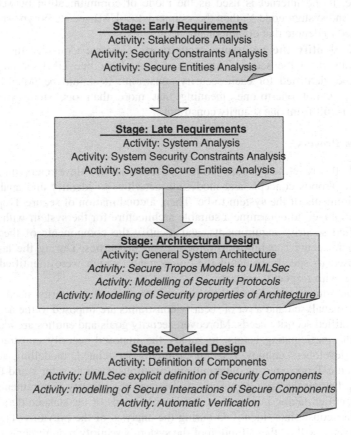

Fig. 2. The redefined development process

4   Case Study

To demonstrate our approach, we employ a case study from the e-commerce domain: The Common Electronic Purse System (CEPS) [4]. CEPS proposes the use of stored value smart cards, called electronic purses or CEP cards, to allow cash-free point-of-sale (POS) transactions offering more fraud protection than credit cards[2].

Amongst others, the following participants are defined in a CEP transaction [4]: the **Scheme Provider**, the authority responsible for establishing an infrastructure for the overall functionality and security of the CEP system and enforcing the operating

---

[2] Credit card numbers are valid until the card is stopped, enabling misuse. In contrast, electronic purses can perform cryptographic operations which allow transaction-bound authentication.

rules and regulations of the scheme; the *Card Issuer*, the organisation responsible for the provision and distribution of smart cards containing a CEP application (electronic purses), and the management of the funds pool; the *Cardholder*, the person who uses the card for making purchases; the *Load Acquirer*, the entity responsible for establishing business relationships with one or more scheme providers to process load and currency exchange transactions, and settle unlinked transactions; the *Merchant*, who is responsible for the use of a POS device to accept CEP cards for payment of goods and services; the *Merchant Acquirer*, the entity responsible for establishing a business relationship with one or more scheme providers to process POS transactions, and settle POS transactions. Moreover, the merchant acquirer is responsible for the provision and distribution of Purchase Secure Application Modules (PSAMs) that interact with terminals for conducting transactions at the point of sale.

4.1 Early Requirements

Initially, the main actors of the system are identified together with their dependencies and their security constraints. In particular, a CEP based transaction, although it provides many advantages, over a cash transaction, for both the buyer and the merchant; it is much more complex. In a normal operating scenario of the CEPS scheme, the *Cardholder* loads his/her card with money. During the post-transaction settlement, the *Load Acquirer* sends the money to the relevant *Card Issuer*. The *Cardholder* buys a product from a *Merchant* using his/her card. In the settlement, the *Merchant* receives the corresponding amount of money from the *Card Issuer*. It is worth mentioning that card issuers can take on the roles of load acquirers. As shown in Figure 3, the *Merchant* depends on the *Buyer* (known as the cardholder on the CEP scheme) to pay using the *CEP Card*, on the *CEP Scheme Provider* to provide the cash free transaction infrastructure and on the *Card Issuer* to collect the money.

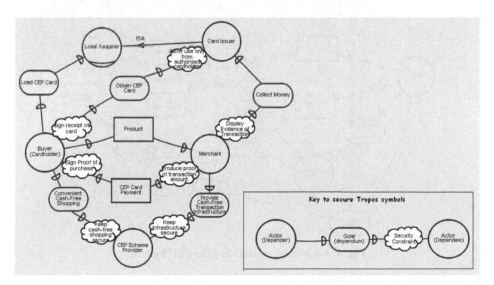

Fig. 3. Actor diagram of the CEP System

On the other hand, the *Buyer* depends on the *Card Issuer* to obtain a CEP enabled card, on the *Load Acquirer* to load the card and on the *CEP Scheme Provider* for convenient cash free shopping. As part of these dependencies, security related constraints are introduced, imposed by the different actors and the environment [13]. For instance, the *Buyer* imposes to the *Card Issuer* the *Allow use only from authorised cardholder* security constraint as part of the Obtain CEP Card dependency. In turn, and in order to satisfy this constraint, the *Card Issuer* imposes two security constraints, one to the *Buyer* (*sign receipt of card*) and one to the *Merchant* (*Display evidence of transaction*). On the other hand, the *Merchant*, to satisfy the security constraint imposed by the *Card Issuer*, imposes two security constraints to the *Buyer* (*sign proof of purchase*) and the *CEP Scheme Provider* (*Keep infrastructure secure*). Apart from defining the dependencies and the security constraints of these dependencies, secure Tropos allows developers to analyse each actor internally[3].

4.2 Late Requirements Analysis

During the late requirements analysis, the system is introduced as another actor who has a number of dependencies with the existing actors, and it accepts a number of responsibilities delegated to it by the other actors. For instance, for the CEP case study, the *CEP Scheme Provider* delegates the responsibility for administering the CEP transactions to the *CEP System*, whereas the *Merchant* delegates the CEP transaction resource to the *CEP System* (cf. Figure 4). With respect to security, since dependencies are delegated from the actors to the *CEP System*, possible security constraints regarding those dependencies are also delegated. In our case study, the *CEP Scheme Provider* actor

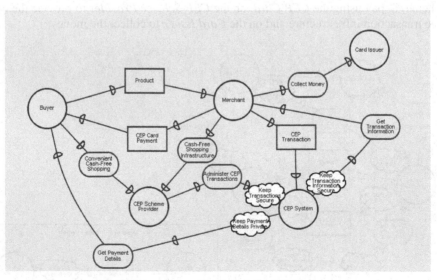

Fig. 4. Actor diagram including the CEP System

---

[3] Due to lack of space we do not illustrate in this paper the internal analysis of the actors. The modelling activities used for this can be found in [13].

together with the administer CEP transactions goal, delegates the *Keep transactions secure* security constraint on the *CEP system* actor. This means, that the *CEP System* is responsible now for satisfying that security constraint.

On the other hand, the introduction of the *CEP system* introduces new dependencies between the system and the existing actors. For example, the *CEP System* depends on the *Merchant* to get information regarding the transactions, such as the product information, the amount and so on. The *CEP System* also depends on the Buyer to get payment details such as the Buyer's card and account number. Moreover, these new dependencies impose extra security constraints on the *CEP System*. For instance, the *Buyer* wants their payment details to remain private so a security constraint is imposed to the *CEP System* from the *Buyer* as part of the *Get Payment Details* secure dependency. Similarly, the *Merchant* imposes a security constraint on the *CEP System* for the *Get Transaction Information* secure dependency.

However, at this stage, the security constraints are defined at a high level which makes it impossible (and impractical) to truly understand the security implications of the imposed security constraints to the *CEP System*. Moreover, the system itself has not been defined in such a detail that it can allow developers to further analyse the security constraints. Therefore, the next step involves the internal analysis of the CEP system actors following the same analysis techniques used during the early requirements stage.

Due to lack of space, we focus our analysis for the rest of the case study to a central part of the *CEP System*, the purchase transaction. This is an off-line protocol that allows cardholders to use their electronic *CEP card* to pay for products. The internal analysis of the system for the purchase transaction results in the identification of the following main goals of the system: *process transaction data, store transaction data, adjust credit balance, display transaction details* and *provide proof of transaction*.

From the security point of view, secure goals are identified to satisfy the security constraints imposed initially from the other actors to the system. Moreover, the internal analysis of the system helps to identify security constraints that were not identified during the previous analysis or define in more details some existing security constraints. For instance, the *Keep transactions secure* security constraint imposed by the *CEP Scheme Provider* to the *CEP System* can now (that the system's goals have been identified) be further defined. For example, related to the purchase transaction, the *Keep transaction secure* security constraint can be further refined to constraints such as *keep transaction private, keep transaction available* and *keep integrity of the transaction*. These security constraints introduce more security constraints on the system such as *obtain user's authorisation details, authenticate all transactions* and so on. When all the goals, secure goals, entities and secure entities have been identified, the next stage of the process is the architectural design.

4.3 Architectural Design

During the architectural design, the architecture of the system is defined with respect to its security requirements, and potential sub-actors are identified and the responsibility for the satisfaction of the system's goals and secure goals is delegated to these actors.

Furthermore, the interactions of the newly identified sub-actors and the existing actors of the system are specified. In our case study, the sub-actors of the system, related to the purchase transaction, are the *Point-Of-Sale (POS) Device, the Purchase Security Application Module (PSAM)*, and the *Display*. Therefore, these actors are delegated responsibility for the system's goals (such as *Adjust Credit Balance, Process Transaction Data* and *Display Transaction Details*) and secure goals (such as *Perform Integrity Checks, Ensure Data Availability* and *Perform Cryptographic Procedures*). Moreover, this process allows developers to identify security constraints that could not be identified earlier in the development process. For instance, the *Merchant* and the *Buyer* now depend on the *POS Device* to deliver the resource *Proof of Transaction*. However, both these actors impose, as part of the *Proof Transaction* dependency, the security constraint *tamper resistant* to the *POS Device*. The *Buyer* imposes that constraint because he/she does not want to be charged more than the transaction amount, and the *Merchant* because he/she wants to make sure they will get the money displayed on the transaction. On the other hand, the *POS Device* actor, in turn, imposes that security constraint to the other actors involved with the resource proof of transaction, i.e. the *PSAM* and the *Display*. Therefore, security goals are introduced to the *PSAM* and the *Display* to satisfy the *tamper resistant* security constraint.

Moreover, a new actor is identified that interacts with the system, the *CEP Card*. In particular, the *Buyer* depends on the *CEP Card* actor to *pay for goods*. However, the *Buyer* imposes two security constraints to the *CEP Card* actor, to *verify the transaction* and to *be tamper-resistant*. Therefore, secure goals are identified for the *CEP Card* actor to satisfy these two security constraints. When all the security constraints and secure goals have been identified the next step in the development process involves the use of UMLsec to define more precisely some of the security related attributes of the identified actors. As indicated in Section 3.1 the first step on this process is to map the Secure Tropos analysis model to the UMLsec class diagram. Following the first four steps described in section 3.1 the UML classes are identified as shown in Figure 5.

In particular, as our analysis has shown, the participants involved in the off-line purchase transaction protocol are the customer's card and the merchant's POS device. The POS device contains a *Purchase Security Application Module* (PSAM) that is used to store new and processed data. As indicated in our analysis, the *PSAM* is required to be tamper-resistant. Moreover, following step 5 of our guidelines, UMLSec stereotypes are identified. For example, the sessions keys *SK* on the *PSAM* object are required to be fresh, therefore this is indicated using the {fresh} tag of UMLsec (see section 2 for {fresh}).

Following the steps of the second guideline provided in section 3.1, the deployment diagram of figure 6 is constructed. To satisfy the security constraint *tamper resistant,* identified during the previous stage, for the *PSAM*, the *Display* and the *POS device*, the communication link between the *PSAM* and the *Display* is secured.

As shown in Figure 6, this is achieved by using a smart card with an integrated display as the *PSAM*. Furthermore, to satisfy the rest of the security constraints of our analysis, our design makes sure that the *PSAM* cannot be replaced without being noticed.

4.4 Detailed Design

The next step on the development involves the detailed design of each of the system components.

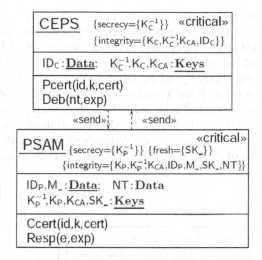

Fig. 5. Partial UMLSec diagram for the presented case study

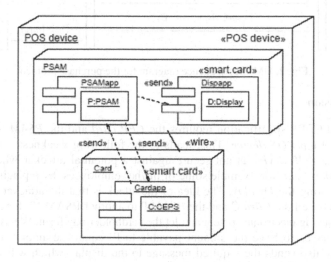

Fig. 6. Deployment diagram of the case study

During this stage each of the components identified in the previous stages is further specified by means of *Statechart Diagrams*, *Activity Diagrams*, and *Sequence Diagrams*[4]. Moreover, the UMLsec stereotypes allow us to specify the security constraints linked to the information flow and the processes carried out by the components.

UMLsec sequence diagrams are used to specify the security issues on the resulting sequences of states and the interaction with the component's environment. As an example, consider the following diagram for the purchase protocol:

---

[4] Due to lack of space we illustrate only sequence diagrams.

At the beginning of its execution in the *POS device*, the *PSAM* creates a transaction number NT with value 0. Before each protocol run, NT is incremented. If a certain limit is exceeded, the *PSAM* stops functioning, to avoid rolling over of NT to 0. Note that here we assume an additional operation, the +, to build up expressions. The protocol between the *Card* C, the *PSAM* P, and the *Display* D starts after the *Card* C is inserted into a *POS* device containing P and D and after the amount M is communicated to the *PSAM* by typing it into a terminal assumed to be secure. Each protocol run consists of the parallel execution of the card's and the PSAM's part of the protocol. Both check the validity of the received certificate. If all the verifications succeed, the protocol finishes, otherwise the execution of the protocol stops at the failed verification.

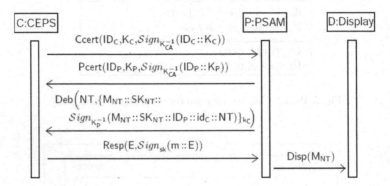

Fig. 7. UMLSec sequence diagram for the purchase protocol

4.5 Discussion

The original CEPS specification requires the *CEP card* and the *PSAM* to be tamper-proof but not the *POS device*. This, leads to the following weakness with respect to security. The *POS device* is not secure against a potential attacker who may try to betray the *Merchant*, for example some of his/her employees, by replacing the *PSAM* and manipulating the *Display*. The idea of the attack is that the attacker redirects the messages between the *Card* C and the *PSAM* P to another PSAM P', for example with the goal of buying electronic content and let the cardholder pay for it. We assume that the attacker manages to have the amount payable to P' equal the amount payable to P. The attacker also sends the required message to the display which will then reassure the merchant that he has received the required amount.

In our design such attack will fail. Our analysis and design improves the initial CEPS specification by securing the communication link between the *PSAM* and the *Display*, and by making sure that the *PSAM* cannot be replaced without being noticed. This will guarantee that the *Display* cannot anymore be manipulated, which means that if the *PSAM* received less money than expected, it would be noticed immediately.

5 Conclusions

Because of their wide-spread use in security-critical applications, information systems have to be secure. Unfortunately, the current state of the art in the development of security-critical information systems is far from satisfactory. A sound methodology to consider the technical as well as the social dimension of security is needed.

Towards this goal, we have presented the integration of two prominent approaches to the development of secure information systems: secure Tropos and UMLsec. The main feature of our proposal is the integration of the strong parts of each of these approaches, namely the socially oriented part of the secure Tropos methodology and the technical part of the UMLsec. This achieves several goals. First of all, developers are able to consider security both as a social aspect as well as a technical aspect. As it was argued in the introduction, this is important when developing information systems. Secondly, the approach allows the definition of security requirements in different levels and as a result it provides better integration with the modelling of the system's functionality. Thirdly, security is not considered in isolation but simultaneously with the rest of the system requirements. Fourthly, the integration allows the consideration of the organisational environment for the modelling of security issues, by facilitating the understanding of the security needs in terms of the security policy and the real security needs of the stakeholders, and then it allows the transformation of the security requirements to a design that is amenable to formal verification with the aid of automatic tools. It is worth mentioning at this point, that advance tool support is provided to assist with our approach [10]. The developed tool can be used to check the constraints associated with UMLsec stereotypes mechanically, and it uses analysis engines, such as model-checkers and automated theorem provers. The results of the analysis are given back to the developer, together with a modified UMLsec model, where the weaknesses that were found are highlighted. There is also a framework for implementing verification routines for the constraints associated with the UMLsec stereotypes.

To demonstrate the practical applicability and usefulness of our approach we have applied it to the CEP case study. The results are promising since our analysis in fact improves the security of the system. A large number of research efforts related to our work has been presented in the literature [2][5][6][8][9][12][19][23]. However, our work is different in two main points. Existing work is mainly focused either on the technical or the social aspect of considering security, and it presented approaches applicable only to certain development stages. In contrast our approach considers security as a two dimensional problem, where the technical dimension depends on the social dimension. Moreover, our approach is applicable to stages from the early requirements to implementation.

References

1. Anderson, R., *Security Engineering: A Guide to Building Dependable Distributed Systems.* John Wiley & Sons, New York, 2001.
2. Basin, D., Doser, J., Lodderstedt, T., Model Driven Security for Process Oriented Systems. In Proceedings of the 8th ACM symposium on Access Control Models and Technologies, Como, Italy, 2003
3. Bresciani, P. Giorgini, P., Giunchiglia, F., Mylopoulos, J., Perini, A., TROPOS: An Agent Oriented Software Development Methodology. In Journal of Autonomous Agents and Multi-Agent Systems, Kluwer Academic Publishers Volume 8, Issue 3, Pages 203-236, 2004

4. CEPSCO, Common Electronic Purse Specifications, Business Requirements ver. 7, Functional Requirements ver. 6.3, Technical Specification ver. 2.2. Available from http://www.cepsco.com [2000].
5. Crook, R., Ince, D., Lin, L., Nuseibeh, B., Security Requirements Engineering: When Anti-requirements Hit the Fan, In Proceedings of the 10th International Requirements Engineering Conference, pp. 203-205, IEEE Press, 2002
6. Cysneiros, L.M. Sampaio do Prado Leite, J.P., Nonfunctional Requirements: From Elicitation to Conceptual Models. IEEE Trans. Software Eng. 30(5): 328-350 (2004)
7. Devanbu, P., Stubblebine, S., Software Engineering for Security: a Roadmap. In Proceedings of ICSE 2000 ("the conference of the future of Software engineering"), 2000.
8. Giorgini, P., Massacci, F., Mylopoulos, J., Requirements Engineering meets Security: A Case Study on Modelling Secure Electronic Transactions by VISA and Mastercard, in Proceedings of the International Conference on Conceptual Modelling (ER), LNCS 2813, pp. 263-276, Springer-Verlag, 2003.
9. Hermann, G. Pernul, G., Viewing business-process security from different perspectives. International Journal of electronic Commence 3:89-103, 1999
10. Jürjens, J., Shabalin, P., Tools for Critical Systems Development with UML (Tool Demo), UML 2004 Satellite Events, Nuno Jardim Nunes, Bran Selic, Alberto Silva, Ambrosio Toval (eds.), LNCS, Springer-Verlag 2004E. [Accessible at http://www.UMLsec.org. Protected content can be accessed as user: Reader, with password: Ihavethebook]. Available as open-source.
11. Jürjens, J., Secure Systems Development with UML, Springer, March-Verlag, 2004
12. McDermott, J., Fox, C., Using Abuse Case Models for Security Requirements Analysis. In Proceedings of the 15th Annual Computer Security Applications Conference, December 1999.
13. Mouratidis, H., A Security Oriented Approach in the Development of Multiagent Systems: Applied to the Management of the Health and Social Care Needs of Older People in England. PhD thesis, University of Sheffield, U.K., 2004
14. Mouratidis, H., Giorgini, P., Manson, G., Integrating Security and Systems Engineering: towards the modelling of secure information systems. In Proceedings of the 15th Conference on Advanced Information Systems (CaiSE 2003), Velden –Austria, 2003
15. Object Management Group, OMG Unified Modeling Language Specification v1.5, March 2003. Version 1.5. OMG Document formal/03-03-01.
16. Saltzer, J., Schroeder, M., The protection of information in computer systems. Proceedings of the IEEE, 63(9):1278–1308, September 1975.
17. Schneider, F., editor. Trust in Cyberspace. National Academy Press, Washington, DC, 1999. Available as http://www.nap.edu/readingroom/books/trust/.
18. Schneier, B., Secrets & Lies: Digital Security in a Networked World, John Wiley & Sons, 2000
19. Schumacher, M., Roedig, U., Security Engineering with Patterns. In Proceedings of the 8th Conference on Pattern Languages for Programs (PLoP 2001), Illinois-USA, September 2001
20. Schumacher, M., Security Engineering with patterns. In LNCS 2754, Springer-Verlag, 2003
21. Shamir, A., Crypto Predictions. In 3rd International Conference on Financial Cryptography (FC 1999), 1999.
22. The Economist, Digital rights and wrongs, July 17, 1999
23. van Lamsweerde, A., Letier, E., Handling Obstacles in Goal-Oriented Requirements Engineering, Transactions of Software Engineering, 26 (10): 978-1005, 2000
24. Viega, J., McGraw, G., Building a Secure Software. Addison-Wesley, Reading, MA, 2002.

Role-Based Modelling of Interactions in Database Applications

Milivoje Petrovic, Michael Grossniklaus, and Moira C. Norrie

Institute for Information Systems,
ETH Zurich,
8092 Zurich, Switzerland
`{petrovic, grossniklaus, norrie}@inf.ethz.ch`

Abstract. Modern information systems interact with a wide variety of users ranging from people with specific roles in business processes to end-users who access information in various ways and in different environments. Therefore, an application has to adhere to a well defined security policy on one hand and be highly adaptable to context on the other. We have extended the OM data model, with its rich support for role modelling, with concepts for modelling interactions between users and applications. In this paper, we show how the resulting interaction model can be used for role-based access control, as well as for modelling interactions in context-aware applications.

1 Introduction

Interaction with users is one of the central aspects of designing an information system. Any interaction between a user and an application has to take care of two things. First, the application should be able to adapt to the users and their environment, and consequently provide only relevant information. Second, only authorised users should be allowed to interact with the application in a particular way. Depending on the type and purpose of a system, one or the other component is dominant. However, in every multi-user environment both context-awareness and security are always present to some extent.

An information system which supports an organisation's business processes has to support interaction with users having different responsibilities. In such systems, it is important to deliver the right information to the right users within given time constraints, and to ensure that only users with certain roles are allowed to perform a task. In contrast, recent developments in mobile information systems focus more on delivering relevant information to users depending on contextual parameters such as location, preferences and client device. In content management systems, these two aspects come together as nowadays they are expected to offer multi-channel and personalised access, while at the same time enforcing strict access control to content authoring based on user roles.

Interaction depends on characteristics of users and application entities. Often the same characteristics are relevant to both security and context-awareness. Moreover, relevant information and services delivered to a user will always be

E. Dubois and K. Pohl (Eds.): CAiSE 2006, LNCS 4001, pp. 63–77, 2006.
© Springer-Verlag Berlin Heidelberg 2006

subsets of the information and services, respectively, that they are authorised to access. For these reasons, it is necessary to reason about interactions on an abstract level, describing them in a way that covers both aspects. Both security and context are orthogonal to the application's functionality and therefore, instead of being modelled in the core application, they should be described in a separate model that enables their influence on runtime behaviour to be handled with well-defined algorithms based on that model.

In this paper, we present such a model and show how it can be used to capture both the context-dependent and access control aspects of information systems. A role-based approach to modelling interactions is used as role hierarchies map well to organisational hierarchies and their expressiveness makes them suitable both for capturing requirements and system design. However, role-based models are rather coarse-grained, and thus should be augmented with means to address fine-grained features.

Section 2 motivates our approach through an example scenario and discusses related work. The OM model and its support for role modelling is described in Sect. 3. Section 4 introduces the interaction model based on OM concepts. Section 5 discusses the role-based access control model obtained from the interaction model, while Sect. 6 discusses modelling interactions in context-aware applications. In Sect. 7 we briefly deal with implementation issues. Concluding remarks are given in Sect. 8.

2   Background

Throughout the paper, we will use a simplified version of an on-line conference management system to explain our approach. The different roles that users may have are Programme Committee (PC) members, some of whom are PC chairs, reviewers and authors. An author submits a paper before the submission deadline and classifies it by topics. PC members register their preference for topics and, given a list of papers associated with these topics, indicate their preferences for papers to review. The PC chairs then assign papers to reviewers who include PC members but may also include other nominated reviewers. Reviews should be submitted before a review deadline, after which, the PC decides whether or not a paper is accepted.

Each of the user roles has clear responsibilities and associated permissions. Reviewers can review papers but the system must ensure that only a reviewer who is assigned to the paper may actually activate review permission on it. Users may have multiple roles as a reviewer can also be an author. In this case, the protection mechanism has to take care of possible conflicts of interest and disallow that a paper is reviewed by its author. Further, permissions change over time according to the phases in reviewing process. For example, authors should not be allowed to submit or update papers after the submission phase is over and reviewers should not be able to change their reviews in the decision phase.

A conference management system not only has to be secure, but also should provide its users with information relevant to their role and task. For example, when a PC member wants to select papers for review, the system should not only exclude the papers that they authored, but also present those which match their preferences by default. The system should also be proactive and push information to the user. For example, one day before the review deadline, the system could automatically send a reminder to reviewers who have not completed all of their reviews.

Probably the most widely used models for capturing interactions between users and applications are UML use case and interaction diagrams [1]. Use case diagrams are used to model the requirements of an application and to clearly define the boundaries of a software system in interaction with actors which can be either humans or other software systems. On the other hand, sequence and communication interaction diagrams model a sequence of messages passed between objects on the level of method calls. The level of abstraction that we need is between those of use case and interaction diagrams. Similar to use case diagrams, our goal is to capture interactions between users and applications. However, to be able to model access control and context requirements, application entities with which the user interacts have to be present in the model. We are not interested at this level in the order of the messages and low level interactions in the implementation of application logic. Rather, we want to focus on characteristics of a user and application entity which influence interaction, and to change the runtime behaviour accordingly.

Research in access control in the past was focused on mandatory (MAC) and discretionary access control (DAC). MAC associates security labels to both subjects and objects and manages access rights in a centralised fashion, whereas DAC leaves the administration of access rights to the object's owner. Role-based access control (RBAC) [2, 3] allows for simplified management of permissions since they are specified on the level of roles and not of individual users. RBAC is policy neutral and can also be used to support MAC and DAC policies [4].

Role hierarchies further simplify the management of permissions by allowing inheritance of access rights. However, as shown in [5], in some cases such inheritance may lead to violation of organisation's control principles, such as separation of duty. In addition to generalisation based role hierarchies described in [2, 3], some other types of role hierarchies have been identified in organisation structures. In [5], activity hierarchies were introduced to model inheritance of the responsibility for activities that are part of larger activities, whereas supervision hierarchies were used to represent user positions in the organisation hierarchy. In [6], contextual and seniority role hierarchies of users and asset hierarchies of accessed objects were introduced. Contextual roles are used to model the fact that, in order to access an asset, a user not only has to posses the required ability, but also needs to be linked to it through some situational role, such as a common project.

In [7], a model-driven security approach is taken where security and a design language are combined to enable automatic generation of access control infrastructures on target software platforms. SecureUML is a security modelling language for role-based access control built as an extension of UML and thus with an intuitive graphical notation. It can be combined using a dialect with any design language in order to introduce access control on its resources. A security design model obtained by merging SecureUML and a structure model enables usage of OCL authorisation constraints to express activation of permissions depending on the state of a system, such as the existence of a relationship between a user and an accessed object.

The roles and properties of individual users and objects may also effect interaction between the user and the system in terms of the form and content of information delivered to the user in a particular context. In web engineering [8, 9], a role-based approach for adaptation to user interests and access control is taken on the navigational and presentational level in a manner similar to adaptive hypermedia [10]. It is usually assumed that the user logs in with one role and navigates through the site view designed for this role. Personalisation is done by querying information associated with a particular user through that role. For our requirements, it is important to integrate access control and context awareness in the core interactions between users and application entities. Further, we need to take all user roles into account when filtering information. Finally, we want to deliver the relevant information by means of an algorithm at runtime based on the model, rather than with queries written in application logic. Note that in this paper, we will not deal with the gathering, representation and interpretation of context information, but rather assume that context is already present in the data model and use it to specify conditions which influence interactions.

There have been several attempts to bring together security and context. In [11], a dynamic access-based control model is presented with the focus on the activation and deactivation of user roles in the session based on changes in user context. In [12], a generalised role-based access control (GRBAC) model is proposed with the notion of environment roles. Environment roles represent conditions which have to hold for some permission to be granted. These approaches are concerned with using context information, such as location and time, to make access control decisions. Our primary goal, however, is to provide a model and an algorithm which can be used to achieve goals focused either on context awareness, access control or both. GRBAC is also interesting because it classifies not only users, but also objects into roles. Such a feature allows for greater flexibility in modelling.

We want to make several points in this paper. Firstly, security and context-awareness are related and consequently can be modelled using the same concepts. They are both system aspects [13] and should be represented in terms of a model rather than in application logic. Further, extensive use of role modelling for both user and application entities can satisfy complicated interaction requirements in a simple way. The modelling of fine-grained behaviour on the level of individual objects can be achieved by the integration of the interaction and structure model. Having users as application entities makes such integration simpler and leads to flexible user management. Finally, querying which takes multiple user and object roles into account can be expressed in such model and can be handled by means of an algorithm.

3   The OM Data Model

The OM data model combines conceptual modelling constructs present in extended entity relationship models with object-oriented constructs, by introducing a clear separation of typing and classification [14, 15]. While types specify the actual representation of objects, collections and associations represent their semantic groupings.

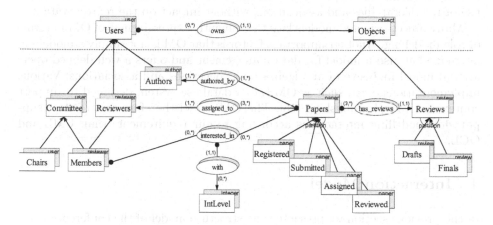

Fig. 1. Conceptual modeling in OM

A simplified OM model of the conference management system is shown in Fig. 1. Shaded rectangles represent semantic collections of objects and ovals associations between the members of collections. Generalisation hierachies are built from subcollection relationships between collections which are represented by directed edges between collections. For example, *Committee*, *Reviewers* and *Authors* are all subcollections of *Users*. The association *authors* captures the relationship between authors and their papers. *Members* is a subcollection of both *Committee* and *Reviewers*, expressing the fact that PC members are both reviewers and members of the committee together with its chair. The subcollections of *Papers* and *Reviews* correspond to the phases in the reviewing process. The *partition* constraint ensures that an object is always in exactly one phase. The system collections *Objects* and *Users* are parent collections for all application and user collections, respectively. The collection *Users* is also a subcollection of *Objects*, but this is not shown in the figure for reasons of clarity. Every application object has its owner, which is represented by the system association *owns*. Associations of interest between different user roles and *Papers* are represented. Since reviewers create reviews, the relationships between them are captured implicitly by the association *owns*.

The separation of typing and classification allows flexible role modelling to be supported as the multiple classification of objects simply corresponds to membership of multiple collections. At the type level, the OM model supports multiple instantiation as objects are dynamically composed from type units depending on a particular type view. Every collection has an associated type which restricts membership to objects of that type and determines the default type view of an object accessed through that collection. Thus, if a user object is accessed through the collection *Reviewers*, the properties of type *reviewer* will be accessible, while if they are accessed through collection *Authors* then it will be the properties of type *author*. Further, associations can be defined between two roles without having to change the types of the associated objects. This allows for extensive use of role hierarchies and associations without impact on the representation.

Many object-oriented models lack the semantic expressiveness of OM in terms of role modelling. Another important factor is that OM is not simply a modelling language but also a model for data management and offers a well defined operational model inclusive of an algebra over collections and associations. Various implementations exist, such as OMSwe, a database system designed to support context-aware web publishing [16]. The OM model therefore offers better support for modelling interactions according to our requirements than UML and OCL.

4   Interaction Model

In the previous section we presented the structure model of the conference management system. Having identified user roles and the most important application entities, we can model interactions based on the requirements presented in Sect. 2. We first introduce the core concepts of the interaction model. An *interaction* represents a set of semantically correlated messages which can be exchanged between a user and an accessed object. An *interaction constraint* is a logical predicate which determines the validity of the interaction. To specify that an interaction is possible between a member of a user role and a member of the object role, we use an *interaction relation* which is a tuple consisting of a user role, an object role, an interaction and a set of interaction constraints. If interaction constraints are defined on the interaction relation, then all of them have to be satisfied for the interaction between two objects to be valid.

The model of interactions between user roles and papers is shown in Fig. 2. An interaction relation is graphically represented as a labelled, directed line between two roles. An interaction constraint is graphically represented as an annotation to the line. From the diagram, we see that a user who possesses the role of a reviewer may issue a *review* interaction for a paper if the interaction constraint *assigned_to* is satisfied for the two objects. Interaction constraints are expressed in terms of the OM collection algebra extended with the keywords `caller` and `callee` to refer to the user and the accessed object, respectively. Interaction constraints may accept additional parameters if they are defined for the interaction as in the case of the interaction *assign_to(member)*. A list of the interaction constraints used for the model is given below. We assume there is a global object *conference* which holds information on *submission_deadline*, whereas parameter *global_time* represents the current system time. We see that

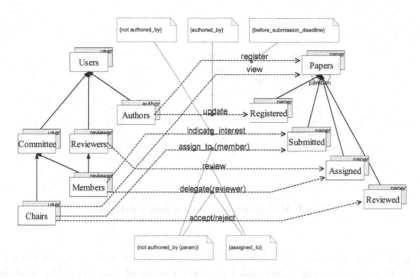

Fig. 2. Interaction model example

some interaction constraints are dependent on relationships between objects in the structure model, while others depend on context information such as time.

```
authored_by(param) := (param, callee) in a"authored_by"
authored_by := (caller, callee) in a"authored_by"
assign_to := a"assigned_to"
before_submission_deadline :=
    global_time < conference[submission_deadline]
```

The relationships in *assigned_to* are created in interaction *assign_to*. Both associations and interactions link two objects. However, associations represent static, persistent relationships between objects, while interactions are dynamic, transient relationships which exist only during the exchange of messages.

Both users and papers are classified into role hierarchies. When an interaction relation is defined between a user and an object role, it is inherited by all combinations of child user and object roles, including the user and object roles themselves. This means that the *view* interaction relation defined between *Chairs* and *Papers* implies that PC chairs can view papers in all phases. Similarly, the *review* interaction relation between *Reviewers* and *Assigned* implies that PC members can also review papers in that phase. In the case that a user or object role is a child of more than one role, then it inherits interaction relations from all of its parent roles. Nevertheless, in some cases, roles need to redefine the interaction relation defined between parent roles because of different interactions or interaction constraints, or both. An example is given in Fig. 3 where the interaction relation *view* between *Reviewers* and *Reviews* is redefined by the interaction relation between *Members* and *Finals*, to allow only PC members to view all other finalised reviews once they have finalised their own.

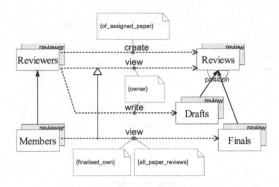

Fig. 3. Redefinition of interaction relations

To model the creation and deletion of objects, we assume that, for each OM type, there is a collection corresponding to the extent of that type. We introduce system interactions *create* and *delete* which are only allowed to be specified on collections that correspond to type extents e.g. *Reviews*. Creation and deletion are considered equivalent to insertion into and removal from such collections. As reviewers create reviews, we define an interaction relation with the interaction *create* between the roles *Reviewers* and *Reviews*, as shown in Fig. 3. Interaction constraints can be specified in combination with the *create* interaction, in which case they are checked after the interaction has been carried out and the object created. In this example, the constraint *of_assigned_paper* given below checks whether the reviewer is assigned to the paper for which the review is created. In the case of instance deletions, all interaction constraints are checked before the interaction. When it comes to other collections, insertion and removal have different semantics as they correspond to granting and revoking roles. The system interactions *grant* and *revoke* are allowed to be used only when the accessed collection does not correspond to the extent of a type.

```
of_assigned_paper :=
    (caller, callee) in inverse (a"assigned_to") compose a"has_reviews"
```

The metamodel of the interaction model is presented in Fig. 4. An interaction relation connects a user role, an object role, an interaction and a set of interaction constraints. Both user and object roles can take part in many interaction relations. An interaction constraint expresses conditions from the structure model and thus can be used for many interaction relations. Since an interaction is just a set of messages, the same interaction can exist between many combinations of user and object roles. Thus, an interaction can be related with many interaction relations. An interaction relation can redefine zero or one interaction relations between parent roles, with the constraint that both the source and target roles are subcollections of the source and target parent roles. Further, an interaction relation can be redefined by many interaction relations defined between different combinations of user and object child roles. Interactions which correspond to a single message are called *atomic interactions*. An interaction may be composed of many interactions which in turn can either be composite or atomic. Any interaction can be part of many interactions. Limitations in composing interactions come only from the evaluation of the interaction constraints in interaction relations. Any interaction constraint which is valid on the parent interaction has to be valid on the child interactions.

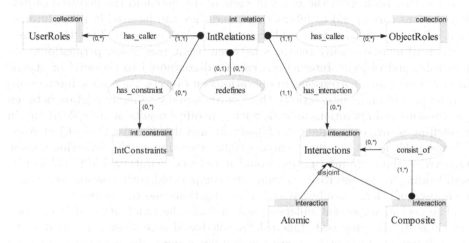

Fig. 4. Interaction metamodel

Both a user and an accessed object are classified into many roles in parallel inheritance paths. The resolution algorithm given below takes this into account to check the validity of interaction i, issued by user u on object o, by passing a set of parameters P. A more general version of the algorithm receives a collection of objects and returns those for which the requested interaction is valid. This is useful when querying for objects which can provide a certain interaction.

1. let R_u and R_o be sets of user and object roles of u and o, respectively
2. let IR be the set of interaction relations IR_k for which $(has\_caller(IR_k), has\_callee(IR_k)) \in R_u \times R_o$ and $i \in has\_interaction(IR_k)$
3. let IR' be the subset of IR obtained by leaving out all IR_k for which exists some IR_j such that $redefines(IR_j) = IR_k$
4. accept if there is $IR_k \in IR'$ for which for all $c \in has\_constraints(IR_k)$, $c(u, o, P) = true$

5   Role-Based Access Control Model

The interaction model of the conference management system is in fact a role-based access control model. We specified which interactions are allowed for user roles in different phases of the reviewing process. In that sense, interactions are permissions that are activated if all interaction constraints evaluate to true for objects in the interaction. Thus, interaction constraints play the role of *authorisation constraints* in this case.

We will show how the concepts of our interaction model relate to those proposed as a possible standard for role-based access control [3]. The first important difference stems from the OM feature that not only user objects, but also objects accessed by them may have multiple roles. This means that our model is role-based both from the point of view of the user and the accessed object. Permissions correspond to interactions, and they can be used in many interaction relations defined between different user and object roles. Thus there exists a chain of many-to-many relations between users, user roles, permissions, object roles and objects. Interactions can be decomposed to the level of atomic interactions which correspond to operations on objects. As atomic interactions can be part of many interactions, there exists a many-to-many relation between permissions and operations as well. Such generality results in great flexibility in modelling security requirements. Especially useful is the usage of object roles. We used this feature to change access rights according to the reviewing phases. Otherwise, the state information would have to be maintained in the object itself, leading to non-intuitive diagrams and complicated authorisation constraints composed of a large number of logical conjunctions and disjunctions.

The second important difference stems from the redefinition of interaction relations. In the proposed standard for role-based access control, a partial order relation exists between roles: senior roles acquire the permissions of their juniors and junior roles acquire users of senior roles. Senior roles correspond to the child roles of the OM model and junior roles correspond to its parent roles. The acquisition of users is achieved using OM subcollections, while the acquisition of permissions is obtained in the interaction model. If a child role has more than one parent role, it inherits the permissions from all of them. Also, a parent role may have many child roles which then inherit its permissions. Thus, role hierarchies are general as they allow multiple inheritance of both users and permissions. The same observations are valid for object role hierarchies. In our model, interaction relations can be redefined by child roles, thus changing permissions and authorisation constraints. This allows for situations where a senior role has less permissions than the junior role. This breaks the partial order but allows for greater flexibility. Without this feature, non-conceptual roles would have to be introduced, as is the case with private roles in [2], thus leading to non-intuitive models.

Authorisation constraints partition objects with the same role into those which are authorised to participate in a given interaction and those which are not. This allows for the expression of fine-grained security requirements. A particularly important authorisation constraint is *owner* since, in many security policies, the object's owner has special rights on it. The *owner* constraint stems from the system association *owns* defined between system collections *Users* and *Objects*. It can be placed on any interaction relation since the user and the accessed object must be members of the corresponding system collections.

The constraint and operational model of OM allows for the specification of complex constraints such as separation of duty, where a task is divided into smaller ones which have to be done by different persons. Simple cases can be handled on the level of the structural model using OM constraints. For instance, the *disjoint* constraint could be used to ensure that a user object cannot possess more than one role from a set of child roles. However, more complex cases require the use of authorisation constraints. Since, in our example, a user may have both the author and the reviewer role, a conflict of interest is prevented by controlling permission activation using authorisation constraints. In similar fashion, authorisation constraints could be used to solve conflicts between control principles and inheritance of access rights posed in [5]. Relationships could be used to track performers of activities. Separation of duty would then be enforced by placing an authorisation constraint which would be negation of the existence of relationship between user and object in the previous activity.

Requirements stemming from the presence of different types of role hierarchies in organisations [6] can be expressed in terms of our model by using associations and authorisation constraints. User and object role hierarchies of our model correspond to functional roles and asset hierarchies, respectively. We do not need to explicitly define seniority and contextual roles that a user needs to possess in addition to functional roles in order to access an asset. Rather, we can introduce an association between user roles to model seniority, and associations between user and object roles instead of contextual roles. Then, we can use authorisation constraints based on these associations to achieve the same effect. Our model is general in the sense that it provides a framework where arbitrary associations between roles can be defined and then used for expression of authorisation constraints in terms of the OM algebra. This enables us to also support delegation and responsibility introduced in [5], since they are in fact based on relationships between user roles and sets of activities.

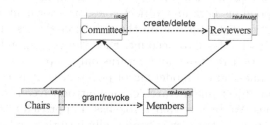

Fig. 5. User management

User objects are not treated differently from any other objects in the OM model. This is convenient for user management and administration as permissions on users can be modelled and controlled in the same way and using the same rules as other objects. The model shown in Fig. 5 states that both PC chairs and members can create reviewers, and that only chairs can promote them to PC members. In this way, we can model and control the creation of users and propagation of privileges in a fine-grained way.

Our model is similar to a security design language obtained by a merging of SecureUML [7] and a static structure design language in that it is graphically intuitive and makes use of authorisation constraints. The difference is that in such a language, users and roles from SecureUML are not part of the structure model, and thus have to be connected with the application entities which represent them using a convention. This complicates the expression of authorisation constraints and, more importantly, prevents the administration of users in the same way as application entities.

6   Context-Aware Interactions

To be able to express context in terms of a model, we generalise the notion of context to any information present in the data and interaction model that is relevant for the interaction between a user and an application. This is in accordance with the definition of context given in [17]. Relevant information and its influence on interaction is expressed in terms of interaction constraints, which, in this case play, the role of *context constraints*. Any property that characterises a user, an accessed object, associated objects or the global environment can be context for a particular interaction. Often the fact that some relationship exists influences the interaction, thus being context itself.

To illustrate how we can support the delivery of relevant information and services based on the interaction model, consider the interaction in which a PC member indicates interests in papers. Although PC members have rights to access any paper, the system should provide them with the list of papers that matches their topic preferences as a default. To achieve this, we can classify PC members into many roles based on their preferences and expertise. Similarly, authors classify papers by topic. Then, we can introduce an interaction which indicates user preferences and specify it using interaction relations between the corresponding user and object roles, as shown in Fig. 6. When a user issues interaction *list_preferred* on the collection *Papers*, the resolution algorithm takes all user roles into account, finds the corresponding object roles through the interaction relations and returns only papers having one of these roles. For further fine-grained modelling of preferences, it is possible to create multilevel user and object role hierarchies, and introduce context constraints on interaction relations. We believe that a role based approach to the modelling of user profiles and object categories is graphically intuitive and allows for multiple user and object roles to be taken into account when querying for preferred objects.

Further, when a PC member accesses a paper, the relevant functionality should be offered to them. If they access a paper in which they have already indicated an interest, the system should offer an update operation. Otherwise, it should offer them the option to indicate their interest. This behaviour is achieved by introducing the interactions *indicate_interest* and *update_interest* in combination with the context constraint *indicated* based on the association *interested_in*.

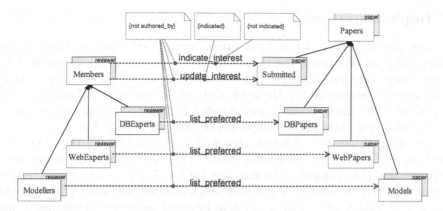

Fig. 6. Context aware requests

We have shown how the runtime resolution algorithm can use the interaction model to adapt the system when a user makes request. Nevertheless, context-aware applications need to be proactive. They should be able to push information to users and execute actions on their behalf when certain conditions are satisfied. Such conditions can be expressed using context constraints. This requires that the application is equipped with an environment that periodically checks all context constraints to trigger proactive interactions. Examples of such proactive interactions in our example are shown in Fig. 7. Interactions which push information are directed from the object to the user role, while interactions which represent automatic execution do not have a direction. In this case, the system will send a reminder to a reviewer one day before the review deadline if a review has not been finalised. The interaction *auto_finalise* states that the system will automatically move the review to the finalised state after the deadline, if a reviewer has set the *automatic_finalise* setting in their preferences.

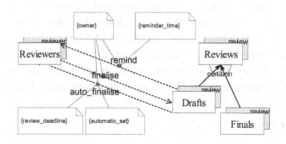

Fig. 7. Proactive behaviour

```
automatic_set := caller[automatic_finalise]
reminder_time := conference[review_deadline] - global_time < 24h
```

7   Implementation

We have shown in Sect. 4 how interactions between roles are modelled on the conceptual level. However, the behaviour of individual objects is specified by the methods of the underlying object-oriented type model. Each interaction can be recursively decomposed to the level of atomic interactions and then mapped to method declarations in an object-oriented language. The interaction model does not deal with the method implementation, and redefinition of interaction relations is fundamentally different from method redefinition. Further, to ensure that interaction constraints are valid, object types need to have the corresponding properties. For example, given the model of Fig. 7, type *review* would need to provide an attribute for *review_deadline* and a common method for interactions *finalise* and *auto_finalise*. Finally, system interactions *create*, *delete*, *grant* and *revoke* correspond to the methods *insert* and *remove* of the collection type.

By developing the interaction model as an extension of OM model, we could integrate it into the core of eOMS, a new data management platform under development based on the OM model. The operational model of eOMS is based on a specially developed object-oriented database programming language OML, which brings together the algebraic operators of the OM query language with procedural constructs. Application logic is provided in OML methods and access control is enforced by the runtime checking of the validity of method calls by applying the resolution algorithm on the application database. To support context-awareness, we are integrating concepts developed in OMSwe, an OM-based platform for web publishing [16].

The interaction model could be also used together with other object-oriented platforms and languages. Similarly to the approach in [7], security infrastructures could be generated for existing software platforms which already support role-based access control to some extent, as is the case with application servers. However, because of the generality of the interaction model, complex mappings would need to be defined in order to bridge the gap between the models. Another approach would be to integrate the interaction model with an existing object-oriented language such as Java. Aspect-oriented frameworks could be used to instrument application code in order to perform security checks on method invocation. However, this would result in issues of how to handle the impedance mismatch arising from the fact that OM supports multiple instantiation and inheritance. Other issues would be how to keep the information on object roles and deal with OM operations in the case of unidirectional Java references.

8   Conclusions

We have shown that it is possible to have a unified role-based interaction model that caters for both the security and context-aware aspects of user interaction with database applications. This was achieved by extending the OM object data model with concepts of interaction relations, interactions and interaction constraints and providing mechanisms for the inheritance and refinement of interactions in role hierarchies.

We plan to facilitate modelling of complex application domains, by providing design patterns to address often occuring requirements. Also, we are working on combining of the interaction model with our extended version model in order to model interactions in collaborative and mobile environments.

References

1. OMG: Unified Modeling Language: Superstructure Version 2.0. (2004)
2. Sandhu, R.S., Coyne, E.J., Feinstein, H.L., Youman, C.E.: Role-Based Access Control Models. IEEE Computer (1996)
3. Ferraiolo, D.F., Sandhu, R., Gavrila, S., Kuhn, D.R., Chandramouli, R.: Proposed NIST Standard for Role-Based Access Control. ACM Trans. Inf. Sys. Sec. (2001)
4. Osborn, S., Sandhu, R., Munawer, Q.: Configuring Role-Based Access Control to Enforce Mandatory and Discretionary Access Control Policies. ACM Trans. Inf. Sys. Secur. (2000)
5. Moffett, J.D.: Control Principles and Role Hierarchies. In: Proc. RBAC. (1998)
6. Crook, R., Ince, D.C., Nuseibeh, B.: Modelling Access Policies Using Roles in Requirements Engineering. Information & Software Technology (2003)
7. Basin, D., Buchheit, M., Doser, J., Hollunder, B., Lodderstedt, T.: Model Driven Security. In: Proc. DACH Security. (2005)
8. Koch, N., Kraus, A., Hennicker, R.: The Authoring Process of the UML-based Web Engineering Approach. In: Proc. Web-Oriented Software Technology Workshop. (2001)
9. Schwabe, D., Guimaraes, R.M., Rossi, G.: Cohesive Design of Personalized Web Applications. IEEE Internet Computing (2002)
10. Brusilovsky, P.: Adaptive Hypermedia. User Modeling and User-Adapted Interaction (2001)
11. Zhang, G., Parashar, M.: Context-Aware Dynamic Access Control for Pervasive Applications. In: Proc. Comm. Networks and Distr. Systems Modeling and Simulation. (2004)
12. Covington, M., Moyer, M., Ahamad, M.: Generalized Role-Based Access Control for Securing Future Applications. In: Proc. Inf. Sys. Sec. (2000)
13. Kiczales, G., Lamping, J., Menhdhekar, A., Maeda, C., Lopes, C., Loingtier, J.M., Irwin, J.: Aspect-Oriented Programming. In: Proc. ECOOP. (1997)
14. Norrie, M.C.: An Extended Entity-Relationship Approach to Data Management in Object-Oriented Systems. In: Proc. ER. (1993)
15. Norrie, M.C.: Distinguishing Typing and Classification in Object Data Models. In: Proc. European-Japanese Seminar on Information and Knowledge Modelling. (1995)
16. Norrie, M.C., Palinginis, A.: Versions for Context Dependent Information Services. In: Proc. CoopIS. (2003)
17. Dey, A.K., Abowd, G.D.: Towards a Better Understanding of Context and Context-Awareness. In: Proc. Context-Awareness Workshop, CHI. (2000)

Conceptual Modelling

Incremental Evaluation of OCL Constraints

Jordi Cabot[1] and Ernest Teniente[2]

[1] Estudis d'Informàtica i Multimèdia, Universitat Oberta de Catalunya
jcabot@uoc.edu
[2] Dept. Llenguatges i Sistemes Informàtics, Universitat Politècnica de Catalunya
teniente@lsi.upc.edu

Abstract. Integrity checking is aimed at determining whether an operation execution violates a given integrity constraint. To perform this computation efficiently, several incremental methods have been developed. The main goal of these methods is to consider as few of the entities in an information base as possible, which is generally achieved by reasoning from the structural events that define the effect of the operations. In this paper, we propose a new method for dealing with the incremental evaluation of the OCL integrity constraints specified in UML conceptual schemas. Since our method works at a conceptual level, its results are useful in efficiently evaluating constraints regardless of the technology platform in which the conceptual schema is to be implemented.

1 Introduction

Integrity constraints (ICs) play a fundamental role in defining the conceptual schemas (CSs) of information systems (ISs) [8]. An IC defines a condition that must be satisfied in every state of an information base (IB). The state of an IB changes when the operations provided by the IS are executed. The effect of an operation on an IB may be specified by means of structural events [18]. A structural event is an elementary change in the population of an entity or relationship type, such as insert entity, delete entity, update attribute, insert relationship, etc.

The IS must guarantee that the IB state resulting from the execution of an operation is consistent with the ICs defined in the CS. This is achieved by ensuring that the structural events that define the operation's effect do not violate any ICs. This process, which is known as *integrity checking*, should be performed as efficiently as possible.

Efficiency is usually achieved by means of *incremental integrity checking*, i.e. by exploiting the information that is available on the structural events to avoid having to completely recalculate the ICs. Hence, the main goal of these methods is to consider as few of the entities in the IB as possible during the computation of IC violations.

For example, a *ValidShipDate* constraint in the CS in Fig. 1.1, which states that "all sales must be completely delivered no later than 30 days after the payment date," may be violated by the execution of the *AddSaleToShipment(s:Sale,sh:Shipment)* operation, which creates a new relationship between sale s and shipment sh, since sh may be planned for a date beyond the last acceptable date for s.

E. Dubois and K. Pohl (Eds.): CAiSE 2006, LNCS 4001, pp. 81–95, 2006.
© Springer-Verlag Berlin Heidelberg 2006

Fig. 1.1. A conceptual schema for sales and their shipments

To verify that *ValidShipDate* is not violated after the execution of the previous operation it is sufficient to consider sale *s* and shipment *sh* of the new relationship, as incremental methods do, rather than carrying out a naive evaluation which must check the previous constraint for all sales and shipments.

In this paper, we propose a new method for coping with the incremental evaluation of ICs at the conceptual level. We assume that CSs are specified in UML [12] and that ICs are defined as invariants written in OCL [11]. For each IC *ic* in the CS and for each structural event *ev* that may violate it, our method provides the most incremental expression that can be used instead of the original IC to check that the application of *ev* does not violate *ic*. By most incremental we mean the one that considers the smallest number of entities of the IB. Our method ensures the most incremental evaluation of the ICs regardless of their specific syntactic definition in the original CS.

If our method were applied to the previous example, it would return an expression whose computation would only verify that the value of the attribute *plannedShipDate* of *sh* does not exceed the value of the attribute *paymentDate* of *s* by more than 30 days.

Since our method works at the conceptual level, it is not technology-dependent. Therefore, the most incremental expressions obtained by our method can be used to efficiently verify the ICs regardless of the target technology platform chosen to implement the CS. Therefore, our results may be integrated into any code-generation method or any MDA-compliant tool to automatically generate an efficient evaluation.

To the best of our knowledge, ours is the first incremental method for OCL constraints. Several proposals have been made for an efficient evaluation of OCL constraints, but with limited results. Moreover, our method is no less efficient than previous methods for the incremental computation of integrity constraints in deductive or relational databases. A comparison with related research is provided in this paper.

The research described herein extends our previous research in [2], in which we proposed a method for computing the entities that might violate an integrity constraint; this method provides partial efficiency results in the evaluation of ICs. The main limitation of that research was that the results were totally dependent on the particular syntactic definition of the IC chosen by the designer, which involved, in the worst case, an almost complete recomputation of the IC after certain structural events. For instance, with the previous definition of *ValidShipDate*, after the *AddSaleToShipment* operation, [2] would verify that the planned date of all shipments of *s* is correct with regards to the payment date (instead of considering just *sh* and *s*, which is achieved using the method we propose here).

The paper is organized as follows. In the subsequent section we present several basic concepts. Section 3 describes our method for incremental integrity checking. Section 4 introduces an optimization for dealing with sets of structural events. An example of the method's application is shown in Section 5. Section 6 compares our approach to related research. Finally, Section 7 presents the conclusions and points out further work.

2 Basic Concepts

Our method assumes that CSs are specified in UML [12]. In UML, entity types and relationship types are represented as classes and associations respectively, while entities are called objects and relationships are referred to as links.

Additionally, the method assumes that textual ICs are defined as invariants written in OCL [11]. Graphical constraints supported by UML, such as cardinality or disjointness constraints, can be transformed into a textual OCL representation, as shown in [6]; therefore, they can also be handled by our method.

As an example, consider the CS in Fig. 2.1, which was designed to (partially) model a simple e-commerce application. The CS contains information on the sales and the products they contain. Sales can be delivered split up into several shipments and shipments can be reused to ship several sales. Finally, sales may be associated with registered customers who benefit from discounts depending on their category.

The CS includes three textual ICs. The first IC (*CorrectProduct*) verifies that all products have a price greater than zero and a max discount of 60% (the maximum discount permitted by the company). The second one is the previous *ValidShipDate* IC, stating that sales must be completely shipped within 30 days after the payment date (and that therefore all shipments of that sale must be planned before that date). Finally, *NotTooPendingSales* holds if customers do not have pending sales for an amount greater than the *maxPendingAmount* value in their category.

Note that an IC in OCL is defined in the context of a specific type[1] or *context type*, and its *body* (the Boolean OCL expression that states the IC condition) must be satisfied by all instances of that type. For example, in *ValidShipDate*, *Sale* is the context type, the variable *self* refers to an entity of *Sale* and the date condition (the body) must hold for all possible values of *self* (i.e. all entities of *Sale*).

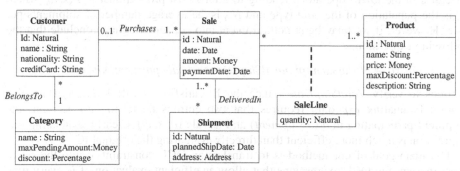

context Product inv CorrectProduct: self.price>0 and self.maxDiscount<=60
context Sale inv ValidShipDate: self.shipment->forAll(s| s.plannedShipDate<=self.paymentDate+30)
context Category inv NotTooPendingSales:
self.customer->forAll(c| c.sale->select(paymentDate>now()).import->sum()<=self.maxPendingAmount)

Fig. 2.1. Our running example

---

[1] In UML 2.0, the context type may be either an entity type or a relationship type since both types are represented in the UML metamodel as subclasses of the *Classifier* metaclass.

As we mentioned above, ICs must be checked after structural events have been applied. In this paper, we consider the following kinds of structural event types:

- InsertET(ET): inserts an entity in the entity type ET
- UpdateAttribute($Attr,ET$) updates the value of attribute $Attr$.
- DeleteET(ET) deletes an entity of entity type ET.
- SpecializeET(ET) specializes an entity of a supertype of ET to ET.
- GeneralizeET(ET) generalizes an entity of a subtype of ET to ET.
- InsertRT(RT) creates a new relationship in the relationship type RT.
- DeleteRT(RT) deletes a relationship of relationship type RT.

3   Determining the Incremental Expressions of an OCL Constraint

In this section, we describe the method we propose for obtaining the most incremental expressions that should be used instead of the original IC, to ensure that the IC is not violated when a structural event is applied to the IB. We start by providing an overview of the method in Section 3.1. Then, in Sections 3.2 to 3.4, we define the three main operators used in our method to obtain these incremental expressions. An implementation of the method is described in [4].

3.1   An Overview of the Method

A direct evaluation of the original OCL definition of an IC, i.e. the one specified in the CS, may be highly inefficient. For example, a direct evaluation of the constraint *ValidShipDate* (as stated in Fig. 2.1) after an event *InsertRT(DeliveredIn)*, which creates a new relationship d between sale s and shipment sh, would require taking into account all sales (because this is the context type) and, for each sale, all its shipments (because of the *forAll* operator), leading to a total cost proportional to $P_s x N_{sh}$, where P_s is the population of the *Sale* type and N_{sh} is the average number of shipments per sale. However, if we take the structural event into account we may conclude that the following expression:

$$exp \equiv d.shipment.plannedShipDate <= d.sale.paymentDate+30$$

suffices to verify *ValidShipDate* (since the IB satisfies *exp* iff *ValidShipDate* also holds). Evaluating *exp* only requires that two entities be taken into account: the shipment participating in d (*d.shipment*) and its sale (*d. sale*). Clearly, evaluating this expression is much more efficient than directly evaluating the original IC.

The main goal of our method is to translate an OCL constraint *ic* into the set of most incremental OCL expressions that allow an efficient evaluation of *ic* every time a structural event is applied over the IB. In general, there will be a different most incremental expression for each IC and each structural event that may violate it.

By incremental we mean that the evaluation of the expression does not need to take all entities of the context type of *ic* and all their relationships into account, since it can reason forward directly from the entities that have been updated by the structural event. The most incremental expression is the one that considers the lowest number of entities of the IB. Obviously, the more entities required to evaluate an expression the less efficient is its computation. We use $inc_{<ic,ev>}$ to denote the most incremental expression for a constraint ic after a structural event ev has been applied. In the previous example, exp is the most incremental expression for *ValidShipDate* after the event *InsertRT(DeliveredIn)* has been applied.

The events that may violate an IC are called *potentially violating structura events* (PSEs) for that IC and may be determined by the method proposed in [1]. Applied to our example, this method would state that only *InsertRT(DeliveredIn)*, *UpdateAttribute(plannedShipDate, Shipment)* and *UpdateAttribute(paymentDate, Sale)* can violate *ValidShipDate*. Note that other events such as *DeleteET(Sale)* or *UpdateAttribute(address,Shipment)* may never violate that IC. The most incremental expressions of an IC must only be defined by events in the set of PSEs of the IC.

Determining the most incremental expressions depends on the given PSE and on the structure of the IC. Moreover, it generally requires changing the context type of the initial IC, since we cannot guarantee that the context chosen by the designer to specify the IC is the most appropriate one as far as efficiency is concerned.

Intuitively, our method works as follows. First, it selects from all possible context types for the constraint (those types referenced in the body of the IC) the most appropriate one with respect to the structural event (i.e. the one that will produce the most efficient expression at the end of the process for that event). Second, it redefines the body of the IC in terms of this new context type ct'. Third, it computes the instances of ct' that may have been affected by the event. Finally, the incremental expression is obtained by refining the body of the IC to be applied only over those relevant instances. This procedure is specified in the following algorithm.

Algorithm. *Obtaining the most incremental expressions*

Given an IC ic, which is defined in terms of a context type ct and an event ev (where ev is a PSE for ic), the following *IncrementalExpression* algorithm returns the $inc_{<ic,ev>}$ expression:

> *IncrementalExpression(ic: Constraint, ev: Event) : Expression*
> > *Type bestContext := BestContext(ic,ev)*
> > *Constraint ic':= Translate(ic,ev,bestContext);*
> > *Expression rel := Relevant (ic', ev)*
> > *return (Merge(rel, ic'))*

where

1. *BestContext(ic:Constraint, ev:,Event)* returns the type that must be used as a context of ic to generate an incremental expression for ic after event ev.
2. *Translate(ic:Constraint, ev:Event, t:Type)* returns an IC ic', which is defined using t as a context type, such that ic' is equivalent to ic regarding ev.
3. *Relevant(ic:Constraint, ev:Event)* returns an OCL expression whose evaluation returns the instances of ct (the context type of ic) affected by ev.
4. *Merge(exp:Expression, ic:Constraint)* creates the final $inc_{<ic,ev>}$ expression by applying b (the body of ic) to all entities reached in exp (the expression computing the relevant instances). If the evaluation of exp returns a single instance (i.e. all navigations included in exp have '1' as a maximum multiplicity), this operator just replaces all occurrences of *self* in b with exp. Otherwise, the final expression is $exp\text{-}> forAll(v|b)$ where all occurrences of *self* in b are replaced with v.

Let us again consider the event *InsertRT(DeliveredIn)* and the constraint *ValidShipDate*. As we have seen their incremental expression is *exp*, which is obtained using our method in the following way:

1. BestContext(*ValidShipDate,InsertRT(DeliveredIn)*) = *DeliveredIn*
2. Translate(*ValidShipDate, InsertRT(DeliveredIn), DeliveredIn*) =
   context *DeliveredIn* **inv** *newIC:*
      self.shipment.plannedShipDate<=self.sale.paymentDate+30
3. Relevant(*newIC,InsertRT(DeliveredIn)*) = *d*, the new relationship created by the *InserRT* event over *DeliveredIn*
4. Merge(*d,newIC*) (i.e. inc$_{<ValidShipDate,InsertRT(DeliveredIn)>}$) =
      d.shipment.plannedShipDate <= d.sale.paymentDate+30

We show in [3] that the expression generated by the previous algorithm is always the most incremental one.

In the rest of this section we formally define the *BestContext, Translate* and *Relevant* operators. To facilitate their definition, our method assumes a normalized representation of the ICs. The normalization reduces the number of different OCL operators appearing in their body (for instance, replacing the *implies* operator with a combination of the *not* and *or* operators or the *exists* operator with a combination of the *select* and *size* operators). This representation is automatically obtained from the initial IC and does not entail a loss of expressive power of the ICs we deal with.

All three operators work with the ICs represented as an instance of the OCL metamodel [11]. According to this representation, they can handle the OCL expression by forming the body of the IC as a binary tree, in which each node represents an atomic subset of the OCL expression (an operation, an access to an attribute or an association, etc.) and the root is the most external operation of the OCL expression. As an example, in Fig. 3.1 the constraint *ValidShipDate* is represented by means of the OCL metamodel. Each node is marked with the set of PSEs produced by that node [1] (i.e. the events that are PSEs of the IC because of that particular node).

3.2 BestContext(ic:Constraint, ev:,Event)

The best context to verify an IC *ic* after applying an event *ev* to the IB is automatically drawn from the node where *ev* is assigned in the tree representing IC. We use *node$_{ev}$* to denote this node (when different *node$_{ev}$* exist we repeat the process for each node). The *BestContext* operator always returns the same result regardless of the original syntactic definition of *ic*, since all possible syntactic definitions of *ic* must contain *node$_{ev}$* (because all of them may be violated by *ev*).

To determine the context type, we must consider whether *node$_{ev}$* participates (i.e. is included) in an *individual condition* or in a *collection condition*. Intuitively, individual conditions must be verified for each individual entity (for instance, each individual product must satisfy the *CorrectProduct* IC). In contrast, collection conditions must be verified by the set of entities affected by the condition as a whole (for instance, in *NotTooPendingSales*, the sum of all sales of a customer must satisfy the *maxPendingAmount* condition). Individual and collection conditions are formalized in Definitions 3.2.1 and 3.2.2.

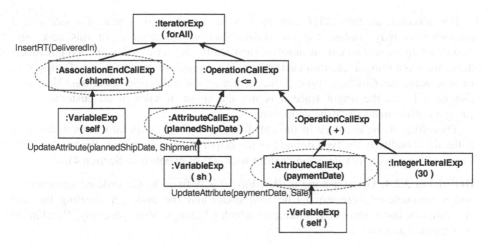

Fig. 3.1. The OCL metamodel of *ValidShipDate* and its set of PSEs

Definition 3.2.1. A node n participates in a *collection condition* when n is used to compute an aggregate operator. Formally, when n verifies that $\{\exists n' | n' \in PathRoot(n)$ and n'.oclIsTypeOf(OperationCallExp) and n'.referredOperation $\in \{size, sum, count\}\}$, where $PathRoot(n)$ is defined as the ordered sequence of nodes encountered between n (the first node in the sequence) and the root of the tree (the last one). *OclIsTypeOf* and *referredOperation* are elements defined in the OCL metamodel.

Definition 3.2.2. A node n participates in an *individual condition* if it does not participate in a collection condition.

Clearly, since individual conditions must hold for each individual entity restricted by the constraint, the most incremental expression will be the one that only takes into account the single entity updated by the event. The original IC must then be redefined in terms of the type of entity to obtain this expression.

Proposition 3.2.3. Let *ev* be an event over an entity *e* (resp. relationship *r*) of type *E* (resp. *R*). If $node_{ev}$ is included in an individual condition, *BestContext* returns the same type *E* (resp. *R*) as the best context.

In our example, the constraint *ValidShipDate* may be violated by three different structural events, all of them included in individual conditions: *InsertRT(DeliveredIn)*, *UpdateAttribute(plannedShipDate,Shipment)* and *UpdateAttribute(paymentDate,Sale)*, as shown in the tree in Fig. 3.1. Their best contexts are therefore *DeliveredIn*, *Shipment* and *Sale* respectively.

The same idea cannot be applied to events included in collection conditions since those conditions must be satisfied by the collection as a whole and not by each single instance. Thus, to consider the modified entity or relationship is not enough to verify it because, after every modification, the whole collection must be recomputed again and the other entities in the collection must also be taken into account. For this reason, in selecting the best context it must be ensured that, after each modification, only the exact set of entities involved in the condition is checked.

For instance, an *InsertRT(Purchases)* event (i.e. the assignment of a sale *s* to a customer *c*) may violate the constraint *NotTooPendingSales*. In this case, the *maxPendingAmount* condition must be satisfied by the set of sales of each customer; thus, after assigning a sale to a customer *c*, it is enough to verify the set of sales of *c*. In this way, the *Customer* type is the origin of the collection condition. Note that *Category* is not the origin since it is not the union of sales of all customers in a category who must satisfy the condition.

Therefore, if the event *ev* in the call to the *BestContext* operator is included in a collection condition, the type defined as the origin of the collection is the best context. This will be especially true when dealing with sets of events (see Section 4).

Definition 3.2.4. Given a node n, *PathVar(n)* is defined as the ordered sequence of nodes encountered between *n* (the first node) and the node representing the *self* variable (the last node) of the subtree to which *n* belongs. More precisely, *PathVar(n)* is computed as follows:

- The first node is *n*.
- For each node included in *PathVar* we also include its child (or the left child if the node has two children), if any.
- When a node *n* included in *PathVar* represents a variable other than *self* (i.e. variables used in *select* or *forAll* iterators), we add as a left child the node pointed to in *n.referredVariable.loopExpr* (i.e. the node representing the iterator; *referredVariable* and *loopExpr* are associations defined in the OCL metamodel).

Definition 3.2.5. Given an integrity constraint *ic*, an event *ev* and the sequence $PathVar(node_{ev})$, $node_{or}$, the node origin of a collection condition is
- The left child of a node $n \in PathVar(node_{ev})$, representing a *forAll* iterator, when a *select* iterator is not encountered between the *self* variable and *n*.
- Otherwise, the last node in $PathVar(node_{ev})$ (i.e. the node representing the *self* variable). If following the *self* variable there is a set of nodes representing navigations $r_1...r_n$ where all r_i have a maximum multiplicity of 1, then the final $node_{or}$ is the node at r_n.

Proposition 3.2.6. Let *ev* be an event included in a collection condition. The type of the entities at $node_{or}$ is then returned as the best context.

In the *NotTooPendingSales* constraint, *Customer* is the origin of the condition since it is the type of the entities accessed in the node previous to the *forAll* iterator (the node navigating to customers from category). Therefore, *Customer* is the *BestContext* for all events included in the collection condition (updates of the *paymentDate* and *amount* attributes and inserts of *Purchases* relationships). The PSEs *UpdateAttribute(maxPendingAmount)* and *InsertRT(BelongsTo)* are included in individual conditions; thus, their best contexts are *Category* and *BelongsTo* respectively (as determined by Proposition 3.2.3).

3.3 Translate(ic:Constraint, ev:Event, t:Type)

Given an IC *ic* that has a context type *t* and an event *ev*, the *Translate* operator returns an IC *ic'* defined over a type *t'*, $t' \neq t$, which is semantically equivalent to *ic* with respect to event ev. Having applied ev over the IB, ic' and ic are semantically equivalent when ic' is satisified iff ic is also satisfied in the new state of the IB.

The $Translate$ operator extends the method we presented in [5] since the context changes required in the work reported here present two particularities that can be used in order to provide a more optimized redefinition than the one in the previous reference.

First, t' is the type returned by the $BestContext$ operator (this implies, for instance, that t' is referenced in the body of ic). Second, ic and ic' need only be equivalent with regards to the particular event ev. Therefore, ic' need not worry about all the literals of ic that cannot be violated by ev.

For instance, given that the body of ic follows the pattern L_1 and L_2 (as $CorrectProduct$ in Fig. 2.1) and that ev can only induce a change in the truth value of L_1, ic' does not need to include the verification of L_2. L_2 was true before ev was executed (since all the states of the IB must be consistent) and, since ev does not affect it, L_2 will still hold after its execution. When it does not hold it is because some other event, ev', has been applied. The incremental expression for ev' will take care of this possible violation.

$Translate$ is defined in two separate steps. First, the tree is pruned to remove the irrelevant conditions. Then the remaining tree is redefined over the context type t' to obtain the final body of the translated constraint ic'.

Definition 3.3.1. Let ev be an event attached to a node $node_{ev}$. A node n_{and} representing an AND condition may be pruned if $\{n_{and} \in PathRoot(node_{ev})$ and $\neg \exists n' |$ $n' \in PathRoot(n_{and})$ and $n'.oclIsTypeOf(IteratorExp)$ and $n'.name="select"\}$. N_{and} nodes are replaced with the child node $n_{child} \in PathRoot(node_{ev})$. Consequently, the other child of n_{and} (i.e. the other condition) is removed from the tree.

Definition 3.3.2. Given a pruned tree tr that represents a constraint ic defined using a context type t, an event ev and the new context type t', the redefined tree tr' that represents an equivalent IC ic' defined over t' is obtained according to the following steps (see [5] for a more detailed explanation and examples):

- Determining the node $node_{t'}$. $Node_t$ is the node $\in PathVar(node_{ev})$ whose evaluation returns entities of type t'. If t' is a relationship type, $node_{t'}$ is the node previous to the navigation through a role of t'.
- Replacing all subtrees that match the sequence $seq=PathVar(node_{t'})$ with a single node representing the $self$ variable.
- Replacing all other nodes that represent $self$ variables with the subtree corresponding to the expression $self.r_1...r_n$ (or $self.r_1...r_n$->$forAll(v|)$ when the maximum multiplicity of some r_i is greater than 1), where $r_1..r_n$ are the roles needed to navigate from t' to t (the roles opposite to the ones used in the ic to navigate from t to t'). Formally, $r_1...r_n = Inverse(PathVar(node_t))$ with $Inverse$ defined as $\{\forall n \in PathVar(node_t) |$ n.oclIsTypeOf(AssociationEndCallExp) $\rightarrow$ OppositeRole(n) $\in$ Inverse(PathVar(node$_t$))$\}$.
- Adding the subtree that corresponds to the expression $self.r_1...r_n$->$notEmpty()$ $implies$ X (where X is the tree resulting from the previous steps) to ensure that only those instances of t' related to a given instance of t are verified (otherwise, they were not involved in the original IC).

The resulting tree can be simplified [5] by, for instance, replacing the subtree $self.r_1...r_n\text{-}>notEmpty()$ with *true* if all multiplicities of $r_1...r_n$ are at least 1 or by removing the *forAll* iterators over single entities.

For example, *Translate(NotTooPendingSales,UpdateAttr(paymentDate,Sale), Customer)* transforms the constraint *NotTooPendingSales*, as defined in Fig. 2.1, in the following *NotTooPendingSales'* constraint defined with the context *Customer*:

context *Customer* **inv:** *self.sale->select(paymentDate>now()).amount>sum()*
$$<\!=\!self.category.maxPendingAmount$$

where, after step one, *self.customer* has been replaced with *self*, the other *self* variable has been replaced with *self.category* (*category* is the role required to navigate from customer to category) and finally, *self.category->notEmpty()* has been simplified (all customers belong to a category) and the *forAll* has been removed.

3.4 Relevant(ic:Constraint, ev:Event)

After issuing a PSE *ev* for an IC *ic* whose context type is *t*, only the instances of *t* that may have been affected as a result of applying *ev* should be verified. The goal of the *Relevant* operator is to return an expression *exp* that returns this set of relevant instances when it is evaluated; *exp* can be automatically derived from the tree representing *ic* [2].

Intuitively, the relevant instances of *t* are the ones related to the instance modified by *ev*. Therefore, the basic idea is that *exp* will consist of the sequence of navigations required to navigate back from the modified instance to the instances of *t*. As in the previous operator, the navigations required are obtained by reversing the navigations used to navigate from the *self* variable to $node_{ev}$.

Definition 3.4.1. Let *ic* be an IC and *ev* a PSE that appears in nodes $node_{ev1}...node_{evn}$. Then, $Relevant(ic,ev) = Inverse(PathVar(node_{ev1})) \cup ... \cup Inverse(PathVar(node_{evn}))$.

As an example, let us consider the *NotTooPendingSales'* IC (as redefined in the previous section). After the event *UpdateAttribute(amount, Sale)* that updates a sale *s*, the IC must be verified over customers returned by *Relevant(NotTooPendingSales', UpdateAttribute(amount, Sale))*. In this case, the operator returns the expression *s.customer*, which implies that we just need to verify the customer that the *sale* is assigned to (at most one, because of the maximum multiplicity specified in *Purchases*). In the expression, *customer* represents the opposite role of the *sale* role of the *Purchases* relationship type (the single role appearing in the *PathVar* sequence of nodes for the $node_{ev}$ of the update event).

4 Dealing with Sets of Events

Up to now we have provided a method that generates incremental expressions for the efficient verification of an IC after issuing a PSE *ev*. Obviously, if an operation consists of several PSEs for the IC, the consistency of the new state of the IB can be verified using the incremental expressions corresponding to each individual event.

However, the efficiency can be improved by taking into account the relationship between the different events when computing the affected instances. This improvement is only relevant to events included in collection conditions (events in individual conditions must be individually verified by each entity).

By way of example, let us assume that the execution of an operation updates the amount of two sales (s_1 and s_2) and assigns a sale s_3 to a customer c. If one (or both) of the updated sales were also assigned to c, we must verify the *NotTooPendingSales* constraint over c several times (once because of the sale assignment and the other times because of the update of sales of c). However, if we first merge the customers affected by each single event and then verify them, we avoid having to verify the same customer several times.

Proposition 4.1. Let $set=\{ev_1,ev_2,...ev_n\}$ be a set of different events for an IC ic sharing the same IC definition ic' after the the *BestContext* and *Translate* operators, and included in the same operation (without loss of generality, we assume that each operation constitutes a single transaction). The *Relevant* operator is then redefined as

$$Relevant(ic',set):= Relevant(ic',ev_1) \cup ... \cup Relevant(ic', ev_{ni})$$

Following the previous example, now the relevant customers (i.e. the ones that will be verified) are computed with the expression

$$c.union\text{-}>(s_1.customer\text{-}>union(s_2.customer))$$

Thus, each relevant customer will be verified only once.

5 Applying the Method

We have applied our method to obtaining the most incremental expressions of all ICs in the CS in Fig. 2.1. The results are shown in Table 5.1. The first column indicates the IC. The second one specifies the structural events[2] that may violate each IC. Finally, the third column shows the most incremental expressions obtained for each IC due to each of the events. In this column, the initial variable represents the entity or relationship modified by the event (d represents the created *DeliveredIn* relationship, sh the updated *Shipment* and so forth).

For instance, Table 5.1 allows us to detect that the application of an event *UpdateAttribute(paymentDate,Sale)* over a sale s may violate the ICs: *ValidShipDate* and *NotTooPendingSales*. The most incremental expressions that allow us to verify that the new state of the IB does not violate any ICs are given by expressions 3 and 7.

As we said, using the most incremental expressions to verify the ICs in the original CS ensures the optimal efficiency of the integrity checking process as far the number of entities involved during the computation is concerned. To illustrate the importance of those results, Table 5.2 compares the cost of the most incremental expressions for *ValidShipDate* (as given by Table 5.1) with the cost of directly evaluating the original IC (see Fig. 2.1).

---

[2] To simplify, we use the notation *UpdateAttr(attr)* when the type is clear from the context.

Table 5.1. Results of applying our method over the example CS

IC	Event	Incremental expression
Valid Ship Date	InsertRT(DeliveredIn)	1. d.shipment.plannedShipDate<=d.sale.paymentDate+30
	UpdateAttr(plannedShip Date)	2. sh.sale->forAll(s| sh.plannedShipDate <= s.paymentDate+30)
	UpdateAttr(paymentDate)	3. s.shipment->forAll(sh| sh.plannedShipDate <= s.paymentDate+30)
NotToo Pend Sales	UpdateAttr(maxPending Amount)	4. c.customer->forAll(cu| cu.sale->select(paymentDate> now()).amount->sum()<=c.maxPendingAmount
	InsertRT(BelongsTo)	5. b.customer.sale ->select(paymentDate>now()).amount- >sum()<=b.category.maxPendingAmount
	InsertRT(Purchases)	6. pur.customer.sale ->select(paymentDate>now()).amount- >sum()<=pur.customer.category.maxPendingAmount
	UpdateAttr(paymentDate) UpdateAttr(amount)	7. s.customer.sale->select(paymentDate>now()).amount- >sum()<=s.customer.category.maxPendingAmount
Correct Prod	UpdateAttr(price)	8. p.price>0
	UpdateAttr(maxDiscount)	9. p.maxDiscount<=60
	InsertET(Product)	10. p.price>0 and p.maxDiscount<=60

Table 5.2. Cost comparisons for *ValidShipDate*

Event	Cost(ValidShipDate)	Cost (Incremental Expression)
InsertRT(DeliveredIn)	P_s x N_{sh}	2
UpdateAttribute(paymentDate)	P_s x N_{sh}	$1+1xN_{sh}$
UpdateAttribute(plannedShipDate)	P_s x N_{sh}	$1+1xN_s$
Other events	P_s x N_{sh}	0

In Table 5.2, P_s stands for the number of instances of *Sale*, N_{sh} for the average number of shipments per sale and N_s for the average number of sales per shipment. Cost comparisons for the evaluation of the other ICs are given in [3].

Designers may use the most incremental expressions to efficiently verify the ICs when they are implementing the CS in any final technology platform. For instance, during code generation for an object-oriented technology, adding expressions 3 and 7 to methods that include the *UpdateAttribute(paymentDate, Sale)* event is enough to ensure that the IB is not violated after the application of the event. Additionally, when we are using a relational database as an IB, we may create a set of triggers that verify both expressions before we apply the change to the *Sale* table data. For example, Fig. 5.1 shows a possible verification of expression 3 in both technologies.

6 Related Work

Two kinds of related research are relevant here: methods devoted to the problem of integrity checking, of which there is a long tradition, especially in the database field (see Section 6.1), and tools that provide code-generation capabilities that may include facilities for improving the efficiency of integrity checking (see Section 6.2).

```
MethodX(Sale s,...)
{  ... s.paymentDate = value;  ...
   //Verification of expression 3
   Iterator setsh = s.shipments.iterator();
   while ( setsh.hasNext() )
   {  Shipment sh = (Shipment) setsh.next();
      If (sh.plannedShipDate>s.paymentDate+30)
         throw new Exception("Invalid date");
   }
}
```

```
create trigger uPaymentDate
before update of PaymentDate on Sale for each row
Declare v_Error NUMBER;
   EInvalidDate Exception;
Begin  --Verification of expression 3
   SELECT count(*) into v_Error
   FROM DeliveredIn d, Shipment sh
   WHERE d.sale = :new.id and d.shipment = sh.id
         and sh.plannedShipDate>:new.paymentDate+30;
   If (v_Error>0) then raise EInvalidDate; end if;
End;
```

Fig. 5.1. Examples of incremental expressions implemented in particular technologies

6.1 Integrity Checking Methods for Deductive or Relational Databases

The most important results of related research of an incremental checking of integrity constraints are provided by methods proposed for integrity checking in deductive databases. In what follows we briefly show that the efficiency of our incremental expressions is equivalent to the incremental rules generated by the most representative proposals in this field (see [7] for a survey).

They define ICs as inconsistency predicates that will be true whenever the corresponding IC is violated. For example, they would represent *ValidShipDate* as (where S stands for *Sale, Sh* for *Shipment, D* for DeliveredIn, *pd* for *paymentDate* and *psh* for *plannedShipDate*)

$$Ic_{ValidShipDate} \leftarrow S(s,pd) \wedge D(s,sh) \wedge Sh(sh, psd) \wedge pd+30 < psd$$

To incrementally check this constraint they would consider the following rules:

1. $Ic_{ValidShipDate} \leftarrow iS(s,pd) \wedge D(s,sh) \wedge Sh(sh, psd) \wedge pd+30 < psd$
2. $Ic_{ValidShipDate} \leftarrow uS(s,pd') \wedge D(s,sh) \wedge Sh(sh, psd) \wedge pd'+30 < psd$
3. $Ic_{ValidShipDate} \leftarrow S(s,pd) \wedge iD(s,sh) \wedge Sh(sh, psd) \wedge pd+30 < psd$
4. $Ic_{ValidShipDate} \leftarrow S(s,pd) \wedge D(s,sh) \wedge iSh(sh, psd) \wedge pd+30 < psd$
5. $Ic_{ValidShipDate} \leftarrow S(s,pd) \wedge D(s,sh) \wedge uSh(sh, psd') \wedge pd+30 < psd'$

where *iX(y)* means that the entity y of type X has been inserted and uX means that it has been updated (those updates are only considered explicitly in [17]).

After applying our method to the same constraint, we obtain the following three incremental expressions (as shown in Table 5.1):

a. s.shipment->forAll(sh|s.paymentDate+30>=sh.plannedShipDate)
b. sh.sale->forAll(s| s.paymentDate+30>=sh.plannedShipDate)
c. d.sale.paymentDate+30>=d.shipment.plannedShipDate

where s is the updated sale, *sh* the updated shipment and d the new *DeliveredIn* relationship. The definitions we get are respectively equivalent to Rules 2, 5 and 3 in those methods. Note that the insertion of a shipment (Rule 4) cannot violate the constraint if it is not assigned to a sale, which is already controlled by our expression c (similarly, for the insertion of sales, Rule 1).

6.2 Tools with Code-Generation Capabilities

Almost all current CASE tools offer code-generation capabilities. However, most of them do not allow the definition of OCL constraints or (more commonly) do no take them into account when they generate the code. This is the case of tools such as *Rational Rose*, *MagicDraw*, *ArcStyler*, *OptimalJ*, *Objecteering/UML* and many more.

All tools that are able to generate code for the verification of OCL constraints depart from the ICs exactly as defined by the designer; thus, their efficiency depends on the concrete syntactic representation of the IC. The differences between these tools lie in how they decide when the IC needs to be checked and the amount of entities they take into account every time the IC is checked.

Tools such as *Octopus* [10] or *OCLE* [16] transform the IC into a Java method; when the method is executed, an exception is raised if the IC does not hold. However, the decision of when to verify the IC is left to the designer. The *OO-Method* [13] verifies all ICs whose context type is t whenever a method of t is executed (even if the changes produced by the method cannot violate a given IC). *Dresden OCL* [15] verifies the ICs only after events that modify the elements appear in the IC body, but it does not consider whether that sort of change can really induce its violation. For instance, *Dresden OCL* would verify *ValidShipDate* after deletions of *DeliveredIn* relationships, although only the latter event can really violate the IC. *OCL2SQL* (included in [15]) transforms each IC into an SQL view so that the view returning data indicates that the IC does not hold. Nevertheless, the view is not incremental. Every time an entity is modified, the view verifies all the entities of the context type.

7 Conclusions and Further Work

We have presented a method that generates the most incremental expressions for OCL constraints defined in UML CSs. These expressions can be used instead of the original IC when the IB is verified after modifications caused by a set of structural events. The method has been implemented in [4].

The most incremental expressions use information on the structural events issued during the operation to optimize the integrity checking process by considering as few entities of the IB as possible. In this way, we ensure an optimal verification of the ICs regardless of the concrete syntactic definition originally chosen by the designer.

The main advantage of our approach is that it works at a conceptual level; therefore, it is not technology-dependent. In contrast with previous approaches, our results can be used regardless of the final technology platform selected to implement the CS. In fact, any code-generation strategy able to generate code from a CS, such as the ones presented in the previous section, could be enhanced with our method for the purpose of automatically generating an optimal integrity checking code for the ICs.

As further work, we could try to further improve the efficiency of the whole integrity checking process by considering, at the conceptual level, additional optimization techniques initially proposed for databases like [9] and [14]. Moreover, we would also like to adapt our method for the incremental maintenance of derived elements specified in a CS.

Acknowledgments

We would like to thank the people of the GMC group J. Conesa, D. Costal, X. de Palol, C. Gómez, A. Olivé, A.Queralt, R. Raventós and M. R. Sancho for their many useful comments in the preparation of this paper. This work has been partially supported by the Ministerio de Ciencia y Tecnologia under project TIN2005-06053.

References

1. Cabot, J., Teniente, E.: Determining the Structural Events that May Violate an Integrity Constraint. In: Proc. 7th Int. Conf. on the Unified Modeling Language (UML'04), LNCS, 3273 (2004) 173-187
2. Cabot, J., Teniente, E.: Computing the Relevant Instances that May Violate an OCL Constraint. In: Proc. 17th Int. Conf. on Advanced Information Systems Engineering (CAiSE'05), LNCS, 3520 (2005) 48-62
3. Cabot, J., Teniente, E.: Incremental Evaluation of OCL Constraints (extended version). UPC, LSI Research Report, LSI-05-12-R (2005)
4. Cabot, J., Teniente, E.: A Tool for the Incremental Evaluation of OCL Constraints. Available at www.lsi.upc.edu/~jcabot/research/tools/caise06 (2006)
5. Cabot, J., Teniente, E.: Transforming OCL Constraints: A Context Change Approach. In: Proc. 21st Annual ACM Symposium on Applied Computing (Model Transformation Track), (2006)
6. Gogolla, M., Richters, M.: Expressing UML Class Diagrams Properties with OCL. In: A. Clark and J. Warmer, (eds.): Object Modeling with the OCL. Springer-Verlag (2002) 85-114
7. Gupta, A., Mumick, I. S.: Maintenance of Materialized Views: Problems, Techniques, and Applications. In: Materialized Views Techniques, Implementations, and Applications. The MIT Press (1999) 145-157
8. ISO/TC97/SC5/WG3: Concepts and Terminology for the Conceptual Schema and Information Base. ISO, (1982)
9. Lee, S. Y., Ling, T. W.: Further Improvements on Integrity Constraint Checking for Stratifiable Deductive Databases. In: Proc. 22nd Int. Conf. on Very Large Data Bases. Morgan Kaufmann (1996) 495-505
10. Klasse Objecten.: Octopus: OCL Tool for Precise UML Specifications. (2005)
11. OMG: UML 2.0 OCL Specification. OMG Adopted Specification (ptc/03-10-14)
12. OMG: UML 2.0 Superstructure. OMG Adopted Specification (ptc/03-08-02)
13. Pastor, O., Gómez, J., Insfrán, E., Pelechano, V.: The OO-Method Approach for Information Systems Modeling: From Object-Oriented Conceptual Modeling to Automated Programming. Information Systems 26 (2001) 507-534
14. Ross, K. A., Srivastava, D., Sudarshan, S.: Materialized View Maintenance and Integrity Constraint Checking: Trading Space for Time. In: Proc. ACM SIGMOD international conference on Management of data, (1996) 447-458
15. Dresden University.: Dresden OCL Toolkit. (2005)
16. Babes-Bolyai University.: Object Constraint Language Environment 2.0.
17. Urpí, T., Olivé, A.: A Method for Change Computation in Deductive Databases. In: Proc. 18th Int. Conf. on Very Large Data Bases. Morgan Kaufmann (1992) 225-237
18. Wieringa, R.: A Survey of Structured and Object-Oriented Software Specification Methods and Techniques. ACM Computing Surveys 30 (1998) 459-527

Object-Relational Representation of a Conceptual Model for Temporal Data Warehouses*

Elzbieta Malinowski** and Esteban Zimányi

Department of Informatics & Networks,
Université Libre de Bruxelles
emalinow@ulb.ac.be, ezimanyi@ulb.ac.be

Abstract. Temporal Data Warehouses (TDWs) allow to manage time-varying multidimensional data by joining the research of Temporal Databases and Data Warehouses. TDWs raise different issues such as temporal aggregations, multidimensional schema versioning, etc. However, very little attention from the research community has been drawn to conceptual modeling for TDWs and its subsequent logical representation. In this paper, we present a mapping transforming our conceptual model for TDW design into the conventional ER and an object-relational models. For the latter, we show some examples using the SQL:2003 standard. We include the mapping for time-varying levels, hierarchies, and measures. We also discuss the inconveniences of a pure relational representation.

1 Introduction

Data Warehouses (DWs) store and provide access to large volumes of historical data supporting the decision-making process. The structure of DWs is usually represented as a *star schema*, consisting of fact and dimension tables. A *fact table* contains numeric data called *measures*, e.g., sales. *Dimensions* are used for exploring the measures from different analysis perspectives. They usually contain hierarchies that allow to analyze detailed and generalized data using the roll-up and drill-down operations of On-Line Analytical Processing (OLAP) systems.

Current DW models include a time dimension that is used for grouping purposes (the roll-up operation) and also serves as a time-varying indicator for measures, e.g., sales in March 2005. However, the time dimension cannot be used for representing changes in other dimensions.

On the other hand, Temporal Databases (TDBs) allow to represent time-varying information. Two different temporal types[1] are considered: *valid time* (VT) and *transaction time* (TT) that indicate, respectively, when the data is

---

* The work of E. Malinowski was funded by a scholarship of the Cooperation Department of the Université Libre de Bruxelles.
** Currently on leave from the Universidad de Costa Rica.
[1] Usually called time dimensions; however, we use the term "dimension" in the multidimensional context.

true in the modeled reality and when it is current in the database. If both temporal types are used, they define *bitemporal time* (BT). Further, the *lifespan* (LS) allows to record changes in time for an object as a whole.

Temporal Data Warehouses (TDWs) join the research achievements of TDBs and DWs in order to manage time-varying multidimensional data. In [6, 8] we proposed MultiDimER, a conceptual model for modeling TDW applications. In this work we give a logical representation for this conceptual model.

Two approaches can be used for logical-level design: using normalization (e.g., [5]) or mapping a conceptual model into a logical model (e.g., [4]). We choose the latter since there are no well-accepted normal forms for TDBs even though some formal approaches exist (e.g., [5, 13]). Further, the purpose of normalization is to avoid the problems of data redundancy, potential inconsistency, and update anomalies. However, the usual practice in DWs is to de-normalize relations to improve performance and to avoid the costly process of joining tables.

In this paper, we present a mapping of a conceptual model for time-varying multidimensional data into a classical ER and into an object-relational (OR) models. The ER representation allows a better understanding of the constructs used in our model. Further, to assist implementers who use our model for conceptual design, we propose general rules for mapping directly our model to the OR model. We consider the particularities of the different elements of a multidimensional model and exploit the features of OR databases for modeling complex objects. In this paper, we do not consider operations in TDWs. There are not easy to cope with since (1) different time granularities between dimension data and measures should be considered, and (2) as demostrated by, e.g., [2, 11], solutions for managing different schema versions should also be included.

Section 2 surveys works related to TDWs. Section 3 briefly presents the main features of the MultiDimER model. Section 4 presents our rationale for using the ER and OR models. Section 5 describes general rules for transforming temporal types to both models. Sections 6 to 8 present, respectively, mappings of temporal levels, temporal links between levels, and temporal measures. Finally, the conclusions are given in Section 9.

2   Related Work

TDWs raise many challenging issues, e.g., the inclusion of temporal types (e.g., [9]) or correct aggregation in the presence of data and structure changes (e.g., [2, 11]). However, very few conceptual models for TDWs have been proposed (e.g., [2, 11, 12]). These models formally describe the temporal support for multidimensional models, nevertheless, they do not consider several aspects proposed in our model, e.g., (non-) temporal relationships between (non-) temporal levels. Further, these models do not provide an associated logical representation.

On the other hand, [1] introduces a temporal star schema that differs from the classical one by the fact that the time dimension does not exist; instead the rows in all tables of the schema are timestamped. They compare this model with the classical star schema taking into account database size and performance.

They conclude that the temporal star schema facilitates expressing and executing queries, it is smaller in size, and it does not keep redundant information.

Since to the best of our knowledge there are not proposed solutions for a logical representation of TDWs, we briefly review logical models for TDBs with the goal to adapt some of these ideas for the logical representation of TDWs.

One approach for logical-level design of TDBs is to use normalization. Temporal functional dependencies have been defined (e.g., [5, 13]). New temporal normal forms (e.g., [13]) or extensions of conventional ones (e.g., [5]) have been also proposed. Most of these approaches rely on the first normal form (1NF), however, the non-first normal form (NF2) was proposed for solving the limitations of the 1NF for modeling complex data. The NF2 allows structured domains, collection domains, and relation-valued domains, which are also included in the SQL:2003 standard under the name of object-relational model [10].

Another approach for logical-level design of TDBs is based on mapping conceptual models. While this is the usual practice for conventional (i.e., non-temporal) database design, to the best of our knowledge only [4] propose such an approach. In general, the mapping of timestamped elements produces a table for each entity type that includes lifespan, a separate table for each timestamped monovalued attribute, and one additional table for each multivalued attribute, whether timestamped or not. This approach gives a significant number of tables since entities and their time-varying attributes are represented separately. Further, it is not intuitive for expressing the semantics of the modeled reality.

3   Overview of the MultiDimER Model

The MultiDimER model is a conceptual model allowing to represent time-varying multidimensional data [6][2]. Figure 1 shows notations used in our model and Figure 2 presents the metamodel. A *schema* is defined as a finite set of dimensions and fact relationships. A *dimension* is an abstract concept representing either a level, or one or more hierarchies. Levels are represented as entity types (Figure 1 a). An instance of a level is called a *member*.

A *hierarchy* contains several related levels (Figure 1 b) that are used for roll-up and drill-down operations. Given two consecutive levels of a hierarchy, the higher level is called *parent* and the lower level is called *child*. A level that does not have a child level is called *leaf*. Hierarchies express different structures according to an analysis *criterion* (Figure 1 c), e.g., geographical location.

Levels have one or several *key attributes* (represented in bold and italic in Figure 1) and may also have other *descriptive attributes*. Key attributes of a parent level define how child members can be grouped. Key attributes in a leaf level or in a level forming a dimension without hierarchy indicate the granularity of measures in the associated fact relationship.

A *temporal level* is a level for which the application needs to keep its time-varying characteristics. We allow support for both temporal attributes and level

---

[2] The non-temporal version of the model is presented in [7].

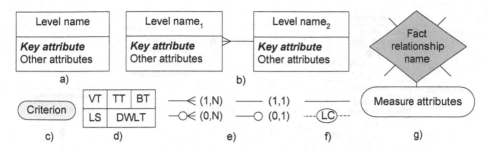

Fig. 1. Notations: a) one-level dimension, b) hierarchy, c) analysis criterion, d) temporal types, e) cardinality ratios, f) cardinality types, and g) fact relationship

lifespan. Figure 1 d) shows the different temporal types. We allow valid time (VT), transaction time (TT), bitemporal time (BT), and lifespan (LS) coming from source systems (if available), and data warehouse loading time (DWLT)[3].

The relationship between two levels is characterized by *cardinalities* (Figure 1 e), which restrict the minimum and the maximum number of members in one level that can be related to a member in another level. This cardinality may be interpreted in two possible ways. The *snapshot cardinality* is valid every time instant whereas the *lifespan cardinality* is valid over the entire members lifespan. The former is represented as a continuous line and the latter as a dotted line with LC symbol (Figure 1 f). The presence of only one cardinality symbol indicates that both cardinalities are the same. Further, the relationship between levels may include different temporal types: VT, TT, BT, and/or DWLT. There is no LS support for relationships since they do not exist by themselves without their participating levels.

A *fact relationship* (Figure 1 g) represents an *n*-ary relationship between leaf levels. It may contain attributes commonly called *measures*. In the MultiDimER model measures are *temporal*, i.e., they always require to include a temporal element (VT, TT, BT, and/or DWLT) [8].

An example of using our notation is given in Figure 3. It represents a schema for analysis of product sales where, for example, changes to products, categories, and relationships between them are kept. Further, changes in measure values are represented using a temporal type (VT in the figure) instead of relying on the conventional Time dimension.

4 Motivation for Mapping to the ER and OR Models

For implementing the MultiDimER model we propose two mappings: to the ER and OR models. The former is a well-known and widely-used model for conceptual modeling. Therefore, the ER representation of the constructs of the MultiDimER model allows a better understanding of their semantics. Further, the

---

[3] In [6, 8] we present our rationale for the inclusion of different temporal types in TDWs.

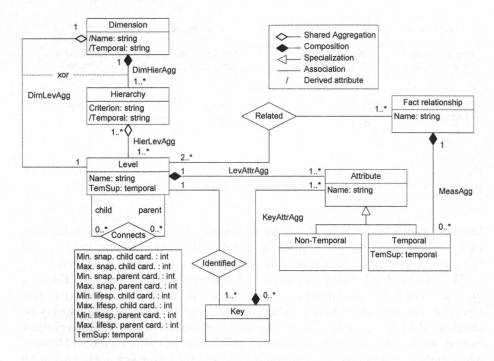

Fig. 2. Metamodel of the temporally-extended MultiDimER model

transformation of the ER model into operational data models is well understood (e.g., [3]) and this translation can be done using usual CASE tools.

On the other hand, in order to better assist the implementers who use the MultiDimER model for conceptual design of TDWs, we propose mapping rules that allow a direct translation of schemas from our model to the OR model. We choose the OR model as logical model since it preserves the foundations of the relational model while extending its modeling power. It also offers upward compatibility with existing relational languages allowing to "flatten" non-atomic data to a conventional 1NF. Further, the OR model allows to better represent the real world by inherently grouping related facts into a single row. In addition, OR features are also included in the SQL:2003 standard [10] and in leading DBMSs, e.g., Oracle or Informix.

5   Mapping of Temporal Types

The temporal support in the MultiDimER model is added in an implicit manner, i.e., the timestamp attributes used for capturing a temporal aspect are hidden using instead pictograms. Therefore, the transformation of the time-related data into classical non-temporal structures of the ER model requires additional attributes for timestamps, which are manipulated as usual attributes.

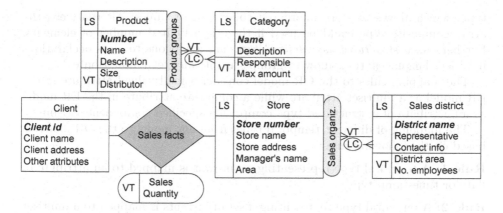

Fig. 3. Example of conceptual schema for a TDW

Further, mapping of temporal types to the ER model depends on whether these types are used for events or states. *Events* represent something that happens at a particular time point whereas *states* something that has extent over time. For the former an *instant* is used, i.e., a time point on an underlying time axis. A state is represented by an *interval* or *period* indicating the time between two instants. Sets of instants and sets of intervals can also be used.

Figure 4 presents different options for mapping VT: a monovalued attribute for an instant (Figure 4 a), a multivalued attribute for a set of instants (Figure 4 b), a simple composite attribute for a period (Figure 4 c), and a multivalued composite attribute for a set of periods (Figure 4 d). Notice that a set of periods or instants are used when the attribute has the same value in different periods or instants of time.

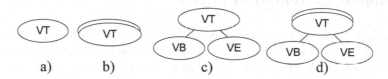

Fig. 4. Different representations of VT in the ER model

As LS can be represented by a period or a set of periods, it is transformed into a simple or multivalued composite attribute, respectively. The latter allows to include discontinuous lifespans, e.g., a professor leaving for sabbatical during some period of time. For representing TT, the usual practice in TDBs is to use a period (or a set of periods) similar to LS. Since DWLT represents the time when data was loaded into a TDW, an instant is used for representing this temporal type, which is transformed into a simple attribute in the ER model.

To specify the mapping rules to the OR model, we use the different elements included in the SQL:2003 standard. For example, we use a multiset composite type, which allows to store unordered collections of values. Alternatively, the array composite type could be used if there is a limited number of elements. Further, since *structured user-defined types* are analogous to class declarations in object languages, they allow to group semantically related attributes[4].

The mapping rules to the OR model consider a multivalued attribute in the ER model as a multiset attribute while a composite attribute in the ER model as an attribute of a structured type comprising specified component attributes.

The mapping of different temporal types from our model to the OR model is based on the following rules:

Rule 1: A temporal type representing an instant is mapped to an attribute of date or timestamp type.

Rule 2: A temporal type representing a set of instants is mapped to a multiset attribute of date or timestamp type.

Rule 3: A temporal type representing a period is mapped to an attribute of a structured type composed of two attributes of date or timestamp type.

Rule 4: A temporal type representing a set of periods is mapped to a multiset attribute of a structured type consisting of two attributes of date or timestamp type.

For example, the different options for VT in Figure 4 can be represented in SQL:2003 as follows:

```
create type InstantT as date;
create type InstantSetT as (InstantT multiset);
create type PeriodT as (Pbegin date, Pend date);
create type PeriodSetT as (PeriodT multiset);
```

6 Mapping of Temporal Levels

Changes in a level can occur either for a member as a whole (e.g., deleting a product) or for attribute values (e.g., changing a product's size). Representing these changes in TDWs is important for analysis purposes, e.g., to discover how the exclusion of some products or the change in their sizes influences sales.

In the MultiDimER model changes to a level member as a whole are represented using the LS symbol next to the level name, e.g., the Product level in Figure 3. For representing changes in attribute values (Size and Distributor in the figure), we use attribute timestamping. We group temporal attributes in our model to ensure that they can be distinguished from non-temporal attributes and to minimize the number of symbols.

A level in our model corresponds to a regular entity type in the ER model. Each temporal attribute is represented in the ER model as a multivalued composite attribute that includes an attribute for the value and another attribute for a temporal type. Notice, that using a multivalued attribute allows to have

---

[4] Due to space limitations, in this paper we do not consider methods.

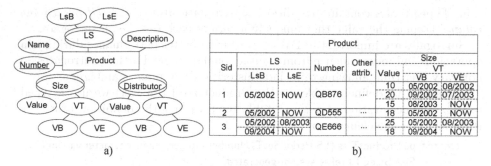

a)   b)

Fig. 5. A temporal level: a) the ER model and b) the OR representation

different values (e.g., sizes or distributors) of the attribute in different periods of time. For example, the transformation of the Product level (Figure 3) to the ER model is shown in Figure 5 a).

Mapping the corresponding ER model to the relational model gives four tables: one with all monovalued attributes and one for each multivalued attribute. This representation is not very intuitive since attributes of a level are stored as separate tables. It also has well-known performance problems due to the required join operations.

An OR representation allows to overcome these drawbacks. It preserves more semantics keeping together in a single table a level and its temporal attributes. The mapping of temporal attributes is straightforward:

Rule 5: An attribute with temporal support is mapped to the OR model as a multiset attribute of a structured type composed of two attributes: one for representing the value and another one for the associated temporal type.

For example, given the declarations for the temporal types in Section 4, the type for the Size attribute[5] is defined as follows: create type SizeT as (Value real, VT PeriodT). Since Size is a multivalued attribute, we represent it as a collection type using either array or multiset, e.g., create type SizeCT as (SizeT multiset).

Mapping a level to the OR model is straightforward once the types for its attributes are defined:

Rule 6: A level is mapped to a relation containing all its attributes and an additional attribute for a key. If a level has LS support, an additional attribute as specified by Rules 3 or 4 should be included.

Figure 5 b) shows the OR schema using a tabular representation containing the member key, the lifespan, and all its attributes represented together in the same table. It corresponds to a so-called temporally-grouped data model, which is considered as more expressive for modeling complex data.

The Product level can be represented in several ways in SQL:2003. For example, two types of tables can be used. *Relational tables* are usual tables while *typed tables* are tables that use structured user-defined types for their defini-

---

[5] For simplicity we do not represent in the figure the Distributor attribute, which can be mapped similarly to the Size attribute.

tion. Typed tables contain in addition an automatically-created *self-referencing column* keeping the value that uniquely identifies each row, i.e., a surrogate.

Surrogates are important in DWs for ensuring better performance during join operations and independence from transactional systems. Further, surrogates do not vary over time allowing to include historical data in an unambiguous way.

Therefore, to define a table for the Product level (Product) we use a typed table[6]. The declaration of a typed table requires first the definition of a type (ProductT) for the elements of the table:

> create type ProductT as (LS PeriodSetT, Number integer, Name character varying(25),
>   ..., Size SizeCT) ref is system generated;
> create table Product of ProductT (constraint prodPK primary key (Number),
>   ref is Sid system generated);

The clause ref is Sid system generated indicates that Sid is a surrogate attribute automatically generated by the system. In SQL:2003 these surrogates can also be generated by the user or derived from one or more attributes.

Until now we have discussed the representations of VT and LS. However, VT and LS can be combined with TT and/or DWLT. They can be mapped according to the explanations given in this section and in Section 5.

7   Mapping of Child-Parent Relationships

7.1   Non-temporal Relationships

Non-temporal relationships indicate that either these relationships never change or if they do, only the last modification is kept. To avoid an incorrect management of hierarchies and dangling references between levels, non-temporal relationships may only link levels that do not keep their LS and do not include VTs for their key attributes, which are used for aggregation purposes [6].

Figure 6 a) represents a hierarchy with a non-temporal relationship. The relationship between child and parent levels corresponds to a usual binary relationship in the ER model as shown in Figure 6 b)[7].

For obtaining the corresponding OR schema, first we represent each level as explained in Section 6. Then, we use the traditional mapping for binary many-to-one relationships.

Rule 7: A non-temporal many-to-one relationship between child and parent levels is mapped to the OR representation by including a parent key in the child level table.

For example, the mapping of the Product level and the Product–Category relationship gives the same relation as the one in Figure 5 b) including an additional attribute in the Product table with the foreign key of the Category table.

---

[6] For simplicity, in the examples we omit full specification of constraints and additional clauses required by the SQL:2003 standard.

[7] For simplicity we do not present level attributes.

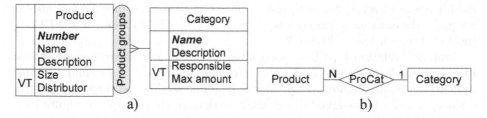

Fig. 6. A hierarchy with a non-temporal relationship: a) the MultiDimER model and b) the ER model

To define the Product table in SQL:2003 first we need to create a typed table Category with the surrogate in the Sid attribute. Then, we specify:

```
create type ProductT as (Number integer, ..., Sizes SizeCT, CatRef REF(CategoryT)
    scope Category references are checked) ref is system generated;
create table Product of ProductT (constraint prodPK primary key (Number),
    ref is Sid system generated);
```

The Product type includes a reference (REF) type that points to the corresponding row in the Category table. In this way, the OR approach replaces value-based joins with direct access to related rows using the identifiers.

7.2 Temporal Relationships

Temporal relationships allow to keep track of the evolution of links between parent and child members. These relationships can link non-temporal levels (Figure 7 a) and 8 a)) or temporal levels (Figure 3). For the former, in order to ensure correct measure aggregations and avoid dangling references, the

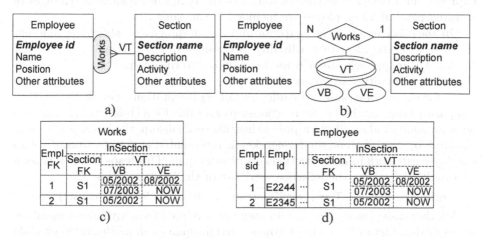

Fig. 7. Temporal relationships linking non-temporal levels: a) the MultiDimER model, b) the ER model, c) and d) alternative OR representations

modifications of levels are not allowed [6]. To represent temporal relationships we place the corresponding temporal symbol (VT, TT, BT, and/or DWLT) on the link between levels (Figure 7 a).

Temporal relationships have associated snapshot and lifespan cardinalities. In the example in Figure 7 a) these cardinalities are the same, many-to-one, indicating that an employee may work only in one section and if he returns after a leave, he must be assigned to the same section. In the example of Figure 8 a), the relationship has a many-to-one snapshot cardinality (continuous line) and a many-to-many lifespan cardinality (dotted line with the LC symbol), i.e., at each instant an employee works in exactly one section, but he may work in several sections over his entire lifespan.

Figure 7 b) shows the ER model for Figure 7 a). We use a multivalued composite attribute for representing VT since an employee can be hired several times in the same section.

For the OR representation we can either create a separate table for the Works relationship (Figure 7 c) or include a multivalued attribute in the child-level table, e.g., include in the Employee table an attribute for the Section surrogates with its temporal characteristics (Figure 7 d).

The definition of the Works relation in SQL:2003 requires that Employee and Section tables have already been declared as typed tables. We do not use a typed table for representing the Works relationship since the relationship does not exist without their levels.

> create type WorksT as (SecFK REF(SectionT) scope Section references are checked,
>   VT PeriodSetT);
> create table Works (EmplFK REF(EmplT) scope Employee references are checked,
>   InSection WorksT);

The SQL:2003 declaration for Employee in Figure 7 d) requires to include the InSection attribute of the WorksT type in the Employee type. This representation expresses in a better way the semantics of the relationship since all changes of working place of an employee are included in the same row.

On the other hand, if the snapshot and the lifespan cardinalities are different (Figure 8 a), the lifespan cardinality is considered when mapping to the ER model. The mapping to the ER model is similar to the one in Figure 7 b) except that the cardinalities are many–to–many.

As for the previous case, two different OR representations may be used: either a separate table for the Works relationship or a table for a child level (Employee) with an additional attribute representing this relationship; the latter is shown in Figure 8 b). Notice, that the foreign key is represented as set of values since an employee can work in many sections over his lifespan. This leads to the inclusion of a multiset type for the InSection attribute of the EmployeeT type:

> create type EmployeeT as (EmplID integer, . . . , InSection WorksT multiset);

Another case arises when a child member is related to many parent members at every time instant[8], i.e., the snapshot and lifespan cardinalities between child

---

[8] Called in [7] *non-strict* hierarchies.

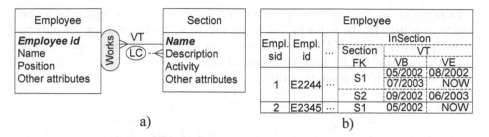

a)   b)

Fig. 8. Temporal relationships linking non-temporal levels: a) the MultiDimER model with snapshot and lifespan cardinalities and b) the OR representation

and parent levels are many-to-many. This situation can be mapped in the same way as the previous one.

Summarizing, for mapping temporal relationships between the child and parent levels to the OR model the following rule is used:

Rule 8: First, a structured type composed of two attributes is defined: one attribute for surrogates of the parent level and another one for the corresponding temporal type. Then, this structured type is used for defining a simple or a multiset attribute depending on whether the cardinality between child and parent levels is many-to-one or many-to-many, respectively. Let us call this attribute TemRel. Finally, one of two possible OR representations can be used:

1. Creating a new relation that contains an attribute for the surrogate keys of the child level and the TemRel attribute.
2. Extending the relation corresponding to the child level with the TemRel attribute.

Even though the second option preserves more semantics, the choice among the alternative OR representations may depend on physical-level considerations for the particular DBMS, such as join algorithms, indexing capabilities, etc. For example, defining the InSection attribute as a nested table in Oracle 10g, will require a join of two tables, thus not offering any advantage with respect to the solution of a separate table for the Works relationship. Notice that for the previous cases, the relational model only offers the option of creating a separate table for the Works relationship.

Additionally, a relationship between levels can include TT and/or DWLT for which the mapping specified in Section 5 can be used.

8   Fact Relationships with Temporal Measures

The MultiDimER model includes temporal support for measures as shown in Figure 3. Notice that the usual Time dimension does not need to be attached to the fact relationship. In fact, temporal support applies to the whole schema of the TDW, i.e., to measures and dimensions.

Depending on analysis needs, time-varying measures may represent either events or states. In the following example, due to space limitations, we only refer to measures whose VT is represented as an instant with granularity month. Nevertheless, the results may be straightforwardly generalized if VT is represented by a period or a set of periods.

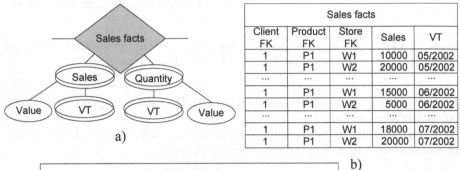

Sales facts				
Client FK	Product FK	Store FK	Sales	VT
1	P1	W1	10000	05/2002
1	P1	W2	20000	05/2002
...	...	...	...	...
1	P1	W1	15000	06/2002
1	P1	W2	5000	06/2002
...	...	...	...	...
1	P1	W1	18000	07/2002
1	P1	W2	20000	07/2002

a)

b)

Sales facts						
Client FK	Product FK	Store FK	Sales		Quantity	
			Value	VT	Value	VT
1	P1	W1	10000	05/2002	100	05/2002
			15000	06/2002		07/2002
			18000	07/2002	150	06/2002
1	P1	W2	20000	05/2002	200	05/2002
				07/2002	50	06/2002
			5000	06/2002	80	07/2002
...	...	...	...	...	...	...

c)

Fig. 9. Temporal measures: a) the ER representation, b) the relational table for the Sales measure, and c) the OR representation

A fact relationship in the MultiDimER model corresponds to an n-ary relationship in the ER model. Measures as attributes of a relationship are mapped to the ER model in the same way as temporal attributes of a level. Therefore, each measure is represented as a multivalued composite attribute (Figure 9 a).

Mapping this fact relationship to the relational model in 1FN gives two tables. In Figure 9 b) we only show the table with the Sales measure since the other table with the Quantity measure has similar structure. However, if additional information is available, this model can be simplified. For example, if all measures are calculated with respect to the same VT, they can be represented in one table and tuple timestamping can be applied.

The OR model creates also a separate table based on the following rule:

Rule 9: A fact relationship with temporal measures is mapped to the OR model by creating a new relation that includes as attributes the surrogate keys of the participating levels. In addition, every measure is mapped into a new temporal attribute according to Rule 5.

An example of the tabular OR representation is given in Figure 9 c).

However, even though the OR model allows to represent the changes in measure values for the same combination of foreign keys, in practice it may be not well suited for aggregations related to time. The objects created for every measure contain two-level nesting: one for representing different measure values for the same combination of foreign keys and another for representing a temporal element. Therefore, it is more difficult to express aggregation statements related to time accessing the second-level nesting. As a consequence, the relational representation is more adequate in order to represent in a more "balanced" manner all attributes that may be used for aggregation purposes.

9 Conclusions

The temporally-extended MultiDimER model [6, 8] is used for modeling time-varying data for DW applications. It is symmetric in the sense that it allows to represent changes for both measures and dimensions. In this paper we presented a mapping of this conceptual model into the ER model and the OR model.

We used an object-relational approach based on the SQL:2003 standard that allows better to represent complex data and preserve as much TDW semantics as possible. We discussed mappings for a temporal level and for hierarchies. Finally, we referred to temporal measures in fact relationships.

The object-relational model allows to better represent time-varying levels and hierarchies than the classical relational model. In the former model a level and its corresponding time-varying attributes are kept together while the relational model produces a significant number of tables with well-known disadvantages for modeling and implementation. Further, for representing a relationship between levels forming a hierarchy the object-relational model gives a designer several alternatives. Thus, he can choose the one considering semantics and physical level features of the particular OR DBMS. On the other hand, the relational model is more adequate for representing time-varying measures. It considers in the same manner all attributes including the ones that represent time, thus it facilitates aggregation procedures.

The proposed mapping shows that TDWs can be implemented using current OR DBMSs. Further, the features of OR databases for representating complex objects facilitate the implementation of attribute timestamping. As opposed to tuple timestamping, which is mostly used in the relational representation of TDBs, attribute timestamping not only allows a better representation of reality (temporal changes are represented only for the specified attributes) but also saves storage space during implementation (the values of attributes that do not vary on time are not repeated).

We have already undertaken a real-scale study in the domain of TDWs to evaluate the usability of our conceptual model and the feasibility of its implementation using Oracle 10g. The results will be reported in a forthcoming paper, but a first analysis has already given encouraging indications that allow us to move to the next research step, i.e., developing a methodology for TDW design.

The proposed mapping may vary according to the expected usage patterns, e.g., data mining algorithms, and specific features of the target implementation system. For example, a user may choose a multidimensional tool-specific storage (e.g., Analytic Workspace in Oracle 10g) instead of relying on more general solutions as the ones proposed in this paper.

References

1. R. Bliujute, S. Slatenis, G. Slivinskas, and C. Jensen. Systematic change mangement in dimensional data warehousing. Technical report, Time Center, TR-23, 1998.
2. J. Eder, C. Koncilia, and T. Morzy. The COMET metamodel for temporal data warehouses. In *Proc. of the 14th Int. Conf. on Advanced Information Systems Engineering*, pages 83–99, 2002.
3. R. Elmasri and S. Navathe. *Fundamentals of Database Systems*. Adison-Wesley, fourth edition, 2003.
4. H. Gregersen, L. Mark, and C. Jensen. Mapping temporal ER diagrams to relational schemas. Technical report, Time Center, TR-39, 1998.
5. C. Jensen and R. Snodgrass. Temporally enhanced database design. In M. Papazoglou, S. Spaccapietra, and Z. Tari, editors, *Advances in Object-Oriented Data Modeling*, pages 163–193. MIT Press, 2000.
6. E. Malinowski and E. Zimányi. A conceptual solution for representing time in data warehouse dimensions. In *Proc. of the 3rd Asia-Pacific Conf. on Conceptual Modelling*, pages 45–54, 2006.
7. E. Malinowski and E. Zimányi. Hierarchies in a multidimensional model: from conceptual modeling to logical representation. Data & Knowledge Engineering. To appear, 2006.
8. E. Malinowski and E. Zimányi. Inclusion of time-varying measures in temporal data warehouses. In *Proc. of the 8th Int. Conf. on Enterprise Information Systems*, 2006. To appear.
9. C. Martín and A. Abelló. A temporal study of data sources to load a corporate data warehouse. In *Proc. of the 5th Int. Conf. on Data Warehousing and Knowledge Discovery*, pages 109–118, 2003.
10. J. Melton. *Advanced SQL: 1999. Understanding Object-Relational and Other Advanced Features*. Morgan Kaufman Publisher, 2003.
11. A. Mendelzon and A. Vaisman. Temporal queries in OLAP. In *Proc. of the 26th Very Large Database Conference*, pages 243–253, 2000.
12. T. Pedersen, C. Jensen, and C. Dyreson. A foundation for capturing and querying complex multidimensional data. *Information Systems*, 26(5):383–423, 2001.
13. X. Wang, C. Bettini, A. Brodsky, and S. Jajodia. Logical design for temporal databases with multiple granularities. *ACM Transactions on Database Systems*, 22(2):115–170, 1997.

Data Translation Between Taxonomies

Sérgio Luis Sardi Mergen and Carlos Alberto Heuser

Universidade Federal do Rio Grande do Sul, Av. Bento Gonalves,
9500 Porto Alegre - RS - Brasil
{mergen, heuser}@inf.ufrgs.br

Abstract. The task of translating data from one schema into another
is usually performed with the help of information stating how the elements between two schemas correspond. Translation mechanisms can use
this information in order to identify how instances of a source schema
must be translated. We claim that a uniform matching approach, where
instances of a source classes are always translated into the same target
classes, may not represent the reality, specially when the schemas involved describe taxonomies. In this paper we demonstrate taxonomies
that support our idea, and propose the usage of a conditional matching
approach to improve the accuracy of taxonomical instances translation.

1 Introduction

Data translation plays a fundamental role in the information integration area.
It is up to a data translation process the task of converting data from its native
storage representation into another representation.

There are several applications where data translation mechanisms represent
a crucial task. In a mediated system[18, 3], when a user submits a query, a
usual approach would be to translate the results coming from the sources into
a format expected by the user. When migrating databases from an old version
to a new version, a commonly faced challenge involves data translation, where
the arising question is how to covert data stored in the old schema into the new
schema, specially when dealing with heterogeneous schemas, or even worse, when
the schemas are represented in different models. Even in data warehouses, the
incoming data must be processed in some way before storage; e.g. data may be
filtered, and relations may be joined or aggregated. As the data is copied from
the sources, it may need to be transformed in certain ways to make all data
conform to the schema at the data warehouse.

Independently of the underlying mechanism that performs the data translation, this processing relies on a general idea that is to identify the matches
between the schemas and apply transformation rules to translate instances of
the source into instances of the target[14, 1, 4, 5] . Figure 1(a) illustrates an abstract example where two schemas are matched. The schemas are represented as
classes with properties. The match is represented by the bold line, which indicates that instances of *Person* in the source should be translated into instances
of *Student* in the target.

E. Dubois and K. Pohl (Eds.): CAiSE 2006, LNCS 4001, pp. 111–124, 2006.
© Springer-Verlag Berlin Heidelberg 2006

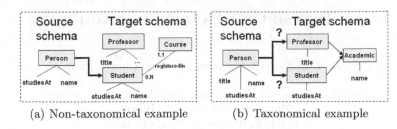

(a) Non-taxonomical example   (b) Taxonomical example

Fig. 1. Matching examples

At this time, there is no fully automatic semantic integration approach[10], which means the user is still responsible for identifying the matches and creating the translation rules. Nevertheless, this often laborious task can be aided with the help of schema matching techniques that suggest to the user the most probable ways to do the matching, and possibly, which transformations to apply on the instances.

However, when it comes to translate data between two taxonomies, there is a gap that neither schema matching techniques nor data translation mechanisms seem to support. Take for instance the taxonomies depicted in figure 1(b). The target schema presents the academic staff in a taxonomical model, where classes are described in terms of specialization and generalization of other classes. In the source schema, the *Person* class is used to store both *Students* and *Professors* instances, undiscriminatingly. Observing the schema level alone it is not clear if an instance of *Person* in the source is in fact a student or a professor.

On the other hand, the instance level may provide some relevant cues on how to translate the instances. For instance, the *studiesAt* and *title* properties of the person class are disjoint by nature. Thus, it is expected that every instance of *Person* contains at most one of these two properties. Taking this reasoning one step further, we conclude that the presence (or absence) of some particular property in an instance may be strong indicators of that instance semantics.

Based on this reasoning, we present an approach to the translation of taxonomies, based on the adoption of a simple mechanism, that we call translation script. A translation script is generated based on pre-computed matches between the schemas.

A translation script is composed of alternative matches for every source class. Each alternative match is associated to a condition that indicates whether the match can be used in the translation of a particular instance or not. During translation, the script can be used to guide the translation process by determining which of the alternative matches should be used when translating a specific instance.

Our contribution is twofold. Firstly, the translation script is a novel method for data translation, that is specifically useful for translating data between taxonomies. Secondly, we demonstrate that the generation of this translation script is straightforward, once it simply requires that pre-computed matches between the schemas involved in the translation are provided.

The rest of the paper is organized as follows: In section 2 we show approaches related to the issue of matching taxonomies along with existing mechanisms used for data translation. Section 3 presents motivating examples that illustrate how alternative matches can be used to improve the translation accuracy. In section 4 we define a translation script and describe the algorithm used to generate a translation script based on pre-computed matches. Section 5 demonstrates a case study where we suggest the use of a translation script on real world ontologies. Section 6 briefly describes a different approach that is also based on a translation script to perform data translation. Final conclusions are presented in section 7.

2   Related Work

When studying translation of taxonomical data, related work can be classified in two groups: Schema matching approaches and data translation approaches.

In general, matching taxonomies can be seen as a broader problem, which is the matching of ontologies. Most of the integrated approaches for ontology matching are based on the idea of combining different strategies and measures of similarity. In the vast literature on ontology matching, we have found several strategies to match taxonomies[6, 11, 12, 15, 9], but none of them seems to worry about the existence of alterative matches to a source class(concept).

The S-Match system [9] takes the process of matching taxonomies one step further by allowing matches with semantic operators other than equivalence. Given two concepts, the algorithm assigns a semantic relation that can be of equivalence ($=$), generalization($\sqsupseteq$),specialization($\sqsubseteq$), mismatch($\perp$), or overlap($\sqcap$). The matches are computed by selecting the strongest semantic relation discovered by the algorithm between two ontology concepts. This kind of matching better describes the semantic of the correspondences between taxonomies, but still presents the drawback of allowing one single match per concept.

In [13] the authors also use several semantic operators when matching schemas. However, they claim that sometimes it is not possible to identify a single match between each pair of concepts of two schemas. They present an approach for schema integration that allows alternative matches for each pair of concepts, where a match is given a level of belief. The matches, referred to as uncertain matches, are computed in the schema matching process and propagated to a schema merging process that is responsible for generating an integrated schema. Similar work is presented in [8], with the limitation that matches can only be done through the equivalence operator. The usage of uncertain matches resembles the usage of the alternative matches suggested in our work, in a sense that both kind of matches are used to dynamically resolve semantic matching problems. However, uncertain matches are applicable for semantic reconciliation of schemas, while our approach is applicable for data translation.

The usage of uncertainty is also present in [17], only this time the uncertainty lies on the data level, instead of the schema level. Their approach, based on the probability theory, allows the user to query for uncertain data in a data integration environment.

As for data translation approaches, most of them [14, 1, 4, 5] rely on the usage of matching rules to perform data translation. Despite some small variations among the approaches, they all share the same idea on what the matching rules should express, which are the matches between the schemas, and the transformations that must be performed when translating the instances. The instances can be transformed either by value modification or by schema restructuring. In [2] the authors introduce a middleware data model that supports the declaration of correspondences between two different representations (schemas). They also describe some practical cases where the correspondences are automatically turned into translation rules. One of the benefits of their approach is that the specification of correspondences can be used to perform translation of data in both directions.

For the best of our knowledge, none of the translation approaches consider the usage of alternative matches, where a match to a given source class may vary during translation. As far as we know, the existing approaches can use the absence of properties inside a given instance only to indicate that the instance should not be translated. Using the presence/absence of properties values of a source instance to decide whether one given class or another should be selected as the target is an entirely new idea.

We claim that our approach to data translation could be incorporated in data translation mechanisms, as a way to dynamically select one of the alternative matches, based on the presence or absence of property values in a given instance.

3 Running Examples of Taxonomy Translation

In order to perform data translation, it is necessary to understand how the source and target schema correspond to each other. Based on this understanding, generally expressed in the form of matchings, it is possible to translate instances of the source schema into instances of the target schema. In this context, we argue that the usage of a uniform matching - where one single match suffices for translating every instance of a source class - is questionable, specially when the schemas describe taxonomies. In such cases, the translation of the instances can vary, according to the values actually being translated.

Next, we show cases where the translation of taxonomical instances may result in an erroneous classification if the translation uses a uniform mapping strategy instead of a flexible one. We also demonstrate how the translation can be semantically improved if the idea of a translation script is used to guide the translation process.

To start, consider the academic staff taxonomies presented in figure 2. Consider a taxonomy-aware matcher able to realize that $\Gamma_2.Tenured$ is a better match to $\Gamma_1.Professor$, instead of its polysemous $\Gamma_2.Professor$. Additionally, the matcher was able to find the properties correspondences, where $nationality$ matches $nationality$, $institution$ matches $lecturesAt$ and $tenuredSince$ matches $isTenuredSince$.

This match solves the problem of translating the instances of professors in Γ_1 without information losses - since all properties of the source are translated - but it does not guarantee there will not be semantic losses. Suppose that some professors stored in Γ_1 are tenured, while others are not. During translation, if the match between $\Gamma_1.Professor$ and $\Gamma_2.Tenured$ is used, every instance of $professor$ in Γ_1 ends up translated into instances of $\Gamma_2.Tenured$.

Fig. 2. Academic staff taxonomies   **Fig. 3.** Bank account taxonomies

However, this is not the expected classification, given that not every professor is tenured. One way to differentiate professors from tenured professors in Γ_2 is that professors lack the definition of properties that are exclusive to tenured professors, such as the property $isTenuredSince$.

In this context, we propose a solution that does not hardwire a match to a specific source class, but allows a range of alternative matches. During instance translation, it is possible to choose one among several alternative matches, by using some inference mechanism that analyzes the presence or absence of properties values in the instance being translated. For the example above, a $Professor$ instance in Γ_1 is translated into a $Tenured$ instance in Γ_2, when the property $tenuredSince$ has a value assigned to it, and is translated into a $Professor$ instance in Γ_2 otherwise. Note that the best that traditional translation mechanisms could do in this case is to invalidate the translation if some of the properties are missing.

We could go even further and say that a professor is a visitor, if we knew that all Γ_2 visitors come from abroad. This kind of information can be embedded in the schema itself, in the form of constraints, if the taxonomy supports this kind of constraint. Another way to obtain additional knowledge from the taxonomies is by discovering data patterns in some sample instances. A data pattern could state the fact that every visitor is actually a professor whose country of origin is different from the country in which the university is located.

Despite the presumable benefits from using existing or computed constraints to improve data translation, this kind of analysis is out of the scope of this paper. Our commitment is on demonstrating that the semantics of the translation can be improved by using an approach that is less sophisticated, but still effective, based solely on the presence/absence of property values in the instances.

Figure 3 shows another example where the presence/absence of property values can eliminate translation ambiguity. In this case the taxonomies describe bank accounts. Notice that the computation of a match for the *Account* class in Γ_3 is even more dubious that the prior example, since the properties declared in the *Account* class in Γ_3 are split across the classes in Γ_4.

Again, exploiting the presence of properties values inside bank account instances could improve the quality of the translation, whereas a traditional translation approach would fail. For instance, an account in Γ_3 with no value for *interestRate* and *borrowingLimit* fits the description of an *Account* in Γ_4.

Moreover, accounts in Γ_3 with all properties defined but *borrowingLimit* could be translated into a *SavingsAccount* in Γ_4. Likewise, accounts in Γ_3 with all properties defined but *interestRate* could be translated into a *CurrentAccount* in Γ_4.

4   The Translation Script Approach

In this section we present the definition of a translation script, along with examples that demonstrate how a translation script can be used during the translation of taxonomies. We start this section with the definition of a taxonomy.

Definition 1 (Taxonomy). *Let $\Gamma = < C, P, Prop(c_i), sup(c_i) >$ be a taxonomy, where C is a set of classes $\{c_i\}$ and P is a set of properties $\{p_i\}$.*

Further, let $Prop(c_i)$ be a function that returns the set of properties of c_i. Additionally, let $sup(c_i)$ be a function that returns the immediate super-class of c_i.

Having defined this, we have that if $f\ c_i = sup(c_j)$, then $Prop(c_i) \subseteq Prop(c_j)$.

A taxonomy is represented as a hierarchy of classes, where each class contains a set of properties. A class shares its properties with each of its sub-classes. For our purposes, it suffices to define properties merely as being part of a class. Additional constraints of a class/property composition, such as the cardinality, are not defined since they are not exploited by our translation mechanism.

For the rest of the paper, we use Γ_s to refer to a source taxonomy, while Γ_t is used to denote a target taxonomy.

The translation script is generated based on an input matching that describes how classes of a source taxonomy correspond to classes of a target taxonomy. The computation of an input matching is out of the scope of this paper, but there are several approaches in the literature that handle class to class matching, as described in section 2. We define the input matching as follows:

Definition 2 (Input Matching). *The input matching M is a set of matches $\{m_i\}$. Let m_i be a tuple $<c_s, c_t, \Psi>$, where:*
  - $c_s \in C_s$, having $C_s \in \Gamma_s$,
  - $c_t \in C_t$, having $C_t \in \Gamma_t$,
  - Ψ is a set of property matchings $\psi = <p_s, p_t>$, where $p_s \in Prop(c_s)$ and $p_t \in Prop(c_t)$. Further, if $\exists\ \psi_i = <p_{si}, p_{ti}> \in \Psi$, than $\not\exists\ \psi_j = <p_{sj}, p_{tj}> \in \Psi$, such that $\psi_i \neq \psi_j$ and $(p_{si} = p_{sj}$ or $p_{ti} = p_{tj})$.

A match is composed by a source class, a target class and a set of correspondences between the classes' properties. Within a single class to class match, only one-to-one property matches are allowed. This restriction is, in fact, an expression of the local one-to-one match cardinality restriction[16], that prevents the occurrence of matches where there is no direct correspondence between elements of the source and target.

This kind of match, also referred to as indirect match[7], occurs, for instance when a source property is actually a composition of two target properties (eg. $name$ in the source and a concatenation of $firstName$ and $lastName$ in the target). Our translation script generation approach currently does not accept indirect matches as part of the input matching. The inability to handle such sort of match is a limitation that we expect to overcome in the near future.

The listing below shows an input matching used to match the taxonomies described in figure 2. Observe that the input matching is valid according to definition 2.

$$m_1 = \{\Gamma_1.Person, \Gamma_2.Employee, [(nationality, nationality)]\}$$
$$m_2 = \{\Gamma_1.Professor, \Gamma_2.Tenured, [(nationality, nationality),$$
$$(institution, lecturesAt), (tenuredSince, isTenuredSince)]\}$$

Listing 1.1. Input matching for the taxonomies of figure 2

The definition 3 describes a translation script. Notice that a translation script is actually an extension of the input matching, where we have κ to express the condition that must be satisfied so that one particular match can be considered valid. A condition is expressed as a set of properties, where all properties belong to the source class. Since the matches are associated to a condition, they are referred to as conditional matches.

Definition 3 (Translation Script). *A translation script M' is a list of conditional matches $[m'_1, m'_2, ..., m'_n]$, where m'_l is a tuple on the form $m'_l =<m, \kappa>$, having κ as a set of properties $\{p_i\}$, such that $p_i \subseteq Prop(m.c_s)$ and $\exists <p_i, p_j> \in m.\Psi$.*

When translating instances, a conditional match can be interpreted as follows: if at least one of the properties within the match κ condition is present (has a value) in an instance, then the κ condition is satisfied, and the match can be used in the translation.

Inside a translation script, the conditional matches that refer to the same source class must be ordered according to definition 4. The matches are sorted with respect to the target class, and go from the more subsumed target class, as the first element, to the less subsumed target class, as the last element. The relation of subsumption between two classes is directly related to the hierarchical relation between the classes. The deeper a target class is in the hierarchy, the higher will be its sorting position.

Definition 4 (Property Presence Sorting). *Having $m'_i =<m_l, \kappa_i> \in M'$ and $m'_j =<m_n, \kappa_j> \in M'$, and having $m_l.c_s = m_n.c_s$, then $i < j$ if $m_l.c_t$ is a subsumption of $m_n.c_t$.*

Furthermore, the conditional matches that refer to the same source class have mutually exclusive κ conditions, as determined in definition 5. It is important that both definitions 4 and 5 are respected so the execution of the translation script may succeed.

Definition 5 (Mutually Exclusive Conditions). *Having $m_i' = <m_l, \kappa_i> \in M'$ and $m_j' = <m_n, \kappa_j> \in M'$, and having $m_l.c_s = m_n.c_s$, then $\kappa_i \cap \kappa_j = \oslash$.*

In listing 1.2 we show an example of a translation script that is based on part of the input matching presented in listing 1.1. The translation script is composed by some conditional matches that can be used for translating instances of the source class $\Gamma_1.Professor$. For clarity reasons, we omit the value of Ψ, whose content is [(tenuredSince, isTenuredSince), (lecturesAt, lecturesAt), (nationality, nationality)].

$$m_1' = \{\{\Gamma_1.Professor, \Gamma_2.Tenured, \Psi\}, [tenuredSince]\}$$
$$m_2' = \{\{\Gamma_1.Professor, \Gamma_2.Professor, \Psi\}, [lecturesAt]\}$$
$$m_3' = \{\{\Gamma_1.Professor, \Gamma_2.Employee, \Psi\}, []\}$$

Listing 1.2. Translation script for instances of $\Gamma_1.Professor$

On the data translation phase, the decision on how to translate an instance can be performed using a rather simple approach. The algorithm starts from the first conditional match to the last and chooses the first match whose κ condition is satisfied.

For instance, the κ conditions expressed in the translation script of listing 1.2 can be used to decide whether a professor in Γ_1 should turn into a tenured professor, a regular professor or an employee in Γ_2. If the source instance has a value for the property *tenuredSince*, then this instance is translated into a $\Gamma_2.Tenured$ instance. Otherwise, if the property *lecturesAt* has a value, than this instance is translated into a $\Gamma_2.Professor$ instance. If the previous alternatives fail, the instance is translated into a $\Gamma_2.Employee$ instance, instead.

Note that the matches agree with definitions 4 and 5. If that was not the case, the processing of the translation script could lead to a misplaced translation, given situations where more than one κ condition can be satisfied regarding a given instance. As an example, if the matches position of listing 1.2 were inverted, tenured professors would be translated into a $\Gamma_2.Employee$ instance.

4.1   Translation Script Generation

In this section we present an algorithm that generates conditional matches based on an input matching. Recall that a translation script is actually the list of conditional matches derived from the matches used as input. This algorithm can be used, for instance, to transform the match for the source class $\Gamma_1.Professor$ specified in listing 1.1 into the translation script presented in listing 1.2.

The algorithm responsible for generating the translation script processes each original match at a time (*processMatches()*). To every original match, the

processMatches()
for $m_i \in M$ do
    conditionBuilder($m_i.c_s, m_i.c_t, m_i.c_t, m_i.\Psi$)
end for

conditionBuilder(c_s, c_t, c_χ, Ψ)
$c'_\chi \leftarrow sup(c_\chi)$
if $c'_\chi \neq NULL$ and $|MatchedProp(c_t)| > 0$ then
    $\kappa \leftarrow MatchedProp(c_\chi) - MatchedProp(c'_\chi)$
    if $|\kappa| > 0$ then
        $createMatch(c_s, c_t, \Psi, \kappa)$
        $conditionBuilder(c_s, c'_\chi, c'_\chi, \Psi)$
    else
        $conditionBuilder(c_s, c_t, c'_\chi, \Psi)$
    end if
end if
$createMatch(c_s, c_t, \Psi, \emptyset)$

Algorithm 4.1. Translation script generation algorithm

recursive algorithm $conditionBuilder()$ is called. As a result of this processing, each original match ($m = \{c_s, c_t, \Psi\}$) generates at least one conditional match in the output. More details about the algorithm $conditionBuilder()$ are given below:

The first and the second parameters represent respectively the source (c_s) and the target class (c_t) of the original match. The third parameter initially represents the target class (c_t), but its value is changed throughout the execution of the recursive calls. This parameter is used to help in identifying the properties of a condition. The fourth parameter is the set of property matches of the source and target class(Ψ). This parameter remains constant throughout the execution of the recursive calls. The function $MatchedProp(c)$ returns all properties of the class c that were matched (are part of Ψ). Observe that the generation of the conditional matches are represented by symbolic calls to the $createMatch$ function.

Given a target class, two kinds of conditional matches can be generated:

Match with an empty condition. A conditional match with an empty κ condition is generated when the target class has no properties, or when it has the same properties as its root class in the taxonomy.

Match with a non empty condition. If the target class has more properties than its top-most parent, a conditional match is generated, where the κ condition is the difference of the properties between the target class and its closest predecessor that has fewer properties. Afterward, the processing starts over using this predecessor as the target class.

The algorithm finishes when the target class is one of the taxonomy roots. The algorithm assures that at least one conditional match is generated for every original match, which will be the match between the source and target class of the original match itself.

All target classes of the generated conditional matches belong to the same branch of the target class of the original match (they are super-classes of the original target class). The match derivation process is performed by climbing the nodes from the target class of the original match until a root is found. Since the algorithm assumes each target class has at most one direct parent, there is currently no support for taxonomies with multiple inheritance.

The set of property matches of a conditional match is equal to the set of property matches of the original match. If the source class of an original match has unmatched properties, such properties are not included in the derived conditional matches. During translation, these properties are ignored.

When more than one conditional match is generated for the same source class, the matches are sorted according to definition 4, except from one special case, when the input matching contains more than one match for the same source class. Take for instance, the listing below, that shows an input match for the taxonomies of figure 3. For clarity reasons, we omit the property matches, whose content is $\Psi_\alpha = [(\text{balance, balance}), (\text{interestRate, interestRate})]$, for m_1, and $\Psi_\beta = [(\text{balance, balance}), (\text{borrowingLimit, borrowingLimit})]$, for m_2. Notice that the input match presents two matches to the source class $Account$.

$$m_1 = \{\Gamma_3.Account, \Gamma_4.SavingsAccount, \Psi_\alpha\}$$
$$m_2 = \{\Gamma_3.Account, \Gamma_4.CurrentAccount, \Psi_\beta\}$$

Listing 1.3. Input matching for the source class $\Gamma_3.Account$

When applying the algorithm to this input matching, we obtain the translation script showed in listing 1.4. Notice that two conditional matches (m'_2 and m'_4) match with the same target class ($\Gamma_4.Account$).

$$m'_1 = \{\{\Gamma_3.Account, \Gamma_4.SavingsAccount, \Psi_\alpha\}, [interestRate]\}$$
$$m'_2 = \{\{\Gamma_3.Account, \Gamma_4.Account, [(balance, balance)]\}, []\}$$
$$m'_3 = \{\{\Gamma_3.Account, \Gamma_4.CurrentAccount, \Psi_\beta\}, [borrowingLimit]\}$$
$$m'_4 = \{\{\Gamma_3.Account, \Gamma_4.Account, [(balance, balance)]\}, []\}$$

Listing 1.4. Translation script for instances of $\Gamma_3.Account$

For this kind of situation, it is necessary to remove redundant matches. In order to preserve the correct match ordering, it suffices to remove all redundant matches whose position within the translation script is higher. In the case of listing 1.4, it would mean to remove the m'_2 conditional match.

An interesting remark about this translation script comes from using it to perform data translation between taxonomies whose instances are inconsistent with respect to each other. For instance, account instances in Γ_3 with all properties defined are not consistent with respect to Γ_4, since in the latter taxonomy the properties $interestRate$ and $borrowingLimit$ are disjoint. In this case both conditional matches m'_1 and m'_3 are valid. Since there is no deterministic way

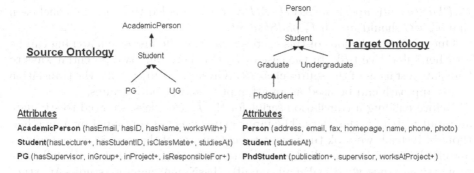

Fig. 4. Ontologies of a research community domain

of sorting these two matches (at least not by our sorting strategy), the instance are always translated into the valid match that is processed first, which is the $\Gamma_4.SavingsAccount$ for the case in question.

5 Case Study

During the explanation of our proposal, we have presented some examples in which conditional matches can be use to improve translation accuracy. In this section, we demonstrate how a translation script behaves when dealing with a translation situation where it is not clear how the instances of a source taxonomy should be translated.

This case study was held using parts of real ontologies we have extracted from the Web. The source ontology(Γ_s) and the target ontology (Γ_t) model a research community, including persons, organizations, and bibliographic metadata. Figure 4 describes the part of the ontologies that were actually used in the experiment. This part represents a taxonomical description of academic people.

Since the ontologies were modelled independently from each other, there is no common agreement on how the classes should match. Given this, we have conducted an exercise with the purpose of establishing a common sense on this subject. In this exercise we asked a group of students from a database research community to identify which classes of the source ontology correspond to which classes of the target ontology. We also asked them to identify the property matches inside each class to class match.

An interesting remark about this exercise is the divergence on the matching of $\Gamma_s.PG$. A significant amount of students (43%) relied more heavily on the semantics of the class names to deduce that $\Gamma_s.PG$ matches $\Gamma_t.Gradute$. The intuition behind the term "graduate" tells that it is a word used to designate students that are beyond the bachelors degree, which is indeed the case of a PG (Post-Graduate) student.

The most significant amount of students (53%) gave more attention to the classes properties to deduce the matches. The students observed that some of the properties of $\Gamma_s.PG(hasSupervisor, inProject)$ are similar to some properties of

$\Gamma_s.PhdStudent(supervisor, worksAtProject)$. This led them to the conclusion that $\Gamma_s.PG$ should match $\Gamma_t.phdStudent$.

One of the conclusions of this exercise was that the instance matching can be a rather subjective task. In the case of $\Gamma_s.PG$ there were two potential ways to translate instances of the source class PG. Given this subjectivity, the translation script approach can be used as an attempt to satisfy both groups.

Before building a translation script for the $\Gamma_s.PG$ class, we need to stipulate an input match for this class. The input match was not computed by a matcher, though. Instead, we took the most frequent answer of the exercise as the correct match. Additionally, we relied on the students opinion to stipulate the following property matches Ψ: [(hasEmail, email), (hasName, name), (studiesAt, studiesAt), (inProject, worksAtProject), (hasSupervisor, supervisor)]. Listing 1.5 shows the resulting input matching.

$$m_1 = \{\Gamma_s.PG, \Gamma_t.PhdStudent, \Psi\}$$

Listing 1.5. Input matching for source class $\Gamma_s.PG$

Given this input match, our translation script generation algorithm produces the following output:

$$m'_1 = \{\{\Gamma_s.PG, \Gamma_t.PhdStudent, \Psi\}, [inProject, hasSupervisor]\}$$
$$m'_2 = \{\{\Gamma_s.PG, \Gamma_t.Graduate, \Psi\}, [studiesAt]\}$$
$$m'_3 = \{\{\Gamma_s.PG, \Gamma_t.Person, \Psi\}, []\}$$

Listing 1.6. Translation script for instances of $\Gamma_s.PG$

Using this translation script, we have three translation possibilities: i) if the properties $\Gamma_s.PG.hasSupervisor$ or $\Gamma_s.PG.inProject$ have a value, the instance is translated into $\Gamma_t.PhDStudent$; ii) if the property $\Gamma_s.PG.studiesAt$ has a value, the instance is translated into $\Gamma_t.Graduate$; iii) the instance is translated into $\Gamma_t.Person$ otherwise.

6   Alternative for the Translation Script

We have devised two alternatives when using conditions for the translation of taxonomical data. So far we have presented the alternative that verifies whether at least one condition property is present in an instance. The second alternative does the opposite, and verifies whether all condition properties are absent. In this case, a match is considered valid only if all its condition properties are absent in a given instance. The listing below shows an example of how the translation script would look like, if the conditions expressed the absence of properties. This translation script regards conditional matches for the source class $\Gamma_1.Professor$, from figure 2.

$m'_1 = \{\{\Gamma_1.Professor, \Gamma_2.Employee, \Psi\}, [lecturesAt, tenuredSince]\}$
$m'_2 = \{\{\Gamma_1.Professor, \Gamma_2.Professor, \Psi\}, [tenuredSince]\}$
$m'_3 = \{\{\Gamma_1.Professor, \Gamma_2.Tenured, \Psi\}, []\}$

Listing 1.7. Translation script for instances of $\Gamma_1.Professor$

Again, during the translation phase, the matches must be analyzed in the correct order to prevent the wrong match from being chosen. As opposed to the approach where a condition tests the properties presence, in this alternative the matches are ordered from the less subsumed target class to the more subsumed target class, as indicated by definition 6.

Definition 6 (Property Absence Sorting). *Having $m'_i = <m_l, \kappa_i> \in M'$ and $m'_j = <m_n, \kappa_j> \in M'$, and having $m_l.c_s = m_n.c_s$, then $j < i$ if $m_l.c_t$ is subsumed by $m_n.c_t$.*

We believe that testing conditions as property presence is faster than testing the opposite. Our conviction is based on the fact that taxonomy instances are expected to have all its properties (or the majority of them) defined. Hence, testing if all properties of a condition are absent may take longer than testing if at least one property of a condition is present.

7   Conclusions

In this paper we address the problem of translating instances between taxonomies. Our approach encompasses a rule-base translation mechanism, that analyzes the presence of properties in the instances to identify the best translation.

Unlike most translations mechanisms, we are not concerned on designing a complete architecture that supports a broad range of translation needs, such as the specification of the transformation rules that must be applied when translating the instances. Instead, we focus our efforts on a simple rule specification, called translation script, that was conceived as a solution for the translating of taxonomical instances.

Since taxonomical instances are becoming increasingly popular with the advent of ontology models, we claim that the general idea hereby presented could be incorporated into more general/complete translation mechanisms, so the overall translation accuracy could be improved when the schemas involved in the translation describe taxonomies.

As future work, we intend to improve our translation mechanism in order to support indirect matches and taxonomies with multiple inheritance. Additionally, we intend to further explore the heuristic that perform data translation based on the absence of properties, and provide a comprehensive comparison between this heuristic and the one based on the presence of properties.

Acknowledgements. This paper was partially supported by projects FAPERGS PRONEX - 0408933, PETROGRAPHER - 360707 and CAPES.

References

1. Serge Abiteboul, Sophie Cluet, and Tova Milo. Correspondence and translation for heterogeneous data. In *Proceedings of the 6th International Conference on Database Theory*, Delphi, Greece, 1997. Springer, Berlin.
2. Serge Abiteboul, Sophie Cluet, and Tova Milo. Correspondence and translation for heterogeneous data. *Theor. Comput. Sci.*, 275(1-2):179–213, 2002.
3. Michael Boyd, Sasivimol Kittivoravitkul, Charalambos Lazanitis, Peter McBrien, and Nikos Rizopoulos. Automed: A bav data integration system for heterogeneous data sources. In *CAiSE*, pages 82–97, 2004.
4. Chen-Chuan K. Chang and Héctor García-Molina. Conjunctive constraint mapping for data translation. In *Proceedings of the Third ACM International Conference on Digital Libraries*, Pittsburgh, Pa., 1998. ACM Press, New York.
5. Sophie Cluet, Claude Delobel, Jérôme Siméon, and Katarzyna Smaga. Your mediators need data conversion! pages 177–188, 1998.
6. M. Ehrig and Y. Sure. Ontology mapping - an integrated approach.
7. David W. Embley, Li Xu, and Yihong Ding. Automatic direct and indirect schema mapping: experiences and lessons learned. *SIGMOD Rec.*, 33(4):14–19, 2004.
8. Avigdor Gal, Ateret Anaby-Tavor, Alberto Trombetta, and Danilo Montesi. A framework for modeling and evaluating automatic semantic reconciliation. *The VLDB Journal*, 14(1):50–67, 2005.
9. Fausto Giunchiglia, Pavel Shvaiko, and Mikalai Yatskevich. S-match: an algorithm and an implementation of semantic matching. In Y. Kalfoglou, M. Schorlemmer, A. Sheth, S. Staab, and M. Uschold, editors, *Semantic Interoperability and Integration*, number 04391 in Dagstuhl Seminar Proceedings, Dagstuhl, Germany, 2005. Internationales Begegnungs- und Forschungszentrum (IBFI), Schloss Dagstuhl, Germany.
10. Sandra Heiler. Semantic interoperability. *ACM Comput. Surv.*, 27(2):271–273, 1995.
11. Y. Kalfoglou and M. Schorlemmer. If-map: An ontology-mapping method based on information-flow theory, 2003.
12. Alexander Maedche, Boris Motik, Nuno Silva, and Raphael Volz. Mafra - a mapping framework for distributed ontologies. In *EKAW '02: Proceedings of the 13th International Conference on Knowledge Engineering and Knowledge Management. Ontologies and the Semantic Web*, pages 235–250, London, UK, 2002. Springer-Verlag.
13. M. Magnani, N. Rizopoulos, P.J. McBrien, and D. Montesi. Schema integration based on uncertain semantic mappings. In *ER'05*, LNCS, pages XX–XX. Springer, 2005.
14. Yannis Papakonstantinou, Héctor García-Molina, and Jeffrey Ullman. Medmaker: A mediation system based on declarative specifications. In *Proceedings of the 12th International Conference on Data Engineering*, New Orleans, La., 1996.
15. Sushama Prasad, Yun Peng, and Tim Finin. A Tool For Mapping Between Two Ontologies Using Explicit Information. In *AAMAS 2002 Workshop on Ontologies and Agent Systems*, Bologna, Italy, July 2002.
16. Erhard Rahm and Philip A. Bernstein. A survey of approaches to automatic schema matching. *VLDB Journal: Very Large Data Bases*, 10(4):334–350, ???? 2001.
17. Maurice van Keulen, Ander de Keijzer, and Wouter Alink. A probabilistic xml approach to data integration. In *ICDE*, pages 459–470, 2005.
18. Gio Wiederhold. Mediators in the architecture of future information systems. In Michael N. Huhns and Munindar P. Singh, editors, *Readings in Agents*, pages 185–196. Morgan Kaufmann, San Francisco, CA, USA, 1997.

Queries

Managing Quality Properties in a ROLAP Environment

Adriana Marotta[1], Federico Piedrabuena[1],and Alberto Abelló[2]

[1] Instituto de Computación, Universidad de la República, Montevideo, Uruguay
[2] Universitat Politècnica de Catalunya, Barcelona, España
{amarotta, fpiedrab}@fing.edu.uy, aabello@lsi.upc.edu

Abstract. In this work we propose, for an environment where multidimensional queries are made over multiple Data Marts, techniques for providing the user with quality information about the retrieved data. This meta-information behaves as an added value over the obtained information or as an additional element to take into account during the proposition of the queries. The quality properties considered are freshness, availability and accuracy. We provide a set of formulas that allow estimating or calculating the values of these properties, for the result of any multidimensional operation of a predefined basic set.

1 Introduction

The use of OLAP systems has become common practice, and in current times enterprise managers have the possibility to analyze the whole enterprise information with a multidimensional visualization. This information is obtained querying many databases, whose data is prepared for this kind of analysis. These databases are called Data Marts (DM). Each DM contains information that is represented in a multidimensional manner, is oriented to certain subject of interest, and comes from other databases, such as enterprise Data Warehouses or operational databases.

The user, who receives the answers of the queries submitted to the DMs, is quite far from the generation of the information (unknowing how and when it was generated at sources and loaded to DMs), therefore it would be extremely useful for him to count with additional information. This meta-information would make him feel more confident about the decisions he is making based on the information retrieved by the queries and, on the other hand, would allow him to eventually reformulate his queries.

Data quality is being deeply studied since some years ago. There exists various quality properties defined in the literature, such as *completeness, accuracy, accessibility, freshness, availability*. In this direction, there is much work for the particular case of information systems that are fed from multiple sources [1] [2] [3]. The possibility to provide a considerable amount of quality information to the users of such systems, and its importance, is globally recognized.

The meta-information associated to the retrieved information from the DMs may consist of a set of values corresponding to certain quality properties. We consider *freshness, availability and accuracy* constitute an interesting group of quality properties for this context, due to functional characteristics of the DMs and intrinsic characteristics of the information received by the user. On one hand, each DM is periodically maintained, which generates constraints in the DM availability and

E. Dubois and K. Pohl (Eds.): CAiSE 2006, LNCS 4001, pp. 127–141, 2006.
© Springer-Verlag Berlin Heidelberg 2006

restricts the freshness of its data. On the other hand, the information obtained by the user is the result of combinations of data coming from different sources, with probably heterogeneous levels of accuracy, thus the accuracy of this information is not a trivial meta-information and is a significant added value for the user.

As an example, consider a director of a multi-national enterprise, who needs information about its sales throughout several countries. For obtaining it, he makes queries over DMs belonging to the different countries' subsidiaries. These DMs follow certain standards of formats, codification, etc., so that their information can be integrated by multidimensional operations. Suppose the director obtains sales amounts corresponding to South-America, discriminated by products, for each month of the current year. We believe that this person would be really grateful if he also obtained meta-information such as when the involved data was loaded in the DMs and how accurate it is. And still more, if previous to the execution of the query he is informed about the availability of the data he is requiring, and alternative DMs for obtaining the non-available information are suggested to him.

Some works about federations of OLAP systems and other technologies can be found in the literature [4] [5]. This work is situated in the context of an environment where multidimensional queries are made over multiple DMs, sometimes combining various DMs in the same query. Our goal is to propose techniques for giving support to users, providing them quality information about the information retrieved, as an added value over the obtained information or as an additional element to consider during the proposition of the queries.

Given a query over DMs, proposed by the user, and the freshness, availability and accuracy values of each DM, the problem we address consists on calculating: (i) availability of the needed DMs' information, and (ii) freshness and accuracy of the information resulting from the executed query. The techniques we propose use existing proposals for quality properties propagation in Relational Algebra operations [1][6][7] as a reference point. Nevertheless, they involve particular criteria that are related with a multidimensional classification of the relational elements and other particularities of the OLAP context.

The contribution of this work is the proposal of: (i) a specific scenario where OLAP-queries results are enriched with quality meta-information, and (ii) techniques for calculating the availability, freshness and accuracy values of information that was obtained through application of OLAP queries to multiple DMs.

The rest of the paper is organized as follows. Section 2 presents the context of the work, Section 3 presents the quality properties we use, in Section 4 we present our proposal for quality evaluation, and finally in Section 5 we present the conclusions.

2   Context

We establish here a concrete scenario, for which we propose the quality management techniques. First, we describe the basic scenario that we consider as starting point for our work. After, we present the enriched scenario, which is the basic one enriched with our proposal.

2.1 Basic Scenario

We consider a ROLAP system (OLAP over RDBMS), where users execute multidimensional queries. These queries are composed by multidimensional operations. In this section we present the scenario and the multidimensional-operations set considered.

OLAP functionality is characterized by dynamic multidimensional analysis of consolidated enterprise data supporting end user analytical and navigational activities (interactively exploring cubes). In an OLAP system each multidimensional operation is a function that takes Cubes (a set of cells placed in an n-dimensional space) as arguments and returns a Cube. "ROLAP" tools automatically generate a SQL query according to the operations performed by the user, see Figure 1. Many times end users navigate from Cube to Cube not just applying isolated operations but performing sequences of operations; this sequence is performed as a sequence of SQL queries.

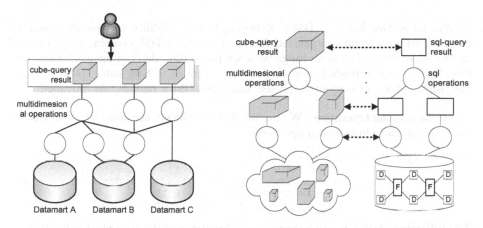

Fig. 1. ROLAP System

Fig. 2. Relational implementation of multidimensional concepts

Given that it does not exist any standard multidimensional algebra or data model, we use YAM^2 [9] multidimensional algebra for the set of operations, because it provides a direct translation to SQL and it allows making any multidimensional query; in [8] this algebra is stated as complete, which assures us the expressiveness offered. Multidimensional operations are represented as SQL queries using a cube-query template that was proposed in [8] for retrieving a Cell of data that conforms to a Cube, from the RDBMS. Figure 2 shows the correspondences between an OLAP and a ROLAP system, each multidimensional operation can be translated to a cube-query and each cube can be translated to a relation.

Each DM in this scenario is a set of cubes that correspond to the same subject of analysis, i.e. to the same fact. These cubes are represented by the Relational Model, through the star (see Figure 3), snowflake (see Figure 4) or a hybrid schema. Completely normalizing each Dimension we get a snowflake schema and not normalizing them at all results in a star schema. We choose the generic approach, like in [10]. With respect to the Fact, it is defined as a set of Cells, which are materializations of different levels of aggregations of the same fact. The Dimension Levels may be materialized according to the materializations of the Cells, since the latter have FKs that must point to the corresponding PKs in the Level relations.

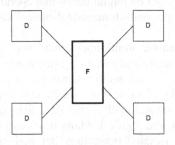

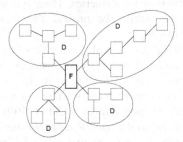

Fig. 3. Star schema   **Fig. 4.** Snowflake schema

We define two kinds of DMs, according to the volatility of their data, and we assume that our system is organized this way: (1) Stable DM, contains only historical information, whose fact-dates range between two certain dates in the past. Therefore, this DM is not refreshed nor loaded any more. (2) Non-stable DM, contains information that comes up to the present date. This DM is periodically refreshed.

Multidimensional Operations. We use the SQL template (Cube-query), for constructing the different multidimensional operations.

Cube-query:
```
RESULT =   SELECT l1.ID, …, ln.ID, c.Measure1, …
           FROM Cell c, Level1 l1, …, Leveln ln
           WHERE c.key1 = l1.ID AND … AND c.keyn = ln.ID
           GROUP BY l1.ID, …, ln.ID
           ORDER BY l1.ID, …, ln.ID
```

The following are the intuitive operations definitions and the associated SQL code.

Dice. By means of a predicate P over a Dimension attribute, this operation allows to choose the subset of points of interest out of the whole n-dimensional space.

```
SELECT l₁.ID, …, lₙ.ID, c.Measure₁, …
FROM Cell c, Level₁ l₁, …, Levelₙ lₙ
WHERE c.key₁ = l₁.ID AND … AND c.keyₙ = lₙ.ID
AND P
GROUP BY l₁.ID, …, lₙ.ID
ORDER BY l₁.ID, …, lₙ.ID
```

Projection. This just selects a subset of Measures from those available in the Cube.

```
SELECT l₁.ID, …, lₙ.ID, c.Measure₁, …
FROM Cell c, Level₁ l₁, …, Levelₙ lₙ
WHERE c.key₁ = l₁.ID AND … AND c.keyₙ = lₙ.ID
GROUP BY l₁.ID, …, lₙ.ID
ORDER BY l₁.ID, …, lₙ.ID
```

Drill-across. This operation changes the image set of the Cube. The n-dimensional space remains exactly the same, only the cells placed in it change.

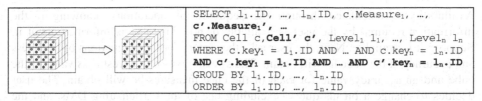

```
SELECT l₁.ID, …, lₙ.ID, c.Measure₁, …,
c'.Measure₁', …
FROM Cell c,Cell' c', Level₁ l₁, …, Levelₙ lₙ
WHERE c.key₁ = l₁.ID AND … AND c.keyₙ = lₙ.ID
AND c'.key₁ = l₁.ID AND … AND c'.keyₙ = lₙ.ID
GROUP BY l₁.ID, …, lₙ.ID
ORDER BY l₁.ID, …, lₙ.ID
```

Roll-Up. It groups cells in the Cube based on an aggregation hierarchy, modifying the granularity of data. Assuming the two levels are materialized separately, suppose $level_1$ and $level_k$ are two contiguous levels from the same dimension (it exists a foreign key from $level_1$ to $level_k$), and we want to roll up from level l_1 to level l_k.

```
SELECT lₖ.ID, …, lₙ.ID, F(c.Measure₁), …
FROM Cell c,Level₁ l₁, …, Levelₙ lₙ, Levelₖ lₖ
WHERE c.key₁ = l₁.ID AND … AND c.keyₙ = lₙ.ID
AND l₁.keyₖ = lₖ.ID
GROUP BY lₖ.ID, …, lₙ.ID
ORDER BY lₖ.ID, …, lₙ.ID
```

Change Base. This operation reallocates exactly the same instances of a Cell in a new n-dimensional space with exactly the same number of points. Thus, it actually modifies the analysis dimensions used.

```
SELECT n₁.ID, …, nₙ.ID, c.Measure₁, …
FROM Cell c, Level₁ l₁, …, Levelₙ lₙ,
NewLevel₁ n₁, …, NewLevelₙ nₙ
WHERE c.key₁ = l₁.ID AND … AND c.keyₙ = lₙ.ID
AND l₁.att₁ = n₁.ID AND … AND lₙ.attₙ = nₙ.ID
GROUP BY n₁.ID, …, nₙ.ID
ORDER BY n₁.ID, …, nₙ.ID
```

Union. We propose a variant of Union operation proposed in [8], because, is very important to consider the possibility of combining cubes, which we know they have the same schema and formats, but we do not know anything about the data they contain. This operation performs the union of two n-dimensional identical cubes.

```
SELECT l₁.ID, …, lₙ.ID, c.Measure₁, …
FROM Cell c, Level₁ l₁, …, Levelₙ lₙ
WHERE c.key₁ = l₁.ID AND … AND c.keyₙ = lₙ.ID
GROUP BY l₁.ID, …, lₙ.ID
ORDER BY l₁.ID, …, lₙ.ID
UNION
SELECT l₁.ID, …, lₙ.ID, c.Measure₁, …
FROM Cell' c, Level₁' l₁, …, Levelₙ' lₙ
WHERE c.key₁ = l₁.ID AND … AND c.keyₙ = lₙ.ID
GROUP BY l₁.ID, …, lₙ.ID
ORDER BY l₁.ID, …, lₙ.ID
```

2.2 Enriched Scenario

We enrich the scenario presented in last section with the quality evaluation of the queries that are posed by the user. In the following, we present the way it would work. The user of the OLAP system poses an OLAP query over various DMs. This query is decomposed into various multidimensional operations and translated to SQL.

Availability is calculated through the sequence of operations, knowing if the information required by the user is available or not. The user is informed about it. Suppose it is available. Next, the user asks the system for the estimations of freshness and accuracy of the cube he will obtain. The system gives him a freshness value of the cube and an accuracy value for each of the cube measures he will obtain. The user decides to change a bit his query, excluding one of the participating DMs, and the estimated values improve. Finally, the user executes the query, obtaining the cube with its associated quality metadata, which was exactly calculated by the system. This metadata includes, the cube freshness value, the accuracy values for each cube measure, and also includes these values for each tuple that can be seen by the user if he is interested in going more in detail.

System Metadata. To provide a comprehensive picture of the overall ROLAP system we use an extension of the Federation Ontology for Multi-Source Information System (MSIS) stated in [11]. It provides six metadata categories of federation information (e.g. quality properties indicators, access control directives topology information), which are highly flexible. In this context we only need two categories:

- Data Quality: This category defines the data quality properties of the DM data and the multidimensional data result.
- Source Quality of Service: This category defines the quality properties of the service of each DM. The DM resolves each multidimensional operation by means of a process or service.

Each DM provides its own metadata to be used by the OLAP system.

3 Quality Properties

The quality properties we have chosen for our scenario are *freshness, availability and accuracy*. This choice is mainly due to two reasons: the usefulness that they may have for the DM users, and the existence of previous work about them that can be applied to our context. Based on existing approaches and definitions of these properties we propose one specific definition for each one, which we think are the most suitable for our needs. Besides each definition we state the level of granularity at which we apply the property, e.g. a whole DM, a cube, a table, each tuple, etc.

3.1 Freshness

Several definitions can be found in the literature for quality properties related to the age of the information. Some of them can be found in [12][13][1], while in [14] they present a summary and classification of a wide set of existing approaches for this property. For this work we propose the definition: *Freshness is the time elapsed since the data was loaded in the DM until it is received by the user through a query.*

We propose for the assignment of freshness values to the system, a DM granularity, a cube granularity and in some cases a tuple granularity. At each DM we do not manage tuple granularity, because we assume it is entirely loaded on a periodic basis, therefore it would be useless to have the possibility of different freshness values in different portions of the DM.

The metadata needed for freshness information at the DM is the following:

- Loading Period (lp): An integer that represents the quantity of hours passed between the starting time of two loading processes (period between loadings).
- Loading Duration (ldur): An integer that represents an approximation of the quantity of hours that passes between the starting time of the loading process (the downing of the DM service) and its ending time (the starting service instant).
- Last Loading Date/Time (lastl): A decimal that represents the date and time when the last loading process was started.
- Stable-or-Not (st): A boolean that indicates if the DM is stable, i.e. if the DM is not refreshed because its information should cover just until certain date (as we explained in Section 2.1).

In the case the DM is stable:

$$lp = ldur = 0 \ . \tag{1}$$

$$lastl = NOW \ . \tag{2}$$

where NOW is a special value, which means the actual moment.

The metadata needed for freshness information in the whole system is the following:

For each fact table (cube):

- Freshness Value (fv): An integer that represents the quantity of hours elapsed since the table data was loaded in the DM.

For each fact table, for each tuple:

- Freshness Value by Tuple (fv_by_tuple): An integer that represents the quantity of hours elapsed since the tuple was loaded in the DM.

The freshness information at the DM allows us to calculate the exact value of freshness at a certain moment at the DM (fv), and also the maximum and minimum freshness values (maxfv and minfv) that are possible at the DM.

We calculate these DM values through the following formulas:

$$fv = round(actual\_datetime - lastl) \ . \tag{3}$$

$$maxfv = lp + ldur \ . \tag{4}$$

$$minfv = ldur \ . \tag{5}$$

Note that for stable DMs:

$$fv = maxfv = minfv = 0 \ . \tag{6}$$

Each fv_by_tuple of each DM fact table is set to the fv of the DM.

3.2 Accuracy

The term accuracy is frequently used to describe many different aspects related to the data itself. Semantic correctness, syntactic correctness, precision and fuzziness are some of the concepts related to accuracy that are used with similar intentions [1], [6], [15], [16]. For this work we propose the definition: *Accuracy is the probability of an attribute value to be correct. A value is correct if corresponds to reality.*

The granularity we use for this property is at attribute level, but we manage accuracy information only for the measure attributes. This is because we consider this kind of attributes is the most relevant for the OLAP analysis, and also this restriction allows us to find solutions that are more specific to certain type of information. For each measure attribute we manage DM, cube and, sometimes, tuple granularity. At each DM we do not manage tuple granularity, because the measurement of accuracy at the DMs could not be made for each value of the attributes, since they are numeric values and cannot be easily verified (considering errors generated by wrong digitations). For example, it is not possible to use tools such as dictionaries or look-up tables, which allow verifying string values belonging to determined domains. Therefore, we suppose that the accuracy values at the DMs are estimated through statistic methods or by people involved in the generation of the data.

The metadata needed for accuracy information is the following:
For each fact table, for each measure attribute:

- Accuracy Value (av): A decimal number between 0 and 1 that represents the probability of being correct for the values of the attribute.

For each fact table, for each measure attribute, for each tuple:

- Accuracy Value by Tuple (av_by_tuple): A decimal number between 0 and 1 that represents the probability of being correct for the value.

At the DMs, each av_by_tuple of each measure of the fact tables is set to the av of the measure attribute.

3.3 Availability

Availability is a measure of a system or service readiness to perform its function when it is needed [17], [12]. For this work we propose the definition: *Availability indicates if a service is ready for use at a given instant.*

We assume that the only factor that influences the availability of the DM is the loading process and that the DM is totally unavailable during this process. We manage a DM granularity and in the rest of the system a cube granularity.

The metadata needed for availability information at the DM is the same as for freshness: i) loading period (lp), ii) loading duration (ldur), iii) last loading date/time (lastl) and iv) stable-or-not (st).

The metadata needed for availability information in the whole system is the following:

- Avalilability Value (vv): A Boolean that represents if the DM is available (vv = TRUE) or not (vv = FALSE).

The metadata at the DM allows us to calculate the availability of the DM at a certain moment (vv). We calculate this value through the following formula:

$$vv = actual\_datetime >= (lastl + ldur) . \tag{7}$$

Note that for stable DMs:

$$vv = true(\text{due to lastl} = actual\_datetime \text{ and } ldur = 0) . \tag{8}$$

4 Quality Evaluation of User Queries' Results

Our goal is to determine how to obtain the quality values of the information retrieved by a query in our defined context. We propose techniques for two kinds of quality evaluation: (i) quality values calculation, after the query is executed, and (ii) quality values estimation, before the query is executed. For the calculation, we need to manage a granularity of tuple, since it takes into account the resulting tuples of each operation. In contrast, for the estimation we manage a cube granularity, since we do not need the information about the obtained tuples in each operation.

We provide a formula for each quality property and operation. For a sequence of operations, the formulas are composed to obtain the quality values of the final cube. The estimations and calculations are done taking into account the SQL specifications for each multidimensional operation given in Section 2.1. The formulas we propose are based on previously proposed formulas for the Relational Algebra (RA) operators [1] [6] [7]. However, they take into account three main aspects that characterize our context: (i) the type of the elements that participate in each operation. Different types of relational elements are distinguished in the operations specifications. A relation can be a *Cell* (or fact table) or a *Level* (a table containing dimension data). An attribute can be a *Measure*, the key of a dimension level or some other dimension attribute. (ii) the relevance that each type of element has in the resulting quality. We state that the quality of the fact tables determines the quality of the user queries results. Therefore the fact tables and measure attributes must have the greatest influence in the quality evaluation formulas. (iii) the granularity managed. The OLAP context particularities suggest us certain granularities for the quality values, which are suitable and useful. We consider the cube granularity because each multidimensional operation result is a cube (in particular the user query result). We also work with the tuple granularity and in the case of accuracy, we manage the granularity at the level of each measure attribute.

For the following sub-sections, consider the SQL specifications for the multi-dimensional operations presented in Section 2.1.

4.1 Estimations

In this section we present, for each multidimensional operation, a general formula for estimating the quality value of the result of its application.

Freshness. In this context, it is not worth considering the cost (duration) of the operations because it is depreciable in comparison to the loading time of a DM and to the period of time between two loadings. We consider facts' freshness relevant only, since we assume dimensions have rather stable information.

Estimations for RA Operations:

- Projection, Selection, Aggregation: The original fv is maintained by these operations.
- Join (R,S), Union (R,S):

$$fv(Result) = max(fv(R), fv(S)) .$$ (9)

Estimations for Multidimensional Operations:

- Dice, Roll-Up, Projection, Change Base: The result has the same freshness value as the input fact table. Dice, Roll-Up, and Change Base operations involve joins between the fact table and dimension tables. However, the freshness of the dimensions does not affect the resulting freshness.

$$fv(Result) = fv(Cell) .$$ (10)

- Drill Across: It involves a join between the fact table of the original cube (Cell) and another fact table (Cell'). The dimensions that are also involved in the join, do not affect the resulting freshness.

$$fv(Result) = max(fv(Cell), fv(Cell')) .$$ (11)

- Union: The union relational operator is applied over two sets of tuples from different fact tables. The formula is the same as (11).

Accuracy. We consider as relevant the facts' accuracy and not the dimensions' one because the dimensions' values are rather stable and we assume they have a good accuracy, while the quantity of measures' values is constantly growing and these values are the main basis for the decision making process.

Estimations for RA Operations:

- Projection, Selection, Aggregation: The original av is maintained by these operations.
- Join (R,S):

$$av(Result) = av(R) * av(S) .$$ (12)

- Union (R,S): A weighted average of input tables' accuracy values, according to the tuple quantity of each input table, is done.

$$av(Result) = (av(R) * |R| + av(S) * |S|) / |R| + |S| .$$ (13)

Note that these estimations are proposed for a relation granularity.

Estimations for Multidimensional Operations: In this case, the join operations never affect the resulting accuracy values due to the granularity we manage, therefore we do not apply the estimation proposed for the RA join. When there is a join between fact tables, each measure attribute maintains its accuracy value.

- Dice, Roll-Up, Projection, Change Base: These operations maintain the accuracy values for each measure attribute.

$$av(Result, Measure_i) = av(Cell, Measure_i) .$$ (14)

- Drill Across: It maintains the accuracy values for each measure attribute.

$$av(Result, Cell.Measure_i) = av(Cell, Measure_i) \, .$$
$$av(Result, Cell'.Measure_j) = av(Cell', Measure_j) \, . \tag{15}$$

- Union: For each measure attribute, we do a weighted average as in (13).

$$av(Result, Measure_i) = (av(Cell, Measure_i) * |Cell| +$$
$$av(Cell', Measure_i) * |Cell'|) / |Cell| + |Cell'| \, . \tag{16}$$

Availability. Given a multidimensional operation, for availability to be true, we need that all necessary data for answering the corresponding SQL query are available. Therefore, in the estimation of this property the dimensions' information has the same incidence as the facts' information.

- Projection, Roll-Up: These operations have as input only one fact table with one associated availability value.

$$vv(Result) = vv(Cell) \, . \tag{17}$$

- Dice: This operation includes a predicate P over an attribute of a dimension table, which may not be its key. Therefore, for executing this operation we need not only the availability of the fact table, but also the availability of the mentioned dimension table. However, all these tables belong to the same DM, therefore, assuring availability of the fact table is enough. The formula is the same as (17).
- Change Base: For this operation not only the fact table must be available, but also the original and new dimension tables, so that the join between them can be done. The new dimension tables may belong to a different DM.

$$vv(Result) = vv(Cell) \text{ AND } vv(NewLevel_1) \text{ AND } \dots \text{ AND}$$
$$vv(NewLevel_n) \, . \tag{18}$$

- Drill Across, Union: In these operations the resulting data comes from both input fact tables, which may belong to different DMs. Therefore, the availability value of the result is equal to the "AND" of the availability values of the input fact tables.

$$vv(Result) = vv(Cell) \text{ AND } vv(Cell') \, . \tag{19}$$

4.2 Calculations

In this section we present, for each multidimensional operation, a general formula for calculating properties values of the result.

For calculations we use a tuple granularity, thus the property values are affected by an operation when it generates one tuple from the combination of two or more tuples. Therefore, the RA operations that can affect calculations are join and aggregation.

We use the ideas of estimations for RA operations existing in the literature for the cases of join and union, but in most cases we propose calculations that are specific for our context and granularity.

Freshness
Calculation of fv_by_tuple. After the application of a multidimensional operation, we can calculate the fv by tuple.

- Projection, Change Base, Dice: These operations do not affect tuples' freshness values. Dice and Change Base operations involve joins between fact table and dimension tables. However, the freshness of dimension tuples does not affect freshness of the resulting tuples.

$$\text{fv\_by\_tuple}(t_1) = \text{fv\_by\_tuple}(t_2) . \tag{20}$$

for all $<t_1,t_2>$, where t_1 is a Result tuple and t_2 is the corresponding Cell tuple.
- Union: The union relational operator is applied over two sets of tuples from different fact tables, however, when managing tuple granularity, the freshness values are not affected.

$$\text{fv\_by\_tuple}(t_1) = \text{fv\_by\_tuple}(t_2) .$$

$$\text{fv\_by\_tuple}(t_3) = \text{fv\_by\_tuple}(t_4) . \tag{21}$$

for all $<t_1,t_2>$ where t_1 is a Result tuple and t_2 is the corresponding Cell tuple, for all $<t_3,t_4>$, where t_3 is a Result tuple and t_4 is the corresponding Cell' tuple.
- Roll-Up: This operation generates tuples that are aggregations from input tuples.

$$\text{fv\_by\_tuple}(t) = \max(\text{fv\_by\_tuple}(u)) . \tag{22}$$

for all t, Result tuple, for all $u \in T$, where T is the tuple set of Cell grouped in t.
- Drill Across: Each resulting tuple is generated by a join that involves two fact tables (Cell and Cell'), therefore its freshness is calculated from the freshness of the corresponding tuples of the input fact tables.

$$\text{fv\_by\_tuple}(t) = \max(\text{fv\_by\_tuple}(u), \text{fv\_by\_tuple}(u')) . \tag{23}$$

for all t, tuple of Result, where $u \in$ Cell, and $u' \in$ Cell', are the tuples whose values participate in t.

Calculation of fv. After the application of a multidimensional operation, we can calculate the fv of a relation from the fv_by_tuple of its tuples.

$$\text{fv(Result)} = \max(\text{fv\_by\_tuple}(t)) . \tag{24}$$

for all t, tuple of Result.

Note that in the case of Projection and Change Base the fv of the cube is maintained, while in the case of the other operations it may change.

Accuracy
Calculation of av_by_tuple. Since the granularity managed for accuracy is of tuple and attribute, the RA join operator does not affect the accuracy of the resulting tuples. The value of each measure attribute of the result comes from only one of the input fact tables, therefore the accuracy of each tuple for each measure attribute is maintained by the join.

- Projection, Change Base, Dice: These operations do not affect the tuples' accuracy values for each measure attribute.

$$av\_by\_tuple(t_1[Measure_i]) = av\_by\_tuple(t_2[Measure_i]) . \tag{25}$$

for all $<t_1,t_2>$, where t_1 is a tuple of Result and t_2 is the matching tuple of Cell.
- Union: Analogously to the case of freshness, the union relational operator is applied but it does not affect tuples' accuracy values. The accuracy of each tuple in each measure of the result is the same it was in the corresponding input table.

$$av\_by\_tuple(t_1[Measure_i]) = av\_by\_tuple(t_2[Measure_i]) .$$

$$av\_by\_tuple(t_3[Measure_j]) = av\_by\_tuple(t_4[Measure_j]) . \tag{26}$$

for all $<t_1,t_2>$, where t_1 is a tuple of Result and t_2 is the matching tuple of Cell, for all $<t_3,t_4>$, where t_3 is a tuple of Result and t_4 is the matching tuple of Cell'.
- Drill Across: It does not affect tuples' accuracy values for each measure attribute.

$$av\_by\_tuple(t_1[Measure_i]) = av\_by\_tuple(t_2[Measure_i]) .$$

$$av\_by\_tuple(t_1[Measure_j]) = av\_by\_tuple(t_3[Measure_j]) . \tag{27}$$

for all $<t_1,t_2,t_3>$, where t_1 is a tuple of Result, t_2 is the corresponding tuple of Cell, and t_3 is the corresponding tuple of Cell'.
- Roll-Up: This operation generates tuples that are aggregations of input tuples. This calculation is made with the same criteria we use in the calculation of the av of a relation (we explain it below).

$$av\_by\_tuple(t[Measure_i]) = (av\_by\_tuple(u_1[Measure_i]) *$$
$$digits(u_1[Measure_i]) + ... + av\_by\_tuple(u_n[Measure_i]) * \tag{28}$$
$$digits(u_n[Measure_i])) / digits(u_1[Measure_i]) + ... + digits(u_n[Measure_i]) .$$

for all t, tuple of Result, for all $u_i \in T$, where T is the set of tuples of Cell grouped in t, where $u_i[Measure_i]$ is the value of the attribute $Measure_i$ in tuple u_i, and digits(n) returns the quantity of digits of number n.

Calculation of av: The av of a relation is calculated from the av_by_tuple of its tuples. For each measure attribute, we make a weighted average, taking into account the values of the measure attribute (multiplying by the number of digits), since we consider that the accuracy of greater values must have more influence on the accuracy of the whole table.

$$av(Result,Measure_i) = (av\_by\_tuple(Cell, Measure_i,t_1) *$$
$$digits(t_1.Measure_i) + ... + av\_by\_tuple(Cell, Measure_i,t_n) * \tag{29}$$
$$digits(t_n.Measure_i)) / digits(t_1.Measure_i) + ... + digits(t_n.Measure_i) .$$

where $t_1 ... t_n$ are all the tuples of Result, $t_i.Measure_i$ is the value of the attribute $Measure_i$ in tuple t_i, and digits(n) returns the quantity of digits of number n.

Note that in the case of Projection and Change Base the av of each measure is maintained, while in the cases of the other operations it may change.

Availability. In our approach, the calculation of this property has no sense because the availability values never depend on the tuples obtained in each operation, but only on the DMs that are involved in the query. Therefore, only estimations can be done.

5 Conclusion

In this work we propose a mechanism for adding quality properties meta-information to an OLAP system. We state a very specific scenario, where the system is implemented as ROLAP and each DM consists of a set of cubes that correspond to the same fact. For the definition of this scenario, we base on the work presented in [8], [10]. The quality properties we manage are freshness, accuracy and availability. We propose a set of formulas for estimating and calculating the values of these properties for any possible multidimensional query posed by the user. Estimations and calculations are both useful for the user. Estimations can be used for changing the query so that a better quality is obtained, and calculations provide a more exact meta-information that may be very valuable at the moment of making decisions.

For the performed study, we focused on a given set of SQL queries and on data with certain given characteristics, e.g. the measure attributes. Such preconditions allowed us to obtain interesting results, such as some formulas for accuracy that take into account the values of the attributes. They also showed how some operations in general do not affect the quality values, while other ones have a great incidence.

This study also shows the feasibility of applying techniques of quality evaluation to an OLAP environment, emphasizing on the main characteristics of these systems.

Future work will focus on considering user quality requirements and managing the system quality for maintaining their satisfaction. This problem leads to extend the scope of our environment, such that the sources of the DMs and the data transformations between them be considered. Another aspect that may be addressed is the extension of the present study to other quality properties.

Acknowledgements

Our work has been supported by the Spanish Research Program PRONTIC and FEDER under project TIN2005-05406, and by Comisión Sectorial de Investigación Científica from Universidad de la República, Montevideo, Uruguay.

References

1. Naumann, F.; Leser, U.; Freytag, J.C.: Quality-driven Integration of Heterogenous Information Systems. VLDB 1999: 447-458
2. Marotta, A.; Ruggia, R.: Quality Management in Muti-Source Information Systems. II Workshop de Bases de Datos, Jornadas Chilenas de Computación (JCC'03), Chile. Nov. 03
3. Marotta, A.; Ruggia, R.: Managing Source Quality Changes in Data Integration Systems. Second International Workshop on Data and Information Quality (DIQ'05) (in conjunction with CAISE). June, 14th. 2005, Porto, Portugal
4. Bach Pedersen, T.; Shoshani, A.; Gu, J.; Jensen, C.: Extending OLAP Querying to External Object Databases. Int. Conf. on Information and Knowledge Management. CIKM 2000.
5. Pedersen, D.; Riis, K.; Bach Pedersen, T.: Query optimization for OLAP-XML federations. ACM Fifth International Workshop on Data Warehousing and OLAP, Nov. 2002, USA.
6. Motro, A.; Rakov, I.: Estimating the Quality of Databases. International Conference on Flexible Query Answering Systems. FQAS 1998: 298-307

7. Peralta, V.; Ruggia, R.; Kedad, Z.; Bouzeghoub, M.: A Framework for Data Quality Evaluation in a Data Integration System. 19° Simposio Brasileiro de Banco de Dados (SBBD'2004). Brasil, October 2004

8. Abelló, A.; Samos, J.; Saltor, F.: Implementing Operations to Navigate Semantic Star Schemas (© ACM). In 6th International Workshop on Data Warehousing and OLAP (DOLAP 2003). New Orleans (USA), November 2003.

9. Abelló, A.; Samos J.; Saltor F.: YAM2 (Yet Another Multidimensional Model): An Extension of UML. International Database Engineering & Applications Symposium, IDEAS'02, July 17-19, 2002, Edmonton, Canada.

10. Romero, O.; Abelló, A.: Improving automatic SQL translation for ROLAP tools. In Proceedings of Jornadas de Ingeniería del Software y Bases de Datos (JISBD 2005). Granada (Spain), September 2005. Pages 123-130. Thomson Editores, ISBN 84-9732-434-X

11. Piedrabuena, F.; Tercia, S.; Vazquez, G.: Federation Ontology for Multi-Source Information Systems. Internal Report. Instituto de Computación, Facultad de Ingeniería, Uruguay. 2005

12. Lee, Y.W.; Strong, D.M.; Kahn, B.K.; Wang, R.Y.: AIMQ: A Methodology for Information Quality Assessment. Information & Management, published by Elsevier Science (North Holland). (Accepted in November 2001)

13. Theodoratos, D.; Bouzeghoub, M.: Data Currency Quality Factors in Data Warehouse Design. In Proc. of the Int. Workshop on Design and Management of Data Warehouses (DMDW'99), Germany, 1999.

14. Bouzeghoub, M.; Peralta, V.: A Framework for Analysis of Data Freshness. 1st Int. Workshop on Information Quality in Information Systems (IQIS). Paris, France, June 2004.

15. Motro, A.: Accommodating Imprecision in Database Systems: Issues and Solutions. ACM SIGMOD Record (Special issue on directions for future DBMS research and development), Vol. 19, No. 4, December 1990, pp. 69--74

16. Strong, D.M.; Lee, Y.W.; Wang, R.Y.: Data Quality in Context. Communications of the ACM. May 1997/Vol.40, No.5

17. Availability. http://availability.com/. Last accessed: Oct. 9, 2005.

Comprehensible Answers to Précis Queries

Alkis Simitsis[1] and Georgia Koutrika[2]

[1] National Technical University of Athens,
Department of Electrical and Computer Engineering,
Athens, Greece
asimi@dbnet.ece.ntua.gr
[2] University of Athens,
Department of Computer Science,
Athens, Greece
koutrika@di.uoa.gr

Abstract. Users without knowledge of schemas or query languages have difficulties in accessing information stored in databases. Commercial and research efforts have focused on keyword-based searches. Among them, précis queries generate entire multi-relation databases, which are logical subsets of existing ones, instead of individual relations. The logical database subset contains not only items directly related to the query selections but also items implicitly related to them in various ways. Earlier work has identified the need of providing the naïve user with meaningful answers to his questions and has suggested the translation of précis query answer in narrative form. In this paper, we present a semi-automatic method that translates the relational output of a précis query into a synthesis of results. We describe a translator engine that uses a template mechanism for generating a précis in a narrative form through a set of reusable templates.

1   Introduction

The need for facilitating access to information stored in databases has been early recognized in the research community with initial efforts dating back to seventies [7]. Emergence of the World Wide Web has made information access possible to a growing number of people. A large fraction of information resides in databases, as libraries, museums, and other organizations publish their electronic contents on the Web. In the same time, most users have no specific knowledge of schemas or structured query languages for accessing information stored in a database. In this context, the need for facilitating access to information stored in databases becomes increasingly more important.

Existing efforts have mainly focused on facilitating querying over relational databases proposing either handling natural language queries [2, 13, 16] or free-form, i.e. keyword-based, queries [1, 18]. In this work, we focus on a relative, still novel, issue of generating meaningful answers to queries and we propose an approach to translate the relational output of a query into a form that resembles narration and is thus more comprehensible to the naïve user.

E. Dubois and K. Pohl (Eds.): CAiSE 2006, LNCS 4001, pp. 142–156, 2006.
© Springer-Verlag Berlin Heidelberg 2006

In particular, we consider the output of précis queries [11]. These are free-form queries that generate entire multi-relation databases, which are logical subsets of existing ones, instead of individual relations. The logical subset of the database generated by a précis query contains not only items directly related to the query selections but also items implicitly related to them in various ways. Logical database subsets are useful in many cases. Given large databases, enterprises often need smaller subsets that conform to the original schema and satisfy all of its constraints in order to perform realistic tests of new applications before deploying them to production. Likewise, software vendors need such smaller but correct databases to demonstrate new software product functionality. Additionally, non-expert users would rather expect a summary or précis of the information contained in a logical subset. For instance, a more meaningful response than the classic "tabular-form" answer to a query that asks about "Woody Allen" might be in the form of the following précis:

"Woody Allen was born on December 1, 1935 in Brooklyn, New York, USA. As a director, Woody Allen's work includes Match Point (2005), Melinda and Melinda (2004), Anything Else (2003). As an actor, Woody Allen's work includes Hollywood Ending (2002), The Curse of the Jade Scorpion (2001)."

A précis may be incomplete in many ways; for example, the abovementioned précis includes a non-exhaustive list of Woody Allen's works. Nevertheless, it provides sufficient information in a comprehensible way to help one learn about "Woody Allen" and possibly identify new keywords for further searching. For example, one may decide to explicitly issue a new query about "*Anything Else*" or implicitly by following underlined topics (hyperlinks) to pages containing more relevant information.

Contributions. This paper deals with the presentation of a précis answer to a keyword query over a relational database. In brief, the contributions of this paper are the following.

– We extend the functionality of précis queries, by enriching the model with labels attached to its constructs. We propose a formal way to compose these labels through a simple to use language.
– We present a mechanism for the definition and instantiation of template labels.
– We present a semi-automatic method that translates the relational output of a précis query into a narrative synthesis of results.

Outline. The rest of the paper is structured as follows. Section 2 discusses related work. Section 3 describes the general framework of précis queries. Section 4 presents a technique for the translation of the information produced by précis queries in a narrative form. Finally, Section 5 concludes our results with a prospect to the future.

2 Related Work

The need for free-form queries has been early recognized in the context of databases [18]. With the advent of the World Wide Web, the idea has been revisited. Several research efforts have emerged for keyword searching over relational [1, 3, 8, 12] and XML data [5, 6, 9]. Oracle 9i Text [19], Microsoft SQL Server [15] and IBM DB2 Text Information Extender [10] create full text indexes on text attributes of relations and then perform keyword queries.

Existing keyword searching approaches focus on finding and possibly interconnecting tuples in relations that contain the query terms. For example, the answer for "Woody Allen" would be in the form of relation-attribute pair, such as (Director, Name). In many cases, this answer may suffice, but in many practical scenarios it conveys little information about "Woody Allen". A more complete answer containing, for instance, information about this director's movies and awards would be more meaningful and useful instead. In the spirit of the above, recently, précis queries have been proposed [11]. These are free-form queries that instead of simply locating and connecting values in tables, they also consider information around these values that may be related to them. Therefore, the answer to a précis query might also contain information found in other parts of the database, e.g., movies directed by Woody Allen. This information needs to be "assembled" -in perhaps unforeseen ways- by joining tuples from multiple relations. Consequently, the answer to a précis query is a whole new database, a logical database subset, derived from the original database compared to flattened out results returned by other approaches.

As we have already mentioned, logical database subsets are useful in many cases. However, naïve users would rather prefer a friendly representation of the information contained in a logical subset, without necessarily understanding its relational character. In earlier work [11], the importance of such representation constructed based on information conveyed by the database graph, has been suggested. This is inspired by BAROQUE [17] and shields the user from the particularities of the underlying data schema and model in use. BAROQUE uses a network representation of a database and defined several types of relationships in order to support functions that scan this network. However, it only locates the position and the relationships in which an item participates. As the database representation adopted does not include joins, it cannot assemble answers split into several relations.

The problem of facilitating the naïve user has been thoroughly discussed in the field of natural language processing (NLP). For the last couple of decades, several works are presented concerning NL Querying [26, 14], NL and Schema Design [22, 13, 4], NL and DB interfaces [16, 2], and Question Answering [24, 21]. As far as we are aware of, related literature on NL and databases, has focused on totally different issues such as the interpretation of users' phrasal questions to a database language, e.g., SQL, or to the automatic database design, e.g., with the usage of ontologies [23]. There exist some recent efforts that use phrasal patterns or question templates to facilitate the answering procedure [16, 21]. Also, there exists a recent experimental study [26] that compares NL Querying versus keyword search and supports the usefulness of the latter especially in the presence of complex queries.

This paper deals with the generation of meaningful answers from keyword queries and develops an approach to translate the relational output of a query into a form that resembles narration and is thus more comprehensible to a user. The process resembles those involved in handling natural language query over relational databases in that they both involve some amount of additional predefinitions for the meanings represented by relations, attributes and primary-to-foreign key joins. However, natural language query processing is more complex, since it has to handle ambiguities in natural language syntax and semantics whereas our approach uses well defined templates to rephrase relations and tuples. Furthermore, it has the advantage that it is not limited by any dictionary, because it concerns relational databases where the schemata are predictable and familiar to an expert, e.g., the dba; thus the template mechanism introduced later in this paper is sufficient for our aim. Moreover, précis queries are keyword queries which can lead to complex SQL queries whose form is only limited by the database schema graph. Works such [21] use a set of pre-defined question patterns, which cannot claim for completeness, i.e. this set is difficult to capture any possible query over a given database. Furthermore, these works produce pre-specified answers, where only the values in the patterns change. This is in contrast to précis queries, which construct logical subsets on demand and use templates and constructs of sentences defined on the constructs of the database graph, thus generating dynamic answers. This characteristic of précis queries also enables template multi-utilization.

In this paper, we built upon the ideas suggested in [11] and we elaborate on the idea of translating a logical database subset generated by a précis query into a narrative piece of information.

3 The Précis Query Framework

The purpose of this section is to provide essential background information on précis queries. First, we describe how a database can be modeled as a graph, and we introduce an example that we refer to throughout the paper. Next, we describe the précis query model and the system architecture of our framework.

3.1 Preliminaries

We consider the *database schema graph* $G(V,E)$ as a directed graph corresponding to a database schema D. Nodes in V are: (a) *relation nodes, R,* one for each relation in the schema; and (b) *attribute nodes, A,* one for each attribute of each relation in the schema. Edges in E are: (a) *projection edges, Π,* each one connects an attribute node with its container relation node, representing the possible projection of the attribute in the answer; and (b) *join edges, J,* from a relation node to another relation node, representing a potential join between these relations. These could be joins that arise naturally due to foreign key constraints, but could also be other joins that are meaningful to a domain expert. Joins are directed as explained later. For simplicity in presentation, we assume that (a) primary keys are not composite; thus, an attribute from a relation joins to an attribute from another relation, and (b) these attributes have the same name. The common name of the joining attributes is tagged on the respective join edge between the two relations.

Therefore, a database graph is formally defined as a directed graph $G(V,E)$, where: $V = R \cup A$, and $E = \Pi \cup J$. The notation for its graphical representation is given in Fig. 1.

A *weight*, w, is assigned to each edge of the graph **G**. This is a real number in $[0, 1]$ representing the significance of the connection between the nodes involved. Weight equal to 1 expresses strong relationship; in other words, if one node of the edge appears in an answer, then the edge should be taken into account making the other node appear as well. If a weight equals to 0, occurrence of one node of the edge in an answer does not imply occurrence of the other node. Two relation nodes could be connected through two different join edges, in the two possible directions, between the same pair of attributes, but carrying different weights. A directed join edge expresses the dependence of the source relation of the join on the target. The source relation indicates the relation already considered for the answer and the target corresponds to the relation that may be included influencing the final result, if the join is applied. For simplicity, we assume that there is at most one directed edge from one node to the same destination node.

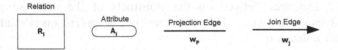

Fig. 1. Representation of graph elements

A directed path between two relation nodes, comprising adjacent join edges, represents the "implicit" join between these relations. Similarly, a directed path between a relation node and an attribute node, comprising a set of adjacent join edges and a projection edge represents the "implicit" projection of the attribute on this relation. The weight of a path is a function of the weight of constituent edges. This function should satisfy the condition that the weight decreases as the length of the path increases, based on human intuition and cognitive evidence.

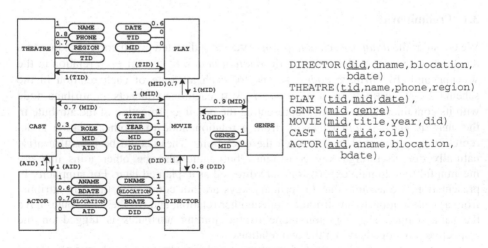

Fig. 2. An example database graph

Example. Consider a movies database[1] described by the schema presented in Fig. 2; primary keys are underlined. For instance, observe the two directed edges between MOVIE and GENRE. Movies and genres are related but one may consider that genres are more dependent on movies than the other way around. In other words, an answer regarding a genre should always contain information about related movies, while an answer regarding a movie may not necessarily contain information about its genres. For this reason, the weight of the edge from GENRE to MOVIE is set to 1, while the weight of the edge from MOVIE to GENRE is set to 0.9.

Using different weights on the graph's edges allows constructing different answers to the same query. Weights may be provided in different ways. They may be set by a user at query time using an appropriate user interface that enables interactive exploration of the contents of a database. A user may explore different regions of the database starting, for example, from those containing objects closely related to the topic of a query and progressively expanding to parts of the database containing objects more loosely related to it. Alternatively, sets of weights corresponding to different queries or groups of users may be stored in the system [20]. For instance, different sets would capture preferences of movie reviewers and filmgoers. The former may be typically interested in in-depth, detailed answers; using an appropriate set of weights would enable these users to explore larger parts of the database around a single précis query. On the other hand, cinema fans usually prefer shorter answers. In this case, a different set of weights would allow producing answers containing only highly related objects. Finally, multiple sets of weights corresponding to different user profiles may be stored in the system. Using user-specific weights allows generating personalized answers. For example, a user may be interested in the region where a theatre is located, while another may be interested in a theatre's phone.

However, the approach presented is general in that it does not depend on a specific weight-model.

3.2 Précis Query Model

Consider a database D properly annotated with a set of weights and a *précis query* Q, which is a set of tokens, i.e. $Q=\{k_1, k_2, ..., k_m\}$. We define as *initial relation* any database relation that contains at least one tuple in which one or more query tokens have been found. A tuple containing at least one query token is called *initial tuple*.

A *logical database subset* D' of D satisfies the following:

- The set of relation names in D' is a subset of that in the original database D.
- For each relation R_i' in the result D', its set of attributes in D' is a subset of its set of attributes in D.
- For each relation R_i' in the result D', the set of its tuples is a subset of the set of tuples in the original relation R_i in D (when projected on the set of attributes that are present in the result).

The result of applying query Q on a database D given a set of constraints C is a logical database subset D' of D, such that D' contains initial tuples for Q and any other tuple in D that can be transitively reached by (foreign-key) joins on D starting from

---

[1] www.imdb.com

some initial tuple, subject to the constraints in C. Possible constraints in C could include the maximum number of joins, the maximum number of tuples in D' and so forth. Using different constraints allows generating different answers for the same query and the same set of weights over the edges of the database graph. Similarly to weights, constraints may be specified at query time, or be pre-stored in the system.

3.3 System Architecture

Given a précis query $Q=\{k_1, k_2, ..., k_m\}$, the following steps are performed in order to generate an answer.

A keyword may be found in more than one tuples and attributes of a single relation and in more than one relations. For this reason, the system uses an inverted index that returns for each term k_i in Q, a list of all its occurrences. A single keyword occurrence is a tuple $<R_j, A_{1j}, Tid_{1j}>$, where Tid_{1j} is the id of a tuple in relation R_j that contains keyword k_i as part of the value of attribute A_{1j}. If no tuples contain the query tokens, the following steps are not executed.

Next, the system maps all initial relations returned from the inverted index on the database schema graph G and tries to find which part of the graph may contain information related to Q. The output of this step is the schema of the logical database subset D' involving initial relations and relations transitively joining to the former and a subset of their attributes that should be present in the result according to the constraints provided.

Finally, the system populates relations in the logical database subset starting from initial relations. More tuples from other relations are retrieved by join queries starting from initial relations and transitively expanding on the logical database subset schema graph. At the end of this phase, the logical database subset is produced.

More technical details for the two steps above, along with the algorithms involved, can be found in [11]. As we have already discussed, in this work, we are mainly concerned with the exploitation of the information stored in the logical database subset. In what follows, we take a step further towards facilitating access of information in databases. This is performed by using information conveyed by the database graph, which may be properly annotated to further enhance its semantics.

4 Translator

In this section, we present a semi-automatic method to render the SQL-like response of a précis query to a more user-friendly synthesis of results. In the context of this work, the presentation of a query answer is defined as a proper structured management of individual results, according to certain rules and templates predefined by a designer or the administrator of the database. Clearly, we do not anticipate the construction of a human-intelligent system; rather, we try to provide a user-friendly response through the composition of simple clauses.

4.1 Preliminaries

In our framework, in order to describe the semantics of a relation R along with its attributes in natural language, we consider that relation R has a *conceptual meaning* captured by its name, and a *physical meaning* represented by the value of at least one of its attributes that characterizes tuples of this relation. We name this attribute the *heading* attribute and we depict it as a hachured rounded rectangle. For example, in Fig. 2, the relation MOVIE conceptually represents "movies" in real world; indeed, its name, MOVIE, captures its conceptual meaning. Moreover, the main characteristic of a "movie" is its "title", thus, the relation MOVIE should have the TITLE as its heading attribute, since the word "title" captures the physical meaning of a "movie".

Heading Attributes. The heading attribute, h_R, of a relation R is defined as the attribute whose name represents the physical meaning of that relation. By definition, the projection edge that connects a heading attribute with the respective relation has a weight 1 and this attribute is always present in the result of a précis query. A domain expert makes the selection of heading attributes, at the initial construction of the database graph.

We do not anticipate that all relations should have a heading attribute. For instance, a relation used only for storing *n-to-m* relationships between different entities (e.g., relation CAST in Fig. 2) does not require a heading attribute. Clearly, this is not a problem, since, in general, these relations are used only for the construction of paths that represent query answers and have no attributes in the logical database subset.

Labels. Each projection edge $e \in \Pi$ that connects an attribute a with its container relation R, is annotated by a label that signifies the meaning, in terms of natural language, of the relationship between this attribute and the heading attribute of the respective relation. For instance, with respect to the design of Fig. 2, a possible label attached to the projection edge between the relation MOVIE and its attribute YEAR may be: "the YEAR of a MOVIE (.TITLE)"; recall, that TITLE is the heading attribute of MOVIE.

If a projection edge is between a relation node and its heading attribute, then the respective label reflects the relationship of this attribute with the conceptual meaning of the relation; e.g., the TITLE of a MOVIE.

Each join edge $e \in J$ between two relations has a label that signifies the relationship between the heading attributes of the relations involved; e.g., the GENRE (.GENRE) of a MOVIE (.TITLE). The label of a join edge that involves a relation without a heading attribute signifies the relationship between the previous and subsequent relations.

4.2 Template Mechanism

The synthesis of query results follows the database schema and the correlation of relations through primary and foreign keys. Additionally, it is enriched by alphanumeric expressions called *template labels* mapped to edges of the database schema graph.

Templates. A *template label*, label(u,z) is assigned to each edge e(u,z)∈**E** of the database schema graph **G(V,E)**. This label is used for the interpretation of the relationship between the values of nodes u and z in a narrative form.

We define as the label l of a node n the name of the node and we denote it as l(n). For example, the label of the attribute node TITLE is "title". The name of a node should be determined by the designer/administrator of the database.

The template label $label(u,z)$ of an edge $e(u,z)$ formally comprises the following elements: (a) a unique identifier for the label in the database graph; (b) the name of the starting node, i.e. $l(u)$; (c) the name of the ending node, i.e. $l(z)$; and (d) several alphanumeric expressions.

A simple template label has the form:

$$label(u,z) = expr_1 + l(u) + expr_2 + l(z) + expr_3$$

where $expr_1$, $expr_2$, $expr_3$ are alphanumeric expressions and the operator "+" acts as a concatenation operator.

In order to use template labels or to register new ones, we use a simple language for templates that supports variables, loops, functions, and macros. A similar approach, but, still, in a totally different environment, can be found in [25] where the authors present a template mechanism for the description of ETL processes in a data warehouse environment. Below, we describe this language.

In a template, when we refer to the conceptual meaning of a node, we simply use its name. When an instance of the node is needed, then we use the node as a variable. There are two kinds of variables: *parameter variables* and *loop iterators*.

Parameter Variables. Parameter variables are marked with a @ symbol at their beginning and are replaced by values at instantiation time. For example, a template label for the projection edge $e(PHONE, THEATRE)$ could be:

$label(PHONE, THEATRE) =$ "The PHONE of the THEATRE @THEATRE.NAME is @PHONE"

where PHONE and THEATRE stand for the conceptual meaning of the nodes (attribute and relation, respectively) PHONE and THEATRE; i.e., $l(PHONE)$ = "phone" and $l(THEATRE)$ = "theatre" respectively. Moreover, @THEATRE.NAME and @PHONE are parameter variables, with possible values "ALPHAVILLE" and "12345". In this case, a valid label for this edge can be the following:

"The phone of the theatre ALPHAVILLE is 12345"

In several cases, the values returned in a query result from a certain attribute could be more than one. Then, we use a list of parameters denoted as:

@<parameter name>[ ]

For such lists, their length should be provided at instantiation time.

Loop Iterators. Loop iterators are implicitly defined in the loop constraint, as we will discuss later. In each round of the loop, all the properly marked appearances of the iterator in the loop body are replaced by its current value (similarly to the way a C preprocessor treats #DEFINE statements). Iterators that appear marked in the loop body are instantiated even when they are part of another string or a variable name. We mark such occurrences by enclosing them between $. This functionality enables referencing all values of a parameter list and facilitates the creation of an arbitrary number of pre-formatted strings.

Functions. We employ a built-in function, arityOf(<list_of_parameters>), which returns the arity of a list of parameters, mainly in order to define upper bounds in loop iterators.

Loops. Loops enhance the genericity of the templates by allowing the designer to handle templates with unknown number of variables and with unknown arity for parameters involved. The general form of loops is:

$$\texttt{[<simple constraint>] \{(loop body)\}},$$

where simple constraint has the form:

$$\texttt{<lower> <operator> <iterator> <operator> <upper>}$$

We consider only linear increase with step equal to 1. Upper bound and lower bound (default value 1) can be arithmetic expressions involving `arityOf()` function calls, variables and constants. Valid arithmetic operators are +, -, /, * and valid comparison operators are <, >, = , all with their usual semantics. During iterations the loop body is reproduced and at the same time all the marked appearances of the loop iterator are replaced by its current value, as described before. Loop nesting is permitted. For instance, consider the following case:

$$\texttt{[i≤arityOf(MOVIE)] \{MOVIE\_\$i\$\}}$$

In this case, the lower bound has the default value (1), and the upper bound is limited by the number (arity) of attributes of the relation MOVIE. Thus, the iterator i takes value between 1 and the total attributes of MOVIE. As far as the loop body is concerned, it contains a parameter list that stores the attributes involved in the relation MOVIE.

For the example database depicted in Fig. 2, with respect to the relation MOVIE, the loop that represents its attributes has the following form:

$$\texttt{[i≤2] \{MOVIE\_\$i\$\}}$$

and at the instantiation of the parameters, we get the following results: MOVIE_1 = TITLE (first attribute) and MOVIE_2 = YEAR (second attribute).

Macros. We introduce macros to ease the definition and to improve the readability of templates. Macros facilitate attribute and variable name expansion. For instance, one major problem in defining a language for templates is the difficulty of dealing with attributes or attribute values of arbitrary arity. At the template level, it is not possible to pin-down the number of (a) attributes that are projected in the précis query, and (b) values of the involved attributes, to a specific value.

For example, in order to find out:

(a) The attributes projected in a certain précis query we need to create a series of attributes like the following:

```
DEFINE MOVIES_LIST as
    [i<arityOf(MOVIE)] {MOVIE_$i$,}
    [i=arityOf(MOVIE)] {MOVIE_$i$}
```

(b) The titles of movies that correspond to a certain query, we need to create a series of values as follows:

```
DEFINE MOVIES_TITLES_LIST as
    [i<arityOf(@MOVIE.TITLE)]  {@MOVIE.TITLE[$i$],}
    [i=arityOf(@MOVIE.TITLE)]  {@MOVIE.TITLE[$i$]}
```

For the example database of Fig. 2, the attribute and value series are:

```
MOVIES_LIST = {TITLE, YEAR}
MOVIES_TITLES_LIST = {"Match Point",
                      "Melinda and Melinda",
                      "Anything Else"}
```

Note the existence of the two loops in each macro in order to avoid the presence of an erroneous ", " after the last value in each list.

4.3 Translation

Additionally, we present a method that parses the result database graph and composes a synthesis of query results in a narrative form.

The translation is realized separately for every occurrence of a token. At the end, the précis query lists all clauses produced. For each occurrence of a token, the analysis of the query result graph starts from the relation that contains the input token. The labels of the projection edges that participate in the query result graph are evaluated first. The label of the heading attribute comprises the first part of the sentence. It becomes obvious that for multiple attributes of the same relation we have to repeat several times the same subject. To avoid this, a domain expert should have attached suitable expressions in the projection edges, in order to allow the construction of complex sentences that make sense.

For instance, consider Fig. 2. Assume that in relation DIRECTOR the labels of the projection edges that connect the heading attribute, DNAME, with attributes BDATE and BLOCATION, which store information about the birth data and birth location of a director, are the following:

```
label(h_R, BDATE) = @DNAME + " was born" + " on " + @BDATE
label(h_R, BLOCATION) = @DNAME + " was born" + " in " + @BLOCATION
```

When both attributes are involved in the answer, then the clause derived from the DIRECTOR relation could be as follows:

```
"@DNAME was born on @BDATE in @BLOCATION"
```

This operation is realized as a simple find-and-replace mechanism, namely resolve_common_expressions, which finds common expressions in the clauses that respond to each label attached to a projection edge. In the example above, the common expressions are @DNAME and " was born ".

The procedure used for the translation of the information stored in a relation is depicted in Fig. 3.

After having constructed the clause for the relation that contains the input token, we compose additional clauses that combine information from more than one relation by using foreign key relationships. Each of these clauses has as subject the heading attribute of the relation that has the primary key. In the example of Fig. 2, the DIRECTOR relation is connected to the MOVIE relation through the DID key. The subject of the respective clause will be the DNAME attribute, while the rest is constructed in a sense similar to the one described before. The procedure terminates

Algorithm Translation of a Relation (TR)
Input: a relation R, a set of tokens T, a database graph G(V,E)
Output: an array of sentences Sentence[]
Begin
 For each token t∈T
    Sentence[t] = ''
    Let R∈V be the container relation of t
    Let h_R be the heading attribute of R
    clause[t,h_R] = l(h_R)
    For each attribute a in R, a≠h_R
       clause[t,a] = label(h_R,a)
    End for
    Sentence[t]=Sentence[t]+resolve_common_expressions(clause[])
 End for
End.

Fig. 3. The algorithm TR

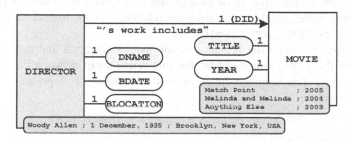

Fig. 4. A part of our example database

when the traversal of the databases graph is complete. In addition, for each attribute projected in the answer, a hyperlink may be created. When a user follows a hyperlink, a new précis query is submitted containing the hyperlink's text.

Consider the case of the database of Fig. 2. Assume that a logical database subset concerning a user's question (e.g., the token "Woody Allen") involves only the relations DIRECTOR and MOVIE, while the schema of the logical subset is depicted in Fig. 4. At first, we consider the case of "Woody Allen" as a director. We construct the template clause that derives from the DIRECTOR relation, as before:

@DNAME + " was born" + " on " + @BDATE + " in " + @BLOCATION

Next, we built the respective template clause that derives from the MOVIE relation:

@TITLE + " (" + @YEAR + ")"

Then, we proceed with the clause composed by the join relationship that connects the relations DIRECTOR and MOVIE. The template label of this relationship is represented with the following formula:

label(DIRECTOR,MOVIE) = expr_1 + @DNAME + expr_2 + MOVIE_LIST

The macro MOVIE_LIST and the expressions may be defined as:

```
DEFINE MOVIE_LIST as
  [i<arityOf(@TITLE)]
      {@TITLE[$i$]+" ("+@YEAR[$i$]+"),"}
  [i=arityOf(@TITLE)]
      {@TITLE[$i$]+" ("+@YEAR[$i$]+")."}
expr_1 ← "As a director, "
expr_2 ← "'s work includes "
```

Therefore, the result of the précis query for the token "Woody Allen" located in the relation DIRECTOR will be:

"Woody Allen was born on December 1, 1935 in Brooklyn, New York, USA. As a director, Woody Allen's work includes Match Point (2005), Melinda and Melinda (2004), Anything Else (2003)."

In the general case, if we enrich the above example with the constraint that only projections with weight equal to or greater than 0.9 should be present in the answer and up to three tuples should be retrieved per relation, then the logical subset contains also the relations GENRE, ACTOR, and CAST.

In this case, we retain the previous result about DIRECTOR and MOVIE, and we proceed with the clause composed by the join relationship between the MOVIE and GENRE relations. The template label of this relationship is represented with the following formula:

```
label(MOVIE,GENRE) = @TITLE + expr_2 + GENRE_LIST
DEFINE GENRE_LIST as
  [i<arityOf(@GENRE)] {@GENRE[$i$]+","}
  [i=arityOf(@TITLE)] {@GENRE[$i$]+"."}
expr_2 ← " is "
```

Therefore, the result of the précis query for the token "Woody Allen" located in the relation DIRECTOR will be:

"Woody Allen was born on December 1, 1935 in Brooklyn, New York, USA. As a director, Woody Allen's work includes Match Point (2005), Melinda and Melinda (2004), Anything Else (2003). Match Point is Drama, Thriller. Melinda and Melinda is Comedy, Drama. Anything Else is Comedy, Romance."

In a similar way, we construct the result of the précis query for the token "Woody Allen" located in the relation ACTOR. Recall that the relation CAST does not have a heading attribute. Thus, the designer should enrich the join edges that interconnect the three relations ACTOR, CAST, and MOVIE with an appropriate label. An example template label could be the following:

"As an actor, @ACTOR's work includes MOVIE_LIST"

and so, given that the label for join relationship between the MOVIE and GENRE relations is constructed as before, the result of the précis query will be:

"As an actor, Woody Allen's work includes Hollywood Ending (2002), The Curse of the Jade Scorpion (2001), Picking Up the Pieces (2000). Hollywood Ending is Comedy, Drama. The Curse of the Jade Scorpion is Comedy, Drama. Picking Up the Pieces is Comedy, Fantasy."

As we mentioned before, if there does not exist any information that both instance values refer to the same physical entity, then, the answer of the précis query comprises two parts, one for each occurrence of the token as shown in the example above. Otherwise, the answers can be merged to produce a fancier result.

5 Conclusions and Future Work

Précis queries are free-form queries that generate entire multi-relation databases, which are logical subsets of existing ones, instead of individual relations. The logical subset of the database generated by a précis query contains not only items directly related to the query selections but also items implicitly related to them in various ways. Earlier work has identified the need of providing the naïve user with meaningful answers to his/her questions and has suggested the translation of a précis query answer in narrative form.

In this paper, we have extended précis queries by presenting a semi-automatic method that turns the relational output of a précis query into a narrative synthesis of results. In the context of this work, the presentation of a query answer is defined as a proper structured management of individual results, according to certain rules and templates predefined by a designer or the administrator of the database. More specifically, we have extended the functionality of précis queries, by enriching the model with labels attached to its constructs. Moreover, we have proposed a formal way to compose these labels through a simple to use language. Also, we have presented a template mechanism for the definition and instantiation of template labels. Finally, we have proposed a semi-automatic method that translates the relational output of a précis query into a narrative synthesis of results.

Clearly, as we have already stressed, we do not anticipate the construction of a human-intelligent system; rather, we try to provide a user-friendly response through the composition of simple clauses, so that a user without any particular knowledge of relational schemas or languages may understand and use the information returned to him/her.

We are currently experimenting with users to solidify the evidence on the effectiveness of our approach. From the feedback obtained, we plan to improve the performance/"intelligence" of the translator presented in this paper. In a similar line of research, a challenging issue is the extension of précis queries to providing ranked or top-k results.

Acknowledgments. This work is co-funded by the European Social Fund (75%) and National Resources (25%) - Operational Program for Educational and Vocational Training II (EPEAEK II) and particularly the Program PYTHAGORAS.

References

1. S. Agrawal, S. Chaudhuri, and G. Das. DBXplorer: A system for keyword-based search over relational databases. In *ICDE*, pp. 5-16, 2002.
2. I. Androutsopoulos, G.D. Ritchie, and P. Thanisch. Natural Language Interfaces to Databases - An Introduction. *NL Eng.*, 1(1), pp. 29-81, 1995.
3. G. Bhalotia, A. Hulgeri, C. Nakhe, S. Chakrabarti, and S. Sudarshan. Keyword searching and browsing in databases using BANKS. In *ICDE*, pp. 431-440, 2002.
4. A. Dusterhoft, and B. Thalheim. Linguistic based search facilities in snowflake-like database schemes. *DKE*, 48, pp. 177-198, 2004.
5. D. Florescu, D. Kossmann, and I. Manolescu. Integrating keyword search into xml query processing. *Computer Networks*, 33(1-6), 2000.
6. L. Guo, F. Shao, C. Botev, and J. Shanmugasundaram. XRank: Ranked keyword search over XML documents. In *SIGMOD*, pp. 16-27, 2003.
7. L. R. Harris. User-Oriented Data Base Query with the ROBOT Natural Language Query System. VLDB 1977: 303-312.
8. V. Hristidis, L. Gravano, and Y. Papakonstantinou. Effcient IR-style keyword search over relational databases. In *VLDB*, pp. 850-861, 2003.
9. V. Hristidis, Y. Papakonstantinou, and A. Balmin. Keyword proximity search on XML graphs. In *ICDE*, pp. 367-378, 2003.
10. IBM. *DB2 Text Information Extender. url:* www.ibm.com/software/data/db2/extenders/textinformation/.
11. G. Koutrika, A. Simitsis, and Y. Ioannidis. Précis: The essence of a query answer. In *ICDE*, 2006.
12. U. Masermann, and G. Vossen. Design and implementation of a novel approach to keyword searching in relational databases. In *ADBIS-DASFAA*, pp. 171-184, 2000.
13. E. Metais, J. Meunier, and G. Levreau. Database Schema Design: A Perspective from Natural Language Techniques to Validation and View Integration. In *ER*, pp. 190-205, 2003.
14. E. Metais. Enhancing information systems management with natural language processing techniques. *DKE*, 41, pp. 247-272, 2002.
15. Microsoft. *SQL Server 2000. url: http://msdn.microsoft.com/library/*.
16. M. Minock. A Phrasal Approach to Natural Language Interfaces over Databases. In *NLDB*, pp. 181-191, 2005.
17. A. Motro. Baroque: A browser for relational databases. *ACM Trans. Inf. Syst.*, 4(2), pp. 164-181, 1986.
18. A. Motro. Constructing queries from tokens. In *SIGMOD*, pp. 120-131, 1986.
19. Oracle. *Oracle 9i Text. url: www.oracle.com/technology/products/text/*.
20. A. Simitsis, and G. Koutrika. Pattern-Based Query Answering. In *PaRMa*, 2006.
21. E. Sneiders. Automated Question Answering Using Question Templates That Cover the Conceptual Model of the Database. In *NLDB*, pp. 235-239, 2002.
22. V.C. Storey, R.C. Goldstein, H. Ullrich. Naive Semantics to Support Automated Database Design. *IEEE TKDE*, 14(1), pp. 1-12, 2002.
23. V.C. Storey. Understanding and Representing Relationship Semantics in Database Design. In *NLDB*, pp. 79-90, 2001.
24. A. Toral, E. Noguera, F. Llopis, and R. Munoz. Improving Question Answering Using Named Entity Recognition. In *NLDB*, pp. 181-191, 2005.
25. P. Vassiliadis, A. Simitsis, P. Georgantas, M. Terrovitis, and S. Skiadopoulos. A Generic and Customizable Framework for the Design of ETL Scenarios. *Information Systems*, 30(7), pp. 492-525, 2005.
26. Q. Wang, C. Nass, and J. Hu. Natural Language Query vs. Keyword Search: Effects of Task Complexity on Search Performance, Participant Perceptions, and Preferences. In *INTERACT*, pp. 106-116, 2005.

An Efficient Approach to Support Querying Secure Outsourced XML Information[*]

Yin Yang, Wilfred Ng, Ho Lam Lau, and James Cheng

Department of Computer Science,
Hong Kong University of Science and Technology
{yini, wilfred, lauhl, csjames}@cs.ust.hk

Abstract. Data security is well-recognized a vital issue in an information system that is supported in an outsource environment. However, most of conventional XML encryption proposals treat confidential parts of an XML document as whole blocks of text and apply encryption algorithms directly on them. As a result, queries involving the encrypted part cannot be efficiently processed. In order to address these problems, we propose XQEnc, a novel approach to support querying encrypted XML. XQEnc is based on two important techniques of vectorization and skeleton compression. Essentially, vectorization, which is a generalization of columns of a relational table, makes use the basic path of an XML tree to label the data values. Skeleton compression collapses the redundant paths into a multiplicity attribute. Our analysis and experimental study shows that XQEnc achieves both better query efficiency and more robust security compared with conventional methods. As an application, we show how XQEnc can be realized with relational techniques to enable secure XML data outsourcing.

1 Introduction

XML has emerged as a new standard for data representation and exchange on the Internet. As more data is expressed in XML, it is increasingly common to find sensitive information in XML, and thus security becomes an important issue. In order to avoid unauthorized access, the confidential parts of the XML document have to be protected. This can be done by *access control* mechanisms, e.g. security views [1] in the XML repository, or by applying encryption. In many cases, the access control components can be bypassed and encryption is a must. For instance, when transmitting data via an untrusted channel, and when the data is stored in vulnerable storage [2], e.g. the hard drive may be stolen.

The heterogeneous nature of XML data raises new requirements for encryption. Specifically, different parts of data need different treatments. Consider the running example of XML snippet given in Table 1(a) in which the details about the customer are confidential and thus must be encrypted, while the names of

---

[*] This work is partially supported by RGC CERG under grant number HKUST6185/03E.

E. Dubois and K. Pohl (Eds.): CAiSE 2006, LNCS 4001, pp. 157–171, 2006.
© Springer-Verlag Berlin Heidelberg 2006

the customers may be accessed by multiple parties and therefore should be kept in plain text. The proposal recommended by W3C [3] addresses this problem. Using the methods described in [3], only details about credit cards are encrypted, resulting in the XML code given in Table 1(b) (some details such as namespaces are omitted for the sake of simplicity in illustration).

Table 1. (a) A running example of XML snippet (b) the Encrypted XML snippet

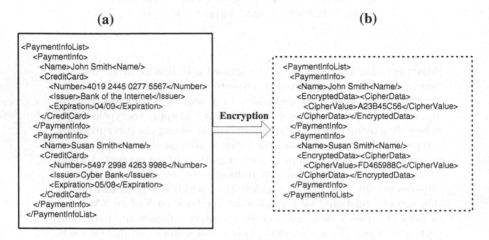

In the above treated XML fragment shown in Table 1(b), the plain text segment from "<CreditCard>" to "</CreditCard>" is encrypted and replaced by an `EncryptedData` node. Note that the protected data is still treated as a whole block of text, and its internal structure is ignored. One problem is that the redundancy introduced by the XML format can be exploited to attack the encryption. For instance, the fact that the encrypted part always ends with the string "</CreditCard>" can be used for cryptanalysis. Another problem is that, since each confidential part is replaced by its corresponding encrypted block, the *context* around it may be exploited by the adversary. In our example, one can judge that the first encrypted block is the credit card information for John Smith. Besides, the fact that John Smith has some secrets (in this case a credit card) in this data file is exposed. When more items are encrypted together, the adversary is able to find out the rough number by judging the length of the cipher text. In other words, some *statistical information* may be exposed.

Apart from these security defects, treating the protected data as a whole inevitably incurs efficiency problems. Consider the following XPath [4] query:

```
//PaymentInfo[//Issuer = "Bank of the Internet"]/Name
```

Among various details of credit cards, only information about issuers is necessary to answer this query. However, since the entire block of sensitive information is encrypted, there is no way to extract the issuer alone from the encrypted blocks. Consequently, a large amount of unnecessary decryption is performed, which may seriously slow down query processing.

Motivated by these security and efficiency drawbacks of existing solutions, we propose XQEnc, a novel XML encryption approach based on recent developments of XML repositories, namely, vectorization and skeleton compression [5], [6], [7]. We show experimentally that compared with existing methods, XQEnc has efficient query processing capability.

Importantly, XQEnc facilitates secure XML data outsourcing, which has not been discussed in the literature. In a nutshell, secure XML data outsourcing makes it possible for organizations to store confidential XML data on untrusted database servers and shift the query workload to the server as much as possible, without revealing the content of the data to the server. From business point of view, organizations following this paradigm are able to enjoy the benefit that their resources can be better invested in their core business but on the other hand, data management is supported by a dedicated service provider.

The rest of the paper is organized as follows: Section 2 surveys related work, focusing on existing XML security schemes and the theoretical foundation of our work: XML vectorization and skeleton compression. Section 3 presents XQEnc with analysis. Section 4 then describes how our XQEnc is able to employ relational technology to enable XML data outsourcing. Section 5 supports our security and efficiency claims by presenting a comprehensive experimental study. Finally, Section 6 concludes the paper with directions for future work.

2 Related Work and Preliminaries

In this section, we present the background of secure data outsourcing and the fundamentals of XML vectorization and skeleton compression.

2.1 XML Encryption

The most influential XML encryption method is the one officially recommended by W3C [3]. Essentially, its emphasis is on providing a mechanism such that different parts of the same document can get different treatments. One of the main virtues of this technique is in its flexibility. Since the encrypted document is still a valid XML document, an XML document can be encrypted for several times by different parties on different parts. An intuitive example of XML encryption using this method has been given in Section 1.

The problems of this approach, and also similar approaches, are apparent. Since the focus is on flexibility, rather than data security or query efficiency, naturally it does not satisfy the requirements of many applications where data security and query efficiency is highly important. In XQEnc, we try to match its flexibility, while at the same time we provide enhanced security and optimized query efficiency.

2.2 XML Vectorization and Skeleton Compression

One technique we adopt in XQEnc is called vectorization. XML vectorization generalizes the well-known technique of *vertical partitioning* in relational databases for optimizing query performance. An extreme form of vertical partitioning, which is called vectorization, is to store each column of a relational table separately. Vectorization means partitioning the document into path vectors in the context of XML. The result of partitioning outputs a sequence of data values appearing under all paths and bearing the same *path labeling*. Applying vectorization on the XML fragment presented in Table 1 of the running example, we obtain the set of vectors (PaymentInfoList is the root node) in Table 2:

Table 2. Path vectors in the "payment information list" document of Table 1

/PaymentInfoList/PaymentInfo/Name	[John Smith, Susan Smith]
/PaymentInfoList/PaymentInfo/CreditCard/Number	[4019 2445 0277 5567, 5497 2998 4263 9986]
/PaymentInfoList/PaymentInfo/CreditCard/Issuer	[Bank of the Internet, Cyber Bank]
/PaymentInfoList/PaymentInfo/CreditCard/Expiration	[04/09, 05/08]

Each of these vectors corresponds to a path of labels that leads to a nonempty text node. This technique has been employed in the recently proposed "semantic compressor" XMILL [8] to achieve optimal compression ratio of XML documents. As we will show in Section 3, XML vectorization can also be utilised to enhance security in addition to compressing XML data in XQEnc.

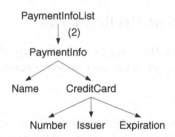

Fig. 1. The compressed skeleton of the running example

Another important technique called "skeleton compression" was originally proposed in [6] for supporting query processing of compressed XML documents. The main idea is to remove the redundancy contained in the XML document tree by sharing common sub branches and replacing identical and consecutive branches with one branch and a multiplicity annotation. The compressed skeleton of our running example in Table 1 is shown in Fig. 1. Note that the two PaymentInfo records are compressed into one branch and one multiplicity annotation, (2). According to the experimental results reported in [6], the compressed XML skeleton is small enough to fit well into main memory. This empirical fact motivates our proposed approach for query processing on outsourced XML data, described in Section 4. Finally, it is worth mentioning that Buneman et al. [5] extend the skeleton compression technique to facilitate the processing of XQuery queries. However, to our knowledge there has been no attempt to apply the technique in querying encrypted XML data in literature.

2.3 Secure Data Outsourcing

Recently, the problem of secure data outsourcing (also referred to as "privacy preserving data outsourcing" in literature) has drawn considerable attention. In the data outsourcing paradigm proposed in [9], data owners store their data on rented servers, and query the server to get desired information. The database server is not trusted, and thus the data must be stored in encrypted form. Meanwhile, the server needs some information about the data (for example the use of "crypto-index" in [10]) in order to process queries. The result of a query is usually an encrypted superset of the actual result and is transferred to the client. There needs second processing on the (trusted) client side by decrypting the data and filtering out those that do not satisfy the query conditions. The goal is to shift query processing as much as possible to the server side while maintaining data security during processing and data transfer. Fig.2 illustrates a simplified

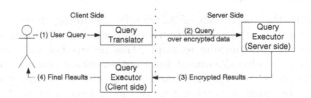

Fig. 2. A simplified architecture of a data outsourcing system

architecture of a typical data outsourcing system. A user query is translated by the query translator into two sub-queries: a query over encrypted data, which is executed at the server side with the help of the crypto-index, and a "filtering" query executed at the client side to select the real answer to the query from the temporary results returned by the server. The temporary results returned by the server are encrypted tuples, and the client needs to do decryption first in order to perform the filtering step.

There are different proposals for defining the crypto-index that provides the helper information for the server to process the queries. The original proposal in [9] is to first partition the entire data space into disjoint buckets, and then stores the bucket IDs on the server. During query processing, the values in the queries are translated into their corresponding bucket IDs. This method reveals information (i.e. bucket IDs) of the original data and the server returns a super set of the actual results. A more efficient way is to use the order preserving encryption algorithm proposed in [2], which guarantees no information leakage and optimal communication overhead. All these proposals, however, consider only the data in relational setting. These proposals are not applicable in XML setting, since the internal structure of the sensitive nodes can also be confidential in XML, thus simply substituting values by crypto-indices may reveal the structural information to the (untrusted) server. In our running example, storing the sensitive credit card details with only values encrypted (e.g. substituted by bucket IDs) exposes the internal structure of the CreditCard node. Therefore, existing methods designed for querying encrypted relational data are not appropriate for XML data outsourcing. This motivates our development of XQEnc.

3   XQEnc: Queriable XML Encryption

Let d denote the plain text XML document to be treated. The goal of XQEnc is to transform d into another XML document d^T such that confidential information is protected and queries and are efficiently processed. For ease of presentation, we first simply assume that all the data contained in d is confidential, and describe the basic ideas of XQEnc in Section 3.1. In Section 3.2 we tackle the more general case in which only some parts of d need to be encrypted. The security and efficiency of XQEnc is analyzed in Section 3.3.

3.1   Basic Ideas of XQEnc

We first illustrate the basic idea of XQEnc by assuming that all textual and structural information in the plain text document d is confidential and needs to be encrypted. In our running example, this means not only the details of credit cards, but also other document information such as names and document structures needs to be encrypted. Hence, the resulting document d^T has only one text node, containing the cipher text of the original document.

```
<EncryptedData><CipherData>
        <CipherValue>2313FB3D980A0</CipherValue>
</CipherData></EncryptedData>
```

Note that this transformation fully complies with the W3C XML encryption standard. The crucial part in the transformation is how to generate the cipher value based on the original document. Traditional methods simply treat the original document as a whole piece of text and apply an encryption algorithm like triple DES on the text. The drawbacks of this methodology have been discussed in Section 1. The basic idea of XQEnc is that we first compute the compressed skeleton and the corresponding set of data vectors, and then encrypt these two entities separately.

In our implementation, XQEnc adopts the approach based on vectorization and skeleton compression for building a structural index called Structure Index Tree (or SIT). The SIT helps to remove the redundant, duplicate structures in an XML document. An example of a SIT is shown in Fig. 4(b), which is the index of the tree in Fig. 4(a), the structure of the sample XML extract in Fig. 3 modelled as a tree. Note that the duplicate structures in Fig. 4(a) are eliminated in the SIT shown in Fig. 4(b). In fact, large portions of the structure of most XML documents are redundant and can be eliminated. For example, if an XML document contains 1000 repetitions of our sample XML extract (with different data contents), the corresponding tree modelling its structure will be 1000 times bigger than the tree in Fig. 4(a). However, the structure of its index tree will essentially have the same structure as the one in Fig. 4(b), implying that the search space for query evaluation is reduced 1000 times by the index.

1. <open_auctions>	7. </bid>	13. <open_auction id = "open2">	19. <date> 11/29/2002 </date>
2. <open_auction id = "open1">	8. <bid>	14. <initial> $500.00 </initial>	20. <increase> $0.50 </increase>
3. <initial> $12.00 </initial>	9. <date> 12/03/2000 </date>	15. </open_auction>	21. </bid>
4. <bid>	10. <increase> $1.50 </increase>	16. <open_auction id = "open3">	22. </open_auction>
5. <date> 12/02/2000 </date>	11. </bid>	17. <initial> $1.50 </initial>	23. </open_auctions>
6. <increase> $2.00 </increase>	12. </open_auction>	18. <bid>	

Fig. 3. A simple Auction XML Extract

Our implementation avoids full decryption by grouping the data (i.e. v.ext in Fig. 4(b)) into many small blocks. We utilize the index to evaluate queries on the encrypted XML data. The novelty is that we apply an encryption algorithm (like triple DES) to encrypt each data block in XQEnc. After that, the encrypted blocks are combined to form the cipher value for the original document. Query processing in XQEnc requires that we first decrypt the relevant encrypted data blocks necessary to answer the query. Our design is not only compatible with compression on the data blocks but also supports a fine-grained encryption as will be discussed later. An immediate benefit of using SIT as in-

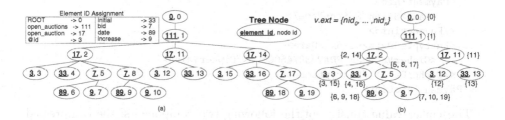

Fig. 4. (a) A simple Auction XML Extract Structure Tree (contents of the exts not shown) of the Auction XML Extract and (b) its corresponding SIT

dexing in XQEnc is that we are able to compress and decrypt the blocks at the same time. During query processing, a retrieved data block is first decrypted and then decompressed. It is clear that there is an overhead of doing compression/decompression, but the overall performance may be better, since compression removes redundancy in the data, the cost of doing encryption/decryption is also reduced. However, a more detailed study of the problem of compression and encryption interaction is not the scope in this paper.

3.2 The General Case in XQEnc

Because of the heterogeneous nature of XML data, in most cases only parts of the original text document d need to be encrypted. These confidential parts may scatter all over d, with or without clear patterns. An intuitive way is to apply the method described in the previous section on each confidential part of the document separately, which complies with the W3C standard. However, there are several drawbacks with this approach as we have illustrated using our running example in Table 1. For example, if we apply XQEnc on the two blocks of credit card information separately, and replace them with their corresponding cipher text, the resulting XML document d^T is similar to the transformed document presented in Section 1, except that the cipher values are generated using XQEnc. The security concern remains that the context can be exploited to attack the encryption and derive statistical information. Moreover, in this example and many other cases, the confidential parts have exactly the same internal structure and the same compressed skeleton is kept multiple times. Meanwhile, the data vectors for a single confidential part are often not large enough to fill a data block, which seriously affects storage utilization and query efficiency.

Rather than encrypting each confidential part individually, XQEnc puts them together and produces one single piece of cipher text, inserted as the last child of the root node. Using our running example, XQEnc generates the result as shown in the following transformed document:

```
<PaymentInfoList>
    <PaymentInfo>
        <Name>John Smith<Name/>
    </PaymentInfo>
    <PaymentInfo>
        <Name>Susan Smith<Name/>
    </PaymentInfo>
    <EncryptedData><CipherData>
        <CipherValue>E7FDA243B745CC586</CipherValue>
    </CipherData></EncryptedData>
</PaymentInfoList>
```

The cipher value consists of the following two components: the compressed skeleton of the *original* document d, and the confidential data partitioned in vectors, both components are in the encrypted form. Keeping the compressed skeleton of d ensures no loss of structural information. The compressed skeleton of a document is usually very small [6], which is much less than 1 megabytes for a document as large as hundreds of megabytes, or much less than 1% of the document size. This memory requirement is not demanding even in lightweight computing devices, given the trend of RAM size has been increasing as technology advances. Furthermore, an alternative is to keep only the "partial" compressed skeleton that is relevant to the confidential data. This makes the cipher value even shorter, at the cost of more complicated query processing. In our current design and implementation version of XQEnc, we adopt the former method (keeping the whole compressed skeleton) though we need to point out that a comparison with the latter is an interesting future work.

For the data vectors, we only include the confidential data, together with their document positions, in the cipher value. To answer an XPath query, first the compressed skeleton of the original document is decrypted from the cipher value. Then, the query processing algorithm of XQEnc described in the previous subsection is executed, treating the unencrypted part of the document and the cipher value as two data sources. When the query processor needs the textual information of a non-confidential text node, it gets that from the plain text part of the document. XQEnc partitions the data vectors into blocks and encrypts each block individually. During query processing the minimum unit of data retrieval is a data block. This technical detail is omitted for the ease of presentation.

In our implementation the unencrypted part is first parsed during preprocessing and the value of a text node can be easily retrieved. When the information contained in a confidential text node is needed, the query processor extracts from the encrypted data vectors according to the document position of the text node . In our running example, the cipher text contains the compressed skeleton shown in Fig. 1, and the last three data vectors in Table 2. During query processing, the names of the card holders are retrieved from the plain text part while confidential details like the issuer of the credit cards are retrieved from the encrypted data vectors.

3.3   Discussion

Using the algorithms described in Section 3.2, there is only one piece of cipher text no matter how many confidential text nodes are scattered through the document, and the cipher text is always appended at the end of the document and affects only one block. This drastically reduces the concern that the context can be exploited to attack the encryption and derive sensitive information. Furthermore, the redundancy of the XML format is eliminated by vectorization, making it even harder to attack the encryption.

The query efficiency of XQEnc can be substantially improved, since rather than retrieving and decrypting the entire confidential part, XQEnc only accesses the data necessary to answer the XPath query, thus the overhead of data retrieval and decryption are reduced to a minimum. As shown in Section 5, XQEnc improves query efficiency by more than an order of magnitude.

4   Secure XML Data Outsourcing Using XQEnc

As discussed in Section 2.3, existing techniques for data outsourcing, which address mainly relational data, can not be applied directly to XML data, in which structural information can be confidential. In this section we propose our solution based on XQEnc, with analysis.

4.1   Assumptions and Setting

We first make several assumptions about the data to be outsourced. First, we assume that the outsourced data is expressed in XML format, and is to be stored in a rented server running a relational database system. This is practical because XML provides flexibility for data expression, while relational database systems are ubiquitous. The main reason for this assumption is that we want to utilize existing data outsourcing techniques by transforming XML data to relational data.

Note that this transformation must not expose the internal structure of the XML data to the server. Therefore, existing XML-to-relational transformation methods, e.g. [11, 12], cannot be applied. Second, for the sake of presentation simplicity we make the assumption that the entire XML data to be outsourced is confidential. The general case that only some parts of the data is confidential can be handled similarly by applying the techniques presented in Section 3.2. For queries, we limit our scope to answering XPath queries. Essentially, the XPath queries on the original document are translated to SQL queries on the transformed relational data by the query translator. Therefore, to handle the more general XQuery queries requires a modified query translator, which is left as future work.

Existing data outsourcing techniques mostly translate a user query on the original data to exactly one query on the encrypted data stored on the server side. In our method the query translator may translate one XPath query into a corresponding set of multiple SQL queries. This is natural because an XPath query can be very complicated and even not expressible in one single SQL query. Moreover, we may need to process the answer returned by the server in order to issue the next SQL query. Therefore, there are interactions between the query translator and the query processor at the client side.

Another issue is that data outsourcing requires stronger security than the core problem of encrypting data. This is because the server owns the knowledge of not only the encrypted data, but also the translated queries. Therefore the security requirement here is that the server cannot derive confidential information, including both textual and structural information, from the encrypted data and all the SQL queries it receives.

4.2   The Solution Based on XQEnc

The solution consists of two parts. The first part is the method to transform a given XML document d to relational data to be stored on the server. The second part is the query answering process. We describe them in sequel.

In order to transform the given document d to relational data, we first compute the compressed skeleton and data vectors of d, as in XQEnc. We denote the compressed skeleton by s, which is small even for very large XML documents as discussed. One key point of our design is that s is not stored on the server; rather, it is stored inside the query translator on the client as metadata. This means that it is impossible for the server to obtain any structural information of d, which is contained in s. Next, we need to transform the data vectors into relational data, and the security requirements in this step is reduced to ensuring confidentiality of textual information.

For each item i in the data vectors, we create a tuple $< V_i, P_i, T_i >$, where V_i is the vector ID that identifies the vector containing i; P_i is the document position of i, and T_i is the textual value of i. This step essentially transforms the data vectors into one single table, which has three columns V (the vector IDs), P (the document positions) and T (the textual data). The primary key of this relation is denoted as the pair $< V, P >$. This transformation is information preserving, in the sense that the original data vectors can be restored using the resulting tuples.

After transforming the data vectors to relational data, the last step is to transform the relational data using existing data outsourcing techniques. Specifically, each tuple $< V_i, P_i, T_i >$ is transformed to another tuple $< etuple, V_i^S, P_i^S, T_i^S >$, where $etuple$ is the encrypted tuple, and X^S is the crypto-index of attribute X. Depending on the data outsourcing techniques used, the crypto-indices can be either bucket IDs using the bucketization technique [9], or encrypted values using the order preserving encryption technique [2].

A potential optimization during this step is to build multiple relations rather than one relation. The problem with cramming everything into one relation is that data in different vectors may have different ranges and distribution, which makes it difficult to compute a good bucketization or order preserving encryption scheme. In order to solve this problem, we devise an optimized cluster to group the vectors according to their sizes and characteristics of their textual values, and establish one relation for each cluster of vectors.

Finally, we support query processing as follows. We run the XQEnc query processing algorithm at the client side, treating the server as an external storage. A query is issued to the server whenever we need to access an item in one of the data vectors. Specifically, when we need the textual value of a data item in vector v and document position p, the following SQL query is sent to the Oracle database server.

$$\text{SELECT } etuple \text{ FROM } R(v) \text{ WHERE } V^S = crypto - index(v)$$
$$\text{AND } P^S = crypto - index(p)$$

The result returned from the server is then decrypted and the textual data is used for further processing. In addition, when the path predicate contains a condition specifying the range or the textual values, e.g. $[issuer = $ "Bank of the Internet"] in our running example, a corresponding selection condition is appended in the WHERE clause of the SQL statement sent to the server. In this example, the condition $T^S = crypto\text{-}index($"Bank of the Internet"$)$ is appended to the SQL query to further reduce the amount of data transmitted from the server to the client.

4.3 Analysis

We now justify that our solution preserves data confidentiality, i.e. both textual and structural information is protected from unauthorized access by the server. First of all, the data stored on the server side does not contain any structural information, and thus the structural information is protected. This is because all structural information is contained in the compressed skeleton s, which is stored only on the client side and not accessible by the server. A single SQL query issued to the server does not contain any structural information either. The only concern is that by analyzing a $sequence$ of queries, the server may derive some pieces of structural information. This can be further avoided by processing a set of multiple XPath queries at the same time, and the client mixes together their translated SQL queries sent to the server.

The confidentiality of textual information is guaranteed by the traditional data outsourcing techniques, e.g. bucketization [9] or order preserving encryption [2]. These techniques are the state of the art techniques for relational data. In other words, that is the best possible robust scheme we can use to protect the textual information. For this reason, we claim that *the structural and textual information is best possible protected in XQEnc.*

Regarding query efficiency, one might think that a possible weakness of our approach is that we need the client to perform the second query processing, in addition to the first processing on the server. With a critical observation of the various factors affecting query efficiency, we argue that our solution is still efficient, despite of having this weakness. The bottleneck of the entire data outsourcing architecture is data transmission between the client and the server. This overhead in XQEnc is reduced to a minimum because the query processing algorithm only retrieves data necessary to answer the query. This also means the decryption work done at the client side is reduced to a minimum, which compensates the computation cost of running the XQEnc query processing algorithm. In general, *all data intensive work is reduced to a minimum on the client, while the amount of undesirable overhead imposed by running the XQEnc query processing algorithm is purely determined by the size of the XPath query.* Therefore, our solution based on XQEnc provides very competitive query efficiency as also supported by the experimental study next section.

5 Experiments

In this section we evaluate the query efficiency of XQEnc through experiments. We have implemented a prototype for XQEnc. All the experiments were run on the Windows XP Professional platform. The CPU was a 1.5 GHz Pentium 4, while the system had 512MB of physical memory. For system parameters, the block size of data vectors is the maximum of 2 megabytes and 1000 data items, which is the empirical optimal block size obtained by the experimental study of [7]. The encryption algorithm chosen is DES.

We carried out the experiments on five different real XML datasets, all of which are well established benchmarks for studying XML query processing algorithms. The sizes of these data sets are listed in Table 3. For more details of the datasets, the readers may refer to [13] describing these datasets.

In order to evaluate the query performance of XQEnc, we need to make practical assumptions about which parts of the XML documents are considered confidential, as well as to choose several representative queries involving confidential parts of the document. Due to limited space we describe the experimen-

Table 3. Five data sets used in the experiments

Dataset	DBLP	SwissProt	LineItem	TreeBank	Shakespeare
Size (MB)	127	109	30.7	82	7.4

tal settings and results in detail for the DBLP dataset. The settings for other datasets are listed in Appendix A.

The document structure for the DBLP dataset is relatively simple. It is basically a fact sheet of various publications. Since the focus here is to test the efficiency of XQEnc, there should be a large part of the document considered confidential. In our experiments we assume all the "inproceedings" nodes, both the internal structures and textual values are confidential. In addition, we make further assumptions that all document URLs, and theses not in public domain are confidential for copyright reasons. The queries used in the experiments are listed below:

(Q1) `/dblp/inproceedings/title`

(Q2) `//mastersthesis/author`

(Q3) `//article[year = "2002"]/url`

(Q4) `//inproceedings[booktitle = "DASFAA"]/url`

(Q5) `//inproceedings[author = "Wilfred Ng"]/title`

The query Q1 is to show that the major factor of query performance is the size of the result, and the most time consuming operation is decryption. Because there is a large number of records for conference papers, the result for Q1 is very large, while the query itself is relatively simple to parse and process. Query Q3 involves both confidential and non-confidential information, and Q4 and Q5 contain highly selective predicates. The conventional method needs to retrieve and decrypt lots of unnecessary data and thus should be much slower than XQEnc, which only retrieves the data needed to answer the query.

We report several aspects of the efficiency of XQEnc. First, we compare the time needed to encrypt the confidential part, using both conventional methods (i.e. treating each part as a whole piece of text) and XQEnc. Second, we show the time needed for decrypting the entire document. In the extreme case, everything in the document is confidential and this time is the lower bound for a conventional method to answer most XPath queries. Third, we report the response time for processing the queries, both the conventional method and XQEnc.

The experimental results are shown in Table 4. All the numbers in the table are response times measured in seconds. For encryption and query response time, we give both the time needed for XQEnc and the conventional method, in the shown query order. In general, the encryption cost of datasets in XQEnc is larger than the conventional method but still within an acceptable range as it is not

Table 4. Experimental results. Here X/C means the ratio of response time by XQEnc to that by Conventional method. The response times are rounded to the nearest second.

Dataset	Encryption time (X/C)	Decryption time (C)	Q1 (X/C)	Q2 (X/C)	Q3 (X/C)	Q4 (X/C)	Q5 (X/C)
DBLP	50/40	38	10/30	1/23	5/23	1/30	1/30
SwissProt	49/35	33	8/30	2/28	2/28	1/28	2/28
LineItem	13/11	10	2/8	1/7	1/8	1/7	1/7
TreeBank	49/27	25	8/18	8/17	8/17	9/17	8/17
Shakespeare	4/3	2	1/2	1/2	1/2	1/2	1/2

frequent. The response time shows that XQEnc is very competitive in answering queries. Another interesting fact is that decrypting the entire dataset is very expensive. Therefore, when the entire dataset is confidential, XQEnc is more than an order of magnitude faster than conventional methods.

The results in the DBLP dataset clearly show that the response time for Q1 is relatively greater than other queries, thought Q1 itself is simple. This can be explained by the fact that the results for Q1 is much larger, and thus decryption becomes the major cost of query processing and XQEnc enjoys less cost-saving benefit as expected. However, XQEnc is much faster for queries Q4 and Q5, which justifies our efficiency analysis.

6   Conclusions

We propose XQEnc, which is a novel XML encryption technique based on XML vectorization and skeleton compression techniques. The technique is useful to support query processing of XML information in an outsourcing environment. Compared with existing solutions, XQEnc provides strengthened security and efficient query processing capability. The resulting document after applying XQEnc complies with the W3C encryption standard, which allows different treatments to be applied on different parts of the XML Document. The techniques can be used together with the existing compression technologies to reduce the data exchange overhead in network.

Throughout, we explain and show how secure XML data outsourcing can be achieved using XQEnc and existing relational data outsourcing techniques. Our solution guarantees robust protection for structural and textual information. Importantly, we demonstrate with a spectrum of XML benchmark datasets that the query performance of our solution is very competitive. Specifically, all data intensive computation and transmissions are reduced to a minimum.

XQEnc gives rise to many interesting topics for future work. At the current stage our design and implementation of XQEnc focus on XPath query support. We plan to extend our solution to more general query languages. For example, Schema-based (e.g. XSchema) validation on encrypted XML data is another promising subject to further study. We also plan to compare our approach with other approaches beside [3]. The analytical study of the relationship between the block parameters, query workload and the encryption efficiency underpinning the cost model is also important to further optimise query processing in XQEnc.

References

1. Fan, W., Chan, C., Garofalakis, M.: Secure XML querying with security views. In: SIGMOD Conference. (2004) 587–598
2. Agrawal, R., Kiernan, J., Srikant, R., Xu., Y.: Order preserving encryption for numeric data. In: SIGMOD Conference. (2004) 563–574
3. Imamura, T., Dillaway, B., Simon, E.: XML encryption syntax and processing. W3C Recommendation (2002)
4. Clark, J., DeRose, S.: XML path language (XPath). W3C Working Draft (1999)

5. Buneman, P., Choi, B., Fan, W., Hutchison, R., Mann, R., Viglas, S.: Vectorizing and querying large XML repositories. In: ICDE. (2005) 261–272
6. Buneman, P., Grohe, M., Koch, C.: Path queries on compressed XML. In: VLDB. (2003) 141–152
7. Cheng, J., Ng, W.: XQzip: Querying compressed XML using structural indexing. In: EDBT. (2004) 219–236
8. Liefke, H., Suciu, D.: XMILL: An efficient compressor for XML data. In: SIGMOD Conference. (2000) 153–164
9. Hacigumus, H., Iyer, B.R., Li, C., Mehrotra, S.: Executing SQL over encrypted data in the database-service-provider model. In: SIGMOD Conference. (2002) 216–227
10. Hore, B., Mehrotra, S., Tsudik, G.: A privacy preserving index for range queries. In: VLDB. (2004) 720–731
11. Bohannon, P., Freire, J., Roy, P., Simeon, J.: From XML schema to relations: A cost-based approach to XML storage. In: ICDE. (2002) 64–76
12. Shanmugasundaram, J., Tufte, K., Zhang, C., He, G., DeWitt, D.J., Naughton, J.F.: Relational databases for querying XML documents: Limitations and opportunities. In: VLDB. (1999) 302–314
13. Miklau, G.: The XML data repository. http://www.cs.washington.edu /research /xmldatasets/ (2006)

A   Appendix: The Datasets for the Experiments

```
Dataset: SwissProt
Confidential Parts: all entries whose class is "standard" and mtype is "PRT"
Q1: //Species
Q2: //Ref[DB = "MEDLINE"]
Q3: //Features[//DOMAIN/Descr = "HYDROPHOBIC"]
Q4: //Entry[AC = "Q43495"]
Q5: //Entry[//Keyword = "Germination"]
Dataset: LineItem
Confidential Parts: all lines whose order key value is between 10000 and 40000
Q1: //table/T/L_TAX
Q2: /table/T[L_TAX = "0.02"]
Q3: /table/T[L_TAX[[. >= "0.02"]]]
Q4: //T[L_ORDERKEY = "100"]
Q5: //L_ DISCOUNT
Dataset: TreeBank
Confidential Parts: everything enclosed by <_QUOTE_> tags
Q1: //_QUOTE_//_NONE_
Q2: //_QUOTE_//_BACKQUOTES_
Q3: //_QUOTE_//NP[_NONE_ = "FTTVhQZv7pnPMt+Eeoe0Sx"]
Q4: //_QUOTE_//SBAR//VP/VBG
Q5: //_QUOTE_//NP/PRP_DOLLAR_
Dataset: Shakespeare
Confidential Parts: all speeches
Q1: //SPEAKER
Q2: //PLAY//SCENE//STAGEDIR
Q3: //SPEECH[SPEAKER = "PHILO"]/LINE
Q4: //SCENE/SPEECH/LINE
Q5: //SCENE[TITLE="SCENE II. Rome. The house of EPIDUS"]/LINE
```

Document Conceptualisation

Wrapping PDF Documents Exploiting Uncertain Knowledge

Sergio Flesca[1], Salvatore Garruzzo[2], Elio Masciari[3], and Andrea Tagarelli[1]

[1] DEIS, University of Calabria
{flesca, tagarelli}@deis.unical.it
[2] DIMET, University of Reggio Calabria
salvatore.garruzzo@unirc.it
[3] ICAR-CNR – Institute of Italian National Research Council
masciari@icar.cnr.it

Abstract. The PDF format represents the de facto standard for print-oriented documents. In this paper we address the problem of wrapping PDF documents, which raises new challenges in the information extraction field. The proposal is based on a novel bottom-up wrapping approach to extract information tokens and integrate them into groups related according to the logical structure of a document. A PDF wrapper is defined by specifying a set of group type definitions which impose a target structure to token groups containing the required information. Due to the intrinsic uncertainty on the structure and presentation of PDF documents, we devise constraints on token groupings as fuzzy logic conditions. We define a formal semantics for PDF wrappers and propose an algorithm for wrapper evaluation working in polynomial time with respect to the size of a PDF document.

1 Introduction

In the context of Information Extraction, *wrapping* is the process of extracting data containing information pertinent to a specific application domain, and organizing such data into a machine-readable format. Traditional wrapping refers to the Web environment; Web wrapping systems (e.g. [1, 2, 3, 4, 5, 6]) exploit markup tags in HTML pages to generate delimiter-based extraction rules [7].

However, HTML and XML are not the only formats to spread and exchange textual information for the purpose of making it accessible to companies and private users. A further and related kind of textual document refers to *print-oriented* formats, whose Acrobat PDF [8] is the de facto standard. A PDF document is described by a *PDF content stream*, which contains a sequence of graphical and textual objects located at precise positions inside the document pages. Such intrinsic print-oriented nature of PDF documents arises many issues that make the information extraction task particularly difficult.

As a motivating application scenario, consider PDF documents describing company balance sheets, like that of Fig. 1. Automatically extracting information from balance sheets is extremely useful to build data warehouses of financial data. Balance sheets are statements of the total assets and liabilities of

E. Dubois and K. Pohl (Eds.): CAiSE 2006, LNCS 4001, pp. 175–189, 2006.
© Springer-Verlag Berlin Heidelberg 2006

Balance Sheet for XYZ Manufacturing Company as of Dec 31 200				
(All Figures in USD)				
Assets	200	Liabilities and Owners' Equity	200
Current Assets	5,000,000	Current Liabilities	
Cash	500,000	Accounts Payable	4,000,000
T-Bills	1,000,000	Dividend Payable	2,000,000
Accounts Receivable	7,000,000	Taxes Payable	3,000,000
Total Current Assets	13,500,000	Total Current Liabilities	9,000,000
Inventory		Long-term Liabilities	
Raw Materials	825,000	Long-term Bank Loan	5,000,000
WIP	750,000	Total Liabilities	14,000,000
Finished Goods	1,200,000	Owners' Equity	
Total Inventory	2,775,000	Capital	20,000,000
Long-term assets		Retained Earnings	28,275,000
Land	30,000,000	Total Net Worth	48,275,000
Machinery	20,000,000		
Depreciation (machinery)	-5,000,000		
Intangible Assets			
Patents	1,000,000		
Total Long-term Assets	46,000,000		
Total Assets	62,275,000	Total Liabilities + Net Worth	62,275,000

Fig. 1. Excerpt of a sample balance sheet

an organization, at a particular date, and are usually available as PDF documents. Each company may encode balance data using different presentation styles (e.g. two-column or four-column layout, different instructions for text formatting etc.). The subjectivity in the layout structure that characterize even thematically similar balance sheets leads to "uncertainty" in the specification of the syntactic extraction rules.

To date, the problem of wrapping PDF documents has not been studied at all, in spite of its applicability to a wide variety of scenarios. No existing wrapper generation system is designed for print-oriented documents. At a first sight, it is evident that while most information extraction approaches can be extended to deal with the characteristics of the PDF format, the main hypothesis enabling most wrapping approaches is lacking: even if documents are yet automatically produced using data coming from company databases, each company can use a different program to encode data in a document and, consequently, the resulting layouts can be different.

In this paper we address the problem of extracting information from PDF documents by focusing on their spatial and content features. We propose a novel bottom-up wrapping approach which considers the complex schema of the information to be extracted and exploits logical fuzzy rule-based conditions on the extracted information. The combined use of bottom-up extraction and fuzzy conditions enables effectively handling uncertainty on the comprehension of the layout structure of PDF documents.

Section 2 introduces basic notions for dealing with PDF documents as sets of spatial tokens, and provides background on spatial relations and fuzzy set theory. Section 3 describes a novel framework for wrapping PDF documents and a semantics for PDF wrappers. Section 4 addresses the PDF wrapper evaluation issue and describes an algorithm for extracting a maximal token group from a source PDF document, which works in polynomial time with respect to the size (number of tokens) of the source document. Section 5 contains concluding remarks.

2 Preliminaries

2.1 Fuzzy Sets

The sharp nature of classic set theory may often lead to scenarios in which the exact assignment of an object to a set is hardly obtained or unfeasible. *Fuzzy set theory* [9] takes into account the uncertainty due to subjective factors in data by introducing a smooth measure to state the place and role in the objects' class assignment. Given a set U, a fuzzy set A is defined by means of its *membership function* $\mu_A : U \mapsto [0..1]$, such that, for any element $x \in U$, the membership value $\mu_A(x)$ is defined as: $\mu_A(x) = 0$ if x does not belong to A, $\mu_A(x) = 1$ if x belongs to A, whereas $0 < \mu_A(x) < 1$ if x partially belongs to A.

A fuzzy atom is a formula $p(t_1, \ldots, t_n)$, where $t_1, \ldots, t_n$ are terms and p is a predicate symbol. Fuzzy predicates can be regarded as fuzzy sets of tuples, that is $\mu(p(t_1, \ldots, t_n)) = \mu_p(t_1, \ldots, t_n)$, where μ_p is the membership function of predicate p. Given an atom a, the truth value $\mu(a)$ ranges in $[0..1]$, and a fuzzy fact is an expression of the form $a \leftarrow \mu(a)$. In our setting, we mainly use built-in predicates, where the truth values of the ground atoms are pre-assigned. Truth value of conjunction and disjunction of atoms can be straightforwardly defined by means of *aggregation operators* [10]. Formally, given two fuzzy atoms $p(t_1, \ldots, t_n)$ and $q(t'_1, \ldots, t'_k)$, we have:

- $\mu(p(t_1, \ldots, t_n) \wedge q(t'_1, \ldots, t'_k)) = min(\mu(p(t_1, \ldots, t_n)), \mu(q(t'_1, \ldots, t'_k)))$,
- $\mu(p(t_1, \ldots, t_n) \vee q(t'_1, \ldots, t'_k)) = max(\mu(p(t_1, \ldots, t_n)), \mu(q(t'_1, \ldots, t'_k)))$,
- $\mu(\neg p(t_1, \ldots, t_n)) = 1 - \mu(p(t_1, \ldots, t_n))$.

As we shall explain in the following, fuzzy formulas enable modelling uncertainty in the wrapping process.

2.2 Spatial Documents

We refer to the concept of *token* as the basic element of a PDF document. A token is an atomic object (i.e. a textual element or an image), which is totally contained within a document page. The graphical representation of a token on the page layout takes up a certain room delimited by the token bounding box. We assume the presence of an alphabet Γ of token values.

Definition 1 (Document token). *A document token is a tuple $\langle v, p, inf_x, inf_y, sup_x, sup_y \rangle$, where $v \in \Gamma$, p is a page number, inf_x and inf_y (resp., sup_x and sup_y) are the coordinates (pixels) of the top-left corner (resp., bottom-right corner) of the token bounding box. A spatial document is a set of document tokens.*

Reasoning about tokens and their relationships lies on the capability of defining suitable predicates to check syntactic as well as semantic properties, and to characterize the spatial properties between pairs of tokens.

Spatial predicates allow for capturing relationships between locations of tokens. We denote with `spatialrelation`(t_1, t_2) a type of predicate that holds if there exists a specific spatial relation between tokens t_1 and t_2. More precisely, spatial predicates include *cardinal direction* predicates, namely *east*, *west*, *north*, *northeast*, *northwest*, *south*, *southeast*, *southwest*, and *topological* predicates such as *precedes* and *follows*.

Cardinal direction predicates are defined as fuzzy predicates, whose truth values depend on spatial relationships between tokens. For instance, the truth value of an atom $north(t_1, t_2)$, defined on tokens t_1 and t_2, depends on the amplitude of the angle formed by a line connecting the center of t_1 to the center of t_2 and the vertical axis of the document. By contrast, topological predicates are more simple since we assume they admit only true or false as truth value.

Content predicates are defined on the content of tokens. Some useful content predicates are listed below:

- $containsStr(t, s)$: holds if string s is contained in the text of token t;
- $isNumber(t)$: holds if token t represents a number;
- $value(t, s)$: holds if string s is the text value of token t;
- $regExp(t, e)$: holds if the text of token t matches a regular expression e;
- $concept(t, c)$: measures the relevance of token t with respect to an ontology concept c.

In the following section, we shall give evidence that spatial and content predicates are the basis for setting constraints on the construction of *token groups*.

3   Wrapping PDF Documents

3.1   PDF Extracted Information Model

In order to extract desired information, individual tokens are hierarchically organized into groups. A *token group* collects logically related tokens. For instance, in Fig. 1, tokens appearing in a line of a balance sheet are to be grouped together to compose a balance item. Balance items of type *Current Assets, Cash, T-bills, Accounts Receivable*, and *Total Current Assets* are then grouped together to compose the current asset group and so on. We assume the presence of a finite alphabet $\mathcal{T}$ of group types.

Definition 2 (Token group). *A token group is a pair* $\langle \tau, \gamma \rangle$, *where* $\tau \in \mathcal{T}$ *is a group type and* γ *is either a sequence* $\gamma = [\langle \tau_1, \gamma_1 \rangle, \dots, \langle \tau_n, \gamma_n \rangle]$ *of token groups, or a single token.*

Given a token group $g = \langle \tau, \gamma \rangle$, we denote with $children(g)$ the set of the groups appearing in γ, and with $subgroups(g)$ the set of the groups that either appear in γ or are recursively contained in $subgroups(g')$ such that $g' \in \gamma$.

As stated in Definition 2, each token group is associated with a group type, and may consist of more subgroups each having a specific type. Thus, a compound token group is characterized in terms of the group types corresponding to its subgroups.

Definition 3 (Group content type). *Given a token group* $g = \langle \tau, \gamma \rangle$, *the content type* $cnt(g)$ *of* g *is either* $\tau_1, \ldots, \tau_n$ *if* $\gamma = [\langle \tau_1, \gamma_1 \rangle, \ldots, \langle \tau_n, \gamma_n \rangle]$, *or symbol* $\epsilon \notin T$ *if* γ *is a single token.*

However, not all the token groups are well-suited to be considered as a result of the extraction task. In particular, we only consider "non-overlapping" groups, that is any group must not contain two identical subgroups. This must be true not only for the children of a group but also for all its descendants. For this purpose, the notion of *well-formed group* is next given.

Definition 4 (Well-formed group). *A token group* $g = \langle \tau, \gamma \rangle$ *is said to be well-formed if and only if there not exist two groups* $g', g'' \in subgroups(g)$, *with* $g' \notin subgroups(g'')$ *and* $g'' \notin subgroups(g')$, *such that* $children(g') \cap children(g'') \neq \emptyset$.

Proposition 1. *Let* $g = \langle \tau, \gamma \rangle$ *be a token group. If* g *is well-formed, each* $g' \in \gamma$ *is well-formed.*

Let $g' = \langle \tau', \gamma' \rangle$ and $g'' = \langle \tau'', \gamma'' \rangle$ be two token groups, where $\gamma' = [g'_0, \ldots, g'_n]$ and $\gamma'' = [g''_0, \ldots, g''_m]$. We say that g' *contains* g'' ($g' \supseteq g''$) if and only if:

- $g' = g''$, or
- $n = m$ and, for each $i \in [0..n]$, $g'_i \supseteq g''_i$, or
- $n > m$ and there exists a sequence of indexes $i_0, \ldots, i_m$ such that, for each $j \in [0..m]$, $i_j < i_{j+1}$ and $g'_{i_j} \supseteq g''_j$.

3.2 PDF Wrappers

In order to define a PDF wrapper we have to specify how to create a group starting from previously recognized subgroups, and which conditions these subgroups must satisfy. However, the print-oriented nature of PDF documents makes it impossible to specify tight conditions. To overcome this limitation we possibly exploit fuzzy conditions on token groupings.

Spatial and content predicates, introduced in Section 2.2 for characterizing properties and relationships between tokens, can be easily extended for token groups. The underlying idea is that a content predicate holds for a group if it holds for all the token within the group. Analogously, a spatial relationship between two groups holds if it holds for all the pairs of tokens within the groups. For instance, given two groups g_1 and g_2, relation $north(g_1, g_2)$ can be formalized as follows: $north(g_1, g_2) \rightarrow \forall t_i \in \gamma_1, t_j \in \gamma_2, \ north(t_i, t_j)$. This guarantees the *monotonicity* property for cardinal direction predicates. Extension of topological predicates to token groups can be made straightforwardly, since such predicates are not defined by means of fuzzy constraints.

A fuzzy constraint is a disjunction of conjunctions of content and spatial predicates. Formally, given a set of variables $\mathcal{V}$, a *fuzzy constraint* $c(\mathcal{V})$ is a formula $\bigvee_{i=0}^{n} c_i(\mathcal{V}_i)$, where each $c_i(\mathcal{V}_i)$ is a conjunction of group atoms $\bigwedge_{j=0}^{k_i} a_{i,j}(\mathcal{V}_{i,j})$ such that $\mathcal{V}_{i,j}$ is the set of all variables appearing in $a_{i,j}$, $\mathcal{V}_i = \bigcup_{j=0}^{k_i} \mathcal{V}_{i,j}$, and $\mathcal{V} = \bigcup_{i=0}^{n} \mathcal{V}_i$.

Let $\mathcal{V}$ and G be a set of variables and a set of groups, respectively, and let θ be a set of pairs x/g such that $x \in \mathcal{V}$ and $g \in G$. θ is a *group variable substitution* if and only if it does not contain two pairs x/g' and x/g'' such that $g' \neq g''$. Moreover, given a conjunction $c(\mathcal{V})$ of group atoms, a group variable substitution θ is said *ground* for $c(\mathcal{V})$ if and only if it contains a pair x/g for each $x \in \mathcal{V}$.

As is usual in standard logic programming, the application of a substitution θ to a variable x returns a group g if $x/g \in \theta$, or x itself otherwise. The result of the application of a substitution θ to an atom $a(x_0, \ldots, x_l)$, denoted with $\theta \circ a(x_0, \ldots, x_l)$, is an atom $a(\theta x_0, \ldots, \theta x_l)$. The application of a substitution to conjunction and disjunction of atoms is defined accordingly.

Proposition 2. *Let c be a conjunction of group atoms, and θ, θ' be ground group variable substitutions for c. If, for each $x/g \in \theta$, there is a pair $x/g' \in \theta'$ such that $g \subseteq g'$ then $\mu(\theta \circ c) \geq \mu(\theta' \circ c)$.*

Group Type Definitions. The specification of group content model requires the conditions, which selected subgroups must satisfy, are defined with respect to the type of a group.

Given an alphabet $\mathcal{T}$ of group types and an alphabet $\mathcal{V}$ of variables, an *annotated element name* is defined as a pair $\tau : x$, such that $\tau \in \mathcal{T}$ and $x \in \mathcal{V}$. An *annotated content model* on $(\mathcal{T}, \mathcal{V})$ is either a *one-unambiguous regular expression* [11] on annotated element names, or a pair $\#TOKEN : x$, where $\#TOKEN$ is the token content model and denotes a simple textual token.[1]

Given a group $g = \langle \tau, \gamma \rangle$ and an annotated content model e, the content type $cnt(g)$ is *valid* for e if:

- $cnt(g) = \epsilon$ and $e = \#TOKEN : x$, or
- $cnt(g) = \tau_1, \ldots, \tau_n \in L(e)$, where $L(e)$ denotes the language generated by e.

Given a group $g = \langle \tau, \gamma \rangle$ and an annotated content model e such that $cnt(g)$ is valid for e, the variable binding of γ with respect to e, denoted with $e(g)$, is a set of pairs $\{g_1/x_1, \ldots, g_n/x_n\}$ such that x_i is the variable implicitly associated to g_i parsing $\gamma = [g_1, \ldots, g_n]$ with e. Moreover, we denote with $\Theta(e, g)$ the set of all the subsets of $e(g)$ that are group variable substitutions. Notice that, in general $e(g)$ is not a group variable substitution, since a variable can be associated to multiple subgroups.

Definition 5 (Group type definition). *Let τ be a group type, e be an annotated content model on $(\mathcal{T}, \mathcal{V})$, and c be a fuzzy constraint on e. A group type definition is a tuple $\langle \tau, e, c \rangle$.*

---

[1] The "one-unambiguous" property for a regular expression allows for determining uniquely which position of a symbol in the expression should match a symbol in an input word, without looking beyond that symbol in the input word. For this reason, it is worth emphasizing that there is only one way by which a string of group types can be "parsed" using an annotated content model, thus an annotated content model implicitly associates a variable x_i to each subgroup $\langle \tau_i, \gamma_i \rangle$ in γ.

Roughly speaking, a group type definition is a complete specification of the content model, together with an additional fuzzy constraint. Moreover, a group type definition $\langle \tau, e, c \rangle$ refers to the type τ. In the following, we characterize the validity of a token group of type τ with respect to a group type definition referring to τ.

Definition 6 (Group validity). *Let $g = \langle \tau, \gamma \rangle$ be a token group and $gtd = \langle \tau', e, c \rangle$ be a group type definition. We say that g is* valid *with respect to gtd if $\tau = \tau'$ and $cnt(g)$ is valid for e.*

The syntactic validity of groups being extracted is not affected by the application of fuzzy constraints. The truth value of a token group can be computed by combining the truth values of its subgroups with the truth values of the fuzzy constraints according to the rules defined in Section 2.1. However, we have to define how a constraint c is grounded by the application of a group variable substitution θ. It may happen that applying θ to c the resulting formula is not ground, i.e. $\theta \circ c$ still contains some variables. In this case, the semantics of constraint intuitively requires that the conjunction in which a variable still appears will not be considered. The following example explains the above intuition.

Example 1. In Fig. 1, consider a group g whose description is as follows:

group	type (τ)	content (γ)
g	Assets	$[g_1, g_2]$
g_1	Current_Assets	t_1
g_2	Intangible_Assets	t_2

where g_1, g_2 are token groups and t_1, t_2 are tokens. Group g is associated with the group type definition $gtd = \langle \tau, e, c \rangle$ such that $\tau = $ Assets, $e = $ Current_Assets : CA, (Inventory : I|Intangible_Assets : IA), and $c = follows(CA, I)$. By parsing g with e, we have $e(g) = \{g_1/CA, g_2/IA\}$, which equals the set $\Theta(e, g)$ since it is a group variable substitution. By applying the substitution to c we obtain the non-ground constraint $follows(g_1, I)$. Thus, the truth value of g is provided by the minimum between the truth values of its subgroups (i.e. g_1, g_2).

Given a fuzzy constraint $c = c_0 \vee \ldots \vee c_n$ and a group variable substitution θ, the grounded version of $\theta \circ c$ is defined as $ground(\theta \circ c) = ground(\theta \circ c_0) \vee \ldots \vee ground(\theta \circ c_n)$, where $ground(\theta \circ c_i)$ is $\theta \circ c_i$ if $\theta \circ c_i$ is ground, $false$ otherwise.

Given a group $g = \langle \tau, \gamma \rangle$ which is valid for a group type definition $gtd = \langle \tau', e, c \rangle$, the truth value of g with respect to gtd is given by the truth value of the formula

$$\mu_{gtd}(g) = \mu \left(\bigwedge_{g' \in \gamma} \mu(g') \; \wedge \; ground(\theta \circ c), \forall \theta \in \Theta(e, g) \right),$$

where for each possible variable binding we compute its truth value with respect to all ground constraints $\theta \circ c$. Once computed the truth value of each conjunct, the overall value is obtained by using the min operator (cf. Section 2.1). Notice that, the truth value of the overall formula propagates starting from the token value. Thus, token truth values bound the overall value of the formula and, as usual in classic logic, if any conjunct evaluates to 0 the overall formula will evaluate to 0 too.

PDF Wrapper Specification and Semantics. Faced with the above definitions, we are now ready to provide the notion of *PDF wrapper*.

Definition 7 (PDF wrapper). *A PDF wrapper is a tuple $W = \langle \tau, G \rangle$, where $\tau \in \mathcal{T}$ is the root group type and $G = \{\langle \tau_0, e_0, c_0 \rangle, \ldots, \langle \tau_n, e_n, c_n \rangle\}$ is a set of group type definitions such that $\tau_i \neq \tau_j$, for each $i, j \in [0..n]$, $i \neq j$.*

Let $W = \langle \tau, G \rangle$ be a PDF wrapper and $\langle \tau_1, e_1, c_1 \rangle$, $\langle \tau_2, e_2, c_2 \rangle \in G$ be two group type definitions. We say that τ_1 *depends on* τ_2 if τ_2 appears in e_1, or there exists a group type definition $\langle \tau_3, e_3, c_3 \rangle$ such that τ_1 depends on τ_3 and τ_3 depends on τ_2. A PDF wrapper is said to be *non-recursive* if it does not contain two group types τ_1, τ_2 such that τ_1 depends on τ_2. In the following we consider only non-recursive PDF wrappers.

Given a wrapper $W = \langle \tau_0, G \rangle$ and a group type τ, we denote with $W(\tau)$ the group type definition of τ in G.

Definition 8 (Valid group). *Let $W = \langle \tau_0, G \rangle$ be a PDF wrapper and doc be a PDF document. A group $g = \langle \tau, \gamma \rangle$ on doc is valid for W if and only if:*

1. *g is well-formed, and*
2. *$\tau = \tau_0$, and*
3. *g is valid with respect to $W(\tau)$, and*
4. *for each subgroup $g' = \langle \tau', \gamma' \rangle$ of g, g' is valid with respect to $W(\tau')$.*

The set of all groups over doc valid for W is denoted as $\mathcal{G}(W, doc)$.

Broadly speaking, a *valid group* is essentially a well-formed group of tokens, which conforms to the schema defined by a wrapper. The reliability of the extracted data that are contained in a group g is substantially fuzzily measured by $\mu_{gtd}(g)$. However, since the truth value of a group depends both on its associated gtd and the truth values of its subgroups, in the following we denote with $\mu_W(g)$ the truth value of a group according to the definition of a wrapper W.

Given a PDF wrapper W and a document *doc*, there can be several different groups that are valid with respect to W. However, not all such groups are desirable as results of the evaluation of W on *doc*. The key-idea is to consider only groups that are "maximal", i.e. groups whose truth value is equal to or greater than a predefined threshold, and which are not contained inside other valid groups that meet the truth value requirement as well.

Definition 9 (Maximal group). *Let $W = \langle \tau_0, G \rangle$ be a PDF wrapper, t be a truth value threshold, and doc be a PDF document. A group $g \in \mathcal{G}(W, doc)$ is said to be* maximal *with respect to t if and only if:*

- $\mu_W(g) \geq t$, and
- there not exists $g' \in \mathcal{G}(W, doc)$ such that $g' \supseteq g$ and $\mu_W(g') \geq t$.

The set of all maximal groups with respect to t is denoted as $\mathcal{M}_t(W, doc)$.

Clearly, it is possible to consider only the maximal groups having the greatest truth value. However, this strategy may be computationally expensive; thus, we rather prefer to adopt a greedy approach for searching a maximal group with the greatest truth value.

4 PDF Wrapper Evaluation

In the proposed approach, the objective of evaluating a wrapper for a PDF document is to compute a maximal token group from that PDF document. We consider a restricted form of wrappers, called $\star$-free wrappers, which do not contain optionals or repeated subgroups in group definitions.

Definition 10 ($\star$-free wrapper). Let $W = \langle \tau_0, G \rangle$ be a PDF wrapper. W is said to be $\star$-free if and only if, for each group type definition $\langle \tau, e, c \rangle \in G$, e does not contain $*$ or $?$.

Given a wrapper W, we denote with $W^\star$ the wrapper obtained by replacing each group type definition $\langle \tau, e, c \rangle$ in W with $\langle \tau, e^\star, c \rangle$, where $e^\star$ is the annotated content model obtained from e by removing each occurrence of symbols $*$ and $?$. This operation allows us to consider the "kernel" of the content model defining W: indeed, as can be easily observed, any expression in $L(e^\star)$ is also in $L(e)$, that is $L(e^\star) \subseteq L(e)$.

The search for maximal groups works by repeatedly trying to add new subgroups to existing groups. This is achieved by expanding optional parts of group definition which have not been previously considered.

Definition 11 (Group expansion). Let $W = \langle \tau_0, G \rangle$ be a PDF wrapper, doc be a PDF document, $g = \langle \tau, \gamma \rangle$ and $g' = \langle \tau, \gamma' \rangle$ be two groups from doc, and $G(\tau)$ be $\langle \tau, e, c \rangle$. We say that g' is an expansion of g if and only if $g \subseteq g'$ and each pair $g_i/x_i \in e(g)$ also belongs to $e(g')$.

Lemma 1. Let W be a PDF wrapper, doc be a PDF document, and g, g' two groups from doc. If g' is an expansion of g then $\mu_W(g) \geq \mu_W(g')$.

Lemma 2. Let W be a PDF wrapper, doc be a PDF document, and t be a truth value threshold. For each group g in $\mathcal{M}_t(W, doc)$, there exists a group g' in $\mathcal{M}_t(W^\star, doc)$ such that g is an expansion of g'.

Lemma 3. Let W be a PDF wrapper, doc be a PDF document, and t be a truth value threshold. $\mathcal{M}_t(W, doc)$ is empty if and only if $\mathcal{M}_t(W^\star, doc)$ is empty.

Theorem 1. Let W be a PDF wrapper, doc be a PDF document, and t be a truth value threshold. Checking if $\mathcal{M}_t(W, doc)$ is empty can be done in polynomial time with respect to the number of tokens in doc.

Theorem 2. *Let W be a PDF wrapper, doc be a PDF document, and t be a truth value threshold. Checking whether a group g is in $\mathcal{M}_t(W, doc)$ is feasible in polynomial time with respect to the number of tokens in doc.*

4.1   A Fuzzy Algorithm for Extracting Maximal Token Groups

In this section we describe a PDF wrapper evaluation algorithm designed to extract a maximal token group from a PDF document (Fig. 2). Given a PDF document *doc* and a wrapper W for it, the maximal token group can be extracted according to the content models specified in W and to a predefined truth value threshold.

Initially, all the elementary token groups (i.e. groups of type *#TOKEN*) are extracted from the source document *doc*. These groups are simply computed by selecting all the tokens that satisfy the truth value threshold with respect to the associated constraints. Then, the $\star$-free wrapper $W^\star$ is applied to *doc* to extract all the $\star$-free token groups; among these, the token group with the maximum truth value is chosen and recursively "expanded" while the group being constructed satisfies the desired truth value threshold.

Expanding a token group consists substantially in adding some subgroups to its content, that is re-defining its original annotated content model including the content of other groups. For this purpose, a *normal form* for annotated content models is exploited.

Definition 12 (Normal form annotated content model). *An annotated content model $e = exp_1, \ldots, exp_n$ is in disjunction-free normal form if and only if, for each $i \in [1..n]$, exp_i is either an annotated element name $\tau : x$ or an expression of the form $exp?$, or $exp\star$, where exp is an annotated content model.*

Given a group g and an annotated content model e in disjunction-free normal form, g is *matched* by e if and only if $cnt(g)$ is valid for $e^\star$. In order to compute the expansion of a group g, the annotated content model e in disjunction-free normal form that matches g is considered. Let $e = exp_1, \ldots, exp_n$ be an annotated content model in disjunction-free normal form. When parsing g with e, each $g_i = \langle \tau_i, \gamma_i \rangle$, such that $\gamma_i \in cnt(g)$, is associated to one subexpression of e which corresponds to a group type; then, a subexpression of the form $exp?$ or $exp\star$ is chosen, and a group sequence $g'_1, \ldots, g'_k$ valid for exp_i is found.

As an example, consider a group $g = \langle \tau, [\langle a, \gamma_1 \rangle, \langle b, \gamma_2 \rangle, \langle c, \gamma_3 \rangle] \rangle$ and an annotated content model in disjunction-free normal form $e = (a : x1, b : x2, (b : x3 \,|\, d : x4)\star, c : x5)$ which matches g. Parsing g with e will result in assigning $x1$ to $\langle a, \gamma_1 \rangle$, $x2$ to $\langle b, \gamma_2 \rangle$, and $x5$ to $\langle c, \gamma_3 \rangle$. g can be expanded by selecting a new group of type b or d, and computing the groups $g' = \langle \tau, [\langle a, \gamma_1 \rangle, \langle b, \gamma_2 \rangle, \langle b, \gamma'_4 \rangle, \langle c, \gamma_3 \rangle] \rangle$ or $g'' = \langle \tau, [\langle a, \gamma_1 \rangle, \langle b, \gamma_2 \rangle, \langle d, \gamma''_4 \rangle \langle c, \gamma_3 \rangle] \rangle$, respectively. Besides groups g' and g'', two annotated content models in disjunction-free normal form that match g' and g'', respectively, can be derived and further used to find new group expansions. For example, with respect to group g', the annotated content model $e' = (a : x1, b : x2, b : x3, (b : x3 \,|\, d : x4)\star, c : x5)$, which is in disjunction-free normal form, can be derived.

Input:
A PDF document doc; A PDF wrapper $W = \langle \tau_0, G \rangle$;
A truth value threshold t.
Output:
A maximal token group g.
Method:
  $dbGroups := extractElementaryTokenGroups(doc, W, t)$;
  $G := buildStarFreeGroups(W, dbGroups, t)$;
  $g := selectMaxTruthValueGroup(G)$;
  do
    /* computes a group g' from g by expanding g itself or one of its subgroups */
    $g' := \textbf{expand}(W, g, dbGroups, t)$;
    if $(g' \neq null)$ **then**
    $g := g'$;
  while $(g' \neq null)$;
  return g;

Function $\textbf{expand}(W, g, dbGroups, t) : g'$;
Method:
  $S := \emptyset$; $g' := null$;
  for each g'' in $descendantOrSelf(g)$ **do**
    $Exp := \textbf{findExpansion}(W, g'', dbGroups, t)$;
    for each $gg \in Exp$ **do**
      $gg' := replace(g, g'', gg)$;
      if gg' is valid for $G(\tau_0)$ and $\mu_W(gg') \geq t$ and gg' is well-formed **then**
        $S := S \cup \{gg'\}$;
  if $(S \neq \emptyset)$ **then**
    $g' := selectMaxTruthValueGroup(S)$;
  return g';

Function $\textbf{findExpansion}(W, g, dbGroups, t) : Exp$;
Method:
  let $g = \langle \tau, \gamma, e \rangle$, with $e = exp_1, \ldots, exp_n$;
  $Exp := \emptyset$;
  for each exp_i of the form $exp?$ or $exp*$ **do**
    $S := instantiate(exp_i)$;
    for each $ex \in S$ **do**
      $SG := selectGroups(ex^*, dbGroups)$;
      for each $sg \in SG$ **do**
        let $ex' = exp_1, \ldots, exp_{i-1}, ex, exp_{i+1}, \ldots, exp_n$;
        if $\langle \tau, compose(ex', \gamma, sg) \rangle$ is valid for $G(\tau)$ and
              $\mu_W(\langle \tau, compose(ex', \gamma, sg) \rangle) \geq t$ and
              $\langle \tau, compose(ex', \gamma, sg) \rangle$ is well-formed **then**
          $Exp := Exp \cup \langle \tau, compose(ex', \gamma, sg), ex' \rangle$;
  return Exp;

Fig. 2. The TokenGroupExtractor algorithm

Let g be a group to be expanded, and $e = exp_1, \ldots, exp_n$ be its matched annotated content model in disjunction-free normal form. The expansion of g can be computed by *instantiating* each expression $exp_i \in e$, that is by computing a set of annotated content models (in disjunction-free normal form) derived from exp_i and such that they do not parse the empty string. We define a function *instantiate* as follows:

- $instantiate(exp*) = instantiate(exp), exp*;$
- $instantiate(exp?) = instantiate(exp);$
- $instantiate(exp_1|exp_2) = instantiate(exp_1) \cup instantiate(exp_2);$
- $instantiate(exp_1, exp_2) = instantiate(exp_1), instantiate(exp_2);$
- $instantiate(\tau : x) = \tau : x.$

The concatenation of two sets of annotated content models E_1, E_2 is the set of annotated content models $\{e_1, e_2 \mid e_1 \in E_1 \wedge e_2 \in E_2\}$. We say that an expression of the form $exp?$ or $exp*$ is an *expandable* expression.

Let $g = \langle \tau, \gamma \rangle$ be a group and $e = exp_1, \ldots, exp_n$ be the annotated content model in disjunction-free normal form that matches g. Let exp_i be an expandable expression, ex_i be an expression in $instantiate(exp_i)$, γ be $[g_1, \ldots, g_n]$, and $g'_1, \ldots, g'_k$ be a sequence of groups matching ex_i. The sequence $[g_1, \ldots, g_j, g'_1, \ldots, g'_k, g_{j+1}, \ldots, g_n]$ matching $ex = exp_1, \ldots, exp_{i-1}, ex_i, exp_{i+1}, \ldots, exp_n$, is denoted as $compose(ex, \gamma, [g'_1, \ldots, g'_k])$.

We are now able to gain an insight into the TokenGroupExtractor algorithm of Fig. 2. We assume that a database *dbGroups* is used to store extracted *annotated groups*. An annotated group is a triplet of the form $g = \langle \tau, \gamma, e \rangle$, where $\langle \tau, \gamma \rangle$ is a group and e the annotated content model in disjunction-free normal form that matches $\langle \tau, \gamma \rangle$.

Once elementary token groups have been extracted and stored into *dbGroups*, function *buildStarFreeGroups* first normalizes the input wrapper by producing, for each $gtd \in G$, group type definitions in disjunction-free normal form; then, following the order derived from the dependence relation between group types, for each normalized group type definition $\langle \tau, e, c \rangle$ it computes $\star$-free groups by invoking $selectGroups(e^*, dbGroups)$, selects those that are well-formed and satisfy the desired truth value threshold, annotates them with the content model e, and finally adds the computed groups into *dbGroups*.

Function expand tries to expand a group g and returns an expanded group if possible, null otherwise. Among all possible ways of expanding g, function expand chooses the one exhibiting the highest truth value. Given three groups g, g', and gg, function *replace* returns a new group obtained by replacing g' with gg inside g if g' is a subgroup of g, or returns gg otherwise. Moreover, function *descendantOrSelf*, given a group g, yields the set of all the subgroups of g and g itself. Finally, function *selectMaxTruthValueGroup*, given a set of groups S, returns the group with the maximum truth value in S.

Function findExpansion computes a set of all the possible expansions of an annotated group with respect to the wrapper, the group database, and the truth value threshold. Function *selectGroups*, given a $\star$-free annotated content model $e = \tau_1 : x_1, \ldots, \tau_n : x_n$ (in disjunction-free normal form) and *dbGroups*, returns the set of group sequences of the form $\{g_1, \ldots, g_n \mid \forall i \ g_i \in \pi_{\tau_i}(dbGroups)\}$, where $\pi_{\tau_i}(dbGroups)$ is the set $\{g \mid g \in dbGroups \land type(g) = \tau_i\}$.

Theorem 3. *Let W be a PDF wrapper, doc be a PDF document, and t be a truth value threshold. If $\mathcal{M}_t(W, doc)$ is not empty, the TokenGroupExtractor algorithm computes a maximal group g in $\mathcal{M}_t(W, doc)$ in polynomial time with respect to the number of tokens in doc.*

5 A Case Study: Wrapping Balance Sheets

To assess the effectiveness of the PDF wrapping framework, we considered a collection of balance sheets made publicly available from Italian companies; it is highly heterogeneous due to the variety of formatting styles used to report the balance assets and liabilities. For the sake of brevity, we describe a significant example of information extraction from a page of the test balance sheet shown in Fig. 3.

Suppose we would like to extract items each containing a balance voice (i.e. the item label) and two currency values referring to different fiscal years. Table 1 summarizes details about the specification of a wrapper suitable to the example balance sheet.

The maximal group to be extracted is of type `item_collection`. This group is composed of token groups `item`, which in turn consist of triplets of type (`balance_voice, amount, amount`). Each group `item` is constrained by a conjunction of two cardinal direction predicates. Once a group `item` has been built,

STATO PATRIMONIALE - ATTIVO	31/12/2003	31/12/2002
B) IMMOBILIZZAZIONI		
I) IMMOBILIZZAZIONI IMMATERIALI		
1) Costi di impianto e di ampliamento	10.739	73.792
3) Avviamento	433.824	495.799
I TOTALE IMMOBILIZZAZIONI IMMATERIALI	444.563	569.591
II) IMMOBILIZZAZIONI MATERIALI		
2) Impianti e macchinari		
a) impianti e macchinari	399.839	336.282
b) f.a impianti e macchinari	169.253-	105.762-
2 TOTALE Impianti e macchinari	230.586	230.520
3) Attrezzature industriali e commerciali		
a) attrezzature industriali e commerciali	63.045	61.845
b) f.a attrezzature industriali e commerciali	47.446-	29.561-
3 TOTALE Attrezzature industriali e commerciali	15.599	32.284
4) Altri beni		
a) altri beni	19.693	18.703
b) f.a.altri beni	11.094-	6.621-
4 TOTALE Altri beni	8.599	12.082
II TOTALE IMMOBILIZZAZIONI MATERIALI	254.784	274.886

Bilancio di esercizio al 31/12/2003   Pagina 1

Fig. 3. Sample page of the test Italian company's balance sheet

Table 1. A wrapper for the balance sheet of Fig. 3

$W = \langle \tau_0, G \rangle$	$\tau_0 = \texttt{item\_collection}$
	$G = \langle gtd_1, gtd_2, gtd_3, gtd_4 \rangle$
$gtd_1 = \langle \tau_1, e_1, c_1 \rangle$	$\tau_1 = \tau_0$
	$e_1 = (\texttt{item} : IT)*$
	$c_1 = True()$
$gtd_2 = \langle \tau_2, e_2, c_2 \rangle$	$\tau_2 = item$
	$e_2 = \texttt{balance\_voice} : BV, \texttt{amount} : N_1, \texttt{amount} : N_2$
	$c_2 = west(BV, N_1) \wedge west(N_1, N_2)$
$gtd_3 = \langle \tau_3, e_3, c_3 \rangle$	$\tau_3 = \texttt{balance\_voice}$
	$e_3 = \sharp TOKEN : X_1$
	$c_3 = concept(X_1, balance\_voice\_object)$
$gtd_4 = \langle \tau_4, e_4, c_4 \rangle$	$\tau_4 = \texttt{amount}$
	$e_4 = \sharp TOKEN : X_2$
	$c_4 = isNumber(X_2)$

```xml
<?xml version="1.0" encoding="UTF-8"?>              <item>
<item_collection>                                     <balance_voice>
  <item>                                                <value>5) Avviamento</value>
    <balance_voice>                                     <page>1</page>
      <value>1) Costi di impianto                       <inf_x>45.7799</inf_x>
             e di ampliamento</value>                   <inf_y>395.8974</inf_y>
      <page>1</page>                                    <sup_x>118.79464</sup_x>
      <inf_x>45.7799</inf_x>                            <sup_y>406.9194</sup_y>
      <inf_y>372.8574</inf_y>                         </balance_voice>
      <sup_x>210.92456</sup_x>                        <amount>
      <sup_y>383.8794</sup_y>                           <value>433.824</value>
    </balance_voice>                                    <page>1</page>
    <amount>                                            <inf_x>420.4875</inf_x>
      <value>10.739</value>                             <inf_y>397.9014</inf_y>
      <page>1</page>                                    <sup_x>475.847</sup_x>
      <inf_x>423.2689</inf_x>                           <sup_y>406.9194</sup_y>
      <inf_y>374.8614</inf_y>                         </amount>
      <sup_x>476.07428</sup_x>                        <amount>
      <sup_y>383.8794</sup_y>                           <value>495.799</value>
    </amount>                                           <page>1</page>
    <amount>                                            <inf_x>502.6391</inf_x>
      <value>73.792</value>                             <inf_y>397.9014</inf_y>
      <page>1</page>                                    <sup_x>557.9986</sup_x>
      <inf_x>505.3864</inf_x>                           <sup_y>406.9194</sup_y>
      <inf_y>374.8614</inf_y>                         </amount>
      <sup_x>558.19183</sup_x>                      </item>
      <sup_y>383.8794</sup_y>                       . . .
    </amount>                                        . . .
  </item>                                          </item_collection>
```

Fig. 4. XML document extracted from the balance sheet of Fig. 3

it is added to the content of the group of type $\texttt{item\_collection}$, without being subject to a real constraint (i.e. constraint c_1 always holds).

Another noteworthy remark concerns c_3. This constraint checks whether a token associated to type $\texttt{balance\_voice}$ really represents a balance voice. To accomplish this, a predicate *concept* evaluates the membership of a given token as an instance of class *balance_voice_object*, according to some functions which compute at what degree a string (token value) conceptually matches a class property (e.g. a domain-specific cue phrase). Figure 4 shows an XML fragment representing the maximal token group of type item_collection extracted by evaluating the wrapper of Table 1, with a truth value threshold set to 0.8.

6 Conclusion

We have presented a novel PDF wrapping framework based on a bottom-up approach, in which the extraction task consists in grouping together document tokens. A wrapper is defined by specifying the content for each type of token group. Annotated content models and fuzzy constraints as the basic elements of group type definitions. Fuzzy constraints are used to impose spatial and logical conditions on the content of each group. We have defined a declarative semantics of PDF wrappers and provided a polynomial time algorithm for extracting maximal groups. We have given evidence that fuzzy constraints are well-suited to capture subjective factors that brand the authorship in logically structuring information into a PDF document.

A system prototype is in advanced phase of development[2] and is currently being applied for extracting information from balance sheets.

References

1. Ashish, N., Knoblock, C.A.: Wrapper Generation for Semistructured Internet Sources. ACM SIGMOD Record 26(4) (1997) 8–15
2. Baumgartner, R., Flesca, S., Gottlob, G.: Visual Web Information Extraction with Lixto. In: Proc. VLDB '01 Conf. (2001) 119–128
3. Crescenzi, V., Mecca, G., Merialdo, P.: RoadRunner: Towards automatic data extraction from large Web sites. In: Proc. VLDB '01 Conf. (2001) 109–118
4. Freitag, D.: Machine Learning for Information Extraction in Informal Domains. Machine Learning 39(2–3) (2000) 233–272
5. Muslea, I., Minton, S., Knoblock, C.: Hierarchical Wrapper Induction for Semistructured Information Sources. Autonomous Agents and Multi-Agent Systems 4(1/2) (2001) 93–114
6. Soderland, S.: Learning Information Extraction Rules for Semistructured and Free Text. Machine Learning 34(1–3) (1999) 233–272
7. Laender, A., Ribeiro-Neto, B., da Silva, A., Teixeira, J.: A Brief Survey of Web Data Extraction Tools. ACM SIGMOD Record 31(2) (2002) 84–93
8. Adobe Systems Incorporated: PDF Reference, 5th edition: Adobe Portable Document Format version 1.6. Available at http://partners.adobe.com/public/developer/pdf (2004)
9. Zadeh, L.: Fuzzy Sets. Information and Control 8 (1965) 338–353
10. Wygralak, M.: Fuzzy Cardinals based on the Generalized Equality of Fuzzy Subsets. Fuzzy Sets & Systems 18 (1986) 143–158
11. Bruggemann-Klein, A., Wood, D.: One-Unambiguous Regular Languages. Information and Computation 142(2) (1998) 182–206

---

[2] http://www.deis.unical.it/tagarelli/pdf-wrapping

Supporting Customised Collaboration over Shared Document Repositories

Claudia-Lavinia Ignat and Moira C. Norrie

Institute for Information Systems, ETH Zurich,
CH-8092 Zurich, Switzerland
{ignat, norrie}@inf.ethz.ch

Abstract. The development of collaborative environments that not only manage information and communication, but also support the actual work processes of organisations is very important. XML documents are increasingly being used to mark up various kinds of data from web content to data used by applications. Often these documents need to be collaboratively created and edited by a group of users. In this paper we present a flexible solution for supporting collaboration over shared repositories containing both XML and text documents. By adopting hierarchical document models instead of linear representations used in most editing systems, the level of conflict granularity and resolution can be varied dynamically and the semantics of the user operations can be easily expressed. Merging of user work is based on the operations performed rather than the document states which provides a less complex and more appropriate way of handling conflicts.

1 Introduction

Collaboration is a central aspect of any team activity and hence of importance to any organisation - be it business, science, education, administration, political or social. The development of collaborative environments that not only manage information and communication, but also support the actual work processes of organisations is therefore very important. While some collaborative activity may involve shared access to databases, a great deal of information central to the operation of organisations is held in documents and support for collaboration is left to file systems, document editors, revision control systems or the users themselves. At the same time, XML documents are increasingly being used to store all kinds of information including not only application data, but also all forms of metadata, specifications, configurations, templates, web documents and even code. While some XML documents are generated automatically from systems, for example database exports, there are many cases where XML documents are created and edited by users either in raw text format or through special tool support.

Although a number of document management and collaborative editing systems have been developed to support collaboration over documents, they tend to focus on a particular form of document or mode of working. For example, some collaborative editors support only synchronous editing of text documents while revision control systems often support only asynchronous editing with support for merging of versions. However, within a single project, it is often the case that different forms of collaboration are used at different stages of the document life cycle and, depending on the activity and mode of working, it should be possible to support both synchronous and asynchronous collaboration and customise the definition and resolution of potential conflicts, as pointed out in [7].

In [8] we described our approach for maintaining consistency for real-time collaboration over text documents. In [5, 6] we described how our approach has been applied to asynchronous collaboration over a repository, the basic unit for collaboration being the text document. In this paper, we focus on asynchronous working over a shared document repository and show how flexible solutions to collaboration over both text and XML documents can be achieved by adopting hierarchical document models instead of the linear representations used in most editing systems. These models enable the level of conflict granularity and resolution to be varied dynamically and capture more of the semantics of user operations. The handling of conflicts is based on the technique of operational transformations applied to different document levels and the merging of user work is therefore based on the operations that they perform rather than the document states which, as we will show, provides a much more appropriate way of detecting and handling conflicts. Rather than providing a full description of the merging algorithms for consistency maintenance, in this paper, we briefly describe the principles of merging and instead focus on the aspects of customisation achieved by our approach in terms of the types of documents supported, i.e. text and XML, and flexibility in the definition and resolution of conflicts.

The paper is structured as follows. We begin in section 2 by presenting the limitations of existing version control systems for collaboration over documents and give an overview of the existing asynchronous collaborative systems for text and XML documents. Section 3 describes the document model that we adopted. In section 4, we present the set of operations that are used to describe the changes performed by the users. In section 5, we show how an existing linear-based merge approach has been used by our tree-based merging approach recursively over the document levels. We then describe in section 6 how conflicts can be defined and resolved in a flexible way in our system. Concluding remarks are presented in section 7.

2   Collaboration over Documents

We start this section with the description of some scenarios showing the set of requirements of a version control system supporting a group of people collaboratively working on set of XML and text documents and the limitations of existing systems. Afterwards we present existing related approaches for asynchronous collaboration on XML and text documents and highlight the contribution of our approach.

Consider the case of a research team in the field of computational physics that wants to publish the results of their simulations in XML documents and also write scientific papers about their research work. The XML format offers a number of advantages for computational physics: clear markup of input data and results, standardised data formats, and easier exchange and archival stability of data. Concurrent editing of the documents containing the data results should be supported as simulations and the gathering of results can be performed in parallel by the members of the group. Documentation for the simulations can be edited and stored in XML or text documents. However, scientific papers should conform to different formats required for publication. Text documents that include formatting instructions cover most of the formats required for publication. For instance, RTF (Rich Text Format) and LaTex documents are text documents including formatting instructions. For the moment, we only consider collaborative editing on raw text documents, but in the future we are going to extend it to text documents that include different formatting instructions.

First consider the editing of XML documents and the case that two researchers concurrently edit the following part of an XML document.

```
<averages>
  <scalar_average name="Energy">
      <mean>-0.9469</mean><error>0.00362</error>
  </scalar_average>
</averages>
```

Assume they concurrently modify the values of the **mean** and **error** elements, with the values -0.9336 and 0.00299. The two changes should both be performed and the final version of the document should be

```
<averages>
  <scalar_average name="Energy">
      <mean>-0.9336</mean><error>0.00299</error>
  </scalar_average>
</averages>
```

In the CVS [1] or Subversion [3] systems merging is performed on a line by line basis with the basic unit of conflict therefore being the line. This means that the changes performed by two users are deemed to be in conflict if they refer to the same line and therefore the concurrent modification of the **mean** and **error** elements is detected as conflict. The user has then to manually choose one of the modifications. If conflicts would be defined at the level of elements both changes could be taken into consideration. Another case is when one user adds some spaces between the **mean** and **error** elements for reformatting purposes, while another user in parallel performs some changes to the **mean** element. Version control systems such as CVS and Subversion will detect conflict since the same line of the document has been modified, even though there is no semantic conflict. Again, such situations can be avoided if the document is structured into elements and separators and the resolution conflict is set at the level of the element. Situations may arise where a user would like to work exclusively on part of a document. The possibility of locking parts of an XML document before an update procedure is performed is not offered by existing version control systems.

Let us analyse next how flexible granularity and policies for the resolution of conflicts could help users in the collaborative editing process. Consider the example of two PhD students from the computational physics group writing a research paper together with their professor. At the beginning, they decide on the structure of the paper and divide the work of writing sections. Initially, after writing different sections, their work is easily merged because the parts that they have been working on do not overlap. Even though they have been assigned separate parts of the document to work on, some parts of the document such as the bibliography or the introduction may be edited together. Moreover, at a later stage, the sections written by one of the authors will be read by the other authors. In early stages of writing the paper, the maximum number of modifications performed in parallel should be kept. In this case, defining the conflict at the word level would be appropriate, i.e. conflict is detected only if modifications have been performed on the same word. But, at a later stage when changes are critical, the conflict granularity can be set at the paragraph level. This means that if two modifications have been performed in the same paragraph, the author committing the changes has to carefully read the two versions of the paragraph and decide which version to keep. Suppose that each version in the repository is associated with the user who committed that version. In the case that the last version from the repository was committed by the professor, the students might choose to synchronise their local workspaces in accordance with the automatic policy of keeping the changes from the repository in the case of a conflict. In this way, in the case of conflict, the changes of the professor included in the last version in the repository are considered rather than the changes of the students.

As seen from the above examples, there is a need to adopt a flexible means of defining conflicts, as opposed to the fixed unit of conflict (the line) adopted by version control systems such as CVS and Subversion. We propose an approach that allows conflicts to be defined using semantic units corresponding to the structure of the document, such as paragraph, sentence or word in the case of text documents or elements, attributes, separators, words and characters in the case of XML documents. Moreover, in our approach, we offer not only manual resolution for conflicts, but also other automatic resolution policies, such as to keep the changes in the repository or in the local workspace in the case of conflict.

Another disadvantage of existing version control systems such as CVS and Subversion is the fact that they adopt state-based merging where only the information about the states of the documents and no information about the evolution of one state into another is used. An operation-based merging approach [15, 10] keeps information about the evolution of one document state into another in a buffer containing a history of the operations performed between the two states of the document. Merging is done by executing the operations performed on a copy of the document onto the other copy of the document to be merged. In contrast to the state-based approach, the operation-based approach does not require documents to be transferred over the network between the local workspaces and the repository. Moreover, no complex differentiation algorithms for XML [17, 2, 9] or diff [14] for text have to be applied in order to compute the delta between the documents. Therefore, the responsiveness of the system is better in the operation-based approach. Merging based on operations also offers better support for conflict resolution by having the possibility of tracking user operations. In the case of operation-based merging, when a conflict occurs, the operation causing the conflict is presented in the context in which it was originally performed. In the state-based merging approach, the conflicts are presented in the order in which they occur within the final structure of the object. For instance, CVS and Subversion present the conflicts in the line order of the final document, the state of a line possibly incorporating the effect of more than one conflicting operation.

In this paper, we propose a merging approach based on the transformation of operations representing the changes performed during editing. By adopting a tree model of the document, different semantic units can be associated to the document levels and the approach offers a flexible way of defining and resolving conflicts. Our approach is general for any document conforming to a hierarchical structure and we show how it can be applied to both text and XML documents.

In what follows we are going to give a very short overview of the existing approaches for the merging of both text and XML documents.

An operation-based merging approach that uses a flexible way of defining conflicts has been used in FORCE [15]. However, the FORCE approach assumes a linear representation of the document, the operations being defined on strings and not taking into account the structure of the document. Another approach that uses the principle of transformation of the operations has been proposed in [11]. However, for the merging of the text documents, the authors proposed using a fixed working unit, i.e. the block unit consisting of several lines of text.

By using a hierarchical model of documents, not only can conflicts be detected and handled in a flexible way, but also the efficiency in terms of the number of transformations performed is improved compared to approaches that use a linear representation of documents, as shown in [8, 6] and shortly explained in what follows. The existing operation-based linear merging algorithms maintain a single log in the local workspace where the locally executed operations are kept. When the operations from the repository need to be integrated in turn into the local log, the entire local log has to be scanned and transformations need to be performed even though the changes refer to completely different sections of the document and do not interfere with each other. In our approach, we keep the log distributed throughout the tree. When an operation from the repository is integrated into the local workspace, only those local logs that are distributed along a certain path in the tree are spanned and transformations performed. The same reduction in the number of transformations is achieved when the operations from the local workspace have to be transformed against the operations from the repository in order to compute the new difference to be kept on the repository. Our merging algorithm recursively applies over the different document levels any existing merging algorithm relying on the linear structure of the document.

A flexible object framework that allows the definition of the merge policy based on a particular application was presented in [13]. The objects subject to the collaboration are structured and therefore semantic fine-grained policies for merging can be specified. A merge matrix defines the merge functions for the possible set of operations. The approach proposes different policies for merging, but does not specify an ordering of concurrent operations, such as the order of execution of two insert operations or an insert and delete. The approach does not describe how the difference between two versions of the hierarchical documents is generated. In our approach, we dealt with both the generation of differences between document versions and the handling of conflicts.

Some state-based approaches for merging XML documents have been proposed in [17, 2, 9]. In contrast, our approach is operation-based and we previously highlighted the advantages of merging based on operations compared to state-based merging.

Another operational-transformation approach for merging hierarchical documents, such as XML and CRC (Class, Responsibility, Collaboration) documents, has been proposed in [12]. The environment provides the user with a graphical interface which allows operations to be performed such as the creation and deletion of a new node, the creation and deletion of a certain attribute and the modification of an attribute. By using the graphical interface, no customised formatting for the elements can be used. Modification of a node involves the deletion of the node and the insertion of a new node containing the modified value. Moreover, for text nodes, a lower granularity such as words or characters does not exist. Our approach offers a more natural way of editing XML documents, as we provide a text interface. We have chosen to rather add some additional logic to the editor to ensure well-formed documents than limit the user with a graphical interface. Moreover, our approach achieves better efficiency since the log of operations is distributed throughout the tree rather than being linear.

3   Model of the Document

We now present our model for text and XML documents and the particular issues concerning consistency maintenance during the editing of well-formed XML documents as defined by W3C. We mention that we did not consider issues of checking the validity during collaborative editing of XML documents according to DTD (Document Type Definition) or XML Schema.

We model a text document as being composed of a set of paragraphs, each paragraph containing a set of sentences, each sentence being formed by a set of words and each word containing a set of characters. In this way, the conflicts can be defined and resolved at different granularity levels, corresponding to the document levels (paragraph, sentence, word and character). For instance, a conflict can be defined at the level of sentence, and, in this way, if two users concurrently modify a sentence, a conflict will be detected. Books, a more general form of text documents, also conform to a hierarchical model being formed by chapters, sections, paragraphs, sentences, words and characters.

XML, the popular format for marking up various kinds of data from web content to data used by applications, is also based on a tree model. We classified the nodes of the document into root nodes, processing nodes, element nodes, attribute nodes, word nodes and separator nodes in order that various conflict rules can be defined. A conflict could then be defined, for example, for the case that two users perform operations on the same word node or for the case that users concurrently modify the same attribute node.

When editing XML content, we encounter problems which do not occur when working with text. Consider the case that a user edits an XML document, e.g. by adding the line '`<test>hello world</test>`' character by character. In this way, the XML document will not be well-formed until the closing tag is completed. The editor should provide support to insert complete elements, so that the operations can be tracked unambiguously at any time in the editing process. Our editor offers auto-completeness of elements. For instance, every time the user inserts a '`<`' character, the insertion of '`<></>`' is performed. Of course an empty tag, such as '`<></>`' is not a valid XML element, but at least it allows the desired operation of creating a new element to be addressed in a valid way.

Additional rules for the deletion of characters have to be provided. A user should be prevented from deleting parts of the structure of an element, such as the begin or end tag, unless the whole element is deleted. For instance, the user cannot delete '`</test>`' from an element '`<test>hello world</test>`'. Another issue regarding the editing of elements is the two different forms that an empty element can take: the form containing both the opening and closing tags such as '`<test></test>`', or the form of an empty element such as '`<test/>`' containing only the closing tag meaning that no further child elements are defined. The user is prevented from directly deleting the closing tag ('`</test>`'). Instead the user can insert a '/' character at the end of the starting tag ('`<test>`' ⇒ '`<test/>`') in order to tell the system that the element should be transformed into an empty element containing only a closing tag. The operation is not performed if the element contains other *child nodes*. On the other hand, the deletion of the '/' character in an empty element leads to the creation of an element containing a begin and end tag.

In the remainder of this section, we discuss detailed handling of each type of node that we used to structure XML documents. The *root node* is a special node representing the virtual root of the document that contains the nodes of the document. The user cannot perform operations on this node.

Processing nodes can be used to define processing instructions in the XML document such as '`<?xml version="1.0"?>`'. In order to keep the XML content valid and to allow insertions of whole elements, the insertion of processing nodes is restricted to complete processing nodes, i.e. '`<??>`' and the deletion of elements referring to the structure of a processing node can be done only if the whole processing node is deleted.

Element nodes represent XML element structures and they consist of an *element name*, as well as some optional *attribute* and *child nodes*. For the following element node '`<test att="val">hello world</test>`', the string '`test`' is the *element name*, '`att="val"`' is an *attribute node* and '`hello world`' is composed of three *child nodes*, namely two *word nodes* and one *separator node*. Similar to processing nodes, in order to ensure well-formed XML documents, only complete element nodes having the form '<></>' are allowed to be inserted, and the deletion of characters modifying the structure of the element node is restricted. Element nodes present a further issue as the element name in the opening and closing tag must be the same. As the update of the element name is an atomic operation, the editor alters the element names automatically whenever the user adds/removes some characters to/from the tag name.

The *attribute nodes* can be used either by the processing nodes or the element nodes and they basically consist of a single attribute string. To support the user, the editor will insert the '="" "' characters automatically whenever the user adds a new attribute.

The *separator nodes* are used to preserve the formatting of the *XML* document and they represent *white spaces* and *quotation marks*.

4   The Set of Operations

In this section, we present the set of operations used to describe the actions performed by users during the editing process of text and XML documents. The set of operations has been chosen to be as minimal as possible, but to allow the flexible definition and resolution of conflicts. Even if the sets of operations for describing the changes performed in the text and XML documents are different, the mechanism for consistency maintenance is the same, as we will show later.

For text editing, the set of operations that can be performed on the model of the document are *insert* and *delete* a semantic unit, such as paragraph, sentence, word or character.

For XML editing, the set of operations contains various forms of insert and delete operations. *INSERT_PROCESSING* inserts a new processing node. *INSERT_ELEMENT* inserts a new element node that can either be a child of the root node or a child of another element node. *INSERT_ATTRIBUTE* inserts a new attribute node that can either be added to a processing or element node. *INSERT_WORD* inserts a new word node that can be added to any element node. *INSERT_SEPARATOR* inserts a new separator node. In order to maintain well-formed documents, the user is not allowed to split the names of processing nodes, elements or attributes by means of separators. *INSERT_CHAR* inserts a character that can be added to update processing or element names, attributes and words. *INSERT_CLOSING_TAG* adds a closing tag. *DELETE_PROCESSING*, *DELETE_ELEMENT*, *DELETE_ATTRIBUTE*, *DELETE_WORD*, *DELETE_SEPARATOR*, *DELETE_CHAR* and *DELETE_CLOSING_TAG* are the delete operations corresponding to the set of insert operations.

5   Operational Transformation Approach

The operational transformation approach [4] is a suitable approach for merging that has been adopted for text documents conforming to a linear structure, such as a sequence of characters. The advantages for merging based on operations compared to state-based merging are, as already pointed out, improved responsiveness and the possibility of tracking the activity of the users.

The basic operations supplied by a configuration management tool are checkout, commit and update. A *checkout* operation creates a local working copy of the document from the repository. A *commit* operation creates in the repository a new version of the document based on the local copy, assuming that the repository does not contain a more recent version of the document than the local copy. An *update* operation performs the merging of the local copy of the document with the last version of that document stored in the repository.

We first illustrate the basic operation of the operational transformation mechanism, called inclusion transformation, by means of an example. The *Inclusion Transformation - IT(O_a, O_b)* transforms operation O_a against operation O_b such that the effect of O_b is included in O_a. Suppose the repository contains the document consisting of one sentence *"We present the merge."* and two users check-out this version of the document and perform some operations in their workspaces. Further, suppose $User_1$ performs the operation $O_{11}=InsertWord$ *("procedure",5)*. It is an operation intending to insert the word *"procedure"* at the end of the sentence, as the 5th word, in order to obtain *"We present the merge procedure."* Afterwards, $User_1$ commits the changes to the repository and the repository stores the list of operations performed by $User_1$ consisting of O_{11}. Concurrently, $User_2$ executes operation $O_{21}=InsertWord("next",2)$ of inserting the word *"next"* as the 2nd word into the sentence in order to obtain *"We next present the merge."* Before performing a commit, $User_2$ needs to update the local copy of the document. The operation O_{11} stored in the repository needs to be transformed in order to include the effect of operation O_{21}. Because operation O_{21} inserts a word before the insertion position of O_{11}, O_{11} needs to increase its position of insertion by 1. In this way the transformed operation will become an insert operation of the word *"procedure"* as the 6th word, the result being *"We next present the merge procedure."*

In what follows, we outline an existing operational transformation approach working on linear structures of documents. Afterwards we present the extension of the linear-based approach working for a hierarchical document structure.

5.1 Linear-Based Merging

First we describe the merging algorithm applied to a linear representation of documents as implemented in [15].

In the commit phase, the repository simply executes sequentially the operations performed in the local workspace in order to generate the state of the latest version from the repository. The list of operations sent to the repository represents the difference between the latest two versions of the document. In the checkout phase, in the case that the requested version number of the document equals the latest version number in the repository, the state of the latest version of the document is sent to the local workspace. In the case that the requested version number is less than the latest version number from the repository, the state of the document that is sent to the local workspace has to be computed. It is obtained by executing on the state of the latest version of the document the inverses of the operations that represent the deltas between the latest version in the repository and the requested version.

In the updating phase, the merging algorithm has to be performed between the list of operations executed in the local workspace LL and the list of operations DL representing the delta between the most recent version from the repository and the version that the local user started working on. Two basic steps have to be performed. The first step consists of transforming the remote operations from DL in order to include the effect of the local operations. These transformed operations are then executed on the local workspace. The second step consists of transforming the operations in LL in order to include the effects of the operations in DL, the list of the transformed local operations representing the new delta into the repository. In the case that operation O_i belonging to DL is in conflict with an operation from LL, O_i cannot be executed in the local workspace and it needs to be included into the delta as its inverse in order to cancel the effect of O_i. Moreover, all operations following it in the list DL need to exclude its effect.

In the case that a user wants to commit the local changes to the repository after performing an update, but in the meantime another user committed his changes to the repository, the first user has to perform a new update.

5.2 Hierarchical-Based Merging

The merging approach presented in the previous section works for a linear representation of documents, the operations being defined on strings, without taking into account the structure of the document. Structuring the document into different semantic units allows the possibility for the user to define and resolve the conflicts in a natural way. The approach that we present is a generalisation of the merging mechanism for a linear structure applied to a hierarchical structure.

The disadvantage of the linear-based merging approach is that all operations in the repository and in the local workspace are kept in a single buffer and, when an operation has to be integrated into one of these buffers, a large number of transformations have to be performed. In our approach, the history buffer is distributed throughout the tree, thereby making the merge more efficient as only certain paths in the tree have to be spanned and few transformations are performed. Using the same model, we were also able to improve the efficiency of real-time collaborative editing as reported in [8]. The model of the document is therefore extended by associating to each node in the hierarchical structure (excluding leaf nodes) a history buffer containing operations associated with its children nodes.

The structure of a text-based document is illustrated in Fig. 1. Each internal node of the tree has an associated history containing operations of insertion or deletion of child nodes.

For the XML document below, its tree representation is illustrated in Fig. 2. The attributes of a node are considered to be children of that node.

```
<?xml version="1.0"?>
<addressBook>
    <person id="p001">
        <name>Smith, John< /name>
    < /person>
< /addressBook>
```

Operations referring to processing nodes, elements, attributes, words and separators are added to the history associated with the parent node. Operations referring to characters are added to the history associated to the processing target, element names, attributes or words to which they belong. The operations referring to the closing tags are added to the history associated with the element to which they belong.

The *commit* and *checkout* phase follow the same principles as described for the linear representation of the documents, with the addition that, in the commit phase, the hierarchical representation of the history of the document is linearised using a breadth-first traversal of the tree. For instance, in the case of text editing, the first operations in the log will be the ones belonging to the paragraph logs, followed by the operations belonging to the sentence logs and finally the operations belonging to the word logs.

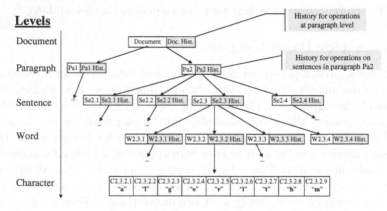

Fig. 1. Structure of a text document

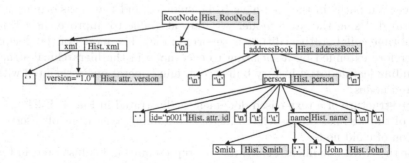

Fig. 2. Structure of an XML document

We now describe the update procedure that we apply for the case of text editing. The *update* procedure achieves the actual update of the local version of the hierarchical document with the changes that have been committed by other users to the repository and kept in linear order in the remote log. It has as its objective the computing of a new delta to be saved in the repository, i.e. the replacement of the local log associated with each node with a new one which includes the effects of all non-conflicting operations from the remote log and the execution of a modified version of the remote log on the local version of the document in order to update it to the version on the repository.

The *update* procedure is repeatedly applied to each level of the document starting from the document level. First the *remote level log* is constructed to contain those operations from the remote log that have the level identical with the level of the operations from the history buffer of the current node. The operations belonging to the remote level log are eliminated from the remote log. The basic merging procedure for linear structures is applied to merge the local log of the current node with the remote level log. As a result of the merging procedure, the new remote log representing the operations that need to be applied on the local document and the new local log representing the operations to be saved on the repository are computed. After the new remote log is applied locally, the operations from the remote log are transformed against the operations in the local log and are divided among the children of the current node. Afterwards, the merging procedure is recursively called for each child. A detailed description of the update procedure is presented in [5].

The same basic ideas underlying the merging of text documents have been applied to the merging of XML documents. While in the case of text editing, transformation functions have been defined between the operations of *insert* and *delete*, in the case of XML editing, transformation functions have been defined for all types of operations targeting processing nodes, elements, attributes, words, characters and separators.

6 Conflict Definition and Resolution

In this section, we show how our approach can be used to define and resolve conflicts in a flexible way.

Due to the tree model of the document, for the case of text editing, the conflicts can be defined at different granularity levels: paragraph, sentence, word or character. In our current implementation, we have defined that two operations are conflicting in the case that they modify the same semantic unit: paragraph, sentence, word or character. The semantic unit is indicated by the conflict level chosen by the user from the graphical interface. The conflicts can be visualised at the chosen granularity levels or at a higher level of granularity. For example, if the user chooses to work at the sentence level, it means that two concurrent operations modifying the same sentence are conflicting. The conflicts can be presented at the sentence level such that the user can choose between the two versions of the sentence. It may happen that in order to choose the right version, the user has to read the whole paragraph to which the sentence belongs, i.e. the user can choose to visualise the conflicts also in the context of the paragraph or at an upper level. Other rules for defining the conflicts could be implemented such as to check if some grammar rules are satisfied. This testing can easily be implemented using the semantic units defined by the hierarchical model.

We allow different policies for conflict resolution, such as automatic resolution where the local changes are kept in the case of a conflict or manual resolution, where the user can choose the modifications to be kept. Concerning manual resolution policies, the user can choose between the operation comparison and the conflict unit comparison policies. The operation comparison policy means that when two operations are in conflict, the user is presented with the effects of both operations and has to decide which of the effects to preserve. In the conflict unit comparison policy, the user has to choose between the set of all local operations and the set of all remote operations affecting the selected conflict unit (word, sentence or paragraph). The user is therefore presented with the two units that are in conflict. The policies for the resolution of conflicts can be specified in the graphical interface. The rules for the definition of conflict and the policies for conflict resolution can be specified by each user before an update is performed and they do not have to be uniquely defined for all users. Moreover, for different update steps, users can specify different definition and resolution merge policies.

In order to better understand how conflicts are defined and resolved, we are going to provide the following scenario. Suppose that two users are concurrently editing a document where the last paragraph consists of the sentence: *"Our algorithm applie a linear merging procedure"*. For simplicity, we are going to analyse the concurrent editing performed on this paragraph. The first user adds the character *"d"* at the end of the word *"applie"* and inserts the word *"recursively"* as illustrated in Fig. 3. The second user adds the character *"s"* at the end of the word *"applie"* and the new sentence *"The approach offers an increased efficiency."* as also shown in the figure.

Suppose that, after performing their modifications, the first user commits their changes to the repository. In order to commit to the repository, $User_2$ has to update their local version. In the case that $User_2$ has chosen the conflict level to be sentence and the policy for merging to be conflict unit comparison, the user is presented with the two sentences that are in conflict, as illustrated in Figure 3. Suppose that they choose the variant corresponding to their local version. After the second user performs a commit, the last paragraph of the new version of the document in the repository becomes: *"Our algorithm applies a linear merging procedure. **The approach offers an increased efficiency.**"*

In the case that the second user would have chosen the word level granularity, the conflict would have been detected for the word *"applie"*. The two words in conflict would be *"applied"* and *"applies"*. Suppose that the variant corresponding to their local version is chosen. After performing a commit, the last paragraph of the new version of the document in the repository becomes: *"Our algorithm applies **recursively** a linear merging procedure. **The approach offers an increased efficiency.**"*

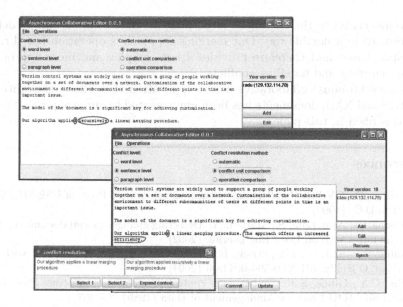

Fig. 3. Conflict resolution

In this example, we see that it is easy to define generic conflict rules involving different semantic units. We mention that, in the case of version control systems such as CVS and Subversion, when $User_2$ is updating the local copy, a conflict between the line *"Our algorithm applied recursively a linear merging procedure."* from the repository and the line *"Our algorithm applies a linear merging procedure. The approach offers an increased"* from the workspace will be detected, as well as the addition of the line *"efficiency."* $User_2$ would have to manually choose between the two conflicting lines and to add the additional line. Most probably, $User_2$ will decide to keep their changes and choose the line they edited, as well as adding the additional line. In order to obtain a combined effect of the changes, $User_2$ has to add manually the word *"recursively"* in the local version of the workspace.

For the case of XML documents, as for the case of text documents, the editor provides a *conflict resolution dialogue* when concurrent changes have been performed on the same granular unit, such as attribute, word or element. The user then needs to decide whether they want to keep the local or the remote version. In the case that a user wants to keep the local version of some parts of the XML document when a merging is performed, they might use the functionality to *lock* nodes of the document.

7   Conclusions

We have presented a customised approach for supporting collaboration over shared repositories containing both text and XML documents. We have shown that, by adopting a hierarchical model of the document, different semantic units can be associated to the document levels and therefore conflicts can be defined and resolved in a flexible way. Our merging approach is operation-based rather than state-based and therefore provides a less complex and more appropriate way of detecting and handling conflicts.

An asynchronous collaborative editor application that allows the editing of both text and XML documents has been implemented in our group based on the ideas described in this paper.

References

1. Berliner, B.: CVS II: Parallelizing software development. Proc. of USENIX, Washington D.C. (1990)
2. Cobena, G., Abiteboul, S., Marian, A.: Detecting changes in xml documents. Proc. of the Intl. Conf. on Data Engineering (2002)
3. Collins-Sussman, B., Fitzpatrick, B.W., Pilato, C.M.: Version Control with Subversion. O'Reilly, ISBN: 0-596-00448-6 (2004)
4. Ellis, C.A., Gibbs, S.J.: Concurrency control in groupware systems. Proc. of the ACM SIGMOD Conf. on Management of Data (1989) 399-407
5. Ignat, C.-L., Norrie, M.C.: Flexible Merging of Hierarchical Documents. Intl. Workshop on Collaborative Editing. GROUP'05, Sanibel Island, Florida (2005)
6. Ignat, C.-L., Norrie, M.C.: Operation-based Merging of Hierarchical Documents. Proc. of the CAiSE'05 Forum, Porto, Portugal (2005) 101-106
7. Ignat, C.-L., Norrie, M.C.: CoDoc: Multi-mode Collaboration over Documents. Proc. of the CAiSE'04, Riga, Latvia (2004) 580-594
8. Ignat, C.-L., Norrie, M.C.: Customisable Collaborative Editor Relying on treeOPT Algorithm. Proc. of ECSCW'03, Helsinki, Finland (2003) 315-334
9. La Fontaine, R.: A Delta Format for XML: Identifying Changes in XML Files and Representing the Changes in XML. XML Europe (2001)
10. Lippe, E., van Oosterom, N.: Operation-based merging. Proc. of the 5th ACM SIGSOFT Symposium on Software development environments (1992) 78-87
11. Molli, P., Oster, G., Skaf-Molli, H., Imine, A.: Using the transformational approach to build a safe and generic data synchronizer. Proc. of Group'03 (2003)
12. Molli, P., Skaf-Molli, H., Oster, G., Jourdain, S.: Sams: Synchronous, asynchronous, multi-synchronous environments. Proc. of CSCWD, Rio de Janeiro, Brazil (2002)
13. Munson, J.P., Dewan, P.: A flexible object merging framework. Proc. of ACM Conf. on CSCW (1994) 231-242
14. Myers, E.: An O(ND) difference algorithm and its variations. Algoritmica, 1(2) (1986) 251-266
15. Shen, H., Sun, C.: Flexible merging for asynchronous collaborative systems. Proc. of CoopIS/DOA/ODBASE (2002) 304-321
16. Vidot, N., Cart, M., Ferrié, J., Suleiman, M.: Copies convergence in a distributed real-time collaborative environment. Proc. of CSCW (2000) 171-180
17. Wang, Y., DeWitt, D.J., Cai, J.Y.: X-Diff: An Effective Change Detection Algorithm for XML Documents. Proc. of ICDE (2003)

Data Conceptualisation for Web-Based Data-Centred Application Design

Julien Vilz, Anne-France Brogneaux, Ravi Ramdoyal, Vincent Englebert, and Jean-Luc Hainaut

Laboratory of Database Application Engineering - University of Namur,
Rue Grandgagnage 21 - B-5000 Namur, Belgium
{jvi, afb, rra, ven, jlh}@info.fundp.ac.be

Abstract. The paper describes the conceptualisation process in the ReQuest approach, a wide-spectrum methodology for web-based information systems analysis and development. This methodology includes a strong involvement of end users in the requirement elicitation process by building prototype user interface fragments of the future application. The paper focuses on the analysis step of these fragments that yields a draft conceptual schema of the application domain. The analysis includes a tree-based representation of the fragments, the detection of shared subtrees through mining techniques, their normalisation and the derivation of the conceptual schema. A short description of a supporting tool is given.

1 Introduction

Despite a large offer of open source and proprietary IDEs for developing web-based applications, the problems of designing and developing quality applications at reasonable cost still are open issues, as testified by the poor quality and the high cost of many e-commerce applications.

The ReQuest framework is a wide spectrum tool-supported methodology for web-based data-centred applications analysis, development and maintenance intended to address these problems. It relies on five principles, namely, (1) intensive user involvement in the requirement collection and analysis phases [1], (2) the induction of the system behaviour from users scenarios [2], (3) the induction of the conceptual data structures from user interfaces [3], (4) the wrapper-based integration of existing data and services [4], and (5) automated validation and generation of major components of the target application. This research is part of ReQuest, a project funded by the Region Wallonne.

This paper concentrates on some important aspects of the database stream of the methodology, and more particularly on principles (1) and (3), that state that a large part of the conceptual data structures can be inferred from the user interface. Whereas existing approaches for modelling web information systems [5] usually produce presentation and navigational models from an existing conceptual schema built using the most traditional approach [6], this elaboration of the conceptual schema is a key part of the ReQuest approach.

E. Dubois and K. Pohl (Eds.): CAiSE 2006, LNCS 4001, pp. 205–219, 2006.
© Springer-Verlag Berlin Heidelberg 2006

According to principle 1, representative users are invited to sketch, through intuitive drawing tools [7], the user interface (comprising windows, dialog boxes, electronic forms and task description) to the intended system that best suits his/her needs. Though this *low-fidelity* description still has to be validated and modified with the help of design experts, it provides a rich description from which the most important components of the database schema can be extracted.

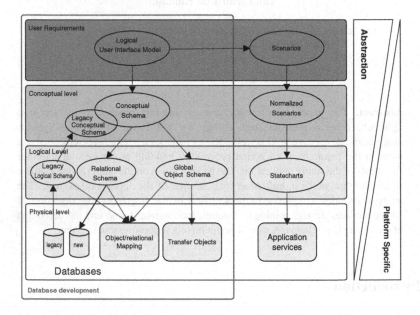

Fig. 1. The ReQuest framework as an MDE-compliant approach. The left area of the schema represents the products of the database development stream. Arrows express derivation processes between design products and artefacts.

Fig. 1 shows the part of the ReQuest framework that copes with database building. The design and development of the application services (behavioural aspects) are only suggested at the right part of the schema while the user interface development (interaction aspects) is not shown.

In the ReQuest approach, prototype interfaces sketched by users are translated into a *Logical user interface model* that, among others, expresses in an abstract way their underlying data structures. This logical interface model is then analysed in order to identify redundant data aggregates that the user naturally exchanges with the system, to reduce these potentially conflicting structures and to produce the conceptual schema. The *Scenario models* (right) and the kernel of the *Conceptual schema* of the database (left) are derived from the Logical interface model. From the latter, we derive the relational schema of the new database as well as the *Object schema* through which the application services will access the legacy and new data.

Integrating existing services is sketched for data only. The logical schema and the conceptual schemas of the *legacy database* are extracted through reverse engineering techniques [8]. The conceptual schema is compared with the global conceptual schema and the subset of the latter that is not covered by the legacy data is translated into the schema of the *new database*. At the physical level, legacy data access is ensured through a wrapper-based interface [4].

These derivation processes heavily rely on the transformational paradigm, which guarantees the propagation of specifications throughout the various levels of abstraction, from user requirements to the application code [9].

Analysing the information underlying corporate forms has long been a part of database design methodologies [6]. Extracting data structures from user interfaces has been proposed in [10] and eliciting knowledge from forms is described in [11]. The former proposal describes structural derivation rules, induction rules from sample data and an expert system that extracts a tentative conceptual schema from a set of forms. The latter proposals is based on a tree representation of forms that allows tree manipulation algorithms to be applied. In the database reverse engineering realm, [12] develops the FORE method to capture the knowledge buried in forms and to derive from it a conceptual object-oriented model.

The specific aspects of Web applications have lead to several specification methodologies that generally are extensions of standard approaches. Entity-relation models have been used and adapted in [13] and in [14] for instance, while [15] proposes an extension of the ORM model. The user-driven dynamic aspects of these systems has lead to enrich these models with behavioural specifications [16]. WebML [17] integrates most pertinent aspects of web applications and makes them available through models, modelling languages, processes and graphical tools. However, inference mechanisms such as those developed have not been developed so far.

Finally, the importance of user involvement in Web application design has been emphasised by, e.g., [18] and [19].

This paper is organised as follows. Section 2 describes the aspects of user interfaces that are relevant to database design and their mapping to the Logical interface model. Section 3 describes the conceptual extraction process, while Section 4 concludes the discussion.

2 User Interfaces as User Requirements Expression

The most abstract level the ReQuest approach is the *User requirements level*. From users viewpoint, electronic forms and dialog boxes appear to be the most natural form of system description. Their use and structure are familiar to end users [11] and the transition to a semantic model has been shown to be tractable [10]. Indeed:

- forms are more natural and intuitive than usual conceptual formalisms to express information requirements;
- the data structures contained in each form can be seen as a user view of the (future) conceptual schema of a database;
- finally, since a form is a kind of physical implementation of a part of the conceptual schema, database reverse engineering techniques can be used to recover that part of the schema [8].

The information on the components of user interfaces, such as the type of the component, explicit labels, semantic names, value type, value size, sample data, default value, and dynamic links, is exploited in two ways.

First, it is analysed to extract *user objects* that are natural data component aggregates that appear in forms. The latter are then transformed into the conceptual schema of the future database. Discovering the semantic of the user objects is similar to a reverse engineering process applied to the underlying data structures of the forms.

Secondly, it is used to specify the task model and to develop and generate the actual user interface of the target application. These aspects are ignored in this paper.

The input of the conceptualisation process is the Logical user interface model, which is extracted from the physical code of the prototype interface. In the ReQuest approach, it consists of a tree representation of restricted web forms.

2.1 User Interface Drawing

Strong involvement of end users in the requirements elicitation process is one of the major objectives of the ReQuest approach: this aspect is materialised by allowing the end users to design a prototype user interface of the future application. To this aim, selected users must have a good knowledge of the application domain and must be familiar with form-based application interface. They are briefly trained in the use of the interface drawing tool and are taught simple guidelines in user interface design. These guidelines aim to ease the automatic analysis of user interfaces and to reuse them in the final application . The guidelines target web-oriented systems. For instance they encourage users to avoid tables for layout purpose in web pages.

The user builds the interface either alone, or with the help of an experienced designer. Empirical studies have shown us that motivated users can quickly design quite valuable prototype interface [20].

Web pages combine specific content and reusable template material [21]. Therefore, the end user designs and annotates the different fragments of the interface according to the context (navigational information, domain application information as well as states of performed tasks), then assembles them to obtain the different complete web pages. Later on, the user can be asked to provide sample data as part of the specification process, which could notably lead to highlight functional dependencies [22].

2.2 Logical User Interface Model

The logical model of an interface comprises controls as well as input and output information for a task that will be performed by the target application. For each interface fragment drawn by the user, the corresponding tree-structured logical user interface model is created, following the translation rules of Table 1.

The data part of the logical interface model is a forest. Leaf nodes are labelled with the user name of the corresponding logical input or output interface components. The (hopefully) semantic name is either extracted from the form labels or explicitly provided by the user when drawing the interfaces. It identifies the concept handled by the component (for instance a *name* or an *address*).

A non-leaf node represents a logical container such as a table and group box. Its subtree gathers the data handled by the graphical components enclosed by this container.

The node representing the user interface fragment (the top container) is the root of the tree. Fig. 2 illustrates the modelling of two user interface fragments. Controls such as buttons add are ignored in this discussion.

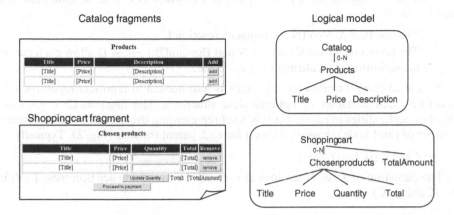

Fig. 2. The logical models of two user interface fragments. The data structures underlying each of them is expressed as a composition tree.

Tools have been developed to extract this model from user interface components written in XUL and XHTML. We have also extended these languages with custom properties to support the necessary annotations described in Section 2.1.

Table 1. Common widgets and their tree translation

Widget	Tree equivalent	Properties
Group box	Node whose children represent the elements contained in the group box.	name
Text input	Leaf node.	name, maximum length, value type, mandatory
Radio button set	Leaf which aggregates the radio buttons of the set.	name, value domain
Check box set	Leaf which aggregates the check boxes of the set.	name, value domain
Selection list	Leaf node.	name, value domain, multiple, mandatory
Table	Node whose children represent the elements contained in the table. The table is dynamic if its content is generated on demand	name, dynamic; if relevant, maximum length, value type, mandatory of the cells

2.3 Formal Definition of the Logical User Interface Model

Each node of a tree in a model is *labelled* with the properties extracted from the widgets, e.g., the semantic name, the size of the input data or the value domain of a selection list. Hence, the formal definition of this model is an extension of the definition of rooted labelled tree as defined in [23].

To cope with the properties of the data structure extracted from the user interface, the labelling function needs to be refined in order to distinguish the two following properties: the semantic name and the value domain of the data.

Therefore, we define the set *Att* of pairs N x D where N is a set of names and D a set of value domains.

- The function A: V$\to$ (N, D) replaces function L.
- The functions NameOf : *Att* $\to$ N and DomainOf : *Att* $\to$ D allow each part of the definition of an attribute to be accessed.

A new labelling function for the edges is also needed to represent repetitive data structures such as tables or optional data structures. The function C: E $\to$ *Card* attaches cardinalities to edges. *Card* is a set representing the minimum and maximum number of child node instances allowed for each parent instance (Fig. 2). Typically,

- *Card* = {0-1, 1-1, 0-N}

The definition of a tree in our logical user interface model hence becomes: T (V, E, Att, Card, A, C).

3 From the Logical User Interface Model to the Conceptual Schema

3.1 Searching for Domain Concepts

A domain concept can appear in several interface fragments. Since a user view describes a user object, we conclude that a user objects is made up of aggregates of domain objects that can appear in other user objects. Hence the idea to identify the subtrees that appear in more than one interface fragment of the logical interface model and to derive from them tentative domain concepts. We call them *shared subtrees*[1].

The basic procedure we will describe consists in (1) identifying the shared subtrees, (2) for each of them, removing all its instances from the source fragment, (3) representing the domain concept subtree by a standalone tree and (4) linking the modified source fragments to this tree. Moreover, the composition relationships that hold among shared subtrees in an interface tree is interpreted as semantic relationships between corresponding domain concepts.

The use of shared subtree limits the search for data structures to redundant tree structures. So a non-connex redundant group of nodes will not be identified in this approach, which can be extended by the use of wildcards in tree labels during the search, as in XML queries [24].

Subtree Definition. There are several types of subtrees, but the most suitable for our purpose are the *induced subtrees*. An induced subtree keeps the parent/child relationship of its source tree. Chi et Al. [25] define the *induced subtree* as follow: "For a tree T with vertex set V and edge set E, we say that a tree T' with vertex set V' and edge set E' is an *induced subtree* of T iff, (1) V' $\subseteq$ V, (2) E' $\subseteq$ E, (3) the labelling of V' and E' is preserved in T'. [...] Intuitively, an induced subtree T' of T can be obtained by repeatedly removing leaf nodes (or possibly the root node if it has only

---

[1] The standard name in the domain of tree mining is "frequent subtree".

one child) in T." Basically, an induced tree is a view on the conceptual schema to be discovered, that is, a subset of its objects.

Identifying Shared Subtrees. Comparing the subtrees that can be derived from the forest of a user interface can be done by *mining* the logical interface model for shared subtrees. Several algorithms have been developed to solve this complex problem [23]. We choose the algorithm *FreqT* [25] since it has a reasonable complexity[2], and the output of the algorithm identifies each occurrence of each shared subtree.

FreqT handles ordered induced subtrees. Since the order of sibling nodes is immaterial, we can, without any information loss, order them as required, for instance according to the lexicographic order on the set N used in the labelling function A.

The algorithm *FreqT* builds potential induced subtrees of the trees extracted from the interface model. These subtrees, also called pattern subtrees, are built using redundant labels. If it exists several occurrences of a pattern subtree in the input trees this pattern is used to create new patterns by adding nodes to it.

According to the definition of induced subtree, the labelling of the source tree must be preserved in T'. As we have redefined the labelling function in our logical user interface model, the equivalence between node labels must also be redefined.

Theoretically, two nodes v_i and v_k are declared identical if the set of input or output data instances in the widgets they represent are identical, or at least, if one set is a non empty part of the other one. However, since the logical interface model is extracted from *unpopulated* interfaces, we can only rely on structural and naming properties.

In the context of conceptualisation, we approximate $v_i = v_k$ with $n_i \cong n_k$ and $d_i \approx d_k$, as follows ($n_p = NameOf(A(v_p))$ and $d_p = DomainOf(A(v_p))$).

1. The *name similarity* relation "$\cong$" defines a non strict equality between names. Since the same domain concept can have different names in several interfaces according to the context, the name equality relation can be refined, for instance to cope with synonyms and homonyms using dictionaries or ontologies. We currently use the *Jaro-Winkler* metrics [26] to compare node names. With this approach, "Chosen products" is similar to "Product" with a distance of 0,68 (two identical strings have a distance of 1). String distance metrics allow to highlight similarly strings according to different criteria. The user validate or invalidate the discovered similarity. As we have a complete control on input trees, a more sophisticated approach has not been felt to be useful so far.

2. The *domain similarity* relation "$\approx$" is also defined as a non strict equality between domain values. It is verified whenever $d_i \subseteq d_k$ or $d_k \subseteq d_i$. This definition is driven by the fact that the logical user interface model does not always provide the precise domain values available for a specific widget. For instance, text fields can typically be used to input several data types such as names, numbers and dates. The user can specify the exact data type through annotations. Otherwise, the usual compatibility rules are used.

For instance, two user interface fragments include a field named "City", that, in the first fragment is defined by a predefined value list and in the second one as a 50

---

[2] $O(fmn)$ with f the number of frequent trees, m the number of nodes in the largest tree and n the number of nodes.

character string. If all the predefined values are no longer than 50, then both domains are considered similar. We do not use the edge labelling function C in the induced subtrees research, but this information will be used later.

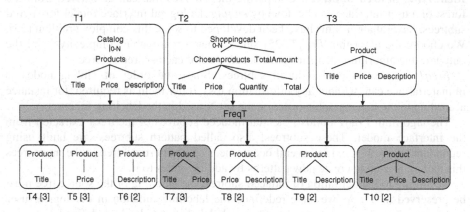

Fig. 3. *FreqT* extracts shared trees T4 to T10 from input trees T1 to T3. The number between brackets indicate in how many input trees the shared tree has been found.

Results of the Induced Subtrees Search. Algorithm *FreqT* produces a list of subtree patterns with the references of the instances that appear in the logical model. According to our goal, which is to isolate domain concepts in user interfaces, we will see that not all results are pertinent.

Fig. 3 shows the results of *FreqT* on the input trees T1, T2 and T3. For simplicity, we only keep the shared subtrees that have more than one node. We get seven subtrees T4 to T10, that all describe the potential domain concept "Product". We first observe that keeping only the *maximal induced subtrees*, i.e., those which are not an induced subtree of another result, is not necessarily appropriate. For instance the maximal induced subtree T10 is shared by two input trees only, while T7 is shared by all of them. We keep T7 and T10 and discard the other ones.

To keep only a set of results that will be useful for the transformation of trees into conceptual structures, we apply the following filter on *FreqT* results. Let

- T_i and T_k be shared subtrees resulting from application of *FreqT*.
- T_i be an induced subtree of T_k.
- I_i be the set of trees in which T_i appears (same for I_k and T_k).

T_i is retained if I_i and I_k are distinct tree sets, so that there is at least a tree in which either T_i or T_k appear.

Applying this filter yields subtrees T7 and T10. This result highlights links between potential domain concepts "Catalog", "Shopping cart" and "Product".

3.2 Representing Trees in the Entity-Relationship Model

Since most database designers are not familiar with abstract graphs, we express the data structures of the logical interface models in a wide-spectrum variant of the popular

Entity-relationship model, called the Generic ER model (GER), that encompasses logical and conceptual structures [9, 27]. In this section, we show how logical interface models and induced subtrees can be described in the GER.

In [27], the GER has been given a *non first normal form* (N1NF) interpretation. Trees as we defined them also are N1NF data structure. For instance,

Shopping Cart (Chosen products[0-N](Title, Price, Quantity, Total), TotalAmount)

is a N1NF relation schema expressing both the tree and the entity type of Fig. 4.

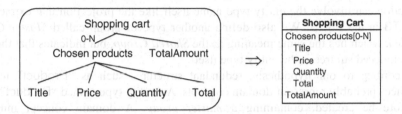

Fig. 4. Expressing a tree as an entity types with compound and/or multivalued attributes

Representing Shared Subtrees. The usual way to extract attributes from a relation is by *projection*. The projection of a N1NF relation seems the natural way to define a subtree from a source tree, provided this operator can still yield a N1NF relation. The standard projection produces *bottom-up subtrees*, as defined in [23]: "A bottom-up subtree T' of T is obtained by taking a vertex v of T together with all the descendants of v and their corresponding edges". For instance, in Fig. 3, we can extract subtree T10 from T1 written as N1FN relation using a projection[3]:

- T10(Products(Price, Title, Description))
- T1(Catalog (Products[0-N](Price, Title, Description))
- T10(Products(Price, Title, Description)) = T1[Products]

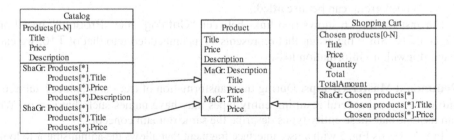

Fig. 5. Induced subtrees in entity types

---

[3] We only use an informal notation that is sufficient for the needs of the presentation. Notation R[I] specifies the projection of relation R on subset I of its attributes. More detail can be found in [15].

However, this operator cannot extract T7 from T1. So we define the *induced projection* to specify induced subtrees by indicating subtrees instead of mere node names. This projection is denoted by a N1FN relation representing the induced subtree to isolate and surrounded by "[ ]".

- T7(Product (Title, Price)) = T1 [Products(Title, Price)]

In the GER, the induced projection is represented by a group of attributes called *Shared Group* (ShaGr) in the third compartment of the representation of an entity type. The group gathers all the attributes involved in the projection[4]. Some induced projection can involve the entity type name itself like the projection that extracts T7 from T3 in the Fig. 3. We also define another type of group called *Master Group* (MaGr), which has the same meaning as the *Shared Group*, but indicates that the root of the induced subtree is the entity type itself.

According to our hypothesis, redundant structures such as "Product" in user interfaces probably represent domain concepts. An entity type named "Product" must therefore be created, containing a *master group*. A domain concept must be represented by one entity type, so that a shared subtree will be represented by one *master group* and one or more *shared groups*.

Fig. 5 represents trees T1, T2 and T3 of Fig. 3 by entity types Catalog, Shopping Cart and Product, and induced subtrees T7 and T10 by shared and master groups. An arrow is drawn from each shared group to its corresponding master group. Conceptually, this link is similar to a N1NF foreign key.

3.3 Logical Model Normalisation

The resulting schema must be processed in order to discard redundant specifications. We describe two techniques : embedded shared groups and redundant master groups.

Embedded Shared Groups. A shared group is embedded into another one when its components also are part of the latter. If they reference the same master group, then the embedded group can be discarded.

For instance Fig. 6 shows two links between "Catalog" and "Product", based on T7 and T10. Since the group that represents T7 is embedded into that of T10, we can discard it with no information loss.

Redundant Master Groups. During the transformation of trees and induced subtrees into entity types, several resulting entity types may have names such that $n_i \cong n_k$. We can assume that these entity types describe the same domain concept.

Fig. 6 extends Fig. 5 with a user interface fragment that allows the administrator to look at the "Shopping Cart" of the connected users. This fragment is called "Shopping cart (Administration)". If we assume that "Shopping cart (Administration)" $\cong$ "Shopping cart", there exists a shared induced subtree having "Shopping cart" as its root. That induced subtree is represented in both entity types by a *master group*.

---

[4] Symbol [*] means that the property holds for each instance of the parent instance.

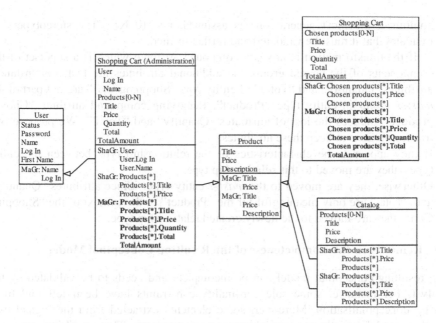

Fig. 6. An unnormalised schema that still includes redundant structures

As only one *master group* may exist for each shared induced subtree, we merge the entity types in which these groups have the *master* status[5]. Entity types integration keeps the *shared groups* of all merged entity types.

The integration consists in adding all the attributes which are not concerned with the redundant *Master Group* into the resulting entity type, as well as the groups involving those attributes. In the example Fig. 6, "User", "Login", "Name" will be added to the new entity type "Shopping Cart", as well as the group linked with the entity type "User".

3.4 Logical to Conceptual Transformation

The representation of trees and shared subtrees provides us with a logical Entity-relationship schema from which a pure conceptual schema must be extracted. This process is a variant of the conceptualisation phase of reverse engineering, through which one attempts to recover the conceptual origin of each technical construct. Transformational techniques have proved particularly powerful to carry out this process. The process is based on three main transformations.

1. Each shared group and its attributes are transformed into relationship type R with the entity type of the Master group. The transformation removes an attribute only if it does not appear in another, still unprocessed, *shared group*. The cardinality constraints of the roles of R are computed from the cardinalities of the attribute in the highest level of the projection that defines the shared group. When the cardinalities of a role cannot be

---

[5] In the future, less strict relationships will be considered, such IS-A relations.

computed, the most general one is assumed, i.e., [0–N]. The stereotype[6] "?" indicates that it must be validated and further refined.

If the transformation removes a compound attribute which is a superset of the components of the shared group, the additional attributes are lost. For instance, attributes "Quantity" and "Total" of entity type "Shopping Cart" are not part of the *master group* in entity type "Product". Removing compound attribute "Chosen products" induces the loss of attributes "Quantity" and "Total". We propose two transformations to keep these attributes.

2. If they appear to be characteristics of the relationship type between the entity types, they are moved to this relationship type.
3. Otherwise, they are moved to the *master* entity type. Since attributes "Quantity" and "Total" are only meaningful for the "Product" in the context of the "Shopping Cart", they are moved to the newly created relationship type.

3.5 Remarks on the Completeness of the Resulting Conceptual Model

The resulting conceptual model can be incomplete and needs to be validated by the analyst. For instance, some role cardinality constraints have been left undefined during conceptualisation. Moreover, some elements extracted from the logical user interface model actually are derived or computed attributes. These attributes appear in the resulting conceptual model but need not be made persistent and can be discarded.

This emphasises the fact that user interfaces analysis, despite its importance, must be complemented by other, more traditional, information sources when required. User interviews and legacy application observation and analysis are popular techniques for requirement elicitation that can be used to validate and complete the conceptual schema obtained so far.

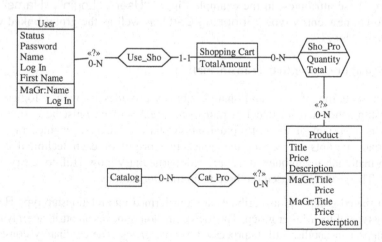

Fig. 7. Partially conceptualised data structures

---

[6] GER stereotype has the same meaning (or absence thereof) as UML's.

4 Conclusions

The process described in this paper is one of the components of the ReQuest framework, the goal of which is to develop a comprehensive environment to specify and generate in a semi-automated way data-intensive applications.

Our contribution to database design in complex web-based application development is threefold. First, it allows a more natural and more intensive user involvement[7] in requirement definition. Second, it gives form-based analysis a clean 3-step architecture derived from database reverse engineering methodologies: (1) physical structure extraction, through XHTML and XUL form parsing, (2) structural enrichment by eliciting shared subtrees through tree mining and normalisation techniques and (3) semantic interpretation or - conceptualisation - of the enriched structures through transformational techniques. Third, specific tools, integrated in the DB-MAIN environment, that support the three steps of this methodology have been developed. In this way, form-based analysis can be integrated in more general tool-supported database design methodologies.

Three case studies have been designed to validate the ReQuest framework, including the requirement elicitation and analysis process. The first one is a *training session management system* with 10 user interface fragments and a schema of 15 entity types. The second one is a *real estate advertising platform* for which 10 user interface fragments have been drawn. The resulting conceptual schema comprises 21 entity types. The last one is a classical *web sales platform* that comprises 20 user interface fragments translating into 4 entity types. Though these studies are recent and limited, we already have drawn interesting information.

1. *Size estimation.* There is no relation between the number of interface fragments and the size of the schema.
2. *Scalability.* The approach is more scalable than expected, but for unexpected reason! Indeed, it appears that a subsystem of 15-30 interface fragments constitutes the ideal work package. This size is manageable in a short time by a motivated user (1-3 days), the result can be visually validated by an expert designer in 2-4 days and the algorithms that extract the redundant substructures and derive the conceptual schemas are still fast despite their complexity (1-5 seconds for *FreqT*). Moreover, the resulting conceptual structures are fairly stable, that is, additional input interface fragments do not significantly improve the quality of the result. Larger systems can be split into subsystems whose conceptual schemas are then integrated through traditional methods [28].
3. *Completeness.* For each case study, the result has been compared with a reference schema elaborated with other methods. It appears that the only missing concepts are processed by well identified non-interactive workflows. Therefore the user model was complete in all cases.

---

[7] The idea to imply end users in the specification of web-based application (e.g., a business-to-customer application) may seem somewhat paradoxical since the real users (the hopefully thousands of customers) cannot be asked to draw their preferred interface. In such cases, representative corporate employees, for instance from the marketing department, can be substituted for these *undefinable* users.

4. *Soundness*. Some concepts were absent from the reference schema. They all were derivable attributes that were erroneously considered basic data by the user. Helping him/her to refine the definition of the fields quickly solved the problems.
5. *Quality*. The resulting schemas were as good as unnormalised schemas extracted through standard techniques. For instance, some ISA relations were left in their physical translation (one-to-one relationship type for instance) and needed further processing. This process is standard and is not specific to our approach.
6. *Acceptance*. The users enjoined being involved in the building of their future tool. In addition, the resulting schema were quite well accepted, since it merely translated in another formalism the information requirements of the users.

Future work will mainly be devoted to (1) enrich the conceptual schema, e.g., by exploiting the dynamic links and information transfer between forms, (2) enhance the validation process through paraphrasing and prototyping techniques, (3) introduce induction reasoning to exploit sample data provided by users.

References

1. The British Computer Society & Royal Academy of Engineering: *The Challenges of Complex IT Projects*. Published by the Royal Academy of Engineering (2004)
2. Damas, C., Lambeau, B., Dupont, P., van Lamsweerde, A. : Generating Annotated Behavior Models from End-User Scenarios, to appear in *IEEE Transactions on Software Engineering*, Special Issue on Interaction and State-based Modeling, 2006.
3. Brogneaux, A-F., Ramdoyal, R., Vilz, J., Hainaut, J.-L.: Deriving User-requirements From Human-Computer Interfaces, in *Proc. of 23rd IASTED Int. Conf.*, Innsbruck, Austria, Feb. 2005.
4. Thiran Ph., Hainaut, J-L., Houben, G-J., Benslimane, D.: Wrapper-based Evolution of Legacy Information Systems, to appear in *ACM Transactions on Software Engineering and Methodology* (TOSEM), 2006.
5. Schewe, K. D., Thalheim, B.: Conceptual modelling of web information systems. *Data Knowl. Eng.* 54(2): 147-188 (2005)
6. Batini, C., Ceri, S., & Navathe, S., B. *Conceptual Database Design*, Benjamin/Cummings. 1992
7. Coyette, J. Vanderdonckt, A.: Sketching Tool for Designing Anyuser Anyplatform Anyplatform, Anywhere User Interfaces, in *Proc. of the 10th IFIP TC 13 Conf. On Human Computer Interaction Interact '05*, Roma, Italy, September 2005.
8. Hainaut, J.-L.: *Introduction to Database Reverse Engineering*, 3rd Edition, LIBD Publish., Namur, 2002 [http://www.info.fundp.ac.be/~dbm/publication/2002/DBRE-2002.pdf]
9. Hainaut, J.-L.: Transformation-based Database Engineering, Chapter in *Transformation of Knowledge, Information and Data: Theory and Applications*, P. van Bommel Editor, IDEA Group (2005).
10. Rollinson, S. R., Roberts, S. A.: Formalizing the Informational Content of Database User Interfaces. Conceptual Modeling - ER'98, in *Proc. of the 17th International Conference on Conceptual Modeling*, Springer-Verlag, (1998) 65-77
11. Choobineh, J., Mannino, M. V., Tseng, V. P.: A Form-Based Approach for Database Analysis and Design. *Com. of the ACM*, Vol. 35, N°2, (February 1992) 108-120
12. Lee, H., Yoo, C.: A Form-driven Object-oriented Reverse Engineering Methodology, *Information Systems*, Vol. 25, No. 3, Elsevier, 2000

13. Ceri, S., Fraternali, P., Bongio, A.: Web Modeling Language (WebML): a modeling language for designing, Web sites. WWW9/Computer Networks 33(1-6): 137-157 (2000)
14. Conallen, J.: Building Web Applications with UML. Addison Wesley (Object Technology Series), 2000.
15. Oaks, P., ter Hofstede, A., H., M., Edmond, D. , Spork, M.: Extending conceptual models for web based applications, in *Proc. of ER Conference 2003*, Springer
16. Brambilla, M.: Extending hypertext conceptual models with process-oriented primitives, in *Proc. ER Conference* 2003, Springer
17. *WebML*, [http://webml.org/]
18. Cato, J.: User-Centered Web Design, Addison-Wesley, 2001.
19. Escalona, M., Koch, N., Requirements Engineering for Web Applications – A Comparative Study, in *Web Engineering Journal*, Vol. 2, No. 3, 2004
20. Jakob Nielsen : User Interface directions for the Web, in *Com. of the ACM*, Volume 42, Number 1 (1999), pp 65-72.
21. Gibson, D., Punera, K., Tomkins, A. : *The Volume and Evolution of Web Page Templates*, David Gibson Center (2005).
22. Collopy, E., Levene, M., Evolving Example Relations to Satisfy Functional Dependencies, in *Issues and Applications of Database Technology*, 1998, pp. 440-447.
23. Chi, Y., Nijssen, Y., Muntz, R., Frequent Subtree Mining - An Overview. *Fundamenta Informaticae* XXI. IOS Press (2001) 1001–1038
24. Yang, L., Lee, M., Hsu, W., Guo, X.: 2PXMiner - An Efficient Two Pass Mining of Frequent XML Query Patterns. In *Proc. of the SIGKDD2004*. 2004.
25. Asai, T., Abe, K., Kawasoe, S., Arimura, H., Sakamoto, H., Arikawa, S.: Efficient Sub-structure Discovery from Large Semi-structured Data. In *Proc. of the 2nd Annual SIAM Symposium on Data Mining*, 2002.
26. Cohen, W. W., Ravikumar, P., Fienberg, S. E.: A comparison of string distance metrics for name-matching tasks. In *Proc. of the IJCAI-2003*. 2003
27. Hainaut, J.-L.: Entity-Relationship models: formal specification and comparison, In *Proc. of the 9th Int. Conf. on the Entity-Relationship Approach*, 1991.
28. Spaccapietra, S., Parent, C., Dupont,Y.: Model independent assertions for integration of heterogeneous schemas. in *VLDB Journal*, 1 (1992) 81–126

Service Composition

Resolving Underconstrained and Overconstrained Systems of Conjunctive Constraints for Service Requests

Muhammed J. Al-Muhammed* and David W. Embley*

Department of Computer Science,
Brigham Young University, Provo, Utah 84602, USA

Abstract. Given a service request such as scheduling an appointment or purchasing a product, it is possible that the invocation of the service results in too many solutions that all satisfy the constraints of the request or in no solution that satisfies all the constraints. When the invocation results in too many solutions or no solution, a resolution process becomes necessary for agreeing on one of the solutions or finding some agreeable resolution. We address this problem by imposing an ordering over all solutions and over all near solutions. This ordering provides a way to select the best-m with dominated solutions or dominated near solutions eliminated. Further, we provide an expectation-based resolution process that can take the initiative and either elicit additional constraints or suggest which constraints should be relaxed. Experiments with our prototype implementation show that this resolution process correlates substantially with human behavior and thus can be effective in helping users reach an acceptable resolution for their service requests.

Keywords: Service requests, underconstrained systems of constraints, overconstrained systems of constraints, ordered solutions and near solutions, dominance, expectation-based resolution.

1 Introduction

We described in a previous paper [AMEL05] a system that allows users to specify service requests and invoke services. This approach is strongly based on conceptual modeling and supports a particular type of service whose invocation involves establishing an agreed-upon relationship in the conceptual model. Examples of these types of services include scheduling appointments, setting up meetings, selling and purchasing products, making travel arrangements, and many more.[1]

---

* Supported in part by the National Science Foundation under grants 0083127 and 0414644.

[1] We intend the word "service" to be thought of in accordance with its typical meaning—"an act of assistance or benefit." Technically, we define a very special type of service (as described herein). We do not intend our services to be thought of in other technical ways such as registering services with a broker so that they can be found by expressing their functionality in terms of inputs, outputs, and capabilities.

E. Dubois and K. Pohl (Eds.): CAiSE 2006, LNCS 4001, pp. 223–238, 2006.
© Springer-Verlag Berlin Heidelberg 2006

It is possible that the invocation of service requests for any of these services results in too many satisfying solutions or in no solution at all although there may be near solutions.

In our approach users can specify services such as the following request for scheduling an appointment with a dermatologist.

I want to see a dermatologist on the 20th, 1:00 PM or after. The dermatologist should be within 5 miles from my home and must accept my IHC insurance.

Our approach uses conceptual-model-based information extraction to map service requests to a domain ontology. This mapping transforms the service request into a formal representation, which consists of concepts along with relationships among these concepts and constraints over the values of these concepts in a domain ontology. Figure 1 shows the formal representation of the appointment request as a conjunctive predicate calculus statement—we added some comments prefixed with "//" to provide more readability and to correlate the request with the predicate calculus statement. To resolve the appointment request, the system tries to instantiate each variable in the formal representation with values such that all the constraints are satisfied. The values come from a databases associated with the domain ontology, or are extracted from the service request, or are obtained interactively from users.[2]

$//I$ want to see a dermatologist
$Appointment(x_0)$ is with $Dermatologist(x_1) \wedge Appointment(x_0)$ is for $Person(x_2)$

$//$on the 20th
$\wedge Appointment(x_0)$ is on $Date("the\ 20th")$

$//1{:}00\ PM$ or after
$\wedge Appointment(x_0)$ is at $Time(x_3) \wedge TimeAtOrAfter(x_3, "1{:}00")$

$//$within 5 miles from my home
$\wedge Dermatologist(x_1)$ is at $Address(x_4) \wedge Person(x_2)$ is at $Address(x_5)$
$\wedge LessThanOrEqual(DistanceBetween(x_4, x_5), "5")$

$//$accept my IHC insurance
$\wedge Dermatologist(x_1)$ accepts $Insurance("IHC")$

Fig. 1. The predicate calculus statement for the appointment request

A *solution* for a request is an instantiation for all the variables that satisfies all the constraints. A *near solution* is an instantiation for all the variables that satisfies a proper subset (maybe empty) of the constraints and, in a way to be made precise later, comes close to satisfying the constraints not (yet) satisfied. Ideally, our system would find just one solution or would find a handful of solutions from which a user could select a desired one. More typically, however,

---

[2] The details of producing formal representations and instantiating them are not the focus of this paper and can be found elsewhere [AMEL05].

	Date	Time	Distance
s_1	the 21th	1:00 PM	6 miles
s_2	the 22th	1:30 PM	8 miles
s_3	the 20th	2:20 PM	20 miles

Fig. 2. Near solutions for the appointment request

	Make	Price	Year	Mileage
s_1	Dodge	$13,999	2005	15,775 miles
s_2	Dodge	$13,999	2004	30,038 miles

Fig. 3. Solutions for the car purchase request

our system may return no solution or too many solutions. When our system returns no solution, the request is *overconstrained*, and when it returns too many solutions, the request is *underconstrained*.

A resolution for overconstrained requests is to offer the best-m near solutions. Figure 2 shows three near solutions for our appointment request. Both s_1 and s_2 violate the date and distance constraints at different degrees in the sense that s_1 is closer to the 20th and violates the distance constraint less than s_2. Consequently, it is reasonable to impose a greater penalty on s_2 than on s_1. Further, the penalty provides a way to recognize dominated near solutions. Near solution s_1 dominates near solution s_2 because s_1 has less of a penalty for each violated constraint. Penalties provide a way to offer the best-m near solutions by ordering the near solutions based on their penalties and discarding the dominated ones. Additionally, suggesting constraints for users to relax provides another way to offer the best-m near solutions. For instance, if prior appointment requests reveal that users are more likely to impose constraints on date and time than on distance, it makes sense to suggest that users relax constraints on distance. Thus, for example, the resolution process can suggest the relaxation of the constraint on distance and possibly offer s_3 as the best near solution in Figure 2.

A resolution for underconstrained requests is to offer the best-m solutions. Consider, for example, the following request for a car purchase.

I want to buy a Dodge, a 2002 or newer. The mileage should be less than 80,000, and the price should not be more than $15,000.

For this request, www.cars.com offered 168 solutions when probed in November 2005, two of which are in Figure 3. Presenting all the solutions or m arbitrarily chosen ones to users is not likely to be very helpful. A way to reduce the number of solutions and offer the best-m solutions is to elicit additional constraints. If prior car purchase requests reveal that users often impose constraints on the car model, for example, it makes sense that a resolution process elicits a constraint on the model of the car. In addition, some solutions satisfy constraints better than others. As Figure 3 shows, s_1 better satisfies the year constraint than s_2 because the car in s_1 is newer. Therefore, we can grant s_1 a reward for better satisfying the request. Further, the reward can provide a way to recognize dominated solutions. As Figure 3 shows, the solution s_2 is dominated by s_1 because the car in s_1 is newer and has less mileage although both have the same price. Rewards provide a way to offer the best-m solutions by ordering the solutions in a decreasing order based on their rewards and discarding the dominated ones.

This paper offers ways to handle underconstrained and overconstrained service requests. First, the paper offers an expectation-based process for eliciting additional constraints for underconstrained requests and for suggesting some constraints for users to relax for overconstrained requests. Second, the paper offers an ordering over solutions and an ordering over near solutions, and a selection mechanism based on Pareto optimality [Par97, Fel80], developed in the late 1800's, to choose the best-m, with dominated solutions or dominated near solutions discarded.

We present these contributions as follows. Section 2 discusses an extension to constraints that allows for ordering solutions based on the degree of satisfiability and for ordering near solutions based on how close they are to satisfying the constraints. For underconstrained requests, Section 3 introduces expectation declarations as domain knowledge and proposes an expectation-based process to select concepts for which to elicit constraints. In addition, we define an ordering of solutions based on the extension to constraint satisfaction introduced in Section 2 and use it along with Pareto optimality to select the best-m solutions. For overconstrained requests, Section 4 shows how to define an ordering over near solutions and use it along with Pareto optimality to select the best-m near solutions. It also introduces an expectation-based process to suggest constraints for users to relax. We evaluate our proposed techniques in Section 5, and give concluding remarks and directions for future work in Section 6.

2 Constraints

A *constraint* is an n-place predicate, which for a tuple t of n values evaluates to either *true* or *false* depending on whether t satisfies or violates the constraint. This *true-false* binary view of a constraint allows us to only differentiate tuples based on whether they satisfy or violate a constraint. Researchers have extended this view to differentiate between tuples that violate a constraint by assigning to these tuples increasing positive real numbers that represent different degrees of violation [LHL97, Arn02]. Although this extension allows for distinguishing between tuples that violate a constraint, it does not allow for distinguishing between tuples that satisfy a constraint because this extension lacks the notion of degree of satisfiability. A constraint evaluates to zero for all tuples that satisfy that constraint, which means all the tuples necessarily have the same degree of satisfiability. We, therefore, further extend the binary view to not only consider degree of violation, but also to consider degree of satisfiability by granting tuples increasing rewards based on how well they satisfy a constraint.

Definition 1. *Let C be an n-place constraint and let D_i be the domain of the ith place of C, $1 \leq i \leq n$. A constraint is a function $C : D_1 \times ... \times D_n \longrightarrow \mathcal{R}$ that* *maps a tuple $t = \langle v_1, \ldots, v_n \rangle \in D_1 \times \ldots \times D_n$ to a real number in $\mathcal{R}$. An evaluation of the constraint C on a tuple t is defined as $C(t) = \alpha$, where $\alpha \in \mathcal{R}^+ \cup \{0\}$, which is a positive real number $\mathcal{R}^+$ or zero, is the value of the evaluation if t satisfies C, and $C(t) = \beta$, where $\beta \in R^-$, which is a negative real number $\mathcal{R}^-$, is the value of the evaluation if t violates C.*

The value α in Definition 1 represents the *reward* granted to a tuple t for satisfying a constraint C. A higher value for the reward α denotes greater satisfaction. The value β represents the *penalty* imposed on a tuple t for violating the constraint. A lower negative value for α denotes a greater degree of violation. Observe that in Definition 1, we try to capture the intuitive idea behind a reward and a penalty by letting the reward be a non-negative real number (rewards are positive) and the penalty be a negative real number (penalties are negative).

Designers should make domain decisions about the amount of a reward α and a penalty β. For instance, in a car purchase domain, designers may give a greater reward for newer cars. Therefore, they may define the evaluation for a constraint on a year in which a car was made such as "a 2000 or later" as $\geq (y, 2000) = y - 2000$. Observe that a 2001 car has a reward of 1 and a 2002 car has a reward of 2, which means that a 2002 car has a greater satisfiability degree according to this evaluation. Also observe that a 1999 car has a penalty of -1 and a 1980 car has a penalty of -20, which means that a 1999 car has much less of a penalty than a 1980 car.

An evaluation function can also impose a fixed penalty when ordering between values is not obvious. As an example, a constraint of the form "Brand = Canon" on digital camera brands can be defined as

$$BrandEqual(x, ``Canon") = \begin{cases} 0, & \text{if } x = ``Canon"; \\ -1, & \text{otherwise} \end{cases}$$

We imposed a fixed penalty for any brand other than "Cannon", as Arnal suggested [Arn02], because it is not obvious how we can order penalties between brands other than "Cannon".

For equality constraints over which a penalty ordering is possible, designers can declare penalties. For instance, a designer may choose the evaluation for *EqualAppointmentTime(t, 10:00 AM)* to be $-(f(t) - f(10{:}00 \ AM))^2$, where f is a function that converts a time to a unitless number. For example, the time 2:15 PM, which is the military time 14:15, could be converted to the integer 1415. For illustration purposes, we have assumed that the designer has chosen to square the difference to give proportionally less of a penalty to times close to 10:00 AM.

3   Underconstrained Service Requests

Underconstrained service requests admit too many solutions. In this section, we discuss two ways to provide users with the best-m solutions out of n solutions. First, we propose an expectation-based elicitation process to elicit additional constraints and apply them to solutions. Applying additional constraints to solutions may reduce the number of solutions and may also make the resulting solutions more desirable [SL01, FPTV04]. Second, we propose an ordering over solutions based on our extension for constraints in Definition 1 along with Pareto optimality based on this ordering to select the best-m solutions.

3.1 Constraint Elicitation Using Expectations

We associate expectations with concepts of a domain ontology. An *expectation* is the probability that value(s) for a concept appear in a service request. The expectation is, therefore, a number in the interval $[0, 1]$, where the low and high extremes of the interval mean, respectively, that a value for the concept is not and is certainly expected to appear in a service request. Values in the open interval $(0, 1)$ represent varying degrees of expectations.

Domain ontology designers estimate the expectations associated with concepts. Although there may be several ways to estimate the expectations, we suggest two general ways. First, designers can estimate the expectation using their knowledge of the domain. Second, designers can analyze service requests in the domain of the ontology and count the frequency of appearance for each concept in the domain ontology. Further, this latter method leads to the possibility that the expectations can be adjusted as the system runs.

Unlike other approaches to constraint elicitation (e.g. [LHL97, SL01, PFK03]), which are built on an assumption that users can impose additional constraints if they review some examples of solutions, we let the resolution process take the initiative and suggest the concepts on which to impose constraints according to the associated expectations with these concepts. The intuitive idea is that the resolution process can order the concepts based on their associated expectations and make reasonable suggestions to users to constrain concept values, starting from the concept associated with the highest expectation for which there is, as of yet, no constraint.

The elicitation process terminates when one of the following three conditions holds. First, the most recent elicited constraint is unsatisfiable in which case the service request becomes overconstrained and the resolution process uses the techniques in Section 4 to handle this situation. Second, the solution space is reduced to m or fewer solutions, in which case the system offers these solutions to users to evaluate and choose one. Third, there is no other concept in the ordering of concepts associated with an expectation that exceeds a prespecified threshold.

To demonstrate the idea of constraint elicitation using expectations, note that the car purchase request in Section 1 does not specify a constraint on the model of the car. Assuming that the expectation associated with *Model*, say 0.6, is the highest among the unconstrained concepts and is above the threshold, say 0.5, the resolution process suggests that the user could impose a constraint on the model. If a user wishes to constrain *Model* to be "Stratus" the resolution process can restrict the solutions to Dodge Stratuses.

3.2 Selecting the Best-m Solutions

Our extension to the binary view of constraints (Definition 1) provides a way to impose an ordering over solutions based on rewards granted to each solution for satisfying the service request constraints. Let $S = \{s_1, \ldots, s_n\}$ be a set of solutions each of which satisfies every constraint in the set of constraints $C = \{C_1, \ldots, C_k\}$, which are imposed on a service request. The evaluation of the set of constraints C for a solution $s_i \in S$ returns a set of real numbers $\{C_1(s_i), \ldots, C_k(s_i)\}$, which are the rewards granted to s_i for satisfying the constraints.

Before computing an aggregate reward for a solution s_i over all constraints in C, we first divide each reward $C_j(s_i)$, $1 \leq j \leq k$, by $\max_{1 \leq i \leq n} C_j(s_i)$, the maximum reward value over all solutions for constraint C_j. This normalizes the rewards to the interval $[0, 1]$. The purpose of the normalization is to discard the relative effects of large magnitude rewards across different constraints and thus to make it unnecessary to correlate values across different constraints. Let us denote the set $\{C_1(s_i), \ldots, C_k(s_i)\}$ after doing the normalization by $C^* = \{C_1^*(s_i), \ldots, C_k^*(s_i)\}$. Researchers have suggested several ways to compute combined evaluations (see [MA04] for a thorough survey). We linearly combine rewards in C^* yielding a combined reward ρ for a solution s_i as follows:

$$\rho_{C^*}(s_i) = \sum_{j=1}^{k} C_j^*(s_i); \, for \; i = 1, \ldots, n.$$

Definition 2. *Let s_i and s_j be two solutions and $C = \{C_1, \ldots, C_k\}$ be a set of constraints. We say that s_i is better than or equivalent to s_j, $s_i \succeq_\rho s_j$, with respect to C if $\rho_{C^*}(s_i) \geq \rho_{C^*}(s_j)$.*

To demonstrate the idea of reward-based ordering, let us suppose that we have a set of constraints $C = \{\leq(mileage,\ "30,000\ miles"),\ \leq(price,\ "\$20,000")\}$ and two solutions $s_1 = \{mileage = "29,000\ miles",\ price = "\$19,000"\}$ and $s_2 = \{mileage = "29,900\ miles",\ price = "\$18,000"\}$, then designers might decide to grant a reward of 1000 for s_1 and of 100 for s_2 for satisfying the mileage constraint, and a reward of 1000 for s_1 and a reward of 2000 for s_2 for satisfying the price constraint. Given these rewards, we can normalize them to $[0, 1]$ by dividing the mileage rewards by 1000 and the price rewards by 2000, yielding the normalized rewards 1 and 0.1 for s_1 and s_2 respectively for satisfying the mileage constraint and the normalized rewards 0.5 and 1 for s_1 and s_2 respectively for satisfying the price constraint. Based on Definition 2, $s_1 \succeq_\rho s_2$ because $\rho_{C^*}(s_1) = 1.5$ and $\rho_{C^*}(s_2) = 1.1$.

The ordering $\succeq_\rho$ sorts the solutions according to their combined rewards from the solution with the highest combined reward to the lowest. (Any solutions with identical rewards appear in a random order within their own equality group.) Although this ordering does sort the solutions, it does not necessarily imply that the first m solutions are the best-m solutions. The sorting procedure considers only the combined rewards, but does not consider the rewards granted to the solutions for satisfying each individual constraint. The rewards of the individual constraints, $C_1, \ldots, C_k$, in C provide additional knowledge to differentiate among solutions based on Pareto optimality, which divides solutions into dominating and dominated solutions based on a dominance relation.

Definition 3. *Let* $C = \{C_1, \ldots, C_k\}$ *be a set of constraints and* $S = \{s_1, s_2, \ldots, s_n\}$ *be a set of solutions. Let* s_i, $s_j \in S$ *be any two distinct solutions, we say that* s_i *dominates* s_j *if* $\forall_{p \in \{1, \ldots, k\}} (C_p(s_i) \geq C_p(s_j))$ *and* $\exists_{q \in \{1, \ldots, k\}} (C_q(s_i) > C_q(s_j))$.

Definition 3 says that the solution s_i, which dominates s_j, has rewards from all the constraints that are at least equal to the rewards for s_j and for at least one of the constraints s_i has a strictly higher reward. Observe the that Definition 3 does not explicitly consider the combined reward $\rho_{C*}(s_k)$. However, the combined reward is implicit in this definition in the sense that a solution can never dominate another solution with a higher combined reward.

Definition 3 provides the basis for our variation of Pareto optimality, a concept which Pareto defined over a century ago [Par97].

Definition 4. *Let* $S = \{s_1, s_2, \ldots, s_n\}$ *be a set of solutions for a service request. A solution* $s_i \in S$ *is said to be Pareto optimal if there does not exist an* $s_j \in S$ *such that* s_j *dominates* s_i.

The key idea in Definition 4 is that a solution cannot be Pareto optimal if it is dominated by another solution.

3.3 Resolution of Underconstrained Requests

To demonstrate our resolution procedure, consider our request for a Dodge (in the introduction). The system first uses expectations to elicit additional constraints to reduce the number of solutions. Since the request does not constrain the model of the car and the expectation associated with the model is the highest among all the unconstrained concepts, the system suggests that the user constrains the model. Adding the constraint that the model be a "Stratus" drops the number of solutions to 53, which is still too many. Since there are no more concepts with an expectation higher than the threshold, 0.5, the system uses the ordering $\succeq_\rho$ and Pareto optimality to return the best-m solutions. Figure 4

Solution	Make	Model	Price	Year	Mileage	$\rho_{C*}(s_i)$	Pareto Optimal
s_1	Dodge	Stratus	13,999.00	2005	15,775	2.499	✓
s_2	Dodge	Stratus	11,998.00	2004	23,404	2.497	✓
s_3	Dodge	Stratus	14,200.00	2005	16,008	2.476	×
s_4	Dodge	Stratus	14,557.00	2005	16,954	2.431	×
s_5	Dodge	Stratus	10,590.00	2003	38,608	2.360	✓
s_6	Dodge	Stratus	14,253.00	2004	17,457	2.332	×
s_7	Dodge	Stratus	10,987.00	2004	56,377	2.267	✓
s_8	Dodge	Stratus	13,999.00	2004	30,038	2.230	×
s_9	Dodge	Stratus	12,995.00	2004	40,477	2.226	×
s_{10}	Dodge	Stratus	12,577.00	2003	33,163	2.216	×
s_{11}	Dodge	Stratus	14,620.00	2004	32,406	2.149	×
s_{12}	Dodge	Stratus	8,975.00	2003	75,689	2.140	✓

Fig. 4. Solutions for the car purchase request

shows the top 12 solutions ordered in ascending order based on their combined rewards $\rho_{C^*}(s_i)$. The rightmost column in Figure 4 shows whether a solution is Pareto optimal ($\checkmark$) or not ($\times$). For instance, the solution s_3 is not Pareto optimal because s_1 dominates it—s_1 is cheaper and has a lower mileage, although both have the same year. Since we have chosen $m = 5$, the system returns the first five Pareto optimal solutions, s_1, s_2, s_5, s_7, and s_{12}.

4   Overconstrained Service Requests

Overconstrained service requests admit no solution. As in Section 3, we discuss two ways to provide the best-m near solutions. First, we propose an ordering over near solutions and use it along with Pareto optimality to offer the best-m near solutions. Second, we propose an expectation-based relaxation process that suggests unsatisfied constraints for a user to relax.

4.1   Ordering Near Solutions

We combine the penalties and rewards, if any, of each near solution, and order the near solutions according to their combined penalties and rewards. Let $S = \{s_1, \ldots, s_n\}$ be a set of near solutions each of which violates one or more constraints from a set of constraints $C = \{C_1, \ldots, C_k\}$. The evaluation of a set of constraints C for a near solution $s_i \in S$ returns a set of real numbers $\{C_1(s_i), \ldots, C_k(s_i)\}$, where each $C_k(s_i)$ is either a reward or a penalty. We divide these real numbers $C_j(s_i)$, $1 \leq j \leq k$ by $\max_{1 \leq i \leq n} |C_j(s_i)|$, the maximum absolute reward or penalty value over all near solutions for constraint C_j. This normalizes the rewards and penalties to the interval [-1, 1]. Let us denote the set $\{C_1(s_i), \ldots, C_k(s_i)\}$ after normalization by $C^* = \{C_1^*(s_i), \ldots, C_k^*(s_i)\}$. We combine each $C_j^*(s_i)$ in C^* linearly, as before, yielding a combined penalty/reward ϕ for each near solution s_i as follows:

$$\phi_{C^*}(s_i) = \sum_{j=1}^{k} C_j^*(s_i); \, for \, i = 1, \ldots, n.$$

Greater values of $\phi_{C^*}(s_i)$ indicate lower penalties on s_i and (possibly) higher rewards. Thus, a high value of $\phi_{C^*}(s_i)$ denotes a better near solution s_i.

Definition 5. *Let s_i and s_j be two distinct near solutions and $C = \{C_1, \ldots, C_k\}$ be a set of constraints. We say that s_i is better than or equivalent to s_j, $s_i \succeq_\phi s_j$, with respect to C if $\phi_{C^*}(s_i) \geq \phi_{C^*}(s_j)$.*

We define a dominance relation and Pareto optimality based on the ordering $\succeq_\phi$ in Definition 5 in the same way as we defined them in Definitions 3 and 4.

4.2   Constraint Relaxation Using Expectations

For constraint relaxation we use the same expectation values for constraints as discussed in Subsection 3.1, but consider the lowest expectation values, rather than the highest, to be the candidates for relaxation. In addition, we consider the violation degree when we suggest constraints for relaxation. For instance, it is likely to be better to suggest relaxing a time constraint violated by 10 minutes than to suggest relaxing a distance constraint violated by 50 miles even though a distance constraint is likely to be associated with a lower expectation value. Further, since we should not badger the user with questions, the number of suggested unsatisfied constraints should not exceed a prespecified threshold. Taking all these ideas into consideration, the system selects the constraints to suggest for relaxation based on the following procedure.

1. To avoid overloading the user with suggestions, select only near solutions that violate fewer constraints than a prespecified threshold.
2. To take the expectation values into account, compute the cost of the relaxation for each near solution based on the expectation using the equation $r(s_i) = \sum_k e_k C_k^*(s_i)$, where e_k is the expectation value associated with the constraint C_k and $C_k^*(s_i)$ is the normalized penalty imposed on s_i for C_k.
3. To take the overall degree of violation into account, select the near solution s_i with the lowest absolute value of $r(s_i)$ and suggest relaxing the constraints that s_i violates only to the degree necessary to satisfy the constraints of s_i.

We give an example in the next subsection.

4.3   Resolution of Overconstrained Requests

To demonstrate our resolution procedure, consider our request for an appointment (in the introduction). Figure 5 shows 8 near solutions for the request ordered in ascending order based on the combined penalty/reward $\phi_{C^*}(s_i)$, which appears in the second column from the right. The system tries first to suggest some constraints to relax using the expectations associated with the constraints. Figure 6 shows the constraints along with their associated expectation values and their rewards/penalties for each near solution. The rightmost column in Figure 6 shows the computed relaxation cost $r(s_i)$ for each near solution. Based on our relaxation procedure, the system could consider the near solution s_4 for suggesting relaxation because it has the lowest relaxation cost $r(s_i)$. The system does not, however, because s_4 violates three constraints, which exceeds the threshold we set, namely fewer than three constraints. The near solution s_3 satisfies our procedure requirements in the sense that s_3 violates two constraints and has the next lowest relaxation cost $r(s_i)$. The system therefore suggests letting the time be 12:40 PM instead of 1:00 PM and letting the date be the 19th instead of the 20th. If the user accepts these relaxed constraints, the system can offer s_3 as the best solution.

For the sake of further discussing the possibilities, we assume that the user does not accept the suggestion to relax the time and date constraints. To compute the best-m near solutions, the system sorts the near solutions based on the combined penalty/reward $\phi_{C^*}(s_i)$ and discards the dominated near solutions using the rewards and penalties information in Figure 6, i.e. $\phi_{C^*}(s_1) = -0.160 = -0.076 + 0.167 - 0.250$; $\phi_{C^*}(s_2) = -0.180 = -0.090 + 0.160 - 0.250$; and

Near Solution	Insurance	Distance	Time	Date	$\phi_{C_*}(s_i)$	Pareto Optimal
s_1	IHC	16	1:00 PM	the 19th	−0.160	✓
s_2	IHC	18	1:10 PM	the 19th	−0.180	×
s_3	IHC	4	12:40 PM	the 19th	−0.257	✓
s_4	IHC	6	12:50 PM	the 19th	−0.264	✓
s_5	IHC	20	3:00 PM	the 19th	−0.271	×
s_6	IHC	8	1:40 PM	the 18th	−0.382	✓
s_7	IHC	18	2:20 PM	the 22nd	−0.479	×
s_8	IHC	3	11:30 AM	the 16th	−1.049	✓

Fig. 5. Near solutions for the appointment request

	Insurance="IHC" Expectation=0.4	Distance≤ 5 Expectation=0.3	Time≥("1:00 PM") Expectation=0.8	Date="the 20th" Expectation=0.9	$r(s_i)$
s_1	0.000	−0.076	0.167	−0.250	−0.248
s_2	0.000	−0.090	0.160	−0.250	−0.252
s_3	0.000	0.007	−0.014	−0.250	−0.236
s_4	0.000	−0.007	−0.007	−0.250	−0.233
s_5	0.000	−0.102	0.083	−0.250	−0.256
s_6	0.000	−0.021	0.139	−0.500	−0.456
s_7	0.000	−0.090	0.111	−0.500	−0.477
s_8	0.000	0.014	−0.062	−1.000	−0.950

Fig. 6. Rewards and penalties for the near solutions

so forth. The rightmost column in Figure 5 shows whether a near solution s_i is Pareto optimal (✓) or not (×). Since $m = 5$, the system returns the first 5 Pareto optimal near solutions, which in our example are s_1, s_3, s_4, s_6, and s_8.

A closer look at the results in Figures 5 and 6 reveals that the returned near solutions are better than the ones filtered out. For instance, comparing the near solution s_1 to the discarded near solution s_2, we find that although both violate the date constraint to the same degree and satisfy the time constraint, s_1 violates the distance constraint less than s_2 and is closer to the requested time, 1:00 PM. Therefore, from the Pareto-optimality's viewpoint, given s_1 as a possibility, no user is likely to accept the near solution s_2.

5   Performance Analysis

To evaluate the performance of our system, we conducted a user study. The goal was to test whether there is a statistically significant difference between human choices and system choices. The subjects in our study were from both genders and from different academic disciplines and education levels—professors, graduate students, and undergraduate students at Brigham Young University. We gave every subject a request from a car purchase domain along with 32 cars that each satisfies all the constraints of the request, and another request from an appointment scheduling domain along with 19 near solutions that each satisfies some but not all the constraints of the appointment request. All the solutions and near solutions were randomly shuffled so as not to provide the subjects with any ordering information. We asked each subject to select and order the best-5 solutions out of 32 solutions for cars and the best-5 near solutions out of 19 near solutions for appointments.

To visualize the degree of agreement between system choices and human choices, we counted the number of times each solution was chosen by the 16 subjects for the car experiment and the number of times each near solution was

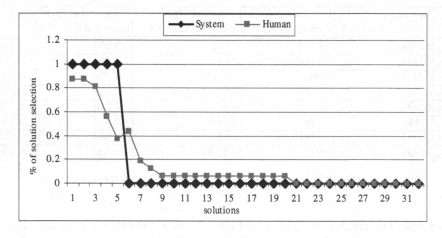

Fig. 7. Human solution selection compared to system solution selection

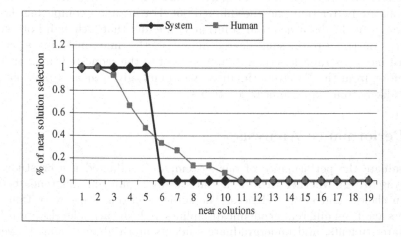

Fig. 8. Human near solution selection compared to system near solution selection

chosen by the 15 subjects for the appointment experiment.[3] Figures 7 and 8 show the percentage of human subjects who chose each solution or near solution respectively. The first five solutions and near solutions are the ordered best-5 Pareto optimal solutions and near solutions. The remaining solutions and near solutions are ordered by decreasing percentage of selection by human subjects. As the figures show there is a high degree of agreement between the system's choices and the human subjects' choices. As Figure 7 shows, over 87% of the subjects chose solutions 1 and 2, and over 81% of the subjects chose solution 3. Figure 8 shows an even higher degree of agreement. All the subjects chose near solutions 1 and 2, and over 96% of them chose near solution 3. The solutions and near solutions that were not chosen by the system as being among the best-5 were also selected less often by our human subjects, with the exception of solution 6 in Figure 7, which was selected by 43% of the human subjects, and the near solutions 6 and 7, which were chosen by the 33% and 26% of the human subjects. Interestingly, the system chose both solution 6 and near solution 6 as the 6th Pareto optimal solution and near solution. Near solution 7, however, is not Pareto optimal. All the other solutions and near solutions were chosen by 20% or fewer of the subjects. Figures 7 and 8 reveal a definite pattern: human subjects chose a high percentage of the best-5 choices and a low percentage for choices not among the best-5 system choices.

To statistically measure the degree of agreement between system choices and human subjects choices, we ran an inter-observer agreement test [LK77] using the MINITAB 14 software package [min05]. The inter-observer agreement per observer pair (system and human) was determined with respect to the dichotomy: the best-5 solutions or the best-5 near solutions and not the best-5. Figures 9 and 10 show the distribution of agreement and disagreement between the system and our human subjects. We disregarded the order in which each subject ordered the best-5 solutions or near solutions, and tallied the number of solutions and near solutions chosen by subjects that belong to the best-5 solutions and the best-5 near solutions selected by the system. We also tallied the number of solutions and near solutions that were not chosen by the system and the subjects as the best-5. For instance, the 16 subjects for the car experiment made 80 choices of which 56 belong to the best-5 system choices and 24 do not. Further, of the 432 solutions not chosen, 24 were among the best-5 system choices while 408 were also not chosen by the system. Figure 11 shows the statistical summary for the car and appointment experiments. The overall agreement, P_o, and the agreement due to chance, P_e, for the car experiment are 0.91 and 0.73 respectively with a Cohen kappa κ value of 0.67, and for the appointment experiment are 0.90 and 0.61 with a κ value of 0.74. Based on the Landis-Koch interpretation for κ values [LK77], the two κ values indicate "substantial" agreement between the system and the subjects. The 95% confidence intervals for κ in Figure 11, however, indicate that the agreement may range from "moderate" (0.58) to "substantial" (0.76) for the car experiment and from "substantial" (0.65) to "almost perfect" (0.83) for the appointment experiment. It is useful also, as suggested

---

[3] One of the subjects did not make choices for the appointment experiment.

Human \ System	The best-5 solutions	Not the best-5 solutions	Total
The best-5 solutions	56	24	80
Not the best-5 solutions	24	408	432
Total	80	432	512

Fig. 9. Human versus system choices for the car experiment

Human \ System	The best-5 near solutions	Not the best-5 near solutions	Total
The best-5 near solutions	61	14	75
Not the best-5 near solutions	14	196	210
Total	75	210	285

Fig. 10. Human versus system choices for the appointment experiment

Agreement index	Type of agreement	Car experiment	Appointment experiment
P_o	overall	0.91	0.90
P_{pos}	the best-5	0.70	0.81
P_{neg}	not the best-5	0.94	0.93
P_e	due to chance	0.73	0.61
Cohen kappa κ	chance corrected	0.67	0.74
95% Confidence interval for κ		[0.58, 0.76]	[0.65, 0.83]

Fig. 11. Statistical summary

in [CF90], to compute two more indices, namely the positive agreement P_{pos} on the best-5 and the negative agreement P_{neg} on those not among the best-5. The positive agreement, P_{pos}, for the car experiment and for the appointment experiment were respectively 0.70 and 0.81 whereas the negative agreement, P_{neg}, were respectively 0.94 and 0.93. All these numbers show a high agreement between the system and human subjects on both the best-5 and not among the best-5 (near) solutions. We next considered how the system and each subject ordered the best-5 solutions and near solutions. The κ values for the car experiment was 0.43 and for the appointment experiment was 0.61, indicating respectively "moderate" and "substantial" agreement between system ordering and subject ordering for the best-5 solutions and the best-5 near solutions.

6   Conclusions and Future Work

We proposed techniques to handle underconstrained and overconstrained systems of conjunctive constraints for service requests. These techniques depend on defining an ordering over the solutions or near solutions along with Pareto optimality to discard dominated solutions or near solutions. From among the ordered

Pareto optimal solutions or near solutions, we select the best-m. We also introduced expectation values as domain knowledge and proposed an expectation-based process to elicit or relax constraints respectively for underconstrained and overconstrained requests. We conducted experiments to test our proposed ordering and Pareto optimality techniques and found substantial agreement between the system and human behavior.

Although still preliminary, the results are promising. As future work, we plan to do more user studies on additional domains with a larger number of subjects. In addition, we need to develop a dialog generation system for user interaction and to conduct a field test for the generated dialog. Finally, we should integrate our resolution techniques into a service request architecture, such as the semantic web.

Acknowledgements

We appreciate Del T. Scott from the Department of Statistics, Brigham Young University, for his help with our statistical analysis. We also appreciate the help of all the subjects who participated in the experiments.

References

[AMEL05]   M. J. Al-Muhammed, D. W. Embley, and S. W. Liddle. Conceptual Model Based Semantic Web Services. In *Proceedings of the 24th International Conference on Conceptual Modeling (ER 2005)*, pages 288–303, Klagenfurt, Austria, October 2005.

[Arn02]   M. T. Arnal. *Scalable Intelligent Electronic Catalogs*. PhD Dissertation, Swiss Federal Institute of Technology in Lausanne (EPFL), 2002.

[CF90]   D. Cicchetti and A. Feinstein. High Agreement But Low Kappa. II. Resolving The Paradoxes. *Journal of Clinical Epidemiology*, 43(6):551–558, 1990.

[Fel80]   A. M. Feldman. *Welfare Economics and Social Choice Theory*. Kluwer, Boston, 1980.

[FPTV04]   B. Faltings, P. Pu, M. Torrens, and P. Viappiani. Designing Example-Critiquing Interaction. In *Proceedings of the 9th International Conference on Intelligent User Interface*, pages 22–29, Funchal, Portugal, November 2004.

[LHL97]   G. Linden, S. Hanks, and N. Lesh. Interactive Assesment of User Preference Models: The Automated Travel Assistant. In *Proceedings of the 6th International Conference on User Modeling (UM97)*, pages 67–78, Vienna, New York, June 1997.

[LK77]   J. R. Landis and G. Koch. The Measurement of Observer Agreement for Categorical Data. *Biometrics*, 33(1):159–174, 1977.

[MA04]   R. T. Marler and J. S. Arora. Survey of Multi-Objective Optimization Methods for Engineering. *Structural and Multidisciplinary Optimization*, 26(6):369–395, 2004.

[min05]   Minitab 14.2 Statitiscal Software. Website, 2005. www.minitab.com.

[Par97]   V. Pareto. *Cours d'économie politique*. F. Rouge, Lausanne, Switzerland, 1897.

[PFK03]   P. Pu, B. Faltings, and P. Kumar. User-Involved Tradeoff Analysis in Configuration Tasks. In *Proceedings of the 3rd International Workshop on User-Interaction in Constraint Satisfaction*, pages 85–102, Kinsale, Ireland, September 2003.

[SL01]   S. Shearin and H. Lieberman. Intelligent Profiling by Example. In *Proceedings of the 6th International Conference on Intelligent User Interfaces*, pages 145–151, Santa Fe, New Mexico, January 2001.

Discovering Remote Software Services that Satisfy Requirements: Patterns for Query Reformulation

Nektarios Dourdas[1], Xiaohong Zhu[2], Neil Maiden[2], Sara Jones[2], and Konstantinos Zachos[2]

[1] SAP, Walldorf, Germany
[2] Centre for HCI Design, City University, UK
NDourdas@gmail.com, XZhu@soi.city.ac.uk,
N.A.M.Maiden@city.ac.uk, S.V.Jones@soi.city.ac.uk,
KZachos@soi.city.ac.uk

Abstract. Developing service-centric applications will require developers to discover candidate services during requirements processes. However such discovery is challenging due to the ontological mismatch between requirement and service descriptions. We propose patterns to re-express requirements-based service queries using classes of solution service, to increase the likelihood of discovering relevant services from service registries. We report a prototype pattern language developed for service-based vehicle fleet management, and demonstrate its use with an example.

1 Introduction

Recent developments in web services and standards have been rapid. Standards such as SOAP and WSDL are well established. Major vendors such as IBM, Microsoft, Sun and HP provide support for services in their development platforms, and many companies are offering web service interfaces to their systems. UDDI offers established directories of service providers. Leavitt [2004] reports that worldwide spending on web services software projects will reach $11 billion by 2008, compared to $1.1 billion in 2003. Given these trends, development of service-centric systems with software services available over the internet is a new research challenge for software engineering – a challenge that we are addressing in the EU-funded SeCSE Integrated Project (secse.eng.it).

Developing service-centric systems has important consequences for how developers determine the requirements of these systems. We conjecture that developers will want to discover candidate services early in the development process, to explore what capabilities are possible, design an architecture compliant with these capabilities, and trade-off quality-of-service requirements [Jones et al. 2005]. To do this, requirements must form elements of service queries with which to discover candidate services for a new application [Schmid et al. 2005].

However, successfully discovering software services using requirements poses research challenges. Requirements express desirable properties of the problem domain

E. Dubois and K. Pohl (Eds.): CAiSE 2006, LNCS 4001, pp. 239–254, 2006.
© Springer-Verlag Berlin Heidelberg 2006

[Jackson 1995] in terms of the goals of the service consumer, for example *repair a fault in a car engine*. In contrast, service specifications describe solution behaviour - what the piece of software does, largely independent of the problem domain, to maximise reuse of the software within and across domains. For example, services to repair an engine fault include *collect and diagnose engine data,* and *locate garages equipped to undertake the repair.* SeCSE's current service discovery environment implements an algorithm for discovering services from requirements specifications using query expansion and word sense disambiguation techniques [Zachos & Maiden 2005] to handle the problem of incomplete requirements.

Alas query expansion alone cannot resolve the mismatch that arises because the problem query and solution service are inevitably expressed using different ontologies. To overcome this ontological mismatch, we are extending the SeCSE algorithm with patterns that encapsulate knowledge about classes of proven service solutions to classes of requirement problems. Knowledge about how service solution classes can solve classes of problem can be applied to change the ontology of the service query to the solution domain, thus increasing the likelihood of discovering services that are compliant with consumer requirements. In the above simple example, the resulting service query will seek services that *collect and diagnose engine data* and *locate garages*, rather than simply *repair an engine*.

In SeCSE we are developing pattern languages in chosen automotive domains. One domain that we have developed a pattern language for is vehicle fleet management in DaimlerChrysler. DaimlerChrysler envisage that company managers of Mercedes car fleets will use remote software services with on-board systems to manage cars that are distributed across the fleet. This paper describes how the pattern language was developed and represented, and demonstrates its usefulness in service discovery using an example from DaimlerChrysler.

The remainder of this paper is in 4 sections. Section 2 describes SeCSE's pattern-based approach to service discovery. Section 3 describes the pattern language for vehicle fleet management elicited from DaimlerChrysler engineers. Section 4 uses an example to demonstrate potential benefits from patterns-based service discovery. The last section describes how we are implementing pattern-based discovery, and outlines future research.

2   Service-Centric Systems and Patterns

Service-centric systems are systems that integrate services from different providers regardless of the underlying operating systems or programming languages of those applications. A software service is a set of operations offered by an application. Users access services through well-defined interfaces independently of where the service is executed. Software services accessed over the internet are called web services. Automotive manufacturers such as DaimlerChrysler can benefit from service-centric applications because software and information used in these applications is not embedded and isolated in cars, but available and up-to-date on remote servers.

Patterns research started with the architect Christopher Alexander, who described over 250 architectural building patterns at different levels of abstraction

[Alexander 1979]. Equivalent software patterns became popular in object-oriented design [Gamma et. al. 1995], and have been applied subsequently to many phases of software development. Our research uses Alexander's [1979] original definition of a pattern as a proven solution to a recurring problem in a context of use. In SeCSE we employ this definition to describe: (i) classes of problem that re-occur during the design of service-centric applications, and: (ii) classes of candidate services proven to solve these problems. Returning to the above example, the problem element of the pattern describes a class of problem in a context, i.e. *a vehicle driving and developing a fault that needs analysis and repair.* The solution element describes classes of service to *collect engine fault data, analyze and diagnose this data*, and *send the data to a parts supplier.* To decouple development of SeCSE patterns from the publication of concrete software services by service providers in heterogeneous service registries such as UDDI, the patterns do not reference concrete services in these registries. Instead, each pattern specifies descriptions of classes of service that an algorithm uses to transform the service query and discover instances of new software services in the registries.

2.1 Previous Work

There has been little research into patterns for service discovery. The only work that addresses service discovery directly was reported by Pärssinen [2004], who introduced a pattern language for service discovery mined from existing discovery protocols. The language describes different aspects of the service discovery process to enable easier comparison of existing approaches.

Elsewhere researchers have posited patterns for service composition. Melloul et al. [2004] expressed high-level patterns as objects that can be specialized to particular applications and reused in the construction of higher-level patterns. Developers write patterns in terms of high-level functions, then decide on the lower-level services to compose. Melloul & Fox [2004] also discussed reuse trade-offs, showing that too much abstraction makes patterns less expressive. To ensure sufficient expressiveness, all patterns must capture what must be guaranteed in every context of invocation, regardless of the selected services. However this work does not address the automatic discovery or dynamic selection of services. It assumes that developers select services manually at pattern-specialization time.

Closer to our work is that of Tut et al. [2002], who also investigated the use of patterns to facilitate the composition of electronic services. Developers use their domain knowledge to instantiate these patterns, which are indexed using classification codes, to different problem domains. During service composition every task in the pattern is mapped to a service or another pattern. However, again, this work does not address service discovery directly.

Our work is also similar to the use of goal refinement patterns in the KAOS requirements method. Goal refinement and operationalization is poorly supported in many requirements methods, therefore Massonet & van Lamsweerde [1996] describe the use of patterns to refine and operationalize goals in the problem domain. Patterns in SeCSE are designed to serve a similar purpose – refine a service consumer goal to determine one or more tasks that can be operationalised using invoked services.

2.2 Service Discovery in SeCSE

To ensure industrial uptake, SeCSE's requirements-based service discovery process formulates service queries from use case and requirements specifications expressed in structured natural language. To achieve this, SeCSE's service discovery environment has 4 main components: (i) UCaRE, which supports web-enabled specification of requirements and use cases, and formulation of service queries from these specifications [Jones et al. 2005]: (ii) EDDiE, which uses service queries to discover service descriptions using different retrieval strategies [Zachos & Maiden 2005]; (iii) SeCSE's service registry – a federated and heterogeneous mechanism for storing service descriptions that is searched by EDDiE; (iv) SeCSE's service explorer environment, which combines text and graphics descriptions of retrieved services to enable selection.

In simple terms, EDDiE uses an analyst-defined service request to generate one or more queries of single or compound natural language terms that it matches to equivalent terms in service descriptions stored in SeCSE's service registries. Distance measures between terms in each query and service description are used to compute the distance between the query and description.

Inevitably, service queries that are derived from incomplete and inconsistent requirements will themselves be incomplete and inconsistent. Therefore EDDiE extends service queries to increase the likelihood of successful service discovery using two core strategies – *query expansion* and *word sense disambiguation* – that are implemented in 4 key components shown in Figure 1. In the first the service query is divided into sentences, then tokenized and part-of-speech tagged and modified to include each term's morphological root (e.g. *driving* to *drive*, and *drivers* to *driver*). In the second the algorithm applies 7 procedures to disambiguate each term by defining its correct sense and tagging it with that sense (e.g. defining a *driver* to be a *vehicle* rather than a *type of golf club*). In the third the algorithm expands each term with other terms that have similar meaning according to the tagged sense, to increase the likelihood of a match with a service description (e.g. the term *driver* is synonymous with the term *motorist* which is also then included in the query). In the fourth component the algorithm matches all expanded and sense-tagged query terms to a similar set of terms that describe each candidate service, expressed using the *service description* facet in the SeCSE service registry. Query matching is in 2 steps: (i) XQuery text-searching functions to discover an initial set of services descriptions that satisfy global search constraints; (ii) traditional vector-space model information retrieval, enhanced with WordNet, to further refine and assess the quality of the candidate service set. This two-step approach overcomes XQuery's limited text-based search capabilities.

The WordNet on-line lexicon fulfills an important role for three of the algorithm's components. WordNet is a lexical database inspired by psycholinguistic theories of human lexical memory [Miller 1993]. It has two important features. Firstly it divides the lexicon into four categories: nouns, verbs, adjectives and adverbs. Word senses for each category are organized into synonym sets (synsets) that represent concepts, and each synset is followed by its definition or gloss that contains a defining phrase, an optional comment and one or more examples. Secondly, WordNet is structured using semantic relations between word meanings that link concepts. Relationships between conceptions such as hypernym and hyponym relations are represented as semantic pointers between related concepts [Miller 1993]. A hypernym is a generic term used to designate a whole class of specific instances. For example, *vehicle* denotes all the things that are separately denoted by the words *train, chariot, dogsled, airplane,* and *automobile,* and is therefore a hypernym of each of those words. On the other hand, a hyponym is a specific term used to designate a member of a class, e.g. *chauffeur, taxidriver* and *motorist* are all hyponyms of *driver.* A semantic relation between word meanings, such as a hypernymy, links concepts.

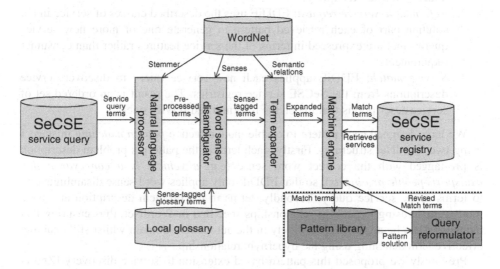

Fig. 1. SeCSE's service discovery algorithm, showing original EDDiE components and our pattern extension to the algorithm below the dotted line

EDDiE implements the WordNet.Net library, the .Net Framework library for WordNet [Crowe 2005]. The library provides public classes that can be accessed through public interfaces. It uses the synonym sets and associated word senses to disambiguate between different meanings of the same word, and semantic relations such hypernym and hyponym as well as synonyms to expand service queries.

Although we treat query expansion and word sense disambiguation as necessary techniques for effective service discovery, we do not believe that, on their own, they are sufficient to overcome the ontological mismatch that will exist between requirement specifications and service descriptions. To deliver this sufficient algorithm, we have developed the pattern extension to EDDiE.

2.3 Pattern-Based Extension to Service Discovery

As Figure 1 shows we implement the pattern-based extension by adding a patterns catalogue and a new component – the query reformulator – to EDDiE. Input to this extension is an expanded and disambiguated set of terms in a service query, and output is one or more new service queries reformulated using retrieved patterns.

Each pattern in the pattern language includes a structured natural language description of a class of problem in context and a structured natural language description of one or more candidate classes of service that are proven solutions to the class of problem. Pattern-based service discovery is in 3 stages:

1. *Pattern match*: EDDiE uses its existing algorithm [Zachos & Maiden 2005] to match the expanded and disambiguated service query to the problem description of each pattern. The result is an ordered set of retrieved patterns that match to the service query;
2. *Reformulate service request*: EDDiE uses the described classes of service in the solution part of each retrieved pattern to generate one or more new service queries that are expressed in terms of the service features rather than consumer requirements;
3. *Service match*: EDDiE applies each new service query to discover service descriptions from the SeCSE service registries. The result is an ordered set of service descriptions that match the reformulated service query.

We have designed each pattern to enable more effective *pattern matching* in stage 1 using two WordNet structures. Firstly, each term in the pattern's problem description is pre-tagged with the correct word sense (e.g. *a vehicle is a conveyance that transports people or objects*), so that EDDiE only applies word sense disambiguation to terms in the service query. Secondly, terms in the problem description are made more generic using hypernym relationships specified in WordNet, thus ensuring that the pattern can be applied more widely in the automotive domain whilst still enabling effective term matching using the hypernym relationship.

Previously we proposed this pattern-based extension to service discovery [Zhu et al. 2005], however both its feasibility and effectiveness were unproven. In the remainder of this paper we report a first evaluation that sought to establish whether: (i) a pattern language could be elicited from domain experts – in our case automotive engineers, and; (ii) the language has the potential to improve service discovery. This paper reports an empirical answer to the first question and an example-based demonstration to begin to answer the second.

3 Developing a Pattern Language for Vehicle Fleet Management in DaimlerChrysler

We worked with SeCSE partners DaimlerChrysler to develop and evaluate a prototype pattern language for their on-board systems for fleet vehicle management. Fleet vehicle management enables DaimlerChrysler to maintain effective customer support after sale or lease, to ensure vehicle quality and support vehicle use. The result was a 40-page specification of a language that contained 7 core patterns. Each pattern was described using 4 facets. The first described background information about the pattern in text form and i^* strategic dependency (SD) and strategic rationale (SR) models [Yu & Mylopoulos 1994] that represent and communicate the essence of each pattern. The SD model depicts dependencies between strategic actors whilst the SR model depicts how actors achieve strategic goals in terms of tasks and resources

[Yu & Mylopoulos 1994]. We had successfully used $i*$ models to elicit, evaluate and communicate patterns on submarine design with BAE SYSTEMS engineers [Pavan et al. 2003], and applied this method again in SeCSE. The second facet described the pattern's problem in context using structured natural language descriptions in use case specifications [Jacobson et al. 2000] and VOLERE requirement statements [Robertson & Robertson 1999]. The third facet described the pattern solution in terms of the behaviour of the service-centric application, again as a use case specification. The fourth facet described classes of service implemented in this application, in terms of structured service descriptions from which EDDiE generates revised service queries [Sawyer et al. 2005].

3.1 Elicitation Method

Elicitation was in three phases. Each focused on a one-day workshop with DaimlerChrysler engineers in Stuttgart. The engineers were experienced system designers from DaimlerChrysler's Research and Development department, and at least 2 engineers participated in each workshop. Throughout each workshop we encouraged the engineers to converse with each other. This technique, known as constructive interaction [Miyake 1986], overcomes the unnatural aspects of other elicitation techniques. All conversation took place in German, the engineer's native language, and the SeCSE researcher was fluent in the language. All results were then translated into English, the language of the project.

The 3 workshops had 3 different goals:

1. **Pattern discovery**, to walk through scenarios that envision how vehicle fleet management might take place, and discover and document design decisions about possible on-board service-centric applications. Results provided an outline pattern language and template for each pattern;
2. **Pattern definition**, to develop and specify complete patterns around the reported design decisions, including the description of possible classes of service that an application might discover and bind to during deployment;
3. **Pattern evaluation**, to evaluate the specified patterns and revise them in light of feedback.

During the first workshop we walked through DaimlerChrysler scenarios that described how fleet vehicle management took place. Engineers selected the scenarios according to business importance, how frequently these scenarios might occur, and the potential use for future software services. They then elaborated these scenarios into sequences of actions that were walked through to discover design decisions that would need to be made to implement the software services. Next we combined brainstorming with laddering, a form of structured interviewing, to elicit knowledge about different candidate architectures, why each was chosen or rejected, and conditions for the use of each. Laddering questions gathered important data about trade-offs between requirements and the feasibility of different architectures. All data was recorded on flipchart sheets. At the end of the workshop we structured knowledge about each pattern in the background facet. We also developed an $i*$

Strategic Dependency (SD) model of the system actors and dependencies described in the pattern.

Prior to the second workshop – pattern definition – we sent each pattern description from the first workshop to the DaimlerChrysler engineers for comment and correction. During the workshop itself we worked with the engineers to develop the $i*$ SR models, gathering data to complete one model for each pattern using brainstorming to discover concepts and laddering to decompose soft goal concepts. We used the $i*$ SR models to decompose modeled tasks into sub-tasks that could be undertaken by remote software services. After the workshop we elaborated the $i*$ models to generate the other 3 facets of each pattern: (i) the problem facet, expressed as classes of behaviour and requirements expressed in a use case specification; (ii) the solution facet, expressed as the use case extended with descriptions of classes of behaviour specific to service-centric applications; (iii) the service classes facet expressed using SeCSE's faceted service specification structure [Sawyer et al. 2005], that was the basis for generating new service queries.

In the third workshop – pattern evaluation – we formally reviewed then evaluated each pattern with the DaimlerChrysler engineers.

3.2 Results

During the first workshop we developed and collected a large number of informal artifacts such the mind maps shown in Figure 2. These artifacts provided the basis for pattern definition in the second workshop. All patterns in the language made reference to onboard vehicle boxes that deliver software services to the driver, software servers that DaimlerChrysler supports to deliver services to vehicles, and service providers from whom services are discovered and deployed. Raw data collected from the 3 workshops is reported in Dourdas [2005].

Fig. 2. The mind maps developed for *Vehicle box update* (on the left) and *Negotiation* (on the right)

At the end of the third workshop the language contained 7 core patterns:

1. **Communication initialization:** Initializing processes prior to data exchange, taking into account requirements from the driver and server;
2. **Authentication:** Determining identities of actors for legal, billing and security purposes, exploring the trade-offs between user-friendliness and security;
3. **Emergency administration:** An administrator accessing the vehicle box to recover from malfunctions;
4. **Vehicle box update:** Updating in response to developer requests and new software versions, taking into account billing and safety requirements;
5. **Language selection:** Services are offered in different languages chosen by the driver, making use of specialized translation services;
6. **Vehicle status sending:** Exploiting vehicle-related services (e.g. detection of the next service station) to transmit data such as position and mileage, trading off keeping information current and up-to-date and communication costs;
7. **Negotiation:** Offering an unlimited amount of service may result in price negotiations with the driver that can lead to usability problems.

Each pattern was described using the background, problem description, solution description and service class facets described earlier. To demonstrate these patterns and the facets, we report the final version of the *Negotiation* pattern.

3.3 The Negotiating Pattern

Background Facet: Drivers use different services from their vehicles, many of which must be paid for. Different service price models and ranges exist, depending on service availability and quality, and the final price must be negotiated by the driver. Pre-defined price preferences speed up the service selection and negotiation but restrict service choice and can lead to driver choice not being met, whilst service providers do not provide transparent and comparable pricing systems. Furthermore, because the driver must accept the price, driver authentication is needed. This leads to a trade-off between the automation of service selection and wider service selection – drivers who accept service prices can benefit from more available services, but this requires more interaction.

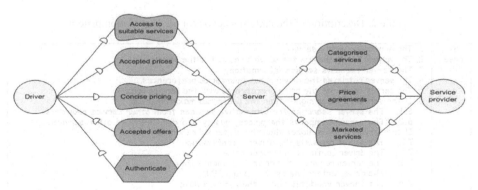

Fig. 3. The i^* SD model for the Negotiating pattern

The SD model in Figure 3 shows two-way dependencies between the *driver* and *server* actors, and between the *server* and *service provider* actors. The supporting SR model, not shown due to lack of space, also models driver tasks such as providing *authentication* and *interacting in negotiations*, and service provider soft goals such as *maximising sale of services*.

Problem Facet: EDDiE matches a service query to the use case and requirement specification in Table 1. Specification terms were selected to minimize the number of possible senses, for example the term *authentication* has just one sense in WordNet. Terms with more than one sense were tagged with WordNet word senses to support query expansion, for example *price* is tagged as a noun with the sense *the amount of money needed to purchase something*. Other service-centric computing term senses were specified in the UCaRE lexicon. One example is *service*, which in WordNet has 15 possible senses as a noun, none of which describe the sense intended in the pattern.

Table 1. Description of the pattern problem for the Negotiation pattern

Use case normal course	1. The driver requests a service. 2. The server offers a suitable service. 3. The driver pays for the service. 4. The driver uses the service.
Requirements	• The driver shall authenticate him/herself before using chargeable services. • The driver shall be able to accept different prices for services. • The services shall be categorised into different price groups. • The driver shall state the price preferences. • The driver shall not directly interact with the services providers. • The server shall be responsible for the B2B negotiations with service providers.

Solution Facet: Table 2 specifies how the service-centric application will negotiate service prices, in the form of a use case specification. Remote software service actions that EDDiE will need to discover are highlighted in **bold**. For example, services will be needed to compare service prices and qualities, as specified in action 6.2. However action descriptions on their own are insufficient for discovering solution services, so the fourth facet, service classes, was specified.

Table 2. Description of the pattern solution for the Negotiation pattern

Use case	1. The driver requests a service.
	2. The vehicle box transmits the service request to the server.
	3. The server requests service information.
	4. The server retrieves the driver's maximum price preferences.
	5. The server compares the price preferences with the service price.
	6. If the service price is higher than the preferred maximum price,
	    6.1. The server searches for alternative services from other service providers.
	    6.2. The server compares the prices, quality and availability of other services.
	7. If the service price is higher than the preferred maximum price,
	    7.1. The server requests the driver's confirmation.
	    7.2. The driver confirms the higher price.
	    7.3. The server requests the driver's authentication.
	    7.4. The driver enters the driver ID and PIN.
	    7.5. The server validates the authentication data.
	8. The server invokes the web service.

Service Class Facet: EDDiE generates new service queries from service classes of the behaviour depicted in bold in Table 2 to discover concrete services from service registries. Table 3 describes one such class – *DriverVehicleAdministration* – to implement behaviour specified in use case actions 6.1, 6.2 and 7.5. The SeCSE service discovery algorithm matches attributes of this facet to equivalent attributes of SeCSE's service description facet in service registries [Sawyer et al. 2005]. Other pattern service classes, for example *ServiceInformation*, are not described in this paper due to lack of space.

Table 3. Description of the *DriverVehicleAdministration* service class

Service	DriverVehicleAdministration
Service Description	The service is able to manage/administrate drivers and vehicles and provides verification/validation of their identification/authentication details.
Service Goal	Provided with the driver's ID and PIN, the service checks the validity of these details. In case of new drivers, the service can register them and provide identify-cation details. The service is also capable of managing vehicles by using their unique vehicle ID. Linking drivers to certain vehicle enables further levels of authentication.
Service Rationale	In order to avoid many different types of authentication, the service manages drivers and vehicles for the server, and equally important, for all different service providers. Otherwise, every single service provider would be responsible for the user authentication and the drivers would be confronted with different authentication procedures when using different services.
Service Consumers	Server, Administrator, Service Provider
Service Operations	Validate driver Validate vehicle Provide driver identification details Manage driver – vehicle combinations

The language's other 6 patterns were structured and described in the same manner [Dourdas 2005]. DaimlerChrysler engineers accepted and signed off the 7 patterns as the basis for a first pattern language with which to evaluate SeCSE's pattern extension to service discovery. The next section demonstrates how service discovery can be enhanced with a simple example that exploits the *Negotiation* pattern.

4 Demonstrating Pattern-Based Service Discovery

In the example requirements analysts use SeCSE's web-based UCaRE tool to specify requirements of service consumers – Mercedes drivers - for an onboard application that provides them with route planning using up-to-date information about traffic conditions. These requirements are expressed as the use cases and VOLERE requirements shown in Figure 4. Each assumes no solution knowledge about journey planner and other services. It is expressed in terms of the problem domain.

EDDiE generates XML service queries from elements in the requirement specification. The query follows an XML schema that defines its structure, content and semantics. EDDiE disambiguates and expands query terms using the components shown in Figure 1 [Zachos & Maiden 2005]. A fragment of the generated XML query with expanded problem domain terms is shown in Figure 5. The first part lists original query terms with their WordNet word types and senses whilst the second lists

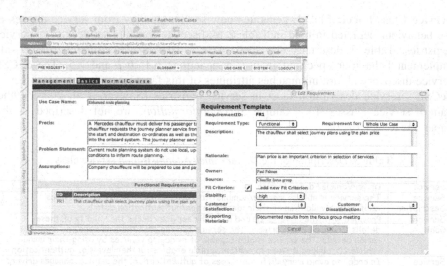

Fig. 4. Use case précis and one requirement for the onboard route planner application, expressed in UCaRE

```
<?xml version="1.0"?>
<Query queryID="459">
  <SubQuery subQueryID="3">
    <UseCase useCaseID="118">
      <Precis>
        <TermStructure>
          <SingleTerm>
            <Term termID="1" occurrence="1" pos="NN" wnsn="1">destination</Term>
            <Term termID="2" occurrence="1" pos="NN" wnsn="1">company</Term>
            <Term termID="3" occurrence="1" pos="NN" wnsn="1">payment</Term>
            <Term termID="24" occurrence="1" pos="VBN" wnsn="1">require</Term>
            <Term termID="26" occurrence="1" pos="JJ" wnsn="1">important</Term>
            .......
            <Term termID="27" pos="NN" refTerm="1" expType="synonym" expWeight="1.3">finish</Term>
            <Term termID="28" pos="NN" refTerm="1" expType="synonym" expWeight="1.3">goal</Term>
            <Term termID="29" pos="NN" refTerm="4" expType="synonym" expWeight="1.3">arrival time</Term>
            <Term termID="30" pos="NN" refTerm="4" expType="synonym" expWeight="1.3">time of arrival</Term>
            .........
```

Fig. 5. Part of the generated XML query from the use case in Figure 4, showing original terms and their WordNet word types and word senses (e.g. *destination*) and expanded terms (e.g. *finish* and *goal*) and expansion weightings

expanded terms and expansion weightings. EDDiE matches original and expanded terms to terms that describe pattern problem facets.

SeCSE's pattern catalogue is implemented in eXist, an Open Source native XML database featuring index-based XQuery processing, automatic indexing, and tight integration with XML development tools. EDDiE queries the catalogue using XQuery, a query language designed for processing XML data. XML queries are transformed into one or more XQueries that are fired at the problem description facets of patterns in the catalogue. Figure 6 shows part of the XML describing the *Negotiation* problem facet. Not shown, again due to lack of space are the tagged word senses (e.g. WordNet sense 1 is tagged to *driver – the operator of a motor vehicle*), whilst other terms are inter-changeable with more generally-applicable WordNet hypernyms, for example *request* with *communicate*, and *offer* with *supply*.

In our example EDDiE retrieves the *Negotiation* pattern reported in Section 3 using the generated XQueries. Matched terms include *<chauffer, driver>*, *<journey planner, service>* and *<authenticate, authenticate>*. As the match to the *Negotiation* pattern is greater than a pre-specified match threshold, EDDiE's query reformulator automatically generates new XML queries and XQueries from information in the *ServiceInformation* and *DriverVehicleAdministration* service classes specified in the facet. A fragment of the XML query for *DriverVehicleAdministration* is shown in Figure 7. In contrast with original query terms in Figure 5, terms describe relevant software behaviour to match to terms describing concrete services in registries.

```
<?xml version="1.0" encoding="utf-8" ?>
<Patterns>
    <Pattern patternID="7" patternName="The Negotiating Pattern">
        <Problem>
            <UseCase>
                <Action acID="1">The driver requests a service.</Action>
                <Action acID="2">The server offers a suitable service.</Action>
                <Action acID="3">The driver pays for the service.</Action>
                <Action acID="4">The driver uses the service.</Action>
            </UseCase>
            <Requirements>
                <Requirement reqID="1" reqType="Functional">
                The driver shall authenticate him/herself before using chargeable services.
                </Requirement>
                <Requirement reqID="2" reqType="Functional">
                The driver shall be able to accept different prices for services.....
```

Fig. 6. Partial XML specification of the Negotiation pattern's problem facet

```
<?xml version="1.0"?>
<Query queryID="460">
    <SubQuery subQueryID="3">
        <UseCase useCaseID="P7">
            <Precis>
                <TermStructure>
                    <SingleTerm>
                        <Term termID="1" occurrence="1" pos="NN" wnsn="1">identification</Term>
                        <Term termID="2" occurrence="1" pos="NN" wnsn="1">validation</Term>
                        <Term termID="3" occurrence="1" pos="NN" wnsn="1">register</Term>
        .......
```

Fig. 7. Part of the reformulated XML query in Figure 5

Next, two things happen. Firstly, UCaRE proposes the pattern solution facet to the requirements analysts to extend the original use case specification shown in Figure 4. Secondly EDDiE fires the reformulated XQuery at the service description facets of services in SeCSE service registries using the existing EDDiE algorithm [Zachos & Maiden 2005]. The reformulated XQueries include new terms not included in the original query, such as *verification*, *validation*, *identification*, *authentication*, *vehicle identifier*, and *register*. Analysts browse and select between retrieved services using SeCSE's service explorer component.

5   Implementation, Discussion and Future Work

We have implemented the vehicle fleet management pattern catalogue as a local SeCSE service registry without implementations of the specified service classes. Each pattern facet is described using an XML data structure in an eXist database. This implementation is the basis for answering our second question in the future – to explore the utility of pattern-based query reformulation in EDDiE.

Results reported in this paper provided an emphatic answer to the first research question, whether a pattern language for service-centric applications can be elicited. Three workshops, each lasting less than one day with 2 DaimlerChrysler engineers, were sufficient to elicit and describe patterns that elaborate on 7 important service-centric design decisions. After the third workshop, DaimlerChrysler signed off the language as an accurate representation of domain knowledge about software services for vehicle fleet management. In this regard, these results supported earlier results [Pavan et al. 2003] that support use of a workshop-based elicitation strategy. An initial analysis of the patterns, demonstrated with the reported example, revealed that service classes linked to each problem class have the potential to reformulate EDDiE service queries with new terms indicative of service ontologies. In the future, an evaluation of EDDiE with service queries for vehicle fleet management based on real automotive requirements is planned to determine the relative effectiveness of EDDiE's pattern-based extension. In particular we will explore different pattern configurations, for example the effectiveness of tagging different terms with WordNet senses, and different hypernym terms to use to express the more abstract pattern. We hope to report results in the near future.

Results gave rise to important discussion points. Although the pattern language was developed for remote software services for vehicle fleet management in DaimlerChrysler, some of the patterns have the potential to generalize beyond both the organization and the domain. The reported *Negotiation* pattern describes classes of candidate service that can reformulate queries in all consumer payment domains including in-car services using more general hypernym relationships, namely *driver* is-a *purchaser*. Similar claims can be made for other patterns in the language, for example *Authentication, Emergency administration* and *Language selection*. This raises important questions about which levels of abstraction afford best pattern matching and reuse [Sutcliffe & Maiden 1998]. Melloul & Fox [2004] report the need for patterns to describe all service invocation contexts, which is neither plausible nor desirable in SeCSE patterns. However deciding what information is needed to describe and discover patterns effectively remains an open question – for example should EDDiE also expand and disambiguate background facet descriptions, and should reformulated queries still include original query terms? During evaluation of EDDiE's pattern-based extension, we will explore these questions with modified pattern versions to other SeCSE domains including telecommunications with other industrial partners Telecom Italia and Telefonica. Finally, the link between the pattern language and emerging standards for semantically enhanced service descriptions such as OWL-S and WSMO warrants some discussion. The language reported in this paper describes DaimlerChrysler expertise using as structured natural language independent of representations needed for implementation in service registries. This is because the design decisions that the engineers make are independent of standards used to represent services. During evaluation of the implemented pattern language we will explore whether use of WordNet as a weak ontology or more formal approaches such as WSDL-S improve the representation, discovery and exploitation of patterns.

The related work revealed that our use of patterns in service discovery is unique in service-centric computing. We plan to advance this work by extending patterns with knowledge about service-centric architectures related to each service class that is expressed using UML message sequence charts and OCL constraints describing service operations and query constraints. This will enable more precise behaviour-based service matching [Spanoudakis et al. 2005] directly from problem requirements expression in UCaRE, potentially shortening the time needed to develop service-centric applications.

Acknowledgements

The work reported in this paper is funded by the EU Framework VI 511680 SeCSE Integrated Project. We wish to thank all partners for their inputs and feedback so far.

References

Alexander C., 1979, 'The Timeless Way of Building', NY: Oxford University Press.

Baeza-Yates, R. & Ribiero-Neto, B., 1999 'Modern Information Retrieval', Addison-Wesley 1999.

Crowe M.,2005, http://opensource.ebswift.com/WordNet.Net

Dourdas N., 2005, 'A Pattern Language for Vehicle Fleet Management in DaimlerChrysler', MSc Thesis, Department Information Science, City University, London, September, 2005.

Gamma E., Helm R., Johnson R. & Vlissides J., 1995, 'Design Patterns – Elements of Reusable Object-Oriented Software', Addison-Wesley.

Jackson M., 1995, 'Software Requirements and Specifications', Addison-Wesley.

Jacobson I., Booch G. & Rumbaugh J., 2000, The Unified Software Development Process, Addison-Wesley-Longman.

Jones S.V., Maiden N.A.M., Zachos K. & Zhu X., 2005, 'How Service-Centric Systems Change the Requirements Process', Proceedings REFSQ'2005 Workshop, in conjunction with CaiSE'2005, 13-14 2005, Porto, Portugal.

Leavitt N., 2004, 'Are Web Services Ready to Deliver?', IEEE Computer, 37(11), 14-18.

Massonet, P. & van Lamsweerde, A., 1996, 'Formal refinement patterns for goal-driven requirements elaboration', Proceedings of FSE-4 - 4th ACM Symposium on the Foundations of Software Engineering, San Fransisco, ACM Press (1996), 179–190.

Melloul L., Fox A. "Reusable Functional Composition Patterns for Web Services", Second International Conference on Web Services (ICWS04), San Diego, CA, July 6-9, 2004.

Miller K., 1993, 'Introduction to WordNet: an On-line Lexical Database' Distributed with the WordNet software

Mijake N., 1986, 'Constructive Interaction and the Iterative Process of Understanding', Cognitive Science 10, 151-177.

Pärssinen J, Koponen, T. and Eronen P. "Pattern Language for Service Discovery", In Proceedings of the 9th European Conference on Pattern Languages of Programs (EuroPLoP '04), 645-660, Irsee, Germany, July 2004.

Pavan P., Maiden N.A.M. & Zhu X., 2003, 'Towards a Systems Engineering Pattern Language: Applying i* to Model Requirements-Architecture Patterns', STRAW'2003, 2nd International Software Requirements and Architectures Workshop, ICSE'2003, May 2003.

Robertson S. & Robertson J., 1999, Mastering the Requirements Process, Addison-Wesley

Sawyer P., Hutchinson J., Walkerdine J. & Sommerville I., 2005, 'Faceted Service Specification', Proceedings SOCCER (Service-Oriented Computing: Consequences for Engineering Requirements) Workshop, at RE'05 Conference, Paris, August 2005.

Schmid K., Eisenbarth M. & Grund M., 2005, 'From Requirements Engineering to Knowledge Engineering: Challenges in Adaptive Systems', Proceedings SOCCER (Service-Oriented Computing: Consequences for Engineering Requirements) Workshop, at RE'05 Conference, Paris, August 2005.

Schütze H. and Pedersen, J.O., 1995 "Information retrieval based on word senses", in Proceedings of the Symposium on Document Analysis and Information Retrieval, 4: 161- 175, 1995.

Spanoudakis G., Zisman A., Kozlenkov A.: 2005, 'A Service Discovery Framework for Service Centric Systems', to appear in IEEE International Conference on Services Computing, IEEE Computer Society Press, 251-259.

Sutcliffe A.G. & Maiden N.A.M., 1998, 'The Domain Theory for Requirements Engineering', IEEE Transactions on Software Engineering, 24(3), 174-196.

Tut M. T. & Edmond, D. 2002 "The Use of Patterns in Service Composition", Revised Papers International Workshop on Web Services, E-Business, and Semantic Web, 28–40, 2002

Yu E. & Mylopoulos J.M., 1994, 'Understanding "Why" in Software Process Modelling, Analysis and Design', Proceedings, 16th International Conference on Software Engineering, IEEE Computer Society Press, 159-168.

Zachos K. & Maiden N.A.M., 2006, 'Discovering Services During Requirements Processes', Technical Report, Centre for HCI Design, City University London.

Zhu H., Maiden N.A.M., Jones S.V., Zachos K., 2005, "Applying Patterns in Service Discovery", Proceedings SOCCER (Service-Oriented Computing: Consequences for Engineering Requirements) Workshop, at RE'05 Conference, Paris, August 2005.

A Library of OCL Specification Patterns for Behavioral Specification of Software Components

Jörg Ackermann and Klaus Turowski

Chair of Business Informatics and Systems Engineering,
University of Augsburg, Universitätsstr. 16, 86135 Augsburg, Germany
{joerg.ackermann, klaus.turowski}@wiwi.uni-augsburg.de

Abstract. One important aspect in building trusted information systems is the precise specification of systems and system parts. This applies even more for information systems built from COTS components. To specify behavioral aspects of software components the UML Object Constraint Language (OCL) is well suited. One current problem in component specifications comes from the fact that editing OCL constraints manually is time consuming and error-prone. To simplify constraint definition we propose to use specification patterns for which OCL constraints can be generated automatically. In this paper we outline this solution proposal and present a library of reusable OCL specification patterns.

Keywords: Component-Based Information Systems, Software Component Specification, OCL Specification Patterns.

1 Introduction

One important aspect in building trusted information systems is the precise specification of systems and system parts: the specification can help to close the (frequently be observable) gap between the expected and the actual behavior of a system. Specifications become even more important if information systems are built from COTS components acquired from a variety of vendors [23]. A precise and reliable specification of COTS components supports sound selection and trust in its correct functioning [10]. Moreover, component specifications are a prerequisite for a composition methodology and tool support [20]. For these reasons the specification of software components is of utmost importance for building trusted information systems out of components.

To specify the behavioral aspects of software components the *UML Object Constraint Language* (OCL) [18] is frequently employed (see Sect. 2). Using a formal language like OCL, however, causes one of the current problems in component specifications: Editing OCL constraints manually is time consuming and error-prone (see Sect. 3). To simplify constraint definition we propose to utilize specification patterns for which OCL constraints can be generated automatically (see Sect. 4). For that we present a library of OCL specification patterns (Sect. 5) and discuss a technique to describe and formally specify them (Sect. 6). We conclude with discussion of related work (Sect. 7) and a summary (Sect. 8). The contribution of the project is the simplification of component specification by utilizing reusable OCL specifications. The

E. Dubois and K. Pohl (Eds.): CAiSE 2006, LNCS 4001, pp. 255–269, 2006.
© Springer-Verlag Berlin Heidelberg 2006

results were developed for software components but are general enough to be interesting for anyone using OCL to specify information systems.

2 Behavioral Specification of Software Components

The appropriate and standardized specification of software components is a critical success factor for building component-based information systems. With *specification* of a component we denote the complete, unequivocal and precise description of its external view - that is which services a component provides under which conditions [22]. Various authors addressed specifications for specific tasks of the development process as e.g. design and implementation [8,9], component adaptation [24] or component selection [14]. Approaches towards comprehensive specification of software components are few and include [7,20,22]. Objects to be specified are e.g. business terms, business tasks, interface signatures, behavior and coordination constraints and non-functional attributes.

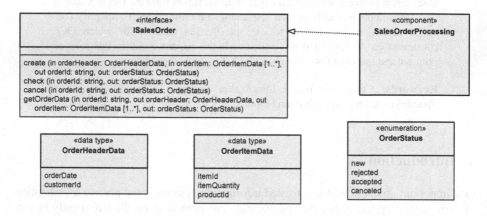

Fig. 1. Interface specification of component *SalesOrderProcessing*

Behavioral specifications (which are topic of this paper) describe how the component behaves in general and in borderline cases. This is achieved by defining constraints (invariants, pre- and postconditions) based on the idea of designing applications by contract [16]. OCL is one of the most used techniques to express such constraints – cf. e.g. [8,9,20,22].

To illustrate how behavioral aspects of software components are specified we introduce a simplified exemplary component *SalesOrderProcessing*. The business task of the component is to manage sales orders. This component is used as example throughout the rest of the paper.

Fig. 1 shows the interface specification of *SalesOrderProcessing* using UML [19]. We see that the component offers the interface *ISalesOrder* with operations to create, check, cancel or retrieve specific sales orders. The data types needed are also defined in Fig. 1. Note that in practice the component would have additional operations and might offer additional order properties. For sake of simplicity we restricted ourselves to the simple form shown in Fig. 1 which will be sufficient as example for this paper.

To specify the information objects belonging to the component (on a logical level) one can use a specification data model which is realized as a UML type diagram and is part of the behavioral specification [5]. Fig. 2 displays such a model for the component *SalesOrderProcessing*. It shows that the component manages sales orders (with attributes id, date of order, status, customer id) and sales order items (with attributes id, quantity, product id) and that there is a one-to-many relationship between sales orders and sales order items.

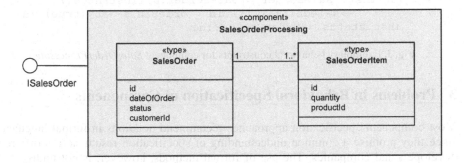

Fig. 2. Specification data model for component *SalesOrderProcessing*

Note that operation parameters for software components are usually value-based (no object-oriented instances are passed). As a consequence the coupling between interface definition (cf. Fig. 1) and specification data model (cf. Fig. 2) is only loose. The operation *ISalesOrder.check* e.g. is semantically an instance method in the sense that it manipulates one specific sales order. Technically, however, the operation is called for the component (and not a sales order instance) and the sales order to be checked is identified by the parameter *orderId*. Therefore the consequences of operation calls on the specification data model must be specified explicitly.

The behavioral specification of a component is based on its interface specification and on its specification data model and consists of OCL expressions that constrain the components operations – for an example see Fig. 3. The first constraint is an invariant for type *SalesOrder*: It guarantees that different sales orders always differ in the value of their id – that is the attribute *id* is a semantic key for sales orders. By defining an invariant this constraint needs only to be formulated once and does not need to be repeated in several pre-and postconditions. The remaining constraints in Fig. 3 concern the operation *ISalesOrder.create*: The precondition demands that the field *customerId* of parameter *orderHeader* must not contain an empty string when calling the operation. The first postcondition guarantees that an instance of class *SalesOrder* (which id equals the value of the output parameter *orderId*) was created by the operation. The second postcondition assures that the newly created sales order instance is in status *new*. Note that Fig. 3 shows only some constraints and does not contain a complete behavioral specification.

```
context SalesOrder
  inv: SalesOrder.allInstances()->forAll(i1, i2 |
                        i1 <> i2 implies (i1.id <> i2.id))

context ISalesOrder::create(orderHeader: OrderHeaderData, order-
Item: OrderItemData, orderId: string, orderStatus: OrderStatus)
  pre:  orderHeader.customerId <> ''
  post: let inst: SalesOrder = SalesOrder.allInstances()
               ->select(i1 | (i1.id = orderId))->any(true) in
        inst.oclIsNew
  post: let inst: SalesOrder = SalesOrder.allInstances()
               ->select(i1 | (i1.id = orderId))->any(true) in
        inst.status = OrderStatus::new
```

Fig. 3. Exemplary behavioral constraints for component *SalesOrderProcessing*

3 Problems in Behavioral Specification of Components

Most component specification approaches recommend notations in formal languages since they promise a common understanding of specification results across different developers and companies. The use of formal methods, however, is not undisputed. Some authors argue that the required effort is too high and the intelligibility of the specification results is too low – for a discussion of advantages and liabilities of formal methods compare [13].

The disadvantages of earlier formal methods are reduced by UML OCL [18]: The notation of OCL has a comparatively simple structure and is oriented towards the syntax of object-oriented programming languages. Software developers can therefore handle OCL much easier than earlier formal methods that were based on set theory and predicate logic. This is one reason why OCL is recommended by many authors for the specification of software components.

Despite its advantages OCL can not solve all problems associated with the use of formal methods: One result of two case studies specifying business components [1,2] was the insight that editing OCL constraints manually is nevertheless time consuming and error-prone. Similar experiences were made by other authors that use OCL constraints in specifications (outside the component area), e.g. [12,15]. They conclude that it takes a considerable effort to master OCL and use it effectively.

It should be noted that behavioral aspects (where OCL is used) have a great importance for component specifications: In the specification of a rather simple component in case study [2], for example, the behavioral aspects filled 57 (of altogether 81) pages and required a tremendous amount of work. For component specifications to be practical it is therefore mandatory to simplify the authoring of OCL constraints.

4 Solution Proposal: Utilizing OCL Specification Patterns

Solution strategies to simplify OCL specifications include better tool support (to reduce errors) and an automation of constraint editing (to reduce effort) – the latter can e.g. be based on use cases or on predefined specification patterns (compare Sect. 7).

To use specification patterns seems to be particularly promising for the specification of business components: When analyzing e.g. case study [2] one finds that 70% of all OCL constraints in this study can be backtracked to few frequently occurring specification patterns.

OCL Constraints Generated from Specification Patterns

1. Select Specification Pattern

Pattern Name: Semantic Key Attributes

Pattern Intent: Specifies that a set of attributes are a semantic key for a class

2. Display Template OCL Constraint

```
context class
inv: class.allInstances()->forAll(i1, i2 | i1 <> i2 implies
(i1.attribute1 <> i2.attribute1) and
(i1.attribute2 <> i2.attribute2))
```

3. Select Pattern Parameter Values

Class: SalesOrder

Number of Key Attributes: 1

Attribute 1: id

    id
    dateOfOrder
    status
    customerId

Generate   Cancel

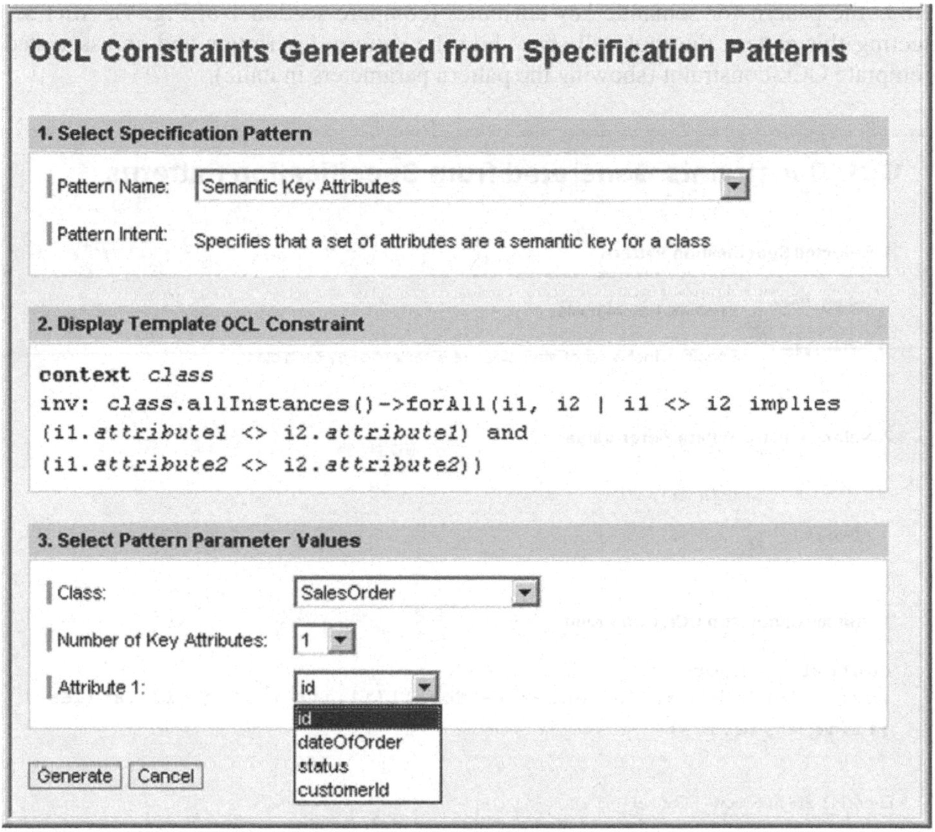

Fig. 4. Selection screen for generating an OCL constraint

Under *(OCL) specification pattern* we understand an abstraction of OCL constraints that are similar in intention and structure but differ in the UML model elements used. Each pattern has one or more *pattern parameters* (typed by elements of the UML metamodel) that act as placeholder for the actual model elements. With *pattern instantiation* we denote a specific OCL constraint that results from binding the pattern parameters with actual UML model elements.

As an example let us consider the pattern *Semantic Key Attributes*: It represents the situation that one or more attributes of a class (in the specification data model – cf. Fig. 2) play the semantic role of a key – that is any two instances of the class differ in at least one value of the key attributes. Pattern parameters are the class and the list of key attributes. A pattern instantiation (for the class *SalesOrder* and its attribute *id*) can be seen in the upper part of Fig. 3.

If such OCL specification patterns are collected, formally described and integrated into a specification tool the specification can be simplified in the following way: Suppose the person who specifies our exemplary component is in the middle of the specification process and wants to formulate the invariant from Fig. 3. He checks the library of predefined specification patterns (which is part of his specification tool) and finds the pattern for semantic key attributes (compare section 1 of Fig. 4). After selecting this pattern the tool will show him the pattern description and an associated template OCL constraint (showing the pattern parameters in italic).

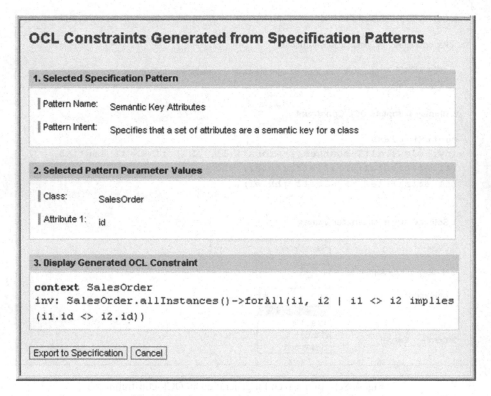

Fig. 5. Display of the generated OCL constraint

The user has to select model elements for the parameters (in section 3 of Fig. 4) – in our example the class *SalesOrder* and its attribute *id* are selected. Note that the tool can be built in such a way that it restricts the input to those model elements that are allowed for a pattern – in section 3 of Fig. 4 for instance you can see that the tool only offers the attributes of class *SalesOrder* for selection.

After providing pattern and parameter values the user can start the generation. The tool checks the input for consistency and then generates the desired OCL constraint (compare section 3 of Fig. 5) which can be included into the component specification.

Applying this approach has the following advantages: For the specification provider maintenance of specifications is simplified because it becomes faster, less error-prone and requires less expert OCL knowledge. For a specification user the understanding of specifications is simplified because generated constraints are uniform and are therefore easier recognizable. Moreover, if the patterns were standardized, it would be enough to specify a pattern and the parameter values (without the generated OCL text) which would make recognition even easier.

5 A Library of OCL Specification Patterns

In this section we introduce a list of OCL specification patterns that are useful for behavioral specification of software components. To obtain this list we first studied several case studies (dealing with business components) and publications about component specifications and identified frequently occurring patterns [3]. In a second step we analyzed the preliminary list and identified additional patterns that are useful but could not be found in the first step. (Reasons to include additional patterns were for instance extending patterns to other relevant UML metamodel elements or symmetry considerations like including a constraint for deleted instances if there is one for created instances.) As result we obtained a library of altogether 18 OCL specification patterns which are subdivided into four categories. The categories and their assigned patterns are shown in Tables 1-4 – the table columns are pattern number (for easier reference), constraint type and pattern name. Note that it is conceivable that the pattern list might be extended in future.

Table 1. Specification patterns concerning only interface specifications

No.	Constraint type	Pattern name
1	Precondition	Value Specification of Input Parameter
2	Postcondition	Value Specification of Output Parameter
3	Precondition	Value Specification of Input Parameter Field
4	Postcondition	Value Specification of Output Parameter Field
5	Precondition	Value Specification of Input Table Parameter Fields
6	Postcondition	Value Specification of Output Table Parameter Fields

The behavioral specification of software components refers to the interface specification (cf. Fig. 1) and the specification data model (cf. Fig. 2). The first pattern category (cf. Table 1) contains patterns that only concern the interface specification.

Pattern 3 (*Value Specification of Input Parameter Field*) for instance is a precondition that allows restricting the value of a field of a structured input parameter of an operation. Pattern parameters are an operation, a parameter, a parameter field, one of the operators (=, <>, <, <=, > or >=) and a value (corresponding to the type of the field). Using this pattern one can e.g. demand that the field must be greater than zero or contain a specific element of an enumeration. An instantiation of this pattern is shown in the precondition of Fig. 3 which requests that the field *customerId* of input parameter *orderHeader* (of operation *ISalesOrder.create*) must not be the empty string.

Analogous preconditions can be formulated for a simple, unstructured input parameter (using pattern 1) and for a field of an input table parameter (pattern 5). Patterns 2, 4 and 6 are similar but represent postconditions assuring that an output parameter (field) has a certain value or value range.

Table 2. Specification patterns concerning only specification data models

No.	Constraint type	Pattern name
7	Invariant	Semantic Key Attributes
8	Invariant	Value Specification of Class Attribute
9	Invariant	Relationship between Class Attribute Values

The second category (cf. Table 2) features patterns that only concern the specification data model. They are independent from operation calls and thus all invariants.

An example is pattern 7 (*Semantic Key Attributes*) which was already discussed before. Pattern parameters are a class and a list of its attributes – a pattern instantiation is given by the invariant in Fig. 3. Note that the pattern is intended for one or more attributes – this is the reason for not using the operator *isUnique* which would be rather constructed for more than one attribute. Additionally it shall be mentioned that the presented patterns are rather static – they allow substituting UML model elements but do not allow structural changes. For structural variations on the pattern (e.g. the attribute *id* of class *SalesOrderItem* in Fig. 2 is only unique in the context of a specific instance of class *SalesOrder*) one has to define additional patterns.

The other patterns in Table 2 allow specifying the value of a class attribute (pattern 8) or the relationship between two attributes of the same class (pattern 9). A possible extension for the last pattern would be the relationship between two attributes of different classes which are connected by an association.

In difference to the patterns presented so far the remaining patterns (in Tables 3 and 4) address the relationship between interface specification and specification data model and are rather specific for software components (more precise: specific for value-based operation calls).

Table 3. Specification patterns concerning the existence of class instances for operation calls

No.	Constraint type	Pattern name
10	Precondition	Class Instance Existing
11	Precondition	Class Instance Not Existing
12	Postcondition	Class Instance Created
13	Postcondition	Class Instance Deleted

The third pattern category (cf. Table 3) contains patterns that deal with the existence of specific class instances for an operation call.

As an example we consider pattern 12 (*Class Instance Created*). This pattern describes a postcondition which specifies that an instance of a class (in the specification data model) was created by an operation call. The pattern parameters are the class *cl* for which an instance was created, the calling operation *op*, and two ordered sets *keyList*, *kparList* of elements identifying the class instance. The parameter *keyList* contains a list of those attributes of *cl* that form together the semantic key of *cl* (compare pattern 7). The parameter *kparList* contains those parameters or parameter fields of *op* in which the key values to identify the required instance are passed. Note that *keyList* and *kparList* must have the same number of elements and must be ordered in such a way, that corresponding entries stand at the same position within *keyList* and *kparList*. A pattern instantiation is given by the first postcondition in Fig. 3 which assures that operation *ISalesOrder.create* created a new instance of class *SalesOrder* which id equals the value of parameter *orderId*. To make the OCL constraint easier to understand first a local variable *inst* is defined for the instance in question and then the actual constraint is formulated in the context of *inst* (cf. Fig. 3).

The other patterns in Table 3 are similar (and have the same pattern parameters) as pattern 12 and can be used to request that a certain instance exists (pattern 10) or does not exist (pattern 11) before the operation call and to assure that a specific instance was deleted (pattern 13) by the operation.

Table 4. Specification patterns integrating interface specification and data model

No.	Constraint type	Pattern name
14	Precondition	Precondition on an Instance Attribute
15	Postcondition	Postcondition for an Instance Attribute
16	Postcondition	Relationship to an Instance of another Type
17	Postcondition	Equivalence of Parameter (Field) Value and Attribute Value
18	Postcondition	Equivalence of Multiline Parameter (Field) Values and Attribute Values

The fourth pattern category (cf. Table 4) collects further patterns that allow specifying prerequisites from model instances for an operation call and consequences of operation calls for model instances.

Pattern 15 (*Postcondition for an Instance Attribute*) describes a postcondition that can be used to assure that an attribute of a given class instance has a certain value (or value range) at the end of an operation call. The second postcondition in Fig. 3 e.g. states that the attribute *status* of the newly created instance of *SalesOrder* (having as id the value of *orderId*) has the value *new* at the end of calling *ISalesOrder.create*. Pattern 15 has pattern parameters for two purposes: On one hand there are the parameters *cl*, *op*, *keyList* and *kparList* which are used to identify the desired class instance (for more details compare pattern 12 as described above). On the other hand the pattern has as parameters the attribute, one of the operators (=, <>, <, <=, > or >=) and a value (corresponding to the type of the attribute) to specify the value or value range of the attribute (compare also pattern 3 described above). Looking at the post-conditions in Fig. 3 one might notice that the instance variable *inst* is defined in both conditions. Behavioral specifications could be simplified if it were possible to reuse local variables like *inst* in several pre- and postconditions. UML OCL, however, only allows declaring reusable variables (via the *define* statement) for invariants and not for operation calls.

Pattern 14 is similar to pattern 15 but represents a precondition which can be used to demand that a class instance attribute has a certain value when calling an operation. Pattern 17 can be used to express that the value of a class instance attribute equals the value of a parameter (or parameter field). Such a condition is useful for create or update operations to show how class instance attributes are filled from parameters or for read operations to show how parameters are filled from instance attributes. To avoid the need to formulate many such constraints if the class has many attributes pattern 17 allows specifying the constraint for a list of attributes and parameters (or parameter fields). Pattern 18 is similar in intention but addresses operation parameters and instance properties of multiplicity greater than one. Pattern 16 is also similar and enables to specify how a parameter (or parameter field) is connected to an instance of a second class which is associated to the first class.

6 Description of OCL Specification Patterns

The specification patterns identified in Sect. 5 need to be described precisely in order to be reusable for component specifications. For that we propose to use on one hand a description scheme and on the other hand a formal specification. The formal specification is done by using OCL itself and addresses OCL experts and tool builders who wish to implement constraint generators. The description scheme addresses users of specification patterns – for this it contains all relevant specification details in a more informal way. To confront a pattern user with the full OCL specification would contradict the goal to support specifications by non-OCL experts as well. In this section we present both description approaches.

Based on the ideas of [3] we developed for pattern users a description scheme that allows displaying all relevant pattern details in a structured and uniform way. As an example Table 5 shows the description scheme for pattern number 7 (*Semantic Key Attributes*).

The first characteristic is the pattern name that identifies the pattern and serves as a short semantic explanation. The characteristic *pattern intent* contains a short statement about intention and rationale of the pattern. The characteristic *pattern parameter* lists the parameters of the pattern together with their type. Parameters can be of elementary type (like *String*) or are elements from the UML metamodel (layer M2 in the four-layer metamodel hierarchy of UML [17]). Parameters of pattern 7 are the class *cl* (of type *Class*) and the list of key attributes *keyList* (of type ordered set of *Property*). The characteristic *restrictions* denotes what conditions the pattern parameters must fulfill. In our case it is required that all elements of *keyList* are attributes of *cl*.

Table 5. Description scheme for pattern *Semantic Key Attributes*

Characteristic	Description
Pattern name	Semantic Key Attributes
Pattern intent	Specifies that a set of attributes are a semantic key for a class
Pattern parameter	cl: Class; keyList: Property [1..*]
Restrictions	Each element of *keyList* is an attribute of *cl*
Constraint type	Invariant
Constraint context	*cl*

Constraint body	`cl.name.allInstances()->forAll(i1,i2 |`
	`i1 <> i2 implies`
	`(i1.keyList[1].name <> i2.keyList[1].name)`
	`and`
	`(i1.keyList[2].name <> i2.keyList[2].name))`

The remaining three characteristics describe the OCL constraint the pattern represents. With *constraint type* we denote if the constraint is an invariant, pre- or postcondition. The characteristic *constraint context* stands for the OCL context of the constraint and is always one of the pattern parameters (in our example class *cl*). The final characteristic *constraint body* shows how the OCL expression to be generated looks like. For that the OCL expression is kept generic: subexpressions in normal typesetting can be left as they are (in our example e.g. `'.allInstances()'`) but subexpressions in italic stand for text that needs to be substituted by a parameter value or a parameters model name (as `cl.name` in Table 5 – because *cl* is a UML meta-model element of type *Class* we need to access its property *name* to retrieve its actual name.) Note that the chosen notation for the characteristic *constraint body* is sufficient to give an idea of the generated OCL expression but has its limitations if patterns are variable: In pattern 7 e.g. an arbitrary number of attributes can be used – in Table 5 the constraint is shown exemplary for two attributes. In this way the use of more complicated constructs (like *loop* or *iterate*) can be avoided which helps in keeping the description easily understandable. Note that the formal pattern description (as discussed below) is powerful enough to enable a precise specification.

Beside the informal pattern description each OCL specification pattern is formally specified. This formal pattern specification is necessary to avoid misunderstandings and is prerequisite for tool builders implementing constraint generators.

The basic idea how to formally describe the specification patterns is as follows: For each OCL specification pattern a specific function (called *OCL pattern function*) is defined. The pattern parameters are the input of the pattern function. Result of the pattern function is a generated OCL constraint which is returned and (if integrated with the specification tool) automatically added to the corresponding UML model element. The OCL pattern functions themselves are specified by OCL – from this specification one can determine the constraint properties (e.g. invariant) and its textual representation. All pattern functions are assigned as operations to a new class *OclPattern* which logically belongs to the layer of the UML metamodel.

As an example we consider again the pattern *Semantic Key Attributes*. For this pattern we define the OCL pattern function *Create_Inv_SemanticKeyAttributes*. Input of the function are the class *cl* and the set of attributes *keyList* – all understood as UML model elements. Result is a UML model element of type *Constraint*. The complete specification of this pattern function is shown in Fig. 6.

```
context OclPattern::Create_Inv_SemanticKeyAttributes (cl: Class,
keyList: orderedSet(Property)): Constraint
(1) pre: keyList->forAll(key | key.class = cl)

(2) post: result.oclIsNew
(3) post: result.namespace = result.context
(4) post: result.specification.isKindOf(OpaqueExpression)
(5) post: result.specification.language = 'OCL'

(6) post: result.stereotype.name = 'invariant'
(7) post: result.context = cl
(8) post: result.name = 'Semantic Key Attributes'
(9) post:
    let lastKey: Property = keyList->any() in
    let keyList1: Set(Property) = keyList->excluding(lastKey) in
  result.specification.body = OclPattern.Multiconcat
   (cl.name,
     '.allInstances()->forAll( i1, i2 | i1 <> i2 implies ',
    keyList1->iterate(key, acc: string '' |
      OclPattern.Multiconcat
       (acc, '(i1.', key.name, ' <> i2.', key.name, ') and ')),
   '(i1.', lastKey.name, ' <> i2.', lastKey.name, ')))')
```

Fig. 6. Specification of pattern function *Create_Inv_SemanticKeyAttributes*

The specification for each pattern consists of three parts: pattern specific preconditions (1), general postconditions (2)-(5) and pattern specific postconditions (6)-(9).

The function specific preconditions describe which restrictions must be fulfilled when calling the pattern function. These preconditions must assure that the actual parameters conform to the specification pattern. The precondition (1) demands for instance that each element of *keyList* is an attribute of *cl*.

The general postconditions (2)-(5) are identical for all OCL pattern functions and represent in a way the main construction details. These postconditions (together with the functions signature) establish the following: The return of each pattern function is a UML model element of type *Constraint*. This constraint is added to the model (2) and is assigned to the model element which is the context of the constraint (3). The actual specification of the constraint is of type *OpaqueExpression* (4) and is edited in the language OCL (5).

The function specific postconditions (6)-(9) establish the following: (6) describes the constraint type (invariant, pre- or postcondition) of the returned constraint. (7) defines the context of the constraint (in our example the operation *cl*). The attribute *name* of *Constraint* is used in (8) to assign the pattern name to the constraint. The textual OCL representation of a constraint can be found in the attribute *body* of the constraint specification. Postconditions like (9) specify this textual representation by combining fixed substrings (e.g. `'.allInstances()'`) with the name of model elements which were supplied as pattern parameter values (e.g. `cl.name`). Note that we used in (9) a help function *OclPattern.Multiconcat* which concatenates a sequence of strings.

By defining OCL pattern functions for the specification patterns it became possible to formally specify the patterns completely and quite elegantly: the pattern parameters can be found as function parameters and the function specification (which uses again OCL) describes the prerequisites to apply the pattern and the properties of the constraint to be generated. One big advantage is that this approach only uses known specification techniques and does not require the invention of new ones. There is only one new class *OclPattern* that encapsulates the definition of all patterns. A more detailed description of the pattern specification, a comparison to other approaches and a discussion about the relationship to the UML metamodel can be found in [4].

7 Related Work

Due to its importance component specifications are discussed by many authors (e.g. [8,9,10,20,22] – for an overview compare e.g. [20]). Most current specification approaches identify the need for behavioral specifications and propose to use pre- and postconditions based on OCL [18]. Problems related with using OCL were so far only reported in the case studies [1,2] and the authors are not aware of any solution to this problem in the area of component specifications.

There are several publications outside the component area discussing the problems of editing OCL constraints manually [6,12,15]. There exist several approaches to simplify constraint writing: [12] develops an authoring tool that supports a developer with editing and synchronizing constraints in formal notation (OCL) and informal notation (natural language). [15] discusses an approach how to generate OCL expressions automatically. They constrain themselves, however, to the single use case of connecting two attributes within a UML model by an invariant. [11] discusses strategies to textually simplify OCL constraints that were generated by some algorithm. [21] develops an algorithm that allows in the analysis phase to transform use cases into class diagrams and OCL specifications. The author suggests that generation of OCL constraints might be possible but gives no details for it. [6] proposes a mechanism to connect design patterns with OCL constraint patterns which allows instantiating OCL constraints automatically whenever a design pattern is instantiated. This idea is very similar to ours but its realization can not be employed for specifying components (for details cf. [4]).

8 Summary

The paper discussed one of the current problems in component specifications: editing OCL constraints manually is time consuming and error-prone. As solution we proposed to utilize specification patterns for which OCL constraints can be generated automatically. For that we identified a collection of OCL specification patterns and presented a way to describe and formally specify these patterns. Such well-defined and formally specified patterns can be reused in component specification tools. Direction of future research include to gain further experience with the identified specification patterns (and extend the library if necessary) and with their usage in our component specification tool.

References

1. Ackermann, J.: Fallstudie zur Spezifikation von Fachkomponenten. In: Turowski, K. (ed.): 2. Workshop Modellierung und Spezifikation von Fachkomponenten. Bamberg (2001) 1-66 (In German)
2. Ackermann, J.: Zur Spezifikation der Parameter von Fachkomponenten. In: Turowski, K. (ed.): 5. Workshop Komponentenorientierte betriebliche Anwendungssysteme (WKBA 5). Augsburg (2003) 47-154 (In German)
3. Ackermann, J.: Frequently Occurring Patterns in Behavioral Specification of Software Components. In: Turowski, K.; Zaha, J.M. (eds.): Component-Oriented Enterprise Applications. Proceedings of the COEA 2005. Erfurt (2005) 41-56
4. Ackermann, J.: Formal Description of OCL Specification Patterns for Behavioral Specification of Software Components. In: Baar, T. (ed.): Proceedings of the MoDELS'05 Conference Workshop on Tool Support for OCL and Related Formalisms - Needs and Trends. Montego Bay, Jamaica (2005) 15-29
5. Ackermann, J., Turowski, K.: Specification of Customizable Business Components. In: Chroust, G.; Hofer, S. (eds.): Euromicro Conference 2003. Belek-Antalya, Turkey (2003) 391-394
6. Baar, T.; Hähnle, R.; Sattler, T.; Schmitt, P.H.: Entwurfgesteuerte Erzeugung von OCL-Constraints. In: Softwaretechnik-Trends 3 (2000) (In German)
7. Beugnard, A.; Jézéquel, J.-M.; Plouzeau, N.; Watkins, D.: Making Components Contract Aware. In: IEEE Computer 7 (1999) 38-44
8. Cheesman, J.; Daniels, J.: UML Components. Addison-Wesley, Boston (2001)
9. D'Souza, D.F.; Wills, A.C.: Objects, Components, and Frameworks with UML: The Catalysis Approach. Addison-Wesley, Reading (1998)
10. Geisterfer, C.J.M., Ghosh, S.: Software Component Specification: A Study in Perspective of Component Selection and Reuse. In: Proceedings of the 5th International Conference on COTS Based Software Systems (ICCBSS). Orlando, USA (2006)
11. Giese, M.; Hähnle, R.; Larsson, D.: Rule-Based Simplification of OCL Constraints. In: Workshop on OCL and Model Driven Engineering at UML'2004. Lisbon (2004)
12. Hähnle, R.; Johannisson, K.; Ranta, A.: An Authoring Tool for Informal and Formal Requirements Specifications. In: Kutsche, R.-D.; Weber, H. (eds.): Fundamental Approaches to Software Engineering, 5th International Conference FASE. Grenoble (2002) 233-248
13. Hall, A.: Seven Myths of Formal Methods. In: IEEE Software 5 (1990) 11-19
14. Hemer, D.; Lindsay, P.: Specification-based retrieval strategies for module reuse. In: Grant, D.; Sterling, L. (eds.): Proceedings 2001 Australian Software Engineering Conference. IEEE Computer Society. Canberra (2001) 235-243
15. Ledru, Y.; Dupuy-Chessa, S.; Fadil, H.: Towards Computer-aided Design of OCL Constraints. In: Grundspenkis, J.; Kirikova, M. (eds.): CAiSE Workshops 2004, Vol. 1. Riga (2004) 329-338
16. Meyer, B.: Applying "Design by Contract". In: IEEE Computer 10 (1992) 40-51

17. OMG (ed.): Unified Modeling Language: UML 2.0 Infrastructure Specification, 2004-10-16 URL: http://www.omg.org/technology/documents, Date of Call: 2005-09-09 (2004)
18. OMG (ed.): Unified Modeling Language: UML 2.0 OCL Specification, 2005-06-06. URL: http://www.omg.org/technology/documents, Date of Call: 2005-09-09 (2005)
19. OMG (ed.): Unified Modeling Language: UML 2.0 Superstructure Specification, 2005-07-04. URL: http://www.omg.org/technology/documents, Date of Call: 2005-09-09 (2005)
20. Overhage, S.: UnSCom: A Standardized Framework for the Specification of Software Components. In: Weske, M.; Liggesmeyer, P. (eds.): Object-Oriented and Internet-Based Technologies, Proceedings of the 5th Net'Object Days. Erfurt (2004)
21. Roussev, B.: Generating OCL specifications and class diagrams from use cases: A newtonian approach. In: Proceedings of 36th Annual Hawaii International Conference on System Sciences (HICSS'03). Big Island (2003)
22. Turowski, K. (ed.): Standardized Specification of Business Components: Memorandum of the working group 5.10.3 Component Oriented Business Application Systems. University of Augsburg (2002). URL: http://www.fachkomponenten.de. Date of Call: 2005-09-09
23. Wallnau, K.C.; Hissam, S.A.; Seacord, R.C.: Building Systems from Commercial Components. Addison-Wesley (2002)
24. Yellin, D.; Strom, R.: Protocol Specifications and Component Adaptors. In: ACM Transactions on Programming Languages and Systems 19 (1997) 292–333

Workflow

Data–Driven Process Control
and Exception Handling
in Process Management Systems

Stefanie Rinderle[1] and Manfred Reichert[2]

[1] Dept. DBIS, University of Ulm, Germany
rinderle@informatik.uni-ulm.de
[2] IS Group, University of Twente, The Netherlands
m.u.reichert@utwente.nl

Abstract. Business processes are often characterized by high variability and dynamics, which cannot be always captured in contemporary process management systems (PMS). Adaptive PMS have emerged in recent years, but do not completely solve this problem. In particular, users are not adequately supported in dealing with real–world exceptions. Exception handling usually requires manual interactions and necessary process adaptations have to be defined at the control flow level. Altogether, only experienced users are able to cope with these tasks. As an alternative, changes on process data (elements) can be more easily accomplished, and a more data–driven view on (adaptive) PMS can help to bridge the gap between real–world processes and computerized ones. In this paper we present an approach for data–driven process control allowing for the automated expansion and adaptation of task nets during runtime. By integrating and exploiting context information this approach further enables automated exception handling at a high level and in a user–friendly way. Altogether, the presented work provides an added value to current adaptive PMS.

1 Introduction

For several reasons companies are developing a growing interest in improving the efficiency and quality of their internal business processes and in optimizing their interactions with customers and partners. Following this trend, in recent years there has been an increasing adoption of business process management (BPM) technologies as well as emerging standards for process orchestration and process choreography [1]. In particular, BPM technologies enable the definition, execution and monitoring of the operational processes of an enterprise.

Currently, one can observe a big gap between computerized workflows and real-world processes [2, 3, 4]. This gap is even increasing during runtime, thus leading to unsatisfactory user acceptance. One reason for this drawback is the inability of existing PMS to adequately deal with the variability and dynamics of real–world processes. For many applications (e.g., logistics, healthcare) process execution cannot be fixed in every detail at buildtime [2, 5]. Regarding a delivery process, for example, the concrete tour for the truck is not known beforehand.

E. Dubois and K. Pohl (Eds.): CAiSE 2006, LNCS 4001, pp. 273–287, 2006.
© Springer-Verlag Berlin Heidelberg 2006

Instead, it should be possible to model the processes only at a coarse–grained level and to dynamically evolve these process skeletons (which set out the rough execution during runtime) at the process instance level.

Another drawback arises from the fact that current PMS do not adequately capture (physical) context data about the ongoing process instances. In particular, real–world data is needed for providing (automated) exception handling support. Due to this missing support in exceptional situations, however, users often have to bypass the PMS. As a consequence, computerized processes do not longer (completely) reflect the real-world processes. For dynamic applications like logistics or healthcare, as mentioned, this fact can quickly lead to a non-negligible (semantic) gap between the processes at the system level and those taking place in the real world. To overcome the discussed limitations one of the greatest challenges is to provide automatic support for expanding and adapting ongoing process instances at runtime by avoiding user interactions as far as possible.

In this paper we provide a formal framework for the automated and data–driven evolution of processes during runtime. This includes data–driven expansion of process task nets as well as data–centered exception handling, i.e., process adaptations necessary to deal with exceptional situations are carried out by modifying data structures (e.g., a delivery list of goods). This data change is then propagated to the running process by the concept of data–driven expansion, and not by directly applying (user–defined) changes on the control flow schema of the concerned process instance. This requires availability of data about real–world processes in order to provide automated support. Particularly, we also have to integrate and exploit process context information (e.g., data about physical objects) in order to automatically derive exception handling strategies at a semantically high level. This paper completes our previous work on the ADEPT framework for adaptive process management [6, 7]. On top of this framework we introduce the concepts mentioned above. However, the described approach could be applied in connection with other adaptive PMS as well (e.g., WASA [8]).

In Section 2 we present a motivating example stemming from the logistics domain. A formal framework for data–driven task net expansion is given in Section 3. In Section 4 we discuss exception handling strategies followed by architectural considerations in Section 5. Section 6 discusses related work. We close with a summary and an outlook in Section 7.

2   Motivating Example (and Basic Concepts)

In this section we introduce our running example used throughout the paper in order to illustrate our approach.

2.1   Example Description

As usual, we distinguish between buildtime and runtime aspects of a business process. This is reflected by the separation of process specifications at the type level (buildtime) and the instance level (runtime).

Process Description at Type Level: We use a logistics process, namely the delivery of a set of furnitures to a number of customers by one truck. Let us assume that a planning component has already determined the list of customers who shall be visited by the truck, and that the order of the list sets out the sequence in which the goods are to be delivered to the customers. Consider this information as input to the logistics process depicted in Fig. 1 (via external data element cust_list). Based on it a delivery_list is built up containing the data needed for delivering the goods (customer name & address, list of the goods to be delivered which have been previously scanned via their bar code). In parallel to this, the truck is prepared. Throughout the processes, the truck position (data element truck_pos) is provided by an external tracking component, whose data are continuously updated by a GPS system – we denote this process data element therefore as *external*. In general, such process context information is stemming from physical objects related to the associated process. Examples for physical objects are truck or good with their associated context information location (by GPS system) or barcode.

The delivery list is handed to the truck driver responsible for the tour who then loads the truck correspondingly. The associated **load truck** activity is a *multiple instance activity*, i.e., at runtime it has to be expanded into several activity instances of which each represents the loading of the items for a certain customer (cf. Fig. 2). The number of running instances and the tour itself (described by multiple instance activity **deliver goods** at type level) are also figured out during runtime according to the order set out by data element cust_list, i.e., this activity is expanded into several activities each of them describing a single customer delivery. We call this data–driven approach *expansion*. Note that, in addition, **deliver goods** is a complex activity (cf. Fig. 2). This results in a runtime expansion into subprocesses each of them consisting of a sequence of the two activities **unload goods** and **sign delivery report** (cf. Fig. 2). Finally, when the truck driver has finished his tour he is supposed to summarize all single delivery reports collected during the tour in order to create a tour delivery report. Afterwards the truck is returned to the truck company.

Process Expansion at Instance Level: Regarding the expansion of the described multiple instance activities **load truck** and **deliver goods** (see Fig. 1), several issues arise. The first one refers to expansion time, i.e., the time when the multiple instance activities are expanded during instance execution (at process instance level). Basically there are two possibilities: either the expansion takes place when the process instance is started or when the multiple instance activity becomes activated. In Fig. 2, for example, in both cases, the expansion time is set to activity activation time. Therefore, for process instance $I1$, **load truck** has been expanded into three activity instances according to the content of the delivery list. These activity instances describe loading the goods for three customers 1, 2, and 3. By contrast, **deliver goods** has not been expanded yet. For process instance $I2$, however, the expansion of activities **load truck** and **deliver goods** (for customer 1 and 2) has already taken place. When expand-

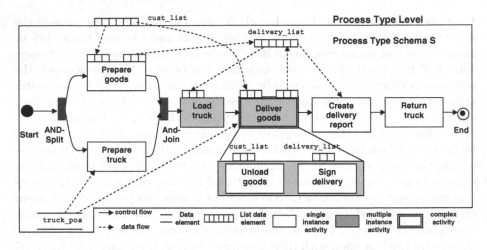

Fig. 1. Logistics Process at Type Level

ing `deliver goods` two activity sequences (consisting of basic activities `Unload goods` and `Sign delivery`) have been inserted at the instance level.

In addition to sequential expansion (as for process instances $I1$ and $I2$ in Fig. 2) parallel expansion will be possible as well if the single activity instances shall be organized in parallel. In addition to this, it is further possible to specifiy in which order the data elements are fetched from the list element responsible for the expansion. Two standard strategies (FIFO and LIFO) are considered in this paper, but others are conceivable as well. More advanced strategies could depend on planning algorithms (especially within the logistics area).

Changes of the process context and the data structures often require process adaptations. The approach of activity expansion during runtime integrates

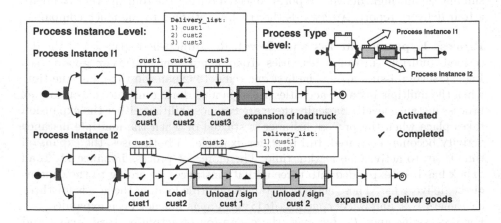

Fig. 2. Expansions of Logistics Process at Instance Level

buildtime flexibility into the process meta model[1]. In the logistics process, for example, an additional delivery can be realised by inserting the associated data into the delivery list before activation time of `load truck` and `deliver goods`. This results in the desired process structure and is based on the expansion mechanism and not on the application of an end–user defined control flow change.

2.2 Exceptional Cases

User acceptance can be further increased by strengthening the data–centered view on processes. In addition to data–driven expansion of activities our approach includes process context information, about "physical objects" (e.g., bar code of the goods to be delivered or the truck position determined by a GPS system). Context information can be extremely helpful when dealing with exceptional situations. Assume that a truck crashes during delivery. Then a solution for this problem can be figured out using the context information about the truck position. Other examples for exceptions comprise a wrong truck load or a rejection of the delivery by the customer (e.g., because of quality problems).

Generally, the provision of automatic exception handling strategies is highly desirable for application processes which are "vulnerable" to exceptions. In addition, it must be possible to define such automatic strategies at a semantically high level in order to increase user acceptance. So far, it has been either not possible to deal with exceptional situation at all or users have been obliged to interfere by adapting the affected process instances. However, such modifications require a lot of knowlegde about the process. Using the concept of data–driven expansion instead, exception handling can be (partially) based on the data (e.g., by changing the customer order within the delivery list). Consequently, the system is enabled to automatically transform these modifications into changes of the process structure.

For finding such auomated, high–level exception handling strategies the ability to exploit context data is indispensable. Consider, for example, process instance I2 depicted in Fig. 2. Assume that during the delivery of goods to customer_2 the truck has a breakdown. In this situation it would be not desirable to interrupt the process and roll it back to the starting point since the other customer(s) have been served properly so far. Exploiting context information, in particular truck positions, it could be a more favorable solution to send an alternative truck to the troubled one, pick up the goods, and deliver them to customer_2. Generally, physical context information is helpful for this (and must therefore be somehow respresented at process type level and be gathered at process instance level). Other examples for exceptional situations during execution of the logistics process comprise an incomplete or incorrect loading / unloading of goods, quality defects (e.g., wrong colour of furniture) resulting in such customer refusal, or absence of the customer when the goods are delivered.

---

[1] We also offer the possibility to adapt process instances ad–hoc by applying instance–specific changes (cf. Section 3).

2.3   Requirements

Altogether, we need a runtime system which allows for a **data–driven** process management. In detail, it must be possible to

- dynamically expand task nets in a data–driven way
- increase process flexibility by automatically translating data structure changes to corresponding process instance adaptations
- integrate context data within the process model
- make use of context information in order to automatically derive exception handling strategies

3   Framework for Dynamically Evolving Process Structures

In this section we present a formal framework for automatically evolving process instances during runtime. The formal foundation is needed in order to present an algorithm for task net expansion, which automatically ensures the correctness of the resulting task net as well as properly working exception handling strategies.

3.1   Process Type Schema

We enrich the standard definition of task nets (like, e.g., activity nets) by introducing the concepts of *list–valued data elements* and the concept of *expansion of multiple instance activities*.

Definition 1 (Process Type Schema). *A tuple $S = (N, D, CtrlE, DataE, EC, Exp)$ is called a process type schema with:*

- *N is a set of activities*
- *D is a set of process data elements. Each data element $d \in D$ has a type $T \subseteq \mathcal{A} \cup \mathcal{L}$, where $\mathcal{A}$ denotes the set of atomic data types (e.g., String, number, etc.) and $\mathcal{L}$ denotes the set of list data types*
- *$CtrlE \subset N \times N$ is a precedence relation (note: $n_{src} \rightarrow n_{dest} \equiv (n_{src}, n_{dest}) \in CtrlE$)*
- *$DataE \subseteq N \times D \times NAccessMode$ is a set of data links between activities and data elements (with $NAccessMode = \{read, write\}$)*
- *$EC: CtrE \mapsto Conds(D) \cup \{Null\}$ assigns to each control edge an optional transition conditions where $Conds(D)$ denotes the set of all valid transition conditions on data elements from D*
- *$Exp \subseteq N \times D \times \{SEQ, PAR\} \times \{LIFO, FIFO\} \times Time$ denotes the subset of multi instance activities from N (expanded during runtime based on the specified configuration parameters). For $e = (n, d, mode, str, time) \in Exp$:*
  - *$n \in N$, $d \in D$ with $dataType(d) \subseteq \mathcal{L}$*
  - *$mode \in \{SEQ, PAR\}$ denotes the multi instantiation mode, i.e., whether the activity instances created at expansion time are carried out in sequence or in parallel.*

- $str \in \{LIFO, FIFO\}$ denotes the strategy in which list data elements are picked (which is relevant if mode $= SEQ$ holds), and
- $time \in Time$ denotes the point in time at which the multi instantiation is carried out; possible configurations are, for example, $time = actT_n$ or $time = sT$. While the former indicates that expansion takes place when activity n becomes activated, the latter configuration states that expansion is done already at process start time. (More configurations are conceivable, but are outside the scope of this paper).

Data elements can be gathered manually or by exploiting context information, e.g., the barcode of goods (cf. Fig. 1). It is also possible to have context data elements which are continuously adapted (but not read) during process execution (e.g., the truck position obtained by a GPS system in Fig. 1). This context data may be used in order to figure out an exception handling strategy (cf. Sect. 4). The process type schema depicted in Fig. 1 comprises multi instance activites Load truck and Deliver goods, i.e., we obtain Exp $= \{($Load truck, delivery_list, SEQ, FIFO, actT$), ($Deliver goods, delivery_list, SEQ, FIFO, actT$)\}$. Note that the specification whether a LIFO or FIFO strategy is used only makes sense if the expansion strategy is set to sequential mode.

In addition, we need a set of change operations defined on task nets with precise semantics in order to provide exception handling strategies as, for example, sending a new truck after a truck crash (what would be carried out by inserting an activity send truck into the affected task net). Table 1 presents a selection of such change operations. As shown in [6, 2] these change operations all have formal pre– and post–conditions based on which the correctness of a task net is automatically ensured when applying the modifications.

3.2 Process Instances

Based on a process type schema S process instances can be created and started at runtime. Due to the dynamically evolving process structure the particular process instance schema may differ from the process type schema the instance was started on. This is reflected by a set Δ_E containing change operations (cf Tab. 1) which may have been applied at different points in time during instance execution and reflect the instance–specific dynamic expansion of S. Furthermore a set of change operations Δ_I is stored which reflects the ad–hoc modifications applied to process instance I (by users) so far. In order to obtain instance–specific schema S_I the merge of the so called change histories Δ_E and Δ_I is applied to S by considering the particular time stamp of each single change operation.

Definition 2 (Process Instance Schema). *A process instance schema S_I is defined by a tuple (S, Δ_E, Δ_I) where*

- *S denotes the process type schema I was derived from*
- *Δ_E denotes an ordered set of change operations which reflect the expansion of S depending on the specified activation time (cf. Fig. 3)*
- *$\Delta_I = (op_1, .., op_n)$ comprises instance–specific change operations(e.g., due to ad-hoc deviations).*

Table 1. *A Selection of High-Level Change Operations on Activity Nets*

Change Operation Δ Applied to Schema S	Effects on Schema S
insertAct(S, X, M_{bef}, M_{aft})	insertion of activity X between activity sets M_{bef}, M_{aft}

Subtractive Change Operations

deleteAct(S, X)	deletes activity X from schema S

Order-Changing Operations

moveAct(S, X, A, B)	moves activity X from current position to position between activities A and B

Data Flow Change Operations

addDataElements(S, dElements)	adds set of data elements dElements to S
deleteDataElement(S, d)	deletes data element d from S
addDataEdge(S, (X, d, mode))	adds data edge (X, d, mode) to S (mode $\in$ {read, write})
deleteDataEdge(S, dL))	deletes data edge dL from S
relinkDataEdge(S, (d, n, [read|write]), n')	re-links read/write data edge from/to data element d from activity n to activity n'

List Data Change Operations

addListElement(S, d, d_{new}, d_i, d_{i+1})	adds element d_i to list data d between elements d_i and d_{i+1}
deleteListElement(S, d, d_{del})	deletes element d_{del} from list data d
moveListElement(S, d, d_{move}, d_i)	moves d_{move} within list data d after list element d_i

The activity set, data set, and edge sets of S_I (i.e., $S_I := (N_I, D_I, CtrlE_I, DataE_I)$) are determined during runtime.

Process instance information consists of the process instance schema and the process instance state expressed by respective activity markings. In Def. 3 we add the runtime information (instance state) to the instance schema and present an expansion algorithm based on the process instance state. As described in Def. 2 the deviation of a process instance I from its original process type schema S is reflected by the merge of change histories Δ_E and Δ_I. In particular, the application of the change operations contained in Δ_E to S results in the expanded process instance schema. How Δ_E is determined is described in the following definition. In addition, there may be instance–specific changes Δ_I, for example, applied to overcome exceptional situations. We include these instance–specific changes within Def. 2 since we want to present semantic exception handling strategies which are mainly based on such ad–hoc changes. As provided in the ADEPT framework certain state conditions have to hold when applying change operations at the process instance level in order to ensure a correct instance execution in the sequel. These conditions mainly preserve the history of the previous instance execution. It is forbidden, for example, to delete an already completed activity. For details we refer to [6].

Definition 3 (Process Instance). *A process instance I is defined by a tuple $(S_I, N^{S_I}, Val^{S_I})$ where:*

- *$S_I := (N_I, D_I, CtrlE_I, DataE_I)$ denotes the process instance schema of I which is determined by (S, Δ_E, Δ_I) during runtime (see Fig. 3 below).*

- NS^{S_I} describes activity markings of I:

  $NS^{S_I} : N_I \mapsto \{\texttt{NotAct, Act, Run, Comp, Skipped}\}$
- Val^{S_I} denotes a function on D_I, formally: $Val^{S_I} : D_I \mapsto Dom_{D_I} \cup \{\texttt{Undef}\}$. It reflects for each data element $d \in D_I$ either its current value from domain Dom_{D_I} (for list data elements we assign a list of data values respectively) or the value $\texttt{Undef}$ (if d has not been written yet).

$\mathcal{I}_{S_I}$ denotes the set of all instances running according to S.

Applying the following algorithm (cf. Fig. 3) leads to the expansion of multi instantiation activities during runtime according to the associated data structures. First of all, we determine all multi instantiation activities. For those with expansion at instance start the expansion is executed immediately (lines 7, 8)

```
1   input: S, M^SI  output: Δ_E
2   Initialization:
3   Δ_E = ∅;
4   Exp_sT := {(n, ..., sT) ∈ Exp};
5   Exp_actT := {(n, ..., act)} ∈ Exp};
6   n_ is start activity of S;
7   // expansion at process instance start
8   NS^SI(n_) = Act ⇒ expInst(S, Δ_E, Exp_sT);
9   // expansion during at activation time
10  while (∃ e := (n,d,[SEQ|PAR],LIFO|FIFO],actT)∈Exp_actT with NS^SI(n)= NotAct){
11      if (∃ e := (n,d,[SEQ|PAR],[LIFO|FIFO],actT) ∈ N_actT with state transition
12          NS^SI(n) = NotAct ⇒ NS^SI(n) = Act) {
13          expInst(S, Δ_E, {e});
14      }
15  }
16  // ----------- Activity Expansion method expInst(S, Δ_E, N') ------------
17  Δ = ∅;
18  for e := (n,d,[SEQ|PAR],[LIFO|FIFO], ...) ∈ N' do {
19      d:= [d_1, ..., d_k]; // d is of list type acc. to definition
20      Δ = Δ ∪ addDataElements{S, {d_1, ..., d_k}};
21      n_succ, n_pred: direct successor / predecessor of n in S;
22      DE_in := {(d, n, read) ∈ DataE} \ {d};
23      DE_out := {(d, n, write) ∈ DataE};
24      // sequential expansion
25      if e:= (n,d, SEQ,[LIFO|FIFO], ...){
26          for i = 1, ..., k do {
27              n_i := n;
28              Δ = Δ ∪ {insertAct(S, n_i, {n_{i-1}}, {n_succ})};
29              // FIFO strategy
30              if e:= (n,d,seq,FIFO, ...){
31                  Δ = Δ ∪ {addDataEdge(S,(d_i, n_i, read)})};
32              // LIFO strategy
33              if e := (n,d,seq,LIFO,...) {
34                  Δ = Δ ∪ {addDataEdge(S,d_i,n_{k-i+1},read)})};
35          }
36      }
37      // parallel expansion
38      if e:= (n,d,PAR, ...) {
39          for i = 1, ..., k {
40              Δ = Δ ∪ {insertAct(S, n_i, {n_pred}, {n_succ})};
41          }
42      }
43      for dE = (d,n,read) ∈ DE_in {
44          for i = 1, ..., k {
45              Δ = Δ ∪ {addDataEdge(S, (d,n_i,read))};
46          }
47      }
48      for dE = (d,n,write) ∈ DE_out {
49          for i = 1, ..., k {
50              Δ = Δ ∪ {addDataEdge(S, (d,n_i,write))};
51          }
52      }
53      Δ_E = Δ_E ∪ Δ;}
```

Fig. 3. Algorithm: Activity Expansion during Runtime

whereas for activities with expansion at activation time method `expInst(S, ..)` is called when their state changes to `Act` (lines 23 – 27). Method `expInst(S, ..)` itself (starting line 16) distinguishes between sequential and parallel expansion. For sequential expansion, moreover, the fetch strategy for data elements (LIFO, FIFO) is taken into account. The expansion itself is realized by adding change operations (cf. Tab. 1) to change transaction Δ_E.

As an example consider process instance I2 (cf. Fig. 2). At first, it is determined that activities `Load truck` and `Deliver goods` are to be expanded at their activation time (what is specified by {(`Load truck, delivery_List, SEQ, FIFO, actT`), (`deliver Goods, delivery_List, SEQ, FIFO, actT`)}). Assume that data element `delivery_List = [cust1, cust2]` contains data for customers 1 and 2. When the state transition NS^{S_I}(`Load truck`) = NotAct $\longrightarrow NS^{S_I}$(`Load truck`) = Act is taking place (i.e., the activation time of `load Truck` is reached), this activity is expanded by a sequential insertion of activities `Load truck` using a FIFO strategy. Using the algorithm the changes necessary to realize the expansion are automatically calculated based on the available change operations (cf. Tab. 1):

$$\Delta_E := \Delta_E \cup \{\text{insertAct}(S_{I2}, \text{load Truck}, \{\text{AndJoin}\}, \{\text{Deliver goods}\}),$$
$$\text{addDataEdges}(S_{I2}, \{(\text{cust1, load Truck, read})\}),$$
$$\text{insertAct}(S_{I2}, \text{load Truck}, \{\text{load Truck}\}, \{\text{deliver Goods}\},$$
$$\text{addDataEdges}(S_{I2}, \{(\text{cust2, load Truck, read})\}),$$
$$\text{addDataEdges}(S_{I2}, \{(\text{delivery\_List, load Truck, write}),$$
$$(\text{delivery\_List, load Truck, write})\})\}$$

The expansion of activity `Deliver goods` is carried out accordingly when the activity state of `Deliver goods` changes from not activated to activated.

4 Intelligent Exception Handling

As discussed in Sect. 2.2 backward process recovery (e.g., [9, 10, 11]) is not always desirable when an exceptional situation occurs. Therefore we want to exemplarily discuss two alternatives for such backward strategies. The first approach refers to data–driven exception handling, the second one is based on exploiting process context information.

4.1 Data–Driven Exception Handling

The expansion of multi instance activities is based on the input data of the particular activity, i.e., a data list setting out the number and order of the activities to be inserted and executed during runtime. This concept provides flexibility since certain process instance changes can be adopted by modifying the input data of multi instance activities what leads, in turn, to changed expansion and execution during rutime. One example is depicted in Fig. 4: Currently, for process instance I the truck is on the way to deliver the goods of customer2 (the goods for customer1 have been already delivered). Then an exceptional situation is arising since customer2 is not present at home wherefore the goods cannot be unloaded. After receiving the truck driver's call the headquarter figures out to solve the problem by first delivering the goods for customer3 and then try to deliver the goods for customer2 again. This solution elaborated at a semantically high level can now be easily brought to process instance I: Changing the order of a data list associated with customer2 and customer3 (by applying change operation moveListElement (S$_I$, ...)) leads to an automatic adaptation of the delivery order within the process (cf. Fig. 4). Note that this is solely based on data flow changes; i.e., by re–linking the connected data elements cust2 and cust3 the delivery order is automatically swapped.

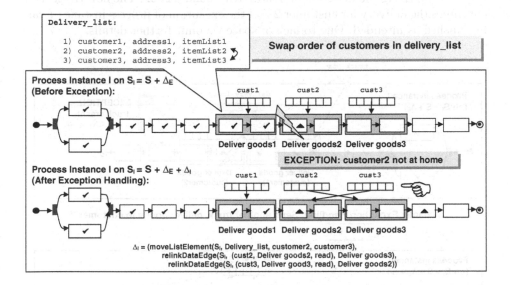

Fig. 4. Data–Driven Change of Delivery Order

For all change operations on data lists like adding, deleting, and moving data elements (cf. Tab. 1), the associated data flow changes (adding and deleting data elements in conjunction with adding, deleting, and moving data edges) can be determined. In this paper, we have exemplarily presented the data flow change operation associated with swapping data list elements. Note that data list modifications as any other change operation can only be correctly applied if certain state conditions hold. For example, for the scenario depicted in Fig. 4 it is not possible to move the list data element for customer1 since associated activity deliver goods1 has been already (properly) completed. Nevertheless the mechanism of data list adaptations and expansion during runtime provides a powerful way for user–friendly exception handling.

4.2 Exception Handling Using Context Information

In addition to data–driven exception handling, context information can be also useful for dealing with exceptional situations. More precisely, context information can be used in order to derive a reasonable forward recovery strategy, i.e., the application of certain ad–hoc changes to the concerned process instance. Assume, for example, the scenario depicted in Fig. 5 where the truck has a crash during the delivery of the goods for customer 2. Cancelling the instance execution (followed by a rollback) is not desired since the goods for customer 1 have been already delivered properly. Therefore a forward strategy is figured out making use of context data `truck position` which is constantly updated by a GPS system. The truck position can be used to send a new truck to the position of the troubled one what can be expressed by dynamic instance change Δ_I (cf. Fig. 5) comprising the insertion of new activity `send truck`. The new truck then continues the delivery for customer 2 and the execution of process instance I can be finished as intended. Due to lack of space we omit further details.

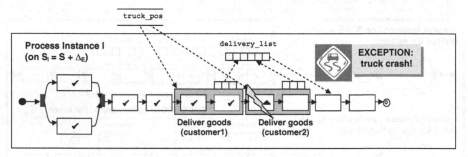

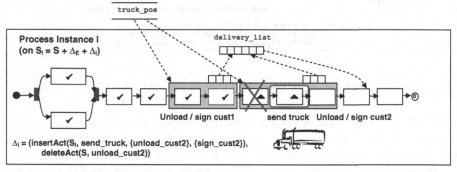

Fig. 5. Exception Handling Using Context Information after Truck Crash

5   Architectural Considerations

We sketch the basic components of our overall system architecture (cf. Fig. 6): Basic to the described features is an adaptive process engine which we have realized in the ADEPT project. It allows for flexible process adaptation at runtime (cf. [12]). In particular, it offers powerful programming interfaces on top of

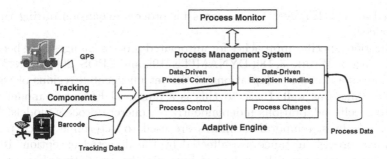

Fig. 6. System Architecture

which data-driven expansion of task nets and automated exception handling can be realized. The former feature requires an extended process execution engine (e.g., implementing the expansion algorithm), the latter one requires additional mechanisms for exception detection and handling.

As illustrated determining the position of a physical object is highly relevant for logistics processes. The incorporation of this kind of context information requires an integrated tracking system. Currently, there are various technologies available which can help to trace the position of an object, such as GPS, GSM, RFID, WiFi and more recently UWB [13]. They have different strengths and weaknesses in terms of resolution, availability, cost etc. Moreover, they differ in how the location is being represented, and in environment applicability. An integrated tracking component must abstract from such details and enable seamless and technology-independent tracking outside and inside buildings.

6   Discussion

Multi instantiation of activities has been addressed by workflow pattern approaches [14, 15]. The most similar patterns are the multi instantiation patterns with and without a priori runtime knowledge as defined in [14]. Although, in [15] the authors suggest a function to compute the number of times an activity is to be instantiated (sequentially or in parallel) the concrete specification of such a function is missing. Therefore the approach presented in this paper can be seen as a first implementation of the multi instantiation pattern without a priori runtime knowledge in practice, i.e., based on associated data structures.

An increase of process flexibility based on a data–centered perspective is offered by the case–handling paradigm [16]. Case–handling enables early review and editing of process data, thus providing a higher degree of flexibility when compared to pure activity-centered approaches. However, it is not possible to dynamically expand process instances during runtime and to use this mechanism for supporting exception handling. A buildtime approach for the automatic generation of processes based on product structures has been presented in [17]. However, no concepts for process expansion during runtime are provided.

Application–specific approaches for automated process changes have been presented in AGENTWORK [3, 18], DYNAMITE [19], and EPOS [20]. AGENTWORK [3, 18] enables automatic adaptations of the yet unexecuted regions of running process instances as well. Basic to this is a temporal ECA rule model which allows to specify adaptations independently of concrete process models. When an ECA rule fires, temporal estimates are used to determine which parts of the running process instance are affected by the detected exception. Respective process regions are either adapted immediately (predictive change) or - if this is not possible - at the time they are entered (reactive change). EPOS [20] automatically adapts process instances when process goals themselves change. Both approaches apply planning techniques (e.g., [4, 21]) to automatically "repair" processes in such cases. However, current planning methods do not provide complete solutions since important aspects (e.g., treatment of loops or data flow) are not considered. DYNAMITE uses graph grammars and graph reduction rules for this [19]. Automatic adaptations are performed depending on the outcomes of previous activity executions. Both DYNAMITE and EPOS provide build-in functions to support dynamically evolving process instances.

Context–awareness is also a hot topic in the area of mobile systems, ad–hoc networks, and ambient intelligence (smart surroundings). These approaches can be used as valuable inspiration and input for future research.

7   Summary and Outlook

We have presented a framework for data–driven process control and exception handling on top of adaptive PMS. This approach is based on two pillars: dynamic expansion of task nets and automated support for exception handling using data–driven net adaptation and exploiting context information. The framework for dynamic task net expansion has been formally defined and illustrated by means of an example from the logistics domain. In particular, our expansion mechanism provides a sophisticated way to implement process patterns representing multiple instances with or without a priori runtime knowledge (cmp. Patterns 14 and 15 in [14]). We have also shown how the presented concepts can be used for automated exception handling by adapting data structures. This allows us to handle certain exceptions in a very elegant and user–friendly manner. Finally, further strategies for exception handling based on context information have been discussed. Future research will elaborate the concepts of exception handling based on context information. In particular we will analzye the question how exception handling strategies can be automatically derived and suggested to the user. Furthermore we want to extend the research on a more data–driven view on process control and exception handling in order to bridge the gap between real–world applications and computerized processes.

References

1. Dumas, M., v.d. Aalst, W., ter Hofstede, A.: Process–Aware Information systems. Wiley (2005)
2. Reichert, M., Dadam, P.: ADEPT$_{flex}$ - supporting dynamic changes of workflows without losing control. JIIS **10** (1998) 93–129
3. Müller, R.: Event-Oriented Dynamic Adaptation of Workflows. PhD thesis, University of Leipzig, Germany (2002)
4. Berry, P., Myers, K.: Adaptive process management: An al perspective. In: Proc. Workshop Towards Adaptive Workflow Systems (CSCW'98), Seattle (1998)
5. Herrmann, T., Just-Hahn, K.: Organizational learning with flexible workflow management systems. In: WS on Organizational Learning, CSCW96. (1996) 54–57
6. Rinderle, S., Reichert, M., Dadam, P.: Flexible support of team processes by adaptive workflow systems. Distributed and Parallel Databases **16** (2004) 91–116
7. Rinderle, S., Reichert, M., Dadam, P.: Correctness criteria for dynamic changes in workflow systems – a survey. DKE **50** (2004) 9–34
8. Weske, M.: Formal foundation and conceptual design of dynamic adaptations in a workflow management system. In: HICSS-34. (2001)
9. Elmagarmid, A.: Database Transaction Models for Advanced Applications. Morgan Kaufman (1992)
10. Schuldt, H., Alonso, G., Beeri, C., Schek, H.: Atomicity and isolation for transactional processes. TODS **27** (2002) 63–116
11. Leymann, F., Roller, D.: Production Workflow. Prentice Hall (2000)
12. Reichert, M., Rinderle, S., Kreher, U., Dadam, P.: Adaptive process management with adept2. In: ICDE'05. (2005) 1113–1114
13. Steggles, P., Cadman, J.: White paper: "a comparison of RF tag location products for real-world applications" (2004)
14. Aalst, W.v., ter Hofstede, A., Kiepuszewski, B., Barros, A.: Workflow patterns. DPD **14** (2003) 5–51
15. Guabtni, A., Charoy, F.: Multiple instantiation in a dynamic workflow environment. In: CAiSE'04. (2004) 175–188
16. v.d. Aalst, W., Weske, M., Grünbauer, D.: Case handling: A new paradigm for business process support. DKE **53** (2004) 129–162
17. v.d. Aalst, W.: On the automatic generation of workflow processes based on product structures. Computer in Industry **39** (1999) 97–111
18. Müller, R., Greiner, U., Rahm, E.: AGENTWORK: A workflow-system supporting rule-based workflow adaptation. DKE **51** (2004) 223–256
19. Heimann, P., Joeris, G., Krapp, C., Westfechtel, B.: DYNAMITE: Dynamic task nets for software process management. In: ICSE'96, Berlin (1996) 331–341
20. Liu, C., Conradi, R.: Automatic replanning of task networks for process model evolution. In: ESEC'93. (1993) 434–450
21. Wilkins, D., Myers, K., Lowrance, J., Wesley, L.: Planning and reacting in uncertain and dynamic environments. Experimental and Theoret. AI **7** (1995) 197–227

Workflow Exception Patterns*

Nick Russell[1], Wil van der Aalst[2,1], and Arthur ter Hofstede[1]

[1] School of Information Systems, Queensland University of Technology,
GPO Box 2434, Brisbane QLD 4001, Australia
{n.russell, a.terhofstede}@qut.edu.au

[2] Department of Technology Management, Eindhoven University of Technology,
PO Box 513, NL-5600 MB, Eindhoven, The Netherlands
w.m.p.v.d.aalst@tm.tue.nl

Abstract. This paper presents a classification framework for workflow exception handling in the form of patterns. This framework is independent of specific modelling approaches or technologies and as such provides an objective means of delineating the exception-handling capabilities of specific workflow systems. It is subsequently used to assess the level of exceptions support provided by eight commercial workflow systems and business process modelling and execution languages. On the basis of these investigations, we propose a graphical, tool-independent language for defining exception handling strategies in workflows.

1 Introduction

Business process management continues to receive widespread focus by technology-enabled organisations offering them a means of optimising their current organisational business processes in a way that aligns with top-level business objectives. In many cases, workflow systems serve as the enabling technology for mission-critical business processes. They offer a means of streamlining such processes by mapping out the key activities, decision points and work distribution directives and then automating much of the overhead that is often associated with managing the various activities which form part of a business process.

Workflow systems are generally based on a comprehensive process model (often depicted in graphical form) that maps out all of the possible execution paths associated with a business process. This ensures that the work activities which comprise each of the likely execution scenarios are fully described. Whilst this approach to specifying business process works well for *well-behaved* cases of a process i.e. those that conform to one of the expected execution paths, it is less successful in dealing with unexpected events encountered during execution.

Deviations from normal execution arising during a business process are often termed *exceptions* in line with the notion of exceptions which is widely used in the

---

* This work was partially supported by the Dutch research school BETA as part of the *PATINT* program and the Australian Research Council under the Discovery Grant *Expressiveness Comparison and Interchange Facilitation between Business Process Execution Languages.*

E. Dubois and K. Pohl (Eds.): CAiSE 2006, LNCS 4001, pp. 288–302, 2006.
© Springer-Verlag Berlin Heidelberg 2006

software engineering community. Because it is difficult to characterise all of the unanticipated situations that may arise during the execution of a program, the notion of exceptions was developed where unexpected events are grouped into classes which are related by similarities that they possess in terms of the conditions under which they might arise. Exception handlers can then be defined in the form of programmatic procedures to resolve the effects of specific events as they are detected. At the lowest level, exceptions can be defined for events such as divide by zero errors and appropriate handling routines can be defined. For business processes, this level of detail is too fine-grained and it is more effective to define exceptions at a higher level, typically in terms of the business process to which they relate.

In this paper, we investigate the range of issues that may lead to exceptions during workflow execution and the various ways in which they can be addressed. This provides the basis for a classification framework for workflow exception handling which we subsequently define in the form of patterns. The patterns-based approach to exception classification is a continuation of previous research conducted as part of the *Workflow Patterns Initiative* which has identified "generic, recurring constructs" in the control-flow [22], data [18] and resource [19] perspectives of workflow systems. These patterns have proven to be extremely intuitive to both practitioners and researchers alike and have been widely utilised for a variety of purposes including tool evaluation and selection, business process modelling, workflow design and education[1]. They also provide the conceptual foundations for the YAWL system [21], an open-source reference implementation of a workflow system.

In line with the broader *Workflow Patterns Initiative*, the motivation for this paper is to provide a conceptual framework for classifying the exception handling capabilities of workflow systems and process-aware information systems more generally in a manner that is independent of specific modelling approaches or technologies. This approach is distinguished from other research activities in this area which seek to extend specific process modelling formalisms and workflow enactment technologies to provide support for expected and unexpected events by incorporating exception detection and handling capabilities. Instead of directly proposing a concrete implementation, we first provide an overview of relevant exception patterns, then we evaluate existing products and languages on the basis of these, and finally we propose a graphical, tool-independent language for exception handling.

2   Related Work

The need for reliable, resilient and consistent workflow operation has long been recognised. Early work in the area [8, 24] was essentially a logical continuation of database transaction theory and focussed on developing extensions to the classic ACID transaction model that would be applicable in application areas requiring the use of long duration and more flexible transactions. As the field

---

[1] Further details are available at www.workflowpatterns.com.

of workflow technology matured, the applicability of exceptions to this problem was also recognised [20] and [7] presented the first significant discussion on workflow recovery which incorporated exceptions. It classified them into four types: basic failures, application failures, expected exceptions and unexpected exceptions. Subsequent research efforts have mainly concentrated on the last two of these classes. Investigations into expected exceptions have focussed previous work on transactional workflow into mechanisms for introducing exception handling frameworks into workflow systems. Research into unexpected exceptions has established the areas of adaptive workflow and workflow evolution [17].

Although it is not possible to comprehensively survey these research areas in the confines of this paper, it is worthwhile identifying some of the major contributions in these areas that have influenced subsequent research efforts and have a bearing on this research initiative. Significant attempts to include advanced transactional concepts and exception handling capabilities in workflow systems include WAMO [6] which provided the ability to specify transactional properties for tasks which identified how failures should be dealt with, ConTracts [16] which proposed a coordinated, nested transaction model for workflow execution allowing for forward, backward and partial recovery in the event of failure and Exotica [2] which provided a mechanism for incorporating Sagas and Flexible transactions in the commercial FlowMark workflow product. OPERA [10] was one of the first initiatives to incorporate language primitives for exception handling into a workflow system and it also allowed exception handling strategies to be modelled in the same notation as that used for representing workflow processes. TREX [23] proposed a transaction model that involves treating all types of workflow failures as exceptions. A series of exception types were delineated and the exception handler utilised in a given situation was determined by a combination of the task and the exception experienced. WIDE [4] developed a comprehensive language – Chimera-Exc – for specifying exception handling strategies in the form of Event-Condition-Action (ECA) rules.

Other important contributions include [13] which identified the concepts of compensation spheres and atomicity spheres and their applicability to workflow systems, [3] which proposed modelling workflow systems as a set of reified objects with associated constraints and conceptualising exceptions as violations of those constraints which are capable of being detected and managed and [15] which first identified the pivot, retriable and compensation transaction concepts widely used in subsequent research.

Identifying potential exceptions and suitable handling strategies is a significant problem for large, complex workflows. Recent attempts [9, 11] to address this have centred on mining execution logs to gain an understanding of previous exceptions and using this knowledge to establish suitable handling strategies. [12] proposes a knowledge-based solution based on the establishment of a shared, generic and reusable taxonomy of exceptions. [14] uses a case-based reasoning approach to match exception occurrences with suitable handling strategies.

Until recently the area of unexpected exceptions has mainly been investigated in the context of adaptive or evolutionary workflow [17] which centre on dynamic change of the process model. A detailed review of this area is beyond the scope of this paper, however two recent initiatives which offer the potential to address both expected and unexpected exceptions simultaneously are ADOME-WFMS [5] which provides an adaptive workflow execution model in which exception handlers are specified generically using ECA rules providing the opportunity for reuse in multiple scenarios and user-guided adaptation where they need refinement, and [1] which describes a combination of "worklets" and "ripple-down rules" as a means of dynamic workflow evolution and exception handling.

3   A Framework for Workflow Exception Handling

In this section we consider the notion of a workflow exception in a general sense and the various ways in which they can be triggered and handled. The assumption is that an exception is a distinct, identifiable event which occurs at a specific point in time during the execution of a workflow and relates to a unique work item[2]. The occurrence of the exception is assumed to be immediately detectable as is the type of the exception. The manner in which the exception is handled will depend on the type of exception that has been detected. There are a range of possible ways in which an exception may be dealt with but in general, the specific handling strategy centres on three main considerations:

- how the work item will be handled;
- how the other work items in the case will be handled; and
- what recovery action will be taken to resolve the effects of the exception.

We discuss the range of possible exception types and the options for handling them in the following sections.

3.1   Exception Types

It is only possible to specify handlers for *expected* types of exception. With this constraint in mind, we undertook a comprehensive review of the workflow literature and current commercial workflow systems and business process modelling and execution languages in order to determine the range of exception events that are capable of being detected and provide a useful basis for recovery handling. These events can be classified into five distinct groups.

Work Item Failure: Work item failure during the execution of a workflow process is generally characterised by the inability of the work item to progress any further. This may manifest itself in a number of possible forms including a user-initiated abort of the executing program which implements the work item, the failure of a hardware, software or network component associated with the work item or the user to whom the work item is assigned signalling failure to

---

[2] We recognise that exceptions may also be bound to groups of tasks, blocks or even entire cases, and in these situations we assume that the same handling considerations apply to all of the encompassed tasks.

the workflow engine. Where the reason for this failure is not captured and dealt within the process model, it needs to be handled elsewhere in order to ensure that both later work items and the process as a whole continue to behave correctly.

Deadline Expiry: It is common to specify a deadline for a work item in a workflow process model. Usually the deadline indicates when the work item should be completed, although deadlines for commencement are also possible. In general with a deadline, it is also useful to specify at design time what should be done if the deadline is reached and the work item has not been completed.

Resource Unavailability: It is often the case that a work item requires access to one or more data resources during its execution. If these are not available to the work item at initiation, then it is usually not possible for the work item to proceed. Similarly, workflow systems are premised on the fact that work items are usually allocated to resources (typically human) who execute them. Problems with work item allocation can arise if: (1) at distribution time, no resource can be found which meets the specified allocation criteria for the work item or (2) at some time after allocation, the resource is no longer able to undertake or complete the work item. Although the occurrence of these issues can be automatically detected, they often cannot be resolved within the context of the executing process and may involve some form of escalation or manual intervention. For this reason, they are ideally suited to resolution via exception handling.

External Trigger: Triggers from sources external to a work item are often used as a means of signalling the occurrence of an event that impacts on the work item and requires some form of handling. These triggers are typically initiated by non-linked work items (i.e. work items that are not directly linked to the work item in question by a control edge) elsewhere within the process model or even in other process models or alternatively from processes in the operational environment in which the workflow system resides. Although a work item can anticipate events such as triggers and provision for dealing with them can be included at design-time, it is not predictable if or when such events will occur. For this reason, the issue of dealing with them is not suited to normal processing within the work item implementation and is better dealt with via exception handling. Generally signals or some other form of processing interrupt indicate that an *out-of-bound* condition has arisen and needs to be dealt with. A general consequence of this is that the current work item needs to be halted, possibly undone and some alternative action taken.

Constraint Violation: Constraints in the context of a workflow system are invariants over elements in the control-flow, data or resource perspectives that need to be maintained to ensure the integrity and operational consistency of the workflow process is preserved. Ongoing monitoring is generally required to ensure that they are enforced. The implementation of routines to identify and handle constraint violations detected within the context of a workflow is similar to the issue of dealing with external triggers. Typically the construct that will detect and need to deal with the violation is a work item although there is no reason why the constraint could not be specified and handled at block or process level. As constraints may be specified over data, resources or other work items within a process model, the approach chosen for handling them needs to be as generic as possible to ensure that it has broadest applicability.

3.2 Exception Handling at Work Item Level

In general an exception will relate to a specific work item in a case. There are a multitude of ways in which the exception can be handled although the specific details will depend on the current state of execution of the work item. Before looking at these options, we first review the execution lifecycle for a work item. Figure 1 illustrates as solid arrows the states through which a work item progresses during normal execution. It is initially *offered* to one or more resources for execution. A resource issues an *allocate* command to indicate that it wishes to execute the work item at some future time, the work item is then *allocated* to that resource. Typically this involves adding the work item to the resource's work queue and removing any references to the work item that other resources may have received, either on their work queues or via other means. When the resource wishes to commence the work item, it issues a *start* command and the state of the work item changes to *started*. Finally, once the work item is finished, the resource issues a *complete* command and the state of the work item is changed to *completed*. Note that there are two possible variations to this course of events shown as dotted arcs in Figure 1: (1) where a work item offered to a resource is *selected* by another resource, it is *withdrawn* from the first resource's worklist and (2) where an executing work item is detected as having *failed*, its state is changed accordingly. This lifecycle map also provides the basis for determining what options exist for handling a work item in a given state when an exception is detected.

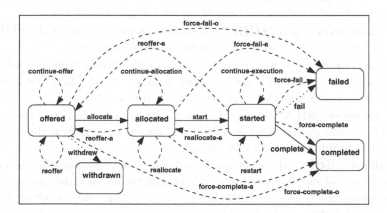

Fig. 1. Work item lifecycle

Figure 1 illustrates fifteen strategies as dashed arcs from one work item state to another. There are subtle differences between each of these transitions, and in order to distinguish between them, we briefly describe each of them:

1. **continue-offer (OCO)** – the work item has been offered to one or more resources and there is no change in its state as a consequence of the exception;
2. **reoffer (ORO)** – the work item has been offered to one or more resources and as a consequence of the exception, these offers are withdrawn and the work item is once again offered to one or more resources (these resources may not necessarily be the same as those to which it was offered previously);
3. **force-fail-o (OFF)** – the work item has been offered to one or more resources, these offers are withdrawn and the state of the work item is changed to failed. No subsequent work items on this path are triggered;
4. **force-complete-o (OFC)** – the work item has been offered to one or more resources, these offers are withdrawn and the state of the work item is changed to completed. All subsequent work items are triggered;
5. **continue-allocation (ACA)** – the work item has been allocated to a specific resource that will execute it at some future time and there is no change in its state as a consequence of the exception;
6. **reallocate (ARA)** – the work item has been allocated to a resource, this allocation is withdrawn and the work item is allocated to a different resource;
7. **reoffer-a (ARO)** – the work item has been allocated to a resource, this allocation is withdrawn and the work item is offered to one or more resources (this group may not necessarily include the resource to which it was previously allocated);
8. **force-fail-a (AFF)** – the work item has been allocated to a resource, this allocation is withdrawn and the state of the work item is changed to failed. No subsequent work items are triggered;
9. **force-complete-a (AFC)** – the work item has been allocated to a resource, this allocation is withdrawn and the state of the work item is changed to completed. All subsequent work items are triggered;
10. **continue-execution (SCE)** – the work item has been started and there is no change in its state as a consequence of the exception;
11. **restart (SRS)** – the work item has been started, progress on the current execution instance is halted and the work item is restarted from the beginning by the same resource that was executing it previously;
12. **reallocate-s (SRA)** – the work item has been started, progress on the current execution instance is halted and the work item is reallocated to a different resource for later execution;
13. **reoffer-s (SRO)** – the work item has been started, progress on the current execution instance is halted and it is offered to one or more resources (this group may not necessarily include the resource that was executing it);
14. **force-fail (SFF)** – the work item is being executed, any further progress on it is halted and its state is changed to failed. No subsequent work items are triggered; and
15. **force-complete (SFC)** – the work item is being executed, and further progress on it is halted and its state is changed to completed. All subsequent work items are triggered.

3.3 Exception Handling at Case Level

Exceptions always occur in the context of one or more cases that are in the process of being executed. In addition to dealing with the specific work item to which the exception relates, there is also the issue of how the case should be dealt with in an overall sense, particularly in regard to other work items that may currently be executing or will run at some future time. There are three alternatives for handling workflow cases:

1. **continue workflow case (CWC)** – the workflow case can be continued, with no intervention occurring in the execution of any other work items;
2. **remove current case (RCC)** – selected or all remaining work items in the case can be removed (including those currently executing); or
3. **remove all cases (RAC)** – selected or all remaining work items in all cases which correspond to the same process model can be removed.

In the latter two scenarios, a selection of work items to be removed can be specified using both static design time information relating to the corresponding task definition (e.g. original role allocation) as well as relevant runtime information (e.g. actual resource allocated to, start time).

3.4 Recovery Action

The final consideration in regard to exception handling is what action will be taken to remedy the effects of the situation that has been detected. There are three alternate courses of action:

1. **no action (NIL)** – do nothing;
2. **rollback (RBK)** – rollback the effects of the exception; or
3. **compensate (COM)** – compensate for the effects of the exception.

Rollback and compensation are analogous to their usual definitions (e.g. [15]). When specifying a rollback action, the point in the process (i.e. the task) to which the process should be undone can also be stated. By default this is just the current work item. Similarly with compensation actions, the corresponding compensation task(s) must also be identified.

3.5 Characterising Exception Handling Strategies

The actual recovery response to any given class of exception can be specified as a pattern which succinctly describes the form of recovery that will be attempted. Specific exception patterns may apply in multiple situations in a given process model (i.e. for several distinct constructs), possibly for different types of exception. Exception patterns take the form of tuples comprising the following elements:

- how the task on which the exception is based should be handled;
- how the case and other related cases in the process model in which the exception is raised should be handled; and
- what recovery action (if any) is to be undertaken.

Table 1. Exceptions patterns support by exception type

Work Item Failure	Work Item Deadline	Resource Unavailable	External Trigger	Constraint Violation
OFF-CWC-NIL	OCO-CWC-NIL	ORO-CWC-NIL	OCO-CWC-NIL	SCE-CWC-NIL
OFF-CWC-COM	ORO-CWC-NIL	OFF-CWC-NIL	OFF-CWC-NIL	SRS-CWC-NIL
OFC-CWC-NIL	OFF-CWC-NIL	OFF-RCC-NIL	OFF-RCC-NIL	SRS-CWC-COM
OFC-CWC-COM	OFF-RCC-NIL	OFC-CWC-NIL	OFC-CWC-NIL	SRS-CWC-RBK
AFF-CWC-NIL	OFC-CWC-NIL	ARO-CWC-NIL	ACA-CWC-NIL	SFF-CWC-NIL
AFF-CWC-COM	ACA-CWC-NIL	ARA-CWC-NIL	AFF-CWC-NIL	SFF-CWC-COM
AFC-CWC-NIL	ARA-CWC-NIL	AFF-CWC-NIL	AFF-RCC-NIL	SFF-CWC-RBK
AFC-CWC-COM	ARO-CWC-NIL	AFF-RCC-NIL	AFC-CWC-NIL	SFF-RCC-NIL
SRS-CWC-NIL	AFF-CWC-NIL	AFC-CWC-NIL	SCE-CWC-NIL	SFF-RCC-COM
SRS-CWC-COM	AFF-RCC-NIL	SRA-CWC-NIL	SRS-CWC-NIL	SFF-RCC-RBK
SRS-CWC-RBK	AFC-CWC-NIL	SRA-CWC-COM	SRS-CWC-COM	SFF-RAC-NIL
SFF-CWC-NIL	SCE-CWC-NIL	SRA-CWC-RBK	SRS-CWC-RBK	SFC-CWC-NIL
SFF-CWC-COM	SCE-CWC-COM	SRO-CWC-NIL	SFF-CWC-NIL	SFC-CWC-COM
SFF-CWC-RBK	SRS-CWC-NIL	SRO-CWC-COM	SFF-CWC-COM	
SFF-RCC-NIL	SRS-CWC-COM	SRO-CWC-RBK	SFF-CWC-RBK	
SFF-RCC-COM	SRS-CWC-RBK	SFF-CWC-NIL	SFF-RCC-NIL	
SFF-RCC-RBK	SRA-CWC-NIL	SFF-CWC-COM	SFF-RCC-COM	
SFC-CWC-NIL	SRA-CWC-COM	SFF-CWC-RBK	SFF-RCC-RBK	
SFC-CWC-COM	SRA-CWC-RBK	SFF-RCC-NIL	SFF-RAC-NIL	
SFC-CWC-RBK	SRO-CWC-NIL	SFF-RCC-COM	SFC-CWC-NIL	
	SRO-CWC-COM	SFF-RCC-RBK	SFC-CWC-COM	
	SRO-CWC-RBK	SFF-RAC-NIL		
	SFF-CWC-NIL	SFC-CWC-NIL		
	SFF-CWC-COM	SFC-CWC-COM		
	SFF-CWC-RBK			
	SFF-RCC-NIL			
	SFF-RCC-COM			
	SFF-RCC-RBK			
	SFC-CWC-NIL			
	SFC-CWC-COM			

For example, the pattern SFF-CWC-COM specified for a work item failure exception indicates that if a failure of a work item is detected after it has started, then the work item should be terminated, have its state changed to failed and the nominated compensation task should be invoked. No action should be taken with other work items in the same case. From the various alternatives identified for each of these elements in Sections 3.2 – 3.4, there are *135 possible patterns*. Not all patterns apply to a given exception type however, and Table 1 identifies those which apply to each of the exception types identified in Section 3.1.

4   Workflow Exception Handling in Practice

The exception patterns identified in Section 3 were used to assess the exception handling capabilities of eight workflow systems and business process modelling languages. The results of this survey[3,4] are captured in Table 2. They provide a salient insight into how little of the research into exception handling has been implemented in commercial offerings. Only deadline expiry enjoys widespread support although its overall flexibility is limited in many tools. Only two of the

---

[3] Full evaluation details are contained in report BPM-06-04 at www.BPMcenter.org
[4] Combinations of patterns are written as regular expressions e.g. (SFF|SFC)-CWC-COM represents the two patterns SFF-CWC-COM and SFC-CWC-COM.

Table 2. Support for exception patterns in commercial offerings

Offering	Exceptions			
	Work Item Failure	Work Item Deadline	External Trigger	Constraint Violation
Staffware Process Suite v9		OCO-CWC-COM ACA-CWC-COM OFF-CWC-COM AFF-CWC-COM SCE-CWC-COM	OCO-CWC-NIL ACA-CWC-NIL SCE-CWC-NIL SCE-CWC-COM	
WebSphere MQ 3.4 (IBM)		OCO-CWC-NIL ACA-CWC-NIL SCE-CWC-NIL		
FLOWer 3.1 (Pallas Athena)		AFC-CWC-NIL SFC-CWC-NIL		AFC-CWC-NIL SFC-CWC-NIL AFC-CWC-COM SFC-CWC-COM
COSA 5.1 (Transflow)	SFF-CWC-RBK	OCO-CWC-COM ACA-CWC-COM SCE-CWC-COM	OCO-CWC-COM ACA-CWC-COM SCE-CWC-COM	
iPlanet Integ. Server 3.1 (Sun)	(OFF|OFC|AFF|AFC|SRS|SFC|SFF)-(CWC|RCC)-(NIL|COM)			
XPDL 2.0 (WfMC)	SFF-CWC-COM SFF-CWC-NIL SFF-RCC-COM SFF-RCC-NIL	SCE-CWC-COM SCE-CWC-NIL SFF-CWC-COM SFF-CWC-NIL SFF-RCC-COM SFF-RCC-NIL	SFF-CWC-COM SFF-CWC-NIL SFF-RCC-COM SFF-RCC-NIL	SFF-CWC-COM SFF-CWC-NIL SFF-RCC-COM SFF-RCC-NIL
BPEL 1.1	SFF-CWC-COM SFF-CWC-NIL SFF-RCC-COM SFF-RCC-NIL	SCE-CWC-COM SCE-CWC-NIL SFF-CWC-COM SFF-CWC-NIL SFF-RCC-COM SFF-RCC-NIL	SCE-CWC-COM SCE-CWC-NIL SFF-CWC-COM SFF-CWC-NIL SFF-RCC-COM SFF-RCC-NIL	
BPMN 1.0 (BPMI)	SFF-CWC-COM SFF-CWC-NIL SFC-CWC-COM SFC-CWC-NIL SRS-CWC-COM SRS-CWC-NIL SFF-RCC-COM SFF-RCC-NIL	SFF-CWC-COM SFF-CWC-NIL SFC-CWC-COM SFC-CWC-NIL SRS-CWC-COM SRS-CWC-NIL SFF-RCC-COM SFF-RCC-NIL	SFF-CWC-COM SFF-CWC-NIL SFC-CWC-COM SFC-CWC-NIL SRS-CWC-COM SRS-CWC-NIL SFF-RCC-COM SFF-RCC-NIL	SFF-CWC-COM SFF-CWC-NIL SFC-CWC-COM SFC-CWC-NIL SRS-CWC-COM SRS-CWC-NIL SFF-RCC-COM SFF-RCC-NIL

workflow systems examined provide support for handling work items failures –
generally via user-initiated aborts. There was also minimal support for external
triggers and constraint violation management amongst the workflow tools with
only Staffware and COSA, and FLOWer respectively supporting these exception
classes. The business process languages (XPDL, BPEL and BPMN) provide
better support across most areas although only for active work items. None
of the offerings examined provided exception support for managing resource
unavailability (and as a consequence this column has been omitted from Table 2
– this reflects other research findings [19] on the lack of support for the resource
perspective in current commercial products.

5   Considerations for a Workflow Exception Language

The insights gained in the previous sections in relation to the identification
and handling of workflow exceptions provide the basis for a general workflow

exception handling language. In this section, we propose a set of primitives for addressing exceptions that might arise during workflow execution and present a mechanism for integrating these primitives with the process model more generally. We then demonstrate the applicability of this approach to exception handling through a working example.

The conceptual model presented in Section 3 identified three key dimensions to handling an exception. These dimensions provide the basis for the primitives in the graphical exception language illustrated in Figure 2. Symbols 1–4, 8 and 12–14 are derived from the actions for dealing with the current work item from Figure 1, symbols 5–7 and 9–11 are derived from the options for dealing with other work items currently active in the same and other cases and symbols 15 and 16 correspond to the two forms of recovery action that can be undertaken. These primitives can be assembled into sequences of actions that define exception handling strategies. These sequences can also contain standard YAWL constructs [21] although we do not illustrate this capability here.

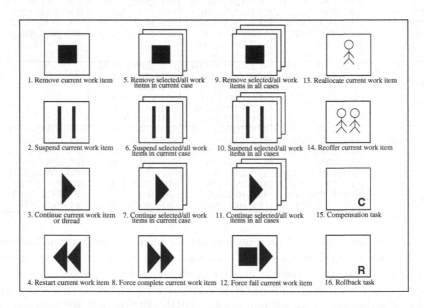

Fig. 2. Exception handling primitives

The interlinkage of exception handling strategies based on these primitives and the overall process model is illustrated in Figure 3. A clear distinction is drawn between the process model and the exception handling strategies. This is based on the premise that the process model should depict the normal sequence of activities associated with a business process and should aim to present these activities precisely without becoming overburdened by excessive consideration of unexpected events that might arise during execution. Exception handling strategies are able to be bound to one of five distinct workflow constructs: individual

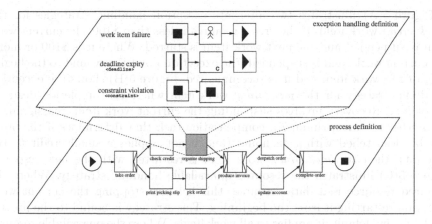

Fig. 3. Exception handling in relation to workflow processes

tasks, a scope (i.e. a group of tasks), a block, a process (i.e. all of the tasks in a process model) and a workflow (i.e. all of the process models in a given workflow environment). The binding is specific to one particular type of exception e.g. work item failure or constraint violation. It may also be further specialised using conditions based on elements from the data perspective e.g. there may be two exception handling strategies for a task, one for work items concerned with financial limits below $1000, the other with limits above that figure.

Exception handling strategies defined for more specific constructs take precedence over those defined at a higher level e.g. where a task has a work item failure exception strategy defined and there is also a strategy defined at the process-level for the same exception type, then the task-level definition is utilised should it experience such an exception. In order to illustrate the application of these concepts, we present an example based on the order fulfillment process illustrated in Figure 4 using the YAWL process modelling notation. In this process, orders are taken from customers, and a picking slip for the required items is prepared and subsequently used to select them from the warehouse. At the same time, the customer's credit is checked and shipping is organised for the order. When all of these tasks are complete an invoice is prepared for the customer and the goods are then packed and despatched whilst the customers account is updated with the outstanding amount. The order details are then finalised and filed.

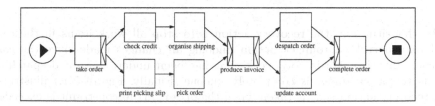

Fig. 4. Order despatch process

Figure 5(A) illustrates two alternate exception handling strategies for the *check credit* work item. If the credit required is less than $100, the current work item is suspended and the next work item is started. Where it is $100 or more, the current work item is suspended, the execution point is rewound to the beginning of the work item and it is recommenced. Figure 5(B) shows the exception handling strategy for the *pick order* work item where its completion deadline is not met. Recovery involves suspending the current work item, reassigning it to another resource, running a compensation task that determines if the order can be despatched within 48 hours (and if not applies a small credit to the account), then the *pick order* work item is restarted with the new resource. Figure 5(C) illustrates the resource unavailable handling strategy. Where the required resource is a data resource, this involves stopping the current work item and restarting it from the beginning. This strategy is bound to the process model i.e. by default, it applies to all work items. Where the unavailable resource is a human resource (i.e. the person undertaking the work item), the recovery action involves suspending the work item, reassigning it to another person and then restarting it from the beginning. Figure 5(D) indicates the approach to handling an *account frozen* trigger received by one of the tasks in the current process.

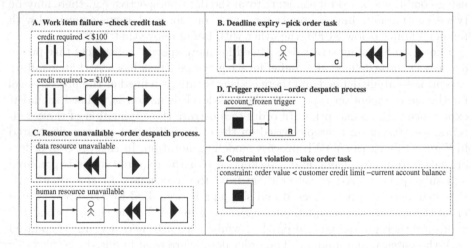

Fig. 5. Exception handling strategies – order despatch process

In this situation, the recovery action is to stop all work items in the case and to undertake a rollback action undoing all changes made since the case started. In other words, any work that has been undertaken on despatching goods to the customer is completely undone. Finally, Figure 5(E) illustrates the recovery action that is taken when the `order value` constraint is exceeded for the *take order* task. This involves stopping all work items associated with the process.

6 Conclusions

This paper has presented a patterns-based classification framework for characterising exception handling in workflow systems. The framework has been used to examine the capabilities of eight workflow systems and business process modelling and execution languages and has revealed the limited support for exception management in these offerings. As a consequence of the insights gained from these investigations, we have proposed a graphical, technology-independent language for defining exception handling strategies in workflows. This language offers the potential to assist in defining and managing deviations from normal process execution and will be the subject of further research in the context of exception handling in the YAWL reference implementation.

References

1. M. Adams, A.H.M. ter Hofstede, D. Edmond, and W.M.P. van der Aalst. Facilitating flexibility and dynamic exception handling in workflows through worklets. In O. Belo, J. Eder, O. Pastor, and J. Falcao é Cunha, editors, *Proceedings of the CAiSE'05 Forum*, volume 161 of *CEUR Workshop Proceedings*, pages 45–50, Porto, Portugal, 2005. FEUP.
2. G. Alonso, D. Agrawal, A. El Abbadi, M. Kamath, G. Gunthor, and C. Mohan. Advanced transaction models in workflow contexts. In *Proceedings of the 12th International Conference on Data Engineering*, pages 574–581, New Orleans, USA, 1996.
3. A. Borgida and T. Murata. Tolerating exceptions in workflows: A unified framework for data and processes. In D. Georgakopoulos, W. Prinz, and A.L. Wolf, editors, *Proceedings of the International Joint Conference on Work Activities Coordination and Collaboration (WACC'99)*, pages 59–68, San Francisco, USA, 1999.
4. F. Casati, S. Ceri, S. Paraboschi, and G. Pozzi. Specification and implementation of exceptions in workflow management systems. *ACM Transactions on Database Systems*, 24(3):405–451, 1999.
5. D.K.W. Chiu, Q. Li, and K. Karlapalem. ADOME-WFMS: Towards cooperative handling of workflow exceptions. In *Advances in Exception Handling Techniques*, pages 271–288. Springer-Verlag, New York, NY, USA, 2001.
6. J. Eder and W. Liebhart. The workflow activity model (WAMO). In S. Laufmann, S. Spaccapietra, and T. Yokoi, editors, *Proceedings of the Third International Conference on Cooperative Information Systems (CoopIS-95)*, pages 87–98, Vienna, Austria, 1995.
7. J. Eder and W. Liebhart. Workflow recovery. In *Proceedings of the First IFCIS International Conference on Cooperative Information Systems (CoopIS'96)*, pages 124–134, Brussels, Belgium, 1996. IEEE Computer Society.
8. A. Elmagarmid, editor. *Database Transaction Models for Advanced Applications*. Morgan Kaufmann, San Mateo, CA, USA.
9. D. Grigori, F. Casati, U. Dayal, and M.C. Shan. Improving business process quality through exception understanding, prediction, and prevention. In P. Apers, P. Atzeni, S. Ceri, S. Paraboschi, K. Ramamohanarao, and R. Snodgrass, editors, *Proceedings of the 27th International Conference on Very Large Data Bases (VLDB'01)*, pages 159–168, Rome, Italy, 2001. Morgan Kaufmann.

10. C. Hagen and G. Alonso. Exception handling in workflow management systems. *IEEE Transactions on Software Engineering*, 26(10):943–958, 2000.

11. S.Y. Hwang and J. Tang. Consulting past exceptions to facilitate workflow exception handling. *Decision Support Systems*, 37(1):49–69, 2004.

12. M. Klein and C. Dellarocas. A knowledge-based approach to handling exceptions in workflow systems. *Journal of Computer-Supported Collaborative Work*, 9(3-4): 399–412, 2000.

13. F. Leymann and D. Roller. Workflow-based applications. *IBM Systems Journal*, 36(1):102–123, 1997.

14. Z. Luo, A. Sheth, K. Kochut, and J. Miller. Exception handling in workflow systems. *Applied Intelligence*, 13(2):125–147, 2000.

15. S. Mehrotra, R. Rastogi, H.F. Korth, and A Silberschatz. A transaction model for multidatabase systems. In *Proceedings of the 12th International Conference on Distributed Computing Systems (ICDCS'92)*, pages 56–63, Yokohama, Japan, 1992. IEEE Computer Society.

16. A. Reuter and F. Schwenkreis. ConTracts – a low-level mechanism for building general-purpose workflow management-systems. *Data Engineering Bulletin*, 18(1):4–10, 1995.

17. S. Rinderle, M. Reichert, and P. Dadam. Correctness criteria for dynamic changes in workflow systems – a survey. *Data and Knowledge Engineering*, 50:9–34, 2004.

18. N. Russell, A.H.M. ter Hofstede, D. Edmond, and W.M.P. van der Aalst. Workflow data patterns: Identification, representation and tool support. In L. Delcambre, C. Kop, H.C. Mayr, J. Mylopoulos, and O. Pastor, editors, *Proceedings of the 24th International Conference on Conceptual Modeling (ER 2005)*, volume 3716 of *LNCS*, pages 353–368, Klagenfurt, Austria, 2005. Springer.

19. N. Russell, W.M.P. van der Aalst, A.H.M. ter Hofstede, and D. Edmond. Workflow resource patterns: Identification, representation and tool support. In O. Pastor and J. Falcao é Cunha, editors, *Proceedings of the 17th Conference on Advanced Information Systems Engineering (CAiSE'05)*, volume 3520 of *Lecture Notes in Computer Science*, pages 216–232, Porto, Portugal, 2005. Springer.

20. D.M. Strong and S.M. Miller. Exceptions and exception handling in computerized information processes. *ACM Transactions on Information Systems*, 13(2):206–233, 1995.

21. W.M.P. van der Aalst and A.H.M. ter Hofstede. YAWL: Yet another workflow language. *Information Systems*, 30(4):245–275, 2005.

22. W.M.P. van der Aalst, A.H.M. ter Hofstede, B. Kiepuszewski, and A.P. Barros. Workflow patterns. *Distributed and Parallel Databases*, 14(3):5–51, 2003.

23. R. van Stiphout, T.D. Meijler, A. Aerts, D. Hammer, and R. Le Comte. TREX: Workflow transaction by means of exceptions. In H.-J. Schek, F. Saltor, I. Ramos, and G. Alonso, editors, *Proceedings of the Sixth International Conference on Extending Database Technology (EDBT'98)*, pages 21–26, Valencia, Spain, 1998.

24. D. Worah and A.P. Sheth. Transactions in transactional workflows. In S. Jajodia and L. Kerschberg, editors, *Advanced Transaction Models and Architectures*, pages 3–34. Kluwer Academic Publishers, 1997.

Dynamic Workflow Modeling and Verification

Jiacun Wang and Daniela Rosca

Department of Software Engineering,
Monmouth University,
West Long Branch, NJ 07762, USA
{jwang, drosca}@monmouth.edu

Abstract. The dynamic nature of incident command systems and their requirement for high flexibility raise a challenge to the research and implementation of
workflows. The significance of applying formal approaches to the modeling and
analysis of workflows has been well recognized and several such approaches
have been proposed. However, these approaches require users to master considerable knowledge of the particular formalisms, which impacts their application
on a larger scale. To address these challenges, we developed an intuitive, yet
formal approach to workflow modeling, enactment and validation. In this paper, we further develop a set of theorems to support dynamic modeling, modification and on-the-fly verification of the workflows. A prototype has been
implemented to demonstrate the feasibility of the theoretical approach.

1 Introduction

The business environment today is undergoing rapid and constant changes. The way
companies do business, including the business processes and their underlying business rules, ought to adapt to these changes rapidly with minimum interruption of the
ongoing operations [9, 13]. This flexibility becomes of a paramount importance in
applications such as incident command systems (ICS) that support the allocation of
people, resources and services in the event of a major natural or terrorist incident.
These systems have to deal with a predominantly volunteer-based workforce and
frequent changes in the course of execution of their workflows, dictated by unplanned
incoming events [19].

Dealing with these issues generates many challenges for a workflow management
system (WFMS). The necessity of making many ad-hoc changes calls for an on-the-
fly verification of the correctness of the modified workflow. This cannot be achieved
without an underlying formal approach of the workflow, which does not leave any
scope for ambiguity and sets the ground for analysis. Yet, since our main users will be
volunteers from various backgrounds, with little computer experience, we need to
provide an approach with highly intuitive features for the description and modification of the workflows.

A number of formal modeling techniques have been proposed in the past decades
for modeling processes and business rules [5, 15, 1, 3, 9]. Petri nets are one of the
most widely used approaches because of its formal semantics as well as graphical
nature [2]. However, they model the loops implicitly, making the decision of whether

E. Dubois and K. Pohl (Eds.): CAiSE 2006, LNCS 4001, pp. 303–318, 2006.
© Springer-Verlag Berlin Heidelberg 2006

a cycle is desired in the workflow, or it is a deadlock, a NP-hard problem. Other than Petri Nets, techniques such as state charts have also been proposed for modeling WFMS [12]. Although state charts can model the behavior of workflows, they have to be supplemented with logical specification for supporting analysis. Singh et al [16] use event algebra to model the inter-task dependencies and temporal logic. Attia et al [7] have used computational tree logic to model workflows.

As indicated in [3], it is desirable that a business process model can be understood by the stakeholders as straightforwardly as possible. Unfortunately, a common major drawback of all the above formal approaches is that only users who have the expertise in these particular formal methods can build their workflows and dynamically change them. For example, in order to add a new task to a Petri-net based workflow, one must manipulate the model in terms of transitions, places, arcs and tokens, which can be done correctly and efficiently only by a person with a good understanding of Petri-nets. This significantly affects the application of these approaches on a large scale. To address this issue, we introduced a new Workflows Intuitive Formal Approach (WIFA) for the modeling and analysis of workflows, which, in addition to the abilities of supporting workflow validation and enactment, possesses the distinguishing feature of allowing users who are not proficient in formal methods to build up and dynamically modify the workflows that address their business needs [19]. In this paper, we further develop a set of theorems to guide the dynamic, well-formed workflow modeling, modification and verification. Since WIFA is a result of the desire of modeling the ICS, it does not make the distinction between workflow schemas and workflow instances. There is only one person executing a dedicated workflow at a particular time in an ICS. However, after undertaking the modeling of other applications, we have noticed the need of introducing this distinction. The discussion of workflow instance migration to new schemas during the workflow execution is outside the scope of this paper.

Although WIFA was designed with a high degree of usability in mind, it has not sacrificed expressive power. As such, WIFA is able to model sequential and concurrent execution of tasks, conflict resolution, synchronization, mutual exclusion and loops. MILANO [6], another tool that claims "simplicity" of use, has sacrificed some expressive power, such as the representation of loops, for the flexibility during enactment. The same deficiency can be noticed in WASA [20]. WIDE [8] proposed a complete and minimal set of primitives that allow the correct transformation of an old workflow schema to a new one. Based on that minimal set, other change primitives can be derived, for both modifying workflow schemas and migrating instances to new schemas. TRAM [11], uses a versioning approach for the modification of workflow schemas. They use a principle similar to WASA's for migrating workflow instances to new schemas, e.g. verifying whether the instance can continue from its current state according to the new schema. In [5], the author proposes an approach where schema modifications should not be migrated to instances that are executed on "change regions". Currently, WIFA does not handle data flow control, as in WASA, Flow Nets [10], ADEPT [14], and other systems. This represents a dimension that needs to be added to our work.

The paper is organized as follows: Section 2 briefly introduces the new workflow formalism WIFA and its state transition rules. A detailed presentation can be found in [19]. Section 3 presents the definition of well-formed workflows and a set of theorems which help build well-formed workflows and dynamically validate workflows after various types of modifications. In Section 4, an example is used to illustrate the use of these theorems. Section 5 presents a brief description of the prototype that supports the WIFA approach, as well as a discussion of the findings of a usability study conducted to assess WIFA's intuitiveness. Finally, Section 6 presents conclusions and ideas for the continuation of this work.

2 The WIFA Workflow Model

In general, a workflow consists of processes and activities, which are represented by well-defined *tasks*. Two tasks are said to have *precedence constraints* if they are constrained to execute in some order. As a convention, we use a partial-order relation <, called a *precedence relation* over the set of tasks, to specify the precedence constraints among tasks. A classic way to represent the precedence constraints among tasks in a set T is by a directed graph $G = (T, <)$, in which each vertex represents a task in T, and there is a directed edge from vertex T_i to vertex T_j if T_i is an immediate predecessor of T_j. The graph is called a *precedence graph*.

The *preset* of a task T_k is the set of all tasks that are immediate predecessors of the task, denoted by $*T_k$; the *postset* of T_k is the set of all tasks that are immediate successors of the tasks, denoted by T_k*. If $|T_k*| \geq 1$, then the execution of T_k might trigger multiple tasks. Suppose $\{T_i, T_j\} \subseteq T_k*$. There are two possibilities: (1) T_i and T_j can be executed simultaneously, and (2) only one of them can be executed, and the execution of one will disable the other, due to the conflict between them. We denote the former case by $c_{ij} = c_{ji} = 0$, and the latter case by $c_{ij} = c_{ji} = 1$.

If $|*T_k| \geq 1$, then based on the aforementioned classic precedence model, the execution of T_k won't start until *all* of its immediate predecessors are executed. This precedence constraint is called *AND precedence constraint*. An extension to this classic precedence model is to allow a task to be executed when *some* of its immediate predecessors are executed. This loosens the precedence constraints to some extent, and the loosened precedence constraint is called *OR precedence constraint*. Obviously, the *OR* precedence model provides more flexibility than the classic *AND* precedence model in describing the dependencies among tasks. In this paper, the *OR* precedence model is adopted. The *AND* precedence model can be viewed as a special case of the *OR* precedence model.

2.1 WIFA Workflow Definition

In WIFA, a workflow is defined as a 5-tuple: $WF = (T, P, C, A, S_0)$, where

1) $T = \{T_1, T_2, \ldots, T_m\}$ is a set of *tasks*, $m \geq 1$.
2) $P = (p_{ij})_{mxm}$ is the *precedence matrix* of the task set. If T_i is the immediate predecessor of T_j, then $p_{ij} = 1$; otherwise, $p_{ij} = 0$.
3) $C = (c_{ij})_{mxm}$ is the *conflict matrix* of the task set. $c_{ij} \in \{0, 1\}$ for $i = 1, 2, \ldots m$ and $j =1, 2, \ldots m$.
4) $A = (A(T_1), A(T_2), \ldots, A(T_m))$ defines *pre-condition set* for each task. $\forall T_k \in T$, $A(T_k): *T_k \rightarrow 2^{*T_k}$. Let set $A' \in A(T_k)$. Then $T_i \in A'$ implies $p_{ik} = 1$.
5) $S_0 \in \{0, 1, 2, 3\}^m$ is the *initial state* of the workflow.

A state of the *WF* is denoted by $S = (S(T_1), S(T_2), \ldots, S(T_m))$, where $S(T_i) \in \{0, 1, 2, 3\}$. $S(T_i) = 0$ means T_i is *not executable* at state S and *not executed previously*; $S(T_i) = 1$ means T_i is *executable* at state S and *not executed previously*; $S(T_i) = 2$ means T_i is *not executable* at state S and *executed previously*; and $S(T_i) = 3$ means T_i is *executable* at state S and *executed previously*.

By the above definition of state values, at any state, only those tasks whose values are either 1 or 3 can be selected for execution. Suppose task T_i at state S_a is selected for execution, and the new state resulted from the execution of T_i is S_b, then the execution of T_i is denoted by $S_a(T_i)S_b$.

At the initial state S_0, for any task $T_i \in T$, if there is no T_j such that $p_{ji} = 1$, then $S_0(T_i) = 1$; otherwise $S_0(T_i) = 0$.

Note that tasks that have no predecessor do not need to wait for any other task to execute first. In other words, these tasks are executable immediately. We assume that there are always such tasks in a workflow. They are the initial triggers or "starting" tasks of workflows.

Fig. 1 shows a workflow model with seven tasks, $T = \{T_1, T_2, \ldots T_7\}$, in which T_1 is the starting task of the workflow. The execution of T_1 triggers both T_2 and T_3, which do not conflict with each other, i.e., $c_{23} = c_{32} = 0$. T_2 can be triggered by either T_1 or T_6, i.e., $A(T_2) = \{\{T_1\}, \{T_6\}\}$. The execution of T_5 triggers both T_6 and T_7, which conflict with each other, i.e., $c_{67} = c_{76} = 0$. T_7 is executable only if both T_3 and T_5 are executed, i.e., $A(T_7) = \{\{T_3\}, \{T_5\}\}$. The initial state is $S_0 = (1, 0, 0, 0, 0, 0, 0)$. After the execution of T_1, the new state will be $S_1 = (2, 1, 1, 0, 0, 0, 0)$. If in the next step we select T_2 for execution, the new state will be $S_2 = (2, 2, 1, 1, 0, 0, 0)$.

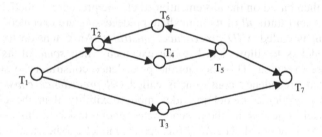

Fig. 1. A seven-task workflow

2.2   State Transition Rules

The dynamics of a WIFA workflow can be captured by state transitions. The state transitions are guided by the following rules:

If $S_a(T_i)S_b$, then $\forall\ T_j \in T$,

1) If $T_j = T_i$ then $S_b(T_j) = 2$;
2) If $T_j \neq T_i$ then the state value of T_j at new state S_b depends on its state value at state S_a. We consider four cases:
   Case A – $S_a(T_j) = 0$:
   If $p_{ij} = 1$ and $\exists A \in A\ (T_j)$ such that $S_b(T_k) = 2$ for any $T_k \in A$, then $S_b(T_j) = 1$; otherwise $S_b(T_j) = 0$.

$Case\ B - S_a(T_j) = 1$
 If $c_{ij} = 0$ then $S_b(T_j) = 1$; otherwise $S_b(T_j) = 0$.
$Case\ C - S_a(T_j) = 2$
 If $p_{ij} = 1$ and $\exists A \in A\ (T_j)$ such that $S_b(T_k) = 2$ for any $T_k \in A$, then $S_b(T_j) = 3$; otherwise $S_b(T_j) = 2$.
$Case\ D - S_a(T_j) = 3$
 If $c_{ij} = 0$ then $S_b(T_j) = 3$; otherwise $S_b(T_j) = 2$.

According to the above state transition rules, for example, a task's state value at a given state other than the initial state is 0 iff one of the following is true:

1) Its state value is 0 in the previous state and it is not a successor of the task which is just executed.
2) Its state value is 0 in the previous state, and it is the successor of the task which is just executed, but for each of its precondition sets there is at least one task that is not executed.
3) Its state value is 1 in the previous state but it conflicts with the task which is just executed.

Note that a state value can increment from 0 to 1, from 1 to 2 or from 2 to 3; it can also decrement from 1 to 0 or from 3 to 2. But it cannot decrement from 2 to 1.

3 Well-Formed Workflow Definitions

In this section, we introduce *well-formed workflows* which have no dangling tasks and are guaranteed to finish. We particularly discuss *confusion-free workflows*, which are a class of well-formed workflows and have some distinguishing properties. We demonstrate how to build confusion-free workflows, and how to ensure a workflow remains confusion-free when it is changed.

3.1 Well-Formed Workflow Definitions

Definition 1 (*execution path*). An execution path is a sequence of tasks that are executable starting from a given state. Denote all possible execution paths starting from a state S by $\Sigma(S)$.

Definition 2 (*reachable set*). A state S_k of a workflow is *reachable* from the initial state S_0 if and only if there exists $\sigma \in \Sigma(S_0)$ such that the execution of σ leads the workflow to state S_k. denoted by $S_0(\sigma)S_k$. The set of all reachable states, including the initial state, is called the reachable set of a workflow, denoted by R.

Definition 3 (*well-formed workflow*). A workflow is *well-formed* if and only if the following two *behavior conditions* are met:

1) $\forall T_i \in T, \exists S \in R$ such that $S(T_i) = 1$. (i.e. there is no dangling task.)
2) $\forall\ S_i \in R, \exists \sigma \in \Sigma(S_i)$ and $S_e \in R$, where $S_e(T_i) \in \{0, 2\}$ for $\forall T_i \in T$, such that $S_i(\sigma)S_e$. (i.e., given any reachable state, there is always a path leading the workflow to finish.)

The example workflow given in Section 2.1 is well-formed, because based on Fig. 1, every task in this workflow is executable, and from each state there is an execution path leading the workflow to one of the two ending states. In general, the validation of a workflow being well-formed requires the reachability analysis of the workflow. Below we introduce *confusion-free* workflows, which are a class of well-formed workflows with some restrictions imposed on their structure.

Definition 4 (*confusion-free workflow*). A well-formed workflow is *confusion-free* if and only if the following two *structural conditions* are met:

1) $\forall T_k \in T$ with $|T_k^*| \geq 3$, if $\exists T_i, T_j \in T_k^*$ such that $c_{ij} = 1$ (or $c_{ij} = 0$), then for $\forall T_a$, $T_b \in T_k^*$ $c_{ab} = 1$ (or $c_{ab} = 0$) (i.e., either all tasks triggered by the task are in conflict, or no pair of them are in conflict. In the former case, the task is called an AND-out task; in the latter case, it is called a XOR-out task.)

2) $\forall T_k \in T$ with $^*T_k = \{T_{k1}, T_{k2}, ..., T_{kn}\}$, $n \geq 2$, either

$$A(T_k) = \{\{T_{k1}, T_{k2}, ..., T_{kn}\}\}, \tag{1}$$

or

$$A(T_k) = \{\{T_{k1}\}, \{T_{k2}\}, ..., \{T_{kn}\}\} \tag{2}$$

(i.e., T_k becomes executable either when all of its predecessor tasks are executed, or when any one of them is executed. In the former case, the task is called an AND-in task; in the latter case, it is called a XOR-in task.)

Based on this definition, the example workflow of Fig. 1 is confusion-free. As will be described next, it is easy to construct and validate a confusion-free workflow.

From the perspective of triggering conditions and relations among triggered tasks, we can classify the tasks in a confusion-free well-formed workflow into four types: *AND-in-AND-out, AND-in-XOR-out, XOR-in-AND-out* and *XOR-in-XOR-out*.

Without loss of generality, a task with only one or no immediate predecessor is treated as an "AND-in" task, and a task with only one or no immediate successor treated as an "AND-out" task. We denote by T_{AP} the set of all AND-in-AND-out tasks, T_{AC} all AND-in-XOR-out tasks, T_{OP} all XOR-in-AND-out tasks, and T_{OC} all XOR-in-XOR-out tasks. For example, for the workflow of Fig. 1, $T_{AP} = \{T_1, T_3, T_4, T_6, T_7\}$, $T_{AC} = \{T_5\}$, $T_{OP} = \{T_2\}$, and $T_{OC} = \varnothing$.

Since the definition of well-formed workflows has a concern over infinite task loop, we formally define a task loop as follows:

Definition 5 (*loop*). Tasks $T_1, T_2, ..., T_s$ forms a loop L iff $p_{s,1} = p_{i,i+1} = 1$ for $i = 1, 2, ..., s-1$. Let $T(L) = \{T_1, T_2, ..., T_k\}$. A task $T_k \in T \setminus T(L)$ is said to be an *entry* of L iff $p_{kj} = 1$ for some $T_j \in T(L)$. A task $T_k \in T \setminus T(L)$ is said to be an *exit* of L iff $p_{jk} = 1$ for some $T_j \in T(L)$.

In the workflow of Fig. 1, for example, there is a loop L where $T(L) = \{T_2, T_4, T_5, T_6\}$. For this loop, T_1 is the only entry task, while T_7 the only exit task. It is obvious that if a loop has no entry task, then all tasks in the loop are dangling tasks; if a loop has no exit task, then the loop is an infinite loop, and the workflow will never be finished. In the rest of the paper, a loop with at least one entry task and one exit task is called a *healthy loop*. Otherwise, the loop is called an *unhealthy loop*.

Discussion: WIFA engine in general allows us to build any control pattern of workflow constructs as mentioned in [4]. However, a well-formed confusion-free WIFA model can only be composed of the five simple control patterns, namely sequence, parallel split, synchronization, exclusive choice and simple merge.

3.2 Build a Well-Formed Workflow

Lemma 1: Given a workflow $WF_A = (T, P, C, A, S_0)$ with $T_k \in T$. As shown in Fig. 2, $WF_B = (T', P', C', A', S'_0)$ is obtained by replacing T_k with T_{k1} and T_{k2}, such that

1) $*T_{k1} = *T_k$, $T_{k2}* = T_k*$, $T_{k1}* = \{T_{k2}\}$ and $*T_{k2} = \{T_{k1}\}$,
2) $A'(T_{k1}) = A(T_k)$, i.e., T_{k1} has the same pre-condition set in WF_B as that of T_k in WF_A;
3) $C'(T_i, T_j) = C(T_i, T_j)$ for $\forall T_i, T_j \in T_k*$, i.e, the conflict property among all T_k's immediate successors remain unchanged in WF_B.

Then WF_B is confusion-free well-formed iff WF_A is confusion-free well-formed.

Proof
Necessity: Assume WF_A is well-formed. Then there exists an execution path which results in reachable state sequence $S_0S_1S_2...S_{a-1}S_a$ with WF_A such that:

$$S_i(T_k) = 0, i = 0, 1, ... a-1;$$
$$S_a(T_k) = 1.$$

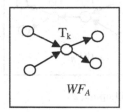 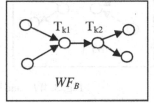

WF_A WF_B

Fig. 2. WF_A and WF_B in Lemma 1

Based on the definition of WF_B, we know there is a corresponding state sequence $S'_0S'_1S'_2...S'_{a-1}S'_a$ with WF_B such that:

$$S'_i = S_i \cup \{S_i(T_{k1})\} \cup \{S_i(T_{k2})\} \setminus \{S_i(T_k)\}, i = 0, 1, ... a;$$
$$S'_i(T_{k1}) = S'_i(T_{k2}) = 0, i = 0, 1, ... a-1;$$
$$S'_a(T_{k1}) = 1, S'_a(T_{k2}) = 0.$$

After the execution of T_{k1} at S'_a, task T_{k2} becomes executable. Then based on conditions 1) and 3), it is obvious that the behavior of WF_B after the execution of task T_{k2} will be the same as that of WF_A after the execution of task T_k. So WF_B is also well-formed.

Sufficiency: Assume WF_B is well-formed. Then there exists an execution path which results in reachable state sequence $S'_0S'_1S'_2...S'_{a-1}S'_aS'_{a+1}$ with WF_B such that:

$S'_i(T_{k1}) = S'_i(T_{k2}) = 0, i = 0, 1, \ldots a\text{-}1;$
$S'_a(T_{k1}) = 1, S'_a(T_{k2}) = 0.$
$S'_{a+1}(T_{k1}) = 2, S'_{a+1}(T_{k2}) = 1.$

Based on the relationship between WF_A of WF_B, there exists a corresponding state sequence $S_0 S_1 S_2 \ldots S_{a\text{-}1} S_a$ with WF_A such that:

$S_i = S'_i \cup \{S_i(T_k)\} \setminus \{S_i(T_{k1})\} \setminus \{S_i(T_{k2})\}, i = 0, 1, \ldots a;$
$S_i(T_k) = 0, i = 0, 1, \ldots a\text{-}1;$
$S_a(T_k) = 1.$

According to conditions 1) and 3), the behavior of WF_A after state S_a will be the same as that of WF_B after S'_{a+1}. So WF_A is also well-formed.

The lemma is proved.   ∎

Lemma 2: Let $WF_A = (T, P, C, A, S_0)$ be a well-formed confusion-free workflow with $T_{k1}, T_{k2} \in T, T_{k1}* = *T_{k2} = \varnothing$, and T_{k2} is not a predecessor of T_{k1}. As shown in Fig. 3, $WF_B = (T', P', C', A', S'_0)$ is obtained by introducing precedence constraint between T_{k1} and T_{k2} such that T_{k1} is an immediate predecessor of T_{k2}. Then WF_B is also well-formed and confusion-free.

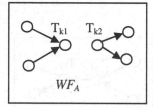 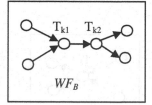

Fig. 3. WF_A and WF_B in Lemma 2

Proof: Since WF_A is well-formed, so T_{k1} is executable. Also because T_{k2} is not a predecessor of T_{k1}, there exists an execution path which results in reachable state sequence $S_0 S_1 S_2 \ldots S_{a\text{-}1} S_a$ with WF_A such that:

$S_i(T_{k1}) = 0, i = 0, 1, \ldots a\text{-}1;$
$S_a(T_{k1}) = 1;$
$S_i(T_{k2}) = 0, i = 0, 1, \ldots a.$

Based on the definition of WF_B, for each such a sequence with WF_A, we know there is a corresponding state sequence $S'_0 S'_1 S'_2 \ldots S'_{a\text{-}1} S'_a$ with WF_B such that:

$S'_i(T_{k1}) = 0, i = 0, 1, \ldots a\text{-}1;$
$S'_a(T_{k1}) = 1;$
$S'_i(T_{k2}) = 0, i = 0, 1, \ldots a.$

After the execution of T_{k1} at S'_a, task T_{k2} becomes executable, and all T_{k2}'s successor tasks in WF_B are executable as they are in WF_A. Because T_{k2} is not a predecessor of

T_{kl}, no new loop is introduced, so there won't be any infinite loop in WF_B, thus WF_B can always finish. This means WF_B is well-formed and confusion free.

The lemma is proved. ∎

Theorem 1: Given a confusion-free well-formed workflow $WF = (T, P, C, A, S_0)$, by adding a new task T_k to it, the obtained new workflow is denoted by $WF' = (T', P', C', A', S_0')$. Then WF' is also a confusion-free workflow if it matches one of the following cases:

1) $*T_k = T_k* = \varnothing$, i.e., $p'_{ki} = p'_{ik} = 0$ for all $T_i \in T' \setminus \{T_k\}$.
2) $*T_k = \varnothing$, $T_k* \neq \varnothing$, and $\forall T_i \in T_k*$, if T_k is an AND-in task in WF, then T_i is also an AND-in task in WF'; If T_i is an XOR-in task in WF, then T_i is also an XOR-in task in WF'.
3) $*T_k \neq \varnothing$, $T_k* = \varnothing$. If T_k is an all-in task in WF, then there exists a $S_a \in \mathrm{R}(WF)$ such that $S_a(T_i) = 2$ for all $T_i \in *T_k$; If T_k is an or-in task in WF, then there exists a $S_a \in \mathrm{R}(WF)$ such that $S_a(T_i) = 2$ for some $T_i \in *T_k$. In addition, $\exists T_i \in *T_k$, if T_i triggers two or more conflicting tasks, then T_k conflicts with each of these tasks, otherwise, $c_{kj} = 0$ for any $T_j \in T_i*$.
4) $*T_k \neq \varnothing$, $T_k* \neq \varnothing$, with all other conditions appear in 2) and 3). Besides, $\forall T_i \in T_k*$, if T_i is also a predecessor of T_k (i.e., T_k introduces a loop), then T_i can only be an XOR-in task, and the loop is a healthy loop.

Proof
Case 1): T_k is an isolated task. Based on Definition 3, T_k will not be in any other task's pre-condition set, so it has no impact to the original workflow WF, and the two structural conditions of confusion-free workflows are all met in WF'. Because T_k has no predecessors, so it is executable in S'_0. Since WF is well-formed, there must be an ending state $S_q \in \mathrm{R}(WF)$, then state $S'_q = S_q \cup \{S(T_k) = 2\}$ is an ending state of WF'. Therefore, WF' is confusion-free.

Case 2): In this case, T_k has no predecessors, so it is executable in S'_0. We need to make sure that all tasks that are successors to T_k are still executable after adding in T_k. As shown in Fig. 7(b), $\forall T_i \in T_k*$, if T_i is an and-in task in WF', then that WF is confusion-free indicates that there is a state S_a in WF such that all tasks in $*T_i$ have state value of 2. Because T_k is unconditionally executable, so there must be a corresponding state S_a' in WF' such that $S_a' = S_a \cup \{S_a'(T_i) = 2\}$. Thus T_i is still executable in WF'. On the other hand, if T_i is an or-in task in WF', then the execution of any task in $*T_i$ in WF' can still trigger T_i as it does in WF, and T_k is just an additional task that triggers T_i. Thus T_i is still executable in WF'.

Now consider the second condition of being well-formed workflows. Since WF is well-formed, $\forall S_i \in \mathrm{R}(WF)$, $\exists \sigma \in \Sigma(S_i)$ and an ending state $S_e \in \mathrm{R}(WF)$, such that $S_i(\sigma)S_e$. If T_i has no occurrence in σ, then for WF' we have

$$S_i \cup \{S(T_k) = 0\} \ (\sigma T_k) \ S_e \cup \{S(T_k) = 2\},$$

where $S_i \cup \{S(T_k) = 0\}$ is the state in WF' which is the S_i extended with the state of T_k, $S_e \cup \{S(T_k) = 2\}$ the state in WF' which is the S_e extended with the state of T_k, and σT_k the execution path of WF'. If T_i has one occurrence in σ, let σ be $\sigma_1 T_i \sigma_2$. Then for WF' we have

$$S_i \cup \{S(T_k) = 0\} \ (\sigma_1 T_k T_i \sigma_2) \ S_e \cup \{S(T_k) = 2\},$$

If T_i has multiple occurrences in σ, we can use the same way to construct the execution path for WF' which leads it to finish.

Case 3): In this case, T_k has no successors. The other conditions already guarantee that task T_k is executable, and the two structural conditions of confusion-free workflows are also met. We only need to prove that the introduction of T_k won't cause other tasks to become non-executable. It is easy to understand that the state transition behavior of WF' from any state S' in which $S'(T_k) = 0$ is not affected due to the introduction of T_k. Suppose that at state S_a' we have $S_a'(T_k) = 1$ and T_k is triggered by T_i ($T_i \in {}^*T_k$). If all tasks triggered by T_i are able to execute in parallel with T_k ($c_{kj} = 0$ for any $T_i \in T_i^*$), then T_k has no impact to the execution of other triggered tasks. The other possibility is that T_k is in conflict with any other task triggered by T_i. In this case, if T_k is not chosen for execution, the state transition behavior from S' will be just like the case in state $S = S' \setminus \{ S'(T_k) = 1\}$ of WF. All these suggests that WF' is also a confusion-free workflow.

Case 4): This case can be viewed as a combination of *Case* 2 and *Case* 3. If T_k doesn't introduce a loop to the workflow, then we can add T_{k1} and T_{k2} to WF first, where T_{k1} satisfies condition 3) and T_{k2} satisfies condition 2). The obtained workflow is like the WF_A shown in Fig.5 and it is well-formed and confusion free as we just proved in Case 2 and Case 3. Then by connecting T_{k1} and T_{k2} and applying Lemma 2, we know obtained workflow, which is illustrated as WF_B in Fig. 5, is well-formed and confusion free. Merging T_{k1} and T_{k2} and applying Lemma 1, we conclude that WF', which is illustrated as WF_A in Fig. 4, is also well-formed and confusion free.

In case T_k introduces a loop to the workflow, since we already restrict that T_i be an or-in task, T_i can be triggered as it is without T_k in place. Adding T_k simply introduces one more trigger to T_i. So the loop does not cause any task un-executable. Moreover, because the loop is healthy, the workflow can finish.

The theorem is proved.   ■

Theorem 1 can serve as a rule in building a well-formed and confusion-free workflow. At the beginning, the task set is empty. When the first task is introduced, the workflow is well-formed, because this single task has no predecessors and successors and it is executable. Then we add a second task. This second task can either be an isolated one (Case 1 of Theorem 1), or be a successor of the first task (Case 2 of Theorem 1), or be a predecessor of the first task (Case 3 of Theorem 1), or even be both a predecessor and successor to the first task (Case 4 of Theorem 1). Since the first task is the only possible successor or predecessor to the second task, the new workflow (with these two tasks) is still confusion-free. When we continue to introduce more tasks to the workflow, as long as we make sure each new task is added in such a way that it satisfies the conditions defined in one of the four cases, then the new workflow is guaranteed to be confusion-free.

3.3 Modify a Well-Formed Workflow

Modifying a workflow can be conducted in three ways: adding new tasks to the workflow, deleting tasks from the workflow, and changing business rules defined on the workflow by adding or deleting precedence arcs between tasks. Theorem 1 considered the case of adding new tasks to a workflow. Now we consider the last two types of modifications. We first discuss deleting a precedence arc from a workflow, then deleting a task, and then adding precedence arcs.

Theorem 2: Let $WF = (T, P, C, A, S_0)$ be a confusion-free well-formed workflow with $T_i, T_j \in T$ and $p_{ij} = 1$. WF' is obtained by deleting the precedence arc between T_i and T_j, i.e. setting p_{ij} to 0. Then WF' is confusion-free well-formed iff the deletion does not introduce any unhealthy loop.

Proof: Because WF is confusion-free well-formed, so T_j is executable in WF. Also because in WF' the precondition of T_j is loosened compared with it is in WF, so T_j is executable in WF' as well. This means the executability of T_j and all its successors are not affected by deleting removing the precedence relation between T_i and T_j. Also because the precedence arc deletion does not introduce any unhealthy loop, the workflow is guaranteed to finish. Therefore, WF' is also confusion-free well-formed.

The theorem is proved. ∎

Theorem 3: Given a confusion-free well-formed workflow $WF = (T, P, C, A, S_0)$, deleting a task $T_k \in T$ and all precedence arcs starting from or ending up to T_k, the obtained new workflow is denoted by $WF' = (T', P', C', A', S_0')$. If the deletion of does not cause an unhealthy loop, then WF' is also a confusion-free well-formed workflow.

Proof: Since the deletion does not cause an unhealthy loop, the workflow is guaranteed to finish. We only need to prove all tasks in the new workflow are executable, Consider the following four cases:

$Case\ 1$: $*T_k = T_k* = \varnothing$.
In this case, T_k is an isolated task, so its presence or absence has no impact on the execution of the rest of the workflow.

$Case\ 2$: $*T_k = \varnothing, T_k* \neq \varnothing$.
In this case, T_k has no predecessors, so we only need to prove that all tasks that are immediate successors of T_k are still executable after removing in T_k.

Suppose $T_i \in T_k*$. If T_i is an AND-in task in WF, then that WF is well-formed implies that T_i is executable, i.e. there is a state S_a in WF such that all tasks in $*T_i$ have state value 2. If $\forall T_j \in *T_i\backslash\{T_k\}$, T_j is not a (either immediate or not) successor of T_k, then T_j is executable in WF', then there must be a corresponding state S_a' in WF' such that $S_a' = S_a \backslash \{S_a'(T_i) = 2\}$, which means T_i is still executable in WF'. If $\exists T_j \in *T_i\backslash\{T_k\}$, T_j is a successor of T_k, then we can always find a task T_l such that $T_l \in T_k*$ and T_j is a successor of T_l. Without loss of generality, we assume that there is no other task that is also an immediate successor of T_k and sits in between T_l and T_j. We have already proved that T_l is executable after removing T_k. So T_j is also executable after removing T_k, which further indicates that T_i is executable in WF'.

Now we consider the case that T_i is an XOR-in task in WF. Again, WF is well-formed implies that T_i is executable, and it also implies that all of its s are executable. So, removing T_k has no impact to the executability of T_i. In other words, T_i is still executable in WF'.

Case 3) $*T_k \neq \varnothing$, $T_k* = \varnothing$.
In this case, T_k has no successors, so removing T_k has no impact to the executability of T_i. Since *WF* is well-formed, all tasks in $T \setminus \{T_k\}$ are executable in *WF*. Thus all tasks in *WF'* are also executable. Moreover, if S_q is an ending state of WF, then $S'_q = S_q \setminus \{S(T_k) = 2\}$ is an ending state of *WF'*. Therefore, *WF'* is confusion-free well-formed. Also, it is obvious that the two structural properties of confusion-free workflow are not affected by removing T_k. So *WF'* is also confusion free.

Case 4) $*T_k \neq \varnothing$, $T_k* \neq \varnothing$.
This case can be viewed as a combination of Case 2 and Case 3. We first split T_k into T_{k1} and T_{k2}, where T_{k1} and T_{k2} are connected as shown in WF_B of Fig. 2, T_{k1} satisfies condition 3) and T_{k2} satisfies condition 2). According to Lemma 1 we know the obtained workflow is well-formed and confusion free. Then we remove the precedence constraint between T_{k1} and T_{k2}, and the obtained workflow, like the WF_A of Fig. 2, is also well-formed and confusion free according to Theorem 2. Finally, applying the proof for Case 2) and Case 3) results in that the obtained workflow after removing T_{k1} and T_{k2}, which is *WF'* stated in this theorem, is well-formed and confusion free.

The theorem is proved. ∎

Theorem 3 shows a distinguishing feature of confusion-free workflows. That is, when we delete any task and its associated precedence arcs from a workflow, as long as it does not cause any unhealthy loop, the remaining workflow is still well-formed and confusion-free. However, it should be pointed out that, if the task to be deleted is not an isolated task, then deleting it will cause changes to the precedence relations among the remaining tasks. So in most cases, after we delete a task, we need to adjust the precedence relations among those tasks that are s or immediate successors.

When adding a precedence arc between two tasks, say T_i and T_j, the relationship between these two tasks in the original workflow has an impact to the well-formedness of the resultant workflow. More specifically, if T_j is not a predecessor of T_i, then setting $p_{ij} = 0$ will not cause a loop. Otherwise, a loop will be introduced. In the latter case, if T_i is an "AND-in" task, then T_i will never be executable because of the existence of deadlock: T_i is not executable until T_j is executed; meanwhile T_j is not executable until T_i is executed. In addition, as a general rule, one should not introduce a precedence arc between two exclusive tasks, because it violates logic consistency. The following theorem addresses adding precedence constraint to a workflow. Due to space limitation, we only give proof sketch to this theorem.

Theorem 4: Let $WF = (T, P, C, A, S_0)$ be a well-formed confusion free workflow with $T_i, T_j \in T$ where $p_{ij} = 0$ and T_i and T_j are not mutual exclusive. *WF'* is obtained by adding a precedence arc between T_i and T_j, i.e. setting p_{ij} to 1. Then *WF'* is confusion-free well-formed if it matches one of the following cases:

1) T_i is of the same type in both *WF* and *WF'*, so is T_j.
2) If the addition introduces a loop, then the loop must be healthy.

Proof sketch: Condition 1) ensures confusion free and task executability. Condition 2) guarantees the new workflow to finish. ∎

The importance of the above theorems is that they allow a progressive workflow well-formedness verification, which significantly reduces the complexity of large-scale model analysis. This is particularly useful in modeling and enacting incident command systems where timing is so critical to mission success. In the next section we will show how to apply these theorems.

4 Example

We illustrate the use of the five theorems through changes to the workflow model shown in Fig. 1.

Suppose that the model is incomplete. Now we add task T_8 to the model such that T_8 is the immediate successor of T_7 and it has no successors. The new model is shown in Fig. 4. Based on Theorem 1, Case 3, the workflow of Fig. 4 is well-formed and confusion-free.

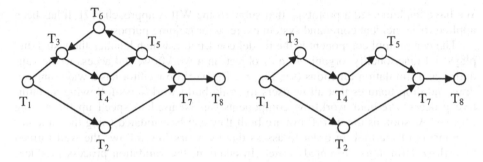

Fig. 4. Add task T_8 **Fig. 5.** Delete task T_6

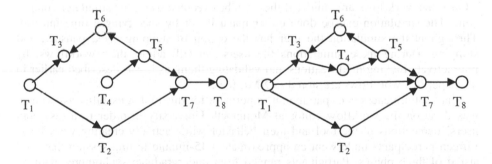

Fig. 6. Delete precedence arc between T_3 and T_4 **Fig. 7.** Add precedence arc between T_1 and T_7

The workflow in Fig. 5 is obtained by deleting task T_6 from Fig. 4. Because the workflow of Fig. 4 is well-formed and confusion-free, based on Theorem 2, the workflow of Fig. 5 is also well-formed and confusion-free. Note that deleting T_7 from Fig. 4 is not allowed, because it will make the loop of T_3, T_4, T_5 and T_6 unhealthy – no exit.

Fig. 6 shows a case where a precedence arc between two tasks that are in a loop is deleted. After deleting the arc between T_3 and T_4, T_4 becomes unconditionally executable. It is not hard to find that there is no dangling task in this model, and the workflow, depending on T_6 or T_7 is chosen to execute, will either end at state (2, 2, 2, 2, 2, 2, 0, 0) or state (2, 2, 2, 2, 2, 0, 2, 2), respectively. So the workflow is well-formed and confusion-free. This conclusion can be drawn immediately by applying Theorem 3, because T_3 is a XOR-in task.

In Fig. 7, a precedence arc between T_1 and T_7 is added, and it is important that T_1 remain as an AND-in task and T_7 remain as an AND-in task. Then based on Theorem 4, the workflow is well-formed and confusion-free.

Note that a change to a workflow may take several atomic steps, and the well-formedness may be violated before the change is complete. We allow this to happen as long as the model after the change is still well-formed.

5 Tool Support

We have implemented a prototype that supports the WIFA approach [17]. It has been applied to an incident command system exercise for training purposes.

The central tool component is the model constructor, which handles the visual displays, UI functionality, organization of objects in a workflow, and access to the validation and simulation functions (see Fig. 8). The workflow editor has a wide range of drag-and-drop features that allow users to easily build workflows following an intuitive process. Pre-built workflow components can be used to speed up the editing process. As soon as the workflows are built they can be validated using the validator component of the tool, in order to assess that the workflow follows the well-formed workflow definitions presented earlier. In addition, the validation process produces two separate outputs. One output is the validation report which includes errors in the workflow design and suggestions on how to fix them. The second output is the workflow reachable states that can be analyzed later.

Once the workflows are validated they can be executed using the simulator component. The simulation can be done either manually or by specifying a time interval. Throughout the simulation the user has the option of stepping back, pausing, and stopping. During these simulations the users can still adjust their workflows, by interactively making modifications and validating them, as it was described earlier in the paper. All workflows are stored as XML files.

Since intuitiveness is of paramount importance for this tool, a usability assessment was done on the workflow editor at Monmouth University in order to assess both users' perceptions of the tool and their behavior while actually creating workflows. Fifteen participants underwent an approximately 45-minute testing session that consisted of three phases. Participants ranged from undergraduate sophomores with no programming expertise to more experienced software engineering graduate students. Afterwards, participants were asked to complete a questionnaire. The results of the questionnaire suggest that, in general, the workflow editor was considered useful and that its usability was acceptable. The only aspect that was considered less intuitive was the four types o tasks that we defined in WIFA. In order to avoid this drawback, we have since incorporated into the tool the capability of using abstract task types that don't require the users to specify the task types. Other minor findings of the usability study are currently being included in the prototype.

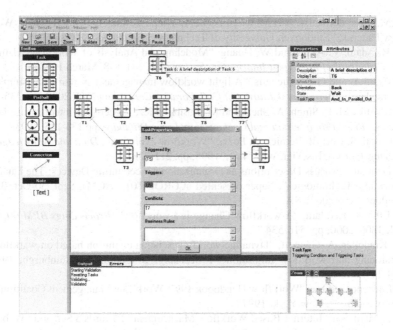

Fig. 8. WIFA prototype

6 Concluding Remarks

In this paper we explored the dynamic properties of the WIFA workflow engine. More specifically, we developed a set of theorems to guide the dynamic modeling, modification and verification of well-formed workflows. The importance of this work relies in these theorems that allow a progressive workflow well-formedness verification, which significantly reduces the complexity of large-scale model analysis. This is particularly useful in modeling and enacting incident command systems where timing is so critical to mission success.

We are also working on extending WIFA with the data dimension, and with capabilities for inter-organizational workflow modeling and analysis, to be able to represent the interactions between different people and organizations that need to work together for achieving different business goals.

References

1. W.M.P. van der Aalst, "Verification of Workflow Nets", *Proceedings of Application and Theory of Petri Nets*, LNCS, Volume 1248, pp. 407-426, 1997.
2. W.M.P. van der Aalst, "Three Good Reasons for Using a Petri Net-Based Workflow Management System", *Proceedings of the International Working Conference on Information and Process Integration in Enterprises* (IPIC'96), pp. 179–201, Nov 1996.
3. W.M.P. van der Aalst, A.H.M. ter Hofstede, and M. Weske, "Business Process Management: A Survey." *International Conference on Business Process Management* (*BPM 2003*), LNCS, volume 2678, pages 1-12. Springer-Verlag, Berlin, 2003.

4. W.M.P. van der Aalst, A.H.M. ter Hofstede, B. Kiepuszewski, and A.P. Barros, "Workflow Patterns," Eindhoven University of Technology, Eindhoven, 2000.
5. N. R. Adam, V. Atluri and W. Huang, "Modeling and Analysis of Workflows Using Petri Nets", *Journal of Intelligent Information Systems*, pp. 131-158, March 1998.
6. Agostini A. and G. DeMichelis, "A light workflow management system using simple process models", *International Journal of Collaborative Computing* (16), 2000, pp. 335-363.
7. P. C. Attie, M. P. Singh, A. Sheth and M. Rusibkiewicz, "Specifying Interdatabase Dependencies," *Proc. 19th International Conf. on Very Large Database*, pp.134-145, 1993.
8. F. Casati, S. Ceri, B. Pernici, G. Pozzi, "Workflow evolution", *Data and Knowledge Engineering Journal*, Elsevier, vol. 24 (3), 1998, pp. 211-238.
9. P. Dourish, "Process Descriptions as Organizational Accounting Devices: The Dual use of Workflow Technologies", Paper presented at GROUP'01, (ACM), Sept. 30-Oct. 3, 2001, Boulder, Colorado, USA.
10. C. Ellis, K. Keddara, "A workflow Change is a workflow", *Proceedings BPM'00*, LNCS, vol. 1806, 2000, pp. 516-534.
11. M. Kradolfer, A. Geppert, "Dynamic workflow schema evolution based on workflow type versioning and workflow migration", *Proceedings of CoopIS'99*, Edinburgh, 1999, pp. 104-114.
12. P. Lawrence, editor, "Workflow Handbook 1997, Workflow Management Coalition", John Wiley and Sons, New York, 1997.
13. D.C. Marinescu, Internet-Based Workflow Management: Towards a Semantic Web, Wiley Series on Parallel and Distributed Computing, vol. 40, Wiley-Interscience, NY, 2002.
14. M. Reichert, P. Dadam, "ADEPT $_{flex}$ – supporting dynamic changes of workflows without losing control", *Journal of Intelligent Information Systems*, 10 (2), 1998, pp.93-129.
15. D. Rosca, S. Greenspan, C. Wild, "Enterprise Modeling and Decision-Support for Automating the Business Rules Lifecycle", *Automated Software Engineering Journal,* Kluwer Academic Publishers, vol.9, pp.361-404, 2002.
16. M.P. Singh, G. Meredith, C. Tomlinson, and P.C. Attie, "An Event Algebra for Specifying and Scheduling Workflows," *Proceedings 4th International Conference on Database System for Advance Application*, pp. 53-60, 1995.
17. M. Stoute, J. Wang, and D. Rosca, "Workflow Management Tool Support for an Incident Command System", accepted for publication in the *Proceedings of ICNSC'06*, Miami, FL, 2006
18. J. Wang, Timed Petri Nets: Theory and Application, Kluwer Academic Publishers, 1998, ISBN: 0-7923-8270-6.
19. J. Wang, D. Rosca, W. Tepfenhart, A. Milewski and M. Stoute, "An Intuitive Formal Approach to Dynamic Workflow Modeling and Analysis," Proceedings of *the 3rd Conference on Business Process Management*, Nancy, France, Sept. 6-8, 2005.
20. M. Weske, "Formal Foundation and Conceptual Design of dynamic adaptations in a workflow management system", *Proceedings of HICSS-34*, 2001.

Business Modelling

On the Notion of Value Object

Hans Weigand[1], Paul Johannesson[2], Birger Andersson[2], Maria Bergholtz[2],
Ananda Edirisuriya[2], and Tharaka Ilayperuma[2]

[1] Tilburg University, P.O. Box 90153,
5000 LE Tilburg, The Netherlands
H.Weigand@uvt.nl
[2] Royal Institute of Technology,
Department of Computer and Systems Sciences, Sweden
{pajo, ba, maria, si-ana, si-tsi}@dsv.su.se

Abstract. It is increasingly recognized that business models offer an abstraction that is useful not only in the exploration of new business networks but also for the design and redesign of operational business processes. Among others, they can be used as input for a risk analysis that is crucial in cross-organizational business process design. However, the notion of value object is up till now not clearly defined. In this paper we investigate the notion of value, value objects and the activities involved when transferring value objects between business actors. We illustrate the proposed value object model by applying it on the well-known conference case.

1 Introduction

Meeting changing customer demands and creating new opportunities makes it necessary for businesses to constantly re-invent themselves. This is often done by changing the processes that produce the goods or services that an organization offers to the market. The changes may take many forms, e.g., the products offered may change, the ways in which the products are produced are changed, or the organization that produces the products may change.

There is an increased recognition that when creating models of new business processes or redefining old ones, the right point of departure in the analysis is not the business processes themselves but notions at a higher level of abstraction. The abstraction can be achieved by focusing on the essential communicative acts [3] rather then the specific message exchanges, on functional and non-functional goals rather than the way they are achieved [13], on commitments and obligations [7] rather than the way these are fulfilled, or on the business models behind a process. In this paper, the point of departure is one kind of business model, the e^3value model introduced by Gordijn [4]. A value model shows the exchanges of values that takes place, for instance, when actors trade goods and services for money. Value models have a special characteristic in that they are formulated declaratively with little or no concern for the order of activities taking place or other forms of dependencies.

When value models are used in the design of business processes, somehow a link must be made between the value model and the process model. A value model focuses on high level and timeless objects like value objects, actors, and value exchanges. In contrast, a process model focuses on procedural details including messages and activities as well as control and data flow. So when moving from one type of model to the other, a significant ontological gap has to be bridged. A problem the arises specifically when using e^3value as a starting point is that the notion of value object in e^3value is defined in general terms only. This may be sufficient when the model is used in discussing business models, but we need to know more about the internal structure of value objects if we want to make the step to the design of operational processes.

The objective of our research is to find a rigorous way of identifying value objects in business models and to explore how these value objects can be used to derive process models in a systematic way. Results of this research will be useful for practitioners, that is, business process analysts and designers who currently lack abstraction mechanisms or, if they do use one like e^3value, lack a systematic way of producing executable process models (e.g. expressed in BPEL [14]). The theoretical relevance is that the research clarifies the relationships between different models used in business process design.

The second part of our research objective is addressed in a separate paper [11]. This paper contributes to the first part by addressing the following research questions:

- What is exactly a value object?
- What is the relationship between value object and value activities?

In the paper, we provide tentative answers to these questions, using the well-known conference example as test case. In section 2, we will introduce the notion of value models and our general approach. Section 3 provides answers to our main research questions. In section 4, our answers are applied to the test case, which raises some new questions, and we conclude with a summary and directions for future research.

2 Background

In this section, we first explain the main concepts from the e^3value model and then present our general framework for the transformation of value models to process models.

2.1 The e^3-$value$ Model

e^3value [4] is a modeling approach that is originally aimed at supporting the explorations of new business networks. For these explorations, process details are not relevant. What is important is whether a collaboration can be set up that provides value to all participants. Recently, e^3value has also been applied for other purposes, such as business/IT alignment [12]. We briefly introduce the basic concepts. An *actor* is an economically independent entity and is often, but not necessarily, a legal entity. Examples: enterprises, end-consumers. A *value object* is something that is of economic value for at least one actor. Examples: cars, Internet access, stream of music. A *value port* is used by an actor to provide or receive value objects to or from other actors. A value port has a direction, in (e.g., receive goods) or out (e.g., make a payment) indicating whether a value object flows into or out of the actor. A *value interface* consists of in and out ports that belong to the same actor. Value interfaces are used to model economic reciprocity. A *value exchange* is a pair of value ports of opposite directions belonging to different actors. It represents one or more potential trades of value objects between these value ports. A *value activity* is an operation that could be carried out in an economically profitable way for at least one actor.

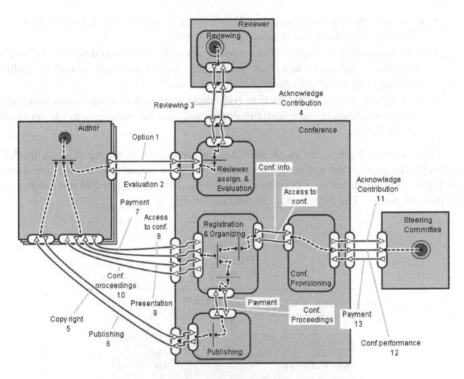

Fig. 1. e^3value model of the conference case

An example of an e^3value model for the well-known conference case is given in Fig. 1, where actors are shown by rectangles, value activities by rounded rectangles, value ports by triangles, value interfaces by oblong rectangles enclosing value ports, and value exchanges as lines between value ports with names of value objects as labels. For example, we see that the value object the reviewer offers is the reviewing – something valuable to both the Conference and the Author, and that she gets acknowledgement in return. The conference itself has several value activities, and corresponding value interfaces. First of all, this means that some value activities that are currently performed by the conference organization could be delegated to other parties as well. For example, the reviewing could be delegated completely to a PC, and the publishing to a commercial publisher. Secondly, the value interfaces could be opened separately to other actors. For example, the conference registration may not be limited to authors, but also to other participants.

2.2 From Value Model to Process Model

When constructing the process model, a number of design decisions have to be taken concerning the ordering and decomposition of activities. Process patterns can be used here to suggest possible transformations. We claim that the design decisions are based on three different aspects of a business case: resource management, communication design, and risk:

- *Resource management* aspect. This aspect concerns the physical flow of resources (logistics) and their capacity planning.
- *Communicative design.* This aspect concerns the coordination between customers and providers that is needed to initiate and complete value exchanges by means of communicative actions.
- *Risk* aspect. This aspect concerns risks that may result in value transactions not being completed or only partially completed, and the various ways to mitigate risks ([2][9]).

All three aspects have to be dealt with and influence the resulting process model. Although the aspects are not completely independent, it is useful to distinguish them. They provide a separation of concerns, thereby facilitating design and traceability of the process model. The approach is summarized in Fig. 2.

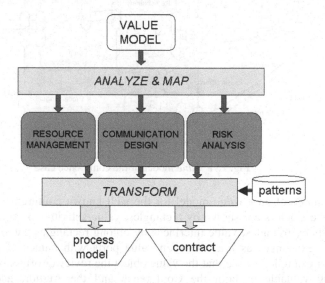

Fig. 2. From value model to process model

3 On the Notion of Value Object

There exists a huge body of knowledge in the area of economics regarding the concept of value. It is commonly defined as "The worth or desirability of something expressed as an amount of money" [15]. This something is often an asset or property of someone. Some assets can quite easily be given a monetary value, e.g., cash and stock, whereas others, like intellectual property or brand value, are harder to measure. The definition highlights the quantitative aspect of value, which is of course quite important from a business perspective. However, it does not say anything about the subjective value experience nor about the internal structure of the value object. In economics, a categorization of what can be described as a tradable property (has a value) is the following list: a) personal property, e.g., cars or tools, b) real property, e.g., buildings or land, c) intangible property, e.g., patents or copyrights.

According to [4], a value object is "a service, a product, or even an experience which is of economic value for at least one of the actors involved". This definition makes clear that value objects are not restricted to goods or money exchanged, but it is rather open. In the work of Holbrook [6] to which Gordijn refers, the focus is on consumer value, and in this framework, *anything* can be of value, as consumer value is supposed to reside in the consumption *experience* rather than in the product or service itself. Consequently, Holbrook remains vague about the internal structure of value objects, but he does offer an interesting framework of consumer values, such as efficiency, aesthetics and status.

3.1 Towards a Value Object Model

We can learn something from the examples of value objects identified in Gordijn's examples such as the Free Internet Provider: "a fee", "internet access", "interconnection", "termination" and "termination possibility". In the contact ad example, we find the value objects: "submitted ad", "possible contact", and "read contact ad" [5]. We refer to the original work for the full description of these examples.

Products and money are obvious value object candidates, although we should realize that the value exchange should not be equated with the logistic transfer: basically, what one acquires when one buys a product is the *ownership* of the product. Ownership can be conceived as a bundle of rights, and other rights can be value objects as well. For example, when borrowing a book from a library, one gets the right to keep and read the book for a certain period of time, and on the Internet, one could acquire the right to use a certain piece of software for a limited number of users.

On the basis of examples like these, we may tentatively identify a value object with a certain right on some resource. A right of one party means obligations for the other party. The customer should be enabled to use the right. For example, a transfer of ownership of a product should be accompanied by a delivery of the product, or at least the customer should get the possibility to pick up the product somewhere. So we may define a value object as a certain right on some resource (of the provider) and the enabling to use that right (a working access route or means to exercise the right on the value object). This definition works not only for goods and money, but also for services mentioned above such as "internet access" (the right to send and receive data to and from Internet, where availability of the network is assumed), or "read ad" (the right to read a contact ad, typically including the right to contact the sender somehow).

We have found that this first definition works for many cases, but not for all. Think for example of services like hairdressing and transportation. What is characteristic of these cases is that some action is performed on an object belonging to the customer that adds value. I prefer myself with my hair cut, or prefer my kid being at school in the morning. Let us call such an action a value transformation. In the Free Internet Example above, "termination" falls in this category: when the internet provider picks up the phone (terminates a call), he does something to the telephone network, owned by the telecompany, that increases its value to its owner, as he can charge costs to the caller. More precisely, the network becomes more valuable to consumers because they can use it now to connect to the Internet provider, and so access the Internet, and therefore it becomes more valuable to the telephone company since the marginal costs of a connection are very low. On the basis of examples like these, an alternative definition of value object is: "the value transformation of some object belonging to (or at least of interest to) the customer". Note that we assume a relationship between the customer and the object in question, and in most cases, including the ones above, this is a relationship of "belonging", but it can be more general. For example, "restoring my town" or even "reducing pollution of my planet" can be viewed as value transformations on things in which I have an interest (my town, my planet), and the fact that I value them can be inferred indirectly from the fact that I may be willing to donate money to a party like Greenpeace that claims to provide this value. To avoid confusion with the term "value object", we will use the term "value subject" for the thing whose value is increased by some transformation process.

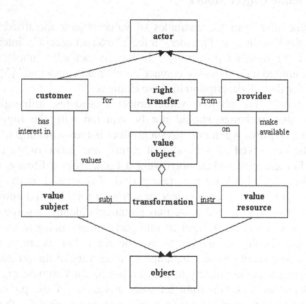

Fig. 3. Value object model

Note that in this second definition, the focus is on the value transformation of the value subject, but this does not exclude that some resource of the provider is involved as well. For example, the transportation service involves the use of a bus or some other vehicle, and the hairdressing service involves the use of a chair and the dedication of a hairdresser for a certain period of time. More generally, the value transformation of the value subject belonging to the customer often involves a right (and the enabling thereof) on some resource owned by the provider. This suggests a unification of the two definitions. In this unified model, we distinguish both a resource and a value transformation in which the resource is instrumental. When the focus is on the resource, the value transformation is not explicit, but still it can be found in many cases. For example, one could say that the borrowed book is used for reading, to teach something, or provide pleasure. However, the value exchange, as economic event in this case, focuses on the resource provided, and leaves unspecified what the customer does with it.

Figure 3 summarizes our value object model. Provider P transfers a value object to customer C when P brings in a resource R for the purpose of a transformation of some subject S in which C has an interest such that the transformation has value for C. "Bringing in" the resource means that P transfers C some right on R and makes R available (enables C to execute the right). The value that C gets could be characterized further by Holbrook's value framework (e.g. status, aesthetic pleasure). Given this background, the value object can be defined as an aggregation of value transformation and the right transfer, where usually but not necessarily both are present.

3.2 Some Remarks on the Value Object Model

We analyze the value object model in some more detail by addressing a couple of issues.

An Experience is Not a Value

Customer and value subject are roles that may be filled by the same entity, such as in the hairdresser case. Similarly, the provider may be a resource himself. Note that the value that the customer gets of the value transformation should be distinguished conceptually from the experience of the value subject, even if the customer is the subject. For example, in the case of watching a movie the *value* could be the pleasure of having watched a good movie, and the experience consists of the emotions that the movie imposes (e.g. pity). The experience (as a special case of value transformation) provides value, but is not a value.

Value Exchange Implies Value Transformation

The value transformation in the centre of our value object model is not an isolated activity, but can be integrated with the value chains of both customer and provider. According to [8] the value chain is a chain of activities, which are the building blocks by which a firm creates a product valuable to its buyers. The resource made available by the provider is either made or bought; if it is made, the provider should perform one or more value transformations that depend on other resources. At the customer's side (either a firm or an individual consumer), the value subject may itself be a resource for another value transformation. For example, a consumer may acquire a hammer, besides other things, to ameliorate his house. Value subjects that are used to raise value somewhere else are called extrinsic value objects by Holbrook, as opposed to intrinsic ones. Note that our model allows us to link the value object directly to the *value activities* in the e^3value model. A value activity is defined as an operation that could be carried out in an economically profitable way for at least one actor. However, in the value model logic, economic profit is only possible if the activity has some value to some actor in the first place, so a value activity (disregarding for the moment the possibility of allowing coordination activities to be value activities) will also be a value transformation, although not every value transformation is necessarily a value activity – it might be impossible to exploit it profitably. Below in section 4, we will argue that a value transformation model may be useful to complement the current e^3value model; the contribution of our current analysis of the value object is that it shows how value transfer and value activity are linked through the notion of value transformation.

In our model, it is not specified who performs the value transformation. In the hairdresser case, the provider, or one of the assistants, is the agent. In other cases, such as the borrowed book, the customer is the agent, as she is the one who does the reading. The more or less active contribution from the customer (Holbrook talks about active versus reactive value) is an interesting distinctive feature, but not so relevant for modeling the provider's responsibilities, as his involvement in the value transformation can be seen as an extension of "making resource available".

The transfer of ownership (goods, money) reappears in this model as a special case where subject and resource coincide: the resource provided by the provider is not only used but disappears as such, and it reappears as a value subject belonging to the customer. The value transfer as such is not a value transformation (it does not add value in the economic sense – note that supporting activities like transport can be value transformations, but the value transfer is not the physical transport). The question can be raised whether this case should be seen as a transfer of rights only, without a value transformation. An argument pro is that the customer can use the acquired resource in many unspecified ways (so it is hard to indicate what the value transformation is) and it falls out of the scope of the value transfer. An argument con is that in many cases, the resource has a specific goal, which sometimes is part of the value transfer or of the value proposition. An example of the former is when the customer buys clothes, these are for wearing (a value transformation of her body); if for some reason the value transformation does not succeed, this can be a reason for rolling back the value transaction – the customer returns the clothes. Examples of the latter are when phone companies sell phones with the slogan "be connected" or educational institutes sell a course with the slogan "improve yourself". So the preliminary answer that we want to give to the question is that the value transformation need not be included, but can be seen as part of the value object when this is deemed relevant.

Value Object is Not Value Proposition
The value object model can be used to analyze value objects, and gives a rather objective basis to the value object identification. However, we should keep in mind that the value proposition of a provider is a particular *view* offered on a value transfer, and hence may highlight certain elements, repress others, and even add elements, such as the indirect value the customer may get in a later stage. The value proposition is extremely important in marketing, but less informative for the design of the operational processes.

A Symbolic Value Object is Different from the Value Object It Points At
The transfer of ownership of symbolic objects needs some special attention. For example, if I buy a ticket for a football match, what is the value object I acquire? Is it the legitimate access to the match (as resource)? Or is it the ticket itself that I can use to get access to the match but that I could also profitably resell to others? Evidently,

there are many symbolic value objects (tickets, stamps, vouchers – also money itself). It is part of the choices to be made in the overall value model whether to introduce symbolic value objects or not. We propose the following rule: only when there is some unique (mostly physical) symbolic token of a transferable right – a right that is not bound to a specific agent but for which it holds that the legal *owner* of the token is the holder of the right, then this token *may* be treated as a value object in the same way as physical goods. So a football match ticket may be a value object, as is money, but an airline ticket is not (which may explain partly why airline tickets are disappearing nowadays). Whether it *should* be modeled as a value object is another question. If the token is only used for control purposes (like a cinema ticket), it is

3.3 A General Format of Value Object Description

Using our analysis of the value object, we propose to use the following general format for describing a value object. The value object is something the actor offers, so we always start with "A offers B".

A offers *B that a value subject is transformed* (by means of giving B | including) the right to *use* a *value resource*

An alternative format is to focus on the customer's value. In that case, the sentence would be something like " For B it has value that <value transformation> (by means of getting | including) the right to <use value resource>". In the case of doubt about a value object, this alternative may be used as a test.

The difference between the two variants "by means of giving" and "including" has to do with the role of the value resource. If the value resource exists before the value transformation, then the first phrase is appropriate. It is also possible that the value resource is created during the value transformation, and in such a case the second phrase is appropriate.

When the formula is instantiated, *A* and *B* will be actors and *use* will express a certain way of using or having access to a resource, e.g., own, lend, read, and copy. This formula captures the two aspects of a value object, i.e., the resource an actor gets access to as well as the transformation of some value subject in which the actor has an interest. When only the transformation is of interest, the second half of the formula can be omitted, while the first part is omitted if only the transfer of resources is of interest (However, we recommend that this should be done only if the other part is really out of the scope). Some examples:

A offers *B that his hair is cut*
A offers *B* the right to *read a contact ad*
A offers *B that he is entertained* by means of giving *B* the right to *access the entertainment park*

As we said in the above, the transfer of ownership is a special case. Using the format above, it would be expressed like:

A offers *B that he can spend money* by means of giving *B* the right to *get that money from him*
A offers *B that he uses product X* by means of giving *B* the right to *get that product X from him*

In some cases, the "use" of the product can be made more specific, as we argued above. However, we also allow a shorthand notation in case details are not deemed to be relevant:

A offers *B* <u>a *value resource*</u>

For example, "A offers B money", "A offers B product X". Note that this abbreviation should be used only when there is really transfer of ownership. It should not be used, for example, for the selling of digital goods, where the buyer only acquires a right to use a copy of the product; and not in the case A only has an intermediary role, like a broker that helps someone to buy a house which is not the broker's property.

4 Application and Discussion

In this section, we apply our value object analysis to a larger case, not for thorough validation but for illustration and to deepen our understanding. We also explore how to model the notions of value resource and value transformation graphically.

4.1 The Conference Case

As an illustration of our analysis of value objects, we have considered the well-known conference case. The e^3value model [4] for this example is shown in figure 1 in Section 2. The numbers in the list below correspond to the numbers on the labels in the e^3value model in Fig. 1.

1. The Author offers the Conference the right to consider publishing her paper
    Value resource = paper
2. The Conference offers the Author <u>that her Paper is evaluated</u> including the right to read the evaluation report
    Value resource = evaluation report
    Value subject = paper
3. The Reviewer offers the Conference <u>that a Paper is reviewed by him</u> including the right to use the review report for evaluation and include it in the evaluation report
    Value resource = review report
    Value subject = paper
4. The Conference offers the Reviewer <u>that he is acknowledged for his Contribution</u>
    Value subject = Reviewer
5. The Author offers the Conference the right to publish/copy her Paper
    Value resource = paper
6. The Conference offers the Author <u>that her Paper is published in the Proceedings</u>
    Value resource = paper
7. The Author offers the Conference Money
    Value resource/subject = money
8. The Conference offers the Author the right to participate in the Conference Event
    Value resource = conference event

9. The Author offers the Conference that the conference program is augmented by means of giving it the right to include the presentation of her paper
   Value resource = presentation
   Value subject = conference program
10. The Conference offers the Author a copy of the Proceedings
    Value resource/subject = copy of the proceedings
11. The Conference offers the Steering Committee that it is acknowledged for its contribution by means of the right to be mentioned in the proceedings
    Value resource = proceedings
    Value subject = Steering Committee
12. The Conference offers the Steering Committee that its conference event is organized
    Value subject = conference event
13. The Steering Committee offers the Conference Money
    Value resource/subject = money

The analysis that we give here is not necessarily the only right one. What we do claim is that our analysis and the format that we use makes the identification process more rigid. However, there is not one unique value model for all conferences. In some cases, the authors get paid for a presentation, whereas in other cases, they have to pay. The Steering Committee may provide financial resources, but it may also try to acquire them. Ultimately, it is not the designer but the stakeholders in the business collaboration who decide on what the value objects are.

Sentence 3 exemplifies a complex right: the Conference not only can use the review report for its evaluation of a paper, but also has the right to include it in the evaluation report, that is, to forward it to the author. Again, conferences may handle review reports in different ways, but our analysis forces the stakeholders to be explicit about the rights rather than posit an unqualified value object "review report". It is our claim that this is valuable for the business network negotiations and also when the value model is used as input for process design. Another interesting question raised by the initial analysis is: what are the resources that are used in the value transformation "organization of the conference event" (sentence 12)? In a further analysis, it may turn out that more parties need to be identfied, such as a conference hotel.

Sentence 4 and 11 exemplify the situation that an actor is also a value subject: the public acknowledgement of the Reviewer and Steering Committee, respectively, adds value to themselves.

4.2 Sourcing

The example of the conference case urges us to say something about the effect of sourcing. Sourcing, or delegation is present here in the form of reviewers performing some task on behalf of the Conference, and would be possible also for other value activities, like the publishing of the papers. Sourcing complicates the value object model because the provider may delegate some of his tasks to a third agent. In that case, the agent has a double orientation [10]: it offers value to the provider's customer, on behalf of the provider, and (thereby) provides value to the provider. To work out the effects of sourcing is beyond the scope of this paper; we limit ourselves to the remark that if necessary, the two value objects the agent provides should be distinguished carefully, and that the B in our format (the one for whom the value object has value) is not necessarily the customer of A but may also be the customer of the agent's principal.

4.3 Modeling Value Transformations

Our analysis of the value object has revealed value resources, value subjects and value transformations - concepts are currently not in the e^3value model. Rather than overload this model, we propose that these concepts are dealt with in a complimentary model. Where the e^3value model focuses on value exchanges, and centers the model around the actors, the complimentary model should focus on value transformations, centering value resources and repressing the actors. A possible candidate for this model is the Activity Dependency Model described in [1] that aims at being half-way between value models and process models. Its purpose is to describe, on a high level, the activities needed for carrying out the value transfers. For that purpose, it includes coordination activities and assignment activities, among others, and flow dependencies. It highlights the activities, corresponding partly to value transformations, but it does not contain the objects on which these activities work. For a graphical representation of the value object sentences, the Activity Dependency Model is not appropriate

It would be possible to define a new graphical format for this purpose, but a more practical solution is to use a combination of standard UML diagrams. More in particular, we can use Class Diagrams for modeling the value resources and Activity Diagrams to model the life cycle of value resources in terms of the value transformations that they undergo. Figs. 4 and 5 contain the initial models for the conference case.

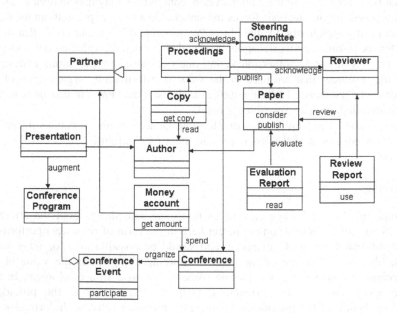

Fig. 4. Class diagram for the Value Resource Model of the conference case

In the class diagram, we include all value subjects and value resources (something can be a value subject in one value transformation and a value resource in another – to simplify, we propose to use the term Value Resource model). In the operation boxes, the operations found in "use rights" parts of the value object sentences are included. For example, in sentence 2 the right of reading the evaluation report is mentioned. If this right is provided to somebody, then it must also be enabled, that is, "read" must be an operation (method) of the class "evaluation report". The named associations should be interpreted as value subject/value resource relationships: that is, the resource plays a role in the named value transformations of the value subject. There are also unnamed associations for the relationship between an object and the actor that brings it in. All in all, the Value Resource Model integrates the information that is known about the value resources and presents it in a concise way.

The Value Resource Model can also be used for validation and further exploration. For example, in our conference example, there is the value transformation "acknowledge" for the subject "reviewer", but no resource was mentioned. In fig. 4, we have filled in this gap by allocating this job to the Proceedings. We have also included some aggregation relationships that were implicit in the sentences, and identified a superclass of author and Steering Committee. We have not added multiplicities yet, but this can also be useful (for example, can a paper have multiple authors?). If our goal is to transform the value model to a process model, the Value Resource Model is an important input for the resource management analysis that has to make choices on e.g. the logistics of papers, review reports, money etc.

In the example above, we have tried to be faithful to the sentences, in order to show that the value resource model is not a result of design but of analysis only. We made an exception with the class Money, as this would lead to a conflict with the OO assumption of identifiable discrete instances, and modeled it as Money account.

The activity diagram (Fig. 5) focuses on the value transformations per value subject. It allows the designer to order them and it may also have a heuristic value, for example, as it leads to the question what is the birth event of the object. In this case, it allows the designer to add the value transformation "write paper" that was not recognized

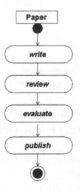

Fig. 5. Activity Diagram (object life cycle) for the Value Transformation Model of the value subject "Paper"

yet as a value transformation. The ordering of the value transformations is to be added by the designer, although some part can be derived from the value subject/value resource relationships. The Value Transformation Model might be useful for deriving flow dependencies in the Activity Dependency Model.

5 Concluding Remarks

The objective of this paper was to analyze the notion of value object, as it has been defined up till now in general terms only as "a goods, a service or even an experience that is of value". We have analyzed that in the case of goods, the value exchange is in fact a transfer of ownership. In the case of a service, we have defined this service more precisely as a value transformation on something (the value subject) that belongs to the customer or is of interest to him. In some cases, the provider only contributes to the value transformation indirectly by providing an access right to some value resource that plays a role in the value transformation. In our analysis, we distinguish value object from value experience (the value the customer gets from the value object). However, it is quite well possible that the customer is also the value subject and that the value transformation consists in offering him some experience.

Our analysis of the value object has brought us to the introduction of the notions of value resource and value subject as roles in a value transformation. We propose to add these concepts to the e^3value model ontology. We have also suggested to model these concepts graphically using UML class diagrams and activity diagrams.

The results of this paper might be useful for designers using the e^3value model as it allows them to define value objects in a more rigorous way. The additional models may also have heuristic value during the design. These suggestions need to be validated in practice of course, which is still to be done.

To achieve the research objective that we described in the introduction, our next step is to work on the mapping from value model to process model, via the three aspect analyses. Besides other things, this work will make clear whether the analysis of the value object presented in this paper is instrumental to the process model mapping or not.

References

[1] Andersson, B., Bergholtz, M., Edirisuriya, A., Ilayperuma, T., Johannesson, P., "A Declarative Foundation of Process Models", Proc. CAISE'05, Springer-Verlag, LNCS, 2005.

[2] Bergholtz, M., Grégoire, B., Johannesson, P., Schmitt, M., Wohed, P., Zdravkovic, J. "Integrated Methodology for linking business and process models with risk mitigation", Proc. REBNITA 05, 2005.

[3] Dietz, J.L.G. "Enterprise Ontology – theory and methodology", Springer-Verlag Heidelberg, Berlin, New York 2005.

[4] Gordijn J., Akkermans J.M. and Vliet J.C. van, "Business Modeling is not Process Modeling", Conceptual Modeling for E-Business and the Web, LNCS 1921, Springer-Verlag pp. 40-51, 2000.

[5] Gordijn, J., H. Akkermans, and H. van Vliet, "Value based requirements creation for electronic commerce applications", in Proceedings of the 33rd Hawaii International Conference On System Sciences, IEEE, 2000.

[6] Holbrook, M. B. "Consumer Value – A Framework for Analysis and Research", Routledge, New York, NY, 1999.

[7] McCarthy W. E., "The REA Accounting Model: A Generalized Framework for Accounting Systems in a Shared Data Environment", The Accounting Review ,1982.

[8] Porter, M. "Competitive Advantage", New York, Free Press, 1985.

[9] Schmitt, M., Grégoire, B. "Risk Mitigation Instruments for Business Models and Process Models", Proc. REBNITA 05.

[10] Weigand, H. and De Moor, A. "Workflow Analysis with Communication Norms". Data & Knowledge Engineering, 47(3), pp.349-369, 2003.

[11] Weigand, H., Johannesson, P., Andersson, B., Bergholtz, M., Edirisuriya, A., Ilayperuma, T. "Value Modeling and the transformation from value model to process model", Proc. INTEROP-ESA'06, (fc).

[12] Wieringa, R.J., J. Gordijn, "Value-Oriented Design of Service Coordination Processes: Correctness and Trust". 20th ACM Symposium on Applied Computing, pp. 1320–1327. ACM Press, March 13-17 2005

[13] Yu E., "Modelling Strategic Relationships for Process Reengineering". PhD thesis, University of Toronto, Department of Computer Science, 1995.

[14] "Business Process Execution Language (BPEL) Resource Guide", Accessed November 2005, http://www.bpelsource.com/

[15] Global Investor Glossary, http://www.finance-glossary.com/pages/home.htm Accessed November, 2005

Inter-organisational Controls as Value Objects in Network Organisations

Vera Kartseva[1], Jaap Gordijn[2], and Yao-Hua Tan[1]

[1] Information Science, Management and Logistics, Vrije Universiteit,
De Boelelaan 1105, 1081 HV Amsterdam, The Netherlands
{vkartseva, ytan}@feweb.vu.nl
[2] Computer Science, Business Informatics, Vrije Universiteit,
De Boelelaan 1105, 1081 HV Amsterdam, The Netherlands
gordijn@cs.vu.nl

Abstract. Inter-organizational controls are measures to ensure and monitor that networked enterprises do not commit a fraud and behave as agreed. Many of such controls have, apart from their control purpose, an inherent *economic value* component. This feature requires controls to pop-up into business value models, stating how actors create, trade and consume objects of economic value. In this paper, we provide guidelines that can be used to decide whether organizational controls should be part of a value model or not. We demonstrate these guidelines by a case study on the Letter of Credit procedure.

Keywords: inter-organizational controls, value modelling, trust.

1 Introduction

Due to the popularity and widespread use of the world-wide-web, information technology (IT) services increasingly become *commercial* services to final customers, rather than just enabling *technical* interoperability (e.g. using UDDI, SOAP, WSDL, etc) between multi-enterprise software components. Examples include the iTunes store of Apple, and Windows Live. Additionally, many commercial IT services are offered by a *partnership* of enterprises rather than just *one* enterprise. Many customer needs are in fact reasonably complex; therefore competencies of a series of companies are needed to satisfy them. It is actually the Internet itself that *enables* enterprises to work closely together on satisfying a complex consumer need.

Obviously, developing and deploying commercial IT-intensive services requires information systems that span multiple enterprises, assuming that such services are offered by a partnership. It is then important to understand first *which* enterprises are involved in the first place, and what they *exchange of economic value* with each other, before starting with a requirements engineering and software design phase for developing information systems, enabling and supporting these value exchanges. To this end, we have proposed the e^3value methodology and ontology (see [11], [12] for an overview). Using this methodology results in a *value model*, stating actors (enterprises and final customers) exchanging *objects* of *economic value*, as well as an

E. Dubois and K. Pohl (Eds.): CAiSE 2006, LNCS 4001, pp. 336–350, 2006.
© Springer-Verlag Berlin Heidelberg 2006

analysis whether these exchanges result in profit for all actors involved. We assume that sustainable profit for all actors is important for a successful value model.

The notion of *value object* is a key concept in value models. A value object is created, traded, and consumed by actors, and is of economic value for at least one of the actors involved. In many cases, value objects can be found quite easily. For instance, a good obtained by a customer to satisfy his needs is a value object, as well as the money he pays for obtaining this value object. However, when we model *inter-organizational controls* [5], [17], [19], [20], [22], it is sometimes difficult to decide when something is a value object or not. Controls are measures to ensure that actors behave honestly: they can be used to prevent fraudulent behavior or can be used to discover that a fraud has been committed afterwards. Controls are of importance to create and enhance trust in execution of value exchanges.

Evidence documents often play an important role in inter-organizational controls; we call them *control documents*. It is argued in [5], [24] that one way to *reduce* uncertainty in the behavior of trading parties is to exchange such documents. Many of such control documents have elements of *economic value*. For instance, consider a cinema ticket. A cashier sells the visitor a ticket which is checked by a controller to enter the theatre. The control purpose here is to prevent that the cashier allows free entrance to the cinema, which is accomplished by checking whether the amount of the tickets obtained by the controller corresponds to the total amount of money collected by the cashier. In this case, a ticket is a control document. Additionally, this ticket can be *sold* by the visitor to others, and the visitor can even earn money by doing so, if he resells the ticket for a higher price than he paid for it. Because of the reselling possibility the control document (the ticket) becomes also a *value* object.

It is, however, sometimes difficult to *decide* whether a control document *is* a value object. Consider e.g. a non-transferable plain-ticket. It is a control document, but is it a value object too? To answer this question, we investigate the notion of a value object. We extend the value object ontology into two directions. First, we take an *economic* perspective on the notion of value object. The economic perspective is of importance because value objects possess economic value for some actors, and thus show why a value model may work at the first place. Second, we take a *legal* perspective. We argue that control documents have properties of a value object, if they represent an element of a *right*, which can be *traded* and is of *value*. We suggest that there is a need to distinguish between (1) *possession* of a value object, (2) *ownership rights* on a value object, and (3) *control documents* that represent these rights. In addition, we argue that transfer of possession is *not* a value exchange, since the fact of possession cannot provide an economic value for someone who has no ownership rights. Finally, we present how our revised conceptualization of 'value object' is of use in a case on the Letter of Credit procedure, a rather complex service for securing payments.

2 The e^3-*value* Ontology

In earlier work [11], [12] we have proposed the e^3-*value* ontology to model and analyze value networks consisting of actors exchanging objects of value. Below, we briefly review the e^3-*value* ontology, using the cinema example as explained in the introduction. Fig. 1 (a) shows a visitor who wants to see a cinema-movie and offers money in return. This can be conceptualized with the following e^3-value constructs (in bold). **Actors**, such as the visitor and the cinema are economically independent entities. Actors transfer **value objects** (movie, money) by means of **value exchanges**. For value objects, someone should be willing to pay, which is shown by a **value interface** being part of an actor. An interface models the principle of *economic reciprocity:* only if you pay, you can obtain the goods and vice versa. A value interface consists of **value ports**, which represent that value objects are offered to and requested from the actor's environment. Actors may have a **consumer need**, such as the need to view a movie, which when following a path of **dependencies,** results in the exchange of objects through a value interface. Exchanges through a value interface may result in other exchanges through another interface of the same actor, or may result in a **boundary element**. The latter means that we do not consider additional value exchanges.

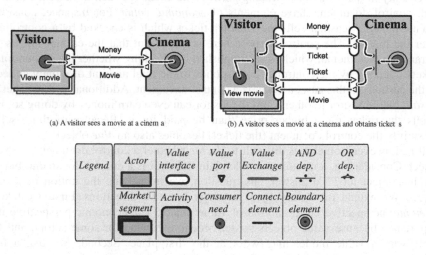

(a) A visitor sees a movie at a cinem a   (b) A visitor sees a movie at a cinema and obtains ticket s

Fig. 1. A visitor going to a cinema in e^3-value

According to the e^3-value ontology [12], a value object is a good, service outcome, or experience, which is of economic value for at least one of the actors in the value model. This is fine for regular value models, but in some cases, it is not so easy to decide whether something is a value object or not. Specifically, consider Fig. 1 (b). Here, we model an organizational control. The purpose of an organizational control is that enterprises cannot commit a fraud. In the cinema example, we want to prevent that a cashier grants entrance to the theatre for free (e.g. for friends). Typically, this is solved by creating a conflict of interest [20], [22]. A cashier sells a ticket, and this ticket is needed to enter the cinema. A controller at the theatre entrance obtains the ticket from the visitor. At the end of the day, the cashier counts the money, and the controller counts the tickets obtained. Obviously, there should be a correspondence between the total amount of money and the number of tickets. Note that the cashier and controller do not show up as actors in the value model, because they are just employees of the cinema and not profit and loss responsible entities.

A modeling question is if we show the tickets as value objects. On the one hand, tickets are just *controls*, and part of e.g. the business *process* of a cinema, and should perhaps therefore not be in a value model, but in a process model, which shows how a value model is *put into operation*. On the other hand, we can argue that tickets indeed show up in the value model, because the ticket is of *value* for its owner (the ticket can e.g. be resold). A similar example can be worked out for personalized airplane tickets, which cannot be resold: are these tickets value objects or not?

3 Extending the e^3-*value* Ontology

The aim of this paper is to provide guidelines that help to decide whether a document, used for organizational control purposes, is a value object or not. To do so, we first extend the e^3-*value* ontology, and more specifically the part dealing with 'value object' (see Fig. 2). This extension includes two perspectives. First, we utilize the original *economic value perspective*, which already exists in the e^3-*value* ontology. One of the aims of using e^3-*value* is to understand how economic value is created, distributed and consumed in a network of enterprises. Additionally, we extend the ontology with a *rights perspective*. Many organizational controls *are* rights [16], which sometimes can be *traded*. This motivates the legal perspective on value objects.

3.1 An *economic value* Perspective on the Notion of Value Object

In a *value* model, objects are only shown if they are of *economic value* to stakeholders. In a *process* model (putting the value model into operation), objects are shown if they serve as required inputs of activities or are produced as outputs. As a consequence, not all objects that are part of a process model need to appear in a value model, because some objects may not be of *direct* value to someone.

Regular Value Object. We distinguish various kinds of value objects. The concepts 'good', 'service outcome', and 'experience' are already covered by the original e^3-*value* ontology. A good is a physical product, a service outcome is product of an intangible nature [14], although a service has in most cases some physical evidence (e.g. a seal – physical evidence - on the toilet of our hotel after it has been cleaned – a service). If there is no physical evidence at all, the value object is an experience. Obviously monetary instruments such as 'money' are also value objects. We have added the notion of 'evidence' as a potential value object which represents a control evidence document. This decision will become clear in the following sections.

Willingness to Pay. To answer the question when an object is a value object, we first look at what is meant by *economic value*. In economics, value is human driven (i.e., it is anthropocentric), meaning that goods and services are not considered to have value unless humans place value on them [1], [21]. This refers to the concept of *willingness to pay*. In the e^3-*value* terms, the expression 'willingness to pay' can be interpreted as some actor is willing to exchange a value object in return for another value object (including money).

The willingness to pay is for every person is *subjective* [15]. Every actor values the same object differently. The subjective component of value makes the value *context-dependent.* For example, a person in a desert values a bottle of water more than a person who has unlimited access to water. Thus, in value model design, an object can be of value or not, depending on the context being modeled. To summaries all the abovementioned arguments, we suggest the following guideline to identify a value object:

*Guideline 1. An object can be considered a value object for a given value model, if there exists at least **one actor**, who depending on his **context**, has a **need** for this value object and is **willing to exchange** this object in return for another value object.*

3.2 A *rights* Perspective on the Notion of Value Object

In some case studies [16], [17], [18], [19] in the non-profit sector, evidence and other control documents are proved to be useful value objects. For example, documentary evidence is useful to model when a service is provisioned by a supplier to a customer (e.g. a healthcare service to a patient), but is paid by a party different than a customer. The supplier (a hospital) has then to prove to the paying party (a government or a representative) that the service has actually been delivered. Since the hospital needs evidence of service delivery to obtain its money, it can be argued that this evidence is of value to the hospital. Further, we look at control documents in more detail.

In simple cases, a physical transfer of an object triggers an exchange of corresponding *rights*. For example, if you buy bread you receive the loaf of bread (you *possess* it), and you receive all the *rights* on it: e.g. you can use it, resell it, etc. In more complicated cases, the possession of a value object is transferred separately from its rights. Suppose that in a local newspaper there are coupons, which give you a right for getting free loaf of bread on Sunday mornings by the local bakery. If you buy the newspaper, you get a coupon that entitles you to all the rights for the bread, but not the bread itself. You can only have the bread, if you present the coupon to the person in the bakery. The coupon in this case is a *control document*, which represents *rights* for bread. In addition, you can resell your control document 'coupon' to someone else, which results in a transfer of the bread rights from you to the buyer, but also makes the coupon a value object for you, because you receive something in return. For capturing the value of such a control documents, we suggest to distinguish between *possession* of an object and *rights* related to the object.

Thinking about the concept of *rights* leads us to property rights theory. Coase [5], whose work is considered as a start of property rights theory in economics, suggests that each asset relates to a *vector of rights* (or a *bundle of rights*). Conventionally, property rights include *use rights*, which define the potential uses of an asset, *income rights*, and *rights to transfer* a value object permanently to another party [1], [8]. Someone who has rights for a value object has it in *ownership*. We speak of *divided ownership*, if two or more actors (people or organisations) own 'different' rights for the 'same' *asset* [1]. In this case, rights for the same asset can be traded separately from each other (e.g. stocks for company assets). In fact, since the fore mentioned rights may comply with our first guideline (willingness to pay for subjective value), on deciding whether something is a value object or not, they *each* can be seen as a *value object*.

Physical possession of an asset is not the same as *ownership*. A person may have rights for an asset (ownership), but may not possess it (as in the coupon example). In property rights theory the concept of possession is omitted [7]; they argue that even if a law defines the ownership, the value of an asset is till available to many others. On the other hand, from legal perspective, if a person possesses an object, but does not have any rights on it (e.g. cannot resell it), the person cannot legally derive value of this object [3]. We chose to take the latter perspective, because it is more realistic for models we made so far, especially when we model fraudulent behavior. Thus, we argue that the transfer of possession alone is not a value exchange, while the transfer of rights is.

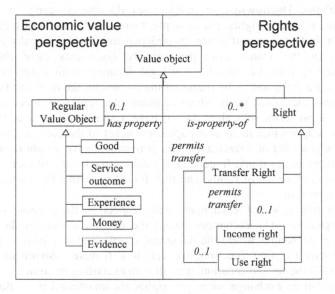

Fig. 2. Extension of the e^3-value ontology

In Fig. 2 we extend the e^3-value ontology based on property rights theory. We introduce the concept of 'Right'. Following property rights theory, rights of ownership can be 'use rights', 'income rights', and 'rights to transfer'. This is not an exhaustive set of rights. For example, there are intellectual property rights, such as copyright, which also can be modeled as rights in this ontology. A right is a property of a 'Regular Value Object'. 'Transfer right' has a relation *permits transfer* with 'income right' and 'use right'. A transfer right is seen as a right that is needed to transfer other rights (use right and income right) from one actor to another. Thus, the transfer right enables a transfer of rights, not a regular value object. Note that in economic literature this distinction is not made explicit: as it is understood in the property rights theory, transfer rights belong to a group of property rights [1], [8].

A right is also a value object itself. This makes it possible to have rights on rights, like, for example, the derivatives financial instruments are rights to buy or sell stocks, while stocks represent rights to companies' assets.

In graphical models, to distinguish rights from regular value objects, we name them differently. Rights are named as properties of the value object they relate to. For example, an income right for a house is stated as *house:income right*.

4 Documentary Controls as Value Objects

Documentary controls can play various roles in value exchanges. To start with, documents can represent *evidence of rights*. These documents are used in two ways. First, a document may enable the *transfer* of rights. Second, a document may enable *claiming (execution of)* rights, which results in a transfer of possession. In addition, there are documents that do not represent any rights, but are just *outcomes* of a service (e.g. a certificate). Below we discuss every type in detail.

Rights Evidence Documents. In many cases documents 'carry' a value. Such documents are related to rights. For example, there is a definition of securities in the legal domain (in Dutch securities are: 'waardepapieren', which literally means 'value document'). In the Dutch law, the security documents have the following characteristics: 1. to be a certain form of legal document with a signature 2. deliver evidence about a right, and 3. by means of the document, the right can be transferred [23]. However, there exist many other documents that represent rights, which are not securities in legal terms (e.g. they do not have a signature); such as the examples above about coupons in a local newspaper or a ticket to the cinema. In earlier times money was also a kind of a right document: a banknote gave a right for golden coins from the Dutch Central Bank. In general, the distinctive feature of such documents is that they are an evidence of rights, and therefore they *enable* the exchange of value these rights represent.

There are two types of exchanges, with respect to the purpose of the rights evidence documents: (1) exchanges where the document enables the *transfer* of rights, and (2) exchanges where the document enables the *execution* of rights. If the document fulfils the first function, we call it a **transfer document**, and if the document fulfils the second function, we call it an **executing document**.

We argue that an exchange where the rights are transferred is a value exchange, and an exchange where the rights are executed is *not* a value exchange, because it implies the transfer of possession of the related value object, and we have argued that that possession is not of value (see section 3). However, in other exchanges, where no transfer or execution occurs, an executing document can be a value object, if it complies with the definition of a value object (guideline 1).

A document transfers rights in an exchange, if in this exchange, actor A transfers the document to actor B, which triggers that actor A gives up or issues the rights for some value object, and B acquires the rights. In Figure 1, if the visitor buys a ticket from the cinema, the rights for viewing a movie are transferred to the visitor; in this exchange, the ticket is a *transfer* document. The rights for a movie are of value to the visitor. We argue that the exchange when the rights are transferred by means of a document in return for a value object is a value exchange, because the rights are always of value:

Guideline 2 (rights transfer value exchange). An exchange is a value exchange if (1) it includes an exchange of a value object (see guideline 1) in return for a document, which represents a set of rights for some other regular value object, and (2) in this exchange a transfer of the rights occurs: the actor who has this document as an outgoing object looses its rights, and some other actor acquires them.

When the visitor transfers the ticket to the cinema, it does not transfer any rights, but *enables execution of the rights* for movie. In this exchange the ticket is an *executing* document. The execution of rights triggers a transfer of possession for some good, or, in case of Movie, the transfer of *access* to a service. Because the possession or access alone is not a value object, we consider that the exchange of execution document in return for a transfer of possession should not be a part of a value model. Basically, we suggest that the exchange of Ticket and Movie in Fig. 1 is an invalid value exchange. The following guideline is suggested:

Guideline 3 (transfer of possession). An exchange, where the document enables an *execution of rights, and its exchange results only in a transfer of possession or access* *to a value object, is not a value exchange.*

Should an executing document be modeled as a value object in other value exchanges, where it does not fulfill the executing function? For example, a bank may use stocks of a customer as collateral in giving a credit (the customer and the bank exchange the stocks for a credit). In this exchange the rights for the stocks are not transferred to the bank, neither they are executed: the bank does not have a right to get income from the stocks (trade them), unless the customer defaults (does not pay). But is this a value exchange? We argue that in such cases the document (stocks) is also of value, because there are other *potential* exchanges (e.g. in case of defaulting), which creates a willingness to pay for the document. So, we suggest the following guideline:

Guideline 4. An executing document can also be a value object in value exchanges, *where it does not fulfill an executing function, as long as it fully complies with* *guideline 1 (willingness to exchange).*

What type of value object is a right evidence document? Is it good, money, service outcome or experience? In the cinema example in Fig. 1, a service for what the visitor is paying is a movie, not a ticket. To our understanding, the ticket and other rights evidence documents are a separate type of regular value objects, which we call *evidence* (see Fig 2).

Documents as Service Outcomes. Some documents are produced as *outcomes* of (commercial) services (e.g. a certification service), they are value objects, but they do not transfer or enable an execution of rights. Therefore, we introduce the following guideline:

Guideline 5. If a document is not a transfer or execution document, it can only be a *value object if this document is a service outcome, and if it complies with guideline 1.*

In the following section we demonstrate the ontology extension and the corresponding guidelines by modeling the "Bill of Lading" from a value perspective.

5   Case "Bill of Lading"

Suppose we have a seller in Hong Kong and a buyer in the Netherlands. The actors are geographically far apart, and the goods have to be transported by a carrier from the seller to the buyer (we assume by sea). On the one hand, the seller does not want to ship the goods onto the carrier's vessel (and thereby lose control over them) without first receiving payment from the buyer. On the other hand, the buyer does not want to pay the seller (and thereby lose control over the money) before the goods have been shipped. In international trade, the risk of non-payment and non-delivery can be prevented by accommodating such an instrument as the document/letter credit procedure (LoC). To secure the risk of non-payment, a contract (*Letter of Credit*) between the seller, the buyer, and the bank is made, in addition to the sales contract between the buyer and the seller.

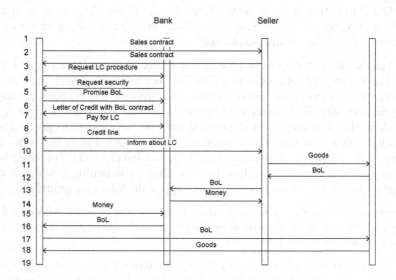

Fig. 3. Time sequence diagram for the Letter of Credit procedure

In Fig. 3, we explain the LoC procedure in detail by using a sequence diagram. In the LoC agreement is stated that that the bank will pay to the seller as soon as the seller will provide the *accompanying documents*. Normally, in international trade goods are accompanied with documents, for example, a Certificate of Origin or Bill of Lading (BoL). These documents are very important control components for the whole process. The bank receives the documents (BoL) from the seller (#11), and in case the documents are fine and comply with the requirements in the LoC, the bank will pay the seller (#12). Further, the buyer has to pay the bank (#13), and the bank then has to transfer the documents to the buyer (#14). The buyer presents the documents (and probably also the LoC and the sales contract) to the carrier (#15), and after that becomes the owner of the goods (#16).

The bank takes the risk that, after the money is paid to the seller, the buyer may default or refuse to pay. Therefore, the bank has to ensure that the money will be always reimbursed. The assessment of the customer's capability to complete the payment is confined to the general reputation of the customer, the type, complexity, and magnitude of the contract, and the country where the contract is to be performed [1]. When it concerns substantial deals, banks require other securities, for example, additional counter-guarantees from other banks. In this model, a BoL plays a role of both accompanying documents, and plays a role as *security*. In the situation when the buyer refuses to accept the BoL, for whatever reason, the bank can use the BoL to obtain the goods. In this specific case study, we consider the situation when the BoL is a tradable, or also called negotiable, document not 'on name', which means that the person who owns the BoL has the rights on the underlying goods.

5.1 A First Value Model for the Letter of Credit

Unlike the time sequence perspective, the value perspective models *only* the exchanges of objects of *value*. There is no notion of time at all. First, we construct a so-called *ideal* value model (see [16], [17]). An ideal value model supposes a perfectly honest world: in e^3-*value* this means that all actors respect the atomicity of the value interfaces (if you get something, you offer something in return). The value model in Fig. 4 shows a simple situation: a customer wants to buy a good and provides money in return.

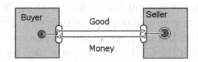

Fig. 4. A customer buys a good from a seller

Second, we now *relax* the assumption that all actors behave ideally. Instead, actors can behave *sub-ideally*, like not paying for a delivered good (the extension of sub-ideality to e^3-*value* is called e^3-*control* and is in detail discussed in [16], [17]). This is where the Letter of Credit (LoC) comes in: to secure that the supplier gets its money, even if the customer *defaults*. This situation is expressed in Fig. 5. Note that we not consider LoC and BoL themselves; they show up in Fig. 6. The customer need begins at the Customer, and the OR-fork splits the path into two paths: an *ideal* path and a *sub-ideal* path. The ideal path is when the buyer pays to the seller, and receives goods in return. The sub-ideal path considers the situation when the buyer does *not* pay to the seller. Sub-ideality is indicated by the *dashed* money exchange between the buyer and seller, representing that this exchange does not happen. As was described above, according to the LoC procedure, the seller will be paid by the bank and the bank receives the goods due to the defaulting of the customer to pay the fee for the goods. (Actually, the bank can never use the goods, but will have to sell them, but we do not model it here, for simplicity reasons).

The LoC procedure is a control mechanism to reduce the risk for the seller. The seller also gets money immediately upon presenting the documents (see Fig. 3, #11 & #12). Note that, we are aware of other sub-ideal situations, for example, when the buyer receives damaged goods. From the buyer's perspective, this procedure is more secure, because he is able to determine, through the LoC, which documents he requires to prove the seller's performance. However, this procedure does not guarantee the buyer that the goods will be delivered. Another control mechanism should be in place, like insurance. We do not consider these situations in his paper due to lack of space.

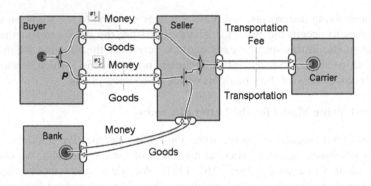

Fig. 5. The Letter of Credit: securing the fee for the supplier

5.2 Introducing the Bill of Lading and the Letter of Credit

The model in Fig. 5 does not present the exchange of the BoL and LoC themselves, and therefore does not yet give a complete picture of control mechanisms from an economic value perspective. In Fig. 5, we model the LoC procedure in more detail.

First, the Letter of Credit (LoC) is a service, provided by the bank to the buyer. In return, the buyer pays the bank money. There is also a document, named Letter of Credit. However, the transfer of the document LoC does not result in an execution of the LoC service. The LoC service consists of many other transfers, and is executed if the BoL is transferred to the buyer by the bank. Thus, the LoC document does not represent the outcome of LoC service and does not comply with guideline 5. We do not model LoC document as a value object. Instead, we model the LoC service outcome as a value object.

According to the ontology of value objects, Goods is a *regular value object*, which has the following rights as properties: use rights, income right, and transfer right. The BoL is a *rights evidence document*, which enables both transfer and execution of the rights for the goods. The BoL is a *regular value object* of type *evidence*.

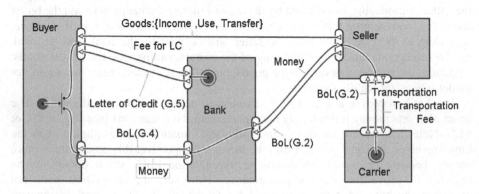

Fig. 6. Document credit procedure with Bill of Lading

The supplier obtains the BoL from the carrier as a part of exchange of Transportation Fee and Transportation, same as in Fig. 5. In this exchange, also the BoL is issued as evidence that the seller has rights for the goods. This is needed because in this exchange the possession of Goods is transferred to the carrier. We consider the BoL in this exchange is a *transfer document* (see guideline 2). Formally speaking, the seller initially has all the rights for the goods. However, because the carrier obtains the *possession* of goods, the BoL is issued as *evidence* of rights. Furthermore, we do not model the transfer of possession of the goods here.

In the exchange where the seller exchanges the BoL with the bank in return for a payment, the BoL is a value object, because it transfers rights and thus, complies with guideline 2. At this point, the seller gives up his rights for goods, which indicates that in this exchange the rights are transferred. According to the LoC agreement, the bank is not allowed to sell the BoL or exchange it for the goods. This means, that although the BoL is transferred physically to the bank, the bank does not receive the rights for the goods. The income, use, and transfer rights *Good:{Income, Use, Transfer Rights}* are received by the buyer. At the buyer, the value object *Good:{Income, Use, Transfer Rights}* is in the same interface as the LoC. This way, we also model that these rights are a necessary component of the customer to get the LoC: they guarantee a creditworthiness of the buyer, and play a collateral role.

This example provides an extension to guideline 2, demonstrating that a transfer document may enable a transfer of rights, between actors different from those exchanging the document physically. If the rights were transferred between the seller and the bank, exactly between actors exchanging the BoL, the rights would not be modelled explicitly, only the BoL that represents them would be modelled.

In the exchange between the bank and the buyer, the bank transfers the BoL to the buyer after the latter pays (see process model #15). No rights are transferred or executed here. However, in this exchange the BoL is presented as value object, because it complies with guideline 4: the buyer needs the BoL to claim the goods, because BoL is an execution document.

In the value model, we do not model the exchange, where the buyer exchanges the BoL with the carrier in return for goods (see #15, #16 in Fig.3). In this exchange, the BoL plays a role of the *executing* document. According to guideline 3, because the executing document BoL is exchanged in return for a transfer of possession of the goods, this exchange is not modelled as a value exchange.

A Sub-ideal Scenario. In Fig. 7, we model the scenario when the buyer refuses to accept the BoL from the bank or when the buyer defaults. This scenario corresponds to the sub-ideal path as explained in Fig. 5.

In case the buyer refuses to pay, the value exchange Money between the bank and the buyer does not occur. Because the bank does not transfer the BoL before the payment by the buyer (see the process model), the value exchange BoL also does not happen (between the bank and the buyer). Hence, according to the process model, we model these exchanges as sub-ideal value exchanges.

If the buyer does not pay, the rights for the goods are transferred to the bank. In the same value exchange as the not transferred credit and BoL, we model that *Good:{Income, Use, Transfer Right}* is exchanged from the buyer to the bank. This corresponds to the sub-ideal exchange of Money between the seller and the bank in

Fig. 5. Note that here the rights are transferred without an exchange of the BoL. Again, we do not model the exchange of Goods and the BoL between the bank and the carrier, because it is a transfer of possession.

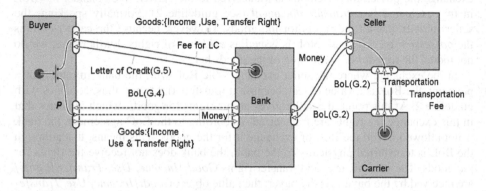

Fig. 7. Document credit procedure with Bill of Lading, sub-ideal scenario

6 Related Research

There are several proposals in the literature that are related to our work. With regards to e^3-value ontology, there have been a few other ontological approaches on business modeling and requirements engineering, among the most related are Tropos, REA, and BMO. Tropos [6] is a methodology that provides an extensive set of tools, including goal modelling, to facilitate early requirements engineering. However, it is not specifically focused on value modelling. Ontologically REA [9] is very similar to e^3-value. From a methodological point of view, REA is not an approach for business development, whereas e^3-value provides a methodology for doing so, e.g. by value model construction and reconstruction, and by profitability-based sensitivity analysis. The BMO ontology was compared with e^3-value ontology in [13], where the merge of the two ontologies was proposed. The main difference is that BMO focuses on one actor, while e^3-value has a focus on the network of actors. The extensions proposed in e^3-control concerning modelling sub-ideality, and the extensions in this paper, with regards to distinguishing legal and economic perspectives, and the relation between value objects, rights, and evidence documents, to our knowledge, have not been proposed until recently.

7 Conclusions and Future Research

In network organisations, the transfer of rights for a value object often occurs apart from the value object itself. Such a transfer is enabled by evidence documents that represent rights, which also play a role of control mechanisms. From the general definition of a value object in the e^3-value ontology, it is not clear when these documents are objects of value. In this paper, we formulated five guidelines that can be used to decide if an evidence document is a value object. We demonstrated the approach with a case study of Letter of Credit procedure. We proposed an extension of the e^3-value ontology with a concept of 'right', and a more precise definition of a concept of value. Value is *subjective* by nature, and an actor considers an object to be of value depending on *needs* of the actor. Thus, an evidence document can be of value for those actors who are *willing to exchange* this evidence for another value object. With regards to rights, we argue that in some cases, when an evidence document has properties of a value object, there is a need to distinguish between modeling (1) possession of a value object, (2) rights on this value object, and (3) control documents that represent the rights. To support this, we extend the ontology of a value object with concepts 'right' and 'evidence'. Furthermore, we distinguish between evidence documents that are outcomes of a service, and documents that represent rights. Within the second type, we distinguish two types of documents: the document that enables the *transfer of rights* and that enables the *execution of rights*. We argue that the transfer of rights is always a value exchange, while the execution is not, because it triggers the transfer of possession of a good or an access to a service, while an actor cannot derive value legally from a possessed object without having ownership rights. Note that we suggest using this approach of modeling the rights explicitly only if the notion of a value object is not sufficient to represent the value of control documents.

Acknowledgements. The authors wish to thank Hans Weigand and Paul Johannessson for the fruitful discussion on the topic of value objects. This research was funded by EDP Audit Education of VUA and by the BSIK Freeband Project FRUX.

References

1. Barbier, E. B., Acreman, M. C., Knowler, D.: *Economic valuation of wetlands: a guide for policy makers and planners*. Ramsar Convention Bureau. Gland, Switzerland (1996).
2. Barzel, Y.: Economic analysis of property rights. Cambridge University Press. Cambridge (1989)
3. Bell, Abraham and Parchomovsky, Gideon, A Theory of Property. U of Penn, Inst. for Law & Econ Research Paper 04-05 (2004) Available at SSRN: http://ssrn.com/abstract=509862 or DOI: 10.2139/ssrn.509862
4. Bertrams, F. R.: Bank guarantees in international trade: the law and practice of independent (first demand) guarantees and standby letters of credit in civil law and common law jurisdictions. ICC Publishing; Kluwer Law International. Paris The Hague (1996)
5. Bons, R.W.H.; Lee, R.M.; and Wagenaar, R.W. Designing trustworthy inter-organizational trade procedures for open electronic commerce, Global Business in Practice, In Gricar, J., Pucihar, T. (eds.), Proceedings of the Tenth International Bled Electronic Commerce Conference. Moderna Organizacija, Kranj (1997)
6. Bresciani, P., Giorgini, P., Giunchiglia, F., Mylopoulos, J., Perini, A.: Tropos: An Agent-Oriented Software Development Methodology. Journal of Autonomous Agents and Multi-Agent Systems. Kluwer Academic Publishers (2004)
7. Coase, Ronald H.: The Problem of Social Cost. Journal of Law and Economics, Vol. 3 (1960) 1-44
8. Foss, K., Foss, N:. Assets, Attributes and Ownership. International Journal of the Economics of Business, Taylor and Francis Journals, Vol. 8(1) (2001) 19-37

9. Geerts, G., McCarthy, W. E.: An accounting object infrastructure for knowledge-based enterprise models. IEEE Intelligent Systems and Their Applications (1999) 89–94
10. Gordijn, J., Akkermans, J.M., van Vliet, J.C.: Business Modelling is not Process Modelling. Conceptual Modeling for E-Business and the Web. Lecture Notes in Computer Science, Vol. 1921. Springer-Verlag. ECOMO 2000, October 9-12, 2000 Salt Lake City, USA (2000) 40-51
11. Gordijn, J., Akkermans, J.M.: e3-value: Design and Evaluation of e-Business Models. IEEE Intelligent Systems, Special Issue on e-Business, Vol. 16(4) (2001) 11-17
12. Gordijn, J., Akkermans, J.M.: Value based requirements engineering: Exploring innovative e-commerce idea. Requirements Engineering Journal, Vol 8(2). Springer Verlag, Berlin Heidelberg New York (2003) 114-134
13. Gordijn, J., Osterwalder, A., Pigneur, Y.: Comparing two Business Model Ontologies for Designing e-Business Models and Value Constellations. Proceedings of the 18th BLED conference (e-Integration in Action), D. R. Vogel, P. Walden, J. Gricar, G. Lenart (eds.). University of Maribor, CDrom (2005).
14. Gronroos. C.: Service Management and Marketing: A Customer Relationship Management Approach. 2nd edition. John Wiley & Sons, Chichester (2000)
15. M. Holbrook.: Consumer value — A Framework for analysis and research. Routledge, New York (1999)
16. Kartseva, V., Gordijn,J., Tan, Y.-H.: Towards a Modelling Tool for Designing Control Mechanisms in Network Organisations. To be published in the International Journal of Electronic Commerce (2005)
17. Kartseva, V., Gordijn,J., Tan, Y.-H.: Designing Control Mechanisms for Value Webs: The Internet Radio Case Study. In Vogel, D.R., Prikko, W., Gricar, J., Lenart, G. (eds.), Proceedings of the Eighteenth International Bled Electronic Commerce Conference (2005) on CD-ROM
18. Kartseva, V. and Tan, Y.-H.: Towards a Typology for Designing Inter-Organisational Controls in Network Organisations. Proceedings of the 38th Annual Hawaii International Conference on System Sciences, IEEE Computer Society Press (2005)
19. Kartseva, V. Tan Y.-H.: Designing Controls for a Marketplace of Health Care services: a Case Study. Proceedings of the 12th Research Symposium on Emerging Electronic Markets, Amsterdam (2005)
20. Starreveld, R.W., de Mare, B., Joels, E.: Bestuurlijke Informatieverzorging (Part 1). 4th edition. Samsom, Alphen aan den Rijn (1994)
21. Ramsay, J.: The real meaning of value in trading relationships. International Journal of Operations and Production Management, Vol. 25(6) (2005) 549-565
22. Ronmey, M.B. and Steinbart, P.J.: Accounting Information Systems. 9th edition. Prentice Hall, Upper Saddle River (2003)
23. Van Emplel G., Huizink ,J.B.: Betaling, waardepapier en documentair credit. Deventer, Kluver (1991)
24. Willams Jr., C.A., Smith, M.L., Young, P.C.: Risk Management and Insurance. 7th edition. McGraw-Hill, New York (1995)

Landscape Maps for Enterprise Architectures

Leendert van der Torre[1], Marc M. Lankhorst[2], Hugo ter Doest[2],
Jan T.P. Campschroer[3], and Farhad Arbab[4]

[1] University of Luxembourg, Luxembourg
[2] Telematica Instituut, Enschede, The Netherlands
[3] Ordina, The Netherlands
[4] CWI, Amsterdam, The Netherlands

Abstract. Landscape maps are a technique for visualizing enterprise architectures. They present architectural elements in the form of an easy to understand 2D 'map'. A landscape map view on architectures provides non-technical stakeholders, such as managers, with a high-level overview, without burdening them with technicalities of architectural drawings. In this paper we discuss the use of and techniques for landscape maps. A formal model for landscape maps is introduced as the basis of visualization and interaction techniques. Moreover, we show how a landscape map can be generated from its underlying model. Finally we show several interaction techniques, for example to build a landscape map from scratch, independently of an underlying model, or to change a landscape map together with its underlying model.

1 Introduction to Landscape Maps

The IEEE 1471-2000 standard [11] promotes the use of viewpoints for architectural description, and it presents as examples the structural, behavioural, physical connect, and the link bit error rate viewpoint. Moreover, to relate to other standards, it includes discussions on the decomposition and allocation, enterprise, information, computational, engineering, and technology viewpoint. Many other viewpoints have been proposed. Also others, such as Finkelstein *et al.* [5], and Lassing *et al.* [9], and Nuseibeh *et al.* [10], have advocated the use of viewpoints for describing architectures.

In this paper we discuss so-called landscape map viewpoints used in decision support of, e.g., information planning. Decision support viewpoints help managers in decision making by offering insight into cross-domain architectural relations. Typically, this is accomplished through projections and intersections of underlying models, but analytical techniques also play a role in construction of landscape maps. Such manipulations of architectural models typically result in lists, tables, matrices and reports. As such, decision support viewpoints create high-level, coherent overviews of enterprise architectures, providing the 'big picture' required by decision makers.

Landscape map viewpoints are used for example to publish an overview for managers and process or system owners, or they are employed by architects as a convenient tool for the analysis of changes or to find patterns in the allocation of resources. A landscape map, as defined by Van der Sanden and Sturm [14], is a matrix that depicts a three-dimensional coordinate system representing architectural relations. Figure 1 is

E. Dubois and K. Pohl (Eds.): CAiSE 2006, LNCS 4001, pp. 351–366, 2006.
© Springer-Verlag Berlin Heidelberg 2006

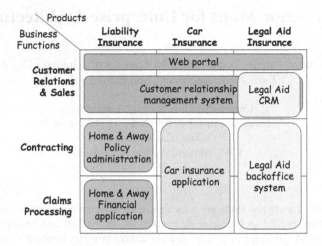

Fig. 1. Example of a landscape map

an example of a landscape map that shows which information systems support the operations of an insurance company. The vertical axis represents the companys business functions; the horizontal axis shows its insurance products. An application rectangle covering one or more cells means that this particular function/product pair is supported by the application, e.g., contracting of a legal aid insurance is supported by the legal aid backoffice system.

The dimensions of the landscape maps can be freely chosen from the architecture that is being modeled. In practice, dimensions are often chosen from different architectural domains, for instance business functions, products and applications, etc. In most cases, the vertical axis represents behavior like business processes or functions; the horizontal axis represents 'cases' for which those functions or processes must be executed. These 'cases' can be different products, services, market segments, or scenarios. The third dimension represented by the cells of the matrix is used for assigning resources like information systems, infrastructure, or human resources. The value of cells can be visualized by means of colored rectangles with text labels.

We propose to use landscape maps as a presentation format (modality) of enterprise architecture models expressed in the ArchiMate language [6, 8]. However, our approach is not restricted to this particular modeling language. In this paper we illustrate how ArchiMate models can be mapped to landscape maps, and how landscape maps can be used as an interactive medium for architecture design. For instance, the landscape map in Figure 1 relates business functions (customer relation and sales, etc.) and products (liability insurance, etc.) to systems (web portal, etc.). The relation between business functions and products is directly supported by the assignment relation. The relation between products and systems is indirectly supported: products are assigned to processes (or functions), which in turn use systems.

The layout of this paper is as follows. In Section 2 we introduce our running example, in Section 3 we give our formal model of landscape maps. In Section 4 we discuss the visual aspects of landscape maps, and we show how a landscape map can be constructed from an underlying model. In Section 5 we discuss interaction with landscape maps, where we distinguish between editing a landscape map from scratch, without reference to an underlying model, and changing the landscape map while simultaneously changing its underlying model as well.

2   Running Example

To illustrate the concept of landscape maps, we introduce an example to be used in the remainder of this paper. Our example involves ArchiSurance, an imaginary though reasonably realistic insurance company. ArchiSurance, originally in the business of home and travel insurance, has merged with PRO-FIT (car insurance) and LegallyYours (legal aid). As a result of this merger, the companys main products are now in home, travel, car, liability, and legal aid insurance. To create high-level insight in ArchiSurances primary operations, the company is described in terms of its main business functions: Customer Relations & Sales, Contracting, Premium Collection, Claims Processing, and Document Processing. Post-merger integration is in full swing. The first step in the integration process has been the creation of a single department for Customer Relations and Sales. However, behind this front office are still three separate back offices:

- Home & Away: this department was the original pre-merger ArchiSurance, responsible for home and travel insurance.
- Car: this department is the core of the old PRO-FIT and handles car insurance, including some legal aid.
- Legal Aid: this is the old LegallyYours, except for the part that has now moved to the Customer Relations & Sales department.

As in many recently merged companies, IT integration is a problem. ArchiSurance wants to move to a single CRM system, separate back-office systems for policy administration and finance, and a single document management system. However, Home & Away still has separate systems for claims handling, premium collection, and payment, and uses the central CRM system and call center. The Car department has its own monolithic system, but uses the central CRM system and call center. The Legal Aid department has its own back- and front office systems (Figure 2).

An important prerequisite for the changes in ArchiSurance's IT is that the IT integration should be 'invisible' to ArchiSurance's clients: products and services remain the same. However, this is not a straightforward requirement. To illustrate the complex relationships among organization, products, business processes and IT support, Figure 3 shows the relations among the Damage Claiming process, its IT support, and the organization. Note that this figure shows these relations for only a single business process. In general, many business processes within the back office link the external products and services with the internal systems. E.g., Figure 3 shows the 'travel insurance' product, comprised of a number of services realized by different business processes.

This web of relations creates a major problem if we want to create insight in the IT support of ArchiSurance. Many systems used by many processes realizing various products and services comprise too much detail to display in a single figure. This is a typical example of where landscape maps can help. As shown in Figure 4, a landscape

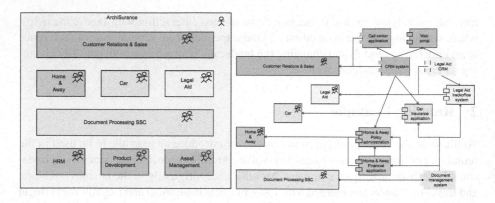

Fig. 2. Actor diagram showing ArchiSurance departments; Applications used by departments

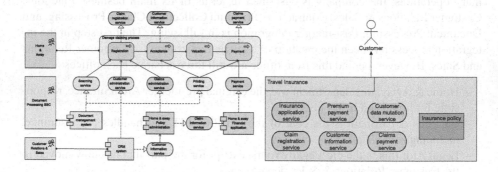

Fig. 3. Relations among Damage Claiming process, its IT support, and the organization; The 'travel insurance' product

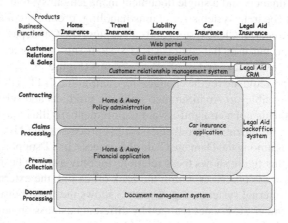

Fig. 4. Landscape map of ArchiSurance

map of ArchiSurance's IT applications in relation to its business functions and products provides a high-level overview of the entire IT landscape of the company.

From this figure, it is apparent that there is an overlap in ArchiSurance's IT support, both in the Car insurance application and in the Legal Aid CRM system. This insight is difficult to obtain from the previous figures. It requires the composition of relations such as 'product contains business service', 'business service is realised by business process', 'business process is part of business function', 'business process uses application service', and 'application service is realised by application'.

3   Definition of Landscape Maps

In this section we give a formal definition of landscape maps, which is used to facilitate the construction of landscape maps from underlying architectural models, the interaction between the visual part of a landscape map and its underlying model, and the analysis of landscape maps. So far landscape maps have been used as a notation without formal underpinnings. Though visualization and interaction techniques can also be developed without a formal model in the background, we believe that the uniform and abstract view on landscape maps given by our formal definition facilitates their design and realization.

The formal definition of a landscape map is based on a well-defined relation to an underlying architectural model and on our notion of the signature of a landscape map, which in turn is loosely based on the notions of architectural description informally defined in the IEEE 1471-2000 standard document [11]. In the subsection below we explain what we mean by a signature of a landscape map. Next, we distinguish symbolic and semantic models, based on this signature. Finally, we discuss landscape map viewpoints, and the distinction between views and visualizations. This terminology is borrowed from formal methods [15], and the use of this terminology in enterprise architecture is discussed in more detail in [3].

3.1   The Signature of a Landscape Map

Intuitively, architectural descriptions such as landscape maps visualize a set of generic concepts and relations. A concept is interpreted as a set, and elements of this set are called concept instances. Of course, in many cases concepts like function and application in our running example are interpreted as objects, not as sets. In such cases we have to add the constraint that the set is a singleton set. Representing concepts by sets is the most general approach, and applied in most modelling languages.

There is a set of concepts on the X-axis (categories, e.g., products), a set of concepts on the Y-axis (functions, e.g., business functions), and one or more sets of concepts displayed on the matrix (e.g., applications). Moreover, there is a ternary relation that represents a landscape map. Thus, the ArchiSurance example contains the following concepts and one relation. Note that the set of concepts does not make explicit which concepts occur on the X-axis, the Y-axis or on the plane.

$$C = C_A \cup C_X \cup C_Y \cup C_Z \qquad\qquad R = \{use\}$$
$$C_A = \{product, function, application\} \qquad C_X = \{home\_ins, travel\_ins, \ldots\}$$
$$C_Y = \{customer\_rel, claim\_processing, \ldots\} \quad C_Z = \{web\_portal, call\_center, \ldots\}$$

Furthermore, we assume an implicit 'is-a' or subset relation on the concepts, since each element of C_X is a product, each element of C_Y is a function, and each element of C_Z is an application.

home_ins $\subseteq$ product, travel_ins $\subseteq$ product, ...

Finally, the relevant information in the landscape map in Figure 4, e.g., that web portal is used by customer relations & sales, but not contracting, can be represented in two ways. First, we may say that the relation is defined on the set of concepts, i.e., use $\subseteq C \times C \times C$. We have product on the X-axis and function on the Y-axis, i.e. use $\subseteq C_X \times C_Y \times C_Z$. Under this interpretation of the relation, the landscape map in Figure 4 can be represented by the following relation.

use $= \{\langle$ home_ins, customer_rel, web_portal$\rangle$, $\langle$ home_ins, customer_rel, call_center$\rangle$,
$\langle$ home_ins, customer_rel, crm$\rangle$, $\langle$ travel_ins, customer_rel, web_portal$\rangle$, ...

Alternatively, inspired by the notion of signature in formal methods [15, 3], we can interpret relations on concept instances use $\subseteq$ product $\times$ function $\times$ application. More precisely, the relation can be interpreted as follows.

use $\subseteq$ home_ins $\times$ customer_rel $\times$ web_portal $\cup$ home_ins $\times$ customer_rel $\times$ call_center
$\cup$ home_ins $\times$ customer_rel $\times$ crms $\cup$ travel_ins $\times$ customer_rel $\times$ web_portal ...

In this paper we use the latter option, which is analogous to the notion of typing information in signatures of formal languages [15]. For the techniques developed in this paper both options could be used, but for other techniques such as analysis and simulation of enterprise architectures, the latter option is preferred [3]. The difference is that in the second case, the relation is not defined on the concepts, but on the concept instances. Consequently, the relation between concepts may be called typing information of the landscape map. This is explained in more detail in the following section, when we discuss the interpretation of a signature, and semantic models. A further discussion can also be found in [3].

The combination of a set of concepts together with the pre-defined is-a relation, and the relation together with typing information, is called the signature of a landscape map.

3.2 Semantic and Symbolic Models

The notion of an architectural model is notoriously ambiguous. The ambiguity becomes clear when we use our formal machinery. First, we have to distinguish between semantic and symbolic (syntactic) models of an architecture. The former are an abstract description of the structure and 'meaning' of the architecture itself; the latter are its denotation, i.e., part of the architectural description. This distinction between the architecture and its description is also made in the IEEE 1471 standard.

A semantic model consists of a domain and an interpretation function. In such a model, each concept is interpreted as a set from a domain, which represents that concepts are generic. The ternary landscape map relation is defined on the concepts instances, not on the concepts themselves. For example, the following describes a simple model. Assume that all concepts that are not mentioned are empty sets. In this example, use is defined on instances of concepts like h_1 and c_1.

home_ins = $\{h_1, h_2, h_3\}$,
customer_rel = $\{c_1, c_2, c_3\}$,
web_portal = $\{w_1, w_2, w_3\}$
use = $\{\langle h_1, c_1, w_1 \rangle, \langle h_1, c_2, w_3 \rangle\}$

Second, the notion of architectural model in the IEEE 1471 standard corresponds to what we call symbolic models, which are logical theories based on a signature. Symbolic models are part of the architectural description, and thus they can describe elements of an architecture. In our formal model, an architectural description is more than just a signature that can be visualized in a view: it also contains constraints and actions which play an important role in analysis and interaction.

Landscape map constraints are logical expressions expressed in terms of the landscape map signature. They further describe the architectures (the semantic models) that fit the signature of the landscape map. For example, there may be constraints that each concept is non-empty, or that concepts are singleton sets. Examples of such constraint languages are OCL for UML [7] and description logics for first-order models [1].

Landscape map actions are descriptions of how a view can be modified, for example due to interaction with the user or as triggered through another view. An action specifies both the interaction dialogue with the user (which kind of information must be obtained from the user when he clicks a button), as well as the consequence of the interaction (e.g., whether and how the underlying model must be modified after interaction with the user).

3.3 Viewpoints, Views and Vizualizations

In the IEEE-1471 standard [11] a view is a representation of a whole system from the perspective of a related set of concerns, that may consist of one or more architectural (i.e., symbolic) models. A viewpoint is a specification of the conventions for constructing and using a view.

In our formal model of landscape maps we abstract away from stakeholders and their concerns, because they are notoriously hard to formalize. Moreover, we distinguish between a view and its visualization. A landscape map viewpoint contains a partial mapping from the signature of the architecture to the landscape map signature, and a landscape map view is the result of applying this mapping to an underlying model. Moreover, the landscape map viewpoint contains a mapping from the view to visual structures.

The visual structure can be formalized in many ways, for example by a signature that expresses in a mathematical way that there is an X-axis, a Y-axis, a plane and rectangles in this plane. Under this formalization, the landscape map viewpoint contains a partial bijective mapping between the signature of the landscape map and the signature of the vizualization. Such a mapping is partial because some elements of the architecture will not be visualized and some elements of the visualization (e.g., colors) may have a meaning outside of the model. However, visual structures can also be formalized in other ways, and we do not constrain ourselves to this particular formalization.

Summarizing, in our model we see a landscape map as a composition of a symbolic model and a visual structure, together with a partial bijective mapping of the model on the visual structure. This is less ambiguous than the informal IEEE standard.

4   Visual Aspects of Landscape Maps

The goal of a landscape map is to give an overview of and insight into some architectural relations. In general, a landscape map represents two relations in one map: on the one hand the relation between the entities along the vertical axis and the entities in the plane, and on the other hand the relation between the entities along the horizontal axis and again the entities in the plane. Through the entities in the plane, an indirect relation is established between the two dimensions of the axes. For instance, if an application supports some business function in relation to a certain product, then the business function can be said to support that product.

4.1   The Axes

An intuitive and easy to understand choice for the axes is essential for landscape maps to be useful. In the infrastructural approach of Ordina [13], the axes are chosen as follows. The vertical axis represents business functions, i.e., business behavior categorized with regard to results and independent of resource or deployment choices. The horizontal axis represents cases, which still can be specialized to different types of entities. For instance, products or services can be considered as cases business functions add value.

To be useful for managing and designing for change, it is important that the choice of axes is stable, i.e., that the same axes can be used for different usages of the map, and for representing different situations over time. Another requirement is that the choice of axes results in a useful decomposition of the domain. The map is useless if all entries are assigned the same value, or if the matrix becomes sparse in all situations.

The axes themselves allow some freedom in how columns (or rows) are ordered. Sometimes this freedom can be used for arranging columns such that the plane consists of nice rectangular regions like in Figure 4. In other cases, there are semantic constraints, like ordering of business functions in time or an ordering according to priority.

Finally, it is possible to add a hierarchical structure to an axis. For business functions or processes this is an obvious approach to allow more detail in a landscape map.

4.2   The Cells

The cells of a landscape map, which are the third dimension of the landscape map, depend on the purpose of the landscape map. If the map is to be used for enterprise application integration, the cells will represent applications or systems; see, for instance, the landscape map in Figure 4. If the purpose is to give insight into the use of data elements, the cells will hold references to data types.

The landscape map in Figure 4 is a view on an underlying model, with its own signature. For example, it may be based on the same sets of concepts, but with two other relations:

$$C = C_A \cup C_X \cup C_Y \cup C_Z \qquad R = \{\text{support, realize}\}$$
$$C_A = \{\text{product, function, application}\} \qquad C_X = \{\text{home\_ins, travel\_ins}, \dots\}$$
$$C_Y = \{\text{customer\_rel, claim\_processing}, \dots\} \quad C_Z = \{\text{web\_portal, call\_center}, \dots\}$$

Figure 2 illustrates how an application supports a business process that spans a number of business functions, and assumes, moreover, that the underlying model specifies how an application realizes a product. Now we have: support $\subseteq C_Y \times C_Z$ and realize $\subseteq C_Z \times C_X$. In this particular case, we can directly find the use relation as the product of support and realize. To be precise, combining support and realize leads to a relation $C_Y \times C_Z \times C_X$, so we still have to reshuffle the order of the parameters to find the use relation. Moreover, as explained in Section 3.1, support, realize and use are defined on concept instances, not on concepts themselves. use = support $\times$ realize

Note that in this case, because the ternary use relation of the landscape map is constructed as a cross product of two binary relations, its components can always be visualized as a rectangle. That is, if there is an application say z, for (x_1, z, y_1), and (x_2, z, y_2), then there are also components for (x_1, z, y_2) and (x_2, z, y_1).

At the first sight, it may seem that the visualization in Figure 4 of the three dimensional use relation is straightforward. However, a closer inspection reveals that several choices must still be made. First, the three dimensional relation does not specify in which order the items on the axes are presented.

Second, the three dimensional relation does not specify how applications are ordered within a cell of the matrix. Consider for example the top right cell, which visualizes the applications used for Customer Relations & Sales, and Legal Aid Insurance. There are four application components in this cell: Web portal, Call center application, Customer relationship management system, and Legal Aid CRM. However, the relation does not specify that the web portal must be on top, that it is bigger than the two others below, etc. This is what we call visual information, which must be deduced and/or produced by a layout algorithm.

4.3 Automatic Layout of Landscape Maps

An important condition for landscape maps to be effective for problem identification is that the visualization must be intuitive and easy to understand. To a large extent, the choice of the axes and the ordering of the rows and columns determine the layout of a landscape map. If adjacent cells in the plane have the same value assigned, they can be merged to form a single shape. If there are no other criteria for ordering the axes such as time or priority, the ordering can be applied to optimize the layout of shapes the plane, and also to limit their number.

Creating the layout of a landscape map can be seen as a search process. We must define the search space, what it means to have a 'good' or 'nice' layout, and we must find smart ways to search.

For the search space, a cell that has multiple values assigned can be visualised by multiple combinations of overlaps and ways to split the cell. The input for an automatic layout algorithm is an empty matrix with a per-cell list of values. A cell that has multiple values assigned may be visualised by using overlaps and/or cell splitting. For instance, the top right cell of Figure 4 has four values assigned and is visualised by splitting the cell in three rows of which the bottom one is overlapped by the fourth value. A layout algorithm should be able to derive such a visualisation (semi-)automatically. Examples of rules that can be used to evaluate possible layouts are to minimize the number of objects on the plane, minimize the number of corners on the objects. maximize the convexity of the objects. make the smallest object as large as possible. We must define also the precedence of the rules in cases of conflict.

For the order of searching the search space, we must find some good heuristics because the search space is huge, already for a simple example as in Figure 4. For instance, assume that a cell has four values assigned, i.e., four applications are used by a particular combination of a product and a business function. The basic layout of this cell can be chosen from 168 possible options:

- 4 overlaps, no cell splitting $\longrightarrow$ 4*3*2 (top bottom order!)
- 4 subcells, no overlaps $\longrightarrow$ 4*3*2 = 24
- 2 subcells with 2x2 overlap $\longrightarrow$ 4*3*2 = 24
- 2 subcells, one with 3 overlaps $\longrightarrow$ 4*3*2 = 24
- 3 subcells, one with 2 overlaps $\longrightarrow$ 4*3*2 = 24
- 3 subcells, one overlapping two $\longrightarrow$ 24
- 3 subcells, one overlapping three $\longrightarrow$ 24

Clearly, the total number of possible visualizations for a landscape map grows exponentially. Therefore, the search space must be constrained by rules. Some rules to guide the search process are to consider only applications that are allowed by the model, for subcells at the border of a cell, choose applications that also occur in neighboring cells, start with borders, then go for corners, and finally choose centers of cells.

A particular kind of search process works as follows. We first try to find a good initial layout and thereafter we try to improve this initial layout. In this case, it is important to find a good initial layout, since improvement is slow. Here we can use variants of the search heuristics mentioned above. The landscape map of Figure 4 has been generated using the following set of rules:

- Choose applications for borders.
- Choose applications for corners.
- For applications that occur only in one cell, put the application in the center of the cell (e.g., top right corner).
- Fill rows and columns (e.g., top three rows of applications).
- Fill neighbors in a 'smart' way.

In the particular case of Figure 4, these construction rules directly yield the presented landscape map without the need for any improvement rules. However, in general there will be room for improvement. Examples of improvement rules are to enlarge one application in a cell, as long as it does not exclude another application from the cell, or to swap two subcells in a cell. The improvements are again measured by the same kind of rules as in the previous case. Now, the additional possibility is not to search the whole search space in an exhaustive way, but to randomly apply the improvement rules, as in evolutionary learning techniques.

5 Interaction with Landscape Maps

So far, landscape maps have been used as a static one-way presentation format, and landscape map tools contain only editors that allow architects to create landscape maps, with no provisions to relate them to more formal underlying architectural models. We use landscape maps as an interactive medium. Landscape maps are used as a starting point for more detailed models and specifications and they can be used for entering relations between the chosen dimensions. Changes in the landscape map can also be analyzed for impact on other elements of the map.

We have developed new techniques to define interactive landscape maps. In this section we discuss the notion of landscape map action, which has already been defined in Section 3.2 as a description of how a view can be modified, for example due to interaction with the user or as triggered through another view.

We say that landscape map actions create new views and visualizations from existing ones, and can therefore be formally described as mappings between views and their vizualizations. At this abstract level, they have something in common with our notion of viewpoint. However, intuitively they are clearly different in important ways, and this is reflected also in our formal definition.

First, when we change the landscape map view we may also have to change the underlying model, and vice versa. For example, consider a stakeholder that works with multiple views at the same time, or multiple stakeholders with multiple viewpoints. In such cases, we visualize the changes directly in all views (with the problem of calculating new visual attributes). On the contrary, when we create a new view from a viewpoint, then existing views do not change. Actions that change the underlying model necessarily have a strict semantics, whereas actions that change only the visualization of a model in a view can be used to make a landscape map more 'suggestive', e.g., by using colors and sizes of objects to signify their relative importance. Although important in practice, we do not discuss visual and psychological aspects of landscape maps here.

Second, actions may be interpreted in different ways, depending on the stakeholder and its viewpoint. For example, some stakeholders may change the underlying model, while others may not. For this reason, we represent actions explicitly in views, in the sense that viewpoints or landscape map actions can also modify the landscape map actions. In this, we use an extended notion of 'view' compared to the IEEE 1471 standard, in which views only relate to the architecture itself.

Third, actions typically require some interaction with the user, before they can be executed. We therefore extend the notion of action by associating an interaction protocol with it. Thus, an action specifies both the interaction dialogue with the user (which kind of information must be obtained from the user when he clicks a button), as well as the consequence of the interaction (e.g., whether and how the underlying model must be modified after interaction with the user).

In this section we discuss two kinds of interactions. In Section 5.1 we describe the creating and navigating a landscape map. In Section 5.2 we discuss the more complex case in which the underlying model can be changed by editing the landscape map.

5.1 Creating and Navigating a Landscape Map

The first contours of a landscape map are usually drawn on a white-board, flip-over or piece of paper. Together with the stakeholders the architect tries to address their concerns. The map should be such that it concentrates on the choices that must be made. The drawing must also be such that consequences are visible. In this interaction the architect chooses the concepts on the axes and on the plane, the level of detail, leaving out the facts that are less important. For the sake of readability, understandability, and acceptance the architect juggles a little bit with the (unwritten) rules of the landscape map. With pen and paper this can obviously be done.

Back at the desk and using the tool we envisage, the landscape map must be constructed in a more formal way. First, the architect needs to select the type of concepts used on the X-axis, on the Y-axis, and on the plane (see Figure 5). In our ArchiSurance example, the X-axis contains products, the Y-axis signifies business functions, and the plane holds applications.

Next, the objects on these axes must be chosen (the $X_1, \ldots, X_m$ and $Y_1, \ldots, Y_n$ in the figure). If a landscape map is used to define a new architecture, these objects can be freely chosen (of course conforming to the type of the axes). Alternatively, if an existing architecture model is visualized they may be selected from this model. By choosing the concepts for the axes the field of play is defined.

After this, the architect must choose the type of assertions that are made by putting an object Z_k somewhere on the plane, i.e., the relations R_1 and R_2. In our example, he chooses business functions on the vertical axis, products on the horizontal axis and applications on the plane. The most obvious, intuitive assertion is that an application is

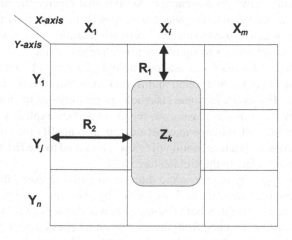

Fig. 5. Elements of a landscape map

used by activities required within the business function in realizing the product, giving us R_1 = support and R_2 = realize. For every object the architect places on the plane, these relations between X_i, Y_j, and Z_k are instantiated.

Furthermore, if the rectangle of the application Z_k is not exactly aligned within a row and/or column, then the relations with the X and Y elements are in a sense 'incomplete'. For example, an application may deliver only some of the functionality needed to support a business function.

In a similar fashion, an existing landscape map can be used as a starting point for navigation. In this case, relevant interactions include:

- Open a rectangle: detailed specifications or detailed models are shown in a separate window.
- Close detailed specification or detailed models.
- Change granularity of an axis; for instance, business processes can be changed to business activities.
- Link two rectangles by a relation supported by the underlying concept. For instance, if rectangles represent systems, use or composition can be used.

5.2 Changing a Landscape Map

If an architect or stakeholder wishes to change an existing landscape map, the effects of this change on the underlying architecture model need to be assessed. Some changes may be purely 'cosmetic' in nature, e.g., changing the color of an object. Other changes need to be propagated to the underlying model, e.g., if an object is added or deleted.

Mapping a seemingly simple change to the map onto the necessary modifications of the model may become quite complicated. Since a landscape map abstracts from many aspects of the underlying model, such a mapping might be ambiguous: many different modifications to the model might correspond to the same change of the landscape map. Human intervention is required to solve this, but a landscape map tool might suggest where the impact of the change is located.

In the example of Figure 4, the architect may, for instance, want to remove the seemingly redundant Legal aid CRM system by invoking a 'remove overlap' operation on this object. This operation influences both the visualization and the architectural model. Figure 6 illustrates the effects of the operation on the underlying model.

First, the architect selects the object to be removed, in this case the Legal Aid CRM system. The envisaged tool colors this object and maps it back onto the underlying object in the architecture model (an element of the set CZ as defined in Section 3.1).

Next, the relations connecting this object to its environment are computed (the second part of Figure 6). Here, this concerns the relations of Legal Aid CRM with the Web portal and the Legal Aid backoffice system. These relations will have to be connected to one or more objects that replace the objects that are to be removed. Since we have chosen a 'remove overlap' operation, the landscape tool computes with which other objects Legal Aid CRM overlaps, in this case the CRM system. The relations formerly connecting Legal Aid CRM are then moved to the other CRM system, unless these already exist (e.g., the relation with the Web portal).

Naturally, this scenario presents an ideal situation with minimal user intervention. In reality, a tool cannot always decide how a proposed change is to be mapped back onto the model, and may only present the user with a number of options. For example, if the functionality of the Legal Aid CRM system would overlap with more than one other system, remapping its relations requires knowledge about the correspondence between these relations and the functions realized by these other systems.

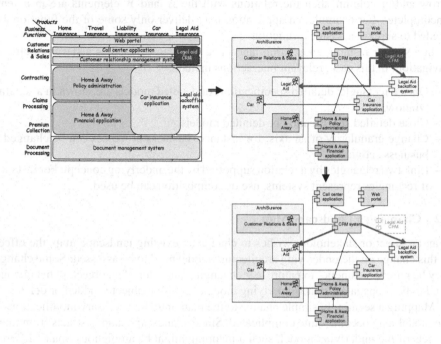

Fig. 6. Editing a landscape map

6   Conclusions and Future Work

In this paper we introduce landscape maps for enterprise architectures, which is an instrument that has proven its value in the architecture and consultancy practice of Ordina. The landscape map is an easy-to-read informative format that provides overview of and insight into architecture relations between different domains. We define a formal semantics for landscape maps based on a mapping to and from the ArchiMate language. We show how landscape maps can be automatically derived from enterprise architectural models and explain how they can be automatically visualised. Finally, we explain how interaction with landscape maps is realised by propagating changes back to the underlying model by means of actions.

The development of landscape maps in this paper carefully balances formalization and informal discussion. Enterprise architectures are often informal, because they must not constrain the architect. However, to provide the architect with useful tools, some formal definitions are necessary. In this paper we only adopt a minimal formalization in terms of the signature of a landscape map, but we do not constrain for example the visual structures, or the landscape map actions. The minimal formalization has been sufficient to define the visualization and interaction techniques.

Based on the formalization of landscape maps presented in this paper, we have developed a prototype that illustrates the added value of the formal semantics of landscape maps and the benefits of interactive landscape maps (based on actions). The prototype serves as a proof of concept of the formalization of, automatic layout of, and interaction with landscape maps. Furthermore, it illustrates to members of the ArchiMate Forum the tool support that we envisage for enterprise architecture. Some of the ideas have been incorporated by BiZZdesign in their ArchiMate-compliant Architect tool.

The use of viewpoints for architecture-level impact analysis (see, e.g., [13, 4, 2, 12]) is a subject for further research. The type of editing illustrated in this paper tends toward this type of analysis. By propagating changes to the landscape map through the architectural model, a high-level impression of the effects of a change can be obtained. Landscape maps can also be used to visualise the results of other types of analysis. For example, a cost or performance analysis may yield quantitative results. Several visual techniques such as colors, line styles, and fonts can be used to highlight these effects within the landscape map.

References

[1] F. Baader, D. Calvanese, D. McGuinness, D. Nardi, and editors P. F. Patel-Schneider. *Description Logic Handbook: Theory, Implementation and Applications*. Cambridge University Press, 2002.

[2] F. de Boer, M. Bonsangue, L. Groenewegen, A. Stam, S.Stevens, and L. van der Torre. Change impact analysis of enterprise architecture. In *Proceedings of IEEE International Conference on Information Reuse and Integration (IRI'05)*, 2005.

[3] F. de Boer, M. Bonsangue, J. Jacob, A. Stam, and L. van der Torre. A logical viewpoint on architectures. In *Proceedings of EDOC'04*, pages 73–83. IEEE, 2004.

[4] F. de Boer, M. Bonsangue, J. Jacob, A. Stam, and L. van der Torre. Enterprise architecture analysis with xml. In *Proceedings of 38th Hawaii international conference on system sciences (HICSS'05)*, 2005.

[5] A. Finkelstein, J. Kramer, B. Nuseibeh, L. Finkelstein, and M. Goedicke. Viewpoints: A framework for multiple perspectives in system development. *International Journal of Software Engineering and Knowledge Engineering*, 2(1):31–57, 1992.

[6] H. Jonkers, M.M. Lankhorst, R. van Buuren, S. Hoppenbrouwers, M. Bonsangue, and L. van der Torre. Concepts for modelling enterprise architectures. *International Journal of Cooperative Information Systems*, 13(3):257–287, 2004.

[7] A. Kleppe and J. Warmer. The object constraint language and its application in the UML metamodel. In *Proceedings UML'98 Beyond the Notation*, Mullhouse, France, 1998.

[8] M. Lankhorst *et al. Enterprise Architecture At Work*. Springer, 2005.

[9] N. Lassing, D. Rijsenbrij, and H. van Vliet. Viewpoints on modifiability. *International Journal of Software Engineering and Knowledge Engineering*, 11(4):453–478, 2001.

[10] B. Nuseibeh, S. Easterbrook, and A. Russo. Making inconsistency respectable in software development. *Journal of Systems and Software*, 56(11), 2001.

[11] IEEE Computer Society. *IEEE Std 1472-2000: IEEE Recommended Practice for Architectural Description of Software-Intensive Systems*. 2000.

[12] A. Stam, J. Jacob, F. de Boer, M. Bonsangue, and L. van der Torre. Using xml transformations for enterprise architectures. In *Proceedings of ISOLA'04*, 2004.

[13] W.A.M. van der Sanden, P. Bergman, J.T.P. Campschroer, and H.R. de Reus. Realisatie van flexibele informatievoorziening (in dutch). *Informatie*, 41:58–65, 1999.

[14] W.A.M. van der Sanden and B.J.A.M. Sturm. Informatiearchitectuur, de infrastructurele benadering (in dutch). 2000.

[15] J. van Leeuwen, Ed. *Handbook of Theoretical Computer Science, vol. B: Formal Methods and Semantics*. Amsterdam, 1994.

Configuration and Separation

Model-Driven Enterprise Systems Configuration

Jan Recker[1], Jan Mendling[2], Wil van der Aalst[1,3], and Michael Rosemann[1]

[1] Queensland University of Technology,
126 Margaret Street, Brisbane QLD 4000, Australia
{j.recker, w.vanderaalst, m.rosemann}@qut.edu.au
[2] Vienna University of Economics and Business Administration,
Augasse 2-6, 1090 Vienna, Austria
jan.mendling@wu-wien.ac.at
[3] Eindhoven University of Technology,
P.O. Box 513, 5600 MB Eindhoven, The Netherlands
w.m.p.v.d.aalst@tm.tue.nl

Abstract. Enterprise Systems potentially lead to significant efficiency gains but require a well-conducted configuration process. A promising idea to manage and simplify the configuration process is based on the premise of using reference models for this task. Our paper continues along this idea and delivers a two-fold contribution: first, we present a generic process for the task of model-driven Enterprise Systems configuration including the steps of (a) *Specification* of configurable reference models, (b) *Configuration* of configurable reference models, (c) *Transformation* of configured reference models to regular build time models, (d) *Deployment* of the generated build time models, (e) *Controlling* of implementation models to provide input to the configuration, and (f) *Consolidation* of implementation models to provide input to reference model specification. We discuss inputs and outputs as well as the involvement of different roles and validation mechanisms. Second, we present an instantiation case of this generic process for Enterprise Systems configuration based on Configurable EPCs.

1 Enterprise Systems and Reference Modeling

Over the last years, Enterprise Systems (ES) have evolved to comprehensive IT-supported business solutions that presumptively support and enhance organizations in their business operations. This, however, only holds true for such systems that are well-aligned with organizational requirements. As Enterprise Systems are developed in a generic manner in order to provide benefits to a wide variety of organizations, industry sectors and countries, their implementation entails the problem of aligning business and IT. Alignment, however, implies extensive configuration and customization efforts in the implementation process and may lead to significant implementation costs that exceed the price of software licenses by factor five to ten [1].

ES vendors are aware of these problems and try to increase the manageability of the implementation process. One respective measure is to deliver ES products

E. Dubois and K. Pohl (Eds.): CAiSE 2006, LNCS 4001, pp. 369–383, 2006.
© Springer-Verlag Berlin Heidelberg 2006

along with extensive documentation and specific implementation support tools. *Reference models* play a central role within such documentation. Vendors provide a set of process models as reference models of their software package [2]. The SAP reference model as such an example includes a large number of process models representing the system processes [3]. However, research shows that reference models still are only of limited use to the ES configuration process [4]. This is mainly due to a lack of conceptual support for configuration in the underlying modeling language. In this context, a *configurable modeling language* should at least support the structured modification and exclusion of model elements or whole parts of a model as well as the definition of constraints on configurability [5]. This is of particular importance for leveraging the main objective of reference models, i.e., streamlining the adaptation of ES. Beyond conceptual support in terms of flexible or configurable modeling languages, see e.g. [5, 6], there is a need for a clearly structured configuration procedure. ES configuration based on configurable reference models is a multi-facetted task requiring guidance to the overall process. It comprises in particular model configuration, validation, translation, deployment, controlling, and consolidation; with each of these subtasks demanding not only profound knowledge of configurable reference modeling but also of the processes of the organization. A dedicated approach is needed to manage the process of model-driven Enterprise Systems configuration all the way from model design to deployment.

Following this line of argumentation this paper reports on the development and application of a generic engineering process for the design and usage of configurable reference models in a model-driven approach towards Enterprise Systems configuration. To be more concise, the *contribution of our paper* is two-fold: First, we introduce an *engineering process* covering the tasks of specification, configuration, transformation and deployment of configurable reference models and the two feedback loops of controlling and consolidation. The engineering process will be described on a generic level to allow for wider uptake in ES contexts beyond the limits of any given modeling language. Second, as an instantiation case, we report on the deployment of this generic engineering process in the development and application of *Configurable EPCs* (C-EPCs) [5, 7] in the context of model-driven ES configuration. We proceed as follows: Section 2 presents the generic engineering process for configurable reference models. Section 3 then reports on the application of the engineering process based on C-EPCs. After discussing related research in Section 4, we conclude the paper in Section 5.

2   A Generic Configurable Reference Modeling Process

This section defines a process for engineering and deploying configurable reference models in the context of Enterprise Systems implementation. This process is generic in that it is not dependent on a specific modeling technique or method. However, a requirement for the application of our engineering process is that the reference modeling language used throughout the process must be configurable as defined in Section 1. Subsection 2.1 gives an overview of the process while subsections 2.2 to 2.7 introduce the six steps of model specification, configuration, transformation, deployment, controlling, and consolidation.

2.1   Overview of the Process

Reference model configuration contrasts with the traditional software development process: during implementation, the scope of the ES system is continuously narrowed down to finally meet the requirements of the organization. This process starts with the overall system capabilities which are then reduced to a relevant subset. Reference models can be used as semi-formal descriptions of such overall capabilities [2] and a configurable reference modeling language provides the means to express configuration alternatives. The lifecycle model introduced by Rosemann and van der Aalst [5] illustrates this continuous 'narrowing down' process by defining different "time" notions: At *design time* the overall capabilities of the ES are captured as a (configurable) reference model. At *configuration time* capabilities that are deemed desirable before the background of organizational requirements are selected from the reference model. This means that irrelevant parts of the model are excluded. At *build time* the configured model is deployed on an ES to serve as a 'template' for how the system support for business will look like during execution. Finally, at *run time* single instances are created for specific cases. Our generic process for model-driven ES configuration is related to these "time" notions, however, we extend this lifecycle with *feedback loops* as described below. The overall process defines four major stages comprising reference model *specification, configuration, transformation,* and *deployment* (see Fig. 1).

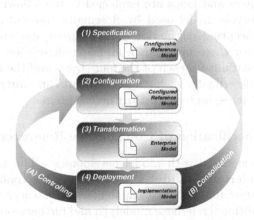

Fig. 1. Engineering process for model-driven ES configuration

The four stages need to be continuously assessed as to their contribution towards fulfilling organizational requirements, which in turn may be subjected to modification due to internal or external changes. As reference models capture knowledge in the form of current best practice descriptions, they form part of an *organizational learning cycle* by (a) being affected by changes within the organizational setting and (b) effectuating such changes via technological or organizational developments. Organizational learning in general can be differentiated in single- and double-loop learning [8]. Single-loop learning can be understood as error minimization in accordance to given objectives and assumptions. Double-loop learning includes a reflection upon these assumptions and may result in completely new objectives, processes and outcomes. Applying these insights to the task of model-driven configuration of Enterprise Systems, we argue that single-loop learning comprises the reflection on a configuration as to its contribution to given organizational requirements. Double-loop learning then is the reflection on the presupposed best practice knowledge captured in the reference models as to whether or not it sufficiently enables organizations to fulfill their objectives. In order to facilitate single- and double-loop learning with configurable reference models, our generic process is extended by two feedback mechanisms, namely *controlling* and *consolidation*. Controlling is understood as the reflection on the implementation of the "best practice" knowledge described in the reference models within the organizational setting, viz., a diagnosis of how well the selected configuration aligns with organizational requirements. Controlling in this sense provides a means to facilitate single-loop learning. Consolidation is understood as a reflection on the specification of the "best practice" knowledge described in the reference models based on current implementation in several organizational settings, viz., a diagnosis of whether the reference model itself (and the ES described within) has to be subjected to refinement or extension due to evolution of technological and/or organizational factors in its domain. Based on this understanding consolidation provides a means to facilitate double-loop learning.

The different stages and loops are explained in the following subsections. In contrast to the lifecycle model used by Rosemann and van der Aalst [5] that merely offers a conceptual distinction of the phases, our engineering process provides guidance for those involved in an ES configuration project by giving detailed recommendations for each of the four stages and the feedback loops. In particular, we will describe for each stage the **inputs** and **outputs**, the different **steps**, **responsibilities**, and **validation mechanisms**.

2.2 Step (1): Specification of Configurable Reference Models

The first step is concerned with model development. The goal is to produce a **configurable reference model** as an output. This configurable reference model captures system functionality, capabilities and structure on a conceptual level (as does a traditional reference model) [2] and furthermore defines *variation points* within the model that capture configurable aspects of an ES. A variation point captures the place of a configuration decision together with the related possible choices and consequences, and thereby serves the concept of variability [9], which empowers constructive model reuse and facilitates the derivation of model variants from the initial model. Concerning input there are basically two options: (1) *Development from scratch*. This means selecting an appropriate configurable modeling technique to develop the reference models. As to methodical guidance, traditional reference model engineering approaches may be followed. The only additional concern here is to place emphasis on the conceptual description of variation points and configuration-related information within the models. (2) *Extension of existing models.* This option refers to the fact that, often, reference models are already available. As an example, the SAP reference model (Version 4.6) [3] covers more than 1,000 business processes. Such existing reference models are, however, usually depicted using traditional reference modeling techniques that do not allow for the description of configuration-related information, for instance the highlighting and selection of different process alternatives [5]. Hence, a configurable modeling language is needed to extend the existing model in order to express variation points and configuration information. It is efficient to stick to the language in which the reference model is expressed and to extend it by annotating the model with configuration concepts, rather than redefining the model in (yet) another modeling language. A potential solution for re-engineering the existing reference model based on process mining techniques is described in [7].

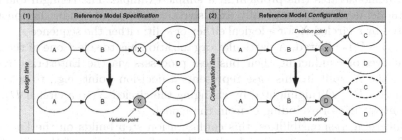

Fig. 2. Specification and configuration of reference model

Part (1) of Fig. 2 illustrates how input and output of the specification step are related. If there is a reference model available, configurable aspects of the system being modeled have to be made obvious in the model by extending it with variation points. In Fig. 2, we exemplarily highlighted such a configurable element by a grey background color.

Concerning responsibilities, the specification step has to rely on ES experts who are familiar both with the functionality of the ES and the support capabilities for an organization's business processes it provides. Furthermore, expertise is required in terms of reference modeling. Usually, such experts are employees of the ES vendor who are responsible for system documentation. If such documentation is not provided by the ES vendor itself, a configurable reference model of an ES might be defined by a consulting company or by an organization using the ES.

Concerning validation mechanisms, existing model quality frameworks (e.g., [10]) can be used in order to ensure the quality of the configurable reference model. This early step and the quality of its output is of crucial importance since as conceptual models used in the requirements specification phase of a system development process determine the acceptability and usability of the product to be built [11]. Not only the configuration alternatives have to be made explicit, but also constraints in terms of interrelations between certain configuration alternatives. Due to this delicate nature, it definitely calls for a deeper investigation in terms of methodical guidance, which in turn we must consider out of scope for this paper. We nevertheless suggest that the result of this task should be validated by at least a second domain expert.

2.3   Step (2): Configuration of Configurable Reference Models

The second step deals with the configuration of a configurable reference model. Taking the reference model defined in the previous step as input, this task defines a set of *configuration decisions* for all configuration aspects of the model and yields a **configured reference model** as an output. Hence, in the configurable reference model for each configurable node a decision on the desired setting has to be taken. Each variation point in the configurable reference model defines a *decision point* at which the reference model user has to specify a configuration parameter while adhering to potential constraints and requirements. Part (2) of Fig. 2 demonstrates this problem in a simple example. The configurable reference model depicts two mutually exclusive alternatives of conducting business, depicted by a circled X for a logical either-or split: either the sequence $A-B-C$ or $A-B-D$ is allowed. A particular organization has to select one of these two alternatives of conducting their business processes via the Enterprise System. Hence, the X split in this case represents a decision point, e.g., to select the option $A-B-D$ (highlighted by changing the circled X to a circled D), with the consequence of excluding C from the model.

Concerning responsibilities, this configuration step builds on the knowledge of ES experts who are familiar both with the functionality of the ES, the requirements of the organization, and the configuration of reference models. In this context, these are most likely members of a configuration/implementation project team involving consultants and experts of the organization itself.

Concerning validation mechanisms, at this stage, the desired configuration needs to be validated against the constraints defined in the configurable reference model. If these constraints have been specified in a formal manner, this task can be conducted automatically. Consider the following example: an organization chooses for its sales & distribution software package not to offer credit card payment to customers. Conclusively, the accounting software package neither needs to provide functionality for credit card authorization and payment. The first configuration decision has a consequence onto the second variation/decision point in that it restrains the possible set of configuration alternatives. Hence, validation at this stage refers to the evaluation of configuration decisions against constraints or configuration requirements.

2.4   Step (3): Transformation of Configured Reference Models

The third step is concerned with the transformation of a configured reference model as input to an **enterprise model** as output. This enterprise model describes conceptually the way the organization will conduct business with the support of the Enterprise System once implemented and running. In short, a "traditional" individual model has to be derived from the configured reference model. If the configuration semantics of the configurable reference modeling language have been defined in a formal way and the activities are supported by applications, this task can be automated by a transformation program. Otherwise, the transformation has to be done manually by an ES expert with modeling expertise. It is recommended to automate the transformation, as a manual execution of this task is both time-consuming and error-prone. Furthermore, instead of validating the enterprise model against the configured model, a validation of the correctness of the transformation program is sufficient, which is much more efficient. As an example, modeling languages that are specified via an XML schema can easily be validated and transformed. Still, at least one ES and business expert should inspect the resulting models to validate that the models (still) meet the requirements of the organization. An automated transformation is especially beneficial when both the configuration decisions have to be translated to the output model and the re-establishment of syntactical correctness of the model becomes necessary [12]. For illustration purposes, consider the example given in Part (3) of Fig. 3. It is assumed that an organization has chosen to implement the sequence $A - B - D$ instead of implementing the sequence $A - B - C$. Thus, the option C - which still exists in the configured reference model - needs to be excluded from the enterprise model. Furthermore, the decision point has to be excluded from the model in order to re-establish syntactical correctness.

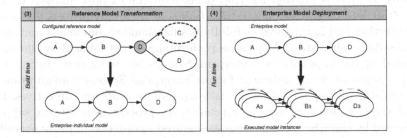

Fig. 3. Transformation to and deployment of enterprise model

2.5   Step (4): Deployment of Enterprise Model

The fourth step is concerned with the deployment of the enterprise model and yields an implement and running enterprise system (which can be understood as an **implementation model**) as output. Part (4) of Fig. 3 shows the principle. There are basically two questions that are important in this context.

First, does a process engine or similar system exist that is able to execute models, in particular the enterprise model, given the modeling language used? It would be desirable if a reference process model that has been transformed to an enterprise model would be directly executable in a workflow engine. A popular example for such an executable process specification is BPEL4WS [13]. If the model is not directly executable, the enterprise model has to be transformed to a modeling language that runs on a dedicated execution engine. If the semantics of the used modeling language are defined in a formal way, this task can be automated by a transformation program. Otherwise, the transformation has to be done manually by an ES or IT expert with modeling expertise.

Second, does the enterprise model already include run time information about data flow and interfaces to applications? If not, the enterprise model or the transformed enterprise model need to be enriched with technical information, and can only be deployed afterwards. Depending on how much technical information still needs to be added to the model, the deployment has to be done by an IT expert or may also be done by an ES expert. Furthermore, testing of the enterprise models is of crucial importance before deployment, especially when run time information is manually added by IT experts. The implementation models are supposed to be instantiated in order to support the operations of the organization. Accordingly, errors in the models may have a direct impact on business performance.

2.6   Loop (A): Controlling of Instance Models

The single-learning feedback loop stems from the notion of process monitoring and controlling. For the purpose of this paper, process *monitoring* deals with the collection of data about workflow instances at run time, mostly in audit trail logs, i.e., an observation of the processes as they are executed in the organization at hand [14]. Process *controlling*, also referred to as *process mining* [15] or *business process intelligence* [16], deals with the ex-post analysis of logged audit trail data of process enactment. It aims at reviewing process performance as to whether and how processes fulfill organizational requirements and support organizational objectives. As process performance is determined by the support provided by the implemented Enterprise System, we argue here that poor process performance is an indicator for an Enterprise System configuration that does not entirely support all organizational requirements and objectives. Based on noted deviations in process performance, the process, as it is being supported or enacted by the ES, needs to be re-configured in order to improve overall performance. Hence, the feedback loop of controlling provides ex-post evaluation of the customized implementation of the Enterprise System based on actual process enactment performance.

To support the single-loop learning feedback look we use recent achievements in process mining [15]. To illustrate the relationship between process mining and reference models we refer to Fig. 4. Essential for process mining is the presence of an *event log* (also referred to as audit trail or transaction log), which log refers to some event, e.g., the start or completion of some activity. The event may bear a timestamp or refer to the person/application executing it. The event may also hold data, e.g., the outcome of a decision activity. Clearly, an information system that is supporting or controlling an operational process is able to monitor such events. We distinguish between two forms of process mining: *process discovery* and *conformance checking* (see Fig. 4).

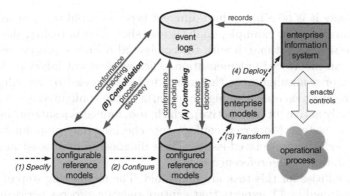

Fig. 4. Process mining approach and relation to configurable reference models

The goal of process discovery is to extract knowledge from event logs in the form of models. These may be process models, e.g., an EPC or Petri net, but also other models such as social networks or time-charts describing the performance (e.g., flow times). Process discovery does not require an a-priori model (such as a reference model), however, the discovered model may be used for delta analysis, i.e., comparing the mined model representing the *actual* process with the reference model representing the *predefined* process. Delta analysis can be used to find parts of the process that are never used or find parts where users deviate from the prescribed procedure. Moreover, the discovered models may refer to other aspects such as time, data and resources. For example, the discovered model may highlight the bottlenecks in the process, reveal the social network (e.g., which people are working together on a frequent basis), or relate properties of cases to their execution (e.g., cases involving more than 1000 euro and handled by the team in Paris tend to be late).

Unlike process discovery, conformance checking *does* require an a-priori model to which it compares the observed behavior as recorded in the log. Using conformance checking one can detect discrepancies but it is also possible to see which parts of the process are really used, where bottlenecks are etc. Clearly, this is very useful for measuring (and quantifying) the "fit" between the real process and some reference model and to pinpoint typical deviations.

To actually measure conformance and to discover a variety of models, we have developed the *ProM framework*[1]. In the context of this framework, several process discovery tools have been developed, e.g., the well-know alpha algorithm [15]. Moreover, the framework offers a *Conformance Checker*, a *Social Network Analyser*, and a variety of other analysis tools.

The dashed lines in Fig. 4 refer to the steps identified in Fig. 1. First, the reference models are specified and then for a particular context (organization and process) they are configured. The configured model is then transformed and deployed. The configured reference model can be compared with the derived models (process discovery) or directly with the event logs (conformance check-

---

[1] Both documentation and software can be downloaded from www.processmining.org

ing). This way it is possible to find different types of problems that may lead to a re-configuration. For example, analysis may show that in reality, the execution of the process does not match with the configured reference process model. This may imply an incorrect implementation, office workers not following the proper procedures, or a misalignment that needs to be addressed by reconfiguring the system. The analysis may also highlight parts of the configured reference model that are rarely active (or over-active), which, too, indicates a suboptimal configuration of the system. Moreover, conformance checking may pinpoint bottlenecks and other performance-related issues. These diagnostics may assist in improving the configuration of the reference model.

Responsibilities for this task are multi-fold. The monitoring step of this stage is best performed by IT experts that capture relevant process performance data in audit trails and have experience in applying process mining techniques. The actual analysis should be done by an analyst having knowledge of process mining and the application domain. It is definitely possible to automate this analysis and offer a kind of "business cockpit" to managers and end-users. Then, the step of controlling is a rather managerial task and merely includes decisions as to how to re-configure the processes in order to increase their performance. Still, based on the assumption that process performance is determined by the support provided by the Enterprise System, an ES expert is recommended to be consulted for this task in order to elicit possible alternatives for supporting existing processes through alternative ES configurations.

2.7 Loop (B): Consolidation of Instance Models

The single-loop learning approach focuses on a specific context (i.e., a given organization and process) and can only result in a reconfiguration. Therefore, it does not aim at improving "best practice" in a broader setting, i.e., it does not reflect on the qualities of the configurable reference model. The double-loop learning approach that we refer to as *consolidation* has a wider scope than controlling. The input of the consolidation feedback loop is a set of instances originating from different configurations, i.e., experiences from multiple applications of the reference model are used as a starting point for the analysis of the reference model itself and not (just) one selected configuration. The result of this analysis can be used to modify the reference model itself. For example, analysis may show that although it is possible to configure a variation point in multiple ways, in reality always the same configuration decision is taken, thus leading to unnecessary configuration work. It is also possible that analysis shows that certain problems (e.g., performance or quality issues) typically occur when a certain configuration is being used. This knowledge can be used to revise the original reference model and the variation points within.

The consolidation phase consists of three smaller steps. First, process mining techniques as described in Section 2.6 are applied in a variety of situations where the reference model has been configured and deployed. For example, situations in different organizational units in the same enterprise or in comparable organizational units across different organizations may be used as input. For each situation, process mining techniques are used to do process discovery and/or conformance checking. This gives insights into the way the system is really being used, helps to identify problems and is used to quantify the performance of the process. Each of these aspects is linked to the selected configuration and external factors such as load and resource availability. Note that compared to Section 2.6 these results are more likely at an aggregate level. The second step uses the results of this first step and compares all situations to discover patterns. This can be done in a qualitative way ("It seems that configuration A only works properly if combined with configuration B.") or in a quantitative way ("There is a positive correlation between the flow time and a particular configuration setting."). In the third and final step these patterns are used to modify the reference model (see Fig. 4). Note that the structure of the reference model may change. However, we envision that more changes will be made to relationships between the different configuration decisions. Moreover, the use of soft constraints in addition to hard constraints seems to be important. Soft constraints can serve as guidelines based on empirical evidence gained from the feedback loop of consolidation.

The responsibility of this task lies with the developers of the reference models guided by input from the organizations involved.

3   An Instantiation Case Using Configurable EPCs

So far, we outlined a generic process that covers the overall reference model lifecycle and applies it to the area of Enterprise Systems configuration. In the following, we will illustrate the technical feasibility of this process by applying it to the case of C-EPCs in the context of ES configuration. C-EPCs have been developed with the clear intention in mind to facilitate a model-driven approach towards ES configuration. In the following, we assume the reader to have some basic knowledge of EPCs. For an introduction, refer to [17].

Event-Driven Process Chains (EPCs) are a frequently used business process modeling language, especially for describing processes on a conceptual level. EPCs have been developed in a joint project by University of Saarland and SAP [17] and SAP has used them as a modeling language for their SAP R/3 reference model [3]. *Configurable EPCs* (C-EPCs) [5] extend EPCs to allow for the specification of variation points, configuration requirements and configuration guidelines in a reference model, including configurable functions that can be switched *on, off* or *optional*; configurable connectors that subsume possible build time connector types, which are less or equally expressive; configuration requirements (must-constraints) and guidelines (should-constraints); and an order relation over the configurable nodes [5]. EPCs have been chosen because they facilitate the usage of the SAP model in *step 1* for the specification of configurable reference models. Respective tool support is available as the ARIS Toolset of IDS Scheer AG is shipped with the SAP model. As a basis for steps 2 to 4, an XML representation of (a) configurable EPCs and (b) configured EPCs based on the EPC Markup Language (EPML) [18] has been specified [19].

This EPML extension serves as an input format for a C-EPC validation tool that has been implemented as a prototype [19]. This tool generates a report on whether a configurable EPC is correct with respect to the C-EPC definition, and whether configuration requirements and guidelines are met. The formal C-EPC definition allows the automation of the validation and, therefore, supports the configuration step (*step 2*). The transformation of C-EPCs to EPC process models bears some challenges which are specific to the syntax and semantics of EPCs [12]. An algorithm has been defined in [20] and implemented to automate this transformation step (*step 3*). This is supposed to speed up the development and grant the correctness of the resulting models. This algorithm is driven by a minimality criterion in order to generate an EPC with as little structure as necessary [20]. In the beginning, it had been an assumption that the generated EPC models can be directly deployed on the ES (*step 4*). As this might not always be the case, a transformation concept from EPCs to executable BPEL [13] process definitions has been developed [21]. As BPEL is a generic language for Web Service composition, this step can only be automated if the data flow and the Web Service endpoints are made explicit in the EPC model. Basically, such information can be included in the configurable model and preserved in the transformation step, so it is still available for deployment. The *two feedback loops* can both be supported by process mining techniques. The ProM framework introduced in Section 2.6 is able to rebuild EPC models from SAP event logs. Also, in [7] it has been shown how process mining can be used to generate C-EPCs from running workflows for controlling or consolidation purposes.

The C-EPC case illustrates that respective tool support for each step of the engineering process has already been established on a prototype basis. The next challenge is to combine the different implementations into a comprehensive configuration framework that can be used by practitioners.

4   Related Work

A number of academic contributions discussing issues related to Enterprise Systems aim at understanding the challenges of ES configuration. For instance, a number of contingencies that potentially impact such projects have been revealed in critical success factor models [22]. Other research claims that ES implementation project failures are likely due to difficulties arising while using specified requirements in the implementation process [23]. Empirical studies, too, tell failure stories [1].

While vendors aim at increasing the chance of ES implementation success by distributing reference models as part of system documentation, these models are at best partly deployed in the configuration of Enterprise Systems. Daneva [4] measured the level of reuse of the SAP reference models in a number of case studies and indicated that full reuse was not achieved in any of them, although sometimes the level of reuse was quite substantial. Some research has focused the field of configurable modeling, good collections of related approaches can be found in [5] and [24]. Some of the discussed approaches are closely related to our ideas of configurable modeling; worthwhile mentioning here is the approach by Reinhartz-Berger et al. [25], who leverage the re-use of reference models for domain engineering using model specialization mechanisms based on generalization and UML stereotypes.

Concerning limitations, model-driven configuration is well suited for deployment of commercial-off-the-shelf software packages but not as a general approach to software engineering, which cannot entirely be described as a 'scoping' exercise. Also, the notion of re-usable models in the software engineering discipline refers to the employment of building blocks of software fragments in multiple contexts rather than the depiction of best practice patterns. There is, however, some related work. As an example, Haugen et al. [26] present an approach to leverage configurable models for system family engineering. In order to capture model variability, they utilize mechanisms of UML 2.0 composite structures and UML association multiplicities. Yet, their approach focusses more on the derivation of individual software systems from system families than on deriving variants from a given models.

5   Contributions and Limitations

This paper reported on the development and application of a generic engineering process for configurable reference modeling. We first presented a process for model-driven Enterprise Systems configuration consisting of the steps *specification*, *configuration*, *transformation*, and *deployment*, as well as the feedback loops *controlling* and *consolidation*. The second contribution of this paper was the application of this generic process to the development and application of C-EPCS for the purpose of configuring Enterprise Systems. We showed how C-EPCs conceptually facilitate a model-driven configuration process in all of our stages.

Our research has a few limitations. First, our approach needs to be empirically validated with business practitioners. This task is currently being conducted. We have already conducted a pilot laboratory experiment with postgraduate IT students on the perceived usefulness and perceived ease of use of C-EPCs in comparison to EPCs, showing that C-EPCs are in fact perceived as more useful and easier to use for the task of reference model configuration [27]. Second, our approach does not strongly consider the challenge of linking configurable models to Enterprise Systems functionality, i.e., how to link model configurations to actual modifications of programmed code. Third, we applied our generic engineering process to a configurable *process* modeling approach. It would be interesting to link it other perspectives such as a data view, refer, for instance, to [28].

Future work will concentrate on (a) an evaluation of our approach via case study application and (b) the development of a sophisticated configuration framework based on our proof-of-concept implementations. The ultimate goal is then to provide comprehensive tool support towards model-driven systems configuration.

Acknowledgement. The research on C-EPCs has been partly funded by SAP Research and Queensland University of Technology with the Strategic Link with

Industry project "Modelling Configurable Business Processes". SAP is a trademark of SAP AG, Germany.

References

1. Davenport, T.H.: Mission Critical: Realizing the Promise of Enterprise Systems. Harvard Business School Press, Boston, MA (2000)
2. Rosemann, M.: Using Reference Models within the Enterprise Resource Planning Lifecycle. Australian Accounting Review 10 (2000) 19–30
3. Curran, T., Keller, G., Ladd, A.: SAP R/3 Business Blueprint: Understanding the Business Process Reference Model. Enterprise Resource Planning Series. Prentice Hall PTR, Upper Saddle River, NJ (1997)
4. Daneva, M.: Practical Reuse Measurement in ERP Requirements Engineering. In Wangler, B., Bergmann, L., eds.: 12th International Conference on Advanced Information Systems Engineering. Volume 1789 of Lecture Notes In Computer Science., Stockholm, Sweden, Springer (2000) 309–324
5. Rosemann, M., van der Aalst, W.: A Configurable Reference Modelling Language. Information Systems **In Press, also available from** www.BPMCenter.org (2006)
6. Soffer, P.: Scope Analysis: Identifying the Impact of Changes in Business Process Models. Software Process Improvement and Practice 10 (2005) 393–402
7. Jansen-Vullers, M.H., van der Aalst, W., Rosemann, M.: Mining Configurable Enterprise Information Systems. Data and Knowledge Engineering 56 (2006) 195–244
8. Argyris, C., Schön, D.: Organizational Learning II. Theory, Method, and Practice. Addison-Wesley, Reading, MA et al. (1996)
9. Halmans, G., Pohl, K.: Communicating the Variability of a Software-Product Family to Customers. Software and Systems Modeling 2 (2003) 15–36
10. Lindland, O.I., Sindre, G., Sølvberg, A.: Understanding Quality in Conceptual Modeling. IEEE Software 11 (1994) 42–49
11. Lauesen, S., Vinter, O.: Preventing Requirement Defects: An Experiment in Process Improvement. Requirements Engineering 6 (2001) 37–50
12. Recker, J., Rosemann, M., van der Aalst, W., Mendling, J.: On the Syntax of Reference Model Configuration. Transforming the C-EPC into Lawful EPC Models. In Bussler, C., Haller, A., eds.: Business Process Management Workshops. Volume 3812 of Lecture Notes in Computer Science. Springer, Berlin, Germany et al. (2006) 497–511
13. Andrews, T. et al.: Business Process Execution Language for Web Services. Version 1.1 (2003)
14. zur Muehlen, M.: Workflow-based Process Controlling. Foundation, Design and Application of workflow-driven Process Information Systems. Logos, Berlin, Germany (2004)
15. van der Aalst, W., Weijters, A., Maruster, L.: Workflow Mining: Discovering Process Models from Event Logs. IEEE Transactions on Knowledge and Data Engineering 16 (2004) 1128–1142
16. Grigori, D., Casati, F., Castellanos, M., Dayal, U., Sayal, M., Shan, M.: Business Process Intelligence. Computers in Industry 53 (2004) 321–343
17. Keller, G., Nüttgens, M., Scheer, A.W.: Semantische Prozessmodellierung auf der Grundlage "Ereignisgesteuerter Prozessketten (EPK)". Technical Report 89, Institut für Wirtschaftsinformatik der Universität Saarbrücken, Saarbrücken, Germany (1992)

18. Mendling, J., Nüttgens, M.: EPC Markup Language (EPML) - An XML-Based Interchange Format for Event-Driven Process Chains (EPC). Information Systems and e-Business Management **In Press, also available from** `wi.wu-wien.ac.at/home/mendling` (2006)
19. Mendling, J., Recker, J., Rosemann, M., van der Aalst, W.: Towards the Interchange of Configurable EPCs: An XML-based Approach for Reference Model Configuration. In Desel, J., Frank, U., eds.: Enterprise Modelling and Information Systems Architectures. Volume P-75 of Lecture Notes in Informatics. German Informatics Society, Klagenfurt, Austria (2005) 8–21
20. Mendling, J., Recker, J., Rosemann, M., van der Aalst, W.: Generating Correct EPCs from Configured CEPCs. In: 21st Annual ACM Symposium on Applied Computing, Dijon, France, ACM (2006) forthcoming
21. Ziemann, J., Mendling, J.: EPC-Based Modelling of BPEL Processes: a Pragmatic Transformation Approach. In: 7th International Conference MITIP 2005, Genova, Italy (2005)
22. Holland, C.P., Light, B.: A Critical Success Factors Model for ERP Implementation. IEEE Software **16** (1999) 30–36
23. Rolland, C., Prakash, N.: Bridging The Gap Between Organisational Needs And ERP Functionality. Requirements Engineering **5** (2000) 180–193
24. Puhlmann, F., Schnieders, A., Weiland, J., Weske, M.: Variability Mechanisms for Process Models. PESOA-Report TR 17/2005, DaimlerChrysler Research and Technology and Hasso-Plattner-Institut, Ulm and Potsdam, Germany (2005)
25. Reinhartz-Berger, I., Soffer, P., Sturm, A.: A Domain Engineering Approach to Specifying and Applying Reference Models. In Desel, J., Frank, U., eds.: Enterprise Modelling and Information Systems Architectures. Volume P-75 of Lecture Notes in Informatics. German Informatics Society, Klagenfurt, Austria (2005) 50–63
26. Haugen, Ø., Møller-Pedersen, B., Oldevik, J., Solberg, A.: An MDA-based Framework for Model-driven Product Derivation. In Hamza, M.H., ed.: Software Engineering and Applications, Cambridge, MA, ACTA Press (2004) 709–714
27. Recker, J., Rosemann, M., van der Aalst, W.: On the User Perception of Configurable Reference Process Models - Initial Insights. In: 16th Australasian Conference on Information Systems, Sydney, Australia, Australasian Chapter of the Association for Information Systems (2005)
28. Rosemann, M., Shanks, G.: Extension and Configuration of Reference Models for Enterprise Resource Planning Systems. In Finnie, G., Cecez-Kecmanovic, D., Lo, B., eds.: Proceedings of the 12th Australasian Conference on Information Systems. Southern Cross University, Coffs Harbour, Australia (2001) 537–546

Configuration Management in a Method Engineering Context

Motoshi Saeki

Dept. of Computer Science, Tokyo Institute of Technology,
Ookayama 2-12-1, Meguro-ku, Tokyo 152, Japan
Tel.: +81-3-5734-2192; Fax: +81-3-5734-2917
`saeki@se.cs.titech.ac.jp`

Abstract. Method Engineering is the discipline for exploring techniques to build project-specific methods for information system development and Computer Aided Method Engineering (CAME) is a kind of computerized tool for supporting the processes to build them. In such method engineering environments, version control and change management for both model descriptions and method descriptions should be seamlessly combined. In addition, when the method being used is changed during a project, we should check whether the current version of a model is still consistent with the newer version of the adopted method. This paper proposes a technique to solve the issues on version control and change management in method engineering processes.

1 Introduction

Development methods for information systems (methods hereafter) and their supporting tools are one of the most significant key factors to success in development projects. To enhance the effect of methods used in a development project, we need to adapt them or build new ones so that they can fit the project. Method Engineering is the discipline for exploring techniques to build project-specific methods for information system development, called situational methods. Computer Aided Method Engineering (CAME) is a kind of computerized tools for supporting the processes to build them [6].

Although we can have a powerful situational method, another difficulty originating from frequent changes of a product still remains. A product is frequently changed due to various reasons, e.g. customer's requirements change, even during its development. Developers should have various versions of a product and manage them in their project. In this situation, the techniques for version control and change management, i.e. for configuration management, are significant to support their tasks by using computerized tools. In [9], we have developed a version control system for model descriptions that are represented in diagrammatic form such as UML diagrams.

In method engineering environments, as well as changes of a model description, the description of the adopted methods may be changed. Therefore the support for version control and change management of methods themselves is necessary. In [10], the changes of methods were classified into a set of patterns, but it did not mention any support for the version control of methods themselves.

In change management, there exist the dependencies among the components of an artifact, and a change of a component may be propagated to other components dependent on it, in order to keep consistency. This kind of change management should be done 1) on model descriptions (product hereafter), 2) on method descriptions (methods or method fragments hereafter) and 3) on both of them. The third case is as follows; when the adopted method is changed, the change is propagated to the model description that was developed with the older version of the method. Model management systems such as Coral [3] and UML repository systems [7, 11] are only for meta models and only for products respectively. They do not consider the support for version control and change management sufficiently from method engineering context, i.e. from both side of products and methods.

To solve above issues, this paper discusses a technique to implement a configuration management mechanism in our CAME tool combined with Version Control System for software diagrams, both of which have been developed before independently [9, 12]. We have two key techniques; the first one is a three-dimensional model to conceptualize the difference between product and method version control [13]. The second is "operation based approach", where change operations that were performed on an artifact[1] are recorded and applied in order to recover a current version of the artifact. The rest of the paper is organized as follows. Our CAME tool and Version Control System is introductorily summarized in the next section. In addition, we illustrate the details of the issues on version control and change management in method engineering context. In section 3, by using a simple example, we discuss the three-dimensional model for conceptualizing version control, it is very useful for getting the solutions to the issues mentioned above. Section 4 discusses how to achieve the change management to maintain consistency in artifacts and clarifies how our technique can solve the issues mentioned in section 2.

2   CAME Tool and Version Control System

2.1   CAME Tool

Our CAME tool is based on a reuse technique similar to the other existing CAME tools such as Decamerone [6], Mentor [14] and MetaEdit+ [8]. Reuse technique is characterized by using reusable method portions, called method fragments or method chunks, which can be extracted from several existing methods. Method fragments are stored in a specific database called method base, and a special engineer, called method, engineer obtains suitable fragments from the method base and assembles them into a new project-specific method. The method engineer, for building a project-specific method, uses a method editor to manipulate

---

[1] We use the term "artifact" for products and methods.

method fragments and assemble them into a new method. The method editor is a kind of diagram editor which allows the method engineer to easily edit method fragments. The method description is called meta model, and we use a Class Diagram to describe it. Our CAME tool generates from a meta model, 1) a diagram editor for supporting inputting and editing products, e.g. a Class Diagram editor, and 2) the schema of a repository to which the generated editors store the developed products. Software engineers may then develop a model of an information system following the project-specific method, by using the generated editors. An example of a meta model of simplified version of Class Diagram is shown in Figure 1. As shown in the figure, the method fragment "ClassDiagram" has the concepts "Class", "Operation" and "Attribute" and all of them are defined as classes on a meta model. These concepts (called method concepts) have associations (called method associations) representing logical relationships among them. For instance, the concept "Class" has "Feature" (a super class of Attribute and Operation), so the association between "Class" and "Attribute" denotes a *has* relationship. We simply call both method concepts and method associations method elements.

In addition, we should consider constraints on the products. Suppose that we define the method "ClassDiagram" as shown in Figure 1. In any class diagram (any instance of "ClassDiagram"), we cannot have different classes having the same name. In order to keep consistency of products, we specify this constraint on the meta model, by using OCL (Object Constraint Language). The OCL expression in the right bottom window "CAMEPackage" of Figure 1 represents the constraint "different names must be attached to different classes".

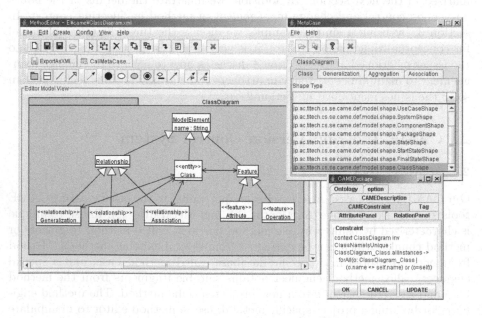

Fig. 1. An Example of Method Fragments

A generated diagram editor deals with a product conceptually as a graph consisting of nodes and edges. Thus we should provide information using which the method concepts in a meta model can be represented with nodes or edges of the graph. The method engineer provides two types of this information; one is the correspondence of method concepts to the elements of the graph, i.e. nodes, edges and text within the nodes or on the edges, and another is notational information of the nodes and edges. Suppose that she or he tries to generate a class diagram editor from "ClassDiagram". The concept Class in the "ClassDiagram" conceptually corresponds to nodes in a graph, while Generalization, Aggregation and Association correspond to edges. She or he provides this information as stereotypes attached to the method concepts in our CAME tool. The right top window "MetaCase" in Figure 1 includes the information for the generator. The readers can find the stereotypes ≪entity≫ and ≪relationship≫" attached to the classes in the meta model of Figure 1. For example, the classes Generalization, Aggregation and Association in the figure have the stereotype ≪relationship≫. The stereotype ≪entity≫ corresponds to a node and ≪relationship≫ corresponds to an edge. In our example of the figure, an occurrence of Class in a class diagram corresponds to a node from the viewpoint of the graph, while an occurrence of Generalization, Aggregation or Association between Classes corresponds to an edge. Note that a generated editor automatically includes commands for creating and deleting the method concepts corresponding to the nodes or the edges.

In addition, the method engineer should specify which figures, e.g. rectangle, circle, oval, dashed arrow etc. are to be used for expressing method elements on the editor screen. Basic figures such as ones used in UML diagrams are built-in and their drawing programs are embedded as Java classes into the generator. In the example in Figure 1, the method engineer tries to use a rectangle (ClassShape) as a figure for Class. Our generator produces a diagram editor by embedding the above information and Java classes into a diagram editor framework.

2.2 Scenario Example

In this sub section, we have the following simple scenario of a development as an example, which will be used throughout this paper. It is very useful to clarify the issues of version control and change management in a method engineering context.

A method engineer constructs a new method by assembling Class Diagram (CI#1) and Sequence Diagram (CI#2) of UML by adding a method association "instance_of" as shown in Figure 2. Each meta model can be considered as a unit of configuration management, i.e. configuration item of method level. Following this new method, a software engineer constructs a class diagram of the system to be developed, and then develops the sequence diagrams, each of which defines a scenario of the interactions among objects belonging to the classes appearing in the class diagram. Figure 3 illustrates a part of Lift Control System developed following this method. Each diagram is a configuration item of product level.

The engineer completes the diagram shown in the left part of Figure 3, and commits it to the repository as version 0. After that, the engineer adds the

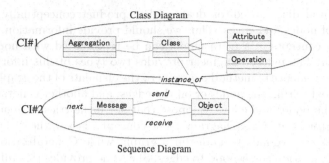

Fig. 2. Assembling Method Fragments

object "Door" to the sequence diagram as shown in the right part of Figure 3, and commits it as version 1. When the engineer adds an object to a sequence diagram, its class should exist in the class diagram in method M0. In this example, since "Door" class does not appear in version 0 of the class diagram, the engineer adds it manually for version 1, as shown in Figure 3. The supporting tool hopefully guides the engineer for this kind of change propagation, and change propagations depend on methods and method assembly.

We continue the example. See Figure 4. The engineer finds that Lift Control System has real-time property, and extends the current method so that the engineer can model timing constraints in sequence diagrams. The engineer modifies the meta model of the Sequence Diagram (M0 : version 0 of the method) by adding the method concept "Timing Constraint", and gets a new version 1 (M1). Although we need the version control of meta models, it is the same as the version control of products, because our meta model is represented with Class Diagram as mentioned in section 2.1. The version control of meta models is called "method version control" to distinguish it from usual version control of products (called "product version control"). Now, the engineer continues her or his activities following the new method M1. Since this change to M1 was adding a new method concept only, it has not impacted the current version of the product, version 1. We continue our example further. As shown in the top part of Figure 4, the engineer adds a timing constraint "b-a< 2 min." (the lift should arrive within 2 minutes after pushing the request button). Suppose that the engineer returns back to the older method M0 after that. Since M0 does not include "Timing Constraint", the existence of "b-a<2min." in the current product causes inconsistency. Thus whenever a current method is changed, we need to check if the new version of the method is consistent with the current version of the product that was made following the older method.

Suppose another change on the method M0 in Figure 2 is applied. What is going to happen in case the engineer deletes the method association *"instance_of"* and tries to commit it as a new version of the method? As a result, the engineer will get the two isolated methods each of which is the same as the already existing method, i.e. Class Diagram and Sequence Diagram, and this result is not meaningful. We should avoid constructing such meaningless versions of the method, and by applying method assembly rules we can check if the resulting method is meaningless or not [5].

To summarize the above discussions, we can categorize our issues on change management into three; 1) for products, 2) for method fragments and 3) for both. How to solve these three issues will be discussed in section 4.

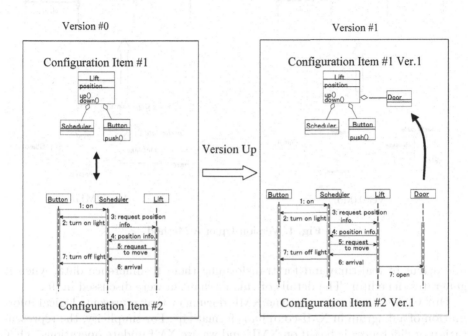

Fig. 3. Lift Control System

2.3 Version Control System

In our version control system, we adopt a technique to store differences between two versions in a repository like CVS [1] and Subversion [2], etc. so that we can recover the older versions that were previously produced. The state of the artifact at a certain time is considered as a baseline, and the version control system stores to the repository the difference between this baseline and each version. To extract a difference between two adjacent versions efficiently, we focus on the developer's activities of editing a product by using an editor. In other words, we generate an element of the difference from an execution of an editor operation such as "create" and "delete" a component. The sequence of such editing operations that developer is performing is captured in real-time during her or his editing activity using the editor. The acquired operation sequence can be considered as the difference between versions, and is stored in the repository. Our CAME tool, which automatically generates a diagram editor from the meta model description, should automatically embed the functions for acquiring performed editing

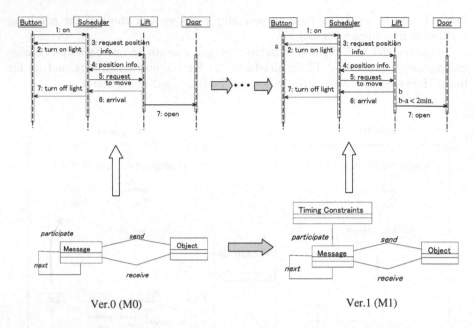

Ver.0 (M0)   Ver.1 (M1)

Fig. 4. Version Up of A Method

operations in real-time and for transforming them to difference data, when it generates the editor. The details of this mechanism were discussed in [9].

Our CAME tool can export the XML document that represents logical information of a diagram in XMI-compliant format [4][2]. For simplicity, the representation of differences is based on XMI, and we use XMI.update operations. They are used for informing about the differences of XMI-compliant documents when the documents are exchanged. We have three operations; XMI.add for adding a component to the older document, XMI.delete for deleting an existing component, and XMI.replace for replacing an existing component element with a new one. Figure 5 illustrates how to represent differences with XMI. A software engineer adds a "Door" class and then an aggregation from "Lift" to it. These change operations performed in the editor are transformed into two XMI.add occurrences and the occurrences are stored as a difference from Version 0 to Version 1. To check-out Version 1 from Version 0, our version control system applies the XMI.add occurrences successively to the XMI document of Version 0.

Our version control system supports version branching and merging branched versions. Suppose that our software engineer produces a new version Ver. 2 by adding a subclass of "Door" to Ver.1 in Figure 3, at the same time the engineer also creates a branched version Ver.1.1 by deleting the class "Door" from Ver.1. When he tries to merge Ver. 2 to Ver. 1.1, a conflict occurs. Since Ver. 1.1 does not have "Door" class any longer, adding automatically the subclass of

---

[2] For comprehensiveness, the XML documents in this paper are made simpler than the real XMI-compliant format.

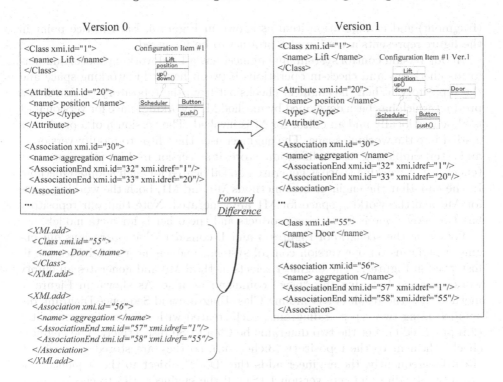

Fig. 5. Representing with XML

"Door" by applying the difference from Ver.1 to Ver. 2, is impossible. In this case, our system asks the engineer to take the alternative of adding "Door" by hand to continue this merge operation, or cancel it. To detect this conflict, each recorded change operation has the pre condition that should be checked before applying it. In XMI.delete, its pre condition is that the object to be deleted should exist in the product. In the above example, the operation "<XMI.add> <Association xmi.id =...> <name> Generalization </name>...</XMI.add>" (adding a Generalization from Door class to a subclass) requires a source object and a destination of the association as a pre condition, i.e. "Door" is required to execute this operation. Pre conditions are automatically generated and attached to change operations to be stored as a difference. Pre conditions maintain consistency not only for merging branched version but also for change propagation, as will be mentioned later in sections 4.2 and 4.3.

3   Conceptual Model for Version Control

In this section, we show a three-dimensional model to conceptualize our version control technique [13] and how to use it. We have "products" and "method fragments" as targets of version control, and each target consists of configuration items. Thus, we can consider version space to have three axes; product, method (fragment) and configuration item as shown in Figure 6. Each lattice point in the figure represents a version of a product to be managed.

In our version control system, an engineer has a local working space, and performs check-out and check-in operations between her or his working space and the repository. When the engineer checks out from the repository version n of a product which has been developed by method M, a working space for version n+1 is allocated locally and an editor for M is invoked. The version n of a product is loaded into the working space. The engineer uses the editor to modify version n, and after completing the modification, stores it as version n+1 into the repository (check-in). A working space is generated and allocated for each adopted method. In the case that the engineer uses methods M0 and M1, both the working space for M0 and the working space for M1 are generated. Note that our repository has two levels: one is for storing products and the other is for meta models.

Following the scenario of Figures 3 and 4, consider what operations our engineer performs on our version control system. The engineer's activities are illustrated in Figure 7. The engineer selects method M0 and generates an empty working space by using the "new" command at first. As shown in Figure 3, method M is the result of assembling Class Diagram and Sequence Diagram, developed using two types of diagrams, each created with its own diagram editor (2:input & edit). Let the two diagrams be C0 and S0 respectively. The engineer checks them in to the repository (3:check-in), so they are stored as version 0 (P0). Consequently, the engineer adds the "Door" object to the sequence diagram S0 (4: edit) and gets version 1 (S1). If the engineer tries to check it in to the repository, she or he fails because the current P0 is not satisfied with the constraint "for each object in the sequence diagram, its class must be included in the class diagram". To get consistency, the engineer adds the Door class to the class diagram C0 and successfully checks it in (5: check-in). The new product comes in the repository as version 1 (P1).

Furthermore, the engineer tries to extend the method M0 to M1 as shown in Figure 4, and checks out M0 from the meta-level part of the repository (6: check-out). The engineer can have a working space for constructing M1, and M0 is loaded in to the space. By using a method editor, as shown in Figure 4, the engineer adds the method concept "Timing Constraint" to M0 (7:edit) and then checks it in as version 1 (M1) to the repository (8:check in). To continue the task by using the new version M1, he or she creates an empty working space for P2 on M1 (9: new), and checks out P1 to this space (10: check-out). After that, the engineer adds a timing constraint "b-a< 2 min." (11: edit) and checks in the resulting product (12: check-in). This product is registered into the repository as version 2 (P2).

Next, suppose that for some reason, the engineer wants to return the used method back to the older version M0. The engineer tries to import M0 into the current working space (13: import). When importing M0, the system checks consistency of the current product with M0 and the import operation succeeds if the consistency check is passed. In our example, since the difference between M0 and M1 includes <XMI.delete> ... "Timing Constraint" ... </XMI.delete> and the current product has its instance "b-a<2 min.", the engineer is notified of the

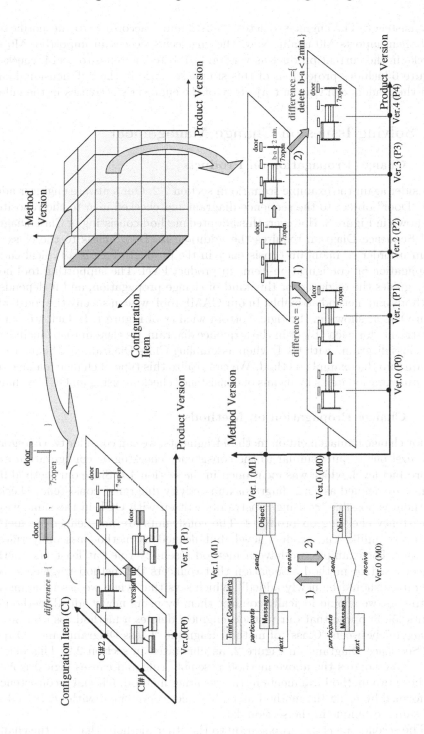

Fig. 6. Three Dimensional Model

inconsistency. The engineer deletes "b-a<2 min." according to the notification and then imports M0 again. Now, the engineer succeeds in importing M0 and checks in the current product as version 3 (P3) to the repository (14: check-in). Figure 6 includes projections of this simple scenario in the 3 dimensional cube, and the readers can trace a trajectory of the engineer's activities in the cube.

4   Solving Issues on Change Management

4.1   Change Propagation on Products

Consider again the example scenario in section 2.2. Our software engineer added the "Door" object to the sequence diagram and checked it in to the repository, as shown in Figure 3. However, this adopted method consisting of Class Diagram and Sequence Diagram requires the addition of "Door" class to the class diagram in order to maintain consistency in the product. This is a typical change propagation on configuration items in product level. The supporting tool hopefully guides the engineer for this kind of change propagation, and it depends on methods and method assembly. In our CAME tool, we can specify the constraints with OCL as shown in the right bottom window of Figure 1. In fact, we put the constraint "for each object in the sequence diagram, its class must be included in the class diagram" with OCL when assembling Class Diagram and Sequence Diagram into the example method. We can realize this type of change management on configuration items by means of consistency checking using an OCL evaluator.

4.2   Change Propagation on Methods

As for change management on method fragments, we can consider two categories. The first one is quite similar to the consistency checking on configuration items of product level, which was mentioned in the section 4.1. Since our method fragments are defined as class diagrams and activity diagrams, consistency checking on them is possible by using constraints written with OCL in the same way as consistency checking on products. The constraints are not defined by method engineers, unlike the product level, but defined as method assembly rules in advance. For example, we have a method assembly rule "at least one method concept and/or method association that connects the method fragments to be assembled should be newly added", which says that when we assemble method fragments, we should logically connect them by using newly added method elements [5]. Suppose that our method engineer deletes a method association "instance_of" between "Class" of method fragment "Class Diagram" and "Object" of "Sequence Diagram" in Figure 2, as illustrated in section 2.2. This deletion operation violates the above method assembly rule and causes logical isolation of these two method fragments in the resulting method. Checking consistency is performed by using the method assembly rules represented with OCL, and it is the same technique in the section 4.1.

The second one is the propagation to the other methods that use the changed method fragments. See Figure 8 and suppose that we have two methods M#1

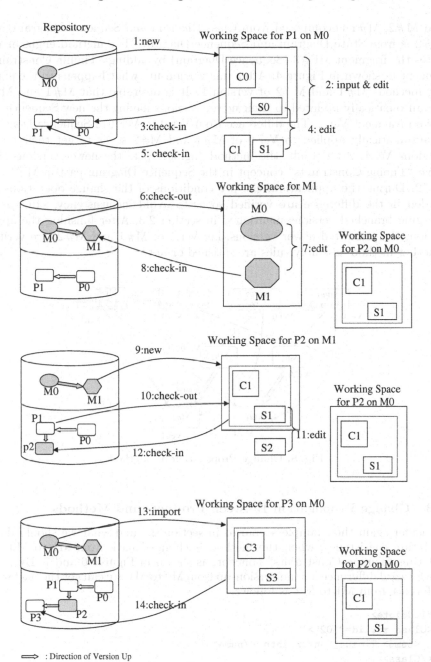

Fig. 7. Version Control System

and M#2; M#1 is composed from Class Diagram and Sequence Diagram, and M#2 is from State Diagram and Sequence Diagram. The method engineer updates the fragment MF#3 (Sequence Diagram) by adding "Timing Constraint" concept as shown in Figure 4. After this version-up, what happens to the existing methods M#1 and M#2 of version 1? It is desirable that M#1 and M#2 are automatically updated to their newer versions having the new Sequence Diagram fragment Ver.1. The difference from Ver.0 to Ver.1 of Sequence Diagram is automatically applied to Ver.0 of M#1 and M#2 so as to get their newer versions Ver.1. As a result, the method engineer gets the newer versions that have "Timing Constraints" concept in the Sequence Diagram part in M#1 and M#2. During the application, the pre conditions of the change operations included in the difference are verified so as to avoid inconsistency, same as in merging branched versions mentioned in section 2.3. After finishing the application, the generated newer versions, i.e. Ver.1 of M#1 and M#2, are verified whether method assembly rules are satisfied or not.

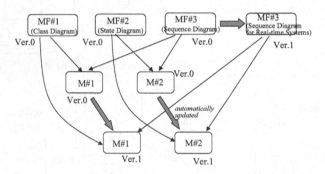

Fig. 8. Change Propagation on Methods

4.3 Change Propagation Between Products and Methods

Consider again the example scenarios in section 2.3 and what we should do to maintain consistency, when the method is changed back from M1 to M0, i.e. deleting "Timing Constraints" concept, as shown in Figures 6 and 7. By using the forward difference for the version-up from M0 to M1, we can get the backward difference from M1 to M0 as follows.

```
<XMI.delete>
  <Class xmi.id="102">
    <name> Timing_Constraints </name>
  </Class>
</XMI.delete>
<XMI.delete>
  <Association xmi.id="103">
    <name> aggregation </name>
    ...
</XMI.delete>
```

It is easy to automatically obtain the above difference, by replacing the occurrences of "add" with "delete" and vice versa in the recorded difference from M0 to M1. In the case that the method engineer deletes a method concept or association from a method fragment and commits it as a new version, we get a difference including "XMI.delete". All that we should do for consistency check of the current method is to look for "XMI.delete" in the difference from the last version to the current one, and extract the method elements included in XMI.delete. And then, in a product we detect the instances whose types are the extracted method elements. In our example, we extract the method element "Timing Constraints" appearing in the above XMI.delete fragment, and then look for those instances, e.g. "b-a<2 min." of the type "Timing Constraints" in the sequence diagram. If the components detected are in the current version of the product, our tool informs the engineer that inconsistency has occurred on account of changing the method. The technique for detecting this kind of inconsistency focuses on the occurrences of XMI.delete in the difference of a method change.

5   Conclusion and Future Work

This paper discussed the problems of configuration management, especially version control and change management in method engineering environments, and proposed an integrated technique to solve them. In particular, in section 4, we clarified various types of change propagations in the method engineering context, and showed that we could solve their issues by our proposed technique.

Although we have implemented basic commands mentioned in section 4 so that our CAME can generate diagram editors having these commands, we need more functions, in particular browsing the repository, displaying the status of products (consistent or not, the newest version or not, etc.), and retrieving a specific version not only by version number but also other, more practical means e.g. tags. And more case studies are necessary to assess our technique and the CAME tool together with version control functions. The support for cooperative tasks by a team is also considered as future work.

Acknowledgements

The author would like to thank Rodion Moiseeiv for his valuable comments to the earlier version of this paper.

References

1. Concurrent Versions System. http://www.cvshome.org/.
2. Subversion. http://subversion.tigiris.org/.
3. The Coral Metamodeling Toolkit. http://mde.abo.fi/tools/Coral/.
4. XML Metadata Interchange. http://www.omg.org/.

5. S. Brinkkemper, M. Saeki, and F. Harmsen. Meta-Modelling Based Assembly Techniques for Situational Method Engineering. *Information Systems*, 24(3): 209–228, 1999.

6. F. Harmsen. *Situational Method Engineering*. Moret Ernst & Young Management Consultants, 1997.

7. R. Keller, J.-F. Bedard, and G Saint-Denis. Design and Implementation of a UML-Based Design Repository. In *Lecture Notes in Computer Science (CAiSE2001)*, volume 2068, pages 448–464, 2001.

8. S. Kelly, K. Lyytinen, and M. Rossi. MetaEdit+ : A Fully Configurable Multi-User and Multi-Tool CASE and CAME Environment. In *Lecture Notes in Computer Science (CAiSE'96)*, volume 1080, pages 1–21, 1996.

9. T. Oda and M. Saeki. Generative Technique of Version Control Systems for Software Diagrams. In *Proc. of the 21st IEEE Conference on Software Maintenance (ICSM'05)*, pages 515–524, 2005.

10. J. Ralyte, C. Rolland, and R. Deneckere. Towards a Meta-tool for Change-Centric Method Engineering: A Typology of Generic Operators. In *Lecture Notes in Computer Science (Proc. of CAiSE'2004)*, pages 202–218, 2004.

11. N. Ritter and H.-P. Steiert. Enforcing Modeling Guidelines in an ORDBMS-based UML-Repository. In *Proc. of International Resource Management Association Conference (IRMA2000)*, pages 269–273, 2000.

12. M. Saeki. Toward Automated Method Engineering: Supporting Method Assembly in CAME. In *Engineering Methods to Support Information Systems Evolution (EMSISE'03 in OOIS'03)*. http://cui.unige.ch/db-research/EMSISE03/, 2003.

13. M. Saeki and T. Oda. A Conceptual Model of Version Control in Method Engineering Environment. In *Proc. of CAiSE Short Paper 2005*, pages 89–94, 2005.

14. S. Si-Said, Rolland C., and G. Grosz. MENTOR : A Computer Aided Requirements Engineering Environment. In *Lecture Notes in Comupter Science (CAiSE'96)*, volume 1080, pages 22–43, 1996.

Why Software Engineers Do Not Keep to the Principle of Separating Business Logic from Display: A Method Rationale Analysis*

Malin Häggmark and Pär J. Ågerfalk

Dept of Computer Science and Information Systems, University of Limerick,
Limerick Ireland; and Dept of Informatics (ESI), Örebro University,
SE-701 82 Örebro, Sweden
malin.haggmark@ul.ie, par.agerfalk@ul.ie

Abstract. This paper presents an investigation into why software engineers do not keep to the principle of separating business logic from display. The concept of method rationale is used to establish what is supposed to be achieved by following the principle. The resulting model is then contrasted with results from in-depth interviews with practicing engineers about what they want to achieve. The difference between what the principle advocates and what engineers consider beneficial holds the answer to why the principle of separating business logic from display is not maintained. The results suggest that many espoused benefits of the principle do not appeal to engineers in practice and the principle is tailored to make it more useful in particular contexts. Tailoring the principle also brought about other benefits, not explicated by the principle, thus reinforcing the idea that method tailoring is crucial to the successful enactment of information systems engineering methods.

1 Introduction

The mantra of most experienced software engineers is the same: *thou shalt separate business logic from display* [19]. Theory maintains that by separating business logic from display, systems will be easier to scale, extend, update and maintain. Also, engineers with different skill sets can work on different parts of a system independently, thus optimizing tasks for each competence. This way of structuring systems, typically with business logic and display structured in different tiers, also facilitates new types of clients to be added with little extra effort [9, 14, 16, 19, 23].

The principle of separating business logic from display can be found in a wide range of information systems engineering (ISE) methods. In general, methods are used in ISE as a means of expressing and communicating knowledge about good (effective and efficient) ISE practice. This way methods encapsulate knowledge of good engineering practice, and by utilizing this, engineers can be more effective, efficient and confident in their work [2]. Basically, a method is a proposed pattern of

---

* This work has been financially supported by the Science Foundation Ireland Principal Investigator projects B4-STEP and Lero, and the EU FP6 Project COSPA.

E. Dubois and K. Pohl (Eds.): CAiSE 2006, LNCS 4001, pp. 399–413, 2006.
© Springer-Verlag Berlin Heidelberg 2006

activities, expressed as a set of prescriptions for action – a.k.a. method prescriptions [3]. When the principle of separating business logic from display is part of an ISE method, keeping to this principle involves following a set of such prescriptions, i.e. following a method. Of course, this principle alone does not provide sufficient support for successful ISE. The point is rather that we can choose to view it as a method fragment [4] – as a set of method prescriptions – in order to draw on previous research on method use in ISE practice. Specifically, this research suggests that if engineers are to follow a method, the method must first and foremost be useful [22], that is, enable them to be more productive and achieve higher levels of performance in their job. For someone to regard a method as useful the knowledge must be possible to rationalize, i.e. the person needs to be able to make sense of it and incorporate it into their own view of the world [2]. It has been stressed that departure from methods is conscious and inevitable in the real world, and that rigorous use of a method does not pay back [6, 25]. Engineers tailor methods to suit their needs in particular situations with awareness of the benefits and drawbacks this causes [6].

By entangling business logic with display the development time may be shortened, but may disadvantageously result in a harder and more tedious maintenance process. This suggests that engineers emphasize short-term benefits [19]. Research has shown that students have difficulties learning how to structure applications [5], suggesting that engineers do not keep to the principle because they have not fully understood how to use it. A possible solution would be to enforce the principle of separation in, for example, the template engine; leaving no possibility to entangle business logic with display [19]. It can be questioned whether enforcement is appropriate, and hence a more thorough investigation of *why* engineers do not keep to the principle is necessary.

To summarize: A method (or any of its parts) has to be useful for engineers to keep to it [22]. Furthermore, engineers must be given the freedom to tailor the method to make it useful in their particular situation [6, 25]. Engineers may not tailor methods in a way that is beneficial for the software produced, but rather to ease and speed up the process of software development, thus, deteriorating the quality of the product (the software) in favour of the personal process goals [19]. Their rationale is rarely explained; they make design decisions with no clear statement of why they do things the way they do [18]. The principle of separating business logic from display does not seem to be an exception from the rule that methods need to be tailored. The principle is espoused as ideal in theory, but practice seems to be a different story altogether [19]. This paper is an empirical enquiry into why engineers do not keep to the principle of separating business logic from display. Answering this question also increases our understanding of the more fundamental question of how and why engineers choose to tailor ISE methods in general.

The contribution of this paper is thus threefold. First, the essence of the principle of separating business logic from display is captured and expressed as a set of method prescriptions. Second, why software engineers do not keep to this principle is investigated. Finally, the usefulness of method rationale as an analytic tool to understand method tailoring is explored.

The paper proceeds as follows. Section 2 covers rationality of methods, and how this can be used to analyse methods. It sets the foundation for the research method, outlined in Section 3. The result of the investigation is presented and analysed in Section 4, preceded by conclusions in Section 5.

2 Methods and Their Rationale

A method is always grounded in a way of thinking [7, 10, 12], which constitutes the foundation for the reasons and arguments behind it. These reasons and arguments can be referred to as *method rationale* [1, 2, 24]. Using method rationale to understand the enactment of ISE methods can be facilitated by discussing it in terms of public and private rationality [26].

Public rationality is about creating an inter-subjective understanding (about the reasons and arguments) of the method. This is a sort of knowledge that is shared by several people as part of their inter-subjective beliefs. Public rationality can be externalized and communicated through written method descriptions (e.g. a method handbook). Public rationality is expressed in an *ideal typical method* [2] or *method-in-concept* [15]. Private rationality, on the other hand, is personal and cannot be externalized in every respect. Private rationality can be found in a person's 'skills and professional ethical and aesthetic judgements' [26]. Private rationality is expressed in a *method-in-action* [2, 15]. In an ideal situation, public and private rationality fully overlap [13]. If so, the method prescription can be carried out to a tee since the engineer fully understands and agrees with everything suggested by the method. This overlap, referred to as *rationality resonance* [26], is depicted in Fig. 1.

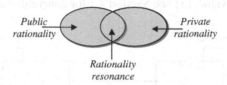

Fig. 1. Rationality resonance [13]

The non-overlap gives rise to a *method usage tension* [15] – a tension between what ought to be done (according to the method creator) and what is actually done. Analysing rationality resonance requires that both private and public rationality are made as explicit as possible to enable comparison [13]. Fig. 2 provides a visual overview of method rationale by showing how its constituent concepts relate.

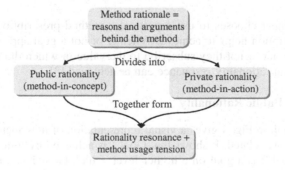

Fig. 2. The constituents of method rationale

2.1 Public Rationality Analysis Through Goals and Values

A methods' public rationality can be analysed with respect to the goals and values it implements. The reasons behind a method prescription can be understood in terms of the goals the prescription is supposed to realize. This way, each method prescription can be related to one or more goals, even though these are not always well articulated in the method descriptions. A goal can be defined as a result, towards which behaviour is consciously or unconsciously directed [3].

Ultimately, public rationality lies in the heads of the people who have developed a method [24]. Accordingly, goals are manifestations of the method creator's value base – all goals are anchored in values. A value can be understood as an ethical judgement like an expression of feeling and attitude and can therefore not be judged as true or false. Goals can be related to each other in goal hierarchies; for example, when a goal is as a means to achieve another (higher) goal. Similarly, values can be anchored in other values. These two properties of method rationale are referred to as *goal achievement* and *value anchoring*, respectively. In addition to goal achievement, there is a possibility that goals contradict rather than complement each other – hence there is an additional *goal contradiction* relation defined over the set of goals. Similarly there is a *value contradiction* relation defined over the set of values. Fig. 3 depicts how every method prescription is related to at least one goal, and each goal is related to at least one value. [3] See Section 4.1 for concrete examples.

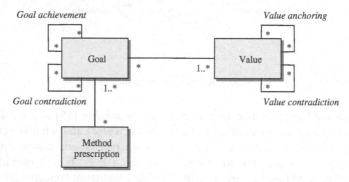

Fig. 3. Method rationale as constituted by goals, values and their relationships [3]

How an engineer chooses to use a particular method prescription depends on the goals this prescription helps to achieve. Whether or not a goal appeals to an engineer depends on whether or not they subscribe to the value in which the goal is anchored; i.e. whether or not rationality resonance can be achieved [3].

2.2 Modelling Public Rationality

The directed graph in Fig. 4 gives a visual representation of how method prescriptions, goals and value are related. It shows that Goal 1 is achieved by following the Method Prescription. Goal 2 is a goal on a higher level, which Goal 1 is a means to achieve [11]. Goal 1 is anchored in Value 1 and Value 2, which in turn are anchored in Value 3 and Value 4. Goal 2 is anchored in Value 5.

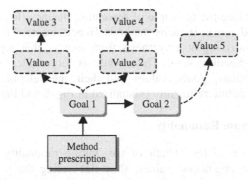

Fig. 4. Visual representation of public rationality through goals and values

3 Research Method

A qualitative research approach with structured interviews [20] was used in this research. A visual presentation of the adopted research approach is shown in Fig. 5 and explored in the remainder of this section.

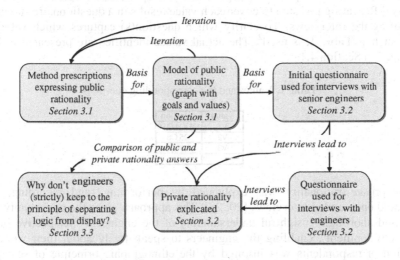

Fig. 5. Research design

3.1 Capturing Public Rationality

As described above, expressed method prescriptions are the foundation for the ideal typical method-in-concept and as such are expressions of public rationality. By analysing these, the goals[1] and values that underpin them can be explicated. The analysis results in a graph, such as the one in Fig. 4. The method-in-concept is in our

---

[1] These are the goals of the method creator(s), which they aim to communicate through method prescriptions [2].

case rather generic since the principle of separating business logic from display does appear, as mentioned above, in many methods. Hence, we need to capture the essence of the principle by arriving at a synthesis from sources that represents frameworks widely used (see Section 4.1). This synthesis constitutes the foundation for elaborating prescriptions, goals, values and their interrelationships, arriving at a model depicting the public rationality (visualized in Fig. 6 and Fig. 7).

3.2 Capturing Private Rationality

The next step is then to test which of the 'public rationality values' that are in accordance with the engineers' values, thus elaborating the private rationality by identifying how they use the method prescriptions. Asking questions that capture those values illuminate the engineers' value base. As explained above, this value base is the foundation for their goals, so focusing the values during interviews will implicitly extend to the goals.

The goal-value-model is the input for designing a questionnaire used in the interviews. One or several questions capture each value in the model. For example, the value 'It is easier to locate and determine problems/bugs in applications composed of well demarcated parts', is captured by the question: 'Do you consider it easier or harder to track down problems/bugs when the application separates logic from display?' Repeating this step to cover each value results in a questionnaire suitable for structuring the interviews. To clarify which question(s) captures which value(s), a table, such as Table 1, is used[2]. The actual values identified are presented in Fig. 6 and Fig. 7 in Section 4.1.

Table 1. Values and the corresponding questions

Value	Question
V1	Q1-Q4 Q10
V2	Q5 Q8
V3	Q3-Q6
...	...

The private rationality was explicated by performing (and recording) semi-structured open-ended interviews [20, 28]. This approach gives the opportunity to get a focused, thorough, insightful understanding of the engineers' perspective on tier-based development[3], enabling the engineers to speak freely about their work. The selection of respondents was inspired by the ethnographic principle of selecting a representative individual for initial enquiry who then suggests further respondents. The number of respondents is then increased until saturation is achieved – that is, until the marginal utility of further interviews are deemed insignificant. Such an approach avoids researcher bias and allows for more objective results. Initially a group interview was carried out with two highly experienced senior engineers/project managers. The questionnaire was here used as a guide, but the aim of this interview was primarily to find weaknesses and improve it for further interviews. This interview

---

[2] For the complete questionnaire and value-question-table used in this research see http://www.csis.ul.ie/staff/paragerfalk/CAiSE2006-Q-V.pdf

[3] Separating business logic from is typically implemented by structuring the software into tiers.

resulted in a questionnaire with more sub-questions and less ambiguity. The improved questionnaire was then used to interview a total of five engineers individually. All respondents were notified of the study in advance, but did not get the questions beforehand. The interviews lasted for 30–50 minutes each.

3.3 Analysing Rationality Resonance

The differences in values (i.e. the method creators' values versus the engineers' values) lead to an understanding of why these engineers do not keep to the principle, thus revealing information about the *method usage tension* in terms of *rationality resonance*. Comparing each 'public rationality value' from the model with the 'private rationality values' from the interviews shows which values differ, thus answering the question why engineers do not follow the principle of separating business logic from display.

3.4 Organizational Context for the Interviews

The interviews took place in the IT department of Statistics Sweden – the Swedish public authority responsible for all official statistics. The IT department provides the organization with applications for gathering and processing data. Typically, data is gathered via web-based clients, which is later processed in windows-based clients.

The organization has previously mainly developed small systems. An application with 1–10 users (method statisticians) has been the most common application. Increasing demands for larger applications, and for integration of various systems, has led the organization to leave their regular Visual Basic environment in favour of the object oriented (OO) multi-tier based .NET-framework. The respondents were all experienced engineers with good knowledge of both environments.

4 Results and Analysis

This section gives a theoretical presentation of the principle of separating business logic from display, explicating the reasons behind the method prescriptions. The goals and values of the method prescriptions are then analysed and presented in Fig. 6 and Fig. 7, followed by the result from the interviews. All references to specific method prescriptions (P), goals (G) and values (V) in this section refer to those figures.

4.1 The Pros and Cons of Separating Business Logic from Display

A most straightforward way to develop a system could be to interweave the display with the business logic. This is probably not a bad idea if the application is relatively small, supports a single type of client, and is not expected to be considerably extended or updated. Dividing an application into different tiers will increase its complexity since extra classes will be required to handle the separation of display and business logic [14, 19, 23, 27].

The idea behind structuring a system in tiers is to achieve separation of concerns (G3, G6, G7, V3–V5, V7, V13); it is much more difficult to change the display if it depends on and is built into the business logic, and vice versa [8, 16, 21]. Separation of these areas of concern generally results in more flexible systems, with the ability to support multiple types of clients (G1–G2, V1–V2) [16, 17]. From this reasoning, the method prescriptions P1 and P2 become apparent.

Dividing the application into separate parts is a kind of encapsulation that enhances the manageability and maintenance [8, 9, 17]. Because each task is contained within its own object, it is easy to locate and determine where a problem exists (G3, V5) [14, 19]. Designers can develop/update the display without the need to contact programmers (V6–V10) [14, 19]. Thus, labour is divided according to different skill sets (G4), as recommended by P4. This encapsulation and breaking down of large tasks into smaller ones also provide for component reuse (G5, V2, V11–V13), either within the project, or in other similar projects, giving rise to P3.

In general, the benefits of tier-separation arise when [14, 19, 27]:

1. The application will support multiple types of clients. Since the display is separated, all that is needed is to create a new type of client, and let it access the business logic.
2. The business logic is likely to be updated or extended throughout its lifecycle.
3. The display is likely to be updated or extended throughout its lifecycle, for example with new 'skins', to improve the looks.
4. The development team develops/maintains more than one application; components can be reused between (but also within) projects.
5. The development team is composed of individuals with different skill sets.

Fig. 6 and Fig. 7 depict a graph representation of the goals and values of the principle of separating business logic from display and how they are related, i.e. it depicts an explicit model of the public rationality.

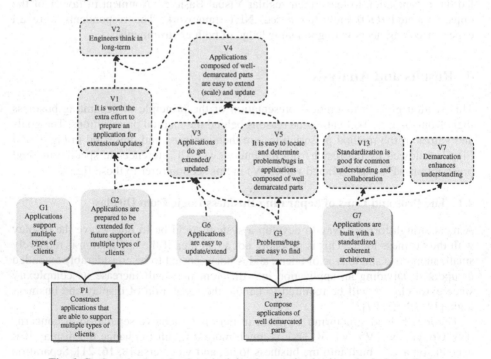

Fig. 6. Goals and values for the principle of separating business logic from display

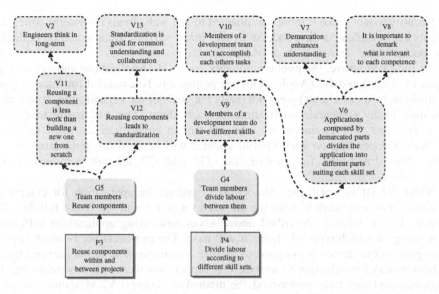

Fig. 7. Goals and values for the principle of separating business logic from display (continued)

4.2 Results from Interviews – Public Versus Private Rationality

This section is a synthesis of the result from the interviews. It is structured along the four method prescriptions (see above) focusing differences and similarities (i.e. method usage tension and rationality resonance) of what is found in the interviews (private rationality) and what the theory/method-in-concept tells us (public rationality).

P1: Construct Applications that are Able to Support Multiple Types of Clients
The organization uses two types of clients, windows clients and web clients in their applications. It is always known beforehand if the application shall have windows clients, web clients or both; a system has never been extended with a new type of client afterwards. It is more common to build two applications instead of one application with two types of clients. They do reuse components in the two different applications. Their aim is to integrate applications, thus having different clients access the same business logic, but so far this has not been achieved. The following goal contradiction came up during the interviews:

'Theoretically, it is possible just to add an extra client to an existing application. In reality though, you need to structure the application differently if it is a windows or web application. With a windows application you can do a lot more, for example, you can keep a big object with a lot of attributes in memory the whole time, there will always be enough memory for this. In a web application you need to be more careful with the resources (like memory), since it is on a server (perhaps a web hotel), and you don't know how many will be using it simultaneously. If you choose to adjust all windows applications for web use, these applications will be a bit "handicapped", and not as advanced as they could be. The windows application functionality will then not be fully utilized.'

Security issues make it more complicated to add web clients to systems, since web clients are not allowed direct access to the 'inner' servers. Data has to be replicated on special 'outer' servers in these occasions.

As indicated above, the public rationality goals G1 (Applications support multiple types of clients) and G2 (Applications are prepared to be extended for future support of multiple types of clients) were not really the goals of the organization. It was more common to do a separate application for each client. This had partly to do with security issues. The engineers also claimed that an application has to be structured differently depending on what kind of client it will be used for; optimizing for one type gives drawbacks for another, etc. G1 and G2 are not achieved in this organization.

Value V1 (It is worth the extra effort to prepare an application for extensions/ updates), does not seem to hold the answer to why G1 and G2 is not fulfilled. The answer lies in what is described above about structuring applications differently depending on which types of clients it will have. The engineers pretty much say that (this part of) the theory is too good to be true; it is impossible to put into practice. It is beyond this investigation to analyse this further, but there is a possibility that the engineers had not fully understood the method-in-concept. V2 (Engineers think in long-term) is a succession of V1, and is therefore not possible to evaluate in this context. However, it will be touched upon in the next section. The value V3 (Applications do get extended/updated (in this case with additional types of clients)), is not consistent with the values in the organization, since the systems were not to be extended with new types of clients.

P2: Compose Applications of Well Demarcated Parts
P2 can be viewed at different granularities: on the higher granularity, there are the different tiers, which constitute the well-demarcated parts. Within each tier (a lower granularity), there is code, preferable well-demarcated pieces of code, for example components. This is actually how the engineers structure their code; in predefined tiers, and in each tier, different components.

The engineers found that the main gain of structuring applications in tiers is that everyone will work and structure the application in a similar way. This results in coherent, homogeneous and stable applications, leading to easier maintenance. The biggest asset is the standardization benefit, namely that it is predefined where different type of code is located, thus enhancing collaboration (like quickly get into each others' applications).

The statement '*it is easier to program if some logic is put into the display tier*', from one of the interviewees, may imply that full understanding of the benefits of tier separation has not been achieved. It is difficult to say though, because other engineers had a more conscious departure from the strict tier-separation, with clear arguments of why they did what they did. They expressed that they would place input controls, such as checking that correct values are filled out in a form, as well as event handling in the display tier. This reduces transfer over the network and increases performance. Sometimes they would do the input controls twice, both in the display and in the business tier, to have all the logic gathered in the same place, and for extra security. A third-part component demanded some logic to be put in the presentation tier; it was not possible to solve it otherwise. This shows that they have done conscious adjustments of the method prescription to achieve some articulated benefits. If there are drawbacks, and whether the engineers are aware of these is beyond the scope of this investigation. For example, if one starts to add logic into the display-tier, it will not be possible to use a designer without programming experience any longer. Since there is no designer role assigned, this drawback is probably not prominent in their situation.

The learning threshold appeared to be the main drawback with tier-based development. The topic came up a few times in each interview when addressing issues of understanding, updating and extending applications. The engineers experienced the learning process as incremental, and in the beginning it was more difficult to understand systems structured in tiers (a necessity for making updates and extensions). It took about a year to achieve proficiency in extending and updating applications using the separation principle. Most engineers thought it would take about the same amount of time to create a tier-based application as one where display and business logic is entangled. They found it a little difficult to compare though, since they had usually developed smaller systems before. As one engineer expressed it *'larger systems require much more planning and structure, especially if they are being updated later on'*. There seems to be a common opinion that the benefits of tier separated applications mainly appears when building larger systems.

The engineers found both advantages and disadvantages with regards to error handling. If it was obvious in which tier the bug was, the tier structure was advantageous, otherwise you have to run up and down in the tiers, actually taking more time, making it a disadvantage.

The engineers apparently aim to fulfil the goals attached to this method prescription, i.e. there is a foundation for rationality resonance. A closer look at the goals shows that the engineers did aim for G3 (Problems/bugs are easy to find), but did not think tier separation always helps achieving it. Tier separation did help achieving G6 (Applications are easy to update/extend). The main gain was G7 (Applications are built with a standardised coherent architecture).

The underlying values also match: The fact that applications did get extended/updated (V3) may have contributed to the engineers' interest in building general reusable components, and their positive attitude to the ones that had been developed so far. They kept to the tier-separation in most cases, even though it took some extra work. This indicates they do think it is worth the extra effort to prepare an application for extensions/updates (V1) and that they do think in long-term (V2). The engineers were of the opinion that applications composed of well-demarcated parts are easy to extend (scale) and update (V4). The largest application developed in this organization so far has a couple of hundred users. Scaling is therefore not relevant to talk about since the applications are too small. When it comes to locating and determining problems/bugs (V5), tier-based applications had both advantages and disadvantages. The main gain of tier-based architecture was considered the standardization benefit, which underpinned common understanding and collaboration (V13) and that demarcation enhances understanding (V7).

P3: Reuse Components Within and Between Projects
This prescription is very closely coupled with the previous one, so the interview findings from the above section contributes to the understanding of this section too.

The engineers experienced that updating the application often led to partly rebuilding it. At this stage they often realized that things could be done in a more general manner. Through this type of development, general reusable components emerged, creating a library of components within the organization. This was a conscious process led by a project group, with the aim to create their own standard.

The engineers definitely aim to reuse components (G5). They certainly also believed that reusing a component is less work than building a new one from scratch (V11). Developing a general component does take a little more time than developing one for a particular application, but is paid back in the next application. It is clear that reuse of components leads to standardization (V12), which is good for common understanding and for collaboration (V13).

P4: Divide Labour According to Different Skill Sets
The engineers had general competence in the different types of skills needed for developing applications. The demarcations into different skill sets appear on the component level, not on the tier level (as in display-designer versus programmer) as the method-in-concept advocates. Some engineers were slightly more specialized in database programming, while others had a bit more feel for user interface programming. There are no designers without programming experience within the organization, so the benefit of being able to use them to create the display-tier could not be explored.

Goal G4 (team members divide labour between them according to different skill sets) is not really a goal of this organization. The values associated with it do not correspond to the engineers' values either. Since the members of the development team do not have different skills (V9), it is not important to demark what is relevant to each competence (V8) and members of a development team actually can accomplish each other's tasks (V10). This is, of course, specific to this organization.

Value V6 (Applications composed by demarcated parts divides the application into different parts, suiting each skill set) must (just as above) be discussed on the two different granularity levels. On the component level, this is partly true, but on the tier level there is no division into skill sets. The same reasoning applies to V7 (Demarcation enhances understanding).

4.3 Discussion

From the above we can see that the engineers in most cases did conscious departures from the method, which is in line with previous research [6, 25]. The method prescriptions did not make sense in their strict form and were therefore not useful, which is a must for successful method tailoring [2, 22].

The statement *'it is easier to program if some logic is put in the display-tier'* may imply that there is a lack of understanding (as suggested in [5]), and also a sign of short-term thinking [19]. This can be viewed as a goal contradiction – that the personal process goal (easy to program) is favoured before the quality of the product (software); aiming for one goal, gives negative results for another. This issue, to actually put logic into the display-tier is a bit contradictive to the result that the main gain of structuring applications this way is that you know where different type of code is located. The actual rules about what should be put where were appreciated since it made it easier to understand each other's applications. Perhaps the idea about enforcing separation [19] would increase this gain even further? The idea that engineers think in short-term does not apply to the bigger picture of this study though.

The fact that the engineers had to balance different factors and prioritized, e.g. security and performance above keeping to the principle is not surprising. The existence of contradictory goals in ISE is well-known, and the trade-offs between the goals and values brought to the fore in this study and other ISE goals and values would be interesting to explore further. Although this is beyond the scope of this study, the same analytic framework could likely be useful in such an endeavour.

5 Conclusion

Generally speaking, engineers do not keep to the principle of separating business logic from display because in some respects it does not help achieving their goals. In these cases, engineers make conscious departures from the method prescriptions, thus tailoring the method to suit their needs.

This study also revealed more specific reasons for tailoring the principle: Business logic was sometimes placed in the display-tier because '*it made it easier to program*', '*it improved performance*', and '*a third part component demanded it*'. All engineers in the study had similar skill sets, so this caused no misunderstandings. Multiple types of clients hardly ever occurred in the study. The engineers were confident that an application could be efficiently optimized for one type of client; a benefit that is lost in case of systems with multiple types of client. This issue is not mentioned in the literature, thus indicating either that the drawbacks are not explicated, or that the engineers have not understood the method-in-concept. If the drawbacks are suppressed in the method-in-concept, this may be the first and foremost answer to why engineers choose not to follow it.

The principle of separating business logic from display is used in a wide range of software engineering efforts today. It is also well known that engineers are 'cheating' with it, thus potentially deteriorating the quality of the software [19]. This investigation contributes to our understanding of why engineers do this, hence holds the key to how this can be overcome. Non-strict use of the principle gave other benefits, not explicated by the method-in-concept, showing that method tailoring is important. The study also shows that the concept of method rationale is a useful tool for addressing these issues.

This qualitative study provides examples of why developers do not keep to the principle of separating business logic from display – and, in line with previous research, suggests that departure from the principle is often conscious and well-motivated. Given the small scale of the study, hard conclusions are obviously difficult to draw. For more generalizable results, a larger study including several more engineers would be required. It would also be interesting to explore to what extent the same results would appear in a different development environment. Perhaps the results from this study are particular for the .NET environment, whereas other issues could be connected to other development environments. For example, the principle obviously relates to the Model View Controller (MVC) pattern which is widely used (it can indeed be seen as subset of the MVC pattern). In order to understand the influence of contradictions between higher level goals, the interplay between this principle and other software engineering principles needs to be studied as well.

References

1. Ågerfalk, P. J., Åhlgren, K.: Modelling the Rationale of Methods. In: M. Khosrowpour, (ed.): Proceedings of the 10th Information Resources Management Association International Conference. (1999) 184-190
2. Ågerfalk, P. J., Fitzgerald, B.: Methods as Action Knowledge: Exploring the Concept of Method Rationale in Method Construction, Tailoring and Use. In: T. Halpin, J. Krogstie, and K. Siau, (eds.): Proceedings of EMMSAD'05. (2005) 413-426
3. Ågerfalk, P. J., Wistrand, K.: Systems Development Method Rationale: A Conceptual Framework for Analysis. In: Proc. 5th International Conference on Enterprise Information Systems (ICEIS 2003) 185–190
4. Brinkkemper, S., Saeki, M., Harmsen, F.: Meta-Modelling Based Assembly Techniques for Situational Method Engineering. Information Systems 24 (1999) 209-228
5. Dewan, P.: Teaching Inter-Object Design Patterns to Freshmen. In: Proc. SIGCSE'05 (2005)
6. Fitzgerald, B.: The Use of Systems Development Methodologies in Practice: A Field Study. Information Systems Journal 6 (1997) 201-212
7. Fitzgerald, B., Russo, N. L., Stolterman, E.: Information Systems Development: Methods in Action. McGraw-Hill, Berkshire, UK (2002)
8. Forsberg, C., Sjöström, A.: Pocket PC Development in the Enterprise. Addison Wesley, London, UK (2002)
9. Gamma, E., Helm, R., Johnson, R., Vlissides, J.: Design Patterns, Elements of Reusable Object-Oriented Software. Addison-Wesley (1995)
10. Goldkuhl, G.: Design Theories in Information Systems: A Need for Multi-Grounding. Journal of Information Technology Theory and Application 6 (2004) 59-62
11. Goldkuhl, G., Röstlinger, A.: Joint Elicitation of Problems: An Important Aspect of Change Analysis. In: D. E. Avison, J. E. Kendall, and J. I. DeGross, (eds.): IFIP WG8.2 on Human, Social, and Organizational Aspects of Information Systems Development. (1993) 107–125
12. Jayaratna, N.: Understanding and Evaluating Methodologies. McGraw-Hill, London (1994)
13. Karlsson, F.: Method Configuration, Method and Computerized Tool Support. Doctoral Dissertation. University of Linköping (2005)
14. Levi, N.: Java 2 Web Developer Cerification Study Guide. SYBEX inc., Alameda, California, USA (2003)
15. Lings, B., Lundell, B.: Method-in Action and Method-in-Tool: Some Implications for CASE. In: Proc. 6th International Conference on Enterprise Information Systems (ICEIS 2004) 623-628
16. Nash, M.: Java Frameworks and Components: Accelerate Your Web Application Development. Cambridge University Press, Cambridge, UK (2003)
17. Parnas, D. L.: On the Criteria to Be Used in Decomposing Systems into Modules. Communications of the ACM 15 (1972) 1053-1058
18. Parnas, D. L., Clements, P. C.: A Rational Design Process: How and Why to Fake It. IEEE Transactions on Software Engineering 12 (1986) 251-257
19. Parr, T.: Enforcing Strict Model-View Separation in Template Engines. In: Proc. WWW2004, ACM (2004)
20. Patton, M. Q.: Qualitative Evaluation and Research Methods. SAGE Publications, Newbury Park California, USA (1990)

21. Pree, W.: Design Patterns for Object-Oriented Software Development. Addison-Wesley (1995)
22. Riemenschneider, C. K., Hardgrave, B. C., Davis, F. D.: Explaining Software Development Acceptance of Methodologies: A Comparison of Five Theoretical Models. IEEE Transactions on Software Engineering 28 (2002) 1135-1145
23. Rogue Wave Software, I.: Distributed MVC: An Architecture for Windows DNA Applications. Boulder, Colorado USA (1999)
24. Rossi, M., Ramesh, B., Lyytinen, K., Tolvanen, J.-P.: Managing Evolutionary Method Engineering by Method Rationale. Journal of the Association for Information Systems 5 (2004) 356-391
25. Russo, N. L., Stolterman, E.: Exploring the Assumptions Underlying Information Systems Methodologies. Information Technology & People 13 (2000) 313-327
26. Stolterman, E., Russo, N. L.: The Paradox of Information Systems Methods: Public and Private Rationality. In: Proc. The British Computer Society 5th Annual Conference on Methodologies (1997)
27. Sun Microsystems, I. Java Blueprints: Model-View-Controller. Sun Microsystems, Inc [Online]. Available: http://java.sun.com/blueprints/patterns/MVC-detailed.html
28. Yin, R. K.: Case Study Research, Design and Methods, 2nd Edition. SAGE, London (1994)

Business Process Modelling

Translating Standard Process Models to BPEL*

Chun Ouyang, Marlon Dumas, Stephan Breutel, and Arthur ter Hofstede

Faculty of Information Technology,
Queensland University of Technology,
GPO Box 2434, Brisbane QLD 4001, Australia
{c.ouyang, m.dumas, sw.breutel, a.terhofstede}@qut.edu.au

Abstract. Standardisation of languages in the field of business process management has long been an elusive goal. Recently though, consensus has built around one process implementation language, namely BPEL, and two fundamentally similar process modelling notations, namely UML Activity Diagram (UML AD) and BPMN. This paper presents a technique for generating BPEL code from process models expressed in a core subset of BPMN and UML AD. This model-to-code translation is a necessary ingredient to the emergence of model-driven business process development environments based on these standards. The proposed translation has been implemented as an open source tool.

1 Introduction

Over the past two decades, developments in the field of workflow and business process management have been hindered by the lack of a lingua franca for describing business processes, whether at the design or at implementation stages of the software lifecycle. Standardisation efforts during the 90s, led by the Workflow Management Coalition (WfMC), failed to be widely adopted for a number of reasons [1]. Recently however, consolidation has led to a single language for business process implementation: the Business Process Execution Language for Web Services (BPEL) [3]. In parallel, two process modelling notations, namely the Unified Modelling Language "Activity Diagram" (UML AD) [10] and the Business Process Management Notation (BPMN) [12], have attained some level of maturity and adoption.

There exist a number of business process execution engines that support BPEL, either natively or through import and export functions. Similarly, a large number of tools provide support for UML modelling, in particular using Activity Diagram, while BPMN, despite being a recent proposal, is already supported by about a dozen tools [5]. It appears however that support for translating models in UML AD and BPMN into BPEL code has received little attention relative to the amount of tools supporting these languages separately. Tools such as Telelogic's System Architect support the generation of BPEL code from BPMN diagrams but only for a limited subset of BPMN. More generally, proposed mappings from UML AD to BPEL [9] and from BPMN to BPEL [12] fail to address some difficult issues as discussed below.

---

* Supported by an Australian Research Council (ARC) Discovery Grant (DP0451092).

E. Dubois and K. Pohl (Eds.): CAiSE 2006, LNCS 4001, pp. 417–432, 2006.
© Springer-Verlag Berlin Heidelberg 2006

Both BPMN and UML AD share a common set of core constructs and for practical purposes, can be treated as variants of the same kernel language. This kernel is essentially an extension of flow charts with parallel splits (fork nodes) and synchronisation points (join nodes). As in flow charts, nodes in BPMN and UML AD (version 2.0) can be linked in arbitrary topologies, making it possible to write models with unstructured cycles. Meanwhile BPEL, which is essentially an extension of structured programming languages, only supports structured loops. Work in the field of structured programming [11] has shown that it is possible to translate from unstructured to structured flow charts and from there to generate code in structured programming languages including "sequence", "if-then-else", and "while" constructs. It turns out however that after adding forks and joins to the flow chart notation these results no longer hold [7].

This paper takes on the challenge of designing a technique for translating BPMN and UML AD models with arbitrary topologies, which we term Standard Process Models or SPMs, into BPEL code. We consider this translation as being necessary to improve the connection between tools supporting process modelling and tools supporting process execution, thus enabling model-driven approaches to business process development based on standard and widely supported languages. The basic idea of the translation is to exploit an underused construct in BPEL, namely *event handlers*. This is the only construct in BPEL that allows one to capture processes with unbounded concurrency (i.e. processes with an unbounded number of threads running concurrently) without having to break down the process into several smaller ones, which may potentially lead to maintenance issues. Since some unstructured cycles in BPMN and UML AD may lead to unbounded concurrency, we argue that using event handlers is the only way to achieve a full translation from any SPM to a self-contained BPEL process. In this respect, the proposed translation goes beyond those in [9] and [12] which are essentially limited to structured models.

The rest of the paper is structured as follows. Sect. 2 gives an overview of BPEL and SPMs (the chosen abstraction of BPMN and UML AD) and reviews related work. Sect. 3 presents an initial approach to translate SPMs into BPEL. This mapping is then illustrated through a case study in Sect. 4. Sect. 5 describes an improvement to the initial translation approach which leads to more structured BPEL code. Finally, Sect. 6 concludes and outlines future work.

2   Background and Related Work

A Standard Process Model (SPM), also known as Standard Workflow Model [6], is constructed from a set of *process elements* and *transitions* connecting process elements. The process elements can be further divided into activities and control nodes which are AND-Split, XOR-Split, OR-Split, AND-Join and XOR-Join. Splits have exactly one incoming transition and at least one outgoing transition, and joins have exactly one outgoing transition and at least one incoming transition. For any split, each of its outgoing transitions has either an explicit guard (i.e. boolean expression) or an implicit "true" guard if none is explicitly given.

Activities have at most one incoming transition and one outgoing transition, and this implies that the use of implicit control nodes is not allowed. Activities with no incoming transitions are *initial activities*, and those with no outgoing transitions are *final activities*. Each SPM has exactly one initial activity and one final activity. It can be described using a process modelling notation such as BPMN or UML AD. In other words, SPMs can be seen as an abstraction of a subset of BPMN and UML AD, wherein constructs corresponding to advanced workflow patterns, e.g. *deferred choice* and *cancellation* [2], are not included.

BPEL [3] is essentially an extension of imperative programming languages (e.g. Pascal, C) with constructs related to the implementation of web service-oriented processes. A BPEL process definition relates a number of *activities*. Activities are split into two categories: *basic activities* and *structured activities*. Basic activities correspond to atomic actions such as: *invoke*, invoking an operation on some web service; *receive*, waiting for a message from a partner; *reply*, replying to a partner; *assign*, assigning a value to a variable; *exit*, terminating the entire process instance; *empty*, doing nothing; and etc. Structured activities impose behavioural and execution constraints on a set of activities contained within them. These include: *sequence*, for defining an execution order; *flow*, for parallel routing; *switch*, for conditional routing; *pick*, for capturing a race between timing and message receipt events; *while*, for structured looping; and *scope*, for grouping activities into blocks to which event, fault and compensation handlers (see below) may be attached.

Event, fault and *compensation handlers* are another family of control flow constructs in BPEL. In particular, *event handlers* are the only construct in BPEL that allows to have multiple simultaneously active instances within a single process instance (initiated by a single case). An event handler is an *event-action rule* associated with a scope. An event handler is enabled when its associated scope is under execution and may execute concurrently with the main activity of the scope. When an occurrence of the event associated with an enabled event handler is registered (and this may be a message receipt or a timeout), the body of the handler is executed. The completion of the scope as a whole is delayed until all active event handlers have completed. *Fault* and *compensation handlers* are designed for exception handling and are not used further in this paper.

SPMs can easily capture control-flow patterns, such as *multi-merge* and *arbitrary cycles*, for which BPEL does not offer direct support [13]. It may also have the facility for spawning multiple *independent* instances of activities within the context of a single case, and so far there has been no solution for mapping such a process to a *single* BPEL process. Hence, translating a process like one of the above into BPEL is not trivial. Below, we discuss this in detail using as an example the mapping from BPMN to BPEL proposed by White [12].

Figure 1 depicts four SPMs described using BPMN. The first three SPMs in Fig. 1(a) to Fig. 1(c) show fundamental issues and limitations in the mapping proposed in [12]. The SPM in Fig. 1(d) involves a livelock and will be mentioned at the end of this section. Note that in BPMN *parallel (forking/joining) gateways*

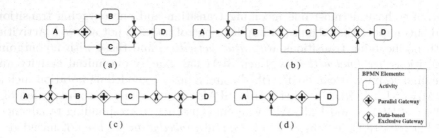

Fig. 1. Four SPMs (described using BPMN) which contain (a) a multiple merge, (b) arbitrary loops, (c) arbitrary loops with a facility spawning multiple independent instances of activities without synchronization, and (d) a livelock

correspond to AND-Splits/Joins, and *data-based exclusive (decision/merge) gateways* correspond to XOR-Splits/Joins.

In Fig. 1(a), an XOR-Join following an upstream AND-Split captures a multi-merge pattern. In this process, activity D is executed twice: once when activity B completes and another time when activity C completes. In White's approach, a parallel gateway is always mapped to a BPEL "flow" activity and a data-based exclusive gateway to a "switch" activity [12]. This mapping assumes that for each AND-split there is a corresponding AND-join and for each XOR-split a corresponding XOR-join. However, in the scenario at hand, the outgoing branches of the AND-split lead to an XOR-Join, thus making White's mapping unapplicable.

In Fig. 1(b), there is a cycle with one entry point before activity B and two exit points – one after activity B, the other after activity C. This scenario cannot be mapped *directly* to a BPEL "while" activity as the "while" activity only captures structured cycles (i.e. loops with one entry point and one exit point). In [12], White considers only two types of cycles: *structured loops* and *interleaved loops*. Interleaved loops are a particular form of unstructured loops wherein two distinct loops can be identified which are not nested one inside the other. The basic idea to map such interleaved loops is to separate the original process into "one or more derived processes that are spawned from a main process and will also spawn or call each other". As a result, the original process will be mapped onto multiple BPEL processes rather than a single BPEL process. The synchronisation between the derived BPEL processes and the main process is achieved through message exchange[1]. While this is an interesting translation, it is not general enough: the scenario in Fig. 1(b) is neither a structured loop nor an interleaved loop (as it is not possible to distinguish two distinct loops on it), so its mapping is not covered by White's approach.

---

[1] A proposed extension to BPEL (`http://www-128.ibm.com/developerworks/webservices/library/specification/ws-bpelsubproc`) includes constructs for defining and invoking sub-processes. These constructs can be used to define multiple inter-related BPEL processes in a single module. However, there are no near-term plans of including these constructs in the BPEL standard. If these constructs were included, they could be used as an alternative to event handlers in our mapping.

Fig. 1(c) illustrates yet another scenario not covered by White's approach. This model differs from the one in Fig. 1(b) in that there is an AND-Split (Fig. 1(c)) rather than an XOR-Split (Fig. 1(b)) between activities B and C. Since this AND-Split is located in a loop and also has another branch leading to activity D outside the loop, it provides a way for spawning multiple instances of D, all of which are independent of each other and no synchronisation is needed. As a new instance of activity D will be created each time the cycle is taken, the number of instances of D becomes unbounded. This captures the pattern of *multiple instances without synchronisation* [2]. Wohed et al. [13] proposes a solution for capturing this pattern in BPEL. The basic idea is to define another process containing activity D, and to invoke this "auxiliary" process multiple times thus spawning multiple instances of D. Again, the original process will be mapped onto multiple BPEL processes. In [12], White proposes a similar solution for mapping a subclass of parallel multiple-instance loops (without synchronisation) onto BPEL, which however does not cover the above scenario.

Sometimes, arbitrary cycles can be converted into structured cycles and these structured cycles can then be mapped directly onto BPEL "while" activities. However, not all non-structured cycles can be converted into structured ones when AND-splits and AND-joins are involved. An analysis of possible conversions and an identification of some situations where they are unapplicable can be found in [7,8]. For example, in Fig. 1(b) it is possible to unfold the arbitrary loops to structured ones, whereas in Fig. 1(c) the arbitrary cycles generate unbounded concurrency (i.e. they may spawn an unbounded number of concurrent instances of an activity) and do not have an equivalent structured form.

In the sequel, we present a technique to translate any SPM into a single BPEL process by exploiting the "event handler" construct in BPEL. The technique can be applied to any SPM so long as it does not involve a livelock (also called *divergence* in the concurrency theory literature) such as the one shown in Fig. 1(d). Livelocks can be detected using model-checking techniques and thus such undesirable SPMs could be excluded during a pre-processing step.

3   From Standard Process Models to BPEL

This section presents an initial approach for translating SPMs to BPEL. The translation focuses on control-flow perspective, and is conducted in three steps. We first generate so-called *precondition sets* for all activities in an SPM. Each precondition set is associated with an activity and encodes a possible way of enabling the activity. Next, all the precondition sets with their associated activities, are transformed into a set of *Event-Condition-Action* (ECA) rules. Finally, we translate this set of ECA rules into BPEL.

3.1   Translating Control-Flow Constructs into Precondition Sets

The term "precondition" is used to capture a conjunction of events and conditions that lead to the execution of an activity in a process. Thus, for each

AllPreCondSets(p: Process):
    let $\{a_1, ..., a_n\}$ = Activities(p) in
        return $\{$PreCondSet(a_1), ..., PreCondSet(a_n)$\}$

PreCondSet(x: Element):
    if IncomingTrans(x) = $\emptyset$ /* initial element */
    return $\{$ProcessInstantiation(Process(x))$\}$
    else let $\{t_1, ..., t_n\}$ = IncomingTrans(x) in   /* non-initial elements */
        return PreCondSetTran(t_1) $\cup$ ... $\cup$ PreCondSetTran(t_n)

PreCondSetTran(t: Transition)
    let x = Source(t)
        if ElementType(x) = "Activity"
        return $\{$Completion(x)$\}$
        else if ElementType(x) $\in$ { "AND-Split", "XOR-Split", "OR-Split" }
            let c = Guard(t),
                $\{prc_1, ..., prc_n\}$ = PreCondSet(x) in
                return $\{c \wedge prc_1, ..., c \wedge prc_n\}$
        else if ElementType(x) = "XOR-Join"
            let $\{t_1, ..., t_n\}$ = IncomingTrans(x) in
                return PreCondSetTran(t_1) $\cup$ ... $\cup$ PreCondSetTran(t_n)
        else if ElementType(x) = "AND-Join"
            let $\{t_1, ..., t_n\}$ = IncomingTrans(x),
                $\{< prc_{1,1}, ..., prc_{1,n} >, ..., < prc_{m,1}, ..., prc_{m,n} >\}$ =
                PreCondSetTran(t_1) $\times$ ... $\times$ PreCondSetTran(t_n) in
                return $\{prc_{1,1} \wedge ... \wedge prc_{1,n}, ..., prc_{m,1} \wedge ... \wedge prc_{m,n}\}$

Fig. 2. Algorithm for deriving precondition sets from an SPM

activity in an SPM, we can compute a precondition set that encapsulates all possible ways of reaching that activity. Fig. 2 shows an algorithm[2] for generating a set of precondition sets for all activities in an SPM. The algorithm is sketched using a functional programming notation. It defines three functions. The first one, namely AllPreCondSets, generates the above set of precondition sets for a process by relying on a second function named PreCondSet. This function takes as parameter a process element (i.e. an activity or a control node). If the element is an *initial* activity, i.e. it has no predecessors, the function returns a singleton set containing a process instantiation event, indicating that the corresponding activity will be executed when a new instance of the process must be started. Otherwise, function PreCondSet generates a precondition set for each of the non-initial elements in the process by relying on a third function named PreCondSetTran. This third function produces the same type of output as PreCondSet but takes as input a transition rather than an element in the process. Before moving on, we introduce the following notations used in the algorithm.

---

[2] This is a variant of an algorithm designed in the context of a method for flexible execution of process-oriented applications [4].

- Activities(p) is the set of activities in process p (defined as an SPM).
- IncomingTrans(x) is the set of transitions whose target is element x.
- Process(x) is the process to which element x belongs.
- ProcessInstantiation(p) is the event signaling to start an instance of process p.
- Source(t) is the source element of transition t.
- ElementType(x) is the type of element x (e.g. "Activity", "AND- Split", etc.).
- Completion(x) is the event signaling that activity x has completed.
- Guard(t) is the guard (i.e. boolean expression) on transition t.

The definition of PreCondSetTran operates based on the type of the source of the transition, which may be an activity or a control node. If the transition's source is an "Activity", a set is returned containing a single completion event for the activity. Intuitively, this means the transition in question may be taken when the activity has completed. Otherwise, if the source of the transition is a control node, the algorithm keeps working backwards through the process model, traversing other control nodes, until reaching activities. In the case of a transition originating from one of the "Split" nodes ("AND-Split", "XOR-Split", or "OR-Split"), which is generally labeled by a guard (or an implicit "true" guard if no guard is explicitly given), this condition is added as a conjunct to all the elements in the resulting precondition set. Finally, in the case of a transition originating from a "XOR-Join" (resp. a "AND-Join"), the function is recursively called for each of the transitions leading to this control node, and the resulting precondition sets are combined to capture the fact that when any (all) of these transitions is (are) taken, the corresponding XOR-Join (AND-Join) node may fire.

3.2 Translating Precondition Sets into ECA Rules

An ECA rule consists of three parts: *event*, which causes the rule to be triggered; *condition*, which is checked when the rule is triggered, and *action*, which is executed when the rule is triggered and its condition is true. An ECA rule can be written in the form of E[C]A: E is a single event or a conjunction of single events (namely a *composite event*); C is a condition; A is a list of actions that can be executed in sequence (denoted as $a_1;a_2$), in parallel ($a_1||a_2$), in conditional branches (if-then-else), in loops (while), or in a combination of any of these block-structured constructs. If an ECA rule allows the use of single events only, it is called a *simple ECA rule*; otherwise, it is a *composite ECA rule*.

It is possible to translate a precondition into an ECA rule. To this end, we use two auxiliary functions GetEvent and GetCond, which extract respectively the events and conditions of a precondition. GetEvent takes as input a precondition prc, and gives as output a composite event equal to the conjunction of all the events appearing in prc (there is always at least one single event in prc). GetCond takes prc as input and gives as output a condition equal to the conjunction of all the conditions appearing in prc (it returns a value of TRUE if there is no condition in prc). A precondition prc for an activity a can be translated into the following ECA rule:

GetEvent(prc) [GetCond(prc)] {do a; invoke Completion(a)}

In the general case, this leads to a composite ECA rule. However, BPEL only supports simple ECA rules. To address this issue, when GetEvent(prc) is a composite event, say $e_1 \wedge ... \wedge e_n$, we translate the above rule into the following simple ECA rule:

$$e_1 \text{ [TRUE]} \{\texttt{receive } e_2 \text{ || } ... \text{ || } \texttt{receive } e_n;$$
$$\texttt{if } \text{GetCond}(prc)$$
$$\texttt{then do } a; \texttt{ invoke } \text{Completion}(a)$$
$$\texttt{else empty}\}$$

The rule specifies that when occurrences for all events e_1 to e_n have been registered, the condition GetCond(prc) can be evaluated. If it evaluates to true, activity a is executed; otherwise, no action is performed.

By applying the above transformation to each precondition in a precondition set, we can translate a precondition set into a set of simple ECA rules. From there, we can generate a set of ECA rules for a given SPM by performing the union of the sets of ECA rules generated for each of the activities in the SPM. However, some of these rules may end up competing for the same event, which may lead to non-deterministic behaviour. For example, in the case of a Split node preceded by activity a_1 and followed by two activities a_2 and a_3, the precondition sets for a_2 and a_3 will both contain event Completion(a_1) and thus the resulting rules will compete for this same event. To avoid this problem, before transforming the precondition sets derived from an SPM into ECA rules, we rename the events shared by more than one precondition to eliminate any overlap between events. For example, the following set of precondition sets:

$\{\{\text{ProcessInstantiation}(p)\}, \{\text{Completion}(a_1) \wedge c_1\}, \{\text{Completion}(a_1) \wedge c_2\},$
$\{\text{Completion}(a_3)\}, \{\text{Completion}(a_3), \text{Completion}(a_1) \wedge c_3\},$
$\{\text{Completion}(a_2), \text{Completion}(a_4) \wedge c_4, \text{Completion}(a_4) \wedge c_5 \wedge \text{Completion}(a_5)\}\}$

can be renamed to:

$\{\{\text{ProcessInstantiation}(p)\}, \{\text{Completion}(a_1)^{(1)} \wedge c_1\}, \{\text{Completion}(a_1)^{(2)} \wedge c_2\},$
$\{\text{Completion}(a_3)^{(1)}\}, \{\text{Completion}(a_3)^{(2)}, \text{Completion}(a_1)^{(3)} \wedge c_3\},$
$\{\text{Completion}(a_2), \text{Completion}(a_4)^{(1)} \wedge c_4, \text{Completion}(a_4)^{(2)} \wedge c_5 \wedge \text{Completion}(a_5)\}\}$

Due to this renaming process, we need to ensure that upon completion of an activity a, one occurrence of each of the completion events associated to a is produced. Coming back in the example above, instead of performing a single action "invoke Completion(a_1)" following the execution of activity a_1, we perform the following actions:

$\texttt{invoke Completion}(a_1)^{(1)} \text{ || } \texttt{invoke Completion}(a_1)^{(2)} \text{ || } \texttt{invoke Completion}(a_1)^{(3)}$

3.3   Translating ECA Rules into BPEL

A simple ECA rule $se\,[C]\,A$ can be realised by a BPEL event handler (onEvent) sketched in Fig. 3(a). As soon as an occurrence of event se is registered, the event handler starts with a *switch* activity in which condition C is evaluated. If C evaluates to true, the activity A is carried out; otherwise, nothing can be done. This event handler may be simplified if C is a boolean constant TRUE. In this case, the switch activity with its conditional branches (drawn in shaded boxes) can be omitted, and activity A is executed once the occurrence of event se is registered. Fig. 3(b) sketches a BPEL event handler capturing a simple ECA rule which is transformed from a composite ECA rule as discussed in Sect. 3.2. Since the rule has a condition TRUE, the event handler executes the sequence of actions immediately upon registering the occurrence of event e_1. This sequence starts with a flow of receive activities waiting for occurrences of events e_2 to e_n, and a switch activity for conditional routings based on evaluation of the condition given by function GetCond(prc). Similarly to Fig. 3(a), if GetCond(prc) is a boolean constant TRUE, the switch activity can be omitted, and once the occurrences of events e_1 to e_n are registered, the event handler executes action a and the activity for invoking a single occurrence of event Completion(a).

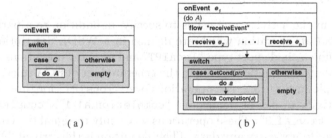

(a)   (b)

Fig. 3. Translating a simple ECA rule into a BPEL event handler

Based on the above, we now translate the set of simple ECA rules derived from the original SPM into a BPEL process. We first introduce some notations. Given a process p, $\{a_1, ..., a_n\}$ is the set of activities in p, and the function InitialActivity(p) returns the initial activity of p. Let $m+1$ be the total number of ECA rules derived from process p, $\{se_1, ..., se_m\} \subseteq \{$Completion($a_1$), ..., Completion($a_n$)$\}$ is the set of (single) events for triggering each of these ECA rules except the one associated with the initial activity. The ECA rule for execution of the initial activity is triggered upon occurrence of the process instantiation

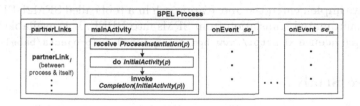

Fig. 4. A BPEL process derived from the set of ECA rules of an SPM

event (ProcessInstantiation(p)). The SPM of process p can be translated into the BPEL process sketched in Fig. 4. The main activity of this process is a sequence of three actions which corresponds to the ECA rule associated with the initial activity of p. Then each of the other (m) ECA rules are mapped onto totally m event handlers within the process. The whole process completes after its main activity and all active event handlers have completed.

The completion events Completion(a_1) to Completion(a_n) are produced by performing a BPEL invoke action via a *local* partner link between process p and itself. A local partner link which allows a process to send a message to itself, can be defined as follows:

```
<partnerLink name="local" partnerLinkType="localLT"
             myRole="localService"/>
</partnerLink>

<partnerLinkType name="localLT">
     <role name="localService" portType="localPT"/>
</partnerLinkType>
```

In a BPEL invoke activity, one needs to specify, in addition to a partner link, a port type and an operation which are defined in a WSDL description. Accordingly, we define a single port type "localPT" and as many operations in this port type as there are completion events in the generated set of ECA rules. In the case of the example in Sect. 3.2, the operations over "localPT" for three completion events of activity a_1 can be defined as: "completion_a1_1", "completion_a1_2" and "completion_a1_3". These operations serve only to signal the completion of activities and do not carry any data. Their definition is thus trivial. For example, the production of event Completion(a_1)$^{(1)}$ is captured in BPEL as follows:

```
<invoke partnerLink="local" portType="localPT"
        operation="completion_a1_1"/>
```

Likewise, completion events are consumed by event handlers and receive activities, referring to the local partner link, port type and the operations described above. For example, the event handler corresponding to event Completion(a_1)$^{(1)}$ can be defined as follows:

```
<onEvent partnerLink="local" portType="localPT"
         operation="completion_a1_1"/>
```

We have implemented the above approach in a tool called SPM2BPEL, which supports automated translation from SPMs into BPEL. It is available under an open-source license at http://www.bpm.fit.qut.edu.au/projects/babel/tools.

4   Case Study

Consider the process for handling complaints shown in Fig. 5. It is described using BPMN. First the complaint is registered (activity *register*), then in parallel a questionnaire is sent to the complainant (*send questionnaire*) and the complaint is processed (*process complaint*). In the upper parallel path, the questionnaire is processed (*process questionnaire*) after it is returned from the complainant (*receive questionnaire*). In the lower parallel path, the complaint is evaluated (*evaluate*). Based on the evaluation result, the processing is either done or continues to activity *check processing*. If the check result is not ok, the complaint requires re-processing. After the complaint has been successfully processed, the complainant is notified of the result. Finally, activity *archive* is executed. Note that the labels *DONE, NEED-CHECK, OK* and *NOK* on the outgoing transitions of each XOR-Split, are abstract representations of guards on these transitions.

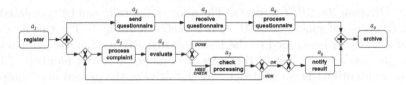

Fig. 5. A complaint handling process described using BPMN

Following the algorithm presented in Sect. 3, we now translate the above process into a BPEL process with event handlers. For simplicity, we assign each activity an activity identifier (placed above an activity rectangle in Fig. 5), and use these identifiers to refer to activities in the following translation.

Step 1: Generating Precondition Sets. Let p denote the process in Fig. 5, then Activity$(p)=\{a_1, ..., a_9\}$. The precondition sets for each of these activities are:

$\text{PreCondSet}(a_1) = \{\text{ProcessInstantiation}(p)\}$
$\text{PreCondSet}(a_2) = \{\text{Completion}(a_1)\}$
$\text{PreCondSet}(a_3) = \{\text{Completion}(a_2)\}$
$\text{PreCondSet}(a_4) = \{\text{Completion}(a_3)\}$
$\text{PreCondSet}(a_5) = \{\text{Completion}(a_1), \text{Completion}(a_7) \wedge NOK\}$
$\text{PreCondSet}(a_6) = \{\text{Completion}(a_5)\}$
$\text{PreCondSet}(a_7) = \{\text{Completion}(a_6) \wedge NEED\text{-}CHECK\}$
$\text{PreCondSet}(a_8) = \{\text{Completion}(a_6) \wedge DONE, \text{Completion}(a_7) \wedge OK\}$
$\text{PreCondSet}(a_9) = \{\text{Completion}(a_4) \wedge \text{Completion}(a_8)\}$

Step 2: Generating ECA Rules. The completion events for activities a_1, a_6 and a_7, each appears twice in the above precondition sets. Thus, it is necessary to rename these events. After the renaming process, all the precondition sets for process p can be translated into the set of simple ECA rules listed below, where "for a_i" is a shortened form of "for execution of activity a_i".

For a_1: ProcessInstantiation(p)[TRUE]
        $\{$do a_1; invoke Completion$(a_1)^{(1)}$ $||$ invoke Completion$(a_1)^{(2)}\}$
For a_2: Completion$(a_1)^{(1)}$[TRUE]$\{$do a_2; invoke Completion$(a_2)\}$
For a_3: Completion(a_2)[TRUE]$\{$do a_3; invoke Completion$(a_3)\}$

For a_4: $\mathsf{Completion}(a_3)[\mathsf{TRUE}]\{\text{do } a_4; \text{ invoke } \mathsf{Completion}(a_4)\}$
For a_5: $\mathsf{Completion}(a_1)^{(2)}[\mathsf{TRUE}]\{\text{do } a_5; \text{ invoke } \mathsf{Completion}(a_5)\}$
$\quad\quad\quad \mathsf{Completion}(a_7)^{(1)}[NOK]\{\text{do } a_5; \text{ invoke } \mathsf{Completion}(a_5)\}$
For a_6: $\mathsf{Completion}(a_5)[\mathsf{TRUE}]$
$\quad\quad\quad \{\text{do } a_6; \text{ invoke } \mathsf{Completion}(a_6)^{(1)} \text{ } || \text{ invoke } \mathsf{Completion}(a_6)^{(2)}\}$
For a_7: $\mathsf{Completion}(a_6)^{(1)}[NEED\text{-}CHECK]$
$\quad\quad\quad \{\text{do } a_7; \text{ invoke } \mathsf{Completion}(a_7)^{(1)} \text{ } || \text{ invoke } \mathsf{Completion}(a_7)^{(2)}\}$
For a_8: $\mathsf{Completion}(a_6)^{(2)}[DONE]\{\text{do } a_8; \text{ invoke } \mathsf{Completion}(a_8)\}$
$\quad\quad\quad \mathsf{Completion}(a_7)^{(2)}[OK]\{\text{do } a_8; \text{ invoke } \mathsf{Completion}(a_8)\}$
For a_9: $\mathsf{Completion}(a_4)[\mathsf{TRUE}]\{\text{receive } \mathsf{Completion}(a_8);$
$\quad\quad\quad\quad\quad\quad\quad\quad\quad\quad \text{do } a_9; \text{ invoke } \mathsf{Completion}(a_9)\}$

Step 3: Deriving the BPEL Process. The above ECA rules can be translated into a BPEL process of which the XML code is sketched in Fig. 6. The rule for execution of activity a_1 is mapped to the last sequence activity, i.e. the main activity of the process, and the rest of the rules are mapped to event handlers. All the events are identified in an abstract way. Intuitively, the arrival of a complaint from a client will initiate a new instance of the process, and thus can be treated as a process instantiation event. The production and consumption of each completion event can be defined in a similar way as that of event $\mathsf{Completion}(a_1)^{(1)}$ described in Sect. 3.3. The receive activity waiting for the process instantiation event, is the "start activity" of the process and thus has the `createInstance` attribute set to `yes`. Activity "register" (a_1) or "archive" (a_9) may be mapped to a BPEL assign activity for recording the relevant information into variables. Activity "sendQuestionnaire" (a_2) corresponds to an invoke activity for sending the questionnaire to the client. For space reasons, we do not describe the mapping in further detail. The interested reader may refer to the testing example of SPM2BPEL (on the tool's website) for a complete list of the BPEL code generated from the complaint handling process in Fig. 5.

5   Improving the Translation Approach

The previous approach in Sect. 3 treats each activity of an SPM as a single unit for translation. This can be improved by taking advantage of structured activities defined in BPEL. For example, in the complaint handling process in Fig. 5, three activities a_2, a_3 and a_4 can be directly mapped onto a "sequence" activity. Hence, if we cluster them into one activity block as a single unit for translation, the complexity of translation can be reduced with less precondition sets, less ECA rules and less event handlers, and the resulting BPEL process will become more compact. However, it is not always the case that a number of activities clustered into an activity block can be directly mapped onto a structured activity in BPEL. Coming back in the example in Fig. 5, the process elements on the lower parallel path constitute an unstructured workflow which cannot be mapped directly onto a structured activity (e.g. a "while" activity). To improve our approach further, we would like to transform unstructured activity blocks to structured ones which can then be mapped onto structured activities. Workflows

```
<process name="complaintHandling">
  <partnerLinks>
    <partnerLink name="local" partnerLinkType="localLT" ... />
    ... </partnerLinks>
  <variables> ... </variables>
  <eventHandlers>
    <onEvent Completion(a₁)⁽¹⁾/>
      <sequence>
        <invoke name="sendQuestionnaire" ... />   <!--do a₂-->
        <invoke Completion(a₂)/>
      </sequence> </onEvent>
    ...
    <onEvent Completion(a₄)/>
      <sequence>
        <receive Completion(a₈)/>
        <assign name="archive"> ... </assign>   <!--do a₉-->
        <invoke Completion(a₉)/>
      </sequence> </onEvent> </eventHandlers>
  <sequence>
    <receive ProcessInstantiation(p) createInstance="yes"/>
    <assign name="register"> ... </assign>   <!--do a₁-->
    <flow>
      <invoke Completion(a₁)⁽¹⁾/>
      <invoke Completion(a₁)⁽²⁾/>
    </flow> </sequence> </process>
```

Fig. 6. An abstract view of the BPEL code for complaint handling process in Fig. 5

that do not contain parallelism have similar semantics as elementary flow charts that are commonly used for procedural program specification. Work in the field of structured programming [11] has shown that any unstructured flow chart can be transformed to a structured one and from there one can generate code in structured programming languages including "sequence", "if-then-else", and "while" constructs. Based on this, we propose to cluster those connected process elements except AND-Splits and AND-Joins into an activity block. Since each activity block will later be treated as a single unit for translation, it cannot have more than one entry point nor more than one exit point. Below, we define *Clusterable Activity Blocks* based on the concept of *Weakly Connected Component* (from MathWorld http://mathworld.wolfram.com/WeaklyConnectedComponent.html).

Definition 1. *A Weakly Connected Component (WCC) is a maximal subgraph of a directed graph such that for every pair of vertices u, v in the subgraph, there is an undirected path from u to v and a directed path from v to u.*

Definition 2. *A Clusterable Activity Block (CAB) is a WCC that has at most one entry point and one exit point in an SPM. It is made up of activities, control nodes except AND-Splits and AND-Joins, and transitions connecting these process elements, such that:* $\forall x \in Elements(CAB)$,

- $ElementType(x) \in \{Activity, XOR\text{-}Split, OR\text{-}Split, XOR\text{-}Join\}$;
- $let\ T_i = \bigcup_{x \in Elements(CAB)} IncomingTrans(x),\ |T_i \setminus Transitions(CAB)| \leqslant 1$; and
- $let\ T_o = \bigcup_{x \in Elements(CAB)} OutgoingTrans(x),\ |T_o \setminus Transitions(CAB)| \leqslant 1$.

Before translating an SPM into BPEL, we pre-process the model by clustering all the original activities into CABs. We start with an arbitrary unclustered activity in the process, then move backwards and forwards from that activity without traversing AND-Splits/Joins (i.e. stop when reaching an AND-Split/Join), and finally cluster all the traversed elements and transitions into a single CAB. This procedure is repeated until no unclustered activities are left in the process. Next, we replace the "Activity" elements with "CAB" elements in the previous algorithm defined in Sect. 3, and apply this updated algorithm to the above pre-processed model. Finally, we map each CAB onto BPEL activities. This may also include transformation from unstructured to structured workflow before the mapping. Note that in the worst case a CAB contains only a single activity.

Example. We apply the improved approach to the translation of the complaint handling process in Fig. 5. Fig. 7 depicts a pre-processed model for this process where the previous *nine* activities with *four* XOR-Splits/Joins are clustered into *four* CABs. CAB_1, which contains just the initial activity a_1, is the initial item, and CAB_4, which consists of only the final activity a_9, is the final item.

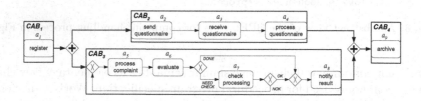

Fig. 7. Pre-processed complaint handling process in Fig. 5

The precondition sets for each of the *four* CABs in Fig. 7 are:

PreCondSet(CAB_1) = {ProcessInstantiation(p)}
PreCondSet(CAB_2) = {Completion(CAB_1)}
PreCondSet(CAB_3) = {Completion(CAB_1)}
PreCondSet(CAB_4) = {Completion(CAB_2)∧Completion(CAB_3)}

The set of simple ECA rules derived from these precondition sets are:

For CAB_1: ProcessInstantiation(p)[TRUE]
      {do CAB_1; invoke Completion(CAB_1)$^{(1)}$‖invoke Completion(CAB_1)$^{(2)}$}
For CAB_2: Completion(CAB_1)$^{(1)}$[TRUE]{do CAB_2; invoke Completion(CAB_2)}
For CAB_3: Completion(CAB_1)$^{(2)}$[TRUE]{do CAB_3; invoke Completion(CAB_3)}
For CAB_4: Completion(CAB_2)[TRUE]{receive Completion(CAB_3);
                do CAB_4; invoke Completion(CAB_4)}

The above ECA rules, except the first one for execution of the initial item CAB_1, can be translated into *three* event handlers. As a comparison, our previous approach yields *ten* event handlers for the same process.

Finally, the improved approach requires an additional step of mapping CABs onto structured activities in BPEL. This does not apply to CAB_1 and CAB_4 as both contain a single activity. CAB_2 can be directly mapped to a sequence activity. CAB_3 exhibits an unstructured workflow which can be transformed into an equivalent structured form shown in Fig. 8. The transformation is done by introducing an auxiliary boolean variable (Q) to carry the evaluation result of the guard represented by OK ($\sim Q$ for NOK). Three activities a_{10}, a_{11} and a_{12} are also added to assign appropriate values to Q. The resulting workflow in Fig. 8 has a structured loop which can be directly mapped to a while activity. Each loop starts if Q has a value of $false$, otherwise the loop will be exit. The main activity of the loop is a sequence of a_5, a_6 and a conditional choice between two branches – one for the guard represented by $DONE$, the other for $NEED\text{-}CHECK$.

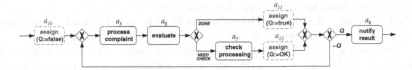

Fig. 8. A structured form of the original unstructured workflow in CAB_3

6   Conclusions

Capturing workflow patterns such as multi-merge, arbitrary cycles and multiple instances in BPEL is problematic. On the other hand, these patterns can be directly captured in standard process modelling notations (i.e. BPMN and UML AD). This mismatch hinders the definition of automated translations from process models to process implementations when using these standards. This paper has presented a technique to translate models captured in a core subset of BPMN or UML AD into BPEL. The technique exploits an interesting and often underused BPEL construct, namely "event handler".

To the best of our knowledge, this is the first attempt at tackling the above patterns in a systematic translation from BPMN or UML AD to BPEL. The proposal has been validated through the implementation of a tool (SPM2BPEL) that automatically translates Standard Process Models into BPEL code. The paper also sketched possible improvements to the technique by clustering activities into activity blocks that can be mapped onto BPEL structured activities, thereby reducing the number of event handlers in the resulting BPEL process.

Ongoing work aims at designing and implementing an algorithm for the improved translation technique. We then plan to extend the technique to cover other workflow patterns, e.g. deferred choice and cancellation. Since the deferred choice captures a race condition between events, the translation algorithm presented in this paper, which excludes race conditions, will need to be revisited. Investigating the expressiveness of BPEL's "pick" and "fault handler" constructs, which allow one to capture race conditions and cancellation in structured settings, may provide a foundation for designing this extended translation.

References

1. W.M.P. van der Aalst. Don't go with the flow: Web services composition standards exposed. *IEEE Intelligent Systems*, 18(1):72–76, 2003.
2. W.M.P. van der Aalst, A.H.M. ter Hofstede, B. Kiepuszewski, and A. P. Barros. Workflow Patterns. *Distributed and Parallel Databases*, 14(3):5–51, July 2003.
3. A. Arkin, S. Askary, B. Bloch, F. Curbera, Y. Goland, N. Kartha, C. K. Liu, S. Thatte, P. Yendluri, and A. Yiu, editors. *Web Services Business Process Execution Language Version 2.0*. Working Draft. WS-BPEL TC OASIS, May 2005.
4. M. Dumas, T. Fjellheim, S. Milliner, and J. Vayssiére. Event-based coordination of process-oriented composite applications. In *Proceedings of the International Conference on Business Process Management (BPM2005)*, volume 3649 of *Lecture Notes in Computer Science*, pages 236–251. Springer-Verlag, 2005.
5. P. Harmon. Standardizing business process notation. URL: http://www.bptrends.com, November 2003.
6. B. Kiepuszewski, A.H.M. ter Hofstede, and W.M.P. van der Aalst. Fundamentals of control flow in workflows. *Acta Informatica*, 39(3):143–209, 2003.
7. B. Kiepuszewski, A.H.M. ter Hofstede, and C. Bussler. On structured workflow modelling. In *Proceedings of 12th International Conference on Advanced Information Systems Engineering (CAiSE 2000)*, volume 1789 of *Lecture Notes in Computer Science*, pages 431–445. Springer-Verlag, 2000.
8. R. Liu and A. Kumar. An analysis and taxonomy of unstructured workflows. In *Proceedings of the International Conference BPM2005*, volume 3649 of *Lecture Notes in Computer Science*, pages 268–284. Springer-Verlag, 2005.
9. K. Mantell. From UML to BPEL. URL: http://www.ibm.com/developerworks/webservices/library/ws-uml2bpel, September 2005.
10. OMG. *Unified Modeling Language: Superstructure*. UML Superstructure Specification v2.0, formal/05-07-04. OMG, August 2005.
11. G. Oulsnam. Unravelling unstructured programs. *Computer Journal*, 25(3): 379–387, 1982.
12. S. A. White. *Business Process Modeling Notation (BPMN) Version 1.0*. Business Process Management Initiative, BPMI.org, May 2004.
13. P. Wohed, W.M.P. van der Aalst, M. Dumas, and A.H.M. ter Hofstede. Analysis of Web services composition languages: The case of BPEL4WS. In *Proceedings of 22nd International Conference on Conceptual Modeling (ER 2003)*, volume 2813 of *Lecture Notes in Computer Science*, pages 200–215. Springer-Verlag, 2003.

Semantic Annotation Framework to Manage Semantic Heterogeneity of Process Models

Yun Lin, Darijus Strasunskas, Sari Hakkarainen, John Krogstie, and Arne Sølvberg

Norwegian University of Science and Technology,
7491 Trondheim, Norway
{yunl, dstrasun, sari, krogstie, asolvber}@idi.ntnu.no

Abstract. Effective discovery and sharing of process models within and/or across enterprises are important in process model management. A semantic annotation approach has been applied for specifying process semantic heterogeneity in the semantic process model discovery in our previous work. In this paper, the approach is further developed into a complete and systematic semantic annotation framework. Four perspectives are tackled in our framework: basic description of process models (profile annotation), process modeling languages (meta-model annotation), process models (model annotation) and the purpose of the process models (goal annotation). Ontologies, including modeling ontology, domain specific ontology and goal ontology, are used for annotation of process models to achieve semantic interoperability. A set of mapping strategies are defined to guide users to annotate process models.

1 Introduction

A considerable amount of business knowledge is put into process models and scattered within and across organizations. Therefore, the possibility to efficiently retrieve and reuse this knowledge is limited. A research problem in process model management is to how cope with semantic heterogeneity of both process models and process modeling languages. The problem of semantic heterogeneity is even more critical in a situation of extensive cooperation and interoperation between distributed systems across different enterprises. The heterogeneity makes it difficult to manipulate the distributed process models in a centralized manner. Ontologies and semantic metadata provide a means to tackle this problem. Thus, we are using ontology-based semantic annotation to tackle the heterogeneous semantics of distributed process models.

In our previous work [10, 11], the semantic heterogeneity problems of process models have been analyzed and the ontology-based semantic annotation approach has been applied in example applications to test the feasibility of the approach. In this paper, the semantic annotation approach is further developed and refined in a semantic annotation framework, which contains profile annotation, meta-model annotation, model annotation and goal annotation.

In order to differentiate process models, we specify a set of metadata to annotate the significant characteristics of process models, terming this the profile. Ontology provides an alignment of the different terminology and conceptualization used in the

E. Dubois and K. Pohl (Eds.): CAiSE 2006, LNCS 4001, pp. 433–446, 2006.
© Springer-Verlag Berlin Heidelberg 2006

models and in modeling languages. Thus, we use ontologies to relate constructs across different modeling languages, as well as to align domain specific terminology used in models. In this way we are able to solve semantic heterogeneity in model management. Furthermore, in order to facilitate goal-driven process model reuse we annotate process models using a goal ontology. This allows discovery of process models used for achieving certain (business) goals.

The contribution of this paper is as follows. First, an extended and refined General Process Ontology (GPO) is presented that constitutes a semantic annotation framework. Second, a process semantic annotation model (PSAM) is developed and presented formally. This explicitly defines all necessary annotation elements. Third, mapping strategies and rules for process model annotation are described to provide a better guidance in model annotation.

The rest of the paper is organized as follows. In section 2, the theoretical basis on modeling and ontology of process models is discussed. Then, the semantic annotation framework and mapping strategies are described in details in section 3. In section 4, we define a process semantic annotation model and formalize it. In section 5 we compare the approach with the related work. Finally, we conclude this paper and outline our future work in section 6.

2   Theoretical Basis of Modeling and Ontology

In this section we will discuss the relationship between process models and ontologies in the context of semantic interoperability and semantic annotation.

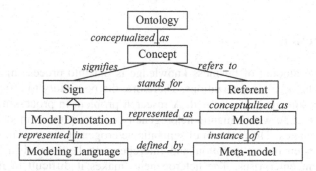

Fig. 1. Relationship between ontology, model, meta-model and modeling language

We adapt the semantic triangle [14] to define the relationships between model, meta-model, modeling language and ontology (see Fig. 1). A model is a conceptualization of referents and it is represented as a set of model denotations in a certain modeling language. Model denotations are signs which signify concepts in the model. The model is an instance of a meta-model, and the meta-model defines a modeling language. Typically, a same concept can refer to different referents in different models. In order for the machine to understand the heterogeneous semantics of the models (e.g. various signs of referents referring to the same concepts or synonymic signs of referents referring to different concepts), a common understanding of concepts has to be formulized in a machine-interpretable way. An ontology is created for this purpose. Here, concepts are conceptualized as an ontology.

A meta-model is also a model – a model of the modeling language. Thus, a meta-model is the conceptualization of modeling referents referred by modeling concepts, and it can be concretized and represented as a specific modeling language. The modeling ontology is a kind of methodology ontology which contains a vocabulary of the modeling concepts (constructs). According to Leppanen's OntoFrame [9], the meta-model can be adapted from the modeling ontology. Accordingly, the heterogeneous modeling languages can be aligned through annotating the meta-model by the modeling ontology.

3   Semantic Annotation Framework

In this section, we will describe our semantic annotation framework for process models in details. Four main annotation sets constitute the framework: namely, profile annotation, meta-model annotation, model annotation and goal annotation. They are discussed in more detail as follows.

3.1   Profile Annotation

The basic and characteristic features of a process model are described by a set of metadata in the profile annotation. We categorize metadata elements for profile annotation according to the types of metadata – administrative, descriptive, preservation, technical and use [4].

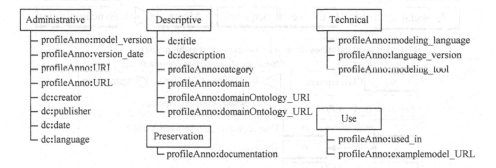

Fig. 2. Profile annotation metadata elements

We reuse some metadata elements from the Dublin Core metadata standard with prefix 'dc' and create also additional metadata with prefix 'profileAnno' to describe the profile of a process model. These metadata elements are classified in Fig. 2.

3.2   Meta-model Annotation

In the meta-model annotation, we use a process modeling ontology as metadata to annotate the semantics of constructs in a modeling language. Therefore, we first introduce our process modeling ontology, and then describe the way of annotating the semantics of meta-models of process modeling languages.

3.2.1 Process Modeling Ontology – GPO

The process modeling ontology is used to align the heterogeneous meta-models of process models. The process modeling ontology should provide a common conceptualization of the concepts typically used in existing process meta-models or process modeling languages. In [10, 11], we built a General Process Ontology (GPO) according to the investigation of some process ontologies and process modeling languages includeing PSL, TOVE, PIF-CORE, CPR, EEML, BPMN and BPML. The visual GPO model is represented in RML (Referent Modeling Language) [17] in Fig. 3. RML is a conceptual modeling language, which can be used to visualize an ontology model.

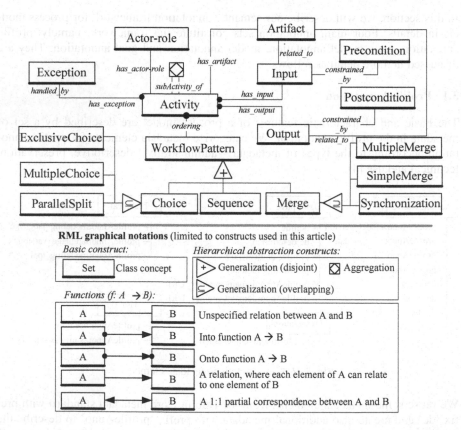

Fig. 3. Visualization of GPO

In our GPO (see Fig. 3 for visual model represented in RML (Referent Modeling Language) [17]), we include the following concepts which are usually modeled as modeling constructs in most process modeling languages: *Activity, Artifact, Actor-role, Input, Output, Precondition, Postcondition, Exception* and *WorkflowPattern*.

Compared with our previous work [10, 11], GPO is updated here by changing the relations between *Precondition, Postcondition* and *Activity* into the relations between *Precondition, Postcondition* and *Input, Output*. Such update is made because the pre- or post- conditions are directly related to inputs and outputs of activities. It is not necessary to make an indirect relationship between pre- or post-condition and input or output through the connection of activity. Another extension of GPO in this paper includes refinement of *WorkflowPattern* into several more specific patterns according to van der Aalst's workflow patterns [19], such as *Choice (Exclusive Choice, MultipleChoice, ParallelSpit), Merge (SimpleMerge, MultipleMerge, Synchronization)* and *Sequence*, which are basic control workflow patterns supported by most process modeling languages with logical symbols like AND, OR and XOR. The aim of including workflow patterns in GPO is for the user to navigate the preceding, succeeding, synchronizing and exclusive activities, because those workflow patterns denote the semantics of process orders.

GPO is implemented as an ontology using Protégé according to the graphical GPO model in Fig. 3. The concepts in GPO will be mapped with meta-models of process modeling languages.

3.2.2 Mapping Rules in Meta-model Annotation

GPO is a mediator for the semantics of process concepts and it should not be seen as a new process modeling language, but a means to annotate the process modeling constructs.

Meta-model annotation has to be done manually by experts who know the process modeling language to be annotated. The procedure of meta-model annotation is actually to set mapping rules between process modeling language constructs or meta-model elements and GPO. The mapping rules consist of both one-to-one and one-to-many correspondences between GPO concepts and modeling language constructs or meta-model elements. There may be more complicated cases: a correspondence between a GPO concept and a combination of some modeling language constructs or meta-model elements. To define the mapping rules for different cases, we categorize three types of modeling constructs – *AtomicConstruct, EnumeratedConstruct* and *ComposedConstruct*. Each single modeling language construct is an *AtomicConstruct*, an *EnumeratedConstuct* is an enumeration set of several *AtomicConstructs*, and a *ComposedConstruct* is composed of several *AtomicConstructs*.

Mapping Rules:

- One-to-one mapping: a GPO concept (e.g. *GPO:Activity*) is referred by an *AtomicConstruct* (e.g. *EEML:Task*);
- One-to-many mapping: a GPO concept (e.g. *GPO:Artifact*) can be referred respectively by several modeling language constructs (e.g. *EEML:Information Object* and *EEML:Material Object*) which are enumerated in an *EnumeratedConstruct*;
- One-to-combination mapping: a GPO concept (e.g. *GPO:WorkflowPattern*) is referred by the combination of those modeling language constructs (e.g. *EEML:Flow* and *EEML:Decision Point*) in a *ComposedConstruct*.

A namespace **metaAnno** is used to encode meta-model annotation in these three mapping cases:

```
<metaAnno:AtomicConstruct rdf:ID="CONSTRUCT_ID">
    <metaAnno:refers_to
        rdf:resource="&GPO_ONTOLOGY#MODELING_ONTOLOGY_CONCEPT"/>
    <metaAnno:modeling_language_construct
        rdf:resource="&MODELNG_LANGUAGE#LANGUAGE_CONSTRUCT"/>
</metaAnno:AtomicConstruct>

<metaAnno:EnumeratedConstruct rdf:ID="CONSTRUCT_ID">
    <metaAnno:refers_to
        rdf:resource="&GPO_ONTOLOGY#MODELING_ONTOLOGY_CONCEPT"/>
    <metaAnno:has>
        <metaAnno:AtomicConstruct rdf:resource="#CONSTRUCT_ID">
            ...
    </metaAnno:has>
</metaAnno:EnumeratedConstruct>

<metaAnno:ComposedConstruct rdf:ID="CONSTRUCT_ID">
    <metaAnno:refers_to
        rdf:resource="&GPO_ONTOLOGY#MODELING_ONTOLOGY_CONCEPT"/>
    <metaAnno:composed_of>
        <metaAnno:AtomicConstruct rdf:resource="#CONSTRUCT_ID">
            ...
    </metaAnno:composed_of>
</metaAnno:ComposedConstruct>
```

Once the mapping rules are defined for a certain process modeling language, the process models in that process modeling language can be described by the GPO concepts, i.e. the GPO concepts are used as metadata to annotate the process semantics. We call the process models described by the GPO metadata as GPO-annotated process model. The GPO-annotated process model will be formulized in the *process semantic annotation model (PSAM)* in Section 4.

3.3 Model Annotation

When a process model is described by the semantic process annotation model, the process model looks similar to a Web service described by OWL-S. The semantics of the process can be interpreted by machine. However, the contents in the semantic process annotation model are only annotated with very abstract concepts like artifact, activity, actor-role, etc. The concrete domain information in the contents needs to be related with domain specific ontology in order to deal with the semantic heterogeneity of model contents. For example, two process models are both about travel booking domain. In one model, a concept called 'client' is annotated as an actor-role; while the concept named 'customer' is also annotated as actor-role in another model. If we map those two concepts to one concept in the travel booking domain ontology (in this case identifying them being synonyms), the machine will know how these two concepts are related, which helps to discover the related process model fragments. Therefore, we need to further annotate the model with domain specific ontologies. The model annotation facilitates the semantic discovery and navigation of process model fragments, which are parts of process models.

3.3.1 Model Annotation Scope
The model annotation can be accomplished with the help of meta-model annotation, because the models related to domain information are usually artifacts, actor-roles,

activities and exceptions in the semantic process annotation models. Artifacts and actor-roles are usually static concepts. Those concepts are defined in a local domain model which provides the context of those concepts. The model annotation is to map the concepts in the local domain model to the concepts defined in the domain specific ontology. If the concepts are not defined in a local domain model, the mapping has to be defined by the user manually. The activities and exceptions are usually related to the task ontology in certain domains. Currently, most domain specific ontologies consist of only static concepts including few concepts about activities or tasks. Task ontologies can be seen as reference processes. One example is SCOR[1] supported by SAP. Another example of task ontology is ontology of *Laboratory Procedures* from [8]: A *LaboratoryProcedure* is a subclass of the class of *Health Care Activities* and a *Chemical* is a subclass of the class of *Substances*; a *Laboratory Procedure* analyzes a *Chemical* and a *Chemical* is analyzed by a *Laboratory Procedure*.

If the task ontology in a certain domain is available, the activities and exceptions can be annotated by concepts defined in the task ontology. If such task ontology can not be found, we can leave this part to the goal annotation, in which a set of predefined goals are linked to the processes or activities.

3.3.2 Mapping Strategies

Different mapping strategies can be used between concepts in the model and the domain specific ontology. It can be simple ones which are applied in meta-model annotation – by referring specific modeling constructs to corresponding domain concepts. It can also be more complicated through refined semantic relationships between concepts used in models and concepts defined in domain ontology.

Simple Reference. If the simple mapping by reference is applied, it assumes that almost all concepts in the model have equal or approximately equal concepts in the ontology. The semantic relationship of mapping can be defined as one type – *refers_to*. We have adopted such mapping strategy in the meta-model annotation to build the correspondences of concepts between modeling languages and the GPO. In the model annotation, users can choose this strategy provided the concepts in the models are very close to the concepts defined in the domain specific ontology. The strategy of simple reference is easy to apply to map the concepts and also make it easy for the machine to infer the mapping relationships without complicated algorithms.

Refined Semantic Relationships. Concepts used in process models are variously defined initially for different projects. Therefore, it might be difficult to find equally defined concepts in the domain specific ontology for process models. However, they are still within one domain, there must be some semantic relationships between concepts in models and concepts in ontology. In order to represent the semantic relationships precisely, we define some refined semantic relationships to link the concepts between models and ontologies for the model annotation.

As described in section 3.3.1 the contents related to artifacts, actor-roles, activities and exceptions are those to be annotated by domain specific ontology concepts. Semantic relationships and the corresponding annotation denotations generally used for the model annotation are listed in Table 1.

---

[1] SCOR(Supply-Chain Operations Reference-model), see www.supply-chain.org

Table 1. Semantic relationships and corresponding annotation denotations

Semantic Relationship	Annotation Denotation
Synonym	*alternative_name* (terminology_level)
	same_as (concept level)
Polysemy	*different_from*
Hypernym	*kind_of*
Hyponym	*superConcept_of*
Meronym	*part_of* (Artifact)
	member_of (Actor-role)
	phase_of (Activity)
	partialEffect_of (Exception)
Holonym	*compositionConcept_of*

Both synonym and polysemy relationships are symmetrical. Hypernym and hyponym are inverse relationships. Concepts in the ontology are more general, while model concepts are relatively concrete for specific projects. Thus, *kind_of* is more often used than *superConcept_ of* when annotating model concepts with ontology concepts. We provide more human sense expressions of meronymic relationship for artifacts, actor-roles, activities and exceptions respectively. For artifacts, we use *part_of*, e.g. 'Engine' is a part of 'Airplane'; for actor-roles, we use *member_of*, e.g. 'Airline' is a member of 'Air Alliance'; for activities, we use *phase_of*, e.g. 'Flying' is a phase of 'Travelling'; for exceptions, we use *partialEffect_of*, e.g. 'Payment is cancelled' is a partial effect of 'Booking has failed'. The inverse relationship of meronym is holonymic relationship, which is seldom used in this framework because of the similar reason described for the hyponym relationship.

We focus on the type level process models in this research, the relationship between instance and class is not included in the framework. We assume that instances are already defined by type-level model constructs in each process model. The contents to be annotated are consequently on the type-level.

Since after the meta-model annotation the model can be described as a GPO-annotated process model, the model annotation can be done directly in the GPO-annotated process model instead of original models. Thereby, the model annotation notations and markup annotation language will be formulized in the *process semantic annotation model* in section 4.

3.4 Goal Annotation

Each process described in a process model is oriented towards achievement of certain goals. Goal analysis is initially separated from process modeling. Nonetheless, there is a relationship between goals and activities. As discussed in [12]: "Goals (desired states of the world) and activities (actions performed to achieve a particular state) are clearly different. However, analyzing activities and goals together makes clear the parallel between decomposing a goal into subgoals to be achieved and decomposing it into primitive activities to be performed".

Some process modeling languages and tools support goal modeling as part of process modeling, such as EEML [7] implemented in the Metis tool[2]. Thus, a set of goals may

---

[2] http://www.troux.com/

be already modeled locally and linked to process models. Having an ontology of goals (global goals) will enable to build the relations between local goals and global goals.

In order to unify the semantics of the links between goals and process models and the relationships between local goal and global goal defined in goal ontology, we extend the annotation framework by additional links as follows. *Achieves_lGoal* relationship between an activity and a local goal and *achieves_gGoal* relationship between an activity and a global goal are used to denote that the activity can achieve the goal. Two types of relationships – *supports* and *contradicts* are defined for relationships between a local goal and a global goal. *Supports* means the achievement of the local goal will help to achieve the global goal; while *contradicts* discloses that achieving the local goal will prevent the realization of the global goal. The above relationships are formalized for the goal annotation in the *process semantic annotation model* in the following section.

4   Process Semantic Annotation Model

As discribed earlier, a process model is represented by GPO concepts in the meta-model annotation. The content annotation and the goal annotation are applied on this GPO represented model. In this section, we formalize the GPO-annotated model together with the content annotation and the goal annotation as a process semantic annotation model.

Definition 1. Process Semantic Annotation Model (*PSAM*) contains concepts of GPO, domain specific ontology and goal ontology and is defined as follows.

$$PSAM = (AV, AR, AF, WP, I, O, \Theta^{pre}, \Theta^{pos}, E, PD, G^l, PG^g) \cdot \tag{1}$$

Where AV is a set of activity composing a process, AR is a set of actor-roles interacting with a process, AF is a set of artifacts participating in a process, WP is a set of workflow patterns, and each workflow pattern denotes an ordering of activities. I is a set of input parameters, O is a set of output parameters, Θ^{pre} is pre-conditions when a process starts, Θ^{pos} is post-conditions when a process ends, E is a set of possible exceptions occurring during a process. PD is a subset of domain ontology (D) concepts, i.e. $PD \subseteq D$, including static ontology concepts and task ontology concepts. G^l is a set of local goals and PG^g is a subset of goal ontology (G^g), i.e. $PG^g \subseteq G^g$.

Definition 2. An activity can be considered as a simple process. Therefore an annotated activity is described as follows.

$$\begin{aligned}AV_i = (&id, model\_fragment, name, alternative\_name, has\_Actor\text{-}role,\\ &has\_Artifact, has\_Input, has\_Output, is\_in\_WorkflowPattern\_of,\\ &has\_Precondition, has\_Postcondition, has\_Exception,\\ &subActivity\_of, same\_as, different\_from, kind\_of, superConcept\_of,\\ &phase\_of, compositionConcept\_of, achieves\_lGoal, achieves\_gGoal).\end{aligned} \tag{2}$$

Each element in PSAM has *id* and *name* to uniquely identify the element. *Model_fragment* is the model fragment id in the original process model for keeping the link between the annotated model fragment and its annotation information. *Alternative_name* provides synonym of the name from terminology level. Elements *has_Actor-role, has_Artifact, has_Input, has_Output, is_in_WorkflowPattern_of, has_Precondition, has_Postcondition, has_Exception, subActivity_of* denote the relationships between the activity and other related elements according to the GPO definition. The *ids* of the related elements are used in those relationships. We use *same_as, different_from, kind_of, superConcept_of, phase_of, compositionConcept_of* to annotate the activities with domain ontology, i.e. using semantic relationship mapping an activity with concepts defined in domain ontology. *Achieves_lGoal* is to link the activity to the *id* of a local goal and *Achieves_gGoal* links the activity to a global goal defined in the goal ontology. Ontology concepts are denoted by URI (Uniform Resource Identifier) in the process semantic annotation model.

Definition 3. An actor-role is the person, agent or organization that interacts with an activity. The annotated actor-role is represented as follows.

$$AR_i = (id, model\_fragment, name, alternative\_name, same\_as, different\_from, \\ kind\_of, superConcept\_of, member\_of, compositionConcept\_of). \tag{3}$$

Definition 4. An artifact is the thing consumed, used or produced in an activity.

$$AF_i = (id, model\_fragment, name, alternative\_name, same\_as, different\_from, \\ kind\_of, superConcept\_of, part\_of, compositionConcept\_of). \tag{4}$$

Definition 5. A workflow pattern represents the type of the ordering of activities.

$$WP_i = (id, model\_fragment, name, alternative\_name). \tag{5a}$$

Refined workflow patterns are defined as follows.

$$Choice_i = (id, model\_fragment, name, alternative\_name, has\_inActivity, \\ has\_outActivity, has\_logicConnector). \tag{5b}$$

Where the cardinality of *has_inActivity* is 1. The *has_logicConnector* element of *Exclusive Choice_i, Multiple Choice_i* and *ParallelSplit_i* has value 'XOR', 'OR' or 'AND' respectively.

$$Merge_i = (id, model\_fragment, name, alternative\_name, has\_inActivity, \\ has\_outActivity, has\_logicConnector). \tag{5c}$$

Where the cardinality of *has_outActivity* is 1. The *has_logicConnector* element of *Simple Merge_i, Multiple Merge_i,* and *Synchronizatione* has value 'XOR', 'OR' or 'AND' respectively.

$$Sequence_i = (id, model\_fragment, name, alternative\_name, has\_inActivity, \\ has\_outActivity). \tag{5d}$$

Where the cardinalities of both *has_inActivity* and *has_outActivity* are 1.

Definition 6. Input and output are defined as parameters of an activity, which include value and data type. They are usually related to artifacts participating in the activity.

$$I_i = (id, model\_fragment, name, alternative\_name, data\_type, related\_artifact), \\ O_i = (id, model\_fragment, name, alternative\_name, data\_type, related\_artifact). \tag{6}$$

If a same artifact related with both input parameter and output parameter of an activity, the state of the artifact must be changed through this activity. We call it transformation.

Definition 7. Precondition and postcondition are presented by expressions to constrain input and output. The constraints are usually used as contract in services or process composition.

$$\Theta_i^{pre} = (id, \ model\_fragment, \ name, \ alternative\_name, \ related\_input) \ ,$$

$$\Theta_i^{pos} = (id, \ model\_fragment, \ name, \ alternative\_name, \ related\_output) \ . \tag{7}$$

Definition 8. Exception happens in an activity and it can be handled by an activity.

$$E_i = (id, \ model\_fragment, \ name, \ alternative\_name, \ handler\_Activity, \ same\_as,$$
$$different\_from, \ kind\_of, \ superConcept\_of, \ partialEffect\_of, \tag{8}$$
$$compositionConcept\_of).$$

Exception will be annotated using predefined exception types in domain ontology. The activity handling the exception is pointed out by *handler_activity*.

Definition 9. Local goals are sometimes defined together with local process models and linked to activities in the process model.

$$G_i^l = (id, \ model\_fragment, \ name, \ alternative\_name, \ supports, \ contradicts). \tag{9}$$

The relationships between a local goal and activities are defined in activity element. Here we only annotate the relationships between a local goal and a global goal with *supports* and *contradicts*.

Domain ontology (D) and goal ontology (G^g) are defined in current Web Ontology Languages, such as OWL. With the semantic process annotation model, the process semantics of different models can be caught and represented by the concepts of GPO, domain ontology and goal ontology which harmonize the semantic heterogeneity of process modeling languages, models and process goals. Based on the above formalizations, we define a markup process semantic annotation language with namespace **psam** by extending GPO ontological definitions in OWL using Protégé. Consequently, the extension includes adding a concept *LocalGoal* and properties for all concepts. An example of this markup annotation language of representing an annotated *Artifact* is below:

```
<psam:Artifact rdf:ID="ID">
    <psam:model_fragment rdf:resource="&MODEL_NAMESPACE#MODEL_ID"/>
    <psam:name>NAME</psam:name>
    <psam:alternative_name>ALTERNATIVE_NAME</psam:alternative_name>
    <psam:same_as
        rdf:resource="&DOMAIN_ONTOLOGY#DOMAIN_ONTOLOGY_CONCEPT"/>
    <psam:different_from
        rdf:resource="&DOMAIN_ONTOLOGY#DOMAIN_ONTOLOGY_CONCEPT"/>
    <psam:kind_of
        rdf:resource="&DOMAIN_ONTOLOGY#DOMAIN_ONTOLOGY_CONCEPT"/>
    <psam:superConcept_of
        rdf:resource="&DOMAIN_ONTOLOGY#DOMAIN_ONTOLOGY_CONCEPT"/>
    <psam:part_of
        rdf:resource="&DOMAIN_ONTOLOGY#DOMAIN_ONTOLOGY_CONCEPT"/>
```

```
<psam:compositionConcept_of
    rdf:resource="&DOMAIN_ONTOLOGY#DOMAIN_ONTOLOGY_CONCEPT"/>
</psam:Artifact>
```

5 Related Work

Semantic interoperability is an active research area caused by the semantic heterogeneity in current information systems. Semantic interoperability is the ability to integrate data sources developed using different vocabularies and different perspectives on data [16]. To achieve semantic interoperability, the semantics of data have to be machine-understandable.

The most popular approach to tackle the semantic interoperability problem is to apply domain ontology. The domain ontology approach uses a machine understandable definition of concepts and relationships between concepts so that there is a shared common understanding within a community [16]. Semantic annotation is a way of linking domain ontology and data to align the semantics defined heterogeneously into agreed machine-understandable semantics. It is initially applied in annotating unstructured Web content and digital documents e.g. Web pages, digital texts or images with formally defined semantic metadata. The semantic annotation helps to achieve more precise and efficient information retrieval on the Web or from Digital Libraries. Later on, the concept of annotation is extended to the structured Web Services to envision the Semantic Web Services. Semantically described services will enable better service discovery and allow easier interoperation and composition of Web Services [15]. The widely used Semantic Web Services Ontology Languages are DAML-S [1] and OWL-S [13] based on a W3C standard. Another emerging proposal for Semantic Web Services is from DERI[3] which comprises WSMO[4] (Web Services Modeling Ontology) and WSML (Web Services Modeling Language). Semantics of services content can be added to the services described either by syntactic Web Service standards or ontology-based description language. The common factor in most of these approaches is relating concepts in Web Services to domain specific ontologies [15], so called the semantic annotation approach.

The semantic annotation approach has been applied and tested on both unstructured and structured artifacts to achieve semantic interoperability. Seldom work is done on the semi-structured artifact, e.g. enterprise/business process models. In traditional information system development the process models were usually defined and used for a specific project within an enterprise. They were seldom reused in other projects or interoperated and integrated with other external process models. It is difficult to reuse models because of lacking of knowledge about the context of models, modeling methodologies, standards of modeling languages and also because of the semantic heterogeneity problem.

Some ongoing European projects like INTEROP [6] and ATHENA [2] aim to achieve the interoperability of heterogeneous systems and applications across networked enterprises. The interoperability of enterprise models is one of important issues dealt with in both projects. They share a common objective of Enterprise Modeling, i.e. pro-

---

[3] http://www.deri.org/
[4] http://www.wsmo.org/

viding a set of core modeling methodology elements or a shared language for supporting collaborative enterprise design and management. In the INTEROP project, a common enterprise modeling language – UEML 2.1 adapted from the UEML project [18] is under development. The UEML comprises languages and techniques that can be used for exchanging information between enterprise modeling tools [3]. Similarly, the POP* methodology is proposed in ATHENA project including a set of common and basic modeling constructs to support model interchange. Although those two proposals are not directly associated with semantic annotation, both UEML and POP* provides common semantic definitions of modeling constructs primarily for model exchange between tools and not for reusing existing models [5].

Our method deals with the heterogeneous semantic definitions of different process modeling languages by meta-model annotation through the General Process Ontology (GPO). Although GPO looks like UEML or POP*, it is defined as an ontology only concerning the process dimension not a modeling language covering all perspectives in the enterprise domain. GPO is defined in OWL in order to make use of semantic Web technology to create a computer-interpretable semantic markup language for process modeling in the Web environment. As a whole, our semantic annotation framework intends to achieve the semantic discovery of process models but not to focus on the enterprise model translation as UEML or POP* mainly do. Therefore, current UEML or POP* methodology only deals with semantic heterogeneity on modeling language level. We have to address the semantic heterogeneity problem on both model and modeling language levels. Additionally the context of process models is also considered in our semantic annotation approach by employing the profile annotation and goal annotation.

6 Conclusions and Future Work

Based on our previous work, we have proposed a semantic annotation framework to manage the semantic heterogeneity of process models from the following perspectives: basic description of process models (*profile annotation*), process modeling languages (*meta-model annotation*), process models (*model annotation*) and the purpose of the process models (*goal annotation*). Three ontologies are used for annotation purposes: *General Process Ontology* used for meta-model annotation, *domain ontology* for model annotation and *goal ontology* for process goal annotation. Furthermore, we have defined a set of mapping strategies for guiding users to annotate models. Nevertheless, the formal process semantic annotation model (PSAM) is the main contribution of this paper.

Further we are going to elaborate on the goal annotation part of the framework. A semantic annotation tool based on the framework is under development. We are looking at the possibility to make it as a Plug-in for Metis, a powerful tool for enterprise modeling and meta-modeling. The techniques of integrating or importing ontologies into modeling tools are a primary interest. The validity of the mapping in meta model annotation and model annotation will be checked using DL (Description Logic) based reasoning mechanisms. The framework is going to be further evaluated by implementing semantic process model discovery applications, and using this on selected case studies.

References

1. Ankolekar, A., Burstein, M., Hobbs, J., Lassila, O., Martin, D., McDermott, D., Mcllraith, S., Narayanan, S., Paolucci, M., Payne, T., Sycara, K.: DAML-S: Web service Description for the Semantic Web. In Proc. of the 1st Int'l. Semantic Web Conf., LNCS 2343, Springer-Verlag (2002) 348-363.
2. ATHENA Project (IST-2003-2004). http://www.athena-ip.org (2005) (Last accessed: 2006 02 15).
3. Bourrieres, J.P., Missikoff, M., Berre, A., Doumeingts, G., Piddington, C.: Deliverable D4.2 INTEROP 2nd Workplan. http://interop-noe.org/deliv/d4.2/attach/D4.2%20V1.pdf (2005) (Last accessed: 2006 02 15).
4. Gill, T., Gilliland-Swetland, A., Baca, M.: Introduction to Metadata: Pathways to Digital Information. Baca, M. (Ed.) Getty Information Institute, Los Angeles, USA (2000).
5. Grangel, R., Chalmeta, R.: A Methodological Approach for Enterprise Modeling of Small and Medium Virtual Enterprises based on UML: Application to a Tile Virtual Enterprise. In Proc. of Doctoral Symposium in the 1st Int'l Conf. on Interoperability of Enterprise Software and Applications, Geneva, Switzerland (2005).
6. INTEROP Project. http://interop-noe.org (2006) (Last accessed: 2006 02 15).
7. Krogstie, J., Jørgensen, D.H.: Interactive Models for Supporting Networked Organisations. In Proc. 16th Intl. Conf. on Advanced Information Systems Engineering, LNCS 3084, Springer-Verlag (2004) 550-562.
8. Kumar, A., Ciccarese, P., Smith, B., Piazza, M.: Context-Based Task Ontologies for Clinical Guidelines. In Pisanelli, D.M. (Ed.) Ontologies in Medicine, Proc. of Workshop on Medical Ontologies. Amsterdam: IOS Press (2004) 81-94.
9. Leppanen, M.: An Ontological Framework and a Methodical Skeleton for Method Engineering: A Contextual Approach. PhD Thesis at University of Jyvaskyla, Finland (2005).
10. Lin, Y., Strasunskas, D.: Ontology-based Semantic Annotation of Process Templates for Reuse. In Castro, J. and Teniente, E. (Eds.): Proc. of the CAiSE'05 Workshops Vol.1 (EMMSAD Workshop). Porto, Portugal (2005) 593-604.
11. Lin, Y., Ding, H.: Ontology-based Semantic Web Annotation for Semantic Interoperability of Process Models. In Proc. of the Int'l Conf. on Computational Intelligence for Modeling, Control and Automation, Vienna, Austria (2005).
12. Malone, T.W., Crowston, K., Herman, G.A.: Organizing Business Knowledge: The MIT Process Handbook. The MIT Press (2003).
13. Martin, D., Burstein, M., Hobbs, J., Lassila, O., McDermott, D., Mcllraith, S., Narayanan, S., Paolucci, M., Parsia, B., Payne, T., Sirin, E., Srinivasan, N., Sycara, K.: OWL-S: Semantic Markup for Web Services. http://www.w3.org/Submission/OWL-S/ (Last accessed: 2006 02 15).
14. Ogden, C., Richards, I.: The Meaning of Meaning. London: Kegan Paul (1923).
15. Patil, A., Oundhakar, S., Sheth, A., Verma, K.: METEOR-S Web Service Annotation Framework. In Proc. of the 13th Int'l. World Wide Web Conf., ACM Press (2004) 553-562.
16. Ram, S., Park, J.: Semantic Conflict Resolution Ontology (SCROL): An Ontology for Detecting and Resolving Data and Schema-Level Semantic Conflicts. IEEE Transactions on Knowledge and Data Engineering 16(2), (2004) 189-202.
17. Solvberg, A.: Data and What They Refer To. In Chen, P., Akoka, J., Kangassalo, H., Thalheim, B. (Eds.): Conceptual Modeling: Current Issues and Future Trends. LNCS 1565. Springer-Verlag (1999) 211-226.
18. UEML Project (IST-2001-34229). http://www.ueml.org (2005) (Last accessed: 2006 02 15).
19. van der Aalst, W.M.P, Barros, A.P., ter Hofstede, A.H.M., Kiepuszewski, B.: Advanced Workflow Patterns. In Proc. of the 7th Int'l. Conf. on Cooperative Information Systems, LNCS 1901, Springer-Verlag (2000) 18-29.

A Study of the Evolution of the Representational Capabilities of Process Modeling Grammars

Michael Rosemann[1], Jan Recker[1], Marta Indulska[2], and Peter Green[2]

[1] Faculty of Information Technology,
Queensland University of Technology,
Brisbane, Australia
{m.rosemann, j.recker}@qut.edu.au
[2] UQ Business School,
University of Queensland,
Ipswich, Australia
{m.indulska, p.green}@business.uq.edu.au

Abstract. A plethora of process modeling techniques has been proposed over the years. One way of evaluating and comparing the scope and completeness of techniques is by way of representational analysis. The purpose of this paper is to examine how process modeling techniques have developed over the last four decades. The basis of the comparison is the Bunge-Wand-Weber representation model, a benchmark used for the analysis of grammars that purport to model the real world and the interactions within it. This paper presents a comparison of representational analyses of several popular process modeling techniques and has two main outcomes. First, it provides insights, within the boundaries of a representational analysis, into the extent to which process modeling techniques have developed over time. Second, the findings also indicate areas in which the underlying theory seems to be over-engineered or lacking in specialization.

1 Introduction

While the general objectives and methods of Business Process Management (BPM) are not new, BPM has only recently received a significant amount of attention and is now perceived to be a main business priority [1]. However, the actual modeling of business processes still presents major challenges for organizations. As graphical presentations of current or future business processes, business process models serve two main purposes. First, intuitive business process models are used for scoping the project, and capturing and discussing business requirements and process improvement initiatives with subject matter experts. A prominent example of such a business modeling technique is the Event-driven Process Chain (EPC). Second, business process models are used for process automation, which requires their conversion into executable languages. These automated techniques have higher requirements in terms of expressive power. Examples include Petri nets or the Business Process Modeling Notation (BPMN), a new Business Process Execution Language for Web Services (BPEL4WS)-conform notation.

E. Dubois and K. Pohl (Eds.): CAiSE 2006, LNCS 4001, pp. 447–461, 2006.
© Springer-Verlag Berlin Heidelberg 2006

Overall, a high number of process modeling techniques have been proposed since Carl Petri published his initial ideas on Petri nets in 1962 [2], and process modeling has become one of the most popular reasons for conceptual modeling [3]. Clearly, a theoretical basis is required to assist in the evaluation and comparison of available process modeling techniques. Given the existence of such theory, it would not only be possible to evaluate these techniques, but also to determine if the discipline of process modeling is building on previous knowledge, and if new techniques denote an actual improvement. A promising candidate of such theories, the Bunge-Wand-Weber (BWW) representation model, uses the principles of *representational analysis* for an investigation of a modeling technique's strength and weaknesses. The BWW representation model denotes a widespread means for evaluating conceptual modeling grammars for information systems analysis and design. We will employ this model as a benchmark and filter through which we will assess comparatively the most popular process modeling techniques. Thus, our research is motivated in several ways:

1. to provide theoretical guidance in the evaluation and comparison of available process modeling techniques;
2. to propose a measure of development of process modeling over time;
3. to highlight representations that process modeling languages do not appear to address; and
4. to add to the development of the BWW theoretical models.

The *aim of this paper* then is to study the development of process modeling techniques over time. As a measurement for the development of these techniques we selected *ontological completeness,* defined as the coverage of constructs as proposed by the Bunge-Wand-Weber representation model. We are very much aware that ontological completeness is not the only relevant criterion for the evaluation of the capabilities of a modeling technique. Thus, the focus on the set of BWW constructs leads to a specific scope in the evaluation. The study of modeling technique development is based on a review of previous published BWW analyses of process modeling techniques. In order to report on a reasonably complete set of modeling techniques, we also conducted our own analysis of two additional prominent modeling techniques, *viz.,* Petri nets and BPMN. Overall, this paper considers twelve common process modeling techniques and extracts the similarities and differences in terms of the ontological completeness of these techniques. The consolidated findings point to common shortcomings of modeling techniques, but also they highlight the main differentiating features. As part of this work, the BWW representation model is also evaluated in terms of appropriateness of its specification within the business process modeling domain.

This paper is structured as follows. The next section provides an overview of the Bunge-Wand-Weber set of models and its previous applications in the area of process modeling, including our analyses of Petri nets and BPMN. Section 3 presents and discusses the findings of the comparison of process modeling techniques from the viewpoint of ontological completeness. Also, it reports on potential issues of the BWW set of models with respect to their application to the area of process modeling. The paper concludes in section 4 with a discussion of results, limitations, and future research.

2 Related Work and Background

2.1 Representation Theory in Information Systems

Over the last few decades many conceptual modeling techniques, used to define requirements for building information systems, have emerged with limited theoretical foundation underlying their conception or development [4]. Concerned that this situation would result in the development of information systems that were unable to capture completely important aspects of the real world, Wand and Weber [5-7] developed and refined a set of models for the evaluation of the representational capability of the modeling techniques and the scripts prepared using such techniques. These models are based on an ontology defined by Bunge [8] and are referred to as the Bunge-Wand-Weber (BWW) models. Generally, *ontology* studies the nature of the world and attempts to organize and describe what exists in reality, in terms of the properties of, the structure of, and the interactions between real-world things [9]. As computerized information systems are representations of real world systems, Wand and Weber suggest that a theory of representation based on ontology can be used to help define and build information systems that contain the necessary representations of real world constructs including their properties and interactions. The *BWW representation model* is one of three theoretical models defined by Wand and Weber [7] that make up the Representation Theory. Its application to information systems foundations has been referred to by a number of researchers [10]. Some minor alterations have been carried out over the years by Wand and Weber [6, 7] and Weber [11], but the current key constructs of the BWW model can be grouped into the following clusters: things including properties and types of things; states assumed by things; events and transformations occurring on things; and systems structured around things (see Appendix 1 for a complete list).

Weber [11] suggests that the BWW representation model can be used to analyze a particular modeling technique to make predictions on the modeling strengths and weaknesses of the technique, in particular its capabilities to provide *complete* and *clear* representations of the domain being modeled. He clarifies two main evaluation criteria that may be studied according to the BWW model: *Ontological Completeness* and *Ontological Clarity*. The focus of our study is ontological completeness only, *i.e.,* the analysis of the extent to which a process modeling technique covers completely the set of constructs proposed in the BWW representation model.

Among other theories that have been proposed as a basis for representational analysis of conceptual modeling in information systems, the approaches of Chisholm [12] and Guizzardi *et al.* [13] are to be regarded as closest to the ideas of Wand and Weber. These upper-level ontologies have been built for similar purposes and seem to be equally expressive [14] but have not yet achieved the popularity and dissemination of the BWW models.

2.2 Previous Representational Analyses of Process Modeling Techniques

Only limited research efforts have been made to compare process modeling techniques based on an established theoretical model, refer, for instance, to [15]. However, these proposals neither appear to have been widely adopted in practice nor do they have an established track record. On the contrary, the BWW representation model has been used in over twenty-five research projects for the evaluation of different modeling techniques (see [10] for an overview), including data models, object-oriented models and reference models. It also has a track record in the area of process modeling, with contributions coming from various researchers. In this section, we briefly summarize these studies that focused on process modeling techniques.

Keen and Lakos [16] determined essential features for a process modeling scheme by using the BWW representation model to evaluate the degree of ontological completeness of six process modeling techniques in a historical sequence. Empirical studies to validate the results have not been conducted. The process modeling techniques examined include the ANSI flowchart notation, the ISO Conceptual Schema Model (ISO/TC97) [17], the Méthode d'Etude et de Réalisation Informatique pour les Systèmes d'Entreprise (MERISE) [18], the Data Flow Diagram (DFD) notation [19], the Integrated Definition Method 3 Process Description Capture Method (IDEF3) [20], and the Language for Object-Oriented Petri nets (LOOPN++) [21]. From their analysis, Keen and Lakos concluded that, in general, the BWW representation model facilitates the interpretation and comparison of process modeling techniques. They propose the BWW constructs of *system*, *system composition*, *system structure*, *system environment*, *transformation*, and *coupling* to be essential process modeling technique requirements. As our analysis will show, however, these findings are not entirely reflected in the leading process modeling techniques we consider.

Green and Rosemann [22] used the BWW representation model to analyze the Event-Driven Process Chain (EPC) notation [23], focusing on both ontological completeness and clarity. Their findings have been empirically validated through interviews and surveys [24]. Confirmed shortcomings were found in the EPC notation with regard to the representation of real world objects, in the definition of business rules, and in the thorough demarcation of the analyzed system.

Green *et al.* [25] also examined the Electronic Business using eXtensible Markup Language Business Process Specification Schema (ebXML BPSS) v1.01 [26] in terms of ontological completeness and clarity. While the empirical validation of results has not yet been performed, the analysis shows a relatively high degree of ontological completeness.

Green *et al.* [27] examined the ontological completeness of four leading standards for enterprise system interoperability, including BPEL4WS v1.1 [28], Business Process Modeling Language v1.0 (BPML) [29], Web Service Choreography Interface v1.0 (WSCI) [30], and ebXML v1.1 [26]. In addition, a minimal ontological overlap (MOO) analysis [7, 11] has been conducted in order to determine the set of modeling standards with a minimum number of overlapping constructs but with maximal ontological completeness (MOC), *i.e.*, maximum expressiveness, between the selected standards. The study identified two sets of standards that, when used together, allow for the most expressive power with the least overlap of constructs, *viz.*, ebXML and BPEL4WS, and, ebXML and WSCI. The results of the analysis remain to be tested empirically.

While there has been further work that concentrates on the representational analysis of dynamic modeling techniques (see, for example, [31, 32]), these particular techniques are not considered in our research. For example, modeling techniques relying on an object-oriented paradigm (like UML, OML, OPM, or LOOPN++) have not been included in this study. These techniques, applied in software engineering rather than process management contexts, have different or extended requirements in terms of representation capabilities and are, therefore, limited in comparability to 'pure' process modeling notations. We believe that the inclusion of such techniques would limit the comparability of the results to process modeling languages that focus on control flow.

2.3 Representational Analysis of Petri nets and BPMN

While the previous representational analyses of process modeling techniques covered the main techniques, we felt that the field should be further extended by at least two more prominent techniques, *viz.*, Petri nets and BPMN.

We conducted our own representational analysis of *Petri nets* in its original and most basic form [2], as we perceive it to be the intellectual birthplace of more rigorous and disciplined process modeling. Petri nets are composed of places, transitions, tokens, and arcs together with an initial state called the initial marking. As places and arcs may be assigned a certain weight of tokens, the notation allows for quite extensive modeling purposes. Special attention is, for example, paid to its capability of business process simulation. Additionally, due to the underlying strict formal foundation, Petri nets provide the capabilities for mathematical analyses and means to be directly executed [33]. Due to this rigorous, yet flexible, specification we found that although the notation originally merely consists of seven constructs, its ontological completeness is quite high. While this apparent flexibility in the interpretation of the Petri net constructs resulted in more than the seven expected mappings, Petri nets still lack ontological completeness. For example, there is no support for the modeling of systems structured around things. Hence, it is problematic to define thoroughly and demarcate the modeled system, a deficit that in turn causes understandability problems in terms of the scope as well as subparts and interrelationships of system elements. Even though our study is based on the notion of ontological completeness, it is important to point out that the same flexibility that affords Petri nets a higher ontological completeness, also results in extensive construct overload [11]. For example, a place construct in a Petri net can be used to represent a *thing*, *class*, or *state*. Such flexibility, while seemingly an advantage, can result in models that are harder to interpret. This weakness can result in ambiguity of the models as extra-model knowledge is required to understand what is meant when a particular construct is used in a model, *e.g.*, whether a place in a given model represents a thing, a class of things, or a state of a thing.

The *Business Process Modeling Notation (BPMN)* [34] is a recently proposed standard that stemmed from the demand for a graphical notation that complements the BPEL4WS standard for executable business processes. Although this gives BPMN a technical focus, it has been the intention of the BPMN designers to develop a modeling technique that can be applied for typical business modeling activities as well. The BPMN specification defines thirty-eight distinct language constructs plus attributes, grouped in four basic categories of elements, *viz., Flow Objects, Connecting Objects, Swimlanes* and *Artefacts* [34]. For example, nine distinct event types and three different event dimensions are included.

As the focus of this paper is on the comparison of different process modeling techniques, we only provide a reduced summary of the outcomes of this analysis. A more complete analysis is discussed in detail in [35]. Our analysis shows that the specification provides a relatively high degree of ontological completeness. However, BPMN is not ontologically complete. For example, states assumed by things cannot be modeled with the BPMN notation. This situation can result in a lack of focus in terms of state and transformation law foundations for capturing business rules. Also, systems structured around things are under-represented. For example, as there is no representation of system structure, problems will arise when information needs to be obtained about the dependencies within a modeled system.

3 Comparison of Representational Analyses

3.1 Research Design and Overview

We reviewed and compared analyses of twelve process modeling techniques with the focus being on the ontological completeness of these techniques. As we are aware that many available process modeling techniques have been designed for distinct purposes, we placed special emphasis on ensuring comparability of the analyses. In order to ensure a reasonably holistic overview of this area, our analysis covered a wide selection of modeling techniques for different purposes, ranging from mere illustration methods (e.g., Flowcharts) to integrated techniques (e.g., EPC), and also covering more recent techniques capable of both process description and execution (e.g., ebXML and BPEL4WS).

As the prior analyses were independently conducted by different research groups and since the representational analyses referred to varied research purposes, effort was put into making the individual analyses comparable. We did neither question nor review the mapping results as proposed by the different research groups. So, our study consolidates existing analyses instead of revising or extending previous research work. The results of our comparison are shown in Table 1, where each tick indicates that the specified BWW construct can be represented by the analyzed technique.

However, due to varying sets of BWW representation model constructs included in the analyses, we had to generalize some constructs of the BWW model in order to stabilize the comparison of the evaluations:

- As some analyses did not entirely differentiate between property types, these types were generalized here to the super-type 'property'. Therefore, if a mapping was found for a sub-type of 'property', then the mapping was recorded as belonging to the super-type 'property'.
- Similarly, as some analyses did not consider the constructs of *stability condition* and *corrective action* in the context of the *lawful transformation* construct, we generalized mappings of these to a mapping of the *lawful transformation* construct.
- As the construct *process* [22] was not specified in the BWW representation model as defined in [6, 7, 11] we did not consider it in our comparison.

Table 1. Comparison of representational analyses of process modeling techniques

BWW Construct	Petri net 1962	ANSI Flow- charts 1970	DFD 1979	ISO TC87 1982	Merise 1992	EPC 1992	IDEF3 1995	ebXML 1.01 2001	BPML 1.0 2002	WSCI 1.0 2002	BPEL4WS 1.1 2003	BPMN 1.0 2004	Construct Coverage
THING	✓			✓	✓		✓					✓	5 / 12
CLASS	✓							✓	✓	✓	✓	✓	6 / 12
KIND												✓	1 / 12
PROPERTY			✓			✓	✓	✓	✓	✓	✓	✓	8 / 12
STATE	✓					✓	✓	✓	✓	✓	✓		7 / 12
CONCEIVABLE STATE SPACE									✓				1 / 12
STATE LAW	✓			✓	✓	✓							5 / 12
LAWFUL STATE SPACE	✓							✓					2 / 12
STABLE STATE							✓	✓					2 / 12
UNSTABLE STATE	✓							✓					2 / 12
HISTORY								✓					1 / 12
EVENT	✓			✓	✓	✓	✓	✓	✓	✓	✓	✓	10 / 12
CONCEIVABLE EVENT SPACE								✓					1 / 12
LAWFUL EVENT SPACE								✓					1 / 12
EXTERNAL EVENT				✓	✓	✓		✓	✓		✓	✓	8 / 12
INTERNAL EVENT	✓			✓	✓	✓		✓	✓	✓	✓	✓	9 / 12
WELL-DEFINED EVENT	✓					✓		✓	✓	✓	✓	✓	7 / 12
POORLY DEFINED EVENT								✓	✓	✓	✓	✓	5 / 12
TRANSFORMATION	✓	✓	✓		✓	✓	✓	✓	✓	✓	✓	✓	12 / 12
LAWFUL TRANSFORMATION	✓			✓	✓	✓		✓	✓	✓	✓	✓	9 / 12
ACTS ON	✓							✓		✓	✓	✓	5 / 12
COUPLING		✓	✓		✓		✓	✓		✓	✓	✓	8 / 12
SYSTEM			✓		✓		✓	✓		✓	✓	✓	7 / 12
SYSTEM COMPOSITION			✓		✓		✓			✓	✓	✓	6 / 12
SYSTEM ENVIRONMENT			✓									✓	2 / 12
SYSTEM STRUCTURE					✓					✓	✓		4 / 12
SUBSYSTEM								✓				✓	2 / 12
SYSTEM DECOMPOSITION			✓			✓						✓	3 / 12
LEVEL STRUCTURE			✓		✓	✓						✓	4 / 12
Representational Coverage	12 / 29	2 / 29	8 / 29	7 / 29	11 / 29	11 / 29	11 / 29	22 / 29	10 / 29	15 / 29	15 / 29	19 / 29	

3.2 Issues in Process Modeling Techniques: Findings and Propositions

The notion of ontological completeness of a particular process modeling technique serves as an indication of its *representational capabilities*, being the extent to which the techniques are able to provide complete descriptions of a real-world domain.

The consolidation of previous representational analyses with our analyses of Petri nets and BPMN leads to several interesting results. A longitudinal study of the ontological completeness shows an obvious increase in the coverage of BWW constructs that can be interpreted as a sign of increasing representational development over time. Fig. 1 visualizes this trend over time, as measured by the number of BWW constructs covered by each technique. We can see that, while the original Petri net specification did not provide exceptionally good representational coverage[1] (41%) as defined by the BWW representation model, it still performed better than more recent grammars such as DFD (28%) or IDEF3 (38%). A noticeable spike in Fig. 1 depicts the high level of development (in terms of ontological completeness) of the ebXML standard (76%). It is interesting to note that ebXML is specified in UML, with a semi-formal construct definition and description, whereas BPEL4WS, WSCI, and BPMN, for example, have textual specifications supplemented by diagrams of examples. As such, the ebXML specification is less subjective in its possible interpretations.

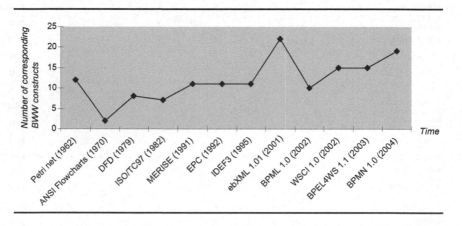

Fig. 1. Comparison of representation mapping analyses

BPMN also appears to perform very well (66%) and hence appears to be quite mature in terms of representation capabilities. This higher level of ontological completeness can perhaps partly be explained by the fact that previous approaches, including EPC and Petri nets, influenced the development of BPMN [34]. Also, this finding is not only supported by the number of identified mappings to BWW constructs, but also by the specialization of the constructs. For example, BPMN has sub-types of *event* and *transformation* that allow a more rigorous and expressive model to be defined. However, this strength can potentially also be its weakness as the varied sub-types of *transformation* and *event* will require thorough understanding by the user in order to appropriately represent the right types of transformations and events, respectively.

It appears that techniques that focus on describing process flow from a business perspective (for instance DFD and IDEF3) are less ontologically complete than those

---

[1] The degree of representational coverage (DrC) is here calculated as the number of BWW constructs found to be represented by language constructs #L divided by the number of constructs defined in the BWW representation model #M = 29. Note here that each BWW construct has the same weight.

that have to cater for more syntactical rigor due to their focus on executability or translatability into executable languages (such as BPEL4WS or ebXML).

In terms of the coverage of BWW constructs, Table 2 shows some occurrences of mappings of BWW representation model constructs within the considered analyses of process modeling techniques.

Table 2. Analysis of construct occurrences

Most supported BWW constructs		Least supported BWW constructs	
Construct	Occurrence ratio (%)	Construct	Occurrence ratio (%)
TRANSFORMATION	100	KIND	8
EVENT	83	HISTORY	8
LAWFUL TRANSFORMATION	75	CONCEIVABLE STATE SPACE	8
INTERNAL EVENT	75	CONCEIVABLE EVENT SPACE	8
EXTERNAL EVENT	67	LAWFUL EVENT SPACE	8
COUPLING	67	LAWFUL STATE SPACE	17
PROPERTY	67	STABLE STATE	17
STATE	58	UNSTABLE STATE	17
SYSTEM	58	SYSTEM ENVIRONMENT	17
WELL-DEFINED EVENT	58	SUBSYSTEM	17

As can be expected in a BPM domain, each of the analyzed techniques has the ability to represent the BWW construct *transformation* – one of the core concepts in process modeling [36]. Seventy-five percent of these techniques also allow differentiation between all possible transformations and a lawful transformation that is allowed under the business rules in a given case. It is also interesting to note that while *transformation* has full support, neither *event* nor *state* have the same occurrence, with *state* being represented in under sixty percent of the modeling techniques. This situation is surprising, given the importance of events and states in process modeling [36].

There is divided support for the cluster *things including properties and types of things*. Closer inspection of Table 1 shows that while earlier process modeling techniques provided a construct for a specific *thing* (overall support: 42%), more recent standards have representation capabilities for *class* (overall support: 50%) rather than *thing*. Therefore, it would appear that, in general, there has been a move to model classes of things rather than actual things, *i.e.*, instances. It is also interesting to note that only BPMN is able to cover all aspects of things, including properties and types of things (see Table 1). In this respect, BPMN appears to denote a considerable improvement compared to other techniques.

Throughout the BPM domain, a lack of support for business rule definitions can be observed (see also [22, 35]). Because *conceivable* and *lawful event spaces* as well as *state spaces* are under-represented – none of these constructs has support of more than seventeen percent – state and transformation modeling is unclear for the modeler who may encounter confusion when determining which set of events and states can occur in the system and which events and states are possible but should not be allowed. A closer look at Table 1 reveals that most techniques achieve a very low degree of representational coverage in the cluster of *states assumed by things*, except for ebXML (100% in this cluster) and – interestingly – Petri nets (52% in this cluster). This situation suggests that the modeling of business rules is heavily dependant on rigorous state and state law specification. The mathematical specification of Petri nets seems to be advantageous in this aspect.

Also, there appears to be inconsistent support for *systems structured around things*. From the list of seven BWW constructs grouped in this cluster, five are represented in under thirty-four per cent of the modeling techniques. Thus, appropriate structuring and differentiation of modeled things, such as business partners, is not well supported, a fact we find quite problematic, especially in light of collaborative business processes and interoperability. Table 1 suggests that DFD, IDEF3 and BPMN models perform best in representing systems structured around things. All these grammars have in common dedicated constructs for decomposing process models into interlinked subsets.

3.3 Focusing the Underlying Theory

A representational analysis of modeling techniques has two facets. On the one side, it provides a filtering lens that facilitates insights into potential issues with a modeling technique. On the other side, it can also contribute to the further development of the selected theoretical basis. In fact, our findings from the longitudinal analysis of process modeling techniques align with some of the previous criticisms of BWW representation model-based analyses [37, 38].

The fact that even the most developed process modeling technique (ebXML) supports only 76% of the BWW constructs suggests that the selected theory of representation might be too demanding. With regard to this potential *lack of relevance* of the BWW representation model, we suggest the development and use of a specialized BWW model for the domain of business process modeling. The current BWW representation model needs to be investigated in order to determine areas that need further specialization, extension, deletion, or renaming. For example, *events* and *transformations* occurring on *things* may require further specialization. BPMN distinguishes between nine event types, representing a differentiation scheme that is not covered by the BWW constructs of *event* and its subtypes. The same situation can be seen in standards such as ebXML, BPEL4WS, BPML, and WSCI. A similar situation holds for the *transformation* construct that we often found to be susceptible to construct redundancy. For example, in BPML there are ten language constructs representing different types of transformations. A similar situation exists in standards like BPEL4WS and ebXML. This situation implies that, just as 'properties' in the BWW representation model are specialized, perhaps transformations should also be specialized for the domain of BPM.

It is interesting also to note that throughout the analyses of process modeling techniques, control flow mechanisms such as logical connectors, selectors, gateways and the like are regarded as construct excess as they do not map to any construct of the BWW model. However, these constructs are deemed to be essential to the BPM domain (for empirical evidence supporting this proposition refer, for example, to [35]). Consequently, we are considering how the BWW model might be extended to better reflect such control flow concepts important to the BPM domain.

Taking a methodological viewpoint to the BWW representation model-based analysis, we found the *lack of objectivity* issue persisting. Significant effort had to be applied in objectifying the different analyses in terms of finding a comparable set of BWW constructs. This situation highlights the need for the use of meta-models in conducting analyses. A meta-model allows for a clearer description of the source representation model constructs as well as less subjective evaluation of the target grammar, partially through pattern matching, assuming the meta-model and the grammar are specified in the same notation. A BWW meta-model has been developed [39] for such a purpose and its use for evaluating grammars with meta model-based specifications has been promoted and discussed in [14, 37].

4 Conclusions, Limitations and Future Research

This paper presents the first comprehensive longitudinal study comparing previous representational analyses of process modeling techniques. The innovative comparative study also includes our outcomes of the initial representational analyses of Petri nets and the new proposed modeling standard, BPMN. The findings clearly show signs of a developing modeling discipline, measured by an increased ontological completeness of process modeling techniques over time. The results also identify the common core constructs of process modeling techniques (for example, *transformation, properties, events*) as well as their key differentiators (for example, *subsystem, system environment, lawful state space*). Furthermore, the findings provide valuable insights for the future application of the BWW representation model as a benchmark for such analyses of modeling techniques. As shown in Table 2, there are some constructs of the BWW representation model that are supported by only one technique of the chosen twelve, for example the constructs *kind* and *history*. While this might indicate an area for improvement in the representation power of process modeling techniques, it might also indicate that, perhaps, the particular BWW construct is not necessary for modeling in the domain of BPM. Such issues require further empirical testing (currently under way) in order to determine whether the theory of representation requires pruning and specialization or whether the techniques require refinement and extensions in order to be able to model what is represented by the BWW construct. Such research might also motivate other researchers to conduct a similar study for data or object-oriented modeling techniques.

Furthermore, the outcomes will be of interest to the developers and users of process modeling techniques. Developers of process modeling techniques should be motivated to examine representational analyses of currently used process modeling tools in order to build upon these grammars and counteract any weaknesses in the newly developed techniques or technique extensions. On the other hand, users of process modeling techniques might be motivated to use ontological completeness as one potential evaluation criterion for the selection of a more appropriate modeling technique.

We identify some limitations in our research. Most notably, we based our study on previous representational analyses that have been conducted by different researchers. Therefore, there may exist issues related to the comparability of the analyses due to the impact of the subjective interpretations of the researcher [37]. Second, we constrained the considered representational analyses to analyses based on the BWW representation model that in turn limits the generalization of the results and also the number of techniques we were able to consider. We believe, however, that the selected set of techniques is representative of the most popular techniques in the BPM field. It also enables us to focus our work and to avoid the necessity to translate between different theoretical bases. Third, we focused on ontological completeness, thereby giving a one-dimensional view of modeling technique development over time.

In our future research, we will extend this analysis to include also ontological clarity as an evaluation criterion. We will then use the outcomes of this study and the extended study to develop a process modeling-specific version of the BWW representation model. This work will be divided into four steps. First, based on the BWW representation model, we will eliminate those constructs that seem to be of no or limited relevance for process modeling. Second, some BWW constructs may need to be renamed so that they better reflect common terminology in the domain of process modeling (for example, *activity* instead of *transformation*). Third, we will extend the BWW representation model by specializing those constructs that are perceived as having too high a level of granularity. Fourth, we may, in exceptional cases, introduce new constructs.

In a related stream of research, the outcome of this research is also used to continue work on a weighted scoring model for the interpretation of the levels of criticality of the results of representational analyses [14, 37].

References

1. Gartner Group: Delivering IT's Contribution: The 2005 CIO Agenda. Gartner, Inc, Stamford, Connecticut (2005)
2. Petri, C.A.: Fundamentals of a Theory of Asynchronous Information Flow. In: Popplewell, C.M. (ed.): IFIP Congress 62: Information Processing. North-Holland, Munich, Germany (1962) 386-390
3. Davies, I., Green, P., Rosemann, M., Indulska, M., Gallo, S.: How do Practitioners Use Conceptual Modeling in Practice? Data & Knowledge Engineering (In Press)
4. Floyd, C.: A Comparative Evaluation of System Development Methods. In: Olle, T.W., Sol, H.G., Verrijn-Stuart, A.A. (eds.): Information System Design Methodologies: Improving the Practice. North-Holland, Amsterdam, The Netherlands (1986) 19-54
5. Wand, Y., Weber, R.: An Ontological Model of an Information System. IEEE Transactions on Software Engineering 16 (1990) 1282-1292
6. Wand, Y., Weber, R.: On the Ontological Expressiveness of Information Systems Analysis and Design Grammars. Journal of Information Systems 3 (1993) 217-237
7. Wand, Y., Weber, R.: On the Deep Structure of Information Systems. Information Systems Journal 5 (1995) 203-223
8. Bunge, M.A.: Treatise on Basic Philosophy Volume 3: Ontology I - The Furniture of the World. Kluwer Academic Publishers, Dordrecht, The Netherlands (1977)
9. Shanks, G., Tansley, E., Weber, R.: Using Ontology to Validate Conceptual Models. Communications of the ACM 46 (2003) 85-89
10. Green, P., Rosemann, M.: Applying Ontologies to Business and Systems Modeling Techniques and Perspectives: Lessons Learned. Journal of Database Management 15 (2004) 105-117

11. Weber, R.: Ontological Foundations of Information Systems. Coopers & Lybrand and the Accounting Association of Australia and New Zealand, Melbourne, Australia (1997)

12. Chisholm, R.M.: A Realistic Theory of Categories: An Essay on Ontology. Cambridge University Press, Cambridge, Massachusetts (1996)

13. Guizzardi, G., Herre, H., Wagner, G.: On the General Ontological Foundations of Conceptual Modeling. In: Spaccapietra, S., March, S.T., Kambayashi, Y. (eds.): Conceptual Modeling - ER 2002. Lecture Notes in Computer Science, Vol. 2503. Springer, Tampere, Florida (2002) 65-78

14. Davies, I., Green, P., Milton, S., Rosemann, M.: Analysing and Comparing Ontologies with Meta Models. In: Krogstie, J., Halpin, T., Siau, K. (eds.): Information Modeling Methods and Methodologies. Idea Group, Hershey, Pennsylvania (2005) 1-16

15. Söderström, E., Andersson, B., Johannesson, P., Perjons, E., Wangler, B.: Towards a Framework For Comparing Process Modelling Languages. In: Pidduck, A.B., Mylopoulos, J., Woo, C.C., Ozsu, M.T. (eds.): 14th International Conference on Advanced Information Systems Engineering. Lecture Notes in Computer Science, Vol. 2348. Springer, Toronto, Canada (2002) 600-611

16. Keen, C.D., Lakos, C.: Analysis of the Design Constructs Required in Process Modelling. In: Purvis, M. (ed.): Proceedings of the International Conference on Software Engineering: Education and Practice. IEEE Computer Society, Dunedin, Ireland (1996) 434-441

17. van Griethuysen, J.J.: Concepts and Terminology for the Conceptual Schema and the Information Base. ISO/TC97/SC5 Report N695. International Organization for Standardization, Geneva, Italy (1982)

18. Tardieu, H.: Issues for Dynamic Modelling through Recent Development in European Methods. In: Sol, H.G., Crosslin, R.L. (eds.): Dynamic Modelling of Information Systems II. North-Holland, Amsterdam, The Netherlands (1992) 3-23

19. Gane, C., Sarson, T.: Structured Systems Analysis: Tools and Techniques. Prentice-Hall, Englewood Cliffs, California (1979)

20. Mayer, R.J., Menzel, C.P., Painter, M.K., de Witte, P.S., Blinn, T., Perakath, B.: Information Integration For Concurrent Engineering (IICE) IDEF3 Process Description Capture Method Report. Interim Technical Report AL-TR-1995-XXXX. Logistics Research Division, College Station, Texas (1995)

21. Keen, C.D., Lakos, C.: Information Systems Modelling using LOOPN++, an Object Petri Net Scheme. In: Sol, H.G., Verbraeck, A., Bots, P.W.G. (eds.): Proceedings of the 4th International Working Conference on Dynamic Modelling and Information Systems. Delft University Press, Noordwijkerhout, The Netherlands (1994) 31-52

22. Green, P., Rosemann, M.: Integrated Process Modeling. An Ontological Evaluation. Information Systems 25 (2000) 73-87

23. Keller, G., Nüttgens, M., Scheer, A.-W.: Semantische Prozessmodellierung auf der Grundlage "Ereignisgesteuerter Prozessketten (EPK)" (in German: Semantic Modeling of Processes based on Event-driven Process Chains). Working Paper 89. Institut für Wirtschaftsinformatik der Universität Saarbrücken, Saarbrücken, Germany (1992)

24. Green, P., Rosemann, M.: Ontological Analysis of Integrated Process Models: Testing Hypotheses. The Australian Journal of Information Systems 9 (2001) 30-38

25. Green, P., Rosemann, M., Indulska, M.: Ontological Evaluation of Enterprise Systems Interoperability Using ebXML. IEEE Transactions on Knowledge and Data Engineering 17 (2005) 713-725

26. OASIS: ebXML Business Process Specification Schema Version 1.01. UN/CEFACT and OASIS (2001), available at: http://www.ebxml.org/specs/ebBPSS.pdf

27. Green, P., Rosemann, M., Indulska, M., Manning, C.: Candidate Interoperability Standards: An Ontological Overlap Analysis. Technical Report University of Queensland, Brisbane, Australia (2004)
28. Andrews, T., Curbera, F., Dholakia, H., Goland, Y., Klein, J., Leymann, F., Liu, K., Roller, D., Smith, D., Thatte, S., Trickovic, I., Weerawarana, S.: Business Process Execution Language for Web Services. Version 1.1. BEA Systems, International Business Machines Corporation, Microsoft Corporation, SAP AG and Siebel Systems (2003), available at: http://xml.coverpages.org/BPELv11-May052003Final.pdf
29. Arkin, A.: Business Process Modeling Language. BPMI.org, (2002), available at: http://www.bpmi.org/
30. Arkin, A., Askary, S., Fordin, S., Jekeli, W., Kawaguchi, K., Orchard, D., Pogliani, S., Riemer, K., Struble, S., Takacsi-Nagy, P., Trickovic, I., Zimek, S.: Web Service Choreography Interface (WSCI) 1.0. BEA Systems, Intalio, SAP, Sun Microsystems (2002), available at: http://www.w3.org/TR/wsci/
31. Opdahl, A.L., Henderson-Sellers, B.: Ontological Evaluation of the UML Using the Bunge-Wand-Weber Model. Software and Systems Modeling 1 (2002) 43-67
32. Soffer, P., Golany, B., Dori, D., Wand, Y.: Modelling Off-the-Shelf Information System Requirements. An Ontological Approach. Requirements Engineering 6 (2001) 183-199
33. Murata, T.: Petri Nets: Properties, Analysis and Applications. Proceedings of the IEEE 77 (1989) 541-580
34. BPMI.org, OMG: Business Process Modeling Notation Specification. Final Adopted Specification. Object Management Group (2006), available at: http://www.bpmn.org
35. Recker, J., Indulska, M., Rosemann, M., Green, P.: Do Process Modelling Techniques Get Better? A Comparative Ontological Analysis of BPMN. In: Campbell, B., Underwood, J., Bunker, D. (eds.): Proceedings of the 16th Australasian Conference on Information Systems. Australasian Chapter of the Association for Information Systems, Sydney, Australia (2005)
36. Soffer, P., Wand, Y.: On the Notion of Soft-Goals in Business Process Modeling. Business Process Management Journal 11 (2005) 663-679
37. Rosemann, M., Green, P., Indulska, M.: A Reference Methodology for Conducting Ontological Analyses. In: Lu, H., Chu, W., Atzeni, P., Zhou, S., Ling, T.W. (eds.): Conceptual Modeling – ER 2004. Lecture Notes in Computer Science, Vol. 3288. Springer, Shanghai, China (2004) 110-121
38. Rosemann, M., Green, P., Indulska, M.: A Procedural Model for Ontological Analyses. In: Hart, D., Gregor, S. (eds.): Information Systems Foundations: Constructing and Criticising. ANU E Press, Canberra, Australia (2005) 153-163
39. Rosemann, M., Green, P.: Developing a Meta Model for the Bunge-Wand-Weber Ontological Constructs. Information Systems 27 (2002) 75-91

Appendix

Appendix 1. Constructs in the BWW representation model, assigned to cluster groups. Adapted from [6, 11] with minor modifications.

BWW Construct	Cluster	Description and Explanation
THING	Things including properties and types of things	A thing is the elementary unit in the BWW ontological model. The real world is made up of things. Two or more things (composite or simple) can be **associated** into a **composite** thing.
PROPERTY in general in particular hereditary emergent intrinsic non-binding mutual binding mutual Attributes		Things possess properties. A property is modeled via a function that maps the thing into some value. For example, the attribute "weight" represents a property that all humans possess. In this regard, weight is an attribute standing for a property **in general**. If we focus on the weight of a specific individual, we would be concerned with a property **in particular**. A property of a composite thing that belongs to a component thing is called a **hereditary** property. Otherwise it is called an **emergent** property. Some properties are inherent properties of individual things. Such properties are called **intrinsic**. Other properties are properties of pairs or many things. Such properties are called **mutual**. **Non-binding mutual** properties are those properties shared by two or more things that do not "make a difference" to the things involved; e.g. order relations or equivalence relations. By contrast, **binding mutual** properties are those properties shared by two or more things that do "make a difference" to the things involved. **Attributes** are the names that we use to represent properties of things.
CLASS		A class is a set of things that can be defined via their possessing a single property.
KIND		A kind is a set of things that can be defined only via their possessing two or more common properties.
STATE	States assumed by things	The vector of values for all property functions of a thing is the state of the thing.
CONCEIVABLE STATE SPACE		The set of all states that the thing might ever assume is the conceivable state space of the thing.
LAWFUL STATE SPACE		The lawful state space is the set of states of a thing that comply with the state laws of the thing.
STATE LAW		A state law restricts the values of the properties of a thing to a subset that is deemed lawful because of natural laws or human laws.
STABLE STATE		A stable state is a state in which a thing, subsystem, or system will remain unless forced to change by virtue of the action of a thing in the environment (an external event).
UNSTABLE STATE		An unstable state is a state that will be changed into another state by virtue of the action of transformations in the system.
HISTORY		The chronologically-ordered states that a thing traverses in time are the history of the thing.
EVENT	Events and transformations occurring on things	A change in state of a thing is an event.
CONCEIVABLE EVENT SPACE		The event space of a thing is the set of all possible events that can occur in the thing.
LAWFUL EVENT SPACE		The lawful event space is the set of all events in a thing that are lawful.
EXTERNAL EVENT		An external event is an event that arises in a thing, subsystem, or system by virtue of the action of some thing in the environment on the thing, subsystem, or system.
INTERNAL EVENT		An internal event is an event that arises in a thing, subsystem, or system by virtue of lawful transformations in the thing, subsystem, or system.
WELL-DEFINED EVENT		A well-defined event is an event in which the subsequent state can always be predicted given that the prior state is known.
POORLY DEFINED EVENT		A poorly-defined event is an event in which the subsequent state cannot be predicted given that the prior state is known.
TRANSFORMATION		A transformation is a mapping from one state to another state.
LAWFUL TRANSFORMATION stability condition corrective action		A lawful transformation defines which events in a thing are lawful. The **stability condition** specifies the states that are allowable under the transformation law. The **corrective action** specifies how the values of the property functions must change to provide a state acceptable under the transformation law.
ACTS ON		A thing acts on another thing if its existence affects the history of the other thing.
COUPLING binding mutual property		Two things are said to be coupled (or interact) if one thing acts on the other. Furthermore, those two things are said to share a **binding mutual property** (or relation).
SYSTEM	Systems structured around things	A set of things is a system if, for any bi-partitioning of the set, couplings exist among things in the two subsets.
SYSTEM COMPOSITION		The things in the system are its composition.
SYSTEM ENVIRONMENT		Things that are not in the system but interact with things in the system are called the environment of the system.
SYSTEM STRUCTURE		The set of couplings that exist among things within the system, and among things in the environment of the system and things in the system is called the structure.
SUBSYSTEM		A subsystem is a system whose composition and structure are subsets of the composition and structure of another system.
SYSTEM DECOMPOSITION		A decomposition of a system is a set of subsystems such that every component in the system is either one of the subsystems in the decomposition or is included in the composition of one of the subsystems in the decomposition.
LEVEL STRUCTURE		A level structure defines a partial order over the subsystems in a decomposition to show which subsystems are components of other subsystems or the system itself.

Agent Orientation

From Stakeholder Intentions to Software Agent Implementations

Loris Penserini, Anna Perini, Angelo Susi, and John Mylopoulos

ITC-IRST, Via Sommarive 18, I-38050, Trento, Italy
{penserini, perini, susi}@itc.it, jm@cs.toronto.edu

Abstract. Multi-Agent Systems have been proposed as a suitable conceptual and technological framework for building information systems which operate in open, evolving, heterogeneous environments. Our research aims at proposing design techniques and support tools for developing such complex systems. In this paper we address the problem of better linking requirements analysis to detailed design and implementation in the *Tropos* agent-oriented methodology with the aim to address adaptability issues. In particular, we revisit the definition of agent capability in *Tropos* and refine the development process in order to point out how capability specification can result from the integration of various analysis strategies. We also show how fragments of an implementation can be generated automatically from an agent capability specification.

1 Introduction

Nowadays, distributed information systems need to operate in open, evolving, heterogeneous environments. Trust in these systems by their owners and users entails ever-increasing expectations for robustness, fault tolerance, security, flexibility and adaptability. Multi-Agent Systems (MAS) have been proposed as a suitable conceptual framework for building such information systems [3, 5, 10, 15, 12]. In this framework, an information system is conceived as an open network of software agents who interact with each other and human/organizational agents in their operational environment in order to fulfill stakeholder objectives. Agent-oriented software engineering projects have been developing novel design techniques and support tools for complex information systems [10]. In particular, the *Tropos* methodology [3, 5] captures early requirements through an analysis of stakeholder goals and strategic dependencies among them. System requirements and design is then derived in a systematic way. System design includes both architectural and detailed design, and is followed by system implementation. Our research is conducted within the context of the *Tropos* project.

In this work, we refine the *Tropos* software development methodology proposed elsewhere [3, 5] by focusing on the concept of agent capability. Agent capability has been defined in agent-oriented programming [20] as the ability of an agent to achieve a goal. This definition has been revised in recent work [15] into a refined notion based on the philosophical idea that 'can' implies both *ability* and *opportunity*. This suggest that the lack of either ability or opportunity implies 'cannot'. More specifically, [15] uses the concept of "capability for a given goal" meaning that the agent has at least one plan —the ability— that can fulfill a given goal. This plan constitutes a necessary condition

E. Dubois and K. Pohl (Eds.): CAiSE 2006, LNCS 4001, pp. 465–479, 2006.
© Springer-Verlag Berlin Heidelberg 2006

for achieving the goal, while the sufficient condition (i.e. the opportunity) is defined in terms of the pre-conditions or the context that can trigger the plan.

In this paper, we illustrate how the above capability definition can be naturally accommodated with the *goal* and *plan* concepts. More precisely, as detailed in [17], an actor capability is always related to a leaf-goal after goal analysis has been completed. Moreover, we revise the *Tropos* design process in order to make capability modelling and analysis more explicit and systematic. This extension allows us to better exploit information on the environment captured during early and system requirements analysis, while conducting design and implementation of a MAS. Our ultimate objective is to define a systematic process for designing software agents able to adapt and extend their capability at run time, through composition mechanisms analogous to those used in web services [21].

In this work, we adopt Model-Driven Architecture (MDA) guidelines and standards proposed by OMG's [14]. Along with an extended Tropos development process, we are developing specific tools that support the proposed methodology by facilitating the construction, analysis, and transformation of models.

The rest of the paper is structured as follows. Section 2 recalls background notions of *Tropos* and of MDA guidelines and standards. Section 3 introduces an example we use to illustrate our approach. Section 4 introduces our definition of capability and proposes a systematic process for capability design. Section 5 presents a toolset for implementing capability in JADE (Java Agent Development Framework [2]) through an automatic transformation of a platform independent model to a platform specific one, while Section 6 describes capability implementation. Section 7 presents related work and Section 8 offers concluding remarks.

2   Background

We adopt the *Tropos* agent-oriented methodology [3, 5] which rests on a model-driven software development process, i.e. it guides the software engineer in building a conceptual model, which is incrementally refined and extended, from an early requirements model to system design artifacts and then to code. The methodology uses a modelling language based on a multi-agent paradigm named i^* [22], which provides concepts of *actor, goal, plan, softgoal, resource* and *capability*. The i^* modelling framework also includes relationships between actors and goals. In addition, the framework provides a graphical notation to depict views of a model, such as *actor diagrams*, which point out dependencies between a set of actors and *goal diagrams*, which depict how actor goals can be decomposed into subgoals[1].

The *Tropos* methodology also includes various analysis techniques which are tool supported[2] and a structured software development process which has been specified in terms of a non-deterministic concurrent algorithm [3]. This process starts with the identification of critical actors ("stakeholders") in a domain along with their goals, and

---

[1] The *Tropos* modelling activities are supported by the TAOM4E tool [18] (see http://sra.itc.it/tools/taom).

[2] The *Tropos* formal analysis, goal-reasoning and security analysis techniques are supported by the T-Tool, the GR- Tool and ST-Tool respectively (see http://www.troposproject.org).

proceeds with the analysis of goals from the perspective of each actor. In particular, given a goal, the software engineer may decide to *delegate* it to an actor already existing in the domain or to a *new actor*. Such delegations result in a network of dependency relationships among actors. Moreover the software engineer may decide to *analyze* a goal producing a set of subgoals. Goal analysis generates a goal hierarchy where the leaves in various combinations represent concrete solutions to the root goal. Finally the software engineer may decide that a certain actor is able to *satisfy* the goal via a plan the actor is able to execute; in this case the goal is assigned to that actor (with no further delegations). The process is complete when all goals have been dealt with.

This iterative process is organized in four main requirements analysis and design phases, each characterized by specific objectives. In particular, during *Early Requirements* the environment (i.e. the organizational setting) is modelled and analyzed; during *Late Requirements*, the system-to-be is introduced and its role within the environment is modelled; during *Architectural Design* the system architecture is specified in terms of a set of interacting software agents; *Detailed Design* is concerned with the specification of software agent capabilities and interactions and provides the input to code generation.

In refining the modelling process algorithm and building tools which can support it [19], we adopted ideas and standards from MDA. MDA conceives system development in terms of a chain of model transformations, namely, from a domain model (Computationally Independent Model — CIM) to a Platform Independent Model (PIM), and from a PIM to a Platform Specific Model (PSM), from which code and other development artifacts can then be straightforwardly derived. In this paper we focus on how to build a PIM for a MAS generic platform in *Tropos* and on how to automatically transform it into a PSM; we consider here the JADE programming platform [2] metamodel. Our framework is compliant with the MDA metamodelling standard called Meta Object Facility (MOF) [13], which defines a set of modelling constructs supporting metamodelling. Moreover, we exploit a Frame Logic-based approach described in [6] to deal with metamodel to metamodel transformations.

3 Example

An example is taken from the on-line selling shop application[3] domain. According to *Tropos*, the early requirements analysis has to define the social actors and their intentions in terms of social dependencies, commitments, and responsibilities among stakeholders. While, the late requirements phase introduces the system-to-be —e.g. the actor Retailer System— relating it to the other stakeholders of the domain. In this case, as depicted by the Fig. 1, some of the Customer needs are delegated to the Retailer System —i.e. softgoals search for the desired product automatically, flexible and automatic payment, and fast delivery— in order to correctly design the system functionalities. For the sake of simplicity, the figure does not depict all the elements a *why* dependency is composed of. Each time a Customer asks for product details, Retailer System can fulfill such a request by achieving the goal provide product info. As illustrated by the goal diagram of Fig. 1, there are two possible (means-ends) alternatives

---

[3] The scenario used is an idealization, intended solely for illustration purposes.

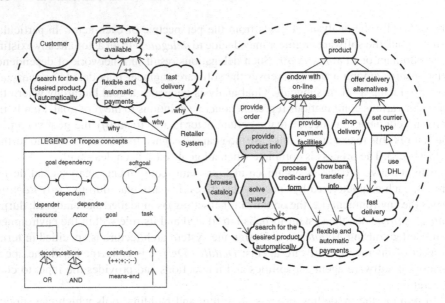

Fig. 1. Late Requirements: Fragment of Retailer System Goal Analysis

to deals with such a goal: browse catalog and solve query. Moreover, in our case, the goal diagram models a class of Customers that need to search for product details as much as possible automatically, i.e. by the softgoal search for the desired product automatically. This non-functional requirement can be used by the Retailer System to drive the plan selection according to the contribution link analysis. Specifically, as illustrated by Fig. 1, the plan solve query gives a positive contribution (+), while browse catalog gives a negative contribution (-) to this softgoal.

Given a characterization of the system-to-be inside its operating environment, e.g. Fig. 1, the methodology allows the designers soft attention to Architectural and Detailed Design. In our case, Fig. 2.(A) depicts a fragment for the Architectural Design phase where the main system components have been identified, i.e., Web Server, Order Manager, and Search Manager. The fulfillment of some of the previous functional and non-functional requirements have been delegated to such actors (hereafter agents). For example, as depicted in Fig. 2.(A), the goal provide product info has to be fulfilled by the agent Search Manager. Again, the plan process credit-card form has been delegated to the external actor Credit Authority. Therefore, architectural design results in a multi-agent system consisting of agents, dependencies among them, as well as environmental constraints these agents have to cope with.

The Detailed Design deals with specification details for each agent, showing and describing how an agent concretely behaves in order to execute a plan or to satisfy a goal. For example, as illustrated by Fig. 2.(B), in order to fulfill the plan solve query, the agent Search Manager relies on three sub-plans interpret ACL performatives, deal with cooperation, and provide results. For the sake of simplicity, only the plan deal with cooperation has been further detailed in three atomic sub-plans search for new acquaintances, get the query, and deal with matching. In our case, to get the query, this agent depends on the actor Web Server responsible for interfacing the

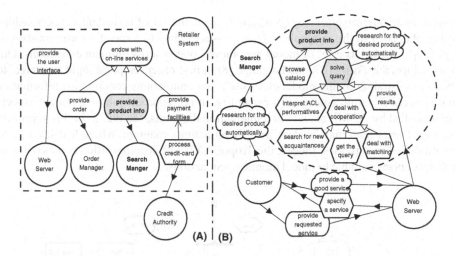

Fig. 2. (**A**) Architectural Design: fragment of the Retailer System sub-actors definition; (**B**) Detailed Design: fragment of the Goal Analysis for the agent Search Manager

system-to-be with external users or other agents (Customer). Therefore, Customer, who models both human users and software agents, depends on the system through the component Web Server for the goal provide requested service. Moreover, softgoals may model stakeholders needs that may be only achieved by means of specific system actor capabilities. Hence, also softgoals (Fig. 1) have to be delegated to specific system components, e.g. Customer depends on Search Manager to satisfy search for the desired product automatically.

To effectively deal with the agent behavior at run-time, the methodology has also to address the dynamic aspects that affect agent activities. This important phase is discussed in detail in the next sections.

4 Capability Design

While we adopt the *Tropos* definition of capability, we propose to extend the way to specify it during design by explicitly describing not only the dynamic part, but also its descriptive and context part. For this, we revise the *Tropos* definition of capability to include both *ability* and *opportunity*, as detailed in [17]. In particular, the *ability* part is described via the *Tropos* means_end relationship between a goal and a plan, while the *opportunity* is described in *Tropos* via plan/softgoal contributions, $\langle plan, softgoal, metric \rangle$ ($metric \in \{+, -, ++, --\}$) and environmental constraints (e.g. temporal constraints between sub-plans) that are specified by model annotations. More formally, the definition of capability is given in terms of a set of basic building blocks that a designer can use to represent its several aspects, namely:

$$Cap = \langle means\_end(goal, plan), \cup_i contribution(plan, softgoal_i, metric),$$
$$\{A_1, \ldots, A_n\} \rangle$$

where $contribution(plan, softgoal_i, metric)$ is the set of contribution relationships of the plan $plan$ to the softgoals $softgoal_i$ —according to a specific metric $metric$— and $\{A_1, \dots, A_n\}$ is a set of model annotations that describe domain constraints. Our work adopts the Formal *Tropos* language [8], a first order temporal logic language, to specify constraints on the model elements[4]. The annotations contain also information that concern dynamic aspects of a capability. In our approach, these dynamic aspects are modelled by AUML activity and interaction diagrams, see Fig. 3. In this approach, each root-level plan may be described by an activity diagram, where leaf-level plans are modelled as activities. Indeed, the Tropos AND/OR decomposition comes out with leaf-level plans suitable to model atomic agent actions.

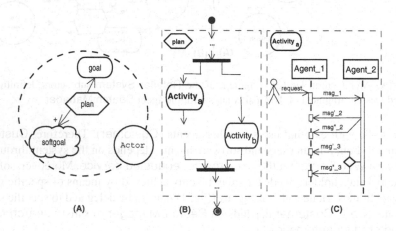

Fig. 3. Focusing on the dynamic dimensions of a capability: (A) actor's view in *Tropos* notation, (B) control-flow structure of the ability $plan$, and (C) agent-interaction for a part of the ability fulfillment, i.e. activity $Activity_a$

Fig. 3.(A) shows the elements and the relationships that characterize a capability from early requirements to detailed design. Fig. 3.(B) describes the activity diagram for the *plan*, while Fig. 3.(C) gives the representation of agent interactions for just one of the activities of the *plan* —$Activity_a$. We can find this pattern in the example shown in Fig. 1; focusing on the goal provide product info the *ability* part of the capability is given by the means-ends relationship with the plan solve query. The ability part only gives a partial description of the capability, that is, it does not provide any information on the influence of the environment on the behavior of the system at run-time. The second part of the definition describes the *opportunity* for the capability, can be given via "softgoal contributions", e.g related to the softgoal search for the desired product automatically that our customer requires. As an example, in Table 1, for Cap_2,

---

[4] We are exploring the possibility to integrate different approaches dealing with the agent intelligence representation, such as, declarative annotations in OWL-S [21, 16], or belief-desire-intention concepts for agent behavior characterization [4, 15]. Therefore, the annotations $A_1, \dots, A_n$, could represent further details of a capability expressed in one of several specification languages.

we specify an annotation named A_1 that is associated with a BDI based semantics as detailed in the next Section.

In order to support the capability design activity, we added a new step to the *Tropos* algorithm described in [3]. The details of a revised version of the proposed algorithm for the Tropos design process can be found in [17]. In particular, during the initialization of the design process, the set of stakeholders and goals is added to the model; goals are then assigned to actors, and therefore become the root goals for those actors. During the analysis, for every goal in the model, a *goal_Analysis* step is carried out, in order to delegate the goal, expand it into subgoals or operationalize each goal, associating it one or more plans, thereby discovering a required capability for the system. According to this strategy, given a certain goal, the *capability_modelling* procedure proposes plans that can fulfill the goal and adds to the current model a means_ends relationship for every discovered goal/plan pair. This pair constitutes the first part of the definition of a capability. For every discovered means_ends links the algorithm collects the set of "softgoals contribution" relationships related to the plan involved in the contribution and discovered during the modelling process. These contributions represent conditions from the domain for that capability. The set of annotations —such as softgoals that model environmental constraints, related to the goals/plans involved in the capability— feeds the "annotation" part of the capability definition, e.g. A_1 for Cap_2. The capability discovery and specification process can be iterated during the whole modelling activity in order to capture new capabilities or new components of capabilities that have been already specified and that gradually emerge during the analysis. The output of the analysis process is a set of capabilities related to a given goal that in our case is partially illustrated in Table 1.

Table 1. Capabilities at Architectural Design phase

Agent	Capabilities	Means_End(goal,plan)	List of Contributions	Annotations
$SearchManager$	Cap_1	provide product Info, browse catalogue	{search the desired prod. autom. -}	...
	Cap_2	provide product Info, solve query	{search the desired prod. autom. +}	A_1
$CreditAuthority$	Cap_3	provide payment facilities, process credit card	{flexib. and autom. pay. +}	...
	Cap_4	provide payment facilities, show bank transfer info	{flexib. and autom. pay. -}	...
$OrderManager$	Cap_5	provide order, manage order form	{null}	...
...	...	....	{...}	...

Focusing on Ability. Taking advantage from the previous capability modelling phase, here we illustrate how the methodology effectively deals with ability aspects. Fig. 4 addresses the dynamic aspects of the capability Cap_2. To effectively deal with such aspects, we consider two dimensions: *(i)* the control-flow structure of the activities that the capability is composed of, and *(ii)* for each activity and for each agent interaction required by its execution, the required interaction protocols. We propose to use AUML activity diagrams for *(i)* —e.g. as illustred in Fig. 4.(A)— and AUML interaction diagrams for *(ii)* —e.g. as illustrated in Fig. 4.(B). In the example, the control-flow for the ability part of Cap_2 is composed of 4 activities —i.e. Fig. 4.(A)— with the following labels and meanings:

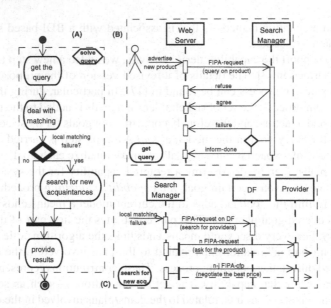

Fig. 4. A fragment of the two dimensions for the capability Cap_2 (Table 1) detailed-design: (A) the control-flow structure and (B) the agent interactions

- **get the query.** As further detailed by the interaction diagram of Fig. 4.(B), **Search Manager** waits for the web-user's request that carries out partial information on the product it is interested in, i.e. such an agent plays the *responder* role within a FIPA-request. The message content carries out the information on the product to look for, structured as follows: <product-category=..>, <product-name=..>, <product-quantity=..>, <product-price-range=(*min,max*)>.

- **deal with matching.** Once the product specifications have been correctly interpreted the **Search Manager** checks such a product in its local repository. Notice that, this phase does not require any external interaction, but the repository is inquired by **Search Manager** using a self FIPA-request IP.

- **search for new acquaintances.** This activity is performed when a failure occurs during the local matching phase (**deal with matching**), e.g., the local stock quantity is not sufficient for the required quantity, the current price does not fit the range, the product does not exist, etc. Therefore, in order to overcome such failures, the **Search Manager** cooperates with other providers, i.e. distributed warehouses. This capability activity is the most complicated as depicted by Fig. 4.(C), indeed, it is composed of three IPs: i) a FIPA-request in order to ask the Directory Facilitator (DF) for the providers; ii) n FIPA-requests targeted to all the providers returned by the DF in order to check the product availability in their warehouses; iii) a FIPA-cfp in order to negotiate the best price with the n-j providers figured out at the previous step.

- **provide results.** At the end, the agent communicates the obtained results by a simple inform message that can be of two types: a failure description (no results) or a list of retrieved products along with their detailed descriptions.

5   From Platform-Independent to Platform-Specific Model

In this section we present a technique to automatically derive the description of the capability of a JADE agent, i.e. a PSM, from the PIM model. In particular, we show how it is possible to map AUML Activity and Interaction Diagrams to JADE structures, using transformation techniques compliant with MDA's Query/View/Transformation requirements, that have been introduced in [9]. We exploit a Frame Logics based approach to model transformation described in [6] and implemented in the Tefkat tool[5]. The language consists of three major concepts: *pattern definitions, transformation rules, tracking relationships. Pattern definitions* are generated in order to identify structures

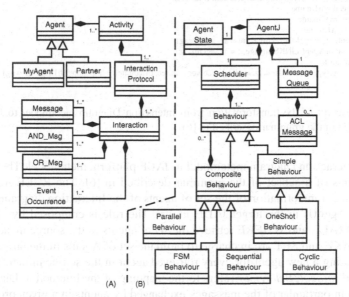

Fig. 5. (A) Fragment of the Interaction Diagram metamodel (part of the PIM model); **(B)** Fragment of the JADE metamodel (the PSM)

that are frequently used in a given transformation. *Transformation rules* map source to target metamodels constructs. *Tracking relationships* allow to maintain the traceability between entities in source and target model instances. The syntax of rules uses clauses such as the *Forall* and *Where* to recognize elements of the instance of the source model, and *Make* and *Set* for building the instance of the target model.

In the following we give an example of the mapping of AUML Interaction Diagrams to a subset of the JADE platform concepts based to the example described in the previous sections. The transformation is based on the metamodels of the two languages. Fig. 5(A) shows a subset of the AUML Interaction Diagram metamodel as described in [1]. From one side the agents involved in the interaction represented by the class Agent, on the other the interaction protocol constituted by a set of interactions (represented by the class Interaction and Interaction Protocols) made of simple messages or more complex structures like the And, Or and Xor composition of messages.

---

[5] More details are available in http://www.dstc.edu.au/Research/Projects/Pegamento/tefkat/

A subset of the target metamodel is shown in Fig. 5(B). Here an agent is described as an aggregation of Message Queue, Agent States and Scheduler behaviors that is an aggregation of behaviors. A behavior can be simple or composite, allowing to specify a composition of several behaviors. Fig. 6 illustrates an excerpt of the mapping rules

```
TRANSFORMATION Interaction2JADE: auml → Jade
RULE Agent2Agent()
    FORALL MyAgent mya
    MAKE AgentJ a
    SET a.name = mya.name, a.role = mya.role;
    LINKING AgentForAgent WITH agent = a, myagent = mya
RULE InteractionProtocol2Behaviour()
    FORALL MyAgent a1, MyAgent a2, InteractionProtocol ip
    WHERE ip.send = a1.name
        AND ip.rec = a2.name
        OR ip.rec = a1.name
        AND AgentForAgent LINKS myagent = a1, agent=ag1
        AND AgentForAgent LINKS myagent = a2, agent=ag2
    MAKE Behaviour b1
    SET b1.type = ip.type, b1.sender = ip.send, b1.receiver = ip.rec, b1.counter = ip.counter, b1.AgentJ = ag1
    ......
```

Fig. 6. An excerpt of the transformation from Interaction Diagram metamodel to JADE metamodel defined in the grammar described in [6]

from the Interaction Diagram metamodel to JADE platform metamodel. They are specified in terms of a subset of the grammar described in [6]. The RULE *Agent2Agent* allows for the transformation of the set of agents of the Interaction diagrams into a set of agents (AgentJ) in the target JADE model. The rule is composed by clauses: the clauses FORALL and WHERE retrieve the set of agents in the source metamodel; the clauses MAKE and SET are in charge to build the set of Agents in the target platform, simply creating a new agent for every retrieved agent in the source model. The RULE *InteractionProtocol2Behaviour* refers to the mapping of the Interaction Diagrams elements, and in particular of the messages exchanged by agents in a given protocol, into the definition of a JADE agent behavior. The target structure is created via the MAKE directive and instantiated via the SET directive in the rule; part the resulting XMI file is shown below.

```
<?xml version="1.0" encoding="ASCII"?>
<xmi:XMI xmi:version="2.0" xmlns:xmi="http://www.omg.org/XMI"
    xmlns:jade_conc="http:///jade_conc.ecore">
  <jade_conc:AgentJ xmi:id="26990772" name="Search_Manager" role="Serch_Manager"/>
  <jade_conc:AgentJ xmi:id="11552137" name="Provider" role="Provider"/>
  <jade_conc:Behaviour xmi:id="10834914" type="req"
      sender="Search_Manager" receiver="Provider" counter="1"/>
  <jade_conc:Behaviour xmi:id="2511137" type="cfp"
      sender="Search_Manager" receiver="Provider" counter="2"/>
  ...
</xmi:XMI>
```

6   Ability and Opportunity Implementation

Let's consider one of the examples of Table 1. Cap_2 is composed of an ability part — i.e. the plan solve query— and an opportunity part —i.e. the softgoal research for the desired product automatically. Since the opportunity aspect is related to the intelligent part of an agent behavior, it naturally fits into a Belief-Desire-Intention (BDI) agent architecture, having adopted the Jadex plug-in for JADE. Although our current prototype only supports the automatic transformation (from detailed design to implementation) for the ability part, we have manually generated the opportunity part as Jadex-based precondition. In this case, the goal provide product info has been assigned specific trigger-messages (FIPA-request) that the agent can satisfy adopting one of the abilities already specified at design-time in Fig. 2.(B) —i.e. plans browse catalog and solve query. Notice that, these trigger-messages may also carry out information about the user's profile —i.e. as a precondition— that enables or disables the achievement of specific softgoals. Specifically, such a precondition for Cap_2 has been annotated in A_1 at design-time, as depicted in Table 1. Therefore, each time a user logs in, the system classifies her/him into a predefined category that also enables or disables ($true$ or $false$) the activation of specific preconditions. For example, if the softgoal research for the desired product automatically is enabled, at the time the agent has to achieve the goal provide product info, the ability solve query will receive a higher selection-priority in respect to browse catalog.

```
import jade.core.*;
...
public class CAP_2 extends FSMBehaviour {
  private DSManager dsManager;
  ...
  public CAP_2(Agent a, DSManager ds) {
    super(a);
    dsManager = ds;
    //* AUTOMATON STATES DEFINITION
    registerFirstState(new Get_The_Query(), ZERO_STATE);
    registerState(new Deal_With_Matching(), ONE_STATE);
    registerState(new Search_For_New_Acq(), TWO_STATE);
    registerLastState(new Provide_Results(), THREE_STATE);
    registerState(new WaitBehaviour(a, 2000), WAIT_STATE);
    //* STATE TRANSITIONS DEFINITION
    registerTransition(ZERO_STATE, ONE_STATE, ZERO_ONE);
    //** NON-DETERMINISTIC CHOICE DEFINITION
    //*** Branch triggered when good_match = true
    registerTransition(ONE_STATE, TWO_STATE, ONE_TWO);
    registerTransition(TWO_STATE, THREE_STATE, TWO_THREE);
    //*** Branch triggered when good_match = false
    registerTransition(ONE_STATE, THREE_STATE, ONE_THREE);
    //** WAIT STATE TRANSITIONS
    registerTransition(ZERO_STATE, WAIT_STATE, ZERO_WAIT);
    registerTransition(WAIT_STATE, ZERO_STATE, WAIT_ZERO);
    ...
    scheduleFirst();
  }
  class Get_The_Query extends OneShotBehaviour (...)
  class Deal_With_Matching extends OneShotBehaviour (...)
  class Search_For_New_Acq extends OneShotBehaviour (...)
  class Provide_Results extends OneShotBehaviour (...)
  class WaitBehaviour extends TickerBehaviour (...)
}
```

(A)

```
class Search_For_New_Acq extends OneShotBehaviour {
  ...
  public void action() {
    ...
    //SEARCH ON DF
    template_df = new DFAgentDescription();
    template_sd = new ServiceDescription();
    template_sd.setType("PROVIDERS");
    template_df.addServices(template_sd);
    try{
      listOfProviders =
          DFService.search(this.myAgent,template_df);
    }catch(Exception fe){()}
    ...
    //FIPA-REQUEST AS INITIATOR
    msg = new ACLMessage(ACLMessage.REQUEST);
    msg.setProtocol(InteractionProtocol.FIPA_REQUEST);
    request_initiator = new RequestInitiator(myAgent, msg);
    for (int i = 0; i < listOfProviders.length; ++i) {
      request_initiator.addRecipient(
          listOfProviders[i].getName().toString());}
    this.myAgent.addBehaviour(request_initiator);
    ...
    //FIPA-CFP AS INITIATOR
    msg = new ACLMessage(ACLMessage.CFP);
    msg.setProtocol(InteractionProtocol.FIPA_CONTRACT_NET);
    cfp_initiator = new CFPInitiator(myAgent, msg);
    cfp_initiator.addRecipient(cfp_receiversList);
    myAgent.addBehaviour(cfp_initiator);
  }
  public int onEnd() {
    if (dsManager.getCounter() == turn) {
      return TWO_THREE;
    }
    else {
      return TWO_WAIT; } } }
```

(B)

Fig. 7. A fragment of the Cap_2 implementation: (A) control-flow as a JADE-based automaton implementation, (B) agent interactions as JADE-based FIPA IPs

The implementation of the ability part of a capability results from a transformation process, previously explained, in terms of a set of Tefkat xmi files, one for each activity of the AUML activity diagram. Consequently, as shown in Fig. 4 Cap_2 is composed of 4 transformation output files that are read and interpreted in order to generate the real Java code, i.e. our agent template for the agent Search Manager. Iteratively the same process applied to the whole table 1 produces the MAS previously designed.

The tool component in charge of performing the last development phase —i.e. code generation— uses very simple rules[6] in order to map the semi-structured information specified by the xmi output files into a JADE-based agent framework. Such rules drive the mapping between the diagrammatic concepts and a flexible agent framework that allows an agent to play different roles along with different capabilities according to specific environmental conditions —i.e. trigger messages that represent stakeholder intentions. The principal rules that have been adopted for our agent framework are the following:

1. Each agent *extends* the class *jade.core.Agent* according to special trigger-messages —i.e. target goals. That is, an agent can sense the environment and consequently switch to a specific role, hence it plays a precise capability. To deliver on such an aim, each agent owns a table that relates each capability to a set of trigger-messages and viceversa.

2. Each capability *extends* the class *jade.core.behaviours.FSMBehaviour*, namely it represents a final states machine (automaton). Thanks to such an implementing choice, each single activity of an activity diagram —i.e. an atomic task of the capability— corresponds to a single state of the automaton.

3. Each state is monitored —in terms of messages exchanged— in order to make the agent aware about the next state-transition. Thanks to such a feature, the agent can handle non-deterministic events at the moment they occur. Moreover, each time a failure occurs, such a strong property may allow the agent to switch in a compensation state[7].

An excerpt of the ultimate Cap_2 development phase is given in Fig. 7. In particular, Fig. 7.(A) shows how is defined in JADE the automaton associated to Cap_2: a states assignment step, e.g. *registerState(new Deal_With_Matching(),ONE_STATE)* and a state transitions step, e.g. *registerTransition(ONE_STATE,TWO_STATE,ONE_TWO)*. Notice that, each single activity of the activity diagram (Fig. 4.(A)) has been mapped in a JADE *jade.core.behaviours.FSMBehaviour* state, while inside each state a FIPA-IP has been mapped in an equivalent JADE FIPA-IP, as detailed by Fig. 4.(B). As illustrated in Fig. 4.(B), the framework allows the agent to monitor the state termination, namely, each IP (JADE behavior) saves its information on a *jade.core.behaviours.DataStore* class that is periodically checked (i.e. by our *dsManager*). This framework property allows the agent to monitor its internal behaviors and to pro-actively react against internal failures.

7 Related Work

There are, two types of research that are relevant to our work, namely research on agent capability and on AOSE methodologies covering agent implementation issues. Along the first line we mention the proposal given in [15], which defines a possible formal

---

[6] Related to the target agent framework building. Moreover, we are still investigating how many of these rules can be delegated to the Tefkat engine.

[7] This issue is not within the scope of this paper. However, we are actively investigating it.

relationship between capabilities and BDI concepts —i.e. beliefs, goals and intentions. This work roots the concept of capability into the philosophical idea that 'can' implies both *ability* and *opportunity*.

As detailed in this paper, our approach adopts the concept of capability as composed of ability and opportunity. Moreover, our approach extends previous capability formalizations principally in two directions. The first one is that it considers the possibility to have an agent ability —i.e. a plan— decomposed in sub-plans that can also be delegated to other agents. While, the second extension takes into account the possibility to have an opportunity, related to a given agent ability, composed of different opportunities that come from other agent perspectives. Moreover by means of our methodology the designer can trace the capability environmental constraints arisen in the early phases down to detailed design and implementation.

An approach which attempts to link the operative part of the capability —i.e. a set of actions embedded in the *behavior* concept— with the intelligence of an agent — i.e. in terms of beliefs and intentions, is proposed in [4]. More precisely, the authors propose an agent-oriented approach to software engineering called Behavior Oriented Design (BOD). By means of their BOD methodology, a complex problem can be decomposed in simple and independently modules that contain the agent actions. In particular, they consider an agent characterized principally with: *goals* —i.e. conditions to be achieved—, *intentions* —i.e. goals and subgoals that are currently chasing—, *beliefs* —i.e. the knowledge basis as partial view of the world—, and the *behaviors* —i.e. set of actions it can take. Thanks to such an approach, each agent can be characterized by behavioral modules. Even if our capability definition seems similar to this behavior concept, the proposed framework is less flexible than our in detailing the single components. In particular, the above mentioned approach, considers the modules as predefined rigid blocks of actions related to specific agent goals and beliefs. On the contrary, our approach also describes how atomic actions (sub-plans) contribute to the stakeholders intentions and beliefs achievements, i.e. by the softgoal contribution link analysis technique.

Along the second line, [11] goes in the direction of adding flexibility to agents and proposes a component based framework that facilitates the domain experts themselves making modification of deployed multi-agent systems with the aim of increasing the capacity of the systems to fit the evolving needs identified in the domain. In particular the framework is based on agent systems composed by well defined components and gives a structured support to the user for modifying or composing existing components, or adding new components in well defined ways; this mechanism, for example, intends to help the experts in specifying new goals and plans for the agents starting from the adaptation of the components that describe the existing one.

Among AOSE methodologies that describe and cover the agent implementation phase, Passi seems to be one of the most flexible and documented [7]. In the Passi methodology the process that guides the agent-based code generation is quite similar to our approach. For example, such methodology adopts activity diagrams to specify agent behaviors (i.e. *Multi-Agent Behaviour Description*), and it characterizes an agent role in terms of its tasks, e.g. see Chapter IV of [10] for details. The main differences with our approach are the followings. While Passi aims to model an agent role in terms of its tasks (i.e. the behavior), we model capabilities in terms of interaction protocols and internal tasks. In this way, the role is only a logical concept that arises when the agent plays a specific set of capabilities. Hence, our agent may play several roles, namely an agent behavior may be composed of several capabilities (composition). Passi does not consider stakeholder intentions and social dependencies —e.g. as illustrated in this paper by the *Tropos* softgoals— as strategic knowledge elements that the agent requires to effectively deal with capability selection. On the contrary, by means of the opportunity concept modelling, we are able to embed in the agent knowledge also environmental constraints figured out at the early phases of the requirements analysis. Notice that, such requirements cannot (easily) emerge by only considering the MAS architectural level.

8   Conclusions and Future Work

This paper focuses on design issues for agent oriented software development, such as requirements traceability and automated code generation. In particular, we revise the *Tropos* capability definition to better trace early and late requirements —e.g. stakeholder intentions and domain constraints— till down the MAS detailed design and implementation phases. Specifically, we have illustrated through examples —supported by prototype tools— that a MDA approach can cope with the automatic mapping between a platform-independent agent-based conceptual model (Tropos) and a platform-specific agent-based model (JADE). Whenever possible, our approach is based on current standards, namely, OMG's MDA for model transformations, IEEE's FIPA for an agent architecture and interaction protocols, and AUML for activity and interaction diagrams. As future work, we propose to deal with monitoring and compensation during capabilities execution to validate the system behavior with respect to design-time requirements. Further validation on real case studies will also be performed.

Acknowledgments

We would like to thank Barbara Tomasi, Loris Delpero, and Alessandro Orler for their precious contribution to accomplish the experiments.

References

1. B. Bauer, J. P. Muller, and J. Odell. Agent uml: A formalism for specifying multiagent software systems. *International Journal of Software Engineering and Knowledge Engineering*, 11(3):1–24, 2001.
2. F. Bellifemine, A. Poggi, and G. Rimassa. JADE: A FIPA Compliant agent framework. In *Practical Applications of Intelligent Agents and Multi-Agents*, pages 97–108, April, 1999.
3. P. Bresciani, P. Giorgini, F. Giunchiglia, J. Mylopoulos, and A. Perini. Tropos: An Agent-Oriented Software Development Methodology. *Autonomous Agents and Multi-Agent Systems*, 8(3):203–236, July 2004.
4. J. Bryson and S. McIlraith. Toward behavioral intelligence in the semantic web. *IEEE Computer - Web Intelligence*, 35(11):48–54, 2002.

5. J. Castro, M. Kolp, and J. Mylopoulos. Towards Requirements-Driven Information Systems Engineering: The Tropos Project. *Information Systems*. Elsevier, Amsterdam, the Netherlands.

6. CBOP, DSTC, and IBM. MOF Query/Views/Transformations, 2nd Revised Submission. Technical report, 2004.

7. M. Cossentino. *From requirements to code with the PASSI methodology*. Chapter 4, In [10], 2005.

8. A. Fuxman, M. Pistore, J. Mylopoulos, and P. Traverso. Model checking early requirements specifications in Tropos. In *IEEE Int. Symposium on Requirements Engineering*, pages 174–181, Toronto (CA), Aug. 2001. IEEE Computer Society.

9. T. Gardner, C. Griffin, J. Koehler, and R. Hauser. A review of omg mof 2.0 query / views / transformations submissions and recommendations towards the final standard. In *MetaModelling for MDA Workshop*, York, England, 2003.

10. B. Handerson-Seller and P. Giorgini. *Agent-Oriented Metodologies*. Idea Group, 2005.

11. G. Jayatilleke, L. Padgham, and M. Winikoff. A Model Driven Component-Based Development Framework for Agents. *Computer Systems Science & Engineering*, 4(20), 2005.

12. N. Jennings, K. Sycara, and M. Wooldridge. A roadmap of agent research and development. *Autonomous Agents and Multi-Agent Systems*, 1(1):7–38, 1998.

13. S. R. Judson, R. B. France, and D. L. Carver. Specifying Model Transformations at the Metamodel Level, 2004. http://www.omg.org.

14. S. J. Mellor, K. Scott, A. Uhl, and D. Weise. *MDA Distilled*. Addison-Wesley, 2004.

15. L. Padgham and P. Lambrix. Formalizations of Capabilities for Bdi-Agents. *Autonomous Agents and Multi-Agent Systems*, 10:249–271, 2005.

16. L. Penserini and J. Mylopoulos. Design Matters for Semantic Web Services. Technical Report T05-04-03, ITC-irst, April 2005.

17. L. Penserini, A. Perini, A. Susi, and J. Mylopoulos. From Stakeholder Intentions to Agent Capabilities. Technical report, ITC-irst, Trento, Italy, October 2005.

18. A. Perini and A. Susi. Developing Tools for Agent-Oriented Visual Modeling. In G. Lindemann, J. Denzinger, I. Timm, and R. Unland, editors, *Multiagent System Technologies, Proc. of the Second German Conference, MATES 2004*, number 3187 in LNAI, pages 169–182. Springer-Verlag, 2004.

19. A. Perini and A. Susi. Agent Oriented Visual Modeling and Model Validation for Engineering Distributed Systems. *Computer Systems Science & Engineering*, 20(4):319–329, 2005.

20. Y. Shoham. Agent-Oriented Programming. *Artificial Intelligence*, 60:51 – 92, 1993.

21. K. Sycara, M. Paolucci, A. Ankolekar, and N. Srinivasan. Automated discovery, interaction and composition of semantic web services. *Journal of Web Semantics*, pages 27–46, 2003.

22. E. Yu. *Modelling Strategic Relationships for Process Reengineering*. PhD thesis, University of Toronto, Department of Computer Science, University of Toronto, 1995.

Modeling Mental States in Agent-Oriented Requirements Engineering

Alexei Lapouchnian[1] and Yves Lespérance[2]

[1] Department of Computer Science, University of Toronto,
Toronto, ON M5S 3G4, Canada
alexei@cs.toronto.edu
[2] Department of Computer Science and Engineering, York University,
Toronto, ON M3J 1P3, Canada
lesperan@cs.yorku.ca

Abstract. This paper describes an agent-oriented requirements engineering approach that combines informal $i*$ models with formal specifications in the multiagent system specification formalism CASL. This allows the requirements engineer to exploit the complementary features of the frameworks. $i*$ can be used to model social dependencies between agents and how process design choices affect the agents' goals. CASL can be used to model complex processes formally. We introduce an intermediate notation to support the mapping between $i*$ models and CASL specifications. In the combined $i*$-CASL framework, agents' goals and knowledge are represented as their mental states, which allows for the formal analysis and verification of, among other things, complex agent interactions and incomplete knowledge. Our models can also serve as high-level specifications for multiagent systems.

1 Introduction

Modern software systems are becoming increasingly complex, with lots of intricate interactions. The recent popularity of electronic commerce, web services, supply chain management and other inter-organizational systems, digital libraries, etc. confirms the need for software engineering methods for constructing applications that are open, distributed, and adaptable to change. This is why many researchers and practitioners are looking at agent technology as a basis for distributed applications.

Agents are active, social, and adaptable software system entities situated in some environment and capable of autonomous execution of actions in order to achieve their set objectives [20]. Furthermore, most problems are too complex to be solved by just one agent — one must create a multiagent system (MAS) with several agents having to work together to achieve their objectives and ultimately deliver the desired application. Therefore, adopting the agent-oriented approach to software engineering means that the problem is decomposed into multiple, autonomous, interacting agents, each with a particular objective (goal). Agents in MAS frequently represent individuals, companies, etc. This means that there is an underlying organizational context in MAS. Like humans, agents need to coordinate their activities, cooperate, request help from others, etc., often through negotiation. Unlike in object-oriented or component-based

E. Dubois and K. Pohl (Eds.): CAiSE 2006, LNCS 4001, pp. 480–494, 2006.
© Springer-Verlag Berlin Heidelberg 2006

systems, interactions in multiagent systems occur through high-level agent communication languages, so these interactions are mostly viewed not at the syntactic level, but at the knowledge level, in terms of goal delegation, etc. [20].

In requirements engineering (RE), *goal-oriented approaches* (e.g, KAOS [3]) have become prominent. In Goal-Oriented Requirements Engineering (GORE), high-level stakeholder objectives are identified as goals and then refined into fine-grained requirements assignable to agents/components in the system-to-be or in its environment. Their reliance on goals makes GORE methods and agent-oriented software engineering a great match. Moreover, agent-oriented analysis is central to requirements engineering since the assignment of responsibilities for goals and constraints to components in the system-to-be and agents in its environment is the main result of the RE process. Therefore, it is natural to use a goal-oriented requirements engineering approach when developing MAS. With GORE, it is easy to make the transition from the requirements to the high-level MAS specifications. For example, strategic relationships among agents will become high-level patterns of inter-agent communication. Thus, it would be desirable to devise an *agent-oriented RE approach with a formal component that supports rigorous formal analysis, including reasoning about agents' goals and knowledge.*

In the above context, while it is possible to informally analyze small systems, formal analysis is needed for any realistically-sized system to determine whether such distributed requirements imposed on each agent in a MAS are correctly decomposed from the stakeholder goals, consistent and, if properly met, achieve the system's overall objectives. Therefore, the aim of this work is to devise an agent-oriented requirements engineering approach with a formal component that supports reasoning about agents' goals (and knowledge), thereby allowing for formal analysis of the requirements expressed as the objectives of the agents in a MAS.

In our approach we integrate the $i*$ modeling framework [21] with CASL [14], a formal agent-oriented programming language supporting the modeling of agent mental states. This gives the modeler the flexibility and intuitiveness of the $i*$ notation as well as the powerful formal analysis capability of CASL. To bridge the gap between informal $i*$ diagrams and formal CASL specifications we propose an intermediate notation that can be easily obtained from $i*$ models and then mapped into CASL. With our $i*$-CASL-based approach, a CASL model can be used both as a requirements analysis tool and as a formal high-level specification for a multiagent system that satisfies the requirements. This model can be formally analyzed using the CASLve [15] tool or other tools and the results can be fed back into the requirements model.

One of the main features of this approach is that goals (and knowledge) are assigned to particular agents thus becoming their subjective attributes as opposed to being objective system properties as in many other approaches (e.g., Tropos [1] and KAOS [3]). This allows for the modeling of conflicting goals, agent negotiation, information exchange, complex agent interaction protocols, etc.

The rest of the paper is organized as follows: Section 2 briefly describes the concepts of $i*$ and CASL; Section 3 discusses our approach in detail and Section 4 concludes the paper.

2 Background

2.1 The *i** Framework

*i** [21] is an agent-oriented modeling framework that can be used for requirements engineering, business process reengineering, etc. *i** centers on the notion of *intentional actor* and *intentional dependency*. Actors are described in their organizational setting and have attributes such as goals, abilities, beliefs, and commitments. In *i**, an actor can use opportunities to depend on other actors in achieving its objectives, at the same time becoming vulnerable if those actors do not deliver. *i** actors are *strategic* in the sense that they are concerned with the achievement of their goals and strive to find a balance between their opportunities and vulnerabilities. Similarly, dependencies in *i** are *intentional* since they appear as a result of actors pursuing their goals.

In this paper, we use a variant of the meeting scheduling problem, which has become a popular exemplar in Requirements Engineering (e.g., [17]). In the context of the *i** modeling framework the process was first analyzed in [21]. We introduce a number of modifications to the meeting scheduling process to make our models easier to understand. For instance, we take the length of meetings to be the whole day. We also assume that in the environment of the system-to-be there is a legacy software system called the Meeting Room Booking System (MRBS) that handles the booking of meeting rooms. The complete case study is presented in [7].

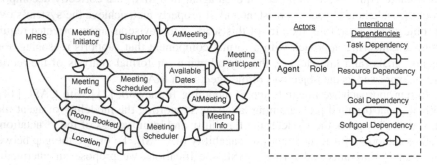

Fig. 1. The Meeting Scheduler in its environment

The *i** framework has two main components: the *Strategic Dependency (SD) model* and the *Strategic Rationale (SR) model*. The former describes the external relationships among actors, while the latter focuses on exploring the rationale behind the processes in organizations from the point of view of participating actors. SD models are networks of actors (which can be agents, positions, and roles) and dependencies. Depending actors are called *dependers* and depended-upon actors are called *dependees*. There can be four types of dependencies based on what is being delegated – a goal, a task, a resource, or a softgoal. Softgoals are related to the notion of non-functional requirements [2] and model quality concerns of agents.

Fig. 1 is an SD diagram showing the computerized Meeting Scheduler (MS) agent in its environment. Here, the role Meeting Initiator (MI) depends on the MS for scheduling meetings and for being informed about the meeting details. The MS, in turn, depends on the Meeting Participant role for attending meetings and for providing his/her available dates to it. The MS uses the booking system to book rooms for meetings. The Disruptor actor represents outside actors that cause changes in participants' schedules, thus modeling the environment dynamics.

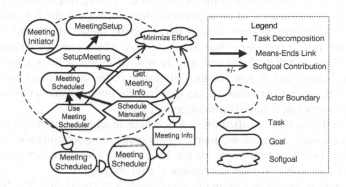

Fig. 2. SR model for the meeting initiator

SR models enable the analyst to assess possible alternatives in the definition of actor processes to better address their concerns. Four types of nodes are used in SR models – goals, tasks, softgoals, and resources – and three types of links – means-ends links, task decompositions links, and softgoal contribution links. Means-ends links specify alternative ways to achieve goals; task decomposition links connect tasks with components needed for their execution. For example, Fig. 2 is a simple SR models showing some details of the MI process. To schedule meetings, the MI can either do it manually, or delegate it to the scheduler. Softgoal contribution links specify how process alternatives affect quality requirements (softgoals), and so softgoals such as `MinimizeEffort` in Fig. 2 are used to evaluate these alternatives.

2.2 The Formal Foundations: CASL

The Cognitive Agents Specification Language (CASL) [13][14] is a formal specification language that combines theories of action [10][11] and mental states [12] expressed in situation calculus [9] with ConGolog [4], a concurrent, non-deterministic agent-oriented programming language with a formal semantics. In CASL, agents' goals and knowledge are modeled formally; communication actions are provided to update these mental states and ConGolog is then employed to specify the behaviour of agents. This combination produces a very expressive language that supports high-level reasoning about the agents' mental states. The logical foundations of CASL allow it to be used to specify and analyze a wide variety of MAS including non-deterministic systems and systems with incompletely specified initial state.

CASL specifications consist of two parts: the model of the domain and its dynamics (the declarative part) and the specification of the agents' behaviour (the procedural part). The domain is modeled in terms of the following entities: 1) *primitive actions* – all changes in the domain are due to primitive actions being executed by agents; 2) *situations*, which are states of the domain that result from the execution of sequences of actions (there is a set of initial situations, with no predecessor, corresponding to the ways agents think the world might be like initially); 3) *fluents*, which are predicates and functions that may change from situation to situation. The fluent Room(meetingID,date,room,s), where s is a situation parameter, models the fact that a room has been booked on some day for some meeting in a situation s.

To specify the dynamics of an application domain, we use the following types of axioms: 1) *action precondition axioms* that describe under what conditions actions can be performed; 2) *successor state axioms* (SSA), which were introduced in [10] as a solution to the frame problem and specify how primitive actions affect fluents; 3) *initial state axioms*, which describe the initial state of the domain and the initial mental states of the agents; 4) *other axioms* that include unique name axioms for actions and domain independent foundational axioms.

Agents' behaviour is specified using a rich high-level programming language with recursive procedure declarations, loops, conditionals, non-determinism, concurrency, and interrupts [4]. A special predicate *Do(Program,s,s')* holds if there is a successful execution of *Program* that ends in situation s' after starting in s.

CASL supports formal modeling of agents' goals and knowledge. The formal representation for both is based on a *possible worlds semantics* incorporated into the situation calculus, where situations are viewed as possible worlds [12]. CASL uses accessibility relations K and W to model what an agent knows and what it wants respectively. $K(agt,s',s)$ holds if the situation s' is compatible with what the agent agt knows in situation s, i.e., in situation s, the agent thinks that it might be in the situation s'. In this case, the situation s' is called K-*accessible*. When an agent does not know the value of some formula φ, it considers possible (formally, K-accessible) some situations where φ is true and some where it is false. An agent knows some formula φ if φ is true in all its K-accessible situations: **Know**$(agt,\varphi,s)= \forall s'(K(agt,s,s') \supset \varphi[s'])$. Constraints on the K relation ensure that agents have positive and negative introspection (i.e., agents know whether they know/don't know something) and guarantee that what is known is true. Communication actions such as inform are used for exchanging information among agents. The precondition for the inform action ensures that no false information is transmitted. The changes to agents' knowledge due to communication and other actions are specified by the SSA for the K relation. The axiom ensures that agents are aware of the execution of all actions. This formal framework is quite simple and idealized. More complex versions of the SSA can be specified, for example, to handle encrypted messages [14] or to provide belief revision [16].

The accessibility relation $W(agt,s',s)$ holds if in situation s an agent considers that everything that it wants to be true actually holds in s', which is called W-accessible. We use the formula **Goal**(agt,ψ,s) to indicate that in situation s the agent agt has the goal that ψ holds. The definition of **Goal** says that ψ must be true in all W-accessible situations that have K-accessible situation in their past. This ensures that, while agents may want something they know is impossible to obtain, the goals of agents must be consistent with what they currently know. In our approach, we mostly use achievement goals that specify the desired states of the world. We use the formula **Goal**$(agt,$**Eventually**$(\psi),s)$ to state that agt has the goal that ψ is eventually true. The request and cancelRequest actions are used by agents to request services from other agents and cancel their requests respectively. Requests are used to establish intentional dependencies among actors and lead to changes in goals of the requestee agent. The dynamics of the W relation are specified, as usual, by an SSA. There are constraints on W and K relations, which ensure that agents' goals are consistent and that that agents introspect their goals.

3 The $i*$-CASL Notation and Process

3.1 A Motivating Example

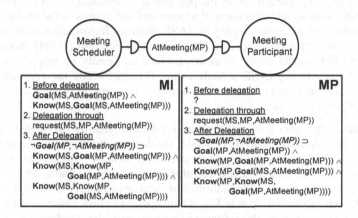

Fig. 3. A motivating example

Suppose that we are employing an approach like Tropos [1], a requirements-driven agent-oriented software development methodology that uses the $i*$ modeling notation, to model a simple goal delegation involving two agents. Fig. 3 shows a goal dependency where the Meeting Scheduler depends on the Meeting Participant for attending a meeting. We would like to be able to analyze this interaction and predict how it will affect the goals and the knowledge of these agents. Using the approach proposed in this paper, one can develop a formal model based on the SD diagram in Fig. 3 and the corresponding SR-level models (as will be shown later), analyze it, and conclude that, for example, before the goal delegation, the MS has the goal AtMeeting(MP) and knows about this fact. After the delegation (and provided that the MP did not have a conflicting goal), the MS knows that the MP has acquired the goal, that the MP knows that it has the goal, that the MP knows that the MS has the same goal, etc. For the Participant agent in Fig. 3, we cannot say what its mental state was before the goal delegation. But, after the request from the MS we know that it has the goal AtMeeting(MP) and knows about it, etc. The MP also knows how it has acquired the goal and thus will be able to trace its intention to achieve AtMeeting(MP) to the Meeting Scheduler's request.

Note that the change in mental state of the requestee agent is the core of goal delegation. Also, in our approach, goals and knowledge are attributes of particular agents. This allows for better models of agent conflicts, interaction, negotiation, etc.

3.2 Increasing Precision with iASR Models

Our aim in this approach is to tightly associate SR models with formal specifications in CASL. The standard SR diagrams are geared to informal analysis and can be very ambiguous. For instance, they lack the details on whether the subtasks in task decompositions are supposed to be executed sequentially, concurrently, under certain conditions, etc. CASL, on the other hand, is a precise language. To handle this precision mismatch we use Intentional Annotated SR (iASR) models that help in bridging the gap between SR models and CASL specifications. Our goal is to make iASR models precise graphical representation for the procedural component of CASL specifications while helping with the identification of axioms and definitions in the declarative one.

The starting point for developing an iASR diagram for an actor is the regular SR diagram for that actor (e.g., see Fig. 2). It can then be appropriately transformed to become an iASR model every element of which can easily be mapped into CASL. The steps for producing iASR models from SR ones include the addition of model annotations and the details of agent interactions, the removal of softgoals, the *deidealization* of goals [17], etc.

Annotations. The main tool that we use for disambiguating SR models is *annotations*. Annotations allow analysts to model the domain more precisely and to capture data/control dependencies among goals and other details. Annotations, proposed in [19] for use with SR models and ConGolog, are textual constraints on iASR models and can be of three types: composition, link, and applicability conditions. Composition annotations (specified by σ in Fig. 4) are applied to task and means-ends decompositions and specify how the subtasks/subgoals are to be combined to execute the supertask and achieve the goal respectively. Four types of composition are allowed: sequence (";"), which is default for task decompositions, concurrency ("||"), prioritized concurrency ("»"), and alternative ("|"), which is the default for means-ends decompositions. These annotations are applied to subtasks/subgoals from left to right. E.g., in Fig. 4, if the "»" annotation is applied, n_1 has the highest priority, while n_k has the lowest. The choice of composition annotations is based on the ways actions and procedures can be composed together in CASL.

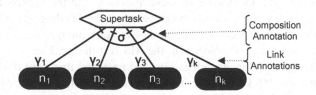

Fig. 4. Composition and link annotations

Link annotations (γ_i in Fig. 4) are applied to subtasks/subgoals (n_i) and specify how/under what conditions they are supposed to be achieved/executed. There are six types of link annotations (corresponding to CASL operators): *while* loop, *for* loop, the *if* condition, the pick, the interrupt, and the guard. The pick annotation (π(variableList, condition)) non-deterministically picks values for variables in the subtask that satisfy the condition. The interrupt (whenever(variableList, condition, cancelCondition)) fires whenever there is a binding for the variables that satisfies the condition unless the cancellation condition becomes true. Guards (guard(condition)) block the subtask's execution until the condition becomes true. The absence of a link annotation on a particular decomposition link indicates the absence of any conditions on the subgoal/subtask.

The third annotation type is the *applicability condition* (ac(condition)). It applies to means-ends links used with goal achievement alternatives and specifies when the corresponding alternatives are applicable (see below for an example).

Softgoals. Softgoals (quality requirements) are imprecise and thus are difficult to handle in a formal specifications language. Therefore, we use softgoals to help in choosing the best process alternatives (e.g., by selecting the ones with the best overall contribution to all the softgoals in the model) and then remove them before iASR models are produced. Alternatively, softgoals can be operationalized or metricized, thus becoming hard goals. Also, applicability conditions in iASR models can be used to capture the fitness of the remaining alternatives w.r.t. softgoals, which is normally encoded by softgoal contributions in SR diagrams. For example, one can specify that phoning participants to notify them of the meeting details is applicable only in cases with few participants (see Fig. 8), while the email option is applicable for any number of participants. This may be due to the softgoal "Minimize Effort".

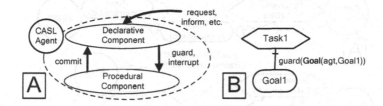

Fig. 5. Synchronizing procedural and declarative components of CASL specifications

Agent Goals in iASR Models. A CASL agent has a procedural and a declarative components. iASR diagrams only model agent processes and therefore can only be used to represent the procedural component of CASL agents. The presence of a goal node in an iASR diagram indicates that the agent knows that the goal is in its mental state and is prepared to deliberate about whether and how to achieve it. For the agent to modify its behaviour in response to the changes to its mental state, it must detect that change and synchronize its procedural and declarative components (see Fig. 5A). Agent mental states are specified declaratively and usually change as a result of communication acts that realize goal delegation and information exchange. Thus, the procedural component of the agent must monitor for these changes. To do this we use interrupts or guards with their conditions being the presence of certain goals or knowledge in the mental state of the agent (Fig. 5B). Procedurally a goal node is interpreted as invoking the means to achieve it.

In CASL, as described in [14], only communication actions have effects on the mental state of the agents. We, on the other hand, would like to let agents change their mental state on their own by executing the action commit(agent,φ), where φ is a formula that the agent/modeler wants to hold. Thus, in iASR diagrams all agent goals must be acquired either from intentional dependencies or by using the commit action.

By introducing goals into the models of agent processes, the modeler captures the fact that multiple alternatives exist in these processes. Moreover, the presence of goal nodes suggests that the designer envisions new possibilities for achieving these goals. By making the agent acquire the goals, the modeler makes sure that the agent's mental state reflects the above intention. In this way the agents would be able to reason about various alternatives available to them or come up with new ways to achieve their goals at runtime. Self-acquired goals add flexibility to system models by preserving within the corresponding formal specifications the variability in the way goals can be achieved and by avoiding early operationalization of goals. Self-acquired goals can be used to "load" goal refinements and AND/OR goal decompositions, which are abundant in GORE and AI, into the mental state of the agent if reasoning about these refinements is required. This is unlike the approach in [19] where agent goals had to be operationalized before being formally analyzed.

Another way of increasing the precision of the iASR model is the addition of parameters to iASR models. For example, in Fig. 6B, all of the nodes in the model have the parameter mid (short for "meeting ID"), a unique meeting identifier. Quite frequently, we replace the conditions in annotations and other model elements (they tend to be long) with suitably named abbreviations, e.g., RequestedDateRange(mid).

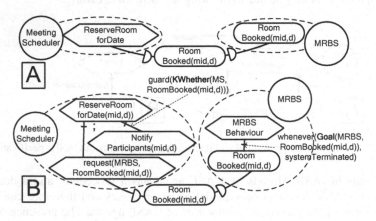

Fig. 6. Adding iASR-level agent interaction details

Providing Agent Interaction Details. $i*$ usually abstracts from modeling any details of agent interactions. CASL, on the other hand, models high-level aspects of inter-agent communication: requests for services or information, the selection of the course of action upon the receipt of the information, etc. Because of the importance of agent interactions in MAS, in order to formally verify multiagent system specifications in CASL, all high-level aspects of these interactions must be provided in the corresponding iASR models. This includes the tasks that request services or information from agents in the system, the tasks that supply the information or inform about success or failure in providing the service, etc. We assume that the communication links are reliable.

For example, the SR model with the goal dependency RoomBooked (see Fig. 1) in Fig. 6A is refined into the iASR model in Fig. 6B showing the details of the requests, the interrupts with their trigger conditions referring to mental states of the agent, etc.

3.3 Mapping iASR Diagrams into CASL

Once all the necessary details have been introduced into an iASR diagram, it can be mapped into the corresponding CASL model, thus making the iASR model amenable to formal analysis.

The modeler defines a mapping **m** that maps every element (except for intentional dependencies) of an iASR model into CASL. This mapping associates iASR model elements with CASL procedures, primitive actions, and formulas so that a CASL program can be generated from an iASR model. Specifically, agents are mapped into constants that serve as their names as well as into CASL procedures that specify their behaviour; roles and positions are mapped into similar procedures with an agent parameter so that they can be instantiated by individual agents; leaf-level task nodes are mapped into CASL procedures or primitive actions; composition and link annotations are mapped into the corresponding CASL operators, while the annotation conditions map into CASL formulas.

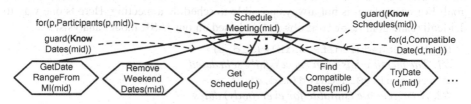

Fig. 7. Example iASR task decomposition

Mapping Task Nodes. A task decomposition is automatically mapped into a CASL procedure that reflects the structure of the decomposition and all the annotations. While the possibility of mapping leaf-level tasks into CASL procedures may reduce model size and increase the level of abstraction, restricting the mapping of these tasks to similarly named primitive actions allows the CASL procedures to be automatically constructed from these actions based on iASR annotations.

Fig. 7 shows how a portion of the Meeting Scheduler's task for scheduling meetings can be decomposed. This task will be mapped into a CASL procedure with the following body (it contains portions still to be (recursively) mapped into CASL; they are the parameters of the mapping **m**):

```
proc ScheduleMeetingProc(mid)
  m(GetDateRangeFromMI(mid));
  guard m(KnowDates(mid)) do m(RemoveWeekendDates(mid))
    endGuard;
  for p: m(Ptcp(mid)) do m(GetSchedule(p)) endFor;
  guard m(KnowSchedules(mid)) do m(FindCompatibleDates(mid))
    endGuard;
  for d: m(CompatibleDate(d,mid)) do m(TryDate(d,mid)) endFor;
...
endProc
```

Note how the body of the procedure associated with the `ScheduleMeeting` task is composed of the results of the mapping of its subtasks with the annotations providing the composition details. This procedure can be mechanically generated given the mapping for leaf-level tasks and conditions.

Mapping Goal Nodes. In our approach, an iASR goal node is mapped into a CASL formula, which is the formal definition for the goal, and an achievement procedure, which encodes how the goal can be achieved and is based on the means-ends decomposition for the goal in the iASR diagram. For example, a formal definition for MeetingScheduled(mid,s) could be: $\exists$d[AgreeableDate(mid,date,s) $\wedge$ AllAccepted(mid,date,s) $\wedge$ RoomBooked(mid,date,s)]. This says that there must be a date agreeable for everybody on which a room is booked and all participants have accepted to meet. This seems correct, but initial formal goal definitions are often too ideal for the goal that cannot always be achieved. Such goals must be *deidealized* [17]. In order to weaken the goal appropriately, one needs to know under what circumstances the goal cannot be achieved. Modeling an achievement process for a goal using an iASR diagram allows us to understand how that goal can fail and thus iASR models can be used to come up with a correct formal definition for the goal. For example, it is not always possible to schedule a meeting. Here is one way to deidealize the goal MeetingScheduled based on our iASR model analysis:

MeetingScheduledIfPossible(mid,s)=
//1. The meeting has been successfully scheduled
SuccessfullyScheduled(mid,s) $\vee$
//2. No agreeable (suitable for everybody) dates
$\forall$d[IsDate(d) $\supset$ ¬AgreeableDate(mid,d,s)] $\vee$
//3. For every agreeable date at least one participant declined
$\forall$d[AgreeableDate(mid,d,s)$\supset$ SomeoneDeclined(mid,d,s)] $\vee$
//4. No rooms available
$\forall$d[SuggestedDate(mid,d,s) $\wedge$ AllAccepted(mid,d,s) $\supset$
    ¬RoomBookingFailed(mid,date,s)]

CASL's support for reasoning about agent goals presented us with an interesting possibility. In the case study, we decided not to maintain schedules for meeting participants explicitly. Instead, we relied on the presence of goals AtMeeting(participant,mid,date,s) in their mental states as indications of the participants' intention to attend certain meetings on certain dates (the absence of meeting commitments indicates an available time slot). Then, we made the participants know that they can only attend one meeting per time slot (a day in our case) with the following initial state axiom (this can be shown to persist in all situations):

$\forall$agt[**Know**(agt,$\forall$p,mid1,mid2,date[AtMeeting(p,mid1,date,now) $\wedge$
    AtMeeting(p,mid2,date,now) $\supset$ mid1=mid2],S_0)]

Thus, the consistency of participants' schedules is automatically maintained since meeting requests conflicting with already adopted AtMeeting goals are rejected.

The achievement procedures for goals are automatically constructed based on the modeled means for achieving them and the associated annotations including the applicability conditions (see Fig. 8). By default, the alternative composition annotation is used, which means that some applicable alternative will be non-deterministically

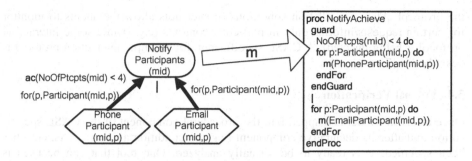

Fig. 8. Generating achievement procedures

selected. Other approaches are also possible, e.g., one can try all appropriate alternatives concurrently or in sequence. Note that the applicability condition (ac) maps into a guard operator to prevent the execution of unwanted alternatives.

Modeling Dependencies. Intentional dependencies are not mapped into CASL per se – they are established by the associated agent interactions. iASR tasks requesting help from agents will generally be mapped into actions of the type request(FromAgt,ToAgt,**Eventually**(φ)) for achievement goals φ. We add a special abbreviation **DoAL**(δ,s,s') (Do At Least) to be used when establishing task dependencies. It stands for **Do**(δ||(πa.a)*,s,s'), which means that the program δ must be executed, but that any other action may occur. Thus, to ask an agent to execute a certain known procedure, the depender must request it with: request(FromAgt, ToAgt,**DoAL**(SomeProcedure)).

In order for an intentional dependency to be established we also need a commitment from a dependee agent to act on the request from the depender. Thus, the dependee must monitor its mental state for newly acquired goals. For example, here is an interrupt that is used by the Meeting Participant to check for a request for the list of its available dates:

```
<mid:Goal(mp,DoAL(InformAvailableDates(mid,MS),now,then) ∧
    Know(mp,¬∃s,s'(s ≤ s' ≤ now ∧
            DoAL(InformAvailDates(mid,MS),s,s'))) →
    InformAvailDates(mid,MS)
until SystemTerminated>
```

Here, if the MP has the goal to execute the procedure InformAvailDates and knows that it has not yet executed it, the agent sends the available dates. The cancellation condition SystemTerminated indicates that the MP always monitors for this goal. Requesting agents use similar interrupt/guard mechanism to monitor for requested information or confirmations. When modeling agent interaction protocols in this approach, for every incoming message an agent will have an interrupt monitoring for it with its body specifying the appropriate response to the message. Since the interrupts fire when changes in the mental state are detected, agents can execute the protocols flexibly by, for example, self-acquiring the goal of buying some urgently required product from a vendor and thus skipping the lengthy price negotiation part of the protocol. Also, cancellation conditions in interrupts allow the agents to monitor for certain requests/informs only in particular contexts (e.g., while some interaction protocol is being enacted). A CASL specification for a simple interaction protocol is described in [7].

3.4 Formal Verification

Once an iASR model is mapped into the procedural component of the CASL specification and after its declarative component (e.g., precondition axioms, SSAs, etc.) has been specified, it is ready to be formally analyzed. One tool that can be used is CASLve [15], a theorem prover-based verification environment for CASL. CASLve provides a library of theories for representing CASL specifications and lemmas that facilitate various types of verification proofs. [13] shows a proof that there is a terminating run for a simplified meeting scheduler system as well as example proofs of a safety property and consistency of specifications. In addition to physical executability of agent programs, one can also check for the *epistemic feasibility* [8] of agent plans, i.e., whether agents have enough knowledge to successfully execute their processes.

Other approaches could be used as well, for instance, simulation or model checking. However, tools based on these techniques work with much less expressive languages than CASL. Therefore, CASL specifications must be simplified before these methods can be used on them. For example, most simulation tools cannot handle mental state specifications; these would then have to be operationalized before simulation is performed. The ConGolog interpreter can be used to directly execute such simplified specifications, as in [19]. Model checking methods (e.g. [5]) are restricted to finite state specifications, and work has only begun on applying these methods to theories involving mental states (e.g., [18]).

If expected properties of the system are not entailed by the CASL model, it means that the model is incorrect and needs to be fixed. The source of an error found during verification can usually be traced to a portion of the CASL code and to a part of the corresponding iASR model since our systematic mapping supports traceability.

3.5 Discussion and Future Work

In the approach presented in this paper and in [7], we produce CASL specifications from $i*$ models for formal analysis and verification. The approach is related to the Tropos framework in that it is agent-oriented and is rooted in the RE concepts. Our method is not the first attempt to provide formal semantics for $i*$ models. For example, Formal Tropos (FT) [5], supports formal verification of $i*$ models through model checking. Also, in the $i*$-ConGolog approach [19], on which our method is based, SR models are associated with formal ConGolog programs for simulation and verification. Additionally, the Trust-Confidence-Distrust approach [6] combined $i*$ and ConGolog to model and analyze trust in social networks. The problem with all these methods is that goals of the agents are abstracted out and made into objective properties of the system in the formal specifications. This is done due to the fact that the formal components of these approaches (the model checker input language for FT and ConGolog for the other) do not support reasoning about agent goals (and knowledge). However, most of the interactions among agents involve knowledge exchange and goal delegation since multiagent systems are developed as social structures. Thus, complementing informal modeling techniques such as $i*$ with formal analysis of agent goals and knowledge is very important in the design of multiagent systems.

We use a version of CASL where the precondition for the `inform` action requires that the information being sent by an agent be known to it (we assume that what is known must be true). This prevents agents from transmitting false information. The removal of this restriction allows the modeling of systems where agents are not always truthful. This can be useful when dealing with security and privacy requirements. However, dealing with false information may require belief revision, which complicates the model somewhat (see [16]). Similarly, the precondition for `request` makes sure that the sender does not itself have goals that conflict with the request. Relaxing this constraint also allows for the possibility of modeling malicious agents.

Other extensions to CASL to accommodate various characteristics of application domains are possible. For example, in many domains one needs to specify whom an agent trusts and to whom it is helpful. In [7] we proposed a simple way to handle trust and helpfulness in CASL. Fine-grained modeling of trust and helpfulness among agents in our approach is future work.

We also point out that CASL assumes that all agents are aware of all actions being executed in the system. Often, it is useful to lift this restriction, but dealing with the resulting lack of knowledge about agents' mental states can be challenging. In future work, we plan to address these issues. We would also like to accommodate reasoning about softgoals in our framework as well as to test the method on more realistic case studies. Additionally, we are developing a toolkit to support requirements engineering using our approach.

While the procedural component of a CASL specification accurately reflects the corresponding iASR model, the model only hints on what has to be in the declarative component of the specification (e.g., the axioms for actions, the definitions of annotation conditions, and so on). We expect that our RE toolkit will be able to significantly simplify the specification of the declarative component of CASL models.

4 Conclusion

In this paper, we have proposed a framework for agent-oriented requirements engineering incorporating both graphical and formal notations. The graphical notation allows for comprehensive modeling of system requirements as well as of its organizational setting including stakeholder goals and goal delegation. These models are then gradually made more precise so that they can be mapped into formal agent specifications where goals are not removed, but are modeled formally and can be updated following requests. This allows agents to reason about their objectives. Information exchanges among agents are also formalized as changes in their knowledge state. In our approach, goals and knowledge are not system-wide properties, but belong to concrete agents. This supports the modeling of conflicting goals, agent negotiation, information exchange, complex agent interaction protocols, etc. The generated formal model can be used both as a requirements analysis tool and as a formal high-level specification for the multiagent system.

References

1. Castro J., Kolp M., Mylopoulos, J.: Towards Requirements-Driven Information Systems Engineering: The Tropos Project. *Information Systems*, 27(6) (2002) 365-389
2. Chung, L.K., Nixon, B.A., Yu, E., Mylopoulos, J.: Non-Functional Requirements in Software Engineering. Kluwer (2000)
3. Dardenne, A., van Lamsweerde, A., Fickas, S.: Goal-Directed Requirements Acquisitions. *Science of Computer Programming*, 20 (1993) 3-50
4. De Giacomo, G., Lespérance, Y., Levesque, H.: ConGolog, A Concurrent Programming Language Based on the Situation Calculus. *Artificial Intelligence*, 121 (2000) 109-169
5. Fuxman, A., Liu, L., Mylopoulos, J., Pistore, M., Roveri, M., Traverso, P.: Specifying and Analyzing Early Requirements in Tropos. *RE Journal*, 9(2) (2004) 132-150
6. Gans, G., Jarke, M., Kethers, S., Lakemeyer, G., Ellrich, L., Funken, C., Meister, M.: Requirements Modeling for Organization Networks: A (Dis-)Trust-Based Approach. Proc. *RE'01* (2001) 154-163
7. Lapouchnian, A.: Modeling Mental States in Requirements Engineering – An Agent-Oriented Framework Based on $i*$ and CASL. M.Sc. Thesis. Department of Computer Science, York University, Toronto (2004)
8. Lespérance, Y.: On the Epistemic Feasibility of Plans in Multiagent Systems Specifications. Proc. *ATAL-2001*, Revised papers, LNAI 2333, Springer, Berlin (2002) 69-85
9. McCarthy, J., Hayes, P.: Some Philosophical Problems From the Standpoint of Artificial Intelligence, *Machine Intelligence*, Vol. 4, Edinburgh University Press (1969) 463-502
10. Reiter, R.: The Frame Problem in the Situation Calculus: A Simple Solution (Sometimes) and a Completeness Result for Goal Regression. Artificial Intelligence and Mathematical Theory of Computation: Papers in Honor of John McCarthy, V. Lifschitz (ed.), Academic Press (1991) 359-380
11. Reiter, R.: Knowledge in Action: Logical Foundations for Specifying and Implementing Dynamical Systems. MIT Press, Cambridge MA (2001)
12. Scherl, R.B., Levesque, H.: Knowledge, Action, and the Frame Problem. Artificial Intelligence, 144(1-2) (2003) 1-39
13. Shapiro, S.: Specifying and Verifying Multiagent Systems Using CASL. Ph.D. Thesis. Department of Computer Science, University of Toronto (2004)
14. Shapiro, S., Lespérance, Y.: Modeling Multiagent Systems with the Cognitive Agents Specification Language - A Feature Interaction Resolution Application. *ATAL-2000*, LNAI 1986, Springer, Berlin (2001) 244-259
15. Shapiro, S., Lespérance, Y., Levesque, H.: The Cognitive Agents Specification Language and Verification Environment for Multiagent Systems. Proc. *AAMAS'02*, Bologna, Italy, ACM Press (2002) 19-26
16. Shapiro, S., Pagnucco, M., Lespérance, Y., Levesque, H.: Iterated Belief Change in the Situation Calculus. Proc. *KR-2000* (2000) 527-538
17. van Lamsweerde, A., Darimont, R., Massonet, P.: Goal-Directed Elaboration of Requirements for a Meeting Scheduler: Problems and Lessons Learnt. Proc. *RE'95*, York, UK (1995) 194-203
18. van Otterloo, S., van der Hoek, W., Wooldrige, M.: Model Checking a Knowledge Exchange Scenario. *Applied Artificial Intelligence*, 18:9-10 (2004) 937-952
19. Wang, X., Lespérance, Y.: Agent-Oriented Requirements Engineering Using ConGolog and $i*$. Proc. *AOIS-01* (2001) 59-78
20. Wooldridge, M.: Agent-Based Software Engineering. *IEE Proceedings on Software Engineering*, 144(1) (1997) 26-37
21. E. Yu. Towards modeling and reasoning support for early requirements engineering. Proc. *RE'97*, Annapolis, USA (1997) 226-235

On the Quantitative Analysis of Agent-Oriented Models

Xavier Franch

Universitat Politècnica de Catalunya (UPC),
C/Jordi Girona 1-3, UPC-Campus Nord (Omega), Barcelona, Spain
franch@lsi.upc.edu
http://www.lsi.upc.edu/~franch/

Abstract. Agent-oriented models are used in organization and information system modelling for providing intentional descriptions of processes as a network of relationships among actors. As such, they capture and represent goals, dependencies, intentions, beliefs, alternatives, etc., which appear in several contexts: business process reengineering, information system development, etc. In this paper, we are interested in the definition of a framework for the analysis of the properties that these models exhibit. Indicators and metrics for these properties are defined in terms of the model elements (e.g., actors, dependencies, scenario paths, etc.) Our approach is basically quantitative in nature, which allows defining indicators and metrics that can be reused in many contexts. However, a qualitative component can be introduced if trustable expert knowledge is available; the extent up to which quantitative and qualitative aspects are intertwined can be determined in every single case. We apply our proposal to the $i*$ notation and we take as main case study a highly-intentional property, predictability of model elements.

1 Introduction

Goal- and agent-oriented analysis methods and languages such as KAOS, $i*$, GRL or TROPOS [1, 2, 3] are widespread in the information systems community for the refinement and decomposition of the customer needs into concrete goals, during the early phase of the requirements specification [4, 5]. This kind of models represents an organization and its processes as a network of actors and dependencies, which may be decomposed into simpler elements.

Once built, the models can be used for different purposes. Two of the most important ones are: analysis of the properties they exhibit, and comparison of alternatives. In the first case, it is checked whether some properties hold in the model; some actors or dependencies exhibit some property (either positive or not) are searched; etc. In the second case, different models, that represent different ways of implementing organizational processes or information systems, are compared with respect to properties that have been considered as crucial. In both cases, evaluation of models is the cornerstone of these analyses, and therefore some suitable metrics to rely upon are needed.

The use of metrics with this purpose is very common in other type of models. For instance, there are some suites of metrics in the field of object-oriented modeling [6, 7], which refer to structural properties like cohesion and coupling. Properties referring to

E. Dubois and K. Pohl (Eds.): CAiSE 2006, LNCS 4001, pp. 495–509, 2006.
© Springer-Verlag Berlin Heidelberg 2006

the system itself, such as security, efficiency or cost, which mainly fall into the category of non-functional or organizational requirements, appear when considering models of the system architecture [8]. These metrics are usually defined in terms of the components, nodes, pipes, etc., that compose the final configuration of the system.

In the case of goal- and agent-oriented modeling, typical approaches analyse models in a qualitative way, especially in conjunction with non-functional requirements [9], by targeting to specific properties such as availability, security and adaptability. These target properties are decomposed into simpler criteria that may be used to evaluate different candidate models for the system-to-be [10]. This evaluation is basically qualitative, which means that the extent up to which a criterion is fulfilled by a candidate model is determined by expert judgement. Although qualitative analysis is a powerful mechanism that is satisfactory in many cases, it may introduce a certain degree of uncertainness because it relies completely on the claims that experts make. The dichotomy among qualitative and quantitative analysis is not new and by no means exclusive of organization or information system modelling, or even the computer science discipline (see [11, p. 40] for an abridged comparison). Some researchers advocate that both types of analysis are exclusive [12], but others believe that they are compatible [13] and even complementary [14]. In goal-orientation, some contributions exist that combine quantitative and qualitative analysis for finding assignment of labels to nodes and determine its propagation in goal graphs [15, 16].

In this paper we are interested in the analysis of agent-oriented models with special emphasis on the quantitative side. To be able to express our approach in detail, we consider agent-oriented models written in the $i*$ language, although we think that the underlying concepts could be adapted to other approaches. More precisely, we want to take profit of the networked structure of $i*$ models to define structural indicators that are quantitative in nature, counting actors, dependencies, and other elements; indicators can be used to define metrics that measure model properties. Our definitions will make it possible to include some expert judgement if considered necessary to obtain more accurate results; in fact, we will see that indicators are highly customizable depending on both the knowledge available on the problem (expert judgement and current state of refinement of the model) and the effort to be invested in this process. Due to its structural nature, our framework is expressed in terms of the OCL [17]; operators such as `allInstances` and `select` suit well for working with model elements.

The paper is structured as follows. In section 2, we define the $i*$ framework using UML. In section 3, we introduce our framework for measuring $i*$ model properties. We analyse one particular property, predictability, in section 4, using the concepts introduced. Finally, we provide some comparison, conclusions and future work in sections 5 and 6.

2   A UML Definition of $i*$

In this section, we introduce the $i*$ framework using the UML for defining rigorously its concepts. We think that this section is necessary because, as reported in [18], there are several variations in the literature for the $i*$ notation and thus we need to make explicit which constructs do we use in this paper and which properties do we assume.

Our i^* framework is based on the seminal Yu's proposal [2] with some minor simplifications. Yu proposes two types of models, each corresponding to a different abstraction level (see fig. 1): a *Strategic Dependency* (SD) model represents the intentional level and the *Strategic Rationale* (SR) model represents the rational level.

A SD model consists of a set of nodes that represent actors, and a set of dependencies that represent the relationships among them, expressing that an actor (*depender*) depends on others (*dependees*) in order to obtain some objective (*dependum*). Altogether form a network of knowledge that allows understanding "why" the system behaves in a particular way [19]. The dependum is an intentional element that can be a *resource, task, goal* or *softgoal* (see [2] for a detailed description).

A SR model allows visualizing the intentional elements into the *boundary* of an actor to refine the SD model with reasoning capabilities. Once SR models are built, the dependencies of the SD model may be linked to the appropriate intentional elements inside the actor boundary. According to their intentional meaning, some restrictions apply: goal dependencies can be assigned to goals and tasks in the dependee side; the same for task dependencies; and resource dependencies just to task dependencies.

The elements inside the SR model are decomposed accordingly to 2 types of links:

- *Means-end links* establish that one or more intentional elements are the *means* that contribute to the achievement of an *end*. The "end" can be a goal, task, resource, or softgoal, whereas the "means" is usually a task. There is a relation *OR* when there are several means, which indicate the different ways to obtain the end. The possible relationships are: *Goal-Task, Resource-Task, Task-Task, Softgoal-Task, Softgoal-Softgoal* and *Goal-Goal*. In *Means-end* links with a *softgoal* as end it is possible to specify if the contribution of the means towards the end is negative or positive; this label may also appear in softgoal dependencies.
- *Task-decomposition links* state the decomposition of a task into different intentional elements. There is a relation *AND* when a task is decomposed into more than one intentional element.

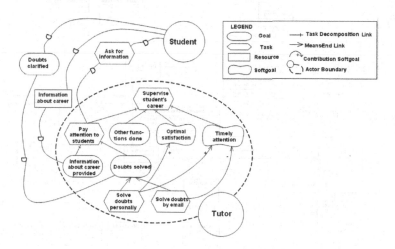

Fig. 1. Example of an i^* model for an academic tutoring system

SR models have additional elements of reasoning such as routines. A *routine* represents one particular course of action to attain the actor's goal among all the existing alternatives. The concept of routine appears in [2] but no notation is provided, so we use the similar notion of *scenario path* as defined in [20] based on the use case map concept appearing in GRL [21].

In Fig. 2 we show the conceptual model in UML, corresponding to our version of the i^* language; OCL constraints are not included for the sake of brevity. It is remarkable that dependencies are not defined as a ternary association; we have opted for composing two binary associations to facilitate the OCL expressions that we will write later in the metrics framework. We remark some modeling elements of interest: the *Model* class (singleton), which gives a name to the model; the *Node* class that provides a key to model elements; the *DependableNode* class, which models the intentional elements for which it is possible define dependencies, that is, actors and intentional elements of the SR model; and the *MeansEndContribution* and *Softgoal-Contribution* classes, that differentiate means-end links and dependencies that involve softgoals.

As an additional point, it may be argued that, in order to formulate metrics to evaluate and eventually compare i^* models, it is necessary not only to rigorously define the semantics of the i^* elements that we use, but also how the models are built, since different people may build correct models very dissimilar in nature and of course too much diversity would make our quantitative framework difficult to apply. We have tackled this point in our previous work, by defining two similar, complementary methodologies for building i^* models, PRiM [22] and RiSD [23], depending on whether we create the model as a process reengineering exercise or from the scratch, respectively. Both methodologies define rules, checkpoints and procedures to guide model construction, therefore we may say that using them we can obtain models in a predictable and repeatable enough manner.

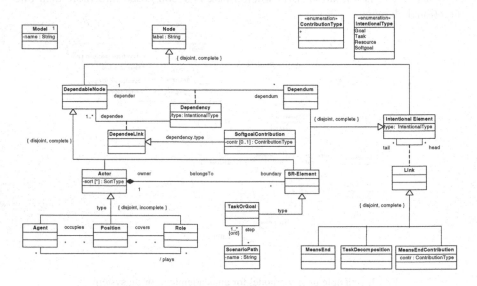

Fig. 2. A UML conceptual model for i^*

3 A Framework for Metrics on $i*$

In this section, we explore the use of *structural indicators* that can be used to define *structural metrics* that measure the *properties* of an $i*$ model, i.e. those properties that depend on the form of the model and the types of its elements. Structural metrics are valuable for both analysing a highly abstract model of a system of any kind, composed basically by roles, and for comparing different feasible realizations of this abstract model (which take the form of actor models too, but composed basically by positions and agents) with respect to the most relevant criteria established in the modelled world. Some examples of properties that appear in the literature are:

- Ability, workability and commitment [2].
- Predictability, security, adaptability, coordinability, modularity and others [10].
- Correctness, completeness, verifiability, modifiability and traceability [24].

For a given property object of measure, it may be the case that all its elements (actors and dependencies) influence the indicator. However, it is also possible that just elements of some particular type affect this property. Furthermore, some individual elements may be identified as especially relevant for the property; in the most general case, all the elements may have a different weight in the indicator. We need then to take into account all these situations if we aim at having a widely applicable metrics framework.

For a given property, different indicators can be defined according to two criteria:

- Returned value. We distinguish among *numerical, logical* and *model-element* indicators. Numerical indicators return a value in the interval [0, 1]; this value measures the degree of accomplishment of some criteria. Logical indicators evaluate true or false, and are used to discern if a property is fulfilled or not. Model-element indicators return a (set of) model element (typically, actors, scenario paths or dependencies) that fulfils a property (e.g., scenario path that maximizes a given criteria, or set of actors that are greater than some threshold).
- Subject of measure. We can measure the whole model, individual elements or even groups of individual elements. In the first case we have *global* indicators, which produce a single value of any type. In the second case, we have *local* indicators, which compute a value for any element of a given type (actor, scenario path, etc., or even dependency of some type). In the third case, we talk about *group* indicators, which compute a value for any combination according to the grouping criteria (e.g., pairs of actors).

Therefore, given a property such as completeness, we may measure completeness of the model, of an element (e.g., an actor) or a group of related elements (e.g., all the actors of the model), with the purpose of deciding if they are complete or not, or to what extent they are complete (e.g., measuring the percentage of undefined elements) or obtaining the elements that are not complete yet. Some of the indicators can be built on top of the others, typically (but not always): logical and model-element indicators are defined in top of numerical ones; global and group metrics are defined on top of local ones.

In the next section we develop as example indicator for one property, predictability, following the concepts introduced in this section.

4 Analysing Predictability of *i** Models

Predictability is used in [10] as one of the properties of interest when analysing organizational styles. Its interest comes from the fact that "actors can have a high degree of autonomy depending on the way they undertake action and communication in their domains. It can be then sometimes difficult to predict individual actor characteristics as part of determining the behaviour of an organization at large" [10]. Therefore, discerning up to what extent the actors of a model are predictable may be useful for knowing more about a model.

From the several points of view we can take to analyse predictability, we opt by an external perception, i.e. how an actor perceives predictability of other actors. To be more precise, an actor is interested to know how predictable is the behaviour of those actors it depends upon, and this yields to select dependencies as the main construct of interest for defining the metrics. In the rest of the section, we first analyse predictability of individual dependencies and then we show several indicators that may be defined upon individual predictability. We will use OCL for measuring predictability on its different forms.

4.1 Predictability of Individual Dependencies

Yu states very clearly which is the degree of freedom bound to dependencies [2]:

- Goal dependencies. The dependee is free to, and is expected to, make whatever decisions are necessary to achieve the goal.
- Task dependencies. The depender makes the decisions, therefore the dependee cannot take a behaviour different than expected.
- Resource dependencies. They represent the finished product of some deliberation-action process, and it is assumed that there are no open issues to be addressed.
- Softgoal dependencies. The depender makes the final decision, but does so with the benefit of the dependee's know-how.

Therefore we may conclude that task and resource dependencies are totally predictable whilst goal and softgoal ones are not. Considering that 1 represents the highest predictability and 0 the lowest, we may define predictability of dependencies as:

```
context Dependency::predictability(): Real
 post: type = Task implies result = 1.0
 post: type = Resource implies result = 1.0
 post: type = Goal implies result = goalPredictability()
 post: type = Softgoal implies result = softgoalPredictability()
```

To define goal and softgoal predictability we may opt among different strategies:

- To assign a fixed weight to every single goal and softgoal dependency of the model. This is a very basic quantitative approach, with the assumption that the factor that rules predictability is the existence of a dependency, whilst its particular meaning or hidden intentionality is not so relevant.
- To provide weights to individual dependencies by expert judgement. This option yields to a qualitative reasoning issue appearing in the context of our quantitative procedure, which aligns with the point of view of [14]. This is the option to choose

when we have just the SD model, which happens in the first stages of organization analysis. For instance, if we apply our RiSD method [23], we build a SD model from the scratch and then perform analysis before proceeding further on. At this stage, we have just the most relevant elements in the model, which means that qualitative analysis is feasible in terms of cost. Experts may use techniques such as laddering [25] or AHP [26] as a help during their assessment.

- To find some suitable rationale for determining predictability. This alternative makes our approach basically quantitative; in fact, it may be defined in a total quantitative manner. This option seems the most appropriate when a SR model is available, which may happen in two ways: a) from the starting SD model, obtained e.g. applying RiSD, dependencies and actors are refined; b) the $i*$ model is synthesised from observation of the current organization and then the SR model exists from the very beginning, as we do in our PRiM method [22].

Fig. 3 summarizes these possibilities. It shows how expert judgement is needed in almost all possible combinations. Expert judgement is represented by underlined elements, i.e. values or functions that must be provided in order to build the metrics.

We focus on the last case, which requires more decisions to take. Considering softgoal dependencies, we decompose their evaluation into two factors. First, a factor bound to the depender actor, which represents how capable it is to take predictable decisions when resolving softgoals; we consider this factor bound to actors' ability and not to individual softgoal dependencies. Second, a factor bound to the dependency, which represents the available know-how with respect to the given dependum. For the OCL expression, we must take into account that the depender can be an actor or an SR element, and in the second case we obtain its owner; a `let` expression makes this easier to write:

```
context Dependency::softgoalPredictability(): Real
pre: type = Softgoal
let ownerActor(x: DependableNode): Actor =
        if x.oclIsTypeOf(Actor) then x else x.owner in
post: result = ownerActor(depender).dependerExpertise()
        * knowHow()
```

Depender expertise may be dealt with by two different strategies: considering expert judgement to weight individual actors, or else to agree a given weight for all the actors. Concerning available know-how, we may define a strategy for measuring predictability using the SR model as follows. We define the know-how as the number of dependees that state a contribution value to the dependum. Then, we need a function such that: 1) when the number of contributions is 0, the function is also 0 (worst predictability because the dependees do not know how to contribute to the softgoal); 2) as the number of contributions grow, the function tends to 1 (best predictability).

An easy, problem-independent way to define the function is $1 - (slope/n+1)$, being n the number of known contributions for the softgoal dependum and $slope$ a constant (defined as an attribute of the model) that determines the slope of the function (see fig. 4, left). Another possibility is to define a utility function [27] such that we define a straight line from 0 to the maximum number of dependee contributions to a softgoal dependum that exists in the model (see fig. 4, right).

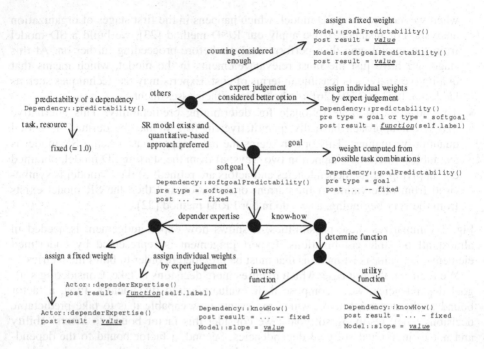

Fig. 3. Procedure for determining the *Predictability* of individual dependencies

Fig. 4. 2 different possibilities of know-how functions: left, inverse function with *slope* = 1; right, utility function (*n* = maximum number of dependee contributions to softgoal dependum)

The resulting OCL definition for the first case is:

```
context Dependency::knowHow(): Real
pre: self.type = Softgoal
let theModel: Model = Model.allInstances()->any() in
let contributionsToSoftgoalDep(d: Dependency): Integer =
      d.dependeeLink.oclAsType(SoftgoalContribution)->
      select(contr->notEmpty())->size() in
post: result = 1 - theModel.slope /
                   (contributionsToSoftgoalDep(self)+1)
```

Fig. 5 presents an example of this case. It is an excerpt of a model for a distance learning environment. The dean has as one of her goals to achieve academic quality, and for this goal she depends on teachers and tutors for having *Good Course Dynamics*.

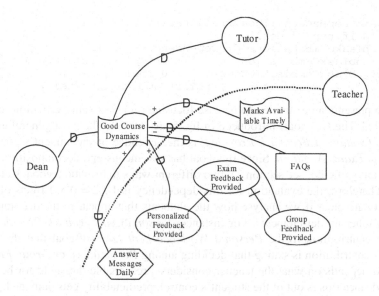

Fig. 5. Distance learning environment model: predictability of softgoal dependencies

There are several ways in which teachers may contribute positively to this softgoal: publishing exams' marks timely, answering students' messages daily and making FAQs lists available. An important issue that influences course dynamics in distance learning is the feedback that teachers provide to students about their exams. There are roughly two strategies: sending personalized messages to students commenting their mistakes, or giving group support by making public the solution and the evaluation criteria, and sending personalized information just on demand. The first strategy is considered to impact positively into the dynamics of the course, but not the second. Concerning tutors, it has not been investigated yet how they contribute to course dynamics. Thus, we have 5 contributions to the softgoal dependency; applying the definition above with `Model.slope` = 1, `GoodCourseDynamics.knowHow()` = 0,83. Since the dean is a highly strategic actor, we may assume that her `dependerExpertise()` = 1,0 and `GoodCourseDynamics.softgoalPredictability()` = 0,83.

Concerning goal dependencies, unpredictability depends on how many ways the dependees have to fulfil the goal. As stated in section 2, a goal dependency may have as intentional elements on the dependee side just goals and tasks. In both cases, the different task combinations that we may find descending by the goal or task, using means-end and tasks decompositions, are computed: the more combinations are found, the less predictable is the dependee with respect to that dependency. It is worth to remark that if the dependency involves more than one dependee, unpredictability appears from the very beginning, because this means that there are many ways to attain the goal dependum. Also we have to deal with the case that the dependee is not a SR element but an actor, which means that the dependency has not been assigned yet to an intentional element and thus unpredictability is maximized (i.e., equals to 0).

Similarly to the case above, a problem-independent function can be defined as the inverse of the number of combinations. We outline the corresponding OCL function, not including the function that computes the number of combinations:

```
context Dependency::goalPredictability(): Real
pre: self.type = Goal
let nbTaskCombinations(d: Dependency) = … in
post: nbTaskCombinations(self) = 0 implies result = 0
post: nbTaskCombinations(self) > 0 implies
                result = 1 / nbTaskCombinations(self)
```

Fig. 6 presents an example of this case focusing on how exam evaluation feedback is provided. The two goals introduced in fig. 5 are refined. The most general goal that appears, *Evaluation Feedback Provided*, is the dependee of the student's goal *Feedback from Exams Acquired*. Since this goal has two means-end decomposition (which are implicitly OR-ed, see section 2), two different ways to provide feedback are being stated. Therefore, the evaluation for this dependency is $1 / 2 = 0,5$. Effects of unpredictability are clear if we analyse how the elements that appear in the decomposition relate to other model elements. For instance, *Personalized Feedback Provided* has a negative contribution to the *Personal Workload kept Low* softgoal that the teacher has. This contribution is stating that deciding among *Personalized* or *Group Feedback Provided* depends on what the teacher considers a reasonable threshold for her workload, and since this is out of the student's control, predictability gets damaged.

As a final remark, we would like to point out that the obtained indicator for dependency predictability is highly customizable (therefore reusable and repeatable); key points are: does the SR model exist or not?, do I really need expert judgement or do I keep my approach purely quantitative?, if expert judgement is chosen, do I prefer to weight individual elements or do I assign the same weight to all of them? The procedure depicted at fig. 3 shows clearly the needed steps; there we represent the information required during the process by underlined italics in the body of OCL expressions.

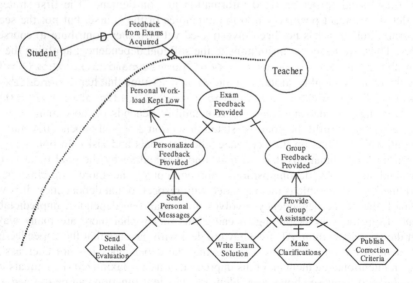

Fig. 6. Distance learning environment model: predictability of goal dependencies

4.2 Indicators for Predictability

Next we talk about the different indicators that may be defined on top of dependency evaluation. The dimensions presented in section 3 can be used. Of particular interest is the dimension about the subject of measure. We present 3 feasible possibilities:

- We may analyse predictability of actors. We may adopt two different points of view: how predictable an actor perceives its environment, and how predictable an actor looks to its environment. In the first case, we group the dependencies in which the actor is a depender, whilst in the second case, we group the dependencies in which an actor is a dependee. For instance, for the first point of view we obtain:

```
context Actor::perceivedPredictability(): Real
   let actorDependencies(a: Actor): Set(Dependency) =
       Dependency.allInstances()->
       select(d | d.depender = a or d.depender.owner = a) in
   post: actorDependencies(self)->size() = 0 implies result = 1
   post: actorDependencies(self)->size() > 0 implies result =
             actorDependencies(self).predictability()->sum()
             / actorDependencies(self)->size()
```

- Another possibility is to concentrate on scenario paths as representative of business processes. A scenario path is composed by steps that are tasks or goals. Each step is either decomposed inside the boundaries of the actor or as depending on external actors; these two cases rule the OCL decomposition below. In both cases, predictability depends on the number of task combinations that exist to carry out the step:

```
context ScenarioPath::predictability(): Real
   post: result = step.predictability()->sum() / step->size()

context TaskOrGoal::predictability(): Real
   let dependsUpon(): Boolean =
                 self.dependency[depender]->notEmpty() in
   post: dependsUpon() implies
         result = dependency[depender].predictability()->sum()
                 / dependency[depender]->size()
   post: not dependsUpon() and nbTaskCombinations() = 0
             implies result = if type = task then 1 else 0
   post: not dependsUpon() and nbTaskCombinations() > 0
             implies result = 1 / nbTaskCombinations(self)
```

being `TaskOrGoal::nbTaskCombinations()` a function that computes the number of task combinations for that task or goal, defined analogously to `Dependency::nbTaskCombinations()` introduced in section 4.1.

- As done in [10], we may define predictability for the whole model, obtaining therefore a single value. They use this property to compare different organizational patterns such as joint venture, structure in 5, and others:

```
context Model::predictability(): Real
   post: result =
             Dependency.allInstances().predictability()->sum()
             / Dependency.allInstances()->size()
```

Concerning the second dimension, we can use these numerical indicators to obtain boolean or model elements ones, allowing e.g.: finding out if strategic actors exceed some threshold; given two models, which one is the most predictable; ordering all the actors in terms of predictability; checking that scenario paths are fully predictable; etc.

5 Comparison with Related Work

In the introduction we have mentioned the existence of qualitative approaches for analysing $i*$ models but, to the best of our knowledge, there is not much related work from a quantitative point of view. The most remarkable proposal in this area is part of the AGORA method [24] that provides techniques for estimating the quality of requirements specifications in a goal-oriented setting. In fact, AGORA puts more emphasis in the analysis of the AND/OR graph resulting from decomposition than in the kind of analysis that has been the focus of this paper. Therefore, comparison is not really possible and in fact, we could think of using AGORA and our approach jointly. Also, it is worth mentioning the work by Sutcliffe and Minocha [28] which proposes the analysis of dependency coupling for detecting excessive interaction among users and systems. They use expert judgement to classify the dependencies of the system in a qualitative scale and then define a metric on the model that use to compare alternative scenario. This metric for coupling is a good example of structural metric and we can check that it is definable using our framework in a straightforward way.

On the other hand, we have already mentioned some work on combining quantitative and qualitative analysis of $i*$ models for finding assignment of labels to nodes and determine its propagation in goal graphs. In [15], qualitative reasoning is based on a sound and complete set of rules that determine backward propagation in a goal-oriented, SR-like graph. The rules combine 4 different types of relationships among goals, depending on whether a goal fully/partially satisfies/denies another goal. Quantitative reasoning consists on assigning weights to those relationships. In [16], assignment of labels to goals, and the use of these labels to propagate values both forward and backwards, become the subject of study. The main difference of these approaches with the work presented in this paper is the interest of the analysis. Whilst [15, 16] focus on goal satisfaction, our work is more interested in the analysis of structural properties of the model. Therefore, we can say again that both approaches are not exclusive but complementary. The way the authors encode the qualitative framework is a good example of how knowledge may be represented in both a simple and accurate way, and it could be thought that this description style of qualitative knowledge may be used also in our context.

6 Conclusions and Future Work

We have presented a framework for the definition of structural metrics for agent-oriented models using the $i*$ language. The metrics are bound to properties of the system model, which usually represent correctness concerns, organizational issues or information systems requirements. The framework considers the definition of indicators organized according to two dimensions (returned value and subject of measure). The indicators are customised to use expert judgement as considered necessary, although we may say that they are basically quantitative in nature. We have shown with an example how these indicators may be used to find out properties of the system.

The most relevant characteristics of our approach are:

- Accuracy. We have provided a UML definition of $i*$ models that is used as a baseline upon which we have build our framework. Indicators and metrics are expressed with the OCL. The approach is complemented with two methodologies to drive the construction of $i*$ models in a consistent way.
- Expressiveness. The use of the OCL allows expressing metrics both in a comfortable and expressive way. Comfortability comes from the easy of structuring inherent to object-orientation, which has been shown in the predictability example.
- Sensitivity. Metrics can be defined more or less accurately depending on: 1) the expert judgement available; 2) the state of refinement of the model; 3) the effort we want to invest in model analysis. Therefore, we have a highly configurable framework that allows defining metrics in several ways (see fig. 3 as an example).
- Easy tool support. The form that our framework takes allows implementation of tool support to drive indicators definition, model edition, generation of alternatives and evaluation of models. We have a first prototype [29] which uses metrics patterns as a way to improve productivity (although it is not based in the OCL). Tool-support may also be used to customise the indicators in a particular setting by means of wizards that basically asks for the required information following a data flow such as the one presented in fig. 3.
- Reusability. The indicators and metrics obtained are independent of the domain and therefore applicable to any model.

The framework presented here has been analysed with a few properties such as the one presented in this paper. However, a proper validation plan has not been yet executed. A long-term goal is to apply the framework to large-scale case studies but, in the meantime, we are validating with respect to some exemplars that are widespread in the $i*$ community, such as the one of predictability presented in this paper. Validation is necessary also to gain more understanding on the property being analysed and then to define more accurately OCL formula. In our example, this kind of validation would help to know if the strategies applied to define goal and softgoals are accurate enough and to compare different strategies. For instance, an alternative to the definition in the case of goals would be to take into account the depth of task decompositions: the deeper the decomposition appears, the less it affects predictability. A thorough validation plan would allow choosing which alternative is better.

It may be said that one of the limitation of our approach is the need to elicit expert judgement at some extent. However, we should remark that the involvement of experts is highly customizable. For instance, we have shown in our case study that this expert judgement may be kept reduced if required by prioritising the quantitative part of our framework (see fig. 3). In any case, we do think that some degree of qualitative reasoning is necessary to obtain information that is accurate with respect to some departing assumptions (which encode the knowledge of the expert). We remark also that expert judgement will usually be necessary in the context of comparison of alternatives that has been cited in the introduction, because given two alternatives, in the general case some metrics will behave better in one model and some in other, therefore expert judgement is needed to prioritize appropriately.

We have identified several ways to proceed along in this line of research. For making our proposal useful, we remark the following:

- Construction of a catalogue of reusable indicators and metrics. Basically in three directions: 1) model-related properties (predictability is one example); 2) organizational-related properties (such as segregation of duties [30]); 3) properties addressing non-functional aspects such as security, efficiency and so on.
- Identification of patterns for indicators and metrics. We have realized that most of the indicators and metrics definitions apply similar rules over and over. In [31] we have identified some patterns that capture some of these situations and we plan to enlarge the catalogue.
- Better tool-support. We plan to enlarge our current prototype and adapt it to the OCL as the language for metrics definition.
- Integration of the framework with other proposals. In particular, we are especially interested in using this framework in the analysis of system architectures [8, 32]. We think that metrics on goal-oriented models may provide first-cut criteria for classifying candidate architectures.

Acknowledgements

This work has been done in the framework of the research project UPIC, ref. TIN2004-07461-C02-01, supported by the Spanish Ministerio de Ciencia y Tecnología. The author wants to thank Gemma Grau for her valuable comments.

References

[1] A. Dardenne, A. van Lamsweerde, S. Fickas. "Goal-directed Requirements Acquisition". *Science of Computer Programming*, 20, 1993.

[2] E. Yu. *Modelling Strategic Relationships for Process Reengineering*. PhD. thesis, University of Toronto, 1995.

[3] J. Castro, M. Kolp, J. Mylopoulos. "Towards Requirements-Driven Information System Engineering: The Tropos Project". *Information Systems*, 27, 2002.

[4] E. Yu. "Towards Modeling and Reasoning Support for Early-Phase Requirements Engineering". *Procs. 3rd Intl. Symposium in Requirements Engineering* (ISRE), 1997.

[5] A. van Lamsweerde. "Goal-Oriented Requirements Engineering: A Guided Tour". *Procs. 5th Intl. Symposium on Requirements Engineering* (ISRE), 2001.

[6] M. Lorenz, J. Kidd. *Object-oriented software metrics: a practical guide*. Prentice-Hall, 1994.

[7] S.R. Chidamber, C.F. Kemerer. "A Metrics Suite for Object-Oriented Design". *IEEE Transactions on Software Engineering*, 20(6), 1994.

[8] L. Baas, P. Clements, R. Kazman. *Software Architecture in Practice, 2nd edition*. Addison-Wesley, 2003.

[9] L. Chung, B. Nixon, E. Yu, J. Mylopoulos. *Non-Functional Requirements in Software Engineering*. Kluwer Academic Publishers, 2000.

[10] M. Kolp, J. Castro, J. Mylopoulos. "Organizational Patterns for Early Requirements Analysis". *Procs. 15th Intl. Conf. on Advanced Information Systems Engineering* (CAiSE), 2003.

[11] M.B. Mile, A.M. Huberman. *Qualitative Data Analysis*. Sage Publications, 1994.

[12] T.A. Schwandt. "Solutions to the Paradigm Conflict: Coping with Conflict". *Journal of Contemporary Etnography*, 17(4), 1989.

[13] M.Q. Patton. *Qualitative Evaluation and Research Methods*. Sage Publications, 1990.

[14] R.B. Johnson, A.J. Onwuegbuzie. "Mixed Methods Research: A Research Paradigm Whose Time Has Come". *Educational Researcher*, 33(7), 2004.

[15] P. Giorgini, J. Mylopoulos, E. Nicciarelli, R. Sebastiani. "Formal Reasoning Techniques for Goal Models". *Procs. 21st Intl. Conference on Conceptual Modeling* (ER), 2002.

[16] R. Sebastiani, P. Giorgini, J. Mylopoulos. "Simple and Minimum-Cost Satisfiability for Goal Models". *Proceedings of 16th Conf. on Advanced Information Systems* (CAiSE), 2004.

[17] Object Management Foundation (OMG). "UML 2.0 OCL Specification", available at www.omg.org/docs/ptc/03-10-14.pdf, 2003.

[18] C. Ayala, C. Cares, J.P. Carvallo, G. Grau, M. Haya, G. Salazar, X. Franch, E. Mayol, C. Quer. "A Comparative Analysis of i*-Based Goal-Oriented Modeling Languages". *Procs. Intl. Workshop on Agent-Oriented Software Development Methodology* (AOSDM), 2005.

[19] E. Yu. "Understanding 'why' in software process modeling, analysis and design". *Procs. 16th Intl. Conference on Software Engineering* (ICSE), 1994.

[20] L. Liu, E. Yu, J. Mylopoulos. "Analysing Security Requirements as Relationships among Strategic Actors". *Procs. 2nd Symposium on Requirements Engineering for Information Security* (SREIS), 2002.

[21] D. Amyot. "Use Case Maps Quick Tutorial Version 1.0". Available at http://www.usecasemaps.org/pub/UCMtutorial/, last accessed Nov. 2005.

[22] G. Grau, X. Franch, N. Maiden. "A Goal-Based Round-Trip Method for System Development as Business Process Reengineering". *Procs. 11th Intl. Workshop on Requirements Engineering: Foundation for Software Quality* (REFSQ), 2005.

[23] G. Grau, X. Franch, E. Mayol, C. Ayala, C. Cares, J.P. Carvallo, M. Haya, F. Navarrete, P. Botella, C. Quer. "RiSD: A Methodology for Building i* Strategic Dependency Models". *Procs. 7th Intl. Conf. on Software Engineering & Knowledge Engineering* (SEKE), 2005.

[24] H. Kaiya, H. Horai, M. Saeki. "AGORA: Attributed Goal-Oriented Requirements Analysis Method". *Procs. 10th Joint Conference on Requirements Engineering* (RE), 2002.

[25] T.J. Reynolds, J. Gutman. "Laddering Theory, Method, Analysis and Interpretation". *Journal of Advertising Research*, vol. 28, 1988, pp. 11-31.

[26] T.L. Saaty. *The Analytic Hierarchy Process*. McGraw-Hill, 1990.

[27] R. Keeney, H. Raiffa. *Decision with Multiple Objectives: Preferences and Value Trade-offs*. Wiley, 1993.

[28] A. Sutcliffe, S. Minocha. "Linking Business Modelling to Socio-technical System Design". *Procs. 11th Intl. Conf. on Advanced Information Systems Engineering* (CAiSE), 1999.

[29] G. Grau, X. Franch, N. Maiden. "REDEPEND-REACT: an Architecture Analysis Tool". *Procs. 13th Intl. Conference on Requirements Engineering* (RE), 2005.

[30] A. Burt. "Internal Controls and Segregation of Duties". *UF Bridges Project*, University of Florida, 2004.

[31] X. Franch, G. Grau, C. Quer. "A Framework for the Definition of Metrics for Actor-Dependency Models". *Procs. 12th Intl. Conf. on Requirements Engineering* (RE), 2005.

[32] P. Grünbacher, A. Egyed, N. Medvidovic. "Reconciling Software Requirements and Architectures - The CBSP Approach". *Procs. 5th Intl. Symposium on Requirements Engineering* (ISRE), 2001.

Requirements Management

An Empirical Evaluation of the $i*$ Framework in a Model-Based Software Generation Environment*

Hugo Estrada[1,2], Alicia Martínez Rebollar[1,3], Oscar Pastor[1], and John Mylopoulos[4]

[1] Valencia University of Technology, Valencia, Spain
{hestrada, alimartin, opastor}@dsic.upv.es
[2] CENIDET, Cuernavaca, Mor. Mexico
[3] ITZ, Zacatepec, Mor. Mexico
[4] University of Trento, Italy
jm@cs.toronto.edu

Abstract. Organizational modelling has been found to be very effective in facilitating the elicitation of requirements for organizational information systems. In this context, the $i*$ modelling framework has been used widely in research and – some – industrial projects. However, no empirical evaluation exists to-date to identify areas of strength as well as weaknesses of the framework. This paper presents the results of an empirical evaluation of $i*$ using industrial case studies. These were conducted in collaboration with an industrial partner who employs an object-oriented and model-driven approach for software development. The evaluation of $i*$ uses a feature-based framework. The paper reports on lessons learned from this experience, both in terms of strengths and detected weaknesses. The results of this evaluation can play an important role in guiding extensions of the $i*$ framework.

1 Introduction

Organizational modelling is a promising approach for early requirements analysis during the development of organizational information systems. In this context, the $i*$ modelling framework [13] offers a well-founded and widely used set of concepts for describing organizational settings made up of social actors who have freedom of action, but also depend on other actors to achieve their goals.

The $i*$ framework and its methodological extensions (such as GRL [4] and Tropos [2]) have been used in a wide range of application domains, such as business modelling, object-oriented software development, software requirements elicitation, agent-oriented software development, modelling and analysis of non-functional requirements, security requirements, trust and privacy requirements, and more. In all these applications, $i*$ concepts have been used to capture social and intentional elements of each specific domain, thereby supporting software development. However, despite well-known theoretical advantages of $i*$, there have been no empirical studies that confirm its usefulness and identify potential weak spots.

---

* This work has been partially supported by the MEC project with ref. TIN2004-03534, the Valencia University of Technology, Spain, Care Technologies Enterprise Inc. and the University of Trento, Italy.

E. Dubois and K. Pohl (Eds.): CAiSE 2006, LNCS 4001, pp. 513–527, 2006.
© Springer-Verlag Berlin Heidelberg 2006

The purpose of this paper is exactly this: to present an empirical evaluation of $i*$, based on industrial case studies. The case studies were conducted in collaboration with Care Technologies Inc. (http://www.care-t.com), a software company that has adopted the OO-Method for software development. OO-Method is a model transformation method that relies on a CASE tool ([7]) to automatically generate complete information systems from object-oriented conceptual models. The OO-Method can be viewed as a computer-aided requirements engineering (CARE) method where the focus is on properly capturing system requirements in order to manage the complete software production process. The resulting conceptual model specifies what the system is (problem space). Then, an abstract execution model is provided to guide the representation of these requirements in a specific software development environment that is focused on how the system will be implemented (solution space).

The transformation from a conceptual to an execution model (implementation) is effected by a Conceptual Model Compiler. The compiler exploits precise transformation rules from conceptual modelling constructs to corresponding software representations. The execution model is based on a component-based architecture in order to deal with the characteristics of component-based systems. The final software product's functionally is equivalent to the requirements specification. Figure 1 presents a graphical representation of the OO-Method.

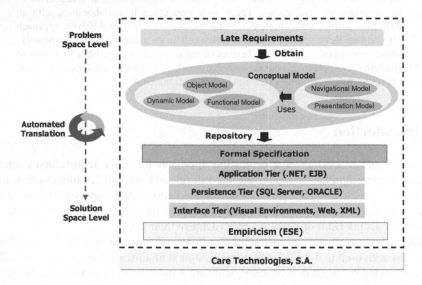

Fig. 1. The OO-Method approach for model-driven software development

Despite the major advantage of the OO-Method in automatically generating information systems, there are disadvantages as well. Specifically, there are currently no mechanisms for acquiring the requirements of an information system. Accordingly, the next step in developing further the OO-Method consists of adding a new phase of organizational modelling as a starting point to determine the correct requirements for the information system-to-be.

In performing the empirical evaluation, our objective was to determine possible extensions to $i*$ that would make it suitable for inclusion in the OO-Method modelling and methodological framework. Consequently, the features selected for measurement in this empirical evaluation are inspired by model-driven approaches.

The rest of the paper is structured as follows: Section 2 presents an overview of the $i*$ framework. Section 3 presents related works. Section 4 describes the evaluation framework we used to assess $i*$, while Section 5 presents the results of the evaluation conducted during the case studies. Section 6 discusses issues to be addressed in future versions of $i*$. Finally, Section 7 concludes and briefly discusses future work.

2 An Overview of the $i*$ Framework

The $i*$ modelling framework [13] views organizational models as networks of social actors that have freedom of action, and depend on each other to achieve their objectives and goals, carry out their tasks, and obtain needed resources.

The $i*$ framework is made up of two models that complement each other: the *strategic dependency model* for describing the network of inter-dependencies among actors, as well as the *strategic rationale model* for describing and supporting the reasoning that each actor goes through concerning its dependencies on other actors. These models have been formalized using intentional concepts from Artificial Intelligence, such as *goal, belief, ability*, and *commitment*.

A strategic dependency model (SD) is a graph involving *actors* who have strategic dependencies among each other. A dependency describes an "agreement" (called *dependum*) between two actors: the *depender* and the *dependee*. The *depender* is the depending actor, while the *dependee* is the actor who is depended upon. The type of the dependency describes the nature of the agreement. Goal dependencies represent delegation of responsibility for fulfilling a goal; softgoal dependencies are similar, but their fulfilment cannot be defined precisely (e.g., because it is subjective and/or partial). Task dependencies require the *dependee* to perform a given activity, and resource dependencies require the *dependee* to provide a resource. In $i*$ diagrams, actors are represented as circles; goals, softgoals, tasks and resources are respectively represented as ovals, clouds, hexagons and rectangles. Dependencies have the form *depender* → *dependum* → *dependee*. In the SD model, the internal goals, plans, and resources of an actor are not explicitly modelled. The focus in such models is on external relationships among actors.

The strategic rationale model (SR) represents through means-ends relationships how stakeholder's goals and softgoals can actually be fulfilled through the contributions of other actors. A strategic rationale model is a graph with four types of nodes -- goal, task, resource, and softgoal -- and two types of links. Means-ends links represent alternative sub-goals/tasks for fulfilling a goal/task, while decomposition links represent necessary sub-goals/tasks for fulfilling a goal/task. A strategic rationale graph explains and accounts for each actor's dependencies on other actors.

3 Related Work

There have been several studies that compare the Tropos agent-oriented software development methodology with others in the same family. Shehory and Sturm [8] propose a feature-based framework for evaluating and comparing agent-oriented methodologies. The framework examines various aspects of each methodology: concepts and properties, notations and modelling techniques, processes, and pragmatics. More recently, the same authors [11] performed an empirical evaluation based on case studies for several agent-oriented methodologies including Tropos (Gaia, Tropos, MaSe, and OPM/MAS). The case studies employed students taking a computer science course. An important contribution of this work is the use of a framework for evaluating and comparing agent-oriented methodologies that is based on a set of pre-defined criteria (features).

Dam and Winikoff [3] also performed an evaluation of agent-oriented software development methodologies (MaSe, Prometheus, and Tropos) using an attribute-based evaluation framework. In this evaluation, a set of summer students developed the same case study using different methodologies. The students then filled out a questionnaire to give feedback about their experience in understanding and using the methodologies based on the selected features. The authors of this evaluation also collected comments from authors of the methodologies using the same questionnaire that the summer students had completed. One of the interesting elements of this work is the attempt to eliminate misconceptions by taking into account comments from the authors of each methodology.

Along similar lines, Sudeikat et al [12] present an evaluation framework for agent-oriented methodologies that takes platform-specific criteria into account. The specific objective of this study was to determine how the methodologies under evaluation (Mase, Tropos and Prometeus) match up with the Jadex agent platform.

Our empirical evaluation is somewhat different than all of the above. Firstly, our evaluation focuses on a modelling framework rather than a software development methodology. Secondly, the object of our study is a specific modelling framework, rather than a comparison of several. Moreover, our evaluation studies how well i^* matches a specific software development context (model-based software generation) in practice, rather than analyze i^* in the abstract. Finally, all the studies mentioned used students working on toy problems. This represents a major limitation of these studies and a major point of difference from our work.

There are also reported studies that use i^* for some application. In most of these studies, the modellers were well-acquainted with i^* concepts and their use. We are only aware of one study [5] where i^* was evaluated (along with other modelling techniques) in practice by modellers who are not researchers working with i^*. In our study, the modellers were practitioners performing organizational modelling in their daily work.

4 A Feature-Based Evaluation Framework

The empirical study of i^* was based on a feature-based framework. Such a framework consists of a set of features that can be properties, qualities, attributes, or characteristics. An evaluation was conducted by *evaluators* who assigned a judgment (*value*) of how well each *feature* was supported by the *subject* of the evaluation. For our study, the features were selected on the basis of their relevance to model-driven software generation.

The empirical evaluation was implemented using three real-life projects that were developed in parallel by three different development teams. The composition of the development teams was as follows: (i) Team 1 consisted of three expert analysts in the use of advanced tools for generating conceptual schemas from requirements models[1]; (ii) Team 2 included three expert analysts in the use of the CASE tool for automatically generating information systems from conceptual models[2]; (iii) Team 3 included two expert analysts in the use of $i*$ for business modelling.

The three case studies were conducted in isolation, i.e., with no exchange of information among participant teams. This was done in order to avoid the empirical analysis being affected by the different levels of knowledge about $i*$ by the teams involved.

The evaluation was conducted in five steps. The first step was devoted to the determination of a set of features (in the context of a model-based transformational approaches) to be measured. The second step consisted of training the three teams, where details about the concepts and proper use of $i*$ were given out, using original $i*$ sources and basic teaching support. In the third step, $i*$ was used to develop the three case studies. The fourth step consisted of evaluating the results of each team. To accomplish this, each participating team evaluated $i*$ for each relevant feature. The final step consisted of analyzing the results and drawing conclusions about the strengths and weaknesses of $i*$.

As indicated, the case studies were real industrial projects. The goal of the development teams was to represent relevant business processes for each project using $i*$. The domains of the three projects were: (i) Technical meeting management: model business processes for organizing technical meetings; (ii) Golf tournament management: model business processes for organizing golf tournaments; (iii) Car rental management: model business processes for a car rental company. For the Technical meeting management case study, the organizational environment involves a large number of interactions among participant actors, and a relatively small number of actors' internal elements[3]. For the Golf tournament management case study, the organizational environment concerns a large number of actors' internal activities and a small number of actor interactions. On the other hand, the Car rental management case study involves an organizational context with a large number of actors' internal activities and actors' interactions. As such, the case studies had rather different organizational characteristics and ensured that our study would be biased because of similarities in the case studies chosen.

The empirical evaluation of $i*$ was based on a set of features that have been considered highly relevant in the context of a model-based software development environment. In this specific context, the modelling primitives of a model must provide precise, bidirectional traceability with subsequent stages of the modelling

---

[1] At the beginning of the evaluation, this team had limited knowledge of $i*$.

[2] At the beginning of the evaluation, this team had no knowledge of $i*$.

[3] The internal elements are those goals, plans, softgoals, and resources (represented inside an actor' boundary) that account for the actor's behavior.

process. It is important to note that the experiment was designed for practicing analysts who are used to dealing with software production concepts such as model-driven architectures, code generation, object-oriented analysis and late (conventional) software requirements specifications, rather than analysts who are familiar with early requirements. After all, we expect that this will be the normal scenario for $i*$ use in software production companies. Therefore the determination of relevant features for the study was perhaps the most critical step in the whole evaluation process.

The features chosen were based on three earlier studies comparing agent-oriented methodologies ([6], [10], [3]). By including features used in three different studies, we have tried to avoid biases that arise from using a single set of features that might be well suited for $i*$.

The evaluation considered two main aspects of $i*$: (i) Modelling Language (Refinement, Modularity, Repeatability, Complexity Management, Expressiveness, Traceability, and Reusability), and (ii) Pragmatics of the Modelling Method (Scalability and Domain Applicability). The features selected for these aspects are listed below.

- **Refinement:** This feature measures the capability of the modelling method to refine a model gradually through stages until the most detailed view is reached [1]. This is a relevant feature because it allows analysts to develop and fine-tune design artefacts at different levels of granularity during the development process [3].
- **Modularity:** the degree to which the modelling language offers well-defined building blocks for building model. The building blocks should allow the encapsulation of internal structures of the model in a concrete modelling construct. This characteristic ensures that changes in one part of the model won't have to be propagated to other parts.
- **Repeatability:** the degree to which the modelling technique generates the same output (i.e., same models), given the same problem. This is a very relevant feature in the context of model-driven approaches, where each modelling element during a specific step of the modelling process corresponds to a modelling element in subsequent steps. Repeatability ensures that a correct result is obtained when a transformation between models is applied. We use this feature to evaluate whether we obtain the same $i*$ model when the same domain is modelled by different modellers.
- **Complexity Management:** This feature measures the capability of the modelling method to provide a hierarchical structure for its models, constructs and concepts. Model management is a fundamental problem in industrial project settings.
- **Expressiveness:** the degree to which the application domain is represented precisely in terms of the concepts offered by the modelling technique. More concretely, this feature measures the degree to which the modelling technique allows us to represent static, dynamic, intentional and social elements of the application domain.
- **Traceability:** the capability to trace modelling elements through different stages of the modelling process. This feature is important because it allows the user to verify that all elements of one model (e.g., capturing requirements) have corresponding elements during the analysis and design stages, and vice versa. Traceability makes it possible for the analyst to move back and forth between models corresponding to different development stages [3].
- **Reusability:** the degree to which models can be reused. As with software code, this feature is causally related to modularity. If the modelling technique allows the definition of modules, general cases (patterns) can be defined for reuse.

- **Scalability:** the degree to which the modelling framework can be used to handle applications of different sizes. Scalability also measures the degree to which the inclusion of new modelling elements leaves unaffected the understandability of models (also known as extensibility). This feature is causally related to refinement and modularity.
- **Domain Applicability:** the degree to which the modelling framework matches modelling requirements for a particular application domain.

It is true that, for some of the features chosen, one can evaluate i^* (or any other modelling framework, for that matter) on theoretical grounds alone. However, in our study of i^*, we wanted to include a practical evaluation as confirmation of any preliminary theoretical suppositions. Moreover, clearly the chosen features interact. For instance, better modularity management, obviously contributes to easier complexity management. Likewise, reusability contributes to scalability. We are studying such correlations and hope to integrate them in the evaluation framework for future studies. For this work, we focus on the application of the proposed set of features in evaluating i^* in practice.

5 Evaluation Results

The evaluation was conducted over a 9-month period. The average size of the models generated by the three teams had as follows: (i) Technical meeting management: 12 actors, 55 dependencies, 70 actors´ internal activities; (ii) Golf tournament management: 8 actors, 42 dependencies, 103 actors´ internal activities; (iii) Car rental management: 13 actors, 143 dependencies, 219 actors´ internal activities.

The evaluation assigned one of three possible values (*Well supported*, *Not well supported*, and *Not supported*) to each feature. Another output of the evaluation was a list of reasons given by the analysts for a judgement passed. In order to make the evaluation consensual, a meeting was held at the end of each case study. In these meetings, produced diagrams and personal evaluations were presented and discussed. The meetings included in-depth discussions for each feature in order to reach consensus and a final judgement.

One interesting result of the evaluation concerns the differences in the models produced by the participating teams. The members of team 1 were experienced in requirements modelling, although not used to modelling in terms of goals, actors and dependencies. They understood well the concepts underlying i^* (after all, requirements concepts match well i* modelling), and were enthusiastic about using i* in practice. In this case, resulting models were partially compliant with i* philosophy. Moreover, the analysts of this team detected several areas where i^* lacked mechanisms to guarantee the usefulness of organizational models in generating system requirements.

In Team 2, the analysts were used to working with class diagrams, state and functional models as part of their on-going modelling activities. In this case, i* social and intentional concepts were rather unfamiliar and the analysts tried to use the concepts in the same way they used the concepts they were accustomed to. In this case, resultant models were less compliant with i* modelling philosophy. Moreover, these analysts had a lot to say about the lack of precise definitions for i^* concepts, and guidelines for generating i^* models.

The analysts for Team 3 were experienced $i*$ modellers. In this case, resulting models were completely compliant with $i*$ modelling philosophy. However, these models were often too abstract for generating software requirements.

Table 1 presents a summary of the results obtained from the evaluation. The first column indicates the type of each feature, the second column lists the feature itself, while the third column indicates the judgement passed on each feature.

Table 1. Results of the empirical evaluation

Evaluation Criteria		Evaluated issue	Evaluation
Modelling Language	1	Refinement	Not Well Supported
	2	Modularity	Not Supported
	3	Repeatability	Not Well Supported
	4	Complexity management	Not well Supported
	5	Expressiveness	Well Supported
	6	Traceability	Not Well Supported
	7	Reusability	Not supported
Pragmatics	8	Scalability	Not supported
	9	Domain applicability	Well Supported

In the following, we present the evaluation and justification for each feature.

1) Feature: **Refinement.** Evaluation: **Not Well Supported**

Explanation: There are two types of refinement supported by $i*$: (i) refinement of strategic dependency models in terms of a more detailed strategic rationale model, where one can see why actors depend on each other; (ii) 2) refinement of actor goals into more concrete subgoals. However, the literature using $i*$ includes many examples where a rationale model is not the result of a refinement of a dependency model. This kind of refinement can be performed in the boundaries of an actor model.

These types of refinement are useful when analyzing small case studies. However, they have severe limitations when the model grows in size and complexity. The dependency model is too concrete to serve as starting point for the analysis of a large enterprise. In such cases, it may contain many actors with a large number of dependencies corresponding to different business processes, whose union constitutes a very complicated model to manage.

The current version of $i*$ does not include modelling primitives that allow one to start the modelling process of an enterprise with abstract concepts. These concepts would allow us to incrementally add more detail -- using other, more specific, modelling primitives -- until we reach concrete models of business processes and their actor dependencies. There are also no concepts to structure the different functional units of a complex organization. As a consequence of this absence of high-level refinement facilities, the modelling of complex systems that involve a large number of dependencies among many different actors is problematic for $i*$.

2) Feature: **Modularity.** Evaluation: **Not Supported**

Explanation: Based on the empirical evaluation, it was concluded that modularity is not supported in $i*$. This is the case because $i*$ doesn't have mechanisms for using building blocks that can be logically composed to represent different organizational fragments (e.g., business processes). In this context, if a new organizational process is added, this may affect all models constructed so far.

The lack of modularity mechanisms in $i*$ can be viewed as a consequence of its focus on actor modelling rather than on business process modelling. The modelling mechanisms of $i*$ are oriented towards the definition of the behaviour of the organizational actors (to satisfy their goals and dependencies) rather than being oriented to the definition of high-level views of the organizational business processes.

Due to this the lack of modularity, rationale models represent a monolithic view where all elements of an enterprise are represented at the same abstraction level without considering any sort of hierarchy. Figure 2 shows an example for the Technical Meeting Management case study where the goal dependency "*obtain quality reviews*" and other dependencies associated with this goal (the task dependency: "*send reviews on time*", and the resource dependency: "*review*") are represented at the same abstraction level. This makes it impossible to distinguish the hierarchical level of these concepts, which are represented as dependencies in the same diagram.

Fig. 2. Representing concepts at same abstraction level

3) Feature: **Repeatability.** Evaluation: **Not Well Supported**

Explanation: One of the key points for ensuring repeatability in a modelling method is the definition of a precise, formal semantics for the modelling constructs. In principle, the modelling constructs of $i*$ have been defined using formal descriptions and meta-modelling diagrams. These definitions are useful for expert analysts in early requirements. However, for those who are not experts in $i*$, these definitions do not provide the necessary, precise support to determine which modelling construct to use when. This problem can also be noted in the $i*$ literature. There are several examples where very similar settings have been modelled using different primitives.

It is also possible to find in the literature examples of dependencies that do not satisfy the basic semantics of an actor dependency (vulnerable actor, actor who decides how to fulfil the dependency, type of *dependum*). For example, we found cases where the *dependee* of a dependency was incorrectly used as the vulnerable actor, instead of the *depender*. In another example, we found cases where the *dependee* of a dependency was incorrectly treated as the actor who prescribes the actions to perform for a delegated task (task dependency), instead of following the guidelines of always placing the *depender* as the actor that prescribes a task dependency. As a consequence of these situations, it is difficult to ensure that a reasonable degree of repeatability is achievable with $i*$.

Figure 3 shows an example of these repeatability problems. In this example, taken from the Golf tournament management case study, the process for "Pay for registration of in tournament" was represented in two different ways by the participating analysts: either as a task dependency, where the focus was placed on the activity to be executed; or as a resource dependency, where the focus was placed on the payment, which was viewed a concrete resource relating the actors involved.

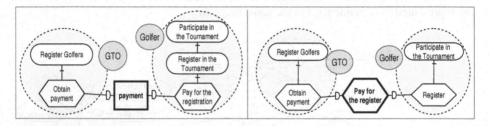

Fig. 3. Example of two different representations for a given single process

4) Feature: **Complexity Management.** Evaluation: **Not Well Supported**

Explanation: In the current version of $i*$, it is possible to analyze an enterprise model using two different viewpoints: the strategic dependency model and the strategic rationale model. These viewpoints are useful for small cases, but they are not adequate for dealing with large and complex problems. There are no mechanisms for defining a high-level view of the whole process executed in the enterprise. This high-level view would be properly decomposed following a model-within-a-model strategy, where lower level descriptions are created separately, incorporating all relevant detail.

The limitation in the mechanisms that are provided for managing the system complexity make modelling in $i*$ unnecessarily complicated. The lack of hierarchies leads to problems such as: a) it is difficult to determine where to start the analysis; b) it is difficult to determine the elements of the model that correspond to each organizational process and/or unit. The lack of hierarchies produces models where several business processes are represented and mixed all together in the same diagram, without any indication of the ownership of each low-level activity nor any information about the boundaries of each individual process (Figure 4).

5) Feature: **Expressiveness.** Evaluation: **Well Supported**

Explanation: There was unanimous agreement among all participants in this experiment that $i*$ indeed provides a very interesting set of conceptual primitives that make it possible to build pure organizational models on top of conventional requirements ones (mostly, use case-based models). Analysts also agreed on the importance of linking early requirements and late requirements, as a way of connecting software engineering practices with organizational design tasks that are too often performed in isolation by consultants.

The i^* framework was deemed adequate for capturing the relevant concepts of the enterprise, providing mechanisms for representing: a) the social structure of the enterprise, b) the intentional aspects of the organizational actors, c) the activities needed to satisfy the goals of the business actors, d) the relevant resources in the business processes, e) the ability to represent roles, positions and agents to describe the organizational actors, f) the architecture of the enterprise and g) the interaction between the system and external agents.

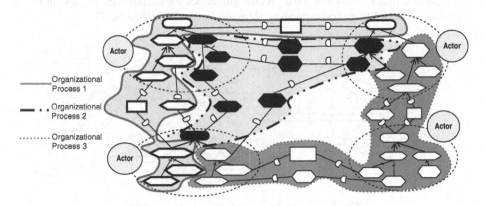

Fig. 4. Representation of different processes in the same diagram

These conclusions account for the difference between i^* and other modelling techniques, which are not as well equipped to represent the social and intentional reasons that underlie the operation of an enterprise. The empirical evaluation allowed us to demonstrate that building an i^* organizational model is very useful for detecting the following problems:

Bottlenecks: This is the case when an actor concentrates a large number of incoming dependencies from other organizational actors. In this case, a failure or delay in this organizational actor could cause a chain reaction in the entire enterprise. The bottleneck problem could be detected by analyzing the dependencies where an actor plays the role of *dependee* of several dependency relationships. We are not aware of other modelling frameworks that account for this kind of analysis.

Vulnerabilities: One of the key advantages of i^* is the explicit representation of vulnerabilities of organizational actors. In this case, if an actor participates in too many dependencies as *depender*, this actor could then become vulnerable if any of the *dependee* actors fail to deliver on their respective dependencies.

Critical Responsibilities: This is the case where an actor concentrates many goal dependencies, which indicate that the actor has many critical responsibilities in the business process. In this case, it may be that the actor has excessive responsibilities and needs help, or at least monitoring.

The explicit representation of these organizational situations is the basis for performing a useful business process reengineering analysis.

6) Feature: **Traceability.** Evaluation: **Not Well Supported**

Explanation: $i*$ provides modelling flexibility for adding elements to individual dependency and/or rational models. This means that new dependencies can be added to a rationale model that were not previously considered in the corresponding dependency model (Figure 5), and vice versa. This is sometimes useful with respect to modelling flexibility. However, it is also true that this could have negative effects for model-driven approaches, where the elements of a model must have counterparts in previous models. We conclude that $i*$ does not have precise guidelines for deriving each element of the dependency model from corresponding elements in the rationale model[4].

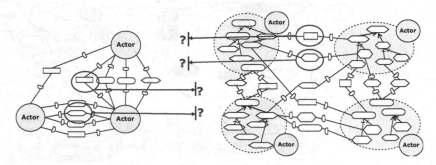

Fig. 5. Representation of problems of traceability

7) Feature: **Reusability.** Evaluation: **Not Supported**

Explanation: $i*$ does not offer clear mechanisms for properly managing reusability of parts of an organizational model. As mentioned earlier, the lack of good reusability capabilities is a consequence of the absence of mechanisms for modularization. The lack of conceptual building blocks with the required granularity makes it very complicated to reuse certain fragments of a model. Moreover, $i*$ lacks view definition mechanisms (in the sense of database views) for selecting parts of a monolithic model that capture new viewpoints.

As a consequence of this weakness, modelling projects using $i*$ must too often start from scratch, without taking advantage of previous projects for similar domains.

8) Feature: **Scalability.** Evaluation: **Not Supported**

Explanation: This is probably the best-known and widely acknowledged problem of $i*$. There are simply no clear mechanisms for managing the scalability of strategic models in $i*$.

For small problems $i*$ clearly works fine. However, when the modelling problem grows in size and complexity, the large number of elements represented in the same diagram makes their systematic use and analysis very complicated, when not completely impossible. The scalability problem is also a direct consequence of the lack of mechanisms for modularization, and the inability to put together an abstract view of the high-level business processes of an enterprise. Consequently, all modelling elements for representing the semantics of a specific business process must

---

[4] Tropos [2] supports such a process that ensures that each element of every dependency model has counterparts in some rational model, and vice versa.

be placed in the same diagram. Figure 6 shows an example of the high number of modelling elements in a diagram for only a fragment of a business process. And this is a very small fragment of the case study.

In summary, the lack of mechanisms for managing scalability is one of the greatest problems for the real applicability of $i*$ modelling.

9) Feature: **Domain applicability.** Evaluation: **Well Supported**

Explanation: $i*$ has an ontology and a corresponding notation that we found well suited for organizational modelling. It is also appropriate for the analysis of late requirements. The conceptual primitives are expressive enough to be applied in different domains, and they are appropriate for expressing properties that an organizational model must include. The semantics of the social concepts could also be applied, for example, to present dependencies within and between communities of systems, or even to represent the dependencies between an information system and its stakeholders.

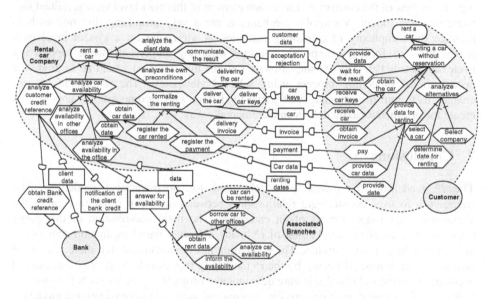

Fig. 6. Fragment of the car renting process in the Car Rental Management case study

6 Discussion

The main conclusion of this empirical evaluation is that $i*$ needs to be extended with mechanisms that manage granularity and refinement in models, as discussed below:

Granularity: Many of the negative results in the evaluation of $i*$ are related to the lack of mechanisms for defining granules of information at different abstraction levels, and composition mechanisms for composing these granules. This problem becomes evident when the modelling problem grows in size and complexity. In these cases, non-expert $i*$ users have difficulties with the scalability of their model. The result of this scenario is usually an overloaded monolithic model that contains all relevant detail of a social and intentional setting. Any activity that tries to extend, analyze, adapt or reuse parts of such a model is bound to be complicated and error-prone. To avoid this problem, it is necessary to provide precise conceptual constructs representing building blocks that break the monolithic structure of $i*$ models, as well as composition mechanisms. Then, encapsulated model units could be created, analyzed and reused in an independent way. The practical implication of the granularity solution is the introduction of viewpoints that go beyond the actor viewpoint. For example, process viewpoints could give an orthogonal view for an organizational model. Note that for this extension, no modifications are needed to the original set of $i*$ modelling constructs.

Refinement: Apart from the definition of abstract primitives as building blocks, analysts must be provided with guidelines that allow them to structure a complete enterprise model. One way to achieve this consists of using concrete specification units to create the models following a refinement-based approach. In this way, the modelling process starts with a high-level view of the enterprise. Then, each element of this high-level view is refined into more concrete model. Viewpoint mechanisms are a very promising direction to help manage the complexity of modelling activities. A viewpoint on a system involves a perspective that focuses on specific concerns regarding the system, while suppressing irrelevant details [9]. A promising strategy towards this direction would be to guide the organizational modelling process using selected viewpoints. The refinement process enables us to join the advantages of social modelling with a compositional approach to create the organizational models in an incrementally way.

7 Conclusions

The $i*$ modelling framework is widely used for organizational modelling. The framework focuses on strategic relationships between actors in order to capture the social and intentional context of an enterprise. The main contribution of this paper consists of an empirical evaluation of $i*$, using a feature-based evaluation framework and three industrial case studies. The evaluation has demonstrated that there is a set of issues that need to be addressed by the $i*$ modelling framework to ensure its successful application within industrial software development projects. These issues boil down to a lack of modularization mechanisms for creating and structuring organizational models.

We propose to extend $i*$ in order to address the weaknesses reported in this paper. Specifically, we are working on a solution for the problems of refinement, modularity, complexity management, reusability and scalability. Our solution is founded on the concept of a Business Service Architecture where organizational units can be encapsulated can only participate in actor dependency networks through well-defined interfaces. Along a different direction, we are developing a proposal to characterize $i*$ modelling primitives based on a multidimensional framework. This makes it possible to clearly differentiate the modelling primitives of $i*$, so that modellers get better guidance on what primitives to use in different situations. With the proposed modifications, our intention is to overcome the current limitations that practitioners face when using i* in its current state. In fact, these modifications are intended to both solve the problems that were detected and to make the practical application of the method easier. It certainly is necessary to evaluate whether these conclusions can be generalized in practice, and this is the direction of our current empirical work.

References

1. Bergenti, F., Gleizes., and Zambonelli, F. Methodologies and Software Engineering for Agent Systems. Kluwer Academic Publishing, 2004.
2. Bresciani, P., Perini, A., Giorgini, P., Giunchiglia, F., and Mylopoulos, J. TROPOS: an agent-oriented software development methodology. Journal of Autonomous Agents and Multiagent Systems, 8 (3): 203-236, July 2004.
3. Dam, K., and Winikoff, M. Comparing Agent-Oriented Methodologies. Proceedings of the Fifth International Bi-Conference Workshop on Agent-Oriented Information System (AOIS 2003), pages 78-93. Melbourne, Australia, July, 2003.
4. Liu, L., and Yu, E. Designing Information Systems in Social Context: A Goal and Scenario Modelling Approach. Information Systems Journal, 29(2): 87-203, 2003.
5. Mavin A., and Maiden N.A.M., 2003, Determining Socio-Technical Systems Requirements: Experiences with Generating and Walking Through Scenarios, Proceedings of the 11th International Conference on Requirements Engineering, pages 213-222, California, USA, September, 2003.
6. Padgham, L., Shehory, O., Sterling, L., and Sturm, A. "Methodologies for Agent-Oriented Software Engineering". Seventh European Agent System Summer School (EASSS 2005), Utrecht, the Netherlands, 2005.
7. Pastor, O., Gómez, J., Infrán, E., and Pelechado, V. The OO-Method approach for information systems modeling: from object-oriented conceptual modeling to automated programming, Information Systems, 26(7): 507-534, 2001.
8. Shehory, O., and Sturm, A. Evaluation of modeling techniques for agent-based systems. Proceedings of the Fifth International Conference on Autonomous Agents, pages 624-631. Montreal, Canada, May, 2001.
9. Sinan, S. Understanding the Model Driven Architecture (MDA). From http://home.comcast.net/~salhir/UnderstandingTheMDA.PDF. October, 2003.
10. Sturm, A., and Shehory, O. A Framework for Evaluating Agent-Oriented Methodologies, Proceedings of the Fifth International Bi-Conference Workshop on Agent-Oriented Information System (AOIS 2003). Melbourne, pages 94-109. Australia, July 2003.
11. Sturm, A., Dori, D., and Shehory, O. A Comparative Evaluation of Agent-Oriented Methodologies, to appear in Methodologies and Software Engineering for Agent Systems, Federico Bergenti, Marie-Pierre Gleizes, Franco Zambonelli (eds): Kluwer Academic Publishers.
12. Sudeikat, J., and Braubach, L., and Pokahr, A & Lamersdorf, W. "Evaluation of Agent-Oriented Software Methodologies Examination of the Gap between Modeling and Platform". Workshop on Agent-Oriented Software Engineering (AOSE-2004). New York, USA, pp. 126-141, July, 2004.
13. Yu, Eric. "Modelling Strategic Relationships for Process Reengineering". Published Doctoral dissertation, University of Toronto, Canada, 1995.

Towards an End-User Development Approach for Web Engineering Methods

Pedro Valderas, Vicente Pelechano, and Oscar Pastor

Department of Information System and Computation,
Technical University of Valencia, Spain
Cami de Vera s/n 46022
{pvalderas, pele, opastor}@dsic.upv.es

Abstract. End-users who are nonprogrammers create web applications by using advanced web development tools. However, these tools are not supported by any methodological process which produces that web applications are of low quality. This paper presents an approach to bring web engineering principles to the end-user community. We complement the web engineering method OOWS with tools that allow end-users to develop web applications by: (1) describing web applications in terms of the end-users' knowledge about the application domain, (2) automatically obtaining a web application prototype by means of the OOWS code generation strategy, and (3) personalizing the web application look and feel by simply selecting a design template. To achieve this, an ontology-based strategy is introduced to support end-users throughout the web application development. We also introduce a strategy that allows us to define domain-independent presentation templates.

1 Introduction

Many advanced web-development tools are continuously being put on sale in the software marketplace. In this context, the creation of web applications has ceased to be an activity for web professionals only. *End-users* who are nonprogrammers are becoming web developers and are creating web applications. End-user tools [3] allow users with little or no programming knowledge to create web applications by means of mechanisms that facilitate the creation of common web page components (at the design level). However, there is no methodological process behind these tools, and end-users do not have the necessary training and experience to develop web applications. Therefore, their web applications are of low quality. W. Harrison refers to this problem as "The Danger of End-User Programming" [4]. In addition, end-users do not have the ability to identify correct and complete web application requirements, which generates web applications that do not always support real end-user needs. All these problems are caused, in part, because the web engineering community [1] does not properly consider end-user development (although authors such as G. Fisher consider it the future of software development [5]). We believe that the web engineering foundations can be brought to the end-user community with an appropriate method and the right tools, preserving the intrinsic complexity of a web application development process, but making it possible for end-users to participate adequately in such a process.

In this work, we present an approach to give support to the end-user development from a web engineering perspective. This approach allows end-users with no programming knowledge and with no web design expertise to develop small and medium-size web applications according to web engineering principles. We define a development process for end-users based on the web engineering method OOWS [6] [7]. This method is based on the principles defined by the Model-Driven Development (MDD) [8] and allows us to automatically obtain fully operative web application prototypes from a requirements specification. We complement the OOWS method with tools that allow end-users to develop web applications by: (1) describing web applications in terms of the end-users' knowledge about the application domain, (2) automatically obtaining an OOWS requirements specification from their description and then generating a web application prototype and (3) personalizing the web application look and feel by simply selecting the most suitable design template from a list of predefined ones. To achieve this, an ontology-based strategy is introduced to give support to end-users throughout the task of developing web applications. We also introduce a strategy that allows us to define domain-independent presentation templates.

Thus, the contributions of this work are:

(1) We properly introduce end-users in a web engineering development process. This provides them with the benefits of the development that is based on engineering principles.
(2) We provide support for developing web applications to those end-users that are experts at a web application domain but have neither programming knowledge nor web design expertise.
(3) We also provide end-users with a method for automatic prototyping (based on the OOWS code generation strategy) that allows them to achieve tasks of testing (over the prototype obtained by the OOWS method).

The rest of the paper is organized as follows: Section 2 presents the related work in web engineering and end-user development. Section 3 introduces an end-user development method based on OOWS. Sections 4, 5 and 6 introduce the tools that give support to this method as well as the OOWS code generation strategy. Finally, conclusions and further work are comment on in Section 6.

2 Related Work

Two different research areas that are focused on web application development are studied. On the one hand, the web engineering community has proposed many different semi-formal approaches (see e.g. OOHDM [10], WSDM [12], WebML [14]) and others based on more formal foundations (see e.g. Schewe et al. [15]) to provide methodological solutions for web application development. These approaches provide analysts with different models to define web applications at a high level of abstraction. Most of these approaches have implemented tools to support their methods. The problem of web engineering approaches is that they provide several abstractions that are difficult for non-professional web developers to understand.

On the other hand, several commercial tools such us Microsoft Frontpage [16] Macromedia Dreamweaver [17] or CodeCharge [18] have been developed to allow end-users to design web applications. Most of these end-user tools present problems when a novice wants to use them. For instance, simple tasks such as implementing the look and feel of the web application become difficult when they have to use HTML-flow-based positioning instead of the more intuitive pixel-based positioning. In addition, none of these tools addresses the entire process of web application development since they mainly focus on graphical design tasks. In order to solve these problems, several approaches that define end-user development as a new research topic have emerged. Tools such us WebFormulate [19], FAR [20], WebSheets [21] or Click [22] provide end-users with mechanisms that facilitate the task of creating a web application. These mechanisms are mainly based on drag and drop techniques as well as spreadsheet concepts or rule-based programming. However, although these tools make the creation of web applications easier, they still require experienced end-users.

3 An End-User Development Method Based on OOWS

We propose an end-user development process based on OOWS, a web engineering method. The OOWS development process is based on the principles defined by MDD and allows us to automatically obtain fully operative web application prototypes from the requirements specification (See [6] and [7] for detailed information).

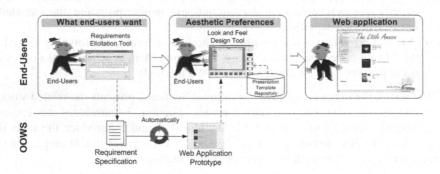

Fig. 1. The end-user development process based on OOWS

The OOWS development process is automatically achieved, and we think that it can be fully transparent to end-users if we provide them with the right tools. Thus, in this work we complement OOWS with the following end-user tools (see Figure 1):

– *End-user requirements elicitation:* This tool queries end-users by means of a guided process to systematically obtain *what they want* and specify it (transparently) as an OOWS requirements specification. Next, a web application prototype is automatically obtained from this specification by following the OOWS development process.

– *End-user look and feel design:* This tool allows end-users to define the aesthetic aspects (such as colours, font size and face, or element positions) of the web application prototype obtained by the OOWS method. To do this the tool allows end-users to select the most suitable presentation template (according to their preferences) from a set of templates stored in a repository. Next, the selected presentation template is applied in the web application prototype to obtain the final web application.

The main benefits of this end-user development process are the following:

- Programming knowledge and web design experience are not required for end-users. The *End-user requirements elicitation* tool hides the complexity of programming software. The *look and feel design* tool allows end-users to apply pre-designed presentation templates.
- The OOWS automatic code generation strategy avoids what W. Harrison calls "The Danger of End-User Programming" [4]: software of low quality is obtained when people with little or no experience use the web programming languages that are in "fashion" (such as PHP, ASP or Perl).
- Web applications are implemented according to web engineering principles (following the OOWS development process).
- Proximity to the end-user mental model. End-users develop web applications by describing *what they want* (the requirements of the system) which is closer to the user's own experiences and goals.
- Clear separation of layout and behaviour. End-users can focus first on what the system must do and then on what the application look and feel must be.
- Easy to extend. If users require a new functionality, they simply need to describe the new requirements by means of the *requirements elicitation* tool.

4   The End-User Requirements Elicitation Tool

The *End-user requirements elicitation* tool targets end-users who want to develop small and medium-size web applications and who have neither programming knowledge nor web design experience. This tool hides the complexity of defining an OOWS requirements specification from end-users by means of the following steps:

1. *Web Application Type Recognition.* The requirements elicitation tool requests end-users to briefly describe the web application using natural language. Next, the tool attempts to recognize the web application type from this description. The tool extracts information from the end-user description and matches the information against known *type ontologies* to find the proper ontology.

   A type ontology defines concepts and relationships between concepts that describe the main features of web applications of a specific type (such as E-commerce applications, web portals, directories, etc). These features represent general features that are shared by every web application of the same type (e.g. E-commerce applications must allow users to purchase products).

2. *Web Application Description.* There exists information that is needed to obtain a full web application description and cannot be systematically extracted from type ontologies. This information is related to domain-dependent features such as the kinds of products that must be on sale in an E-commerce application (e.g. CDs, DVDs, Books, etc.).

3. The tool checks the recognized web application ontology to detect this missing information and asks end-users for it by means of *questions patterns*. A question pattern defines an abstract interface to query end-users about domain-dependent information. Question patterns are type-independent and can be used with any type ontology. The set of applied question patterns defines a wizard that end-users interact with to describe the web application.

4. *Requirements Specification Generation*. First, the tool defines a preliminary version of the requirements specification from the features defined in the type ontology. Next, this specification is progressively refined from the end-user information. To do this, we propose a *generation strategy* that is based on a set of high-level operations defined from the elements of the OOWS requirements specification meta-model.

4.1 Web Application Type Recognition

The goal of this step is to determine what type of web application must be developed. As commented above, we use type ontologies to achieve this goal. These ontologies are presented in Section 4.1.1. Section 4.1.2 introduces the strategy to determine which ontology matches the end-user's web application description.

4.1.1 Type Ontology

A type ontology specifies the concepts and the relationships between concepts that represent a web application of a specific type (E-commerce applications, web portals, directories, etc). To determine the different web application types, we have used the categorization proposed in [24]. We use the OWL language [2] to define a type ontology. Figure 2 shows a partial view of the type ontology for E-commerce applications[1]. This ontology defines concepts such as *On-Line Purchase, Shopping Cart,* or *Products* (concepts that characterize E-commerce applications).

To define ontologies of this kind, we use the approach presented by Al-Muhammed et al [9]. According to this approach, two kinds of concepts can be defined, namely lexical concepts (enclosed in dashed rectangles) and nonlexical concepts (enclosed in solid rectangles). A concept is *lexical* if its instances are indistinguishable from their representation. *Date* (see Figure 2) is an example of lexical concept because its instances (e.g. "21/05/2005" and "04/09/2004") represent themselves. A concept is nonlexical if its instances are object identifiers, which represent real-world objects. *User* (see Figure 2) is an example of nonlexical concept because its instances are identifiers such as "ID1", which represents a particular person in the real world who is a user. The main concept in a type ontology is marked with "->•". We designate the concept *On-line Purchase* in Figure 2 as the main concept because it represents the main purpose of an E-commerce application.

---

[1] In practice, we would need a richer ontology for E-commerce Applications. For instance, other kinds of on-line purchases such as *second hand purchase* must also be defined. Relationship restrictions must also be defined (i.e. we must be sure that a user has a shopping cart assigned only in the case of a direct purchase). We have limited our ontology to those concepts that allow us to introduce a representative example.

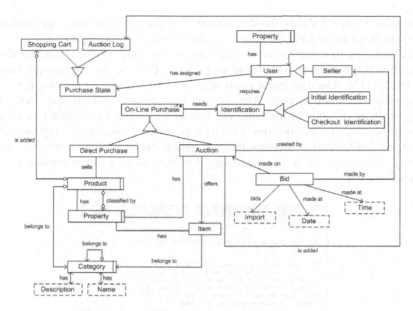

Fig. 2. Type ontology for E-commerce Applications

Figure 2 also shows a set of relationships among concepts, represented by connecting lines, such as *Product has Property*. The arrow connection represents a one-to-one relationship or a many-to-one relationship (the arrow indicates a cardinality of one), and the non-arrow connection represents a many-to-many relationship. For instance, *Auction offers Item* is a many-to-one relationship (i.e. in each auction only an item can be offered but an item can be offered in several auctions) and *Product has Property* is a many-to-many relationship (i.e. a product can have several properties, and a property can be defined for several products). A small circle near the source or the target of a connection represents an optional relationship. For instance, it is not obligatory for a category to belong to another category. A triangle in Figure 2 defines a generalization/specialization with a generalization connected to the apex of the triangle and a specialization connected to its base. For instance, *Direct Purchase* is a specialization of *On-Line Purchase*.

Finally, we have extended this notation by introducing *abstract concepts*. An abstract concept is a concept that depends on the domain of the web application and must be instantiated by end-users. For instance, *Product* is an abstract concept because we know that every E-commerce application must allow users to purchase products; however, we do not know what kind of products they are (they can be CDs, Books, software, etc.). This information depends on the E-commerce application domain and must be instantiated by end-users. These concepts are marked with a vertical line on the right side (see Figure 2, concepts *Product*, *Property* and *Category*).

4.1.2 Recognising Type Ontologies from End-User Descriptions
In order to describe a web application, as a first step, the requirements elicitation tool requests end-users to introduce a brief description (in natural language) of the web

application. Figure 3 shows the description of a small E-commerce application like Amazon (which is used as a running example in the rest of the paper).

The tool uses this description to determine which type ontology matches the web application that end-users want to develop. To do this, we use a technique based on data frames [13]. The data frame approach allows us to describe information about a concept by means of its contextual keywords or phrases, which may indicate the presence of an instance of the concept. Although the data frame approach proposes the specification of other information (such as external and internal representations, operations that transform between internal and external representations, etc.) to fully describe a concept, it is not necessary for our purpose (to recognise the web application type).

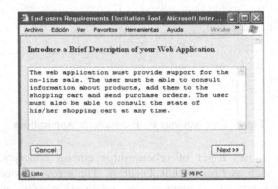

Fig. 3. Brief description of a Web application

We define data frame contextual information for web application types. The tool uses this contextual information to recognize the web application type and select the proper ontology. For instance, Figure 4 shows the contextual keywords and phrases that we associate to E-commerce applications. The tool can determine that end-users want to develop an E-commerce application if words such as *on-line sale, product,* or *shopping cart* appear in the end-user description.

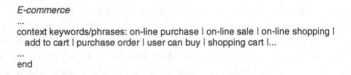

Fig. 4. Context information for the E-commerce type recognition

4.2 Web Application Description

Once the type ontology has been identified, we know the main features of the web application. However, to obtain a full web application description, the tool needs information that cannot be systematically extracted from a type ontology. This information must be introduced by end-users and is the following:

– *Abstract concepts.* As commented above, abstract concepts must be instantiated by end-users (e.g. we define that an E-commerce application must allow users to purchase products, but we do not define the kind of products).
– *Relationships between abstract concepts.* If a relationship connect two abstract concepts, end-users must indicate which instances are related (after instantiate both abstract concepts).
– *Specialized concepts.* Specializations define different kinds of a same concept. For example, in the E-commerce ontology (see Figure 2), an E-commerce application can provide two kinds of *on-line purchases*, *direct purchases* or *auctions*. The tool does not have enough information to decide which option use. End-users must take these decisions.

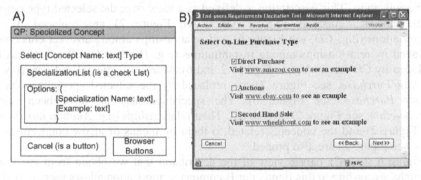

Fig. 5. A question pattern and the HTML interface obtained from it

To ask end-users for this missing information, the tool checks the selected type ontology and looks for abstract concepts, relationships between abstract concepts, and specialized concepts. When the tool finds one of these elements, it selects the proper *question pattern*. A question pattern defines an abstract interface to ask end-users for the missing information. We have defined question patterns for query end-users about abstract concepts, relationships between abstract concepts, and specialized concepts. To do this, we use a strategy based on the Abstract Data View (ADV) design approach [25]. Figure 5A shows the definition of the question pattern associated to specialized concepts. According to this pattern, the tool must provide end-users with a list of options (the different specializations) in order to allow them to select one (check list). Notice that this pattern attaches an example to each specialization in order to help end-users to take the decision. To allow the tool to work with these definitions, they are stored in XML documents.

The tool uses the selected question patterns to automatically implement a wizard that end-users interact with to describe the web application. We have developed a strategy that allows the tool to automatically obtain HTML-Based wizards from question patterns (see Figure 5B). First, the tool reads each question pattern from the XML document. Second, the tool instantiates the question patterns to the corresponding type ontology concept (question pattern terms that are represented between brackets are replaced by ontology concepts). Third, the tool applies an XSL transformation to obtain HTML code. Finally, the tool executes the wizard to allow end-users to introduce information. The entire process is completely transparent to end-users.

Figure 5B shows the HTML interface that allows us to select the on-line sale type of the running example. It has been implemented by instantiating the concept *On-Line Sale* into the question pattern associated to specialized concepts (see Figure 5A). To fully describe the E-commerce application of the running example, we must answer additional questions, such as what products must be on sale, what properties each product must have, what kind of identification must be implemented, whether or not products must be categorized, etc.

This *wizard* allows end-users to introduce features that depend on the specific web application domain. This information, together with the features of the application type (defined in the type ontology), allows the tool to obtain a full description of the web application. This description is defined as a view over the selected type ontology where abstract concepts (e.g. *Product*, see Figure 2) are replaced by their instantiations (e.g. *CD*, see Figure 6) and relationships among abstract concepts are replaced by relationships among instantiations (e.g. *Product has Property* has been replaced by *CD has Title*, see Figures 2 and 6). Moreover, specialized concepts (e.g. *On-line Purchase*, see Figure 2) are replaced by the selected specializations (e.g. *Direct Purchase*, see Figure 6). The specializations that have been rejected (e.g. *Auction*, see Figure 2) are pruned. Their relationships (e.g. *Auction has Property* see Figure 2) and the concepts related to them by means of arrow connections (e.g. *Item*, see Figure 2) are also pruned.

Figure 6 shows a partial view of the description that we obtain from our running example. According to this figure, our E-commerce application allows users to purchase CDs and books through a direct purchase. A shopping cart is available, and users must identify themselves before proceeding with the payment (checkout identification).

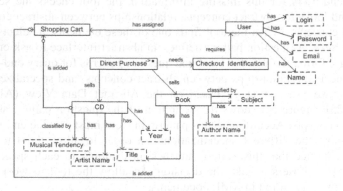

Fig. 6. Final description (partial) of the running example

4.3 Requirements Specification Generation

In this section, we introduce the requirements specification generation step. In this step, the tool obtains an OOWS requirements specification from an end-user web application description. First, we briefly explain the main elements of an OOWS requirements specification. Next, we explain the strategy to obtain it from the end-user description.

4.3.1 Understanding an OOWS Requirements Specification

To define an OOWS requirements specification we must create first a task taxonomy (see Figure 7, zone 1). The task taxonomy specifies in a hierarchical way the tasks that users should achieve when interacting with the web application.

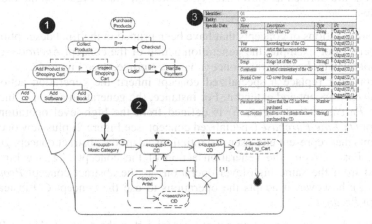

Fig. 7. An OOWS requirements specification

Once the task taxonomy is defined, each leaf task is described by analyzing the interaction that users require from the web application. To do this, a strategy based on activity diagrams is proposed (see Figure 7, zone 2). Each activity diagram is defined from system actions (nodes depicted by dashed lines) or interaction points (nodes depicted by solid lines) that represent the moments during a task where the system and the user exchange information.

Finally, we must specify a set of information templates where the information that the system must store is described (see Figure 7, zone 3). We also use these templates to describe the information exchanged in each interaction point in detail. See [26] for more detailed information about the OOWS requirements specification.

4.3.2 Obtaining an OOWS Requirements Specification

To obtain an OOWS require-ments specification we extend our type ontologies by augmenting each concept with a *generation action*. A generation action describes a sequence of high-level operations what are based on the elements of the OOWS requirements specification meta-model. Taking into account that OOWS requirement specifications are stored in XML documents, these operations allow us to create OOWS requirements specification by generating the proper XML code. We have defined operations such as *createTaxonomy*, *decomposeTask*, *addIP*, *createTemplate*, etc.

Generation actions are associated to type ontology concepts in order to give support to any web application of a specific type. For instance, the type ontology for E-commerce applications presents concepts whose generation action gives support to buy products by means of auctions as well as by means of a direct purchase. However, final web application descriptions do not present every feature defined in the type ontology. For example, the E-commerce application of our running example must only provide support to the direct purchase. Thus, in order to obtain a correct OOWS requirement specification not all generation actions of a type ontology must be achieved. The tool must decide which generation action is considered from the final web application description. Taking into account that web application descriptions are defined as views over type ontologies (see Figure 6), the tool follows these rules:

- Generation actions of concepts that have been pruned in the final description are not considered. For example, the generation action of the concept *Auction* (see Figure 2) is not relevant because this concept has been pruned (see Figure 6).
- Concepts that replace a specialized concept inherit the generation action of the specialized concept and extend it. For instance, the generation action of the concept *Direct Purchase* (see Figure 6) is defined from the high-level operations of the concept *On-Line Purchase* (specialized concept, see Figure 2) plus new ones.
- Concepts that represent end-user instantiations adapt the abstract concept generation action. For example, the generation action of the concept *CD* (see Figure 6) is defined from the same high-level operations as the abstract concept *Product* (see Figure 2); however, it adapts the operations to use the concept *CD* instead of the concept *Product*.

Figure 8 shows the generation actions associated to the concepts *Direct Purchase*, *Checkout Identification*, *Shopping Cart*, *Book* and *CD*. For each generation action, Figure 8 only shows the high-level operations that progressively define the task taxonomy of the running example. The operations that define both the information templates and the activity diagrams have been omitted due to problems of space.

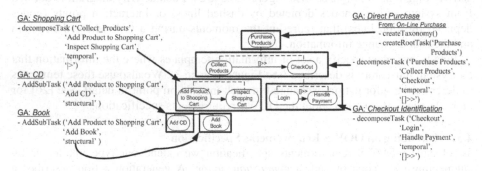

Fig. 8. Generation action examples

From the concept *Direct Purchase*, the tool creates the task taxonomy and the taxonomy root (operations inherited from the specialized concept *On-Line Purchase*). This generation action also defines how users must purchase products (collecting them first, and then making the checkout). From the concept *Checkout Identification*, the tool makes users login before handling the payment (in the checkout). The concept *Shopping Cart* indicates that the web application must provide users with a shopping cart. Then, products are collected by adding them to the shopping cart. Users can also inspect the shopping cart while they are collecting products. Finally, from the concepts *CD* and *book*, the tool knows which products can be added to the shopping cart.

5 Obtaining a Web Application Prototype

As commented above, the OOWS method allows us to automatically obtain a web application prototype from a requirement specification. First, different model-to-model transformations are achieved to derive the web application conceptual schema from the requirements specification. The OOWS conceptual schema is defined from several models that describe the different aspects of a web application: The system static structure and the system behaviour are described in three models (*class diagram* and *dynamic*-and *functional* models) that are borrowed from an object-oriented software production method called OO-Method [23]. The navigational aspects of a Web application are described in a *navigational model* [6].

Next, a strategy of automatic code generation is applied to the web conceptual schema to obtain code. The information and functionality of the web application is generated by the Olivanova Tool [11] from the OO-Method models (structural and behavioural model). The navigational structure of the Web application is generated by the OOWS case tool following directives specified in design templates [6].

The OOWS development process is automatically achieved, and then, it is fully transparent to end-users. The web application prototype is generated according to the information provided by end-users (by means of the end-user requirement elicitation tool). The aesthetic properties of this prototype are extracted from a default presentation template. The next section introduces a tool that allows end-users to easily change the web application look and feel.

6 The End-User Look and Feel Design Tool

The *End-user look and feel design* tool allows end-users without web design expertise to define the aesthetic aspects of a web application. To do this, the tool is based on the *area-based* OOWS code generation strategy. Thus, before presenting the tool itself, we briefly introduce this strategy.

6.1 The Area-Based OOWS Code Generation Strategy

The OOWS code generation strategy allows us to obtain a fully operative web application prototype from a task-based requirements specification. This prototype is made up of a set of interconnected web pages. OOWS divides each web page into three main logical *areas* (see Figure 9A as an example):

- The *information* area presents the data that is provided to users (see box number 1).
- The *navigation* area provides navigation meta-information. It is divided into the next sub-areas:
  - *Location* (see box number 2): Shows the situation of the user (the web page that is currently being shown).
  - *Followed Path* (see box number 3): Shows the navigational path that has been followed to reach that page.

- *Navigational Links* (see box number 4): Provides links to the web pages that can be accessed by users.
- The *corporative* area provides information about the organization such as the name, the contact email, logo, etc. (see box number 5).

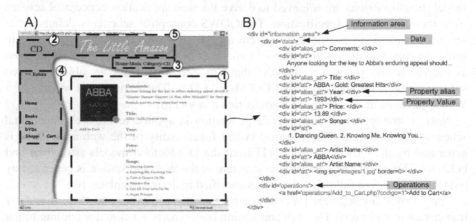

Fig. 9. Logical areas of a web page

Figure 9A shows a web page that provides information about a CD. This page has been implemented from the requirements specification that we have obtained in Section 4. Figure 9B shows the HTML code that implements the information area of this page. This code is based on the **<div>** label. Each area is defined by means of a div block. In addition, each div block is divided into sub-blocks that provide us with a great control to define the aesthetic aspects of web applications. The *information_area* block in Figure 9B is divided into two sub-blocks: *data*, which defines the properties of the selected CD and *operations*, which define the operations that users can activate. Finally, each property is implemented by means of two blocks: one that defines the property alias (for instance, "Year") and another that defines the property value (for instance, "1993").

The area-based strategy allows us to define *general* CSS templates. By *general templates*, we mean CSS templates whose styles are defined without considering the web application domain. Styles are not defined by means of domain-specific terms such as *CD*, *client,* or *invoice*. Styles are defined by means of area-based terms such as *information area*, *data,* or *operations*. Then, these presentation templates can be applied to any web application developed by following the OOWS method.

6.2 Allowing End-Users to Define the Web Application Look and Feel

End-users can easily associate presentation templates (defined by means of area-based terms) to their web applications (developed by means of the end-user requirements elicitation tool) by means of the *End-user look and feel design* tool.

Figure 10A shows a snapshot of the *End-user look and feel design* tool. This tool is divided into three frames. Frame 1 shows the page tool. This tool provides users with a list of web pages (depicted by rectangles with the file name) that make up the loaded web application. Frame 2 shows the template tool. This tool provides users with the list of presentation templates that are stored in a template repository. Currently, we have defined more than fifty templates that provide end-users with different presentations. Frame 3 is the rendering zone. In this zone, users can see the page selected in the page tool with the aesthetic aspects defined by the template selected in the template tool.

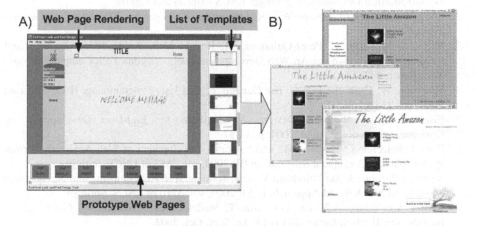

Fig. 10. Look and Feel Design Tool

Thus, the aesthetic aspects of a web application are defined as follows: (1) End-users load the web application into the *End-user look and feel design* tool. (2) End-users select the different presentation templates from the template tool. To see the look and feel of each web page, they can select it from the page tool. (3) Once the end-users have decided on a presentation template, the tool automatically associates it to each web page. Figure 10B shows a web page, which provides a list of movies, with different look and feel designs.

7 Conclusions and Further Work

We have presented an approach that is based on the OOWS method to bring the web engineering principles to the end-user community; it focuses specifically on those end-users that have neither programming knowledge nor web design expertise.

To do this, we have complemented the OOWS method with two end-user tools: (1) The *end-user requirements elicitation*, which allows end-users to obtain an OOWS requirements specification from the description of the application they want, and (2) the *end-user look and feel design*, which allows end-users to define the aesthetic aspects of the web application by simply selecting a presentation template.

As further work, we are studying different kinds of web applications to improve our type ontologies. We are also defining more templates to provide end-users with a wider selection of presentations. Finally, we are extending our approach to define a multidisciplinary method where end-users can work together with web professionals.

References

1. Muruguesan, S., Desphande, Y. Web Engineering. Software Engineering and WebApplication Development. Springer LNCS - Hot Topics (2001).
2. OWL Web Ontology Language. W3C Recommendation 10 February 2004. http://www.w3.org/TR/owl-features/
3. Rode, J., Howarth, J., Perez-Quiñones, M, Rosson M.B. An End-User Development Perspective on State-of-the-Art Web Development Tools. Virginia Tech Computer Science Tech Report #TR-05-03.
4. Harrision, W. From the Editor: The Dangers of End-User Programming. IEEE Software 2004, vol. 21 (4). pp 5-7.
5. Fischer, G., et al. Meta Design: A Manifesto for End-User Development, in Communications of the ACM. 2004. p. 33-37.
6. Fons J., Pelechano V., Albert M., and Pastor O. Development of Web Applications from Web Enhanced Conceptual Schemas. In ER 2003, vol. 2813 of LNCS. Springer
7. Valderas P., Fons J. and Pelechano V. Transforming Web Requirements into Navigational Models: An MDA Based Approach. In ER 2005, vol. 3716 of LNCS. Springer.
8. Mellor, S.J., Clark, A.N. and Futagami, T. Model-driven development - Guest editor's introduction. IEEE Software, 20 (5):14- 18, Sept.-Oct. 2003.
9. AL-Muhammed, M., Embley, D.W., and Liddle, S. Conceptual Model Based Semantic Web Services. In ER 2005, volume 3716 of LNCS. Springer.
10. D. Schwabe, G. Rossi, and S. Barbosa. Systematic Hypermedia Design with OOHDM. In ACM Conference on Hypertext, Washington, USA, 1996.
11. Olivanova Model Execution System. Care technologies (www.care-t.com).
12. O. De Troyer and C. Leune. WSDM: A User-centered Design Method for Web sites. In World Wide Web Conference, 7th International Conference, WWW'97, pages 85-94, 1997.
13. Embley D.W. Programming with Data Frames for every Items. Proceedings of AFIPS Conference, Anheim, California (1980). 301-305
14. S. Ceri, P. Fraternali, A. Bongio. Web Modeling Language (WebML): a Modeling Language for Designing Web Sites. In Proc. of the 9th WWW, Elsevier (2000) 137-157.
15. K.-D. Schewe and B. Thalheim. Conceptual modelling of web information systems. Data and Knowledge Engineering, 2005.
16. Microsoft Front Page 2003. Http://www.microsoft.com/frontpage/.
17. DreamWeaver 8. Http://www.macromedia.com/software/dreamweaver/.
18. CodeCharge Studio. Http://www.yessoftware.com.
19. Ambler, A. and J. Leopold (1998). Public programming in a web world. Visual Languages, Nova Scotia, Canada.
20. Burnett, M., Chekka S.K., Pandey R. FAR: An end-user language to support cottage e-services. IEEE Symposia on Human-Centric Computing Languages and Environments, 2001.
21. Wolber, D., Y. Su and Y. T. Chiang (2002). Designing dynamic web pages and persistence in the WYSIWYG interface. *IUI 2002*, San Francisco, CA.
22. Rode, J., Bhardwaj, Y., Perez-Quiñones, M, Rosson M.B, Howarth, J. As Easy as "Click": End-User Web Engineering. In ICWE 2005, vol. 3579 of LNCS. Springer. 478-488.

23. Pastor O., Gomez J., Insfran E., Pelechano V. The OO-Method Approach for Information Systems Modelling: From Object-Oriented Conceptual Modeling to Automated Programming. Information Systems 26 (2001) 507-534

24. Ginige, J.A., De Silva B., Ginige A. Towards End User Development of Web Applications for SMEs: A Component Based Approach. In ICWE 2005, vol. 3579 of LNCS. 489-499.

25. Cowan D.D. and Lucena C.J.P. Abstract Data Views, An Interface Specification Concept to Enhance Design for Reuse. IEEE Transactions on Software Engineering, Vol. 21(3), March 1995.

26. Valderas, P., Fons J. and Pelechano V. Developing E-Commerce Application From Task-Based Descriptions. EC-Web 2005, volume 3590 of LNCS. Springer. 65-75

Modeling Volatile Concerns as Aspects

Ana Moreira[1], João Araújo[1], and Jon Whittle[2]

[1] CITI/Dept. Informática, FCT, Universidade Nova de Lisboa, 2829-516 Caparica, Portugal
{amm, ja}@di.fct.unl.pt
[2] ISE Dept., George Mason University, 4400 University Drive, Fairfax VA 22030, USA
jwhittle@ise.gmu.edu

Abstract. A rapidly changing market leads to software systems with highly volatile requirements. These must be managed in a way that reduces the time and costs associated with updating a system to meet these new requirements. By externalizing volatile concerns, we can build a stepping-stone for future management of unanticipated requirements change. In this paper, we present a method for handling volatile concerns during early lifecycle software modeling. The key insight is that aspect-oriented techniques can be applied to modularize volatility and to weave volatile concerns into the base software artifacts.

1 Introduction

Modern systems should be able to cope gracefully with changes in requirements. A key barrier to the success of these systems is the time required to deal with requirements volatility. As Firesmith [7] says: "The more volatile the requirements, the more important it becomes for the requirements process to support the quick and easy modification and addition of requirements." This paper proposes a novel modeling method that copes with requirements change by explicitly externalizing volatile concerns. The key insight is that volatility can be handled in the same way as aspects. In general, volatile concerns may or may not be crosscutting but techniques for modeling aspects may be reused because both aspects and volatile concerns share the same basic needs – independency, modular representation and composition with a base description. By representing volatile concerns using aspect-oriented techniques, volatility is modularized and requirements modifications can be rapidly composed into an existing system, leading to efficiency gains in handling requirements creep.

Crosscutting concerns (such as security and logging) are properties whose implementation is scattered among several implementation modules, producing tangled systems that are tough to understand, difficult to maintain and hard to evolve. Aspect-oriented software development (AOSD) aims at handling crosscutting concerns by proposing means to their systematic identification, modularization and composition.

In our approach, both volatile and crosscutting concerns are modeled as aspects by using extended pattern specifications and are composed using specialized techniques for pattern specification composition. Pattern specifications (PSs) were proposed in [8] as a way to formalize reuse of models. Volatile concerns can be modeled as PSs and then instantiated and composed with base modeling artifacts in a number of

E. Dubois and K. Pohl (Eds.): CAiSE 2006, LNCS 4001, pp. 544–558, 2006.
© Springer-Verlag Berlin Heidelberg 2006

different ways. Requirements change amounts to replacing a pattern specification and reapplying the composition strategy.

The major contribution of this paper is to demonstrate the value of early externalization of volatile business rules and constraints to support evolution using aspects. This is achieved by proposing an evolutionary model that includes the concepts of aspect-orientation and its advantages [10]. This facilitates the introduction and removal of business rules because it is easier to add a new aspect to a running system than to add a new class or a new method.

The remainder of this paper is structured as follows. Section 2 introduces some background work. Section 3 gives an overview of our method for modeling volatile concerns. Section 4 applies the method to a case study. Section 5 evaluates the presented method according to general and specific criteria. Section 6 discusses related work and Section 7 concludes the work and suggests directions for further research.

2 Background

Pattern Specifications (PSs). PSs [8] are a way of formalizing the reuse of models. The notation for PSs is based on the Unified Modeling Language (UML) [13]. A pattern specification describes a pattern of structure or behavior defined over the roles which participants of the pattern play. Role names are preceded by a vertical bar ("|"). A PS can be instantiated by assigning concrete modeling elements to play these roles. A role is a specialization of a UML metaclass restricted by additional properties that any element fulfilling the role must possess. Hence, a role specifies a subset of the instances of the UML metaclass. A model conforms to a PS if its model elements that play the roles of the PS satisfy the properties defined by the roles. Thus, a conforming diagram must instantiate each of the roles with UML model elements, multiplicity and other constraints. Note that any number of additional model elements may be present in a conforming diagram as long as the role constraints are maintained. As in [14], we extend the notion of pattern specification from that of [8] by allowing both role elements and concrete modeling elements in a PS. This provides greater flexibility in reuse as often one may wish to reuse a partially instantiated model rather than a model only containing role elements.

The Role of *Roles*. Our approach uses roles to typify concerns in terms of their volatility, genericity and aspectuality. Volatile concerns represent business rules that the stakeholders would like to be able to change quickly, at any time, depending on the market demands. Examples of such volatile business rules are *"Customers whose transactions amount to at least five million euros annually are awarded a position on the company executive board"* or *"Off-peak customers get a 5% discount"*. In traditional software development approaches, the specification, and consequent implementation, of these volatile requirements is hard-wired to core modules that cannot be changed without having to recompile the application. By externalizing these volatile concerns and specifying them as role elements (or, more generally, role models) we are offering a mechanism to instantiate each business rule differently whenever needed (genericity). For example, a volatile concern can be given as a use case role and later be instantiated to a concrete use case.

Roles are also used to represent crosscutting concerns. The advantage is that the resulting role model can be instantiated and composed differently depending on which model it crosscuts. In general, both volatile and crosscutting concerns can be modeled as a PS, and this can be done at multiple levels of abstraction – e.g., a crosscutting use case can be refined into an APS.

Crosscutting Models. We define an aspect-oriented model to be a model that crosscuts other models *at the same level of abstraction*. This means, for example, that a requirements model is an aspect if it crosscuts other requirements models; a design model is an aspect if it crosscuts other design models. In particular, a use case is not necessarily an aspect. Although a use case always cuts across multiple implementation modules, it is only an aspect if it cuts across other use cases.

In this paper, we restrict the definition of an aspect-oriented model further and say that a model is an aspect only if it crosscuts other models written from the same perspective. For example, a model showing global component interactions does not, according to our definition, crosscut a model showing internal component behavior. Although the models are defined at the same level of abstraction, they are written from different perspectives – a global and a local perspective. In terms of UML, this means that we are only interested in crosscuts defined over diagrams of the same type. We therefore do not consider, for example, sequence diagrams that crosscut state machines or use cases that crosscut class diagrams.

Composition Models. Keeping separate the definition of the rules that indicate how base and aspect models are weaved together is as important as representing crosscutting models in a modular fashion. Separating aspects is good for improved modularization and evolution, and composition is necessary to facilitate reuse of both base and aspectual models, to understand the overall picture and to reason about the necessary tradeoffs between conflicting properties.

Composition is achieved through composition rules. These rules weave together compatible models by means of specific operators. Compatible models are those at the same level of abstraction and that were built from the same perspective. Composition operators function as the glue that keeps together aspectual and base models. They are similar to *advices* (*before, after* and *around*) in AspectJ [10] except that here operators are specific to UML diagrams.

3 Modeling Volatility

Volatile requirements are business rules that the stakeholders would like to be able to change quickly, at any time. The key insight is that volatility can be handled in the same way as aspects, since both concepts share the same basic needs – independency, modular representation and composition with a base description. By representing volatile requirements using aspect-oriented techniques, volatility is modularized and requirements modifications can be rapidly instantiated and composed into an existing system. Therefore, the process we propose focuses on requirements evolution, where classification, composition and instantiation form the most important tasks to achieve the adequate flexibility needed for evolvable systems (see Fig. 1).

The process starts with the identification of the main problem domain concerns (step 1). A concern refers to a matter of interest that the future system needs to address to satisfy the stakeholders' needs. Each concern is then classified (step 2) in terms of being either a service or a constraint and either enduring or volatile. Each concern is described in terms of its main elements in a template as shown in Tables 1 and 2. Classification and description of concerns may lead to their refactoring (step 3). Concerns may therefore be iteratively identified, classified, described and refactored.

Concerns are represented (step 4) using UML diagrams or pattern specifications. Enduring services are modeled using UML in the usual way. During this task, crosscutting elements in a model, or crosscutting models can be identified. Volatile concerns, crosscutting concerns and constraints are defined as role elements in the representation models. The representation of these concerns as roles requires that the original concern definition is modified to become non-specific, thus allowing several concrete instantiations (step 5).

Concern evolution (step 7) allows new concerns to be identified, classified, refactored and represented, iteratively. At this stage, the outcome of the process is a specification where core concerns and concern roles are kept separate. Instantiation and/or composition (steps 5 and 6) can take place at the level of granularity of elementary concerns or models. While instantiation offers the opportunity to make concrete decisions regarding volatile concerns, which have been marked as role elements, composition serves to weave the instantiated concerns into a base model consisting of enduring services. Composition can act as a basis for identifying conflicts solved by means of trade-off analysis. In this paper we will ignore conflict analysis and focus on composition using a set of generic directives and a technique similar to the one in [8].

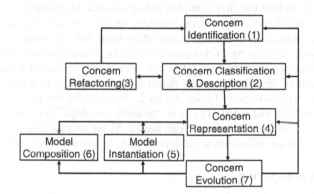

Fig. 1. Aspect-oriented evolutionary model for volatile concerns

We now illustrate the process outline in Fig. 1 using an automated transport system[1] in which transport contractors bid to fulfill passenger transport orders.

3.1 Concern Identification

The identification of concerns starts with the identification of the stakeholders and follows by inspecting existing documents that describe the problem, existing catalogues [2], stakeholders' interviews transcripts and searching techniques [11].

---

[1] Shuttle system description found at http://scesm04.upb.de/case-study-1/ShuttleSystem-Case Study-V1.0.pdf

For example, in the automated transport system, passenger orders can be bid on by all transport contractors and the lowest bid wins. In the event of two lowest bids, the first arriving bid wins. Successful completion of an order results in a monetary reward for the shuttle involved. In case an order has not been completed in a given amount of time, a penalty is incurred. The following two concerns can be identified from this example: (C1) Passenger orders can be bid for by all transport contractors and the lowest bid wins. In the event of two lowest bids, the first arriving bid wins. (C2) Successful completion of an order results in a monetary reward for the shuttle involved. In case an order has not been completed in a given amount of time, a penalty is incurred.

3.2 Concern Classification and Description

Concerns are classified according to their type. This depends on two factors: (i) longevity, which can be enduring or volatile and (ii) conceptual nature, which can be services or constraints. Enduring concerns are "relatively stable requirements which derive from the core activity of the organization and which relate directly to the domain of the system" [12]. Volatile concerns "are likely to change during the system development or after the system has been put into operation" [12]. Constraints are properties that the system must satisfy. Services define functionalities that the system must offer. This information is collected in a bi-dimensional table (see Table 4) where each cell contains the list of concerns that satisfy a combination of those two factors.

For example, concern C1 above is a service that might be classified as both enduring and volatile. While the first sentence refers to something stable as it is likely that shuttles will always have to bid for business in this system, the second implies a choice process which is likely to change depending on organization policies. This leads to a natural refactoring of this concern into two separate concerns – one to capture the enduring part and one to capture the volatile part (cf. section 3.3 below).

Each concern is described in more detail using a template that collects its contextual and internal information. Tables 1 and 2 illustrate the templates for concern C1 (refactored into C1a and C1b). The row "Interrelationships" lists the concerns that a given concern relates to. (The reader can see [2, 6] on several kinds of relationships.) A responsibility is an obligation to perform a task, or know certain information.

3.3 Concern Refactoring

Attempts to assign the enduring/volatility categorization lead to a refactoring of the requirements, thus increasing the granularity. For example, in the automated transport system example, the concern "(C1) Passenger orders can be bid for by all transport contractors and the lowest bid wins. In the event of two lowest bids, the first arriving bid wins." could instead be represented as two separate concerns – one for the bidding (C1a) and one for the decision on who wins in the event of two equal lowest bids (C1b). Identified volatile concerns may be redefined to represent a more generic concern. For example, C1b if originally defined as *Choosing From Equal Bids*, can be generalized to *Choose Bid*. Such a generalization promotes evolution since you may want to change the bidding policies in the future.

The classification process helps to refactor the list of concerns into a list with consistent granularity level. This is because increased granularity is often needed to be able to specify the fact that part of a concern is enduring or volatile. As an example, for concern (C1) above, one would like to say that the first part of the concern (the bidding process) is enduring whereas the second part (dealing with two lowest bids) is volatile – one might, for example, later wish to use a different selection strategy in which bidders with strong performance histories win equal bids. Such a classification would lead naturally to splitting concern (C1) into two concerns (C1a) and (C1b). Applying a classification strategy consistently across a set of concerns leads to a consistent level of granularity in concern representation.

Table 1. *Order Handling* description

Concern #	C1a
Name	Order Handling
Classification	Enduring service
Stakeholders	Shuttle, Passenger
Interrelationships	C1b, C2
List of pre-conditions	
(1) There is a new order	
List of responsibilities	
(1) Broadcast order (2) Receive bids (3) Store bids	

Table 2. *Choose Bid* description

Concern #	C1b
Name	Choose Bid
Classification	Volatile service
Stakeholders	Shuttle
Interrelationships	C1a
List of pre-conditions	
(1) There should be at least one order	
List of responsibilities	
(1) Get offers (2) Select winning bid (3) Store Choice (4) Make decision known	

3.4 Concern Representation

Our approach represents concerns using UML use case and activity models. Elements in a model representing crosscutting concerns or volatile constraints and services are marked as roles and the model becomes a pattern specification model. Thus, we may use Use Case Pattern Specification (UCPS) and Activity Pattern Specifications (APSs).

Build Use Case Models. A UCPS is a modified use case model with use case roles, each one representing volatile constraints and services. It incorporates use case roles, where concerns are mapped into use cases, volatile constraints and services are mapped into use case roles, stakeholders are mapped into actors and interrelationships help in identifying relationships between use cases. Fig. 2 summarizes the process of building a UCPS.

Most use case relationships are given in the usual manner (with <<include>> and <<extend>>). Those that are derived from constraints will, however, be related with other use cases by using the new relationship <<constrain>>, meaning that the origin use case restricts the behavior of the destination use case. (Origin and destination are indicated by the direction of the arrow representing the relationship.) Some of the use cases derived from constraint concerns are typically global properties, such as non-functional requirements. Fig. 3 illustrates an example of a UCPS for the transport system, where C1a (described in Table 1) and C1b (described in Table 2) are represented by use cases. Note how C1b is given as a role use case, pointing out the clear distinction between enduring and volatile concerns – a reader of the model can immediately see where the volatility lies.

Input: a list of stakeholders and classified concerns
Output: a UCPS
For each concern C:
    Create a new use case or use case role corresponding to C
      If C is enduring, describe C as a concrete use case
      If C is volatile, describe C as a use case role
      If C is crosscutting, describe C as a use case role
    If C has a relationship, R, to concern C' in its template description, create a relationship between the use cases or use case roles corresponding to C and C'
      If C is a constraint, attach the <<constrain>> stereotype to this relationship
    Map Stakeholders that interact with the new use cases into actors

---

Fig. 2. Guidelines to map concerns to a UCPS   **Fig. 3.** Transport UCPS

Identify Crosscutting Concerns. Crosscutting concerns are those that are required by several other concerns. This information can be found in the concerns' templates, or by analyzing the relationships between use cases in the UCPS. For example, one use case that is included by several other use cases is crosscutting.

Build Activity Models. Activities describe use cases and activity roles describe use case roles or crosscutting use cases. Fig. 4 gives the process for creating an activity pattern specification from the UCPS. Each responsibility listed in the concern's template corresponds to an activity in an activity diagram or an activity role in an APS. The nature of the concern (crosscutting, enduring or volatile) decides whether activities or activity roles are used. For example, C1b is volatile; therefore, one or more of its responsibilities will correspond to activity roles in the activity diagram. Activity roles are those that correspond to the responsibilities that are primarily responsible for making the concern volatile. In this case, responsibility 2 of C1b will correspond to a role activity (Fig. 5).

Input: a UCPS and the list of concern templates
Output: an APS for each use case role or crosscutting use case;
          an activity diagram for each use case
For each use case U corresponding to a concern C:
    If U is a use case, create a new activity diagram:
      U's activity diagram is a set of activities, one for each responsibility in C, connected by appropriate transitions
    If U is a use case role or crosscutting use case, create an APS:
      U's APS is a set of activities and activity roles that represent responsibilities in C, connected by appropriate role transitions

---

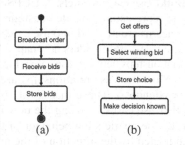

Fig. 4. Guidelines to map UCPS to activity diagrams or APSs

Fig. 5. *Order Handling* (a) and *Choose Bid* APS (b)

3.5 Model Instantiation

Model elements can be instantiated by a rule of the form:

```
<step #.> Replace |<modelElement A>
          with <modelElement B>
```

This means that *modelElement A* is eliminated and substituted by *modelElementB*, including its context. Instantiation is done for each particular configuration of the system. For example, consider our concern (C1b), represented in the UCPS as |Choose Bid. The instantiation rule is as follows:

1. **Replace** |Choose Bid
   with Choose From Bids (Equal Bids Choice Based On Arrival Time)

An instantiation for APS in Fig. 5 (b) is:

2. **Replace** |Select Winning Bid
   with Select Lowest Bid (Equal Bids Choice Based On Arrival Time)

Note that only volatile concern roles will need instantiation. The remaining roles elements might be used as "join points" for composition (section 3.6).

3.6 Model Composition

For the purpose of this paper we define two basic composition operators: *insert* and *replace*. The *insert* operator can be used together with the two clauses *after* and *before*, meaning that a particular model element can be inserted after or before a certain point in the base model, respectively. The *replace* operator, on the other hand, can be used together with the simple *with* clause, meaning that a model element replaces another (similar to an instantiation), together with a *choice* ([ ]) clause, meaning that more than one alternative is possible, together with a *par* (| |) clause, meaning parallelism, etc. The clause *Compose* encapsulates a composition rule (c.f section 4.3 for concrete examples).

Composition and instantiation can be applied independently from each other in an incremental fashion, leading to consecutive refinements of abstract requirements models into more concrete analysis models, supported by a set of guidelines and heuristics. Composition is achieved by defining composition rules that explicitly specify how two or more models of the same type (e.g. activity diagrams and APSs) are weaved together. In a more traditional aspect-oriented view, only crosscutting concerns would be composed with base modules. Here, we use composition to weave aspectual or volatile models to base models. A composition rule consists of a set of instantiation steps, where PS elements are replaced with concrete elements or other PS elements:

```
Compose <PS A> with <PS B>
    <step #.> Replace |<A> with <B>
    <step #.> Insert <A> {after, before} <B>
    <step #.> Insert <A> {after, before} <B>
                    where <statement>
```

where "A" and "B" may be model elements (or models in the case of the *Insert* operator). A composition rule can, of course, be more complex than this, involving, for example, decision and parallel operators. The full description of a composition language is beyond the scope of this paper, and we leave it for future work.

For our example, an obvious composition rule is to put together the activity diagram *Order Handling* and the APS *Choose Bid* (Fig. 6(left)). The resulting model is illustrated in Fig. 6 (right) where transitions (1) and (2) represent the effect of the two *insert* operators. In this particular case, the choice of a particular method for choosing the winning bid would be performed after this composition. When the requirements change (i.e., volatile concerns change), composition can be used to update the model in an efficient and modular way.

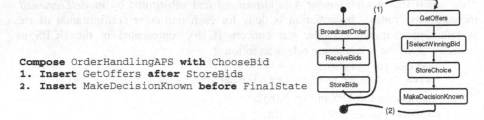

```
Compose OrderHandlingAPS with ChooseBid
1. Insert GetOffers after StoreBids
2. Insert MakeDecisionKnown before FinalState
```

Fig. 6. Composition rule (left); Resulting composed (right)

3.7 Concern Evolution

Evolution should cope with changes in concerns that are already part of the system and with new functionalities or constraints not yet part of the existing system. In the former, the system is prepared to handle the change, by either defining a new instantiation rule, or else by changing one or more composition rules. For example, a change in the process used to select the winning bid (C1b) is easily handled at all levels by choosing different rules (i.e. rule 1 for the UCPS and rule 2 for the APS):

```
1. Replace |Choose Bid
        with Choose From Bids (Equal Bids Choice Based On History)
2. Replace |Select Winning Bid
        with Select Lowest Bid (Equal Bids Choice Based On History)
```

In cases where we have to remove a concern, we need to remove all dependencies on this concern from all the composition rules. Coping with new requirements or constraints requires the reapplication of the method to identify the corresponding new concerns. These are integrated with the existing system by adding or changing existing composition rules.

4   Case Study

This section validates the approach described in the previous section by means of a case study based on the Washington subway system, described as follows:

"To use the subway, a client uses a card that must have been credited with some amount of money. A card is bought and credited in buying machines available in subway stations. The card is used in an entering machine to initiate a trip. When the destination is reached, the card is used in an exit machine that debits it with an amount to be paid. If the card has not enough credit the gate will not open."

4.1   Concerns Identification

Client and passenger are the final users of the system (client is a potential passenger). There are, however, other important stakeholders that provide key information about the system. These are, for example, the owner and the system administrators. The concerns discovered (C1, C3-C5) are listed in Table 3. Each one reflects a set of coherent sub-requirements that the future system must perform and were extracted directly from the short description above. C2, on the other hand, is a security concern needed to access the subway: we must guarantee that the card is a valid one and also that it is the right type of card. This is information we get from the knowledge we have from other application domains that use cards for similar purposes.

Table 3. List of concerns for the subway system

Concern #	Concern description
C1	A client buys a card in a buying machine
C2	A client must own a valid card
C3	Clients credit cards with minimum amounts of money in buying machines
C4	A client enters a subway station using a card in an entry machine
C5	A client leaves the subway station using his card in an exit machine that debits it with the cost of the trip. If the card has not enough credit the gate will not open
C6	The system is used for several passengers simultaneously
C7	The system needs to react in time to avoid delaying passengers while they are entering or leaving the subway, or crediting their cards
C8	The system must be available for use

During the development process of requirements discovery, modeling, design and implementation, a developer needs to assess the quality conditions, or constraints, under which the services of the system will function. Stakeholders that have organizational goals in mind will give most of these "quality attributes" that need to be satisfied by the system. Therefore higher-level stakeholders, such as system administrator and owner, are good sources to identify broadly scoped properties. For example, it is common knowledge that subways have opening and closing hours. Therefore, our system must be available at least during that period. This is guaranteed by C8. Another important characteristic is to serve several passengers at the same time. This is covered by C6. Finally, another condition for the good use of the system is to avoid long queues of passengers. Concern C7 handles this issue. Of course, other concerns may appear later, during the next stages of the development.

The number of concerns identified depends on the decomposition criteria used. For example, instead of C1-C5 we could have one concern to handle each machine (entry machine, exit machine and buying machine).

4.2 From Classification to Refactoring

Concerns in Table 3 are classified according to characteristics defined in Table 4. Constraints impose conditions on services. For example, constraints C6-C8 are global properties that C1-C5 must satisfy. Note that C3 appears in two cells of the table and C5 appears in two cells. C3 is classified both as enduring service and volatile constraint while C5 is classified as enduring and volatile service, and also as volatile constraint. This leads to a refactoring of the list of concerns, which divides C3 and C5 into separate concerns:

- C3A (*enduring service*): Clients credit cards in buying machines
- C3B (*volatile constraint*): Check if card is credited with a minimum amount

- C5A (*enduring service*): Client leaves the subway station using his card in an exit machine that debits it. If the card has not enough credit the gate will not open
- C5B (*volatile service*): Exit machines calculate trip fare to be debited in cards

The reason why we are externalizing the minimum amount (C3B) and the formula to calculate fares (C5B) is because those represent behaviors that we may want to change in the future. For example, to calculate the cost of the trip there are several options, which range from fixed prices to a prices depending on number of zones traveled to special discounts if promotions are available to encourage the usage of the system during periods of low usage. By delaying such a decision, we do not have to "hard wire" the formula that calculates the amount to a certain entity of the system. Instead, we are free to instantiate the behavior with whatever is appropriate at deployment time. Table 5 gives the refactored list of concerns with their identifications and names.

Table 4. System concerns' classification

	Enduring	Volatile
Services	C1, C2, C3, C4, C5	C5
Constraints	C6, C7, C8	C3

Table 5. Refactored list of concerns

Concern #	Concern name
C1	Buy card
C2	Validate card
C3A	Credit card
C3B	Check minimum amount
C4	Enter subway
C5A	Exit subway
C5B	Calculate fare
C6	Multi-access
C7	Response time
C8	Availability

Table 6. Template for "Exit subway"

Concern #	C5A
Name	Exit subway
Classification	Enduring service
Stakeholders	Passenger
Interrelationships	C2,C5B,C6-C8
List of pre-conditions	
(1) Card is valid	
List of responsibilities	
(1) Check balance	
(2) Debit card	
(3) Register trip	
(4) Open gate	
(5) Eject card	

Table 7. Template for "Validate card"

Concern #	C2
Name	Validate card
Classification	Enduring service
Stakeholder	Passenger
Interrelationships	C3A,C4,C5A, C6-C8
List of responsibilities	
(1) Insert card	
(2) Read card	
(3) Check card	

Table 8. Template for "Calculate fare"

Concern #	C5B
Concern name	Calculate fare
Classification	Volatile service
Stakeholder	
Interrelationship	C6-C8
List of responsibilities	
(1) Get entry station	
(2) Get exit station	
(3) Calculate price	

In earlier iterations, the requirement "If the card has not enough credit the gate will not open" of C5 was classified as volatile constraint, since it seems to be a precondition on C5. Later we realized that it was not worth to externalize such a property, as we could not devise a situation where the owner of the system could see (or want) this condition changed. It seems common sense to admit that the client will always have to pay for the trip. If, for some reason, we want to let him/her travel for free, that is another possible instantiation of C5B.

Concerns are described using templates (Section 3.3). From now on, we will use the three concerns C5A, C5B and C2 (tables 6-8) to illustrate our discussions.

4.3 Concern Representation

Build the Use Case Models. A UCPS is obtained by applying the guidelines offered in Fig. 2. Fig. 7 illustrates part of the resulting model.

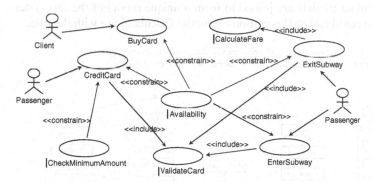

Fig. 7. Partial UCPS

By analysing all the concerns' templates we can identify that ResponseTime, Multi-access, Availability and ValidateCard are crosscutting. This is so since the first three concerns have to be satisfied by several other concerns (e.g., ExitSubway, EnterSubway, CreditCard). On the other hand, ValidateCard is crosscutting because it is included by several use cases.

Build Activity Models. Following the rules given in Fig. 4, activity diagrams and APSs can be derived from use cases and use case roles. Fig. 8 shows one activity diagram each for ExitSubway, ValidateCard and CalculateFare. Fig. 8(b) corresponds to the template defined in Table 7. The three first activities correspond to the responsibilities listed therein. The last two role activities represent the two potential returns after the condition.

4.4 Instantiation and Composition

The UCPS use case role |CalculateFare, for example, can be instantiated with a rule of the type:

```
Replace |CalculateFare
     with CalculateFareBasedOnZones
```

But it could also be instantiated at a finer granularity level by using a similar rule for the APS activity role |CalculatePrice.

Composition can be accomplished using the *replace* and *insert* operators to bring together APSs and/or activity diagrams. An example of a composition rule joining ExitSubway with ValidateCard is:

```
Compose ExitSubway with ValidateCardAPS
  1. Insert InsertCard after InitialState
  2. Replace |CardOk with CheckBalance
  3. Replace |CardNotOk with EjectCard
```

The resulting composed model (Fig. 9) can be automatically generated. If needed, the composition process can be applied again to join more models to this resulting model until all models are joined to form a unique model of the full system. For example, we could add to this composed model CalculateFare with the rule:

```
Compose ExitSubwayValidCard with CalculateFareAPS
  1. Insert CalculateFareAPS before CheckBalance
```

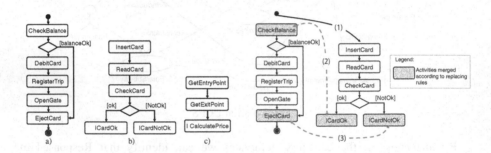

Fig. 8. (a) ExitSubway activity diagram; (b) ValidateCard APS; (c) CalculateFare APS

Fig. 9. Composed activity model

5 Method Evaluation

The evaluation criteria used here were proposed in [15]. There, four general comparison criteria are defined (evolvability, composability, traceability and scalability) as well as five other specific criteria (homogeneity concern treatment, trade-off analysis, verification and validation, handling functional and non-functional crosscutting requirements, mapping requirements to later stages) for assessing requirements engineering approaches.

General Criteria. The main drive to define our method was to offer improved support for *evolution*. Volatile concerns cannot be disregarded as time-to-market is a major concern of leading companies when developing their systems. Our instantiations and compositions facilitate rapid changes in requirements (see Section 3.7). By using aspect-oriented concepts combined with role-based models, *composability* is assured at several different levels of abstraction (concern, use case and activity levels) through the definition of simple composition rules. *Traceability* is supported by concern templates and model derivation guidelines. Finally, the modeler has to specify the instantiations and compositions and these will be, in the worse case, different for each base model crosscut by the aspect. We are now studying how to overcome this *scalability* problem by, for example, reusing instantiations and compositions.

Specific Criteria. Core, volatile, or aspectual concerns are all treated homogeneously by using the same set of techniques. While identifying, describing and classifying concerns, we do not distinguish between *functional requirements, non-functional requirements*, and crosscutting requirements. The method provides several guidelines that support *mappings* across several models. As we follow a UML-based approached, most of the resulting artifacts have a direct map to the analysis phase. However, we need to invest more on this, maybe basing our research on MDD. *Trade-off analysis* has been addressed in our previous work, but not here. *Verification and validation* techniques are not handled in this paper.

6 Related Work

Our pattern specifications are based on [8], where an aspect is defined through role models to be composed into UML diagrams. However, the approach does not allow concrete modeling elements in role models. In this paper, we define a model that integrates UCPSs and APSs in a systematic way, allowing similar composition rules for concrete and role elements.

Jacobson agrees that use case extensions are a way to handle aspects during requirements [9]. However, his work does not include broadly scoped properties nor does he handle evolution through volatile services.

Clarke describes composition patterns [3] to deal with crosscutting concerns as patterns at the design level. Pattern binding is used, and sequence and class diagrams illustrate compositions. The compositions, however, are rigid as they concentrate on pattern instantiations.

The idea to externalize volatile concerns is in some respects similar to the notions of product line architectures [4] and generative programming [5]. They model a family of related applications and then configure particular instances. Our work is similar but focuses on volatility. Although our work is less general, it does not require the huge investment associated with modeling a related family of application.

7 Conclusions and Future Work

Volatile concerns and aspects share the need for independency, modular representation and composition. Along the paper we discussed why those three characteristics were important to support evolution, which is constrained by volatile requirements, and how aspect-orientation and pattern specifications can help in handling it. To address this we proposed the externalization and consequent modularization of constraints and volatile services to cope with change on requirements. This is supported by an evolutionary method, where concern classification, requirements refactoring, model instantiation and model composition play a major role. Composition and instantiation can be applied independently from each other in an incremental manner, where guidelines drive subsequent refinements of abstract requirements models into more concrete analysis models.

For future work we plan to (1) create a specification language to define composition rules; (2) address conflicting emergent behavior that may appear when two or more candidate aspects are allowed to co-exist; (3) handle the scalability problems identified; and (4) develop a tool that supports the identification of concerns, their specification and composition.

Acknowledgments

This work has been partially supported by the Portuguese FCT Grant POSC/EIA/ 60189/2004.

References

1. E. Baniassad, S. Clarke, "Theme: An approach for aspect-oriented analysis and design", ICSE'04, Scotland, 2004.
2. L. Chung, B. Nixon, E. Yu, J. Mylopoulos, *Non-Functional Requirements in Software Engineering*, Kluwer Academic Publishers, 2000.
3. S. Clarke and R. J. Walker, "Composition Patterns: An Approach to Designing Reusable Aspects", ICSE'01, 2001.
4. P. Clements and L. Northrop, *Software Product Lines: Practices and Patterns*, Addison Wesley, 2002.
5. K. Czarnecki and U. Eisenecker, *Generative Programming*,"Addison Wesley, 2000.
6. Å. Dahlstedt and A. Persson, "Requirements Interdependencies - Moulding the State of Research into a Research Agenda", REFSQ'03, Austria, pp 71-80, 2003.
7. D. G. Firesmith, "Creating a Project-Specific Requirements Engineering Process", in *Journal of Object Technology*, vol. 3, no. 5, 2004, pp. 31-44.
8. R. France, D. Kim, S. Ghosh and E. Song, "A UML-Based Pattern Specification Technique," IEEE Transactions on Software Engineering, Volume 30(3), 2004.
9. I. Jacobson, P. Ng, *Aspect-Oriented Software Development with Use Cases*, Addison-Wesley, 2005.
10. G. Kiczales, E. Hilsdale, J. Hugunin, M. Kersten, J. Palm, and W. Griswold, "An overview of AspectJ", ECOOP'01, Budapest, Hungary, 2001, pp. 327–353.
11. A. Sampaio, R. Chitchyan, A. Rashid, P. Rayson, "EA-Miner: A Tool for Automating Aspect-Oriented Requirements Identification", ASE'05, IEEE Computer Society, 2005.
12. I. Sommerville, *Software Engineering*, Addison-Wesley, 7th edition, 2004.
13. UML Specification, version 2.0, August 2005, in OMG, http://www.omg.org
14. J. Whittle, J. Araújo, "Scenario Modeling with Aspects", in *IEE Proceedings Software*, Vol. 151, no. 04, 2004, pp. 157-172.
15. "Survey on Aspect-Oriented Analysis & Design Approaches", http://www.aosd-europe.net/

Author Index

Lecture Notes in Computer Science

For information about Vols. 1–3909

please contact your bookseller or Springer

Vol. 3965: M. Bernardo, A. Cimatti (Eds.), Formal Methods for Hardware Verification. VII, 243 pages. 2006.

Vol. 3964: M. Ü. Uyar, A.Y. Duale, M.A. Fecko (Eds.), Testing of Communicating Systems. XI, 373 pages. 2006.

Vol. 3962: W. IJsselsteijn, Y. de Kort, C. Midden, B. Eggen, E. van den Hoven (Eds.), Persuasive Technology. XII, 216 pages. 2006.

Vol. 3960: R. Vieira, P. Quaresma, M.d.G.V. Nunes, N.J. Mamede, C. Oliveira, M.C. Dias (Eds.), Computational Processing of the Portuguese Language. XII, 274 pages. 2006. (Sublibrary LNAI).

Vol. 3959: J.-Y. Cai, S. B. Cooper, A. Li (Eds.), Theory and Applications of Models of Computation. XV, 794 pages. 2006.

Vol. 3958: M. Yung, Y. Dodis, A. Kiayias, T. Malkin (Eds.), Public Key Cryptography - PKC 2006. XIV, 543 pages. 2006.

Vol. 3956: G. Barthe, B. Gregoire, M. Huisman, J.-L. Lanet (Eds.), Construction and Analysis of Safe, Secure, and Interoperable Smart Devices. IX, 175 pages. 2006.

Vol. 3955: G. Antoniou, G. Potamias, C. Spyropoulos, D. Plexousakis (Eds.), Advances in Artificial Intelligence. XVII, 611 pages. 2006. (Sublibrary LNAI).

Vol. 3954: A. Leonardis, H. Bischof, A. Pinz (Eds.), Computer Vision – ECCV 2006, Part IV. XVII, 613 pages. 2006.

Vol. 3953: A. Leonardis, H. Bischof, A. Pinz (Eds.), Computer Vision – ECCV 2006, Part III. XVII, 649 pages. 2006.

Vol. 3952: A. Leonardis, H. Bischof, A. Pinz (Eds.), Computer Vision – ECCV 2006, Part II. XVII, 661 pages. 2006.

Vol. 3951: A. Leonardis, H. Bischof, A. Pinz (Eds.), Computer Vision – ECCV 2006, Part I. XXXV, 639 pages. 2006.

Vol. 3950: J.P. Müller, F. Zambonelli (Eds.), Agent-Oriented Software Engineering VI. XVI, 249 pages. 2006.

Vol. 3947: Y.-C. Chung, J.E. Moreira (Eds.), Advances in Grid and Pervasive Computing. XXI, 667 pages. 2006.

Vol. 3946: T.R. Roth-Berghofer, S. Schulz, D.B. Leake (Eds.), Modeling and Retrieval of Context. XI, 149 pages. 2006. (Sublibrary LNAI).

Vol. 3945: M. Hagiya, P. Wadler (Eds.), Functional and Logic Programming. X, 295 pages. 2006.

Vol. 3944: J. Quiñonero-Candela, I. Dagan, B. Magnini, F. d'Alché-Buc (Eds.), Machine Learning Challenges. XIII, 462 pages. 2006. (Sublibrary LNAI).

Vol. 3943: N. Guelfi, A. Savidis (Eds.), Rapid Integration of Software Engineering Techniques. X, 289 pages. 2006.

Vol. 3942: Z. Pan, R. Aylett, H. Diener, X. Jin, S. Göbel, L. Li (Eds.), Technologies for E-Learning and Digital Entertainment. XXV, 1396 pages. 2006.

Vol. 3941: S.W. Gilroy, M.D. Harrison (Eds.), Interactive Systems. XI, 267 pages. 2006.

Vol. 3940: C. Saunders, M. Grobelnik, S. Gunn, J. Shawe-Taylor (Eds.), Subspace, Latent Structure and Feature Selection. X, 209 pages. 2006.

Vol. 3939: C. Priami, L. Cardelli, S. Emmott (Eds.), Transactions on Computational Systems Biology IV. VII, 141 pages. 2006. (Sublibrary LNBI).

Vol. 3936: M. Lalmas, A. MacFarlane, S. Rüger, A. Tombros, T. Tsikrika, A. Yavlinsky (Eds.), Advances in Information Retrieval. XIX, 584 pages. 2006.

Vol. 3935: D. Won, S. Kim (Eds.), Information Security and Cryptology - ICISC 2005. XIV, 458 pages. 2006.

Vol. 3934: J.A. Clark, R.F. Paige, F.A. C. Polack, P.J. Brooke (Eds.), Security in Pervasive Computing. X, 243 pages. 2006.

Vol. 3933: F. Bonchi, J.-F. Boulicaut (Eds.), Knowledge Discovery in Inductive Databases. VIII, 251 pages. 2006.

Vol. 3931: B. Apolloni, M. Marinaro, G. Nicosia, R. Tagliaferri (Eds.), Neural Nets. XIII, 370 pages. 2006.

Vol. 3930: D.S. Yeung, Z.-Q. Liu, X.-Z. Wang, H. Yan (Eds.), Advances in Machine Learning and Cybernetics. XXI, 1110 pages. 2006. (Sublibrary LNAI).

Vol. 3929: W. MacCaull, M. Winter, I. Düntsch (Eds.), Relational Methods in Computer Science. VIII, 263 pages. 2006.

Vol. 3928: J. Domingo-Ferrer, J. Posegga, D. Schreckling (Eds.), Smart Card Research and Advanced Applications. XI, 359 pages. 2006.

Vol. 3927: J. Hespanha, A. Tiwari (Eds.), Hybrid Systems: Computation and Control. XII, 584 pages. 2006.

Vol. 3925: A. Valmari (Ed.), Model Checking Software. X, 307 pages. 2006.

Vol. 3924: P. Sestoft (Ed.), Programming Languages and Systems. XII, 343 pages. 2006.

Vol. 3923: A. Mycroft, A. Zeller (Eds.), Compiler Construction. XIII, 277 pages. 2006.

Vol. 3922: L. Baresi, R. Heckel (Eds.), Fundamental Approaches to Software Engineering. XIII, 427 pages. 2006.

Vol. 3921: L. Aceto, A. Ingólfsdóttir (Eds.), Foundations of Software Science and Computation Structures. XV, 447 pages. 2006.

Vol. 3920: H. Hermanns, J. Palsberg (Eds.), Tools and Algorithms for the Construction and Analysis of Systems. XIV, 506 pages. 2006.

Vol. 3918: W.K. Ng, M. Kitsuregawa, J. Li, K. Chang (Eds.), Advances in Knowledge Discovery and Data Mining. XXIV, 879 pages. 2006. (Sublibrary LNAI).

Vol. 3917: H. Chen, F.-Y. Wang, C.C. Yang, D. Zeng, M. Chau, K. Chang (Eds.), Intelligence and Security Informatics. XII, 186 pages. 2006.

Vol. 3916: J. Li, Q. Yang, A.-H. Tan (Eds.), Data Mining for Biomedical Applications. VIII, 155 pages. 2006. (Sublibrary LNBI).

Vol. 3915: R. Nayak, M.J. Zaki (Eds.), Knowledge Discovery from XML Documents. VIII, 105 pages. 2006.

Vol. 3914: A. Garcia, R. Choren, C. Lucena, P. Giorgini, T. Holvoet, A. Romanovsky (Eds.), Software Engineering for Multi-Agent Systems IV. XIV, 255 pages. 2006.

Vol. 3911: R. Wyrzykowski, J. Dongarra, N. Meyer, J. Waśniewski (Eds.), Parallel Processing and Applied Mathematics. XXIII, 1126 pages. 2006.

Vol. 3910: S.A. Brueckner, G.D.M. Serugendo, D. Hales, F. Zambonelli (Eds.), Engineering Self-Organising Systems. XII, 245 pages. 2006. (Sublibrary LNAI).